Encyclopedia of Extreme Sports

Encyclopedia of Extreme Sports

KELLY BOYER SAGERT

GREENWOOD PRESS
Westport, Connecticut • London

Library of Congress Cataloging-in-Publication Data

Encyclopedia of extreme sports / Kelly Boyer Sagert.
    p. cm.
  Includes bibliographical references and index.
  ISBN 978-0-313-34472-5 (alk. paper)
  1. Extreme sports—Encyclopedias. I. Sagert, Kelly Boyer.
  GV749.7.E53 2009
  796.04′6—dc22   2008037869

British Library Cataloguing in Publication Data is available.

Library of Congress Catalog Card Number: 2008037869
ISBN: 978-0-313-34472-5

First published in 2009

Greenwood Press, 88 Post Road West, Westport, CT 06881
An imprint of Greenwood Publishing Group, Inc.
www.greenwood.com

Printed in the United States of America

The paper used in this book complies with the
Permanent Paper Standard issued by the National
Information Standards Organization (Z39.48–1984).

10 9 8 7 6 5 4 3 2 1

As there is no sport more extreme than that of being a mother and raising a child, I want to dedicate this volume to my mother, Jere Lee Taaffe Boyer.

Contents

Alphabetical List of Entries

ALPHABETICAL LIST OF ENTRIES

Guide to Related Topics

Skateboarding
Video Games
X Games

HOFFMAN, MAT (1972–)
Carmichael, Ricky (1979–)
Motocross (Extreme MotoX)
Nyquist, Ryan (1979–)
X Games

HOLMENKOLLEN SKI FESTIVAL: HOME OF THE HOLMENKOLLDAGEN (SKI JUMP)
Skiing, Extreme and Freeride
Ski Jumping

HOTTER 'N HELL HUNDRED: CENTURY BICYCLE RACING
Adventure Racing
Ironman Triathlon
Stamstad, John (1966–)

ICE CLIMBING
Alpine Scrambling
Csizmazia, Kim (1960–)
Mountain Climbing
X Games

ICE YACHTING (ICE BOATING)
Land Yachting (Land Sailing)

INDOOR SPORTS
Artificial Wall Climbing
BMX (Bicycle Motocross)
High-Wire Act/Tightrope Walking (Funambulism)
Inline Skating
Roller Derby
Skateboarding

INLINE SKATING
da Silva, Fabiola (1979–)
Roller Derby

IRONMAN TRIATHLON
Adventure Racing
Hotter 'N Hell Hundred: Century Bicycle Racing
Stamstad, John (1966–)

JUMPING/DIVING SPORTS
BASE (Building/Antenna tower/Span/Earth) Jumping
Bungee Jumping
Pogo Jumping, Extreme
Sky Diving
Sky Surfing

KITE SURFING (KITEBOARDING OR FLYSURFING)
Barefoot Water Skiing
Wakeboarding
Windsurfing

LAND YACHTING (LAND SAILING)
Ice Yachting (Ice Boating)

MANAGING RISK FACTORS OF EXTREME SPORTS
Psychology of Risk

MOTOCROSS (EXTREME MOTOX)
BMX (Bicycle Motocross)
Carmichael, Ricky (1979–)

MOUNTAIN BIKING
BMX (Bicycle Motocross)

MOUNTAIN CLIMBING
Alpine Scrambling
Ethics and Extreme Sports
Ice Climbing

MOUNTAIN SPORTS
Alpine Scrambling
Mountain Biking
Mountainboarding
Mountain Climbing
Skiing, Extreme and Freeride
Ski Jumping

MULLEN, RODNEY (1966–)
Burnside, Cara-Beth (1968–)
Hawk, Tony (Birdman) (1968–)
Skateboarding

NOLL, GREG (1937–)
Lava Sledding
Yoga Surfing

SNOWBOARDING
Palmer, Shaun (1968–)
Shaw, Brooke (1991–)
White, Shaun (1986–)
X Games

SPONSORSHIPS AND ADVERTISING, EXTREME SPORTS
Children and Extreme Sports
Sponsorships, Extreme Sports Mountain Dew
Sponsorships, Extreme Sports: Red Bull
Sponsorships, Extreme Sports: Vans
X Games

SPONSORSHIPS, EXTREME SPORTS: MOUNTAIN DEW
Sponsorships and Advertising, Extreme Sports
Sponsorships, Extreme Sports: Red Bull
Sponsorships, Extreme Sports: Vans
X Games

SPONSORSHIPS, EXTREME SPORTS: RED BULL
Sponsorships and Advertising, Extreme Sports
Sponsorships, Extreme Sports: Mountain Dew
Sponsorships, Extreme Sports: Vans
X Games

SPONSORSHIPS, EXTREME SPORTS: VANS
Sponsorships and Advertising, Extreme Sports
Sponsorships, Extreme Sports: Mountain Dew
Sponsorships, Extreme Sports: Red Bull
X Games

STAMSTAD, JOHN (1966–)
Adventure Racing
Mountain Biking

TRACK SPORTS
BMX (Bicycle Motocross)
Inline Skating
Motocross (Extreme MotoX)

URBAN CLIMBING
Free Running
Parkour
Robert, Alain (1962–)

VALERUZ, TONI (1951–)
Skiing, Extreme and Freeride

VIDEO GAMES
Children and Extreme Sports
Gender and Extreme Sports
Hawk, Tony (Birdman) (1968–)

WAKEBOARDING
Barefoot Water Skiing
Kite Surfing (Kiteboarding or Flysurfing)
Windsurfing

WATER SPORTS
Barefoot Water Skiing
Canoeing and Kayaking
Kite Surfing (Kiteboarding or Flysurfing)
Wakeboarding
Windsurfing

WHITE, SHAUN (1986–)
Skateboarding
Snowboarding
X Games

WINDSURFING
Barefoot Water Skiing
Kite Surfing (Kiteboarding or Flysurfing)
Wakeboarding

X GAMES
BMX (Bicycle Motocross)
Gravity Games
Motocross (Extreme MotoX)
Skateboarding
Snowboarding
Sponsorships and Advertising, Extreme Sports
Sponsorships, Extreme Sports: Mountain Dew
Sponsorships, Extreme Sports: Red Bull
Sponsorships, Extreme Sports: Vans

Introduction

What is an extreme sport and how does it differ from a traditional sport? Numerous ways attempt to divide sports into an extreme category and a nonextreme category, but none of them perfectly addresses the demarcation line.

Perhaps the most intuitive answer to the two questions listed above is that an extreme sport is more extreme than traditional sports in the amount of danger inherent in the activity, whether the danger comes from speed, height, tricks performed, physical exertion required, or something else entirely. Moreover, in extreme sports, uncontrollable variables often are involved in regards to the weather or other factors in the natural environment, such as large waves to conquer or even avalanches to avoid.

When looking at activities that have been labeled as extreme sports, there are many in which the degree of danger is quite high. Sky surfing, wherein an athlete jumps out of a plane and surfs on a board before activating a parachute, or free diving, wherein athletes take only one breath of air before diving, are only two of multiple examples of extreme sports with significant elements of danger; experienced athletes have in fact died pursuing these sports.

The element of danger, though, does not by itself create a dividing line between extreme sports and traditional ones. Traditional sports such as boxing, bull fighting, and NASCAR race driving are also fraught with potential risks that are quite significant, and people have died pursuing these sports as well. Yet, none of those activities are generally categorized as an extreme sport.

Interestingly enough, when sports are categorized based on the degree of risk for insurance purposes, professional sports in general have been rated as category six, which is the riskiest category, while hang gliding, rock climbing, and mountaineering up to 14,763.8 feet (4,500 meters), among others, are rated category five. Some category four sports include snowboarding and scuba diving deeper than 98.4 feet (30 meters), while category three sports include hot air ballooning, skateboarding, and whitewater rafting, and category two sports include high diving and mountain biking.

Another distinction sometimes made between extreme sports and traditional ones is that an extreme sport is an individual sport, whereas traditional sports rely on the concept of teams and teamwork. At first glance, this seems like a more clear-cut method of distinguishing between extreme sports and nonextreme sports. Activities such as skateboarding, snowboarding, BMX (bicycle motocross) riding, and so forth are generally performed solo, while more traditional sports such as baseball, football, soccer, and basketball are team oriented.

Again, this distinction is not perfect. There are traditional sports, such as tennis, golf, and horse racing, in which an individual athlete competes. Moreover, extreme sports are not entirely free of the team concept. In mountain climbing, for example, a person's life may depend on the team with which he or she is climbing; the same applies for people who explore caves deep in the earth, perhaps even scuba diving in them in complete darkness. Furthermore, some sports labeled as extreme—snowboarding, ski jumping and BMX riding, for example—have become part of the Olympic sport experience. Although medals are awarded for individual performances, these athletes are part of the United States team—or part of a team from another country around the globe. As yet another example of teamwork and extreme sports, many extreme sports athletes depend on their sponsors to fund their activities and, in a competition, several athletes may be performing thanks to the financing and support of the same company. These athletes therefore may tour together to put on performances as required by the sponsors.

Another distinction made is that extreme sports athletes are able to express themselves creatively by adding new spins, twists, jumps, or stunts to their performances, while traditional athletes have far less flexibility; need to follow rules more closely; and do not rely on their creativity to win. Although extreme sports athletes can and do create new tricks, stunts, and moves, and put their individual stamps on their sports, this is also true to a degree with gymnasts, ice skaters, ice dancers, and high divers, among others in traditional sports—and gymnastics, ice skating, ice dancing, and diving are not considered extreme sports. Furthermore, extreme sports that are included in the Olympics and X Games are judged, however subjectively. So, if an athlete wants to win, he or she must perform in a manner that will earn the points needed to do so. Winning medals and competitions and setting records help lure or keep sponsors, which is vital for extreme athletes who wish to keep competing.

Extreme sports are not a free-for-all for the athletes, either; in nearly every case, some rules need to be established and followed, at least in competitions. Some extreme athletes get thrown out of a competition for not following rules, just as in traditional sports. In 1992, for example, John Stamstad, an Ultramarathon mountain biker, was tossed out of the Trans-Australia Off-Road Challenge after debating the race setup with the organizer; he kept riding unofficially, though, after persuading some tourists to serve as his support crew.

Perhaps, some have suggested, the colorful personalities of extreme sports athletes contribute to the extremeness of their sports—and there is merit to this suggestion. Stamstad, after discovering that a particular race required a team, submitted different versions of his own name several times, thereby creating his "team." Snowboarder Shaun White is better known as the "Flying Tomato" because of his wild red hair and, for a while, he wore headbands adorned with flying tomatoes; he told *Rolling Stone* magazine that he'd like to be called "Sir Shaun of Shaunalot." Snowboarder Shaun Palmer has been known to jump out of hotel windows; throw a hot dog at an event organizer; and toss his snowboard into a sacred Japanese bath. There is no question that some extreme athletes have bold and extroverted personalities.

How does this differ, though, from former National Basketball Association (NBA) player Dennis Rodman, who has dyed his hair in multiple colors, including lime green, orange, and a mixture of several different colors all at once? He covered his skin with tattoos; sometimes wore nail polish and eye makeup; and, while promoting a book that he wrote, appeared in a wedding dress and later claimed that his intentions were to marry himself. In 2005, Rodman was named commissioner of the Lingerie Football League (LFL), in which female models played football in their underwear.

Rodman cannot easily be dismissed as a freak show, either. Two teams on which he played won a combined five NBA titles and, during the 1991–92 season, he averaged 18.7 rebounds per game, right below the incredible 19.2 rebound mark set by the legendary Wilt Chamberlain. So, although it is true that some extreme sports athletes have colorful personalities, athletes with extreme personalities exist within the boundaries of traditional sports, as well.

Many extreme sports can be partially characterized by the fact that athletes are attempting to set records by doing something faster, higher, lower, or more often than anyone else has done in the past, and it does seem as though extreme athletes are actively pursuing and frequently obtaining records. However, perhaps it is because extreme sports are relatively new and because multiple subdisciplines of extreme sports are appearing that so many extreme records are being set. In other words, a sport that has existed for only 10 or 20 years will most likely have more achievable records to break than a sport that has existed for many more decades; plus, sports with multiple subdisciplines automatically create more opportunities for records to be set. For example, in boomerang throwing, an athlete might win or set a record in fast catch, endurance, trick catch, doubling, Aussie round, or accuracy. It is even possible, in some tournaments, to win or set a record in boomerang juggling.

Furthermore, because extreme sports are more or less unregulated, an athlete can publicize a feat that, prior to his or her accomplishment, few had thought to attempt; athletes in traditional sports rarely have that luxury.

Moreover, important records in traditional sports often take a season—or even a career—to establish. For example, baseball players must commit decades to the goal of breaking a home run record (currently at 73 for a single season and 762, overall, both held by Barry Bonds) to have even a slim hope of achieving that record, and basketball players also need to spend entire seasons and careers trying to break points scored records; the highest number of points scored in a single season is 4,029, accomplished by Wilt Chamberlain in the 1961–62 season. Over his career, Kareem Abdul-Jabbar scored 38,387 points, which is the current all-time scoring record.

Another criterion sometimes mentioned is that extreme sports are dominated by the youth subculture; it is true that extreme sports are appealing to this demographic, with white males, from the ages of approximately 15 to 24, serving as the primary target audience for action sports. Youth participation, though, is not a characteristic that distinguishes extreme sports from traditional ones. Youth begin playing traditional sports at an early age, with leagues starting for those age five or even younger. Conversely, winners of extreme sporting competitions are not always teenagers or young adults. As one example, 32 top-ranked BMX riders competed in the Red Bull Elevation competition in 2007—and the winner was Ryan Nyquist. At the age of 38, he would be older than most athletes in professional sports such as football or basketball.

Extreme sports have been defined as "newer" than traditional sports and there is some truth to this assertion. Some people claim that the term "extreme sports" came into existence during the 1970s or the 1980s, while others believe that it was first used in the 1990s when ESPN began forming and then promoting the Extreme Games (changed to the X Games) competitions. No matter which of those assertions is correct, the term of "extreme sports" is less than 40 years old. Plus, new extreme sports do seem to be appearing on a fairly regular basis, with extreme pogo sticking, as just one example, having its first national competition in 2004. That said, extreme pogo sticking is not entirely new; rather, it is a new adaptation of a child's game that is nearly 100 years old in the United States and perhaps twice that old in Germany. Another example of a newer extreme sport that evolved from a traditional sport is extreme golf, wherein both the score and time needed to complete 18 holes are factored together to determine the winner; extreme golf was first played in 1979, but traditional golf has its origins in a fifteenth-century game first played in Scotland.

Extreme sports, then, are not as "new" as it might first appear—at least not when examining their roots. In fact, some extreme sports, such as lava sledding, and canoeing and kayaking, are believed to be thousands of years old, while scientists have uncovered a boomerang that is more than 20,000 years old. In comparison, many traditional sports are in fact relatively new. Baseball, the traditional sport of the United States, had its birth around 1845; even if one traces the origins of baseball back to bat and ball games in England, it seems quite unlikely that the sport is anywhere near as old as lava sledding—and certainly not as old as boomerang throwing. As another example, basketball was created in 1891, with the NBA being organized in 1946, making both of these traditional sports much newer than some extreme ones.

DEFINITION OF EXTREME SPORTS

How, then, can we define extreme sports? As shown above, no single characteristic differentiates extreme sports from more traditional ones. Taken together, though, a pattern emerges. Extreme sports contain an element of danger; are generally individualistic attempts to master an activity, often through unexpected or creative ways, with these individuals oftentimes interested in breaking records or exceeding previous limitations of human endeavor; and are closely connected to a young and alternative subculture. The sports often evolve in new and exciting ways, perhaps borrowing elements of already established sports to craft new adventures. The quirky personalities of some of the extreme sports athletes add another dimension to the radical nature of extreme sports competitions.

HISTORY OF EXTREME SPORTS

Accepting those parameters as the definition of extreme sports, the question becomes this: when did the first extreme sport take place? Although the roots of some extreme sports reach thousands of years back, these activities were not initially intended as recreation; rather, the activities involved satisfying a basic need, such as obtaining food. Boomerangs, for example, most likely were used as hunting decoys wherein a whirling stick in the sky resembled a predatory eagle; ducks would huddle together for protection beneath the boomerang, allowing hunters to more easily capture them for food. Perhaps this is why boomerangs were found in the pyramid of King Tutankhamun—or perhaps the ancient Egyptian boomerangs were part of a religious ritual that the Egyptians believed their pharaoh would need to undergo in the afterlife.

Other modern-day extreme sports activities have evolved from ancient transportation methods. These include canoeing and kayaking down rivers—and, according to Chinese legend, parachuting. Still other activities may have combined a physical activity with ritual, just as boomerangs probably did; these include lava sledding down volcanoes in ancient Hawaii; boarding down sand dunes in ancient Egypt; and dragon boat racing in ancient China.

Here is just one example of how a need for transportation was fulfilled in ancient times, and then the activity was later modified for recreational purposes. People used skis to transport themselves as long ago as 4,500 years ago, with rock paintings of skis suggesting that this method is even older. By the early 1700s, people in Norway were creating skiing competitions and, in 1892, a ski jumping competition took place in Oslo, Norway, that continues there today as an annual event, attracting modern-day extreme sports athletes who attempt increasingly extreme jumps and stunts.

The search for exceptional ways to travel continues today; in 2008, for example, a U.S. man in Oregon named Kent Couch wanted to fly 300 miles (482.8 kilometers) to Idaho in his lawn chair, which would be powered by 150 latex balloons filled with helium; the name of the sport is "cluster ballooning." As is common in the modern extreme sporting world, Couch obtained corporate sponsorship to finance his adventure.

The takeoff was successful. If he needed to lower the height of his flying chair, Couch planned to pop a few balloons; if the chair was flying too low, he could ditch some of his water overboard. Although this lawn chair did not come equipped with a safety belt, a finger clip monitored his oxygen level and he carried an oxygen tank in case of emergencies. One Global Positioning System (GPS) unit was attached to his chair, and another in his pocket. His emergency kit contained duct tape and zip ties for repairs to his chair; extra clothing; a blanket to fight off the chill found in high altitudes; and food—beef jerky, boiled eggs, and chocolate—for sustenance. Couch successfully completed his trip and intends to continue to seek financing for future travels.

MODERN-DAY EXTREME SPORTS

At what point, though, did the first set of people begin considering themselves as athletes and associating their activities with the extreme sporting movement? None of the ancient peoples engaging in boomerang throwing, lava sledding, or ice yachting would have identified with the extreme sports label, nor would other athletes and adventurers prior to the twentieth century.

The beginning of extreme sports as a cultural phenomenon took place somewhere between the 1950s and the 1990s, depending on the perspective of the person answering that question. Although specific extreme sports were founded in places around the globe, the United States has served as a key location for their overall emergence—and then, perhaps just as important, with their marketing. So, when specifically did the extreme sports movement emerge?

EXTREME SPORTS: 1950S

Suggesting that extreme sports as a cultural movement began in the 1950s is a less commonly given answer but, in that decade, *National Geographic* photographer Charles Lagus photographed villagers in Bunlap in the Pentecost Island; these villagers were participating in a form of bungee jumping. More important, at least when positing how the 1950s could have been the birth of extreme sports as we know them today, is that people began participating in the modern form of skateboarding during that decade. Skateboarding is one of the most popular and well known of all extreme sports and has served to inspire athletes in other extremes sports, including BMX and snowboarding.

EXTREME SPORTS: 1960S

It is easier to make the case that the extreme sports movement began in the 1960s, the decade when surfing became part of the popular culture, in large part because of the songs sung by the Beach Boys and Jan and Dean. These songs brought awareness of that sport to a mainstream audience. Furthermore, it was during the 1960s that surfer Greg Noll rode a nearly 25-foot (7.6-meter) wave in Hawaii, believed to be the largest wave tackled by humans. Furthermore, during the 1960s—

- People began sandboarding down large dunes of sand
- Captain Joseph Kittinger sky dived from a height of 102,800 feet (31,334 meters), which was the world's first "supersonic" jump
- The first artificial climbing walls were built in the United Kingdom
- The Wallenda clan created a seven-person human pyramid for a high-wire act
- The "snurfer," the precursor to the snowboard, was invented
- The first-known motocross race was organized

EXTREME SPORTS: 1970S

The 1970s are often named as the beginning of extreme sports. This decade witnessed a growth of rock climbing and marathon running. Moreover, more than 40 million skateboards were sold, as the activity became increasingly associated with the alternative punk rock movement, and as Florida skater Alan Gelfand—in 1978—accidentally discovered how to become airborne on his board. The latter accomplishment is what allowed skateboarders to begin creating and executing tricks on their boards.

During this decade, several organizations were formed to advance a particular extreme sport, including the following:

- The U.S. Snowmobile Association, which was formed in 1970, and sanctioned more than 250 races that year that took place on frozen waterways
- The Bicycle United Motocross Society (BUMS), which was formed by 13-year-old Scott Breithaupt that same year
- The U.S. Hang Gliding Association, which was created in 1971
- The North American Land Sailing Association (NALSA), which was formed in 1972

Several groups have tried to claim that they invented street luge in the 1970s; these groups were from Oregon, California, and Oklahoma—and even as far away as Austria. On October 26, 1976, the first mountain biking race took place in Fairfax, California, down Repack Road, which was a dirt road that plummeted 1,300 feet (396.2 meters) in just 2.1 miles (3.4 kilometers). In 1977, George Willig climbed the World Trade Center South Tower, signing his name on the observation deck; on February 18, 1978, the first Ironman Triathlon was held, with 15 competitors; in November 1978, Australia hosted the first barefoot water skiing world championships; and, in 1979, Minnesota brothers Scott and Brennan Olson modified an old pair of skates from the Chicago Skate Company, adding a boot and calling them "Rollerblades." Clearly, a good case could be made to state that extreme sports became part of popular culture in the United States and perhaps in several other places, worldwide, as well, in the 1970s.

EXTREME SPORTS: 1980S

The momentum continued throughout the 1980s. Sky surfing began around 1980, when sky divers from California started freefalling while on boards. In 1981, the National Skateboard Association (NSA) was formed; Phil Smith, Phil Mayfield, and Carl and Jean Boenish created the rules for BASE (Building/Antenna tower/Span/Earth) jumping; and the first international boomerang tournament, held between the United States and Australia, took place in Australia.

In 1982, the 100-mile (160.9-kilometer) race Hotter 'N Hell was created to celebrate the centennial of Wichita Falls, Texas; plus another race, the Ironman Triathlon, became part of mainstream news when competitor Julie Moss, who was in first place in the race, became so dehydrated that she collapsed and needed to crawl to cross the finish line. The image of Moss struggling to reach that line began serving as a symbol of determination for extreme athletes, especially those competing in the Ironman event.

In 1983, The National Off-Road Bicycle Association (NORBA) was formed to oversee mountain biking races; plus the United States hosted the first world championships in snowboarding. In 1984, wheelchair athletes participated in exhibition track events during the Summer Olympic Games held in Los Angeles, California, and windsurfing became part of the Olympics. That same year, Mat Hoffman rode up the curved, bowl-shaped half-pipe used by skateboarders, opening up brand new possibilities for BMX riders and transforming the sport. That year also spotlighted the very real dangers of some of these sports, as Carl Boenish, a founder of BASE jumping, died in Norway while participating in a jump.

In 1985, a San Diego, California, surfer named Tony Finn invented the "skurfer," a board that was the precursor of wakeboarding. The following year, Mountain Dew spotlighted Tony Hawk and skateboarding in one of its commercials, one of the earliest combinations of extreme sports and commercial promotion of a product. In 1987, the first Bridge Day festival was held, wherein people could legally jump off of the 876-foot-high (267-meter) New River Gorge Bridge as part of a BASE jumping competition; that same year, the United Sates got its first artificial climbing wall. In 1989, the first adventure race, the Raid Gauloises, was held in New Zealand.

EXTREME SPORTS: 1990S

Without question, extreme sports as a cultural movement had arrived by the 1990s. In 1993, Ron Semiao, the program director for ESPN2, conceived of an Olympic-like competition to showcase extreme sports; these games came to fruition in 1995 as the "Extreme Games" held in Rhode Island and Vermont, and were renamed in 1996 as the "X Games." In 1997, ESPN added the Winter X Games to its programming mix, televising them in 198 countries and translating them into 21 languages. The X Games, both summer and winter, continued to grow in attendance and awareness throughout the 1990s and into the twenty-first century.

In 1999, the first Gravity Games were held in Providence, Rhode Island. Although these games never achieved the prominence of the X Games, the Gravity Games also brought extreme sport competitions to the public's attention.

Some extreme sporting events became part of the Olympics during this decade, including mountain biking in 1996 in Atlanta, Georgia, and snowboarding in 1998 in Nagano, Japan. Also in this decade, extreme sports continued to evolve—and they continued to be created.

REASONS FOR THE POPULARITY OF EXTREME SPORTS

Regardless of the date chosen to represent the beginning of modern-day extreme sports, the reality is that, some time between the 1950s and 1993, a plethora of individualistic sports that had a significant element of risk were created and became much more popular. Although this happened in various spots around the world, the United States served as a core location for these activities.

Theories as to why this phenomenon occurred when and where it did include these three:

- We live in a world in which we must wear seat belts to obey the law; products come with numerous warnings and cautions; and liability suits are filed at an alarming level. Extreme sports, according to this theory, are a reaction to this ultra-buffered world, giving people the chance to explore freedom from restriction.
- White males felt challenged during the 1960s and 1970s, both by the civil rights movement and the feminist movement; to reclaim their sense of pride, they became involved in daring exploits. Through these endeavors, they were recapturing their sense of rugged individualism (Wheaton 2004).
- During the latter part of the twentieth century, technology had advanced to the degree that sporting equipment and protective gear caused activities to become safer than in the past; moreover, airplanes could transport athletes to the far reaches of the globe, whether that meant at the peak of a mountain or some other remote locale.

Another factor involves the media. During the latter part of the twentieth century, information about extreme sports was often spread through media, whether the form was a documentary about a particular sport, a video game promoting an athlete in the sport, televised coverage of an event or events, YouTube videos capturing extreme moments and then posting them on the Internet, or general news stories. In particular, starting in the 1990s, the *New York Times* began publishing in-depth articles about extreme sports, in general, and about specific extreme sports, in particular. Without these multiple forms of media, the notion of extreme sports could not have spread as widely and as quickly as it did.

Moreover, extreme sports "fit" the television format in a way that, for example, a slower moving baseball game does not. People who want to be engaged in a traditional game must commit more time and attention to watching or listening to that game, while the viewer can view an incredible extreme activity in a matter of minutes—or, sometimes, even in seconds. Watching a skateboarder nail a complex trick in the X Games requires far less time and attention than following a football team throughout a season. Even if we isolate one day—say, Super Bowl Sunday—the time commitment needed to watch an extreme sports athlete perform is significantly shorter than watching that game and, in today's sound-bite, short-attention-span world, that is a plus.

MAINSTREAMING OF EXTREME SPORTS

The creation of the X Games and the Gravity Games, and the incorporation of some extreme sports into the Olympics, has raised other questions: Is it possible to organize and regulate an extreme activity without the sport losing its edge? Can, for example, sports such as skateboarding and snowboarding, which have been associated with the free-wheeling, rebellious punk movement, survive mainstreaming efforts and still keep their creative spark? Can this type of sports-related lightning be captured in a bottle and still remain fluid and full of energy?

An article published by the *New York Times* in August 2007, "Dramatic Fall Exposes the Risk in Extreme Sports," suggests that extreme sports are not becoming tamer or more confined. In fact, their position is that "action sports have become more advanced and dangerous," pointing out that athletes on camera will most likely go for the wildest tricks, as they are "not rewarded for restraint" (Higgins 2007).

FUTURE OF EXTREME SPORTS

Finally, what will the future bring for extreme sports? It seems likely that increasing numbers of extreme sports will join snowboarding and BMX in becoming Olympic sports. Because the International Olympic Committee (IOC) does not wish to add new sports to their roster without removing an equal amount of games already included, it is possible that, over time, the Olympics will become more like the contemporary X Games.

If an increasing number of extreme sports are included as Olympic sports, this may spur the creation of more new, even more radical, extreme sports. A contingent of extreme sports athletes want their sports to remain on the fringe and do not wish to participate in sports that have mainstream components to them. Olympic inclusion would be considered mainstreaming by them and could therefore drive this class of athletes into pursuing even more extreme activities. In fact, some athletes would even perceive X Games inclusion as a form of mainstreaming.

Improved technology surely will continue to change the way in which people participate in extreme sports. Further improvements in parachute design, as just one example, could significantly change the way in which people sky dive, sky surf, and BASE jump, and add even more daredevil elements to those sports.

It seems likely that women will have an ever-increasing amount of participation in extreme sports, as well, in part because of the Olympics' inclusion of sports in which they participate and in part because of advocacy groups such as the Action Sports Alliance (ASA) founded by skateboarder Cara-Beth Burnside. Because of Burnside's work with the ASA, she and another ASA member became members of the X Games selection committee that, to date, had been entirely male. Moreover, the upcoming generation of females have role models to follow and emulate, including Burnside; snowboarders Brooke Shaw, Shannon Dunn, and Barrett Christy; surfers Lisa Andersen and Rachelle Ballard; and mountain bikers Alison Sydor and Alison Dunlap, among others.

OVERVIEW OF THE *ENCYCLOPEDIA OF EXTREME SPORTS*

The *Encyclopedia of Extreme Sports* takes a comprehensive look at the world of extreme sports and its athletes, and at how this phenomenon has changed modern-day sports and contributed to popular culture, overall; to accomplish this, the encyclopedia probes the questions included in this introduction in depth. This volume shares the history of each extreme sport included, along with the potential risks and injuries associated with a particular sport, plus the techniques required to master the sport. The accomplishments of top athletes who have spearheaded these extreme events are highlighted, along with information about the relevant competitions, associations, and organizations. This volume is targeted to high school and undergraduate students, as well as to a general readership.

Because the great majority of extreme athletes are male, we analyze how women fit into this cultural and sociological trend in an in-depth entry that focuses on gender-related challenges connected to extreme sports, including pay disparity; we also include a detailed look at the female-dominated sport of roller derby. We provide bios of female extreme sports athletes, including skateboarding pioneer and advocate Cara-Beth Burnside; paragliding world champion and parahawking pioneer Louise Crandal; ice climbing champion Kim Csizmazia; eight-time inline skating world champion Fabiola da Silva; and up-and-coming junior championship snowboarder Brooke Shaw.

We discuss how extreme sports athletes, both male and female, can manage their levels of risk, and we present the psychological explanations for risk-taking behavior in relationship to extreme sports. We analyze how closely marketing campaigns and sponsorships are intertwined with the world of extreme sports, and how this partnership has affected the athletes, the sponsors, and the overall perception of extreme sports.

Ethical questions raised include the Mount Everest controversy, wherein approximately 40 climbers walked past a dying man, and the degree of ethical responsibility that can be attributed to event organizers when a tragedy occurs. We discuss the relationships between music and extreme sports, and video games and extreme sports, as well as the role that performance art can play in some extreme sports, from extreme ironing to free running. This volume covers the formation and history of the X Games and the Gravity Games, and how they have transformed extreme sports from an alternative subculture activity to an important part of modern-day popular culture.

The *Encyclopedia of Extreme Sports* contains 81 full-length entries, along with six sidebars and an extensive timeline detailing the history and highlights of extreme sports, starting at 18,000 BCE and continuing through contemporary times, with the great majority of the timeline focusing on the 1970s through 2008. Although the prime focus is on extreme sports in the United States, information is included about extreme sports in other countries and continents around the globe. A bibliography containing recommended readings is included, along with photos placed in strategic locations throughout the encyclopedia; in the center of the volume, an eight-page spread of color photos illustrates some of the most intriguing aspects of extreme sporting.

As the world of extreme sports keeps growing, new sports—or subdisciplines of established sports, both extreme and traditional—are created, making it impossible to create a definitive work on extreme sports. To fairly present the current spectrum of activities, the *Encyclopedia of Extreme Sports* contains a mixture of more established extreme sports and less established extreme sports. Some extreme sports that are well known in this volume include skateboarding and snowboarding, while others—such as parkour, adventure racing, and free diving—are less well known, as they are still part of a niche subculture. For many of the niche sports, little information has previously been recorded, outside of blogs, Web sites, and Internet-based forums.

Sports covered in this volume range from water sports, such as barefoot water skiing, kitesurfing, and canoeing and kayaking, to snow sports, including extreme and freeride skiing, snowboarding, and snowmobiling (snocross); air sports such as bungee jumping, sky diving, and sky surfing; bicycle and motorcycle sports; running events, such as the

Ironman Triathlon and the Hotter 'N Hell Hundred; special days, such as Bridge Day for BASE jumpers, and the Holmenkollen Ski Festival for ski jumpers; and more. Entries are presented alphabetically, with cross-references to other pertinent entries listed at the end of the entry for ease of use.

Acknowledgments

I wish to acknowledge the multitude of quirky and talented boomerang throwers who welcomed me into their extreme universe 14 years ago. They gave me my first up close look at a niche sport and its participants by inviting me into their homes, their tournaments, and their lives.

Although there are too many people to thank specifically—and so perhaps I shouldn't try—I want to especially thank boomerang experts Ted Bailey and Gary Broadbent for their patience, knowledge, and time.

Timeline of Extreme Sports

18,000 BCE	Boomerangs were being crafted; one was found in a cave in Krakow, Poland.
2250 BCE	Chinese legend states that Emperor Shun performed the first parachuting act in history.
2000 BCE	Boomerangs—golden-capped ivory sticks and gilt-tipped ebony sticks—were placed in King Tutankhamun's Egyptian pyramid.
2000 BCE	Hawaiians were lava sledding.
2000 BCE	Ancient Egyptians may have boarded down dunes using planks of hardened pottery and wood, which is similar to today's sandboarding.
277 BCE	Dragon boat racing gained a deeper meaning for the Chinese people after they tried to rescue a man named Qu Yuan.
12th century	Indonesian and Polynesian fishermen began powering their canoes with kites.
1600	Flemish engineer Simon Stevin of Bruges, Flanders, created a massive land yacht with two masts.
1760	Belgian ice skater Joseph Merlin introduced the quad skate, the precursor to inline skates, to people in London, England.
1786	Michel-Gabriel Paccard and Jacques Balmat climbed Mont Blanc—the earliest record of mountain climbing.
1797	Andre-Jacques Garnerin flew in a basket that was attached to a parachute, which in turn was attached to a hydrogen balloon.
1859	French acrobat Charles Blondin strung a rope across the Niagara River Gorge located below the falls—and then walked across the wire.
1861	Sondre Norheim of Telemark, Norway, developed a loose heel binding for cross-country skiing (also known as Nordic skiing).
1866	Poughkeepsie, along the Hudson River, was the center of ice yachting in the United States; this area was known as Millionaire's Row.
1870s	Canoe races became an approved sport for the British royalty.
1880	The American Canoe Association formed to serve as an international organization for sporting activities.

1881	The American Challenge Pennant was first held on the Hudson River; today this race is generally considered the most prestigious ice yachting race.
Early 1890s	German inventor Otto "Glider King" Lilienthal created the early form of a hang glider.
1899	Geoffrey Winthrop Young published a book with W. P. Spalding called *The Roof Climber's Guide to Trinity*; from this activity arose urban climbing.
1903	Samuel Cody crossed the English Channel in a canvas boat fueled by a kite that he had invented.
1905	The National Ski Association was founded at Ishpeming, Michigan.
1912	In the first ice climbing competitions, athletes climbed in Courmayeur on the Brenva glacier, located on Mont Blanc in the Italian Alps.
1919	Pogo sticks were imported from Germany into the United States.
1924	Ski jumping was an event in the first Winter Olympics, held in Chamonix, France.
1924	American Motorcyclist Association (AMA) formed to represent the interests of motorcycle riders across the country and to oversee competitions.
1930s	A U.S. citizen named Tom Blake wanted to find an easier way to surf, so he created a device that was the precursor to windsurfing.
1930	The first known parachuting competition took place in Russia.
1932	The mountain-climbing association the *Union Internationale des Associations d'Alpinisme* formed.
1935	Film publicist Leo Seltzer created the first roller derby event, calling it the Transcontinental Roller Derby.
1936	Flatwater racing, using canoes and kayaks, became an Olympic sport.
Late 1940s	Competitive wheelchair sporting events were held, when war veterans who were disabled during World War II began playing basketball in hospitals.
1947	On March 6, Dick Pope was the first person photographed barefooting, which is water skiing while barefoot.
1950s	*National Geographic* photographer Charles Lagus took pictures of a form of bungee jumping in village of Bunlap in the Pentecost Island in the South Pacific.
1950s	This decade saw the beginnings of skateboarding.
1953	In May, Sir Edmund Hillary and Sherpa Tenzing Norgay were the first mountain climbers to successfully scale the summit of Mount Everest at 29,035 feet (8,850 meters).
1960s	People began to go sandboarding down dunes of sand.
1960	Captain Joseph Kittinger jumped from a height of 102,800 feet (31,334 meters), making that the first "supersonic" jump.
1962	On January 30, the Wallenda clan formed a seven-person high wire human pyramid.

1964	Jan and Dean's hit "Sidewalk Surfing" brought skateboarding to the attention of music lovers across the country.
1965	Sherman Poppen, an engineer in Michigan, wanted his daughter Wendy to be able to surf down a snowy slope, so he invented a "snurfer," the precursor of the snowboard.
Late 1960s	The first artificial climbing walls were built in the United Kingdom.
1968	On May 12, Tony Hawk, perhaps the best-known extreme sports athlete, was born in San Diego, California.
1969	Organizers in southern California began setting up dirt courses so that riders could "motocross," using their Sting Ray bicycles; this was the beginning of BMX (bicycle motocross).
1969	On December 4, Greg Noll rode a nearly 25-foot (7.6-meter) wave at Makaha, Hawaii; this ride had been believed impossible to master.
1970s	More than 40 million skateboards were sold and the sport became increasingly associated with punk rock music and the overall punk movement.
1970s	Several groups claimed to invent street luge during this decade; groups were located in Oregon, Oklahoma, California, and even as far away as Austria.
1970	On May 23, the U.S. Snowmobile Association was formed, sanctioning more than 250 races that winter that took place over frozen lakes.
1970	Thirteen-year-old Scott Breithaupt formed the first BMX organization: the Bicycle United Motocross Society (BUMS).
1971	The U.S. Hang Gliding Association was formed.
1972	The North American Land Sailing Association (NALSA) was formed.
1976	On October 26, the first mountain biking race took place in Fairfax, California, down Repack Road, a dirt road that plummets 1,300 feet (396 meters) in less than 2.1 miles (3.4 kilometers).
1977	George Willig climbed the World Trade Center in 1977; he signed his name on the observation deck on the South Tower.
1978	A Florida skater, Alan Gelfand, accidentally discovered how to become "airborne."
1978	On February 18, the first Ironman Triathlon was created, with 15 men competing.
1978	In November, Australia hosted the first barefoot water skiing world championships.
1979	Minnesota brothers Scott and Brennan Olsen modified a pair skates to create a wheeled boot they called "Rollerblades."
1980s	Motocross riders began incorporating trick moves into their competitions; this style of riding is often called freestyle motocross.
1980	The origins of sky surfing began around this time, when sky divers in California started doing freefalls while lying flat on boogie boards.

1981	The National Skateboard Association (NSA) formed.
1981	Phil Smith, Phil Mayfield, and Carl and Jean Boenish create the rules for BASE (Building/Antenna tower/Span/Earth) jumping.
1981	The first international boomerang tournament, between Australia and the United States, was held in Australia.
1982	Ironman Triathlon competitor Julie Moss became severely dehydrated during the race and needed to crawl to the finish line.
1982	The 100-mile (161-kilometer) race Hotter 'N Hell was created to celebrate the centennial of Wichita Falls, Texas.
1983	The National Off-Road Bicycle Association (NORBA) formed to oversee the multitude of mountain biking races.
1983	The United States hosted the first world championships for snowboarding.
Mid-1980s	Between 80 and 90 percent of ski resorts now allowed snowboarders to use their hills.
1984	During the Summer Olympic Games, held in Los Angeles, California, wheelchair athletes performed exhibition track events.
1984	Windsurfing became part of the Olympics in Los Angeles.
1984	Mat Hoffman rides up the curved, bowl-shaped half-pipe used by skateboarders, transforming the sport of BMX.
1984	One of the founders of BASE jumping, Carl Boenish, died in Norway while participating in the sport.
1985	A surfer from San Diego, California, named Tony Finn invented the "skurfer," a board that was the precursor of wakeboarding.
1986	Mountain Dew featured Tony Hawk in one of its commercials.
1987	Bridge Day—the day wherein it is legal to jump off the 876-foot (267-meter) New River Gorge Bridge—was held for the first time.
1987	The United States got its first artificial climbing wall.
1987	Bungee jumping was banned in France after three deaths occurred.
1989	The earliest adventure race, the Raid Gauloises, was held in New Zealand.
1990	The first world championship in mountain biking was held in Purgatory, Colorado, in 1990.
1990	World Freestyle Championships for sky surfing were held in Texas.
1991	The first artificial climbing wall world championships were held in Frankfurt, Germany.
1992	A snowboarding duo from the United States and a surfer from Australia were credited with inventing a board specifically for mountainboarding.
1992	The first extreme wakeboarding competition was held in Orlando, Florida; competitors from around the globe participated, and ESPN televised the competitions.

1993	The National Skateboard Association (NSA) became the World Cup Skateboarding (WCS), organizing events in multiple countries, worldwide.
1993	Bungee jumping was introduced in the United States via a road show.
1993	Ron Semiao, the program director for ESPN2, conceived of the idea of the Extreme Games, soon called the "X Games."
Mid-1990s	The sports of snowboarding and skiing merged to create freeride skiing.
1994	Mountainboarding competitions began in the United States.
1995	The Eco-Challenge race was held for the first time.
1995	The first Extreme Games were held from June 24 to July 1, 1995, in Rhode Island and Vermont.
1996	On June 30, it was announced that the first Winter X Games would be held at the Snow Summit Mountain Resort, located in Big Bear Lake in California.
1996	The name of the Extreme Games was changed to the X Games.
1996	Mountain biking became an Olympic event, when the Olympics were held in Atlanta, Georgia.
1996	Newport, Rhode Island, again served as the venue for the X Games.
1996	The International Free Skiers Association (IFSA) formed.
1996	On May 10, eight people died while attempting to climb Mount Everest.
1996	John Stamstad wanted to ride solo in a team mountainbiking Ultramarathon, so he entered four versions of his own name, beating about half of the teams.
1996	Wheelchair rugby was an exhibition sport at the Summer Paralympic Games.
1997	Mountainboarding competitions began in the United Kingdom.
1997	The first Winter X Games were televised in 198 countries, and translated into 21 languages.
1997	The Summer X Games were held from June 20–28 in San Diego and Oceanside, California; approximately 221,000 people attended the games.
1997	Extreme ironing invented by Phil Shaw in Leicester, England.
1997	Jay Larson and other speed golfers formed the International Speed Golf Association.
1997	Dominique and Bruno Legaignoux created the modern-day kitesurfing launch system.
1997	Felix Baumgartner won the only BASE jumping world championship held to date.
1998	Winter X Games were held at the Crested Butte Mountain Resort in Colorado, adding three new sports: freeskiing, snowmobile snocross, and skiboarding.

1998	Attendance at the Summer X Games continued to rise, as more than 233,000 traveled to Mariner's Point to watch the games.
1998	Tony Hawk started a clothing line for children.
1998	Snocross (extreme snowmobiling) was added to the Winter X Games.
1998	Snowboarding was added to the Winter Olympics, which were held in Nagano, Japan.
1998	Championship parachutist Patrick de Gayardon was killed April 13 when his parachute did not open during a jump.
1999	Activision released *Tony Hawk's Pro Skater* for the PlayStation game system.
1999	The Winter X Games were held at Crested Butte again, with women's free-skiing added to the mix; more than 30,000 fans attended the games.
1999	The Summer X Games were held in San Francisco, California, with nearly 275,000 spectators.
1999	In September the first summer Gravity Games were held in Providence, Rhode Island.
2000	An artificial sand dune park, Sand Master Park, was opened in Florence, Oregon.
2000	The gold medalists in street luge from the previous five X Games raced against one another to determine who was truly King of the Hill.
2000	From February 3–6, the Winter X Games were held in Mount Snow, Vermont, with the largest crowd ever: 83,500.
2000	The Sixth Summer X Games were held from August 17–22 in San Francisco.
2001	Sky surfing was removed from the X Games; from 1995 to 2000, this sport had been the most expensive for X Games organizers.
2001	The Winter X Games were held from February 1–4, again in Mount Snow; motocross big air was added.
2001	The Seventh Summer X Games were held from August 17–22 in Philadelphia, Pennsylvania, with downhill BMX added to the roster of events.
2002	The first World Championships for extreme ironing were held in Munich, Germany.
2002	Members of the United States team swept the men's superpipe event, the first sweep in the Winter Olympics for the United States since 1956.
2002	The Winter X Games were held in Aspen, Colorado, at Buttermilk Mountain; new events were ski slopestyle and ski superpipe.
2002	The Eighth Summer X Games were held in Philadelphia on August 15–19; new events included women's skateboarding and motocross.
2002	Tony Hawk created the Tony Hawk Gigantic Skateboard Tour for ESPN and started the Boom Boom HuckJam Tour.

2002   The Winter Olympics featured extreme sports that were not included in the Olympic Games in their advertising, to attract a younger demographic.

2002   On October 12, Audrey Mestre died while attempting to set an International Association of Free Divers (IAFD) world record.

2003   Cara-Beth Burnside became the first female athlete to have a gold medal in both the Winter and Summer X Games—in snowboarding and skateboarding, respectively.

2003   July 31, Felix Baumgartner completed an unpowered flight across the English Channel in 6 minutes and 22 seconds.

2003   By this time, Ryan Nyquist had won every major BMX dirt competition.

2003   The Seventh Winter X Games were held in Aspen, Colorado, from January 30–February 5; featured sports included motocross, skiing, snowboarding, and snowmobiling.

2003   The Summer X Games were held at Los Angeles, California, on August 14–17; total attendance was 187,141.

2003   Freestyle and street skateboarder John Rodney Mullen, known as "Mutt" or "King," was chosen as the greatest extreme sports athlete ever.

2004   The Rowenta Tour was the first extreme ironing competition held in the United States.

2004   The 10th annual Summer X Games were held in Los Angeles from August 5–8; this year, a new finals-only format was broadcast live.

2004   The Eighth Winter X Games were held in January at Buttermilk Mountain in Aspen, Colorado; the events included motocross, skiing, snowboarding, and snowmobiling.

2004   Dan Brown organized the first-known national pogo stick event, Pogopalooza.

2004   The Women's Flat Track Derby Association (WFTDA) was organized to oversee and promote roller derby events.

2005   The Winter X Games were held in Aspen, Colorado, from January 29–February 1, with ESPN's telecasts reaching 33 percent more households than the year before.

2005   Held in Los Angeles from August 4–7, ESPN broadcast the Summer X Games to more than 75 countries.

2005   The Action Sports Alliance (ASA) formed to "enhance action sports and increase opportunities for women."

2005   Mountain Dew debuted the annual Dew Action Sports Tour (Dew AST) competition.

2006   The Winter X Games were held in Aspen, Colorado, from January 28–31.

2006   The Summer X Games were held in Los Angeles from August 3–6; new sports included rally car racing and BMX big air.

2006	Skateboarding champion Cara-Beth Burnside challenged ESPN in relation to pay disparity between men and women at the X Games.
2006	*Rolling Stone* magazine called snowboarder Shaun White the "coolest kid in America."
2006	Controversy erupted when approximately 40 people climbing Mount Everest did not stop to help a climber in distress; the climber did not survive.
2007	Tom Stone organized the He'enalu/He/eholua Surfing Series, with traditional Hawaiian sledding and surfing.
2007	The Winter X Games were held in Aspen, Colorado, from January 25–28; attendance records were broken with 76,150 spectators.
2007	The Summer X Games were held in Los Angeles from August 2–5.
2007	100 parachutists formed the largest diamond pattern to date, over Lake Wales.
2007	In October, Red Bull sponsored the World's First Freerunning Competition in Vienna, Austria.
2008	Nearly 300 roller derby leagues were active in the United States; leagues also formed in Canada, Australia, Scotland, New Zealand, and Hong Kong, China.
2008	By April, Alain Robert—known as "Spiderman" and the "Human Spider"—had successfully climbed 80 buildings.
2008	For the first time, BMX events were included in the Summer Olympics, held in Beijing, China.

ADVENTURE RACING

Adventure racing is typically a team sport wherein teams race through grueling terrain, attempting to pass through as many checkpoints as possible at the fastest speed possible. In most instances, adventure racers are not provided with information about the course, other than the starting point, before they begin. Therefore, they must be fully prepared to climb mountains, cross rivers, bicycle downhill, run through uneven terrain, rely on ropes to climb or descend, and more. Some races have elements of orienteering included, wherein teams must use compasses and other navigational tools to chart their course. In some cases, support teams are allowed; in other cases, they are not; and in still other cases, support teams are required.

Because participants do not have knowledge about what they will face, most adventure racers analyze what they do know about the region and environment involved, and then they make educated guesses about what challenges lie ahead—and about what gear and equipment to pack.

An international course is generally 500 kilometers (310.7 miles) in length, while national and regional races could be anywhere from 60 to 200 kilometers (37.3 to 124.3 miles). All international racing requires that teams have athletes of both **genders**. Although international races generally have four to five participants on a team, national or regional races may allow one person to participate by himself or herself, or sometimes a team can be as small as two people.

In adventure racing, if one person from a team cannot finish the race, then the entire team is disqualified. Therefore, it is in the best interests of the team to ensure the health and safety of each individual team member. Teams generally do not choose to sleep through the night, as they would lose precious time; choosing when and how long to rest is a crucial decision that the team must make together.

Inherent in adventure racing is the concept of taking care of the environment, with racers focusing on green concepts and taking personal responsibility for their part of protecting the environment. Litter, food waste, and human waste must all be collected and carried with the team to preserve the ecology of the area; what to eat and drink is therefore carefully planned and followed. Adventure racing in the United States is overseen by the United States Adventure Racing Association (USARA), and they strongly advocate that athletes should have a minimal impact on the land and waterways upon which they travel.

People interested in participating in adventure races generally start out by participating in smaller wilderness races, perhaps those that last only 6 hours. Once these athletes are fit enough to complete those races, they then choose races that are longer in distance. Once they can endure a race that lasts an entire day, they then begin training to compete in races that last into the night. And once they can complete a race that lasts 24 hours, they can then begin to compete in adventure racing.

PRECURSORS TO ADVENTURE RACING

It is difficult if not impossible to determine the first adventure race. Races that have many of the same facets as adventure racing occurred at least 15 years before the term of "adventure racing" was used.

One such race is the Karrimor International Mountain Marathon, the first of which took place in 1968. In this race, two people formed a team and then ran a double marathon while carrying along any supplies needed to get through this mountainous region. Inspired by the orienteering championships previously held in Scotland, a mountaineer and orienteer named Gerry Charnley was largely responsible for organizing and overseeing this event.

Adventure racing is a culmination of several different extreme sports that can take place in the wilderness; a similar concept is the wilderness triathlon. In these triathlons, competitors need to race through rough, uncharted territory using three different

Adventure racers tackle a grueling week-long race in Dublin, Ireland. (AP Photo/Valerie Sullivan)

athletic skills. An example is the 1980 Alpine **Ironman Triathlon** held in New Zealand; participants were required to run, paddle, and ski to the finish line. Also in New Zealand is the annual Coast to Coast Race, which began in 1983 and continues to this day. The original race had 79 competitors; by 2007, there were 840 participants.

In 1982, the Alaska Mountain Wilderness Classic began. This race lasts six days over 150 miles (241.4 kilometers) of terrain; the course location changes every three years. Participants are required to carry with them all that they need to survive and to complete the race.

ROGAINE

Adventure racing bears a close resemblance to a little-known extreme sport called "rogaine." In rogaine, a team may need to cross more than 40 miles (64.4 kilometers) of off-trail terrain in a 24-hour period; some elite teams can surpass 60 miles (96.6 kilometers) in a day's race. This distance of 40 to 60 miles of hiking may involve 5,000-plus feet (1,524 meters) of elevation gain. Maps are handed out 2 hours before the start of a particular rogaine, and teams can use this time to chart their course; a key consideration is where and how a team could most easily travel through approximately 8 hours of darkness.

Typically, team members will each carry a backpack containing about 10 pounds (4.5 kilograms) of gear and supplies. This includes apparel, such as a sun hat, sunglasses, a rain coat, new pairs of socks, and an extra pair of hiking shoes. Other important items include a watch, a whistle, a headlamp and extra batteries, one or two compasses, first aid items (such as ankle supports/Ace bandages, ibuprofen, sunscreen, lip balm, Vaseline, blister pads, and water purification tablets), and more.

Although rogaine is a race, the purpose of rogaine is not just to finish as quickly as possible, but also to be cognizant of the beauty of nature. One rogaine athlete puts it this way: "Hear the nighttime call of the owls and the dawn warble of the meadowlarks, be mesmerized by the wind's rhythmic ripple in the tall spring grasses, take a moment to look into the center of the blooming wildflowers, admire the deer antler you found next to the water hole" (Godino and Bartholomew n.d., 1).

EVOLUTION OF ADVENTURE RACING

Although it is nearly impossible to pinpoint the first race that could truly be called an adventure race, many sources consider the Raid Gauloises in New Zealand to be that race. In 1989, some French advocates of wilderness sports, including journalist Gérard Fusil, discussed creating a wilderness race with assistance from people in New Zealand. This led to the organization of a wilderness race in the Raid Gauloises (or the Grand Traverse) region of New Zealand, a remote and beautiful landscape. New Zealanders and French athletes worked together to design this race; coed teams of five people each participated, with New Zealand athletes winning first, second, and third places in the race.

Two years later, the New Zealanders charted a different course following the Southern Traverse; the course was more than 400 kilometers (248.5 miles) in length and this race became an annual event. By the late 1990s, teams from a variety of countries were participating.

Eco-Challenge

Perhaps the best-known adventure race, the Eco-Challenge, was held in Utah in 1995. Before the event began, its founder Mark Burnett collaborated with the Discovery Channel to ensure media coverage of this race. Burnett, who was British, had participated in two of the New Zealand events, and he knew that he wanted to emphasize the importance of preserving the wilderness via the Eco-Challenge.

Burnett also wanted people to recognize and honor the cultural differences among race participants from various countries; he believed that was far more important than winning—or perhaps even completing—the race. The following year, the course was located in British Columbia, Canada; this terrain was so challenging that only 14 teams—out of the 70 that had entered—completed the course.

The term "adventure racing" began to be used for this type of wilderness racing after the Eco-Challenge, when a journalist named Martin Dugard first used that term to describe what had occurred.

Primal Quest

In 2002, a new adventure race debuted in the United States, called the Primal Quest. It was first held in Telluride, Colorado. The 2003 race was held at Lake Tahoe on the border between California and Nevada; in 2004, it was held on San Juan Island in Washington. The 2003 and 2004 races were televised.

A tragic accident occurred during the 2004 race when a top-rated rogainer, Nigel Aylott from Australia, was killed while his team was leading the race. The race was to last between 5 and 10 days, covering 400 miles (643.7 kilometers) that required trekking, mountain biking, skating/scootering, ocean kayaking, ropes, mountaineering, river paddling, and orienteering. Two and a half days into the race, it was reported that Aylott's team had not yet stopped to sleep. The team began using ropes to climb a rocky slope when a boulder loosened and struck Aylott in the head; he was not wearing a helmet, as they were only required to do in the biking portion of the race, and he was killed.

The athlete who had been standing on the boulder was seriously injured and airlifted off the mountain. Another competitor suffered minor injuries.

Primal Quest was not held in 2005. In 2006, the 420-mile (675.9-kilometer) race was located in a Utah desert where temperatures exceeded 110° Fahrenheit (43.3° Celsius). Organizers of this race did not permit support teams; athletes were involved in mountain biking, trekking, horseback riding, technical rope skills, mountaineering, kayaking, and whitewater swimming.

The 2008 race will be held by Bozeman, Montana. This race will cover 450 miles (724 kilometers) with more than 100,000 feet (30,480 meters) of elevation gain; support crews are required in this race.

Adventure Racing Risks and Injuries

The most common injuries and conditions experienced by adventure racers include dehydration, overheating, and chilling, along with blisters, bleeding, and infections. Some athletes may experience injuries to joints or tissues. In many instances, other team members may decide to help the injured or weakened racer until he or she recovers enough to continue. When a team member experiences diarrhea, however, it often weakens the person to the degree that he or she cannot continue any further.

Because of the grueling nature of adventure racing, some racers experience panic attacks and even hallucinations. Exhaustion plays a role, which may affect the judgment of the team members and prevent them from observing all safety rules. If team members do not trust one another or work well with one another, the chances for successfully completing the course drop considerably, while the likelihood of injuries may rise.

A study, *Epidemiology of Injuries in Adventure Racing Athletes*, was conducted to determine the demographics of adventure racers in the United Kingdom, plus the number of injuries that occur during this activity. For this research, 300 adventure racing participants were asked to report injuries that had occurred over the past 18 months. Seventy-three percent of the athletes reported some injuries; the most common injuries were as follows: knee (30 percent), ankle (23 percent), lower back (12 percent), shin (12 percent), and Achilles' tendon (12 percent). Sixty-one percent of these injuries occurred while running, with 22 percent of them attributed to cycling.

Acute injuries were sustained by the following: advanced athletes (44 percent), intermediate athletes (35 percent), and beginning athletes (19 percent). Chronic injuries were sustained by the following: advanced athletes (59 percent), intermediate athletes (54 percent), and beginning athletes (56 percent). Chronic injuries were sustained as follows: the knee was most often affected (30.6 percent), the shin was affected (12.1 percent), the lower back was affected (12.1 percent), and the Achilles' tendon was affected (12.1 percent).

Adventure racers believed that 74 percent of chronic injuries occurred because of running and 9 percent of these injuries were attributed to cycling.

Overall, acute injuries occur because of the terrain involved or because the athletes were not receiving adequate rest days, or not enough time was spent strengthening core muscles or on flexibility exercises. Acute injuries caused an athlete to lose an average of 28 training days, while chronic or overuse injuries caused downtime of 24 days. The athletes received medical assistance for 44 percent of the injuries.

See also Hotter 'N Hell Hundred; Stamstad, John

ALPINE SCRAMBLING

Alpine scrambling is a form of off-trail mountaineering that involves quickly climbing what are often vertical sections of a mountain. Scrambling is an activity that is between hiking and climbing; a difficult hike up the mountain, for example, may also be described as an easy scramble, and a difficult scramble may be described as an easier form of rock or **mountain climbing**. If a person is able to climb a section of the mountain without needing to use his or her hands, then the activity is considered hiking, rather than scrambling. If full-fledged climbing gear is required, then the activity is considered rock or mountain climbing, rather than scrambling.

Alpine scrambling allows people to access remote areas that are seldom seen by other humans. For many scramblers, their goal is to ascend a mountain to be in a position to appreciate that beautiful scenery. To be successful in this endeavor, a scrambler needs stamina, an ability to climb rocks, and to swim, if necessary. If heights bother a person, then he or she is not a good candidate for scrambling.

According to the Yosemite Decimal System, on a difficulty scale of one to five, scrambling rates a three; hiking is considered a one, while technical free climbing is considered a five. In the United Kingdom, scrambling routes are rated from Grade 1 to Grade 4, with the level of difficulty rising as the numbers do.

Experienced scramblers caution beginners that scrambling is not "easy." It is a physically demanding activity as climbers are exposed to the elements and its dangers.

Before beginning a climb, scramblers should memorize landmarks that will help orient them on their excursion, including the return to level ground. Loose rocks can be hazardous; so can water, as slipping can lead to a fatal fall. It is recommended that people scramble in groups for safety reasons; in some locales, less experienced scramblers may need to be "spotted"—or given assistance—by another person. Moreover, one scrambler can give advice to another to help the group scramble over an especially tricky spot on the mountain.

Scramblers who have ascended a particular mountain sometimes post information about that site on the Internet for other scramblers to access and use. Guide books that provide this type of information are also available.

ALPINE SCRAMBLING EQUIPMENT

Scramblers should own a pair of hiking boots; waterproof boots are advised if scrambling near water. A rain jacket is recommended, as weather in the mountains can change quickly. A map and compass or a Global Positioning System (GPS) device are also recommended.

Scramblers can choose between summer and winter scrambles, the latter of which requires snowshoes and perhaps some **ice climbing** gear; avalanches are a danger during winter scrambling.

Some scramblers will not take along a rope for emergency situations, believing that this taints the sport; for some, the feeling of ascending a mountain without outside aid is the essence of scrambling. For those who are willing to take a rope, one with a minimum length of 98.4 feet (30 meters) and a minimum diameter of 0.35 inches (9 millimeters) is advised. If intending to use a rope in scrambling emergencies, harnesses and climbing accessories would also be needed.

ALPINE SCRAMBLING RISKS AND INJURIES

Scramblers need to be aware of weather conditions and should choose climbing days with less hazardous weather. Injuries sustained can include sprains, strains, and fractures and, although not frequent, fatalities do occur. On one mountain, An Teallach in Inverness in the United Kingdom, four people were killed and one seriously injured within a period of a few short years, all in the same area of the mountain. In 2004, a man was killed in Boulder County, Colorado, after falling more than 200 feet (61 meters) by a waterfall in Boulder Canyon; his companion was critically injured, and it took the efforts of two dozen rescue team members and 20 volunteer firefighters to get the injured man off the mountain and to the hospital.

ARTIFICIAL WALL CLIMBING

Artificial climbing walls (ACWs) are indoor structures, crafted out of brick, wood, reinforced board, steel, or aluminum, with grips for hands and feet so that people can climb up them; these walls are covered in material that gives them the appearance of outdoor rock. Climbers are usually tethered to prevent falls and injuries; if climbing on a relatively low bouldering wall, ropes are not always used, but padding is then placed on the floor to break a fall.

Rock climbing novices use these walls to practice climbing and to develop their balance and climbing finesse, as well as their flexibility and strength. Experienced outdoor climbers may use these walls to climb during inclement weather. There are also ACW competitions held with athletes ascending laid-out routes; athletes are not allowed to see the routes ahead of time; cannot watch competitors climb; and are usually judged on their speed and the height they reach. These routes are generally between 49 to 60 feet (14.9 to 18.3 meters) high.

DEVELOPMENT OF THE SPORT

Artificial wall climbing began in the United Kingdom when, in the late 1960s, climbers stuck rocks onto an outdoor wall. Although this provided climbers with a venue, this activity suffered from the same weather-related disadvantages as those found when climbing natural rock. Therefore, indoor climbing walls began to be built and used, often in clubs and schools in England.

Emergency personnel are on the scene of a fatality after a young woman falls from a climbing wall. (AP Photo/*Columbia Daily Tribune*, Jenna Isaacson)

In 1987, an indoor climbing wall was created in Seattle, Washington. There, teenagers such as Katie Brown, Chris Sharma, and Charlotte Durif gained attention for their skill. Over the next decade, more than twenty-five American universities added indoor climbing walls to their facilities and other indoor facilities were also built in the United States.

In 1987, the Soviet Union started holding speed climbing events; in 1988, a world championship event was organized, with the first competition being held in Frankfurt, Germany, in 1991. These events are now held in Germany every other year. The World Youth Championships were established in 1992 and were first held in Basel, Switzerland. Artificial wall climbing is also part of the **X Games**.

Usually, competitors race in rounds, with the winner moving on to another round and the loser being eliminated; often there is a double elimination rule. In World Cup races, the winner hits a buzzer at the top of the route and then jumps off the wall; their fall is stopped after a descent of 5 to 6 meters (16.4 to 19.7 feet).

Indoor **ice climbing** facilities are also being built, including the Tiso Glasgow in Glasgow, Scotland, and the Vertical Chill Tower House in London, England.

ARTIFICIAL WALL CLIMBING EQUIPMENT

Artificial wall climbing equipment includes rock climbing shoes; a climbing harness with a belay device; and a chalk bag to hang around the waist and use to create hand traction.

See also Mountain Climbing

BAREFOOT WATER SKIING

In the sport of barefoot water skiing—or barefooting—participants water ski behind a motorboat without using water skis. The boat must travel at greater speeds than in traditional water skiing, generally at about 40 to 45 miles (64.4 to 96.6 kilometers) per hour compared with a maximum of 24 miles (38.6 kilometers) per hour in traditional water skiing. The skiers wear padded "barefoot suits" to protect them whenever they slam into the water.

When preparing to barefoot, most skiers lie back in the water while holding onto a rope with a handle that is attached to the boat. As the boat begins to accelerate, the skier digs his or her heels into the water while pointing his or her toes upward, while being secured by a water line at the insteps of their feet. From the moment that they rise to a standing position in the water, they must diligently maintain their balance.

According to Natalie Angley, spokesperson for USA Water Ski, approximately 5,800 people water ski barefoot in the United States, when including both competitive and recreational skiers (Kim 2006). USA Water Ski is the national governing body for barefooting.

HISTORY OF BAREFOOTING

According to the Water Ski Hall of Fame, the original barefoot water skiers were A. G. Hancock and Dick Pope, Jr. Pope began performing in ski shows at the Cypress Gardens in Florida at the age of 12. His parents owned the facility and, when soldiers asked when the next water ski show started, his family had Pope put one on for them. Prior to that, the park did not have a water ski show. Pope won four consecutive national water skiing titles, starting in 1947, and, in 1950, he won the world championship. What he perhaps is remembered for most, though, is being photographed on March 6, 1947, as he water skied—without skis.

Evidence suggests that the 17-year-old A. G. Hancock had actually tried barefooting before Pope's performance, but the photograph of Pope was solid evidence of the activity. It is also possible that water skier Chuck Sligh, Jr. had initially conceived of the idea to ski barefoot and passed that idea along to Hancock to try. Sligh is better known for having set the first water ski jump record of 49 feet (14.9 meters).

The sport of barefooting gained popularity and the first competition was held in 1950 in Cypress Gardens, Florida, with the person who skied the longest being named the winner. Pope was in the lead, but Emilio Zamudio from Mexico ended up winning the competition.

Innovations came about quickly while this sport was still new. Ken Tibado of Lake Wales, Florida, created the beach start in 1956; in 1958, Joe Cash succeeded with the first deepwater start. In 1960, when Don Thompson and Terry Vance were performing a routine together in the Ozarks in Missouri, Vance began to fall; after his feet spun around, Thompson helped him stand back up—thereby inventing the "tumbleturn" by sheer accident. In 1961, Randy Rabe of St. Petersburg, Florida, began incorporating backward stunts into his skiing. In about 1967, Australians began adding jumps to their barefooting routines.

The first national-level competition was held in Australia in April 1963. The first European championships were held in London in August 1976, with 18 men and one woman participating. At the time, national championships were already being held in England, the Netherlands, Italy, Belgium, South Africa, New Zealand, and Australia.

A U.S. water skier, John Hacker, visited Australia in 1977 and returned with the knowledge of barefoot jumping, expanding the scope of that subdiscipline of barefooting. In 1978, five regional competitions were held in the United States and the first U.S. Nationals were held in Waco, Texas. That same year, the American Barefoot Club (ABC) was formed as an affiliate of the American Water Ski Association.

Australia hosted the first world championships in the city of Canberra in November 1978. At the world championships, 54 people from 10 countries competed, performing jumps and tricks, and skiing wake slalom—or, in other words, skiing around the waves created by the motorboats.

In 1980, the president of ABC published a book on barefooting, *Barefooting: John Gillette's Complete Guide to Barefoot Water Skiing.*

In 1987, Dick Pope and four others created the first five-person pyramid in their sport and slow but steady growth continued to occur in the sport of barefooting. By 2006, approximately 180 skiers from 16 countries participated in the world championships. In the 2007 World Barefoot Water Ski Championships, the U.S. athletes captured three of the top five positions for women; two men from South Africa—Heinrich Sam and Andre de Villiers—were top in the world for men, with Keith St. Onge from the United States coming in third.

The 2008 World Barefoot Water Ski Championships will be held in Otaki, New Zealand; world competitions are now overseen by the International Water Ski Federation.

BAREFOOTING COMPETITIONS

Slalom Event

Skiers are given two opportunities of 15 seconds each to cross between the first and second wakes (waves generated by the motorboats). A one-footed full crossing is worth a full point; a two-footed full crossing is worth a half point; and various partial crossings are worth various fractions of points.

Mario Moser takes first place in the Male Jump competition of the 10th World Barefoot Water Skiing Championship. (AP Photo/Ann Heisenfelt)

Trick Event

The skiers are given two 15-second opportunities to perform flips and turns and other tricks that judges rate; judges also award points based on the startup trick performed (the trick that the skier used to stand up).

Jumping Event

Skiers jump off ramps that are only about 18 inches (45 centimeters) high compared with the 5 to 6 feet (1.5 to 1.8 meters) in traditional water ski jumping. Competitors get three opportunities to complete the longest jump; a distance of 95 feet (29 meters) has already been achieved.

Jumping has been a controversial part of barefoot competitions since the earliest days. Gillette, author and former president of ABC, has lobbied to have jumping removed from any sanctioned competitions, believing it dangerous. Although some members agreed with him, he did not succeed in removing the jumping element of barefooting.

In 1978, U.S. jumper William Farrell began "bum jumping," which meant that he slid up the ramp on his buttocks; the bum jumps achieved were long but unpredictable. After the 1988 world competitions, it was ruled that barefoot jumping must be performed by foot; Rod Trevillian of Australia won the last bum jumping contest.

Mike Seipel of the United States invented the inverted jump move by sheer accident; his feet slipped on the ramp and went out behind him, resulting in a longer jump. In 1984, Seipel set a world jump record of 65.9 feet (20.1 meters); he broke his own record in 1988, jumping 69.2 feet (21.1 meters). In 1990, he broke his record again, this time with a 72.8-foot (22.2-meter) jump. Other athletes recognized how successful Seipel was with his inverted jump and they began to imitate him. By the mid-1990s, a 90-foot-plus (27.4-meter) jump was needed to win a major tournament, with a 100-foot (30.5-meter) jump seen as the next major goal to achieve.

Some barefoot competitions feature endurance events, including figure eight events. In figure eight events, pairs of competitors are towed behind one boat, crossing wakes until one of the competitors either falls or drops out of the competition because of fatigue. The winner moves on to another round of competition until a final winner is determined.

In team endurance events, the goal is to ski long distance, up to about 45 miles (72.4 kilometers). Each team has a boat and skiers take turns skiing down the river in a relay race format. The first team that crosses the finish line wins. According to Doug Winters, who has participated in endurance events, "It's agonizing during the race. You don't experience the joy until the end. Then everybody walks away saying, 'That was awesome. I can barely stand up, but that was awesome'" (Bleyer 2006).

Barefooting was included in the Summer **X Games** from 1995 through 1998, with Justin Seers winning in 1995, Ron Scarpa winning in 1996, and Peter Fleck winning in 1997 and 1998.

BAREFOOTING EQUIPMENT

Before competing, an athlete must have a boat approved by ABC's Towboat Committee. Some boats are specifically made for barefooting, while others have a more general use but are still approved for the sport. Barefoot boats need stronger engines than boats used for traditional water skiing, meaning 400 horsepower rather than 250; these boats require 50 percent more fuel, which makes this sport more costly.

Skiers wear a padded wetsuit with built-in flotation devices, which costs approximately $150, along with padded shorts, which adds about $50 to the price. Ropes used by barefooters have handles with plastic tubing. Beginning athletes can train with booms, which are long poles that hang out of the boat.

Barefoot skiers carry a tube of Super Glue, used to glue shut any cuts on their feet that are sustained during competition. Some participants have been caught breaching the rules, putting duct tape on their feet to protect them against injuries caused by floating debris.

BAREFOOTING RISKS AND INJURIES

Risks are higher in barefoot skiing than in traditional water skiing, in large part because of the higher speeds needed in barefooting. The most common minor complaint is that a skier had the "wind knocked out of him." Ruptured eardrums are another common injury, as is shoulder damage caused by holding on to a rope after a fall. Toes need to be pointed upward to avoid broken foot bones. To avoid common injuries, skiers should drop their ropes as soon as a fall begins; avoid waves; and stay away from high-traffic areas in the water. It is nearly impossible for skiers to avoid the debris and pollutants found in modern-day waterways, and feet sliced by these objects can be painful.

According to "A Review of Water-Skiing Safety in the USA," a paper presented at the Tenth International Symposium on Skiing Trauma & Safety in Austria in May 1993, severe neck injuries can occur in barefoot water skiing (Roberts 1993). Skiers refer to the type of fall that sometimes results in serious neck injuries as the "scorpion fall." The skier falls forward and his or her feet hit the back area; this move can damage the back, the spinal cord, and the neck.

Competitive barefoot skiers sustain significant injuries but generally continue to participate after the injuries have healed. Water skiing champion Sherri Morse has suffered from several injuries, including two back fractures, a split knee, shoulder injuries, and ruptured eardrums. Another female champion, Tenley Cederstrand, has cracked her sternum, injured both of her knees, and torn her hamstring twice.

See also Kite Surfing; Wakeboarding; Windsurfing

BASE (BUILDING/ANTENNA TOWER/SPAN/EARTH) JUMPING

What is more dangerous than leaping off of a tall building? Jumping off a structure that is much closer to the ground, perhaps only 100 to 200 feet (30.5 to 61 meters)—and that is exactly what many BASE (Building/Antenna tower/Span/Earth) jumpers regularly do. The risks involved in this sport—malfunctioning parachutes, landing on rocks, running into electrical wires, and more—are significant.

Throughout much of modern history, people have attempted jumps off of buildings and natural outcroppings. As early as 1879, H. P. Peer jumped off the Upper Suspension Bridge near Niagara Falls and, in 1912, Frederick Law jumped off the Statue of Liberty. In the mid-1950s, an Italian dentist jumped off cliffs while wearing a parachute. In 1966, a jumper leapt off of the south World Trade tower—and was promptly arrested. Also in 1966, experienced sky divers Michael Pelky and Brian Schubert leapt off El Capitan in the Yosemite Valley. Pelky broke his ankle after colliding with the cliff and Schubert was more seriously injured when his parachute malfunctioned 15 feet (4.6 meters) above ground.

In 1978, Carl Boenish filmed a 3,000-foot (915-meter) jump off the El Capitan cliff over Yosemite National Park, which remains a popular jumping site today. In 1980, Kenneth Swyers was dropped off the top of the St. Louis Arch; Swyers planned to jump but instead slid down to his death. In 1992, John Vincent successfully jumped off of the arch. Although controversy remains over whether he was dropped off the top of the arch by a pilot or whether he used suction cups to ascend the arch, he did indeed survive his jump. He was then arrested by the Federal Bureau of Investigation for jumping off of a national monument and he spent 90 days in prison.

The name (and parameters) of BASE jumping was created by Phil Smith, Phil Mayfield, and Carl and Jean Boenish in 1981. A "span" jump must take place off of a bridge or arch, while an "Earth" jump must occur off of a cliff or another type of natural formation. Most jumpers would concur that a "building" must be a structure that can be occupied by people. When a BASE jumper leaps from a fixed object, his or her parachute is not inflated; rather, he or she must activate the parachute while freefalling. Moreover, a BASE jumper does not have a default parachute in case of malfunctions.

It therefore is recommended by BASE jumpers that a new participant to the sport should have successfully completed 100 sky dives before trying BASE jumping, as freefall skills are vital to prevent serious injury or death.

Smith and Carl Boenish created the BASE Association and, whenever a person completes all four types of jumps, he or she receives an official BASE number. Other than the assignment of a BASE number, though, this sport is much less regulated than many others. BASE associations, such as the Cliff Jumpers Association of America and the Alliance of Backcountry Parachutists, advocate for jumpers rather than regulate their activities. That said, in 2005, a group of French jumpers created an organization that was merged into the French Federation of Alpine Clubs (FFCA); this affiliation has given these BASE jumpers access to personal injury insurance coverage and some coverage of legal fees if arrested in a national park while involved in a BASE jumping activity.

A significant challenge faced by BASE jumpers worldwide is to avoid crashing into the building, antenna tower, span, or Earth from where the athlete has just jumped. BASE jumpers have therefore adopted the tracking strategy used by sky divers. Tracking refers to body positions that encourage forward motion in freefall that would take them away from the fixed object as they fall. Jumpers also use the rectangular ram-air parachutes used by sky divers, rather than the older rounder parachutes. Jumpers face challenges in climbing buildings in pursuit of their sport, because most buildings have security features in places to prevent people from reaching the roof.

Moreover, the risk involved with BASE jumping is significant, as highlighted in an article published by Monica A. Seff, Viktor Gecas, and James H. Frey, "Birth Order, Self-Concept and Participation in Dangerous Sports" in the *Journal of Psychology* (Seff et al. 1993). In this survey, extreme sports participants were asked to rank activities from zero (0), meaning little risk, to nine (9), meaning dangerous/risk to life. Results were as follows: BASE jumping (7.5), **hang gliding** (6.6), motorcycle racing (6.3), **mountain climbing** (6.0), parachute jumping (5.0), scuba diving (4.1), piloting a plane (3.2), and snow **skiing** (2.9).

BASE jumping often involves trespassing on private property and perhaps picking locks to climb a building. Moreover, innocent passersby can be injured during the landing, which could lead to criminal charges. In 2006, Jeb Ray Corliss IV dressed up in a fat suit to disguise himself as a tourist visiting the Empire State Building. His true intention was to jump off the roof; although he reached that spot, he was arrested before he could jump, and charged with criminal trespassing, reckless endangerment, and assault while resisting arrest. If a jumper is caught BASE jumping in a National Park in the United States, the fine is $2,500 and the equipment will most likely be impounded.

Since 1981, nearly 100 deaths have been recorded of BASE jumpers—in large part because the parachute used must deploy quickly to prevent a deadly impact upon hitting the ground. One of these deaths occurred in Norway in 1984—that of Carl Boenish, one of the sport's founders. Although no-one witnessed his death, it is believed that he crashed into a cluster of rocks.

Although there is no "safe" way to BASE jump, experienced jumpers have found ways to make the sport safer. Safety equipment includes a parachute that most likely has been modified to open more quickly than originally intended. Modern-day jumpers choose ram-air parachutes that give them more control over their speed and direction. In 1978, however, jumpers used the old-fashioned round parachutes that were not as easily controlled. A parachute that is specially designed for BASE jumping generally costs between $1,200 and $1,500.

The pilot chute that deploys the main parachute is either kept in the jumper's hand or placed in an easily accessible pocket; in BASE jumping, athletes generally use larger pilot chutes than those used in sky diving. They seldom bother with a backup parachute, however, because if the main chute does not work, there is probably not time to deploy another. The BASE jumper then scans the area for potential hazards, which might include electrical wires or jutting rocks, and she chooses the best "exit point" by visualizing the safest trip down—and then the jump takes place.

To put this sport into perspective, a sky diver generally leaps from an airplane about 2,000 feet (610 meters) above ground. If a BASE athlete jumps from a point only 250 feet (76 meters) from the Earth, then he or she literally only has seconds to land; therefore parachute deployment must occur almost instantaneously. If, however, the jumper chooses a spot such as the Angel Falls in Venezuela or El Capitan, the distance to the ground is 3,000 feet (915 meters) and the jumper can enjoy the luxury of stowing the pilot chute in a nearby pocket.

The majority of BASE jumpers live in North America, Europe, the United Kingdom, Australia, the Russian Federation, and South Africa. Because of the illegal nature of much of BASE jumping, participant numbers are not well known. It is known, however, that more than 1,000 people have received a BASE number and some estimates suggest that there are 5,000 to 10,000 jumpers around the world. It is also estimated that one in every seven BASE jumpers either becomes injured or killed while pursuing the sport and, by 2006, the number of recorded fatalities reached 97.

Perhaps the most popular BASE bridge is the New River Gorge Bridge, where U.S. Route 19 spans the New River by Fayetteville, West Virginia. Once a year, the city opens the bridge up for legal BASE jumping and celebrates the sport with a festival. The event is collectively known as Bridge Day. Another popular location is the Perrine Bridge over the Snake River in Twin Falls, Idaho, where jumping is legal, year-round.

Perhaps because of the sheer audacity of the athletes, BASE jumping has been covered by major television networks, including the Australian Broadcasting Corporation, the Outdoor Life Network, and the American Broadcasting Company. This sport has also been featured in several James Bond movies.

See also Baumgartner, Felix; Bridge Day; de Gayardon, Patrick

BAUMGARTNER, FELIX (1969–)

Felix Baumgartner is an accomplished and experienced **BASE (Building/Antenna tower/Span/Earth) jumper** who is known for his daring, dramatic—and even death-defying—feats; he is also known as "BASE 502," as he was the 502nd person to complete jumps in all four arenas: building, antenna tower, span, and Earth. His nicknames include "Fearless Felix" and "God of the Skies." He has also been called the "Human Fly."

Baumgartner, who is a stunt coordinator, a sky diver, a helicopter pilot, and the operator of a freefall camera to record sky dives accomplished by others, is best known for setting world records. These records include setting the world's highest BASE jump and the world's lowest BASE jump, both achieved in 1999—and then breaking the high jump world record again in 2007. In general, Baumgartner does not ask permission from property owners before jumping from a site, believing that he generates more media attention when he performs without permission.

His main sponsor is Red Bull, the energy drink that lists the following benefits on its Web site: "improves performance, increases concentration and reaction speed,

Felix Baumgartner jumps from the arm of the giant Jesus statue above the Brazilian metropolis Rio de Janeiro. (AP Photo/Wolfgang Luif)

increases endurance and stimulates metabolism." Interviews with Baumgartner are posted on this site; one question posed to him asks why he has advised people to stop worrying about death.

He responds by saying that—

> Every one of us has to die at some point—so there's no point living in fear of it. Unfortunately it's easier said than done when you're waiting for three hours at a cave in Oman for the ideal conditions to make the jump—and thinking about the twelve B.A.S.E Jump colleagues who died last year; or that the nearest hospital is five driving hours away. (http://www.redbull.com/en/ArticlePage.1175169684381-957931423/htmlArticlePage.action)

Baumgartner was born in Salzburg, Austria, on April 20, 1969. He worked at Porsche as a machine fitter until drafted into military service; for the military, he served as a tank driver and helicopter pilot until deemed to be a troublemaker who was not fit for the military. He began parachuting in 1986, while still a teenager. In 1996, he leapt from the New River Gorge Bridge on **Bridge Day**, completing his first ever BASE jump.

In 1997, he became the world championship BASE jumper after winning the only world championship competition held to date; out of the approximately 350 participants, Baumgartner was the only European. In 1999, Baumgartner wanted to set the record for the world's highest jump by jumping off of the Petronas Twin Towers located in Kuala Lumpur, Malaysia; the jump was from 1,479 feet (451 meters). Baumgartner disguised himself as a businessman and carried forged identification in case he was stopped while attempting to ascend to the top of the towers; his briefcase hid his parachute and video camera. Baumgartner successfully reached the top, jumped, and set the world record.

In 1999, he also leapt from the statue of Christ the Redeemer in Rio de Janeiro, Brazil, to set the world record for the shortest distance between the spot of the jump itself and the ground; the distance was 95 feet (29 meters). To reach the spot from where he wished to launch, he shot an arrow over the right arm of the statue with a crossbow; the arrow carried a steel cable to which Baumgartner attached ropes so that he could climb the statue. Because of the relatively short distance between the top of the statue and the ground, Baumgartner had only 1.5 seconds to open his parachute; he later said that it was scary to know that only 1 second stood between him and his death. He also knew that he needed to avoid the visitor's platform on the statue on his way down, as well as the edge of the Corcovado Mountains.

In 2000, he and Ueli Gegenschatz from Switzerland completed a successful jump from the Forth Road Bridge located in the United Kingdom; because BASE jumping was not legal there, the pair escaped in a dinghy, fleeing before being captured by police.

When Baumgartner wished to jump 343 meters (1,125 feet) from a bridge spanning the Parne River by Millau, France, he climbed up a 230-meter (755-foot) column, without securing himself to the bridge in any way. He climbed in the early morning hours to escape detection by the guards who watched over the bridge. He then hid until his camera operator told him it was safe to jump without detection.

Baumgartner spent years developing an aerodynamic suit that would protect him from extreme cold. The suit had a 6-foot (1.8-meter) carbon wing that provided the ultimate in freefall, and this gear came equipped with an oxygen tube so that Baumgartner could breathe under extreme conditions. The wing was designed by Rudiger Kunz, a leading aerodynamics expert. Baumgartner tested out this suit and wing while strapped to a Porsche that traveled 199 miles (320 kilometers) per hour. His ultimate goal was to cross the English Channel without using powered flight.

His actual freefall flight across the English Channel took place on July 31, 2003; it began over Dover and lasted 6 minutes, 22 seconds. (Before his unpowered flight, air traffic controllers agreed to give him a 30-minute window to complete his journey.)

He traveled across the 22-mile (35-kilometer) section of the channel after being dropped from a height more than 30,000 feet (9,000 meters); this is higher than the peak of Mount Everest. During this short time, he endured temperatures of $-40°$ Fahrenheit ($-40°$ Celsius) and traveled at speeds up to 225 miles (360 kilometers) per hour. Upon landing safely, he gave photographers the two-fingered peace sign.

The carbon wing that powered this flight had the logo and name of Red Bull splashed across the center; the ends of the wings were reserved for advertising Intertops.com, a popular casino on the Internet.

In September 2004, Baumgartner jumped 355 feet (108 meters) from the Bridge of the Americas, which connects North and South America. Upon landing, he and his photographer were arrested by Panamanian police; they remained in prison for one week. Also in 2004, he jumped from the 193-foot (59-meter) bridge on the Greek Corinth Canal.

He considers his 7.5-second headfirst jump into the Mamet Cave, located in the Velebit National Park in Croatia, to perhaps be the most dangerous feat of his attempted and accomplished. He prepared for 10 months for this 2004 jump and he relied on a 40-person support team throughout the jump. To prepare, Baumgartner would jump from a hot air balloon that was at a height that precisely duplicated the distance of the Mamet Cave jump.

Baumgartner has visited several other places around the globe, to set records in various other countries. As one example, he has jumped from the highest building in Sweden, the Turning Torso that stands at 190 meters (623 feet). The building itself represents the human torso, and it twists 90 degrees from the bottom of the structure to the top.

On January 30, 2006, he jumped from the highest building in Latin America, the 738-foot (225-meter) Torre Mayor located in Mexico City, Mexico. Afterward, he left in a Hummer to avoid potential arrest. Mexico City officials did levy a fine against Red Bull, the company that sponsored this jump; the fine was 7,154 pesos, which would equate to a $682 fine in the United States or a 565€ fine in Europe. The fine was given because the proper permits were not obtained; Red Bull had, however, offered to provide insurance in case of any accidents to the jumper or to spectators.

In 2007, Baumgartner tackled the largest cave in the Middle East, the "Seating of the Spirits" in the Sultanate of Oman, which is also the second largest cave in the world. Several legends center on this cave, one believed by some to be haunted by spirits. This Seating of the Spirits is located at the top of the Selma Plateau at an altitude of 3,937 feet (1,200 meters), and reaching its summit is extremely challenging. Baumgartner timed his jump to begin precisely at 10:55 A.M. to capture the largest amount of sunshine in the cave, and he completed his 394-foot (120-meter) jump in just 6 seconds; it is believed that Baumgartner is the first person to have jumped into that cave.

This jump took significant preparation over a period of several months. His team would illuminate the bottom of the cave with flares in the shape of an arrow so that, when it became time for Baumgartner to jump into darkness without the aid of outside illumination, he would already have his bearings. Using a specially designed parachute in this jump, Baumgartner also needed to know exactly when to change the direction of his fall to follow the curve of the cave.

On December 11, 2007, Baumgartner planned to jump off the world's tallest building, the 509-meter (1670-foot) Taipei 101 Tower, located in Taiwan (China). He first needed to climb past a security barrier. To ensure his success, he investigated the building's security cameras, and then had a friend hide his parachute in the ceiling of a bathroom in the building. Another friend created a distraction so that Baumgartner could slip past the observation deck unnoticed. He reached the top of the building and leapt off; after a 5-second freefall, he opened his parachute and then landed safely on the roof of a multistoried car park.

Baumgartner says that he has "never enjoyed one of my extreme projects. On the contrary, I experience incredible fear—but I can control it and overcome it. Fear is my friend; it reminds me to be cautious and prevents me from doing anything rash" (http://www.redbull.com/en/ArticlePage.1175169684381-957931423/htmlArticle Page.action).

See also de Gayardon, Patrick; Sky Diving

BMX (BICYCLE MOTOCROSS)

BMX is shorthand for "bicycle motocross." The term "motocross" refers to motorcycle racing, and that term was adopted by youth and adults who incorporated facets of motorcycle racing into their sport using bicycles. An earlier term, "pedal-cross," has faded from use.

There are several different styles of BMX. In the initial style or discipline, the goal is to race around a dirt track, approximately 300 meters (984 feet) in length; there may be obstacles to jump over and sharp turns to make, and the person with the fastest completion time wins.

Freestyle BMXers, unlike BMX racers, are not concerned with the speed in which they can complete a course. Instead, they perform tricks and stunts on and with their bikes, often adding pegs on their bicycles' back wheels so that they can stand on them during stunts. There are several subdisciplines within the freestyle BMX discipline, including the following:

- Vert BMX: These riders perform tricks on the same quarter- and half-pipe constructs that skateboarders use; riders may jump as high as 3 to 4.5 meters (9.8 to 14.8 feet) into the air, performing spins, twists, and tricks before they land. Other riders perform tricks while riding then jumping on dirt.

- Street BMX: These riders use the same urban landscape that street skaters use as their playing field: rails, steps, curbs, trees, and so forth. This is an informal, unregulated sport.
- Park BMX: These riders use the ramps and obstacles created for skateboarders in skateboard parks as their course.
- Flatland BMX: These riders spin and pivot their bikes, and otherwise perform tricks on level ground. A common venue for flatland BMX practice is the parking lot. Some observers say that flatland BMX riders look as though they are dancing with their bicycles.

DEVELOPMENT OF THE SPORT

In southern California, starting in 1969, race organizers began setting up dirt courses so that riders could "motocross" using their Sting Ray bicycles. Some people credit a movie, *On Any Sunday*, for inspiring the motocross movement. In this movie, motorcycle racer Mert Lawwill performed outrageous stunts, and it is said that youth wanted to imitate him. In one scene in the movie, California youth are jumping through terrain on their bicycles.

During the early days of the sport, riders

BMX rider and Olympic hopeful Arielle Martin gets up high coming off a jump at the new BMX training track at the Olympic Training Center in Chula Vista, California. (AP Photo/Lenny Ignelzi)

used the smaller, more maneuverable bicycles built in the 1960s and 1970s. Because the bikes were so much lighter than the motorcycle, the riders could get much more "air" in their jumps.

In 1970, a 13-year-old rider, Scott Breithaupt, formed the first BMX organization: the Bicycle United Motocross Society (BUMS), founded in Long Beach, California. Breithaupt organized races and charged participants $0.25 to enter. In 1973, the National Bicycle Association (NBA) formed, created by Ernie Alexander and Suzanne Claspy, uniting numerous smaller BMX leagues. The following year, George Esser, Sr., formed the National Bicycle League (NBL) in Pompano Beach, Florida; this organization absorbed the NBA. In 1997, the NBL became part of USA Cycling. The American Bicycling Association (ABA) is the main sanctioning BMX organization throughout North America. Currently, there are more than 40 countries with BMX sanctioning bodies, making this organization what is said to be the largest sanctioning body worldwide.

During the late 1970s and early 1980s, BMX was the fastest-growing youth sport globally. When it was replaced in popularity by **mountain biking**, it was difficult to impossible for a few years to get BMX bikes outside of California. Only a small group of dedicated riders kept the sport alive during that down time.

These riders created dirt trails in the woods, with anywhere from 3 to 23 jumps; each jump had a takeoff point and a landing point, with a gap to be cleared in between the two. It is an unspoken BMX law that a rider does not ride on another person's track without first asking permission; sometimes, permission is granted and, other times, not.

Modern-day BMX races take place on 1,000-foot (304.8-meter) dirt tracks, with spirals, jumps, and sharp turns. These races generally last less than 1 minute; riders sometimes place both feet on pedals to get a quicker start, and this is known as a "track stand."

As early as the 1970s, some BMX riders performed tricks on their bicycles in between races; this is said to be the origins of the "freestyle" nonracing BMX movement. In 1974, Thom Lund performed a no-handed wheelie in a BMX race; this was captured on film, probably the first to be so documented. Meanwhile, other BMX riders rode alongside skateboarders; John Palfryman rode in an empty swimming pool, as did Stu Thomsen.

In 1984, **Mat Hoffman** began to ride up the curved, bowl-shaped half-pipe used by skateboarders. His innovations are largely credited for inspiring a new generation of riders, including Dave Mirra, Jamie Bestwick, Simon Tabron, and Zach Shaw. These riders and the riders that they themselves have inspired have created tricks such as the flare, wherein athletes perform a backflip by jumping into the air, spinning around once, and sticking the landing; the bunny hop, where the bike is hopped into the air; and much more.

Hoffman has suffered numerous injuries throughout his motocross career, including a concussion that left him flat lining, a ruptured spleen, and more than 100 broken bones. Yet, at one point, he became so bored with BMX that he removed the brakes from his bike to up the ante.

Bob Haro is credited by many as the first flatland rider. He later designed innovative BMX bicycles.

On February 9, 1980, the first sanctioned BMX freestyle show took place in Chandler, Arizona, as part of the ABA Winter Nationals. By the late 1980s, BMX experienced another lull; in 1995, the sport was featured in the **X Games** (then still called ESPN's Extreme Games), with events held in vert, park, and flatland BMX. Vert BMX maintains a strong presence in the games to this day.

According to the International Cycling Union, BMX as a sport reached Europe in 1978; the International BMX Federation was created in 1981, with the first world championships being held in 1982. BMX is also a popular sport in Australia, with interest growing in South America, as well. Although it is impossible to know how many people ride BMX, worldwide, more than 60,000 riders are licensed through the International Cycling Union, 35,000 of whom live in the United States. That said, there are 40,000 BMX riders associated with the ABA; how much cross-over exists in membership is unknown.

BMX Risks and Injuries

There are risks in BMX riding, from bumps and bruises to broken bones, head injuries, paralysis, and even death. On June 22, 2007, BMX rider Stephen Murray was critically injured while racing in the BMX Dirt finals of the Panasonic Open during the Dew

Action Sports Tour (AST). After the accident, Murray was rushed to a Baltimore-area hospital where he received treatment. He has undergone several operations since, along with physical therapy at the International Spinal Cord Injury Center of the Kennedy Krieger Institute.

BMXer Chad Kagy, who has a reputation as being especially daring, has undergone 11 surgeries and knocked out seven teeth; he has suffered 16 concussions, four of which knocked him out for longer than 30 seconds, and a broken neck that required a year of recovery before he regained full mobility.

BMX EQUIPMENT

Initially, BMX riders used Sting Ray bicycles by Schwinn. As the sport developed, riders made modifications to the frame, pedal cranks, and handlebars of the bicycles. In the mid-1970s, manufacturers began mass producing specially designed BMX bikes; the first was the Mongoose.

BMX riders use bicycles with 20-inch (51-cm) wheels; compare these to the 26-inch (66-cm) wheels used on mountain bikes.

In 2006, the cost of a quality BMX bicycle was approximately $300.

SAFETY PRECAUTIONS

Before riding, athletes need to tighten all bolts, remove their kickstands and reflectors (unless street riding; then the reflectors stay on), and ensure that pads cover the cross-bar of the handlebars and handlebar stem, as well as the top tube of the bike frame. Helmets are a vital piece of protective gear.

See also Motocross; Nyquist, Ryan

BMX in the 2008 Olympics

On June 29, 2003, in Prague, Czech Republic, the International Olympic Committee (IOC) voted to add a BMX racing event for both men and women to the Summer Olympics held in Beijing, China, in August 2008. Initially, it was determined that 32 men and 16 women would qualify for competition. On February 6, 2005, however, the IOC announced that, to forward the equality of women in the Olympics, more female athletes would be added. This formula, which nearly causes an even gender split at the Olympics, added 20 more women to the BMX competitions.

Because the IOC does not want the Olympics to become larger in scope and size, two cycling events will be eliminated to make room for BMX.

A dirt obstacle course suitable for multiple competitors will be created for the BMX events; a number of heats will take place, with BMX athletes racing against one another and winners moving on to the next round. Each race should take less than 1 minute.

The *Union Cycliste Internationale* (UCI) will be the overseeing body; USA Cycling will be the governing body for the U.S. team.

BMX is one of 17 sports for which the Beijing hosts will provide cheerleaders; others are hockey, archery, table tennis, athletics (including marathon and race walking), football, handball, water polo, modern pentathlon (equestrian, running, and swimming), bicycling, baseball, basketball, volleyball, boxing, weightlifting, and beach volleyball.

Stunt Bicycle Riding (Freestyle BMX)

By the time that BMX racing was well established, around 1980, some racers started incorporating trick moves that resemble **skateboarding** tricks into their competitions and performances. Tricks could be performed while on flat land or while in air after jumping off a ramp. Other racers did not approve of stunt bicycle riding, also known as freestyle BMX; nevertheless, after Mongoose began manufacturing bikes appropriate for freestyle moves in 1983, competitions began to be held.

By 1985, some contests had cash prizes and the sport spread. The sport got its biggest boost yet when, in 1995, it was included as an event in the inaugural Extreme Games. Approximately 5 percent of BMX racers are involved in freestyle; the most well known is **Mat Hoffman**, who retired in 2002.

Competitions may include ramps, to allow athletes to perform tricks in midair, or the athletes may perform moves on the flat ground. Street competitions take place in venues similar to skateboarding street contests, wherein riders use rails and pipes and whatever is available in the urban environment to perform their tricks. Still other athletes ride vert, using half-pipes similar to those used in skateboarding and **snowboarding**.

Some events are run by the Aggressive Skaters Association (ASA); freestyle BMX is also promoted by ESPN as part of the X Games. ASA incorporates freestyle BMX into their LG Action Sports World Championship, which runs from July to November. Other sports included in these events are skateboarding, inline skating, snowboarding, and freestyle motocross. As part of this competition, ASA will hold the Big-Air BMX Triples, wherein athletes compete in BMX box jumping and dirt jumping with the mini-mega ramp. Sixteen athletes are expected to participate in the 2008 contest, which was added to the LG Action Sports World Championship in 2007.

BOOMERANG THROWING

Boomerang throwers compete to see who can throw the boomerang the fastest, the longest, and the most accurately. Throwers also compete to make predetermined trick catches, among other specified goals. Boomerang throwing tournaments typically include three divisions—novice, intermediate, and advanced—as well as individual events, team events, and informal events. Although boomerang throwers occasionally strike a **sponsorship** deal, most athletes compete with the understanding that no compensation—other than applause and perhaps trophies—will be awarded.

Winning teams are often from the United States, Germany, and France, with other contenders coming from Australia, New Zealand, Canada, Sweden, and other places worldwide. Approximately 25 countries have their own boomerang teams.

One extreme boomerang event is called "Suicide." Throwers—sometimes as many as 80 or more—line up to throw and catch their boomerangs; the competition goes on until all but one thrower has missed his or her catch.

Additional extreme elements were introduced into the sport in the 1990s, in part because of skateboarders from California, most notably Michael "Gel" Girvin, and Seattle throwers, including Stevie Kavanaugh. Kavanaugh, who has experimented with trick maneuvers and extreme venues, was once photographed doing a one-handed handspring on a mountain top, catching his returning boomerang with the other hand.

DEVELOPMENT OF THE SPORT

Although the aborigines of Australia are credited with creating the first boomerangs, the reality is that no one knows with certainty when and where the first boomerang was crafted. There are in fact two different types of carved throwing sticks—kylies, which do not return to the thrower, and boomerangs, which do. Although it is almost certain that kylies were created first, it is nearly impossible to know when the first returning stick—the boomerang—came full circle.

In Australia, aborigines were whittling throw sticks anywhere from 10,000 to 20,000 years ago. These sticks did not have a planed edge and therefore did not return to the thrower. Kylies were used as weapons, and boomerangs more likely were used as decoys.

The oldest throwing stick found to date was discovered in a cave in Krakow, Poland; it is more than 20,000 years old. It was carved out of a mammoth's tusk, and a man's thumb bone was found with the throwing stick.

Boomerangs have been found around the world, including a 5,000-year-plus Swiss boomerang; golden-capped ivory sticks and gilt-tipped ebony sticks found in King Tut's

Perhaps the world's best female boomeranger, Betsylew Miale-Gix throws at the 2007 national tournament. (AP Photo/*Eau Claire Leader-Telegram*, Alex Uncapher)

Egyptian pyramid, circa 2,000 BCE; and a multitude of other boomerangs discovered in South America, Africa, Asia, Europe, and North America.

In 1770, Captain James Cook arrived in Australia; while there, he learned about boomerangs and brought them back to the Western Hemisphere. In 1838, the Dublin University magazine published material about boomerangs, and Mark Twain also wrote about them in 1897. In 1904, a boomerang factory opened in the United States; from that date until the plant's closing in 1924, owners claimed to sell $1 million worth of boomerangs.

In 1969, American Ben Ruhe, who had spent years in Australia, held the first of 13 annual boomerang tosses at the Smithsonian Institution in Washington, D.C. In 1981, a team coached by Ruhe traveled to Australia for a three-match tournament, the first known international match; the Americans won, but lost a rematch in 1984. After that, the U.S. team won all international matches until the world championships held in New Zealand in 1996, when Germany, led by Fridolen Frost, took first place and the American team took second.

MODERN-DAY EVENTS

In boomerang throwing, men and women compete together without handicaps. Although the majority of boomerang competitors are men, Betsylew Miale-Gix of Washington state has regularly competed against males, winning or placing well in events. The most common events include the following:

Accuracy

Athletes attempt to land their boomerangs in the bull's-eye of a target painted on a grassy field.

Aussie Round

Factors of distance and catching ability are added to this accuracy event.

Fast Catch

An athlete throws a boomerang out 20 meters (65.6 feet) and catches it, five times in a row; the world record for five completed catches is 14.6 seconds, held by Adam Ruhf of the United States.

Endurance

This event features 5 minutes of nonstop fast catch.

Maximum Time Aloft

Throwing your boomerang up into the thermals and catching after it returns to Earth; the world record for a nontournament throw is 17 minutes and 6 seconds, held by John Gorski of Avon, Ohio.

Trick Catch

The athletes catch their boomerangs behind their backs, under their legs, and with their feet. In doubling throws, athletes need to throw two boomerangs at once and then catch them in quick succession in predetermined ways.

The U.S. Boomerang Association formed in 1980 to oversee tournaments and to provide resources for interested throwers. American throwers host several sanctioned tournaments per year, with one designated as the national tournament. Several other countries do the same and, every other year, boomerang throwers gather for a world tournament. Once a year, throwers in the United States hold Toss Across America events, where experienced throwers introduce the sport to novices.

In 1996, American boomerang thrower Chet Snouffer of Delaware, Ohio, won his 10th world championship; no other thrower, around the world, has come close to his accomplishments. Snouffer, a gymnast, threw in the first international tournament held in Australia in 1981; to warm up, he threw his boomerang, and then did a backflip from a standing position, landing just in time to snag the boomerang behind his back.

BOOMERANG EQUIPMENT

The most important pieces of equipment are the boomerangs themselves. Competitors throw different types for different events; for fast catch, for example, a compactly carved three-bladed boomerang is used and, for maximum time aloft, a hockey-stick shaped boom is thrown.

Boomerangs are carved differently for right-handed throwers and left-handed throwers, and athletes choose different boomerangs for varying wind conditions. Throwers often carry pennies and tape to tournaments to weight the boomerangs appropriately for the weather.

Fast catch competitors often wear a soccer glove while catching, as these boomerangs can go as fast as an estimated 80 miles (129 kilometers) per hour. Eye protection is recommended but not always used by throwers.

Boomerang champion Gary Broadbent from Canton, Ohio, has the world's largest boomerang collection, having surpassed 10,000 boomerangs several years ago. He decorates his house, the rafters on his roof, and his mailbox with boomerangs carved in the shape of cartoon characters, Michael Jordan dunking a basketball, and more.

Michael "Gel" Girvin of California created a brightly colored four-winged boomerang with a hinged box at the center; he places handwritten poetry in that box and then throws the boomerang to create poetry in motion. Other throwers have flown in a jet across the international dateline to throw a boomerang on one day, but catch it on another.

Boomerang Risks and Injuries

Eye injuries and strained shoulders are among the more common injuries among throwers. As in any sport, though, the more risks that are taken, the more likely it is that some injuries will occur. American thrower Barnaby Ruhe, cousin of the organized sport's founder, Ben Ruhe, performs a William Tell trick that has left him scarred. After sharpening the edge of a boomerang to a knife-like intensity, Ruhe then places an apple on his head and throws the boomerang, hoping to slice the apple in half. Ruhe has both failed and succeeded in performing this extreme toss; his forehead is scarred as proof of earlier attempts.

BRIDGE DAY

Bridge Day is held annually on the third Saturday of October in Fayetteville, West Virginia. For 6 hours, jumpers can legally leap from the 876-foot-high (267-meter) New River Gorge Bridge, which, according to event organizers, is the world's second longest single-arch bridge.

In general, jumpers are—or want to become—BASE (Building/Antenna tower/Span/Earth) jumpers. To receive an official BASE number, a person must successfully complete a leap from a building, an antennae tower, a span, and a natural Earth formation such as a cliff. Because **BASE jumping** often involves trespassing on private property, participants frequently face conflicts with the law, but, for one day a year—Bridge Day—jumps are legal off the New River Gorge Bridge. A successful jump fulfills the "span" requirement to become a BASE jumper. Because this bridge is higher than many other jumping venues and because a significant number of boats patrol the region and assist jumpers out of the water, many sky divers attempt their first BASE jump at this event.

October 20, 2007, was the 29th annual Bridge Day, and approximately 155,000 people attended to watch 377 jumpers from 10 countries make a record 876 jumps during a 6-hour period. Twenty-three rappel teams also attended, with more than 300 people making more than 800 rappels. Mark Seyfang from Ohio was the first person to complete a rappel, an ascent, and a BASE jump. The oldest rappeller, Robert Handley, was 79 years old.

In 2008, once again, a 16-foot (4.9-meter) aluminum diving board will be attached to the bridge. The diving board allows BASE jumpers to spring off the bridge in a manner similar to an Olympic diver and then perform flips and twists before deploying their parachutes, which have no backup system. Teams from Australia and the Russian Federation have announced their intentions to participate in this event in 2008. There will also be a landing accuracy content with cash prizes.

During the first 29 years of Bridge Day celebrations, there were three fatalities. The most recent occurred in 2006, when 388 jumpers participated, 128 of them first-time BASE jumpers from more than one dozen countries. Because of a late parachute deployment, Brian Schubert, described as a "BASE jumping pioneer," died.

Vendors at Bridge Day events sell items from homemade crafts to food, and the event receives national media coverage. Visitors also can enjoy the beautiful scenery along the New River, which is one of the oldest rivers in North America. **Bungee jumping** is banned at Bridge Day festivities.

See also Baumgartner, Felix; de Gayardon, Patrick

BUNGEE JUMPING
Bungee jumpers leap from fixed structures, such as tall buildings, cranes, towers, and bridges, as well as from hot air balloons and other movable objects that may be as high as 1,500 feet (457 meters) from the ground. Before jumping, the athlete attaches

Air National Guard Captain Dan Schilling leaps off the Perrine Bridge in Twin Falls, Idaho, July 8, 2006. The military parachutist set a new world record by jumping 201 times in 24 hours. (AP Photo/*South Idaho Press*, Meagan Thompson)

himself or herself to the fixed structure or movable object with a stretchable cord, which expands and contracts based on the jumper's weight. When the jumper reaches the end of the cord, it snaps back up, causing the jumper to return partway into the air in ever-decreasing increments; this continues until the energy in the cord has expired. At that point, the jumper may be released at the low point of the jump or raised back to the starting point.

DEVELOPMENT OF THE SPORT

In the village of Bunlap in the Pentecost Island in the South Pacific, there is a legend wherein a woman flees from her abusive husband. To hide from him, she climbs a tall banyan tree—and then she ties a vine around her ankle. When her husband catches up to her and tries to grab her, she leaps from the tree; he follows her but, because he was not tied to a vine, he plunges to his death.

Because of this legend, men on the island began learning how to jump in this manner from 30-meter (98.4-foot) towers perhaps as early as the 1500s, briefly touching the ground. Only men were allowed to perform this act, and it became a harvest ritual that was said to increase the fertility of yams being planted. The natives built a jumping tower on a hill, clearing away the rocks and softening the dirt below and this April/May ritual became known as "N'gol."

In the 1950s, *National Geographic* photographer Charles Lagus took pictures of this ritual. On April 1, 1977, the Dangerous Sports Club (DSC) of Oxford mimicked the ritual, jumping from the 245-foot (75-meter) Clifton Suspension Bridge in Bristol, England, while formally dressed. Since then, the club has coordinated jumps in 40 countries.

In 1987, A. J. Hackett from New Zealand (who was a member of DSC) jumped off the Eiffel Tower. Although he already had jumped 91 meters (299 feet) in Tignes, France, it was his Eiffel Tower jump that garnered significant attention. In 1989, New Zealand published its Bungee Code of Practice, and the standards of New Zealand and Australia are now followed by jumpers in many other parts of the world.

To add additional excitement to the sport, jumpers can jump backward or by hanging from their hands and feet. They can also hold weights to accelerate their freefall, which causes them to snap back up higher than the original starting point. Some jumpers "sandbag" by using another person as the additional weight; jumpers can be seriously injured or even killed if their timing is off. To make the challenge more difficult, jumpers may grab prespecified objects from the ground before snapping back up or may perform some other predetermined stunt.

Other athletes jump with a cord tied to two pillars; this is known as the "twin tower thrill."

In 1993, a road show demonstrated the sport of bungee jumping in the United Kingdom, and the sport garnered interest there. The following year, bungee jumping sites were created in Las Vegas, Nevada, and Kissimmee Bay, Florida, in the United States. Other early jumping sites included the Golden Gate Bridge in San Francisco and a bridge spanning the Royal Gorge in Colorado. California became an early center for the sport.

Bungee jumping from a crane is an activity sometimes seen at carnivals and fairs; fairgoers pay a small fee for a single jump. A modified version of bungee jumping is even available for **children** indoors at malls and other venues.

At the end of the 1990s, the sport spread to Germany and Acapulco, Mexico.

Dan Osman took the sport to a new extreme level, called "rope free flying" or "flossing the sky" (Osman's preferred phrase). In rope free flying, the athlete jumps out, away from a fixed object such as a cliff; a rope with less elasticity than those used in regular bungee jumping is first attached to the jumper by use of a harness. This rope does not cause the jumper to rebound back in the air; rather, the jumper spins in huge arcs. This less elastic rope prevents the jumper from feeling the pull of the rope before he or she has completed a freefall, which adds to the excitement of the sport.

COMMERCIALIZATION OF BUNGEE JUMPING

A. J. Hackett of Eiffel Tower fame created a commercial bungee jumping product, as did Peter and John Kockelman in the United States. Hackett used a rubber cord that could be shortened or lengthened by the height and weight of the jumper. A towel is wrapped around the ankle of a jumper and then a cord is attached; another option is to attach a static safety line.

The Kockelman version uses a nylon-wrapped cord that uses rock climbing harnesses and locking carabineers. Users can add or subtract cords to accommodate the weight of jumpers; one cord is used for every 50 pounds (22.7 kilograms), and each cord has the static strength of 1,500 pounds (680.4 kilograms). Jumpers use two harnesses—waist and shoulder, and ankle—for additional security.

The U.S. system is more costly and more technical to use. There is a 2:1 stretch ratio, which provides a longer time to freefall and greater deceleration before the cord catches—or extends fully. The New Zealand product has a 4:1 stretch ratio, which means that the cord is shorter and "catches" earlier; this is a more comfortable system to use.

BUNGEE JUMPING RISKS AND INJURIES

In 1987, three jumpers died in France, causing the sport to become banned in that country while safety studies were conducted. It was determined that most fatalities occur because of human error, which includes improper use of any harness or rope, poor choices of the jump-off site, and jumping with inexperienced people.

People with certain medical conditions, including high blood pressure and epilepsy, should not jump; the same caveat applies to pregnant women. Jumpers may experience neck or back pain, or blurred vision, but these symptoms should be temporary.

BUNGEE JUMPING AND POPULAR CULTURE

Pierce Brosnan, in the character of James Bond, bungee jumped from a 220-meter (721.8-foot) dam in what was to appear to be Angelsk, the Russian Federation; in reality, it was in Verzasca, Switzerland. This 7-second fall was filmed for the 17th James Bond film, *Goldeneye* (1995).

BURNSIDE, CARA-BETH (1968–)

Cara-Beth Burnside, known as "CB," is one of today's best-known female extreme sports athletes, winning medals in both **skateboarding** and **snowboarding**. Burnside is the only female to date who has won a gold medal in both the winter and summer

Cara-Beth Burnside poses with her gold medal after winning the Skateboard Vert Women's final at X Games 12 in Los Angeles on August 3, 2006. (AP Photo/Jae C. Hong)

versions of the **X Games**. She has worked as an advocate for equal treatment for female athletes, founding the Action Sports Alliance, often called the Alliance; this organization serves as a voice for female skateboarders. Burnside has also served as a role model for younger female athletes; the EXPN.com Web site quotes her as saying that, "These girls have had a standard set for them, and I set that standard" (Fenton 2005).

Born on July 23, 1968, in California, her mother, Mary, received a call when Burnside was in third grade, informing her that girls in their school wore dresses, not jeans. Her mother pulled her from that school and enrolled her in a private one with a more casual dress code. Influenced by her two older brothers, Burnside roller skated, rode a **BMX (bicycle motocross)** bike, and had a pony. When she tried skateboarding, though, around the age of 12, she became focused on that sport. She continued to practice at a local skate park until that park shut down because of liability issues; friends of hers then created a quarter-pipe on their property, and she began skating there.

Burnside ran track while attending Santa Rosa Junior College. While studying human development at the University of California–Davis, she played soccer and began snowboarding at Lake Tahoe. She would sleep on the floors of friends who lived near the mountain; collect aluminum cans to pay for her mountain lift tickets; and even alter dates on passes for the lift. She earned a bachelor's degree at UC Davis.

Burnside earned a spot on the 1998 Olympic snowboarding team for the United States, ranking fourth in the competition. She has won numerous X Games medals, including the following:

- Winter 1997: silver medal, snowboarding slopestyle
- Winter 1998: gold medal, snowboarding half-pipe
- Winter 1999: bronze medal, snowboarding half-pipe
- Summer 2003: gold medal, vert skateboarding
- Summer 2004: silver medal, vert skateboarding
- Summer 2005: gold medal, vert skateboarding
- Summer 2006: gold medal, vert skateboarding

In 2001, she won the Vans Triple Crown for skateboarding and, in 2002, she won the Philips Fusion Soul Bowl tournament, also in skateboarding. In 2004, World Cup Skating named her the Female Vert Skater of the Year. She also won skateboarding titles in the All Girl Skate Jam and the Slam City Jam, along with snowboarding titles in the Grand Prix and Vans Triple Crown. When she was 35, she was named *Transworld* magazine's female skateboarder of the year.

In the 2005 Summer X Games, it was a close competition for the vert gold, with Burnside beating out the up-and-coming young athlete Lyn-Z Adams Hawkins.

Burnside appeared in the movie *Our Turn: An All Girls Film: White Knuckle Extreme*; this movie documented professional female skateboarders, snowboarders, and surfers, with Burnside demonstrating action on huge skate ramps located in southern California.

Burnside has received endorsement deals with Vans, Hurley, and Independent, and she was the first female skateboarder to have her name on a signature shoe. In 2003, Bell Helmets announced collaboration with Burnside to market a Barbie helmet to encourage young girls to participate in action sports. She has appeared on the cover of *Thrasher* and *SG* magazines, and has been featured in the *New York Times*, *Women's Sport and Fitness*, *Sports Illustrated for Women*, *Outside*, and *Transworld Snowboarding*, among others.

In 2005, Burnside received $2,000 for her vert gold medal from the X Games, while the winner of the male event won $50,000. She met with X Games officials to discuss pay disparity between men and women skateboarders, insisting that the prize money be increased for women; if not, she, along with other members of the Alliance, would boycott the 2006 games. Although ESPN initially intended to increase the pay to $5,000 for the gold medalist, after meeting with Burnside, the prize amount for the winner increased to $15,000; more television coverage of female athletes was also promised. Burnside and another member of the Alliance, Jen O'Brien, became members of the X Games selection committee that, to date, had been entirely male.

In 2006, she was nominated as an ESPY candidate—the television channel ESPN gives out ESPY awards for numerous accomplishments in sports. In 2007, Burnside was the winner of the ProTec pool party, held in Orange, California, in the skateboarding event.

See also Gender and Extreme Sports; Hawk, Tony; Mullen, Rodney

CANOEING AND KAYAKING

Canoeing and kayaking are two popular paddling sports, wherein participants sit in a water craft and then propel their boats through the water with paddles. Some people enjoy these sports as forms of relaxation while on vacation; others participate in competitive activities, some of which can be labeled as extreme.

A canoe is a long and narrow boat measuring between 23 feet to 39.4 feet (7 and 12 meters). It is propelled by one or more people who are sitting in the canoe; they use single-bladed paddles, facing the direction in which they are traveling, and they paddle on one side of the canoe for a period of time before they switch to paddling on the other side. Canoes are open on top and are pointed at both ends. Kayaks are smaller, between 13.1 and 16.4 feet (4 and 5 meters), and the kayakers sit with their legs extended and covered. "Sit on top" kayaks also are available for those who are uncomfortable with their legs being covered up. The paddles that kayakers use have a blade on each end and they row one stroke on one side of the boat, and then one stroke on the other.

Kayaking and canoeing have numerous subdisciplines, as well as related sports, including whitewater rafting. Although each subdiscipline has unique features, many other features cross over, blurring the distinctions among them. Some of the more extreme versions of these sports are labeled as "whitewater." When canoeing or kayaking participants travel through rapidly moving shallow water, there is significant frothy turbulence, which makes the river's water seem white. Under these conditions, the river is considered to be whitewater. A creek or river that has a number of rapids also may be called whitewater.

According to a study released by the University of Nevada School of Medicine, nearly 10 million people participate in whitewater sports, with more than 3 million of them labeled as "enthusiasts" who participate in the sport more than two times per year. The Outdoor Industry Association estimated that, in 2000, there were 6.5 million kayakers, and the association describes the growth of this activity as "explosive." Out of the 6.5 million kayakers, between 1.4 and 2.8 million are whitewater kayakers; the participation growth rate is estimated to be nearly 15 percent (Fiore 2003). From 1998 through 2003, 5.7 million people tried a paddling sport for the first time, which caused a 235.7 percent increase in participants. It is believed that nearly 2 million paddle sports enthusiasts live in Britain, as well.

Approximately 70 percent of kayakers are male; 55 percent of the rafters in the United States are male and 45 percent of them are female, with 90 percent of rafters and kayakers being white (Fiore 2003). Female participation is increasing, however; out of the 5.7 million people who tried a paddle sport for the first time between 1998 and 2003, 2.5 million were female. The average age of a canoeist or kayaker is 31, and they participate in this sport an average of seven days per year. The most active groups are those between the ages of 12 and 17 for both sports; the second most active group is the 45- to 54-year-old kayakers; and then the 35- to 44-year-old canoeing group.

Eighty-six percent of paddle sport participants choose rivers as their venue; others select seas, lakes, canals, and even artificial whitewater sites.

The wide variety of paddling sports include flatwater racing (often called "canoe ballet"), slalom racing, wildwater racing, and marathons, as well as extreme versions of kayaking and canoeing, which include creeking, extreme racing, and playboating.

Rivers are rated according to the International Scale of River Difficulty. Advocates of more leisurely activity would choose rivers that are Class I or perhaps Class II. As the class number increases, so does the extreme nature of the sport:

- Class I: easy; few obstacles
- Class II: moderate, with small rapids and waves that can be easily navigated
- Class III: challenging rapids, hazards, and waves; requires complex maneuvering
- Class IV: very difficult with large rapids, falls, and hazards; rescue would be difficult
- Class V: extremely difficult, dangerous hazards; for experts only
- Class VI: nearly impossible; only attempted by a team of experts

The International Canoe Federation (ICF) was formed in 1924 and oversees international races. There are 117 national federations, as well, with 43 associations in Europe, 24 in the United States, 15 in Africa, and six in Oceania. The ICF organization is located in Madrid, Spain.

History of Canoeing and Kayaking Sports

People have been using canoes and kayaks to navigate the waters for thousands and thousands of years, and modern-day designs still bear a resemblance to ones from more than 5,000 years ago. People in North America, Greenland, Scandinavia, and Russia created kayaks by stretching seal skin, or walrus or caribou skin around carefully crafted wooden frames; they used bones, antlers, and other natural substances to attach the skins to the wood. They waterproofed the craft with whale fat. The Inuits of Greenland went so far as to create different types of craft for different water and weather conditions.

Kayaks generally measured 11.8 to 15.75 feet (3.6 to 4.8 meters) in length, and they were used to hunt walruses, whales, and other water animals. The smaller sizes of the kayaks made them easier to maneuver while hunting. Canoes were larger than kayaks, ranging from 25 to 40 feet (7.6 meters to 12.1 meters); these were designed to carry larger groups of men, as well as cargo. Although kayaks were used solely by men, women would use canoes when moving to a new location. The canoes used by the

Inuits, called umiaks, have been included in Norwegian paintings that were created around 5000 BCE.

It is believed that paddle boat races existed even before recorded history and that they may have been an important ritual for ancient cultures. As history unfolded, people continued to use kayaks and canoes, using the materials that were most accessible in a particular place and time.

In more modern times, a Scotsman named John MacGregor crafted a boat that he named the "Rob Roy," modeling it after an Eskimo kayak. MacGregor explored European waterways using his kayak between 1845 and 1869; he wrote about and lectured on his experiences, bringing kayaking to the attention of many. In 1866, MacGregor formed the Canoe Club, with the Prince of Wales serving as Commodore until he was named king; this club was renamed the Royal Club in 1873. The New York Canoe Club was formed in 1871, inspired by the English group.

Modern races became a sport approved of by British royalty in the 1870s, and these activities became part of their military training. The American Canoe Association formed in 1880 to serve as an international organization for the sporting activities.

After World War I, canoeing and kayaking blossomed, becoming demonstration sports for the Olympics in 1924 and full medal Olympics sports in Berlin, Germany, in 1936. During World War II, the sport stopped expanding, but it returned full force after the war ended, including in western and eastern European nations, and in countries associated with the Soviet Union. The boats now were being made of fiberglass and aluminum.

FLATWATER

Recreational kayaking and canoeing are the easiest sports for new participants to learn, and many people use this style of kayaking and canoeing to enjoy the outdoors and to exercise in a pleasant manner. Flatwater racing is governed by the ICF, as the athletes race on straight courses in calm water for distances of 200 meters (656.2 feet), 500 meters (1,640.4 feet), and 1,000 meters (3,280.8 feet).

Flatwater racing has been an Olympic sport since 1936 for men, in events using both kayaks and canoes. Events for women were added to the Olympics in 1948, using kayaks only. Olympic courses do not include the 200-meter race, and they are set up so that each athlete has his or her own lane. Flatwater events use elimination rounds to determine the winners; initially, championship females were from Germany and the Soviet Union, but winners now come from a broader scope of nations. European and World Championships do include the 200-meter race in their events.

There are three types of flatwater racing kayaks—or sprint boats: single paddler (K1), double paddler (K2), and the four person paddle (K4). In the Olympics, men compete in K1 and K2 for the 500-meter races, and K1, K2, and K4 for the 1,000-meter races. Women compete in K1, K2, and K4 for the 500-meter race. Men also compete in the 500-meter and 1,000-meter races using canoes, both singles and doubles (C1 and C2).

In world championship events, there are three distances: 200 meters, 500 meters, and 1,000 meters. Women and men compete in K1, K2, and K4 events for each distance, and men compete in C1, C2, and C4 events for each type of canoe, as well.

Flatwater kayaks are extremely lightweight, crafted from fiberglass, carbon fiber, and synthetic fiber, and can be used only in flatwater conditions. A K1 or K2 kayak of a competitive grade costs between $2,000 and $4,000. Their exceptionally narrow construction reduces drag and allows for quick handling. A K1 kayak is 17 feet (5.2 meters) and a K2 is 20 feet (6.2 meters) in length; these boats have a rudder, as well, that is controlled by foot.

SLALOM

Slalom is a whitewater sport wherein kayakers and canoeists negotiate 18 to 25 gates, both upstream and downstream, in a course that is 300 to 600 meters (974.2 to 1,968.5 feet) in length. Downstream gates are green and upstream gates are red.

This type of racing started in Europe and the slalom world championships were first held in Switzerland in 1949. Currently, championships are held every other year.

Expert paddlers usually can complete a course in 80 to 120 seconds, although more complex courses may take up to 200 seconds. Penalties are assigned for missing gates (50 seconds) or touching them (2 seconds). Each athlete goes on two runs, and the scores are added together for a final score; the person with the shortest combined time is the winner. Some smaller competitions, it should be noted, use the faster of the two completion times to declare the winner. Men's and women's courses are equal in length, although gates may not be placed in identical spots.

Slalom has been an Olympic sport for the games in 1972, 1992, 1996, 2000, and 2004; not all locations have had appropriate slalom facilities, which explains the gap between the 1972 and 1992 games. The four Olympic events include C1 for men, C2 for men, K1 for men, and K1 for women.

Horace Holden, Jr., who competed in the 1996 Olympics, said this about slalom: "Like skiing, it's pure thrill going down the hill. One of the unique things is that you're on a dynamic playing field. You get drops, freefall, splashing, speed. And then the precision of going through the gates. You're inches, even millimeters from the poles" (http://gorp.away.com/gorp/activity/paddling/olympic.htm).

The average age of a U.S. Olympian in the 1996 games was 33. New racing boats cost $1,200 to $2,500.

WILDWATER

According to *River Runner Magazine*, quoted at USAWildwater.com, "Wildwater racing is pure whitewater paddling, often called the race of truth" (Beavers n.d.). In wildwater racing, participants race downstream, using kayaks or canoes. Paddlers must find the fastest current in this whitewater sport, and then avoid obstacles while attempting to finish the race in the shortest amount of time. Wildwater races typically take place in Class II, III, or IV rivers.

France hosted the first world championships for wildwater in 1959; initially, courses took 50 minutes or more to complete. Courses have since been shortened to engage spectator interest and, in 1988, the ICF divided events into classic races and sprint races. In classic races, the course is 2.5 to nearly 3.75 miles (4 to 6 kilometers); sprint races are 500 to 1,000 meters (1,640.4 to 3,280.8 feet). Men compete in K1, C1, and C2 events; women compete in K1 events. There are mixed teams with both men and women, as well, and they compete in C2 events.

Competitors are ranked, with rankings being calculated by using results from previous races; the best paddler goes last in wildwater competitions, with competitors starting the race sequentially at 1-minute intervals. In team events, each member of a team must have the same competition ranking.

According to USAWildwater.com,

> Wildwater is at once one of the most physically demanding of paddlesports, because it requires its participants to be strong over the course of four to five miles of class three to four whitewater, yet it also requires strategic acuity to balance raw power and speed with execution and timing: zen-like cognition mixes with the burning in the furnace. (Beavers n.d.)

MARATHON

Canoeing marathons are popular in Europe, although they are also held in other locations. Denmark hosts the Kronberg event and the Tour du Gudena; Great Britain, the Devizes to Westminster race; Spain, the Sella Descent; and Ireland, the Liffey Descent. The first marathon world championship took place in 1988, with K1, K2, C1, and C2 events for men, and K1 and K2 events for women. The world championships helped spread interest in this discipline, with significant participation now existing in the United States, Canada, Australia, and South Africa.

Potential obstacles for athletes include shallow areas of water; jutting rocks or rocks beneath the water's surface; waterfalls and so forth. Sometimes, the athletes need to get out of their canoes or kayaks and walk the boat to a safer place. The ICF dictates that international races must be at least 12.4 miles (20 kilometers) for men and 9.3 miles (15 kilometers) for women. World Cup and world championship racing are usually 21.75 to 24.9 miles (35 to 40 kilometers).

Some of the longer marathons include the following:

- Devizes to Westminster Marathon in England (125 miles/201 kilometers): held every year at Easter since 1948
- International Descent of the River Sella in Spain (12.4 miles/20 kilometers): based on a trip made by Dionisio de la Huerta in 1929; his course became the basis of the River Sella races
- Liffey Descent in Ireland (18 miles/29 kilometers): this race began in 1959 and has included up to 1,000 competitors racing in a single year
- Tour du Gudena in Denmark (74.5 miles/120 kilometers): established in 1967, the 40th anniversary of the event was temporarily halted because of weather conditions
- Texas Water Safari (262 miles/421.6 kilometers): bills itself as the "World's Toughest Boat Race," the annual event was started in 1963
- AuSable River Canoe Marathon (120 miles/193 kilometers, nonstop): held in Michigan in the United States, this race was established in 1947
- Berg River Canoe Marathon in South Africa (154.1 miles/248 kilometers): established in 1962, the race lasts for four days, not counting the day of time trials
- Red Cross Murray Marathon in Australia (251 miles/404 kilometers): begun in 1969, the race lasts five days
- Yukon River Quest (461 miles/742 kilometers): this Canadian race is billed as the "Race to the Midnight Sun"
- Missouri River 340 (340 miles/547 kilometers): organizers warn potential racers that "[t]his ain't no mama's boy float trip" (http://rivermiles.com/mr340/page2.html)

DRAGON BOAT RACING

More than 20 million people in China participate in dragon boat racing, a sport that has spread to Europe, where 50,000 people participate. A dragon boat generally can seat about 20 paddlers and is decorated to resemble the ancient Chinese vision of a dragon, with the following features:

- An oxen's head, deer antlers, and horse mane at the head
- Scales of a python in the middle
- Hawk claws on the paddles
- Fish fins and tail at the end of the boat

Two boats typically race against one another in a traditional dragon boat race; the Chinese believe that team unity is as important as strength and endurance when racing. Each time that dragon races occur, the Chinese in fact are commemorating an historical event that occurred more than 2,000 years ago.

Around 277 BCE, dragon boat racing gained a deeper meaning in Chinese culture when a diplomat named Qu Yuan was banished after giving the king advice that angered others in the government. Postbanishment, Qu Yuan filled his pockets with rocks and drowned himself in the Mi Lo river; locals tried to rescue him, beating drums to scare the fish away from the body. If they could not rescue him, they at least wanted to retrieve his body, so they also tossed rice dumplings wrapped in bamboo into the river so that the fish would eat those, rather than the body of Qu Yuan.

From that point on, the dragon boat races commemorated the moment when the Chinese people raced to try to save Qu Yuan. Modern-day racers beat drums and toss rice cakes to honor him.

Twenty-first-century dragon boats tend to be 32.8 to nearly 40 feet (10 to 12 meters) long, with 10 rows of seats. Two people fit on each seat; a drummer sits in the front and a steersman sits in the back. Before the race starts, a Taoist priest or someone important to the community daubs the dragon eyes with red paint to bring it to life; once the race beings, the paddlers move in time with the drummer's beat.

The organization that governs this activity is the International Dragon Boat Federation (IDBF). These races are generally 500 meters (1,640.4 feet) long, but they can be 250 meters (820.2 feet), 1,000 meters (3,280.8 feet), 2,000 meters (6,561.7 feet), and even longer.

This sport started gaining international attention in the 1970s, and dragon boat races are now held in 50 countries around the world. North American teams generally can paddle 60 to 85 times per minute, but some Asian teams have paddled 100 times or more each minute.

Koreans have had their own dragon boating tradition for more than 1,000 years. Swan boat racing is important in Thai culture, and the Vietnamese have Ba Trao rowing, which arose from ancient worship of the whale god (Ong), the river god, and the Earth god. In parts of India, snake boat races are held; these boats can carry up to 100 paddlers.

EXTREME KAYAKING

Extreme kayaking tends to take place in rivers that are ranked as Class IV, Class V, and sometimes even Class VI. Subdisciplines of extreme kayaking include creeking and extreme racing.

In creeking, sometimes called "steep creeking" or "treetop boating" or "creekboating," athletes tackle rivers with rapids in the Class IV to Class VI range. There is often a gradient of 100 feet (30.5 meters) per mile, although it is not unusual for creeking enthusiasts to tackle gradients of 250 to 300 feet (76.2 to 91.5 meters) per mile.

To participate in creeking, paddlers need to know how to handle falling down a waterfall and then deal with the rush of water overhead. Paddlers who go creeking need to "make almost instantaneous choices on the proper routes down narrow, precipitous chutes and slides, over vertical water falls and through tight, boulder strewn passages, while remaining constantly vigilant for potentially life-threatening hazards" (Chase 2006).

Creeking requires specialized boats and gear. Creeking kayaks are bulbous in shape and crafted from thick, durable plastic. This design allows them to ride closer to the surface of the water and also allows the kayak to more quickly resurface if submerged after a steep fall. Their banana-like shape enables paddlers to turn and react more quickly than they could in a traditional kayak. Occasionally, creekers use canoes that are shorter than usual and that come with airbags and pedestal seats so that the paddler can see more of his or her surroundings.

Helmets and life jackets are necessary, and many athletes also wear elbow pads and face guards. Throw bags that contain coiled up ropes are essential for rescue attempts of those who have fallen out of their boats. Breakdown paddles and rescue kits are advisable.

Creeking teams should have at least three people, as two people are required for rescue purposes. The groups should not be too large, however, as the athletes need to be able to account for everyone else at all times.

In extreme racing, participants race on Class V rivers, with dangerous waterfalls and rapids. The participants may be individually timed or may start the race en masse. Some locations for extreme racing include the following:

- Nevis in Scotland
- Ulla in Norway
- Russell Fork in the United States
- Green River Narrows in the United States
- Upper Gauley River in the United States
- Upper Youghiogheny River in the United States
- Great Falls of the Potomac in the United States

PLAYBOATING

This is the most creative of the kayaking and canoeing sports. Playboaters first choose a particularly challenging spot in a river (a "playspot"). Then, rather than traveling down the river, they stay in their playspot to perform tricks and maneuvers (such as cartwheels and spins) and aerial movements after having gained air from a rough bounce off the waves. In the United States, this activity might be called "whitewater rodeo" or "squirt boating" and, in Europe, it is called "freestyle."

In competitions, paddlers get about 45 seconds to demonstrate their abilities to judges, performing gymnastic tricks such as the "McNasty," "donkey flip," and the "space godzilla." Kayaks used in playboating are shorter than average and they float below the water's surface to engage the undercurrents.

Examples of playboating tricks include the following:

- "Enders": the bow of the boat goes into the water and the kayak becomes vertical
- "Popup": after performing an ender, the paddler causes the boat to pop out of the water and then right itself
- "Pirouette": the boater turns around while performing an ender

- "Surfing": involves staying at a certain point of the river, rather than being forced downstream; there are front surf, back surf, side surf, and carving moves in surfing; carving involves moving back and forth in a particular area of the river
- "Spinning": rotating the boat at least 180 degrees

Some of the most popular playspots include the Hurley Weir on the Thames River near London; the Skookumchuck Narrows in Canada; the Horseshoe on the Ottawa River in Canada; the Rabioux wave on the Durance in France; and the Golden Kayak Park in Golden, Colorado, in the United States.

WHITEWATER RAFTING
A sport closely related to certain forms of kayaking and canoeing is whitewater rafting. In this sport, which has increased in popularity since the 1970s, a group of people use a raft to navigate a whitewater river.

CANOEING AND KAYAKING RISKS AND INJURIES
A recent study indicates that the risk for whitewater canoeing and kayaking is 4.5 injuries for every 1,000 days of paddling. This can be compared to Alpine **skiing**, for which there are 3.2 injuries for every 1,000 days of participation, and **windsurfing**, for which there is only 1 injury per 1,000 days (Gullion 2007, 362). Kayaking injuries often are caused by the transferred force of the water, while rafting injuries are more commonly caused by inadvertent contact with another person's paddle. An estimated 25 to 40 percent of kayaking injuries lead to chronic difficulties with shoulders and wrists. Fatalities occur at a rate of 0.55 per 100,000 user days for rafters, and 2.9 per 100,000 user days for kayaking (Fiore 2003).

Typical injuries from whitewater sports occur to the back, shoulders (approximately 6 percent of paddlers deal with shoulder injuries), wrists, hands, elbows, and forearms. Head and facial injuries are relatively common and sometimes fatal.

Canoeing and kayaking rank second to motor boating as the cause of water-related sports deaths in the United States and one study indicated that nearly 1 in every 10 paddlers has experienced near drowning. Alcohol is a factor in 25 percent of canoeing deaths; other reasons for fatalities include inexperience, hazardous water, and weather.

In 2003, there were 57 canoeing and kayaking deaths in the United States. In September 2006, the 50th death occurred for that year, making 2006 the third year out of the past 12 when 50 or more deaths were caused by whitewater sports (Griffin and Polk 2006).

CANOEING AND KAYAKING SAFETY EQUIPMENT
The American Canoe Association (ACA) emphasizes the importance of wearing safety jackets, as well as avoiding extreme weather conditions. Sobriety is key, as is minimizing the movement inside the canoe while paddling. Helmets and other protective gear are recommended, including elbow pads and face guards. Throw bags with coiled-up ropes, breakdown paddles, and rescue kits are also important. For the most extreme varieties of canoeing and kayaking, such gear is a necessity.

CARMICHAEL, RICKY (1979–)
Ricky Carmichael began racing motorcycles at the age of 5 and has since won numerous **motocross** and supercross tournaments and championships, including 15 American

Motorcyclist Association (AMA) national championships. He is known as G.O.A.T., which stands for "Greatest of all Times." Other nicknames include "RC," "Angry Little Elf," and the "Flying Freckle." He is married to Ursula Holly.

Carmichael was born on November 27, 1979, in Clearwater, Florida. In 1984, at the age of 5, he began competing in amateur motocross races; in his 12 years as an amateur, he won 67 championships. He turned professional in 1996 and, that year, he won every race in the Supercross Series; he also won the AMA Motocross Rookie of the Year Award in the 125 cubic centimeter class.

In 2000, he won first place in the THQ U.S. Open, winning $100,000, along with 9 out of 12 wins at the AMA Motocross Series; the latter accomplishment allowed him to break a 22-year-old record for the most wins in a season. In 2001, he beat Jeremy McGrath for both the supercross and the outdoor motocross titles.

Carmichael started working with **video game** manufacturers to create games that focus on motocross racing. The following games have been released:

- Championship Motocross featuring Ricky Carmichael for PlayStation
- MX 2002 featuring Ricky Carmichael for the PlayStation2
- Championship Motocross 2001 featuring Ricky Carmichael for Game Boy Color
- MX Superfly featuring Ricky Carmichael for Xbox
- CMX 2002 featuring Ricky Carmichael for Game Boy Advance

To date in his professional career, he has been on Team Kawasaki but, in 2001, he was wooed to Team Honda in a deal that reportedly earned him $2 million. In 2002, he rode a perfect season in the 250-cc national championship, the first person to do so.

Because of surgery in December 2003 for a torn ACL (anterior cruciate ligament), he did not race during the indoor season in 2004. That year, though, at Budds Creek Motocross Park, Carmichael celebrated an unprecedented 100th career victory. He won both 250cc heats, becoming the first racer in AMA's 80-year history to hit the 100 mark. He accomplished this after winning four consecutive 250cc series championships; he celebrated his 100th win by waving his arms in the air three times while still at the finish line, and then he made a victory lap in front of a crowd of 16,433 people. Moreover, he swept the entire 2004 outdoor season, another perfect performance.

In 2005, he switched to Team Makita Suzuki Racing, where he won the following:

- World Supercross GP Championship
- AMA Supercross Championship
- AMA Motocross Championship
- U.S. Open of Supercross
- Title of AMA Rider of the Year

Carmichael also participated on Team USA at the Motocross de Nations, where the U.S. team won.

By 2006, he was talking about retiring. He had already won four supercross titles and nine motocross titles; in 2007, he did retire. Before one of his last races began, the Hangtown race director, John Konkle, reminisced about Carmichael, telling the *Sacramento Bee* that, "Some of the things Ricky has done at Hangtown are just amazing. One moto, he fell down, got passed by all the other riders, got up and still won. And he's just the nicest guy, too" (Arrington 2007).

In March 2007, he and his wife Ursula had twins: a son, Kadin, and a daughter, Elise. Also in 2007, Carmichael signed a lucrative three-year contract to drive a National Association for Stock Car Auto Racing (NASCAR) stock car for MB2 Motorsports. The goal is for Carmichael to be racing full time by the Busch Series in 2009.

CAVING, EXTREME (BASEMENT OF THE WORLD)

Dedicated participants refer to their sport as "caving," "sport caving," or "wild caving." They may even say that they "do cave" or that they are "extreme cavers." Serious cavers, however, do not say that they are "spelunking," as spelunking is a term for hobbyist-level cave exploration. In fact, one humorous bumper sticker reads, "Cavers Rescue Spelunkers" (Crookshanks n.d.). An offbeat term for the sport is "potholing."

Some caves are largely above ground, while others go deep into the Earth, often partially under water. Most caves are formed from limestone, but others are formed from gypsum, granite, sandstone, loess, and marble. Ice caves can form beneath glaciers and lava caves—or "tubes"—are found in some locales. The Mammoth Cave in Kentucky has 363.5 miles (585 kilometers) of passageways for cavers; this is almost the distance between New York City and Washington, D.C.

Skills needed to explore caves often resemble the skills needed for mountain climbing, including strength and endurance, plus enough flexibility to maneuver through small spaces. Upon entering a cave, cavers will notice a drop in temperature; by the time they are 20 feet (61 meters) deep into the cave, the only light source is generally one that they have brought with them. Inside a cave, it is often dark and muddy, with jutting rock, tunnels, caverns, streams, and waterfalls; creatures found inside of caves include bats, rats, and crickets.

The preeminent organization for cavers is the National Speleological Society, located in Alabama, with 12,000-plus members. The society advocates that people cave in pairs or in groups, never alone. Throughout the country, there are regional clubs (known as "grottos") wherein more experienced cavers teach novices how to safely pursue caving, what reliable equipment and protective clothing to buy, and what to expect while caving. More experienced cavers also often demonstrate safe climbing techniques to novices. Globally, people of both **genders** and a wide range of ages participate in this year-round sport, although white males are the most prominent participants; 41 countries have Web sites focusing on caving.

CAVING EQUIPMENT

Cavers typically buy their safety equipment piecemeal, as it can become costly. A key piece of safety equipment is a hard helmet, which can cost anywhere from $15 to $70, while an acetylene gas lamp for the helmet (similar to what a miner might use) costs an additional $50. Fuel is also needed for that light. Battery lamps for helmets cost around $30 and electrical models are also available. Cavers often take along two to three different light sources, including candles and flashlights, to ensure that they have backup illumination.

Cavers are advised to take along light sources that will last 12 hours past their anticipated return. They should also check weather forecasts to anticipate additional weather-related challenges, and they should let designated noncavers know where they are going and when they expect to return. Caving is one of the few sports that has no spectators, so it is especially difficult to know when cavers need outside aid.

Other recommended safety equipment includes sturdy boots, kneepads, a backpack, gloves, rope, and other climbing harnesses and gear, plus a water bottle. Clothes will get muddy and dirty, so some waterproofing characteristics are helpful. A map of the cave, if one exists, or a compass if it does not, is essential. Those who dive to deep underwater caves also need appropriate wetsuits, and those that go ice caving need equipment tailored for ice climbing in addition to the traditional gear.

American Caving Accident, a journal that is generally published annually, reports on caving accidents in North America, including when they occurred, where, in what cave, by what specific type of incident, and the result of that incident. As one example, during 2004–2005, there were 52 caving accidents reported, along with 11 cave diving accidents and 30 caving-related accidents. The most common causes of accidents are falling, being struck by falling rock, and hypothermia. People may get lost, get stuck, or become too weak or disoriented to climb out of a cave.

A *Washington Times* article points out that most caving fatalities occur during scuba caving, a sport popular in Florida. Out of the 4 million annual caving excursions in the United States, fatalities generally number between 30 and 35. "Scuba caving," the article reads, "has to be handled by absolute professionals. If people are interested in it, they have to hang out with professional scuba cavers, or they'll get killed" (Mizejewski 1996, 4). Other caving deaths occur because of starvation, falls, asphyxiation, drowning, or hypothermia.

Cavers can struggle with feelings of severe claustrophobia. One caver who has documented this sensation is Barbara Hurd, author of *Entering the Stone: On Caves and Feeling Through the Dark.* In her first caving attempt, she entered a 2-foot-high, tunnel-like passage, scooting on her stomach and using her elbows to propel herself forward. Hit with a panic attack, she needed to push herself backward into the open. Ten years later, however, after many caving experiences, Hurd entered the same cave with friends; propelling herself downward 12 feet, she communed with the darkness for 30 minutes. Hurd writes about caving as a mental challenge, even more so than a physical one. She also speaks of the great darkness as being a powerful equalizer, where no one is more attractive than another (Burnham 2004, 240).

Cavers sometimes attempt to expand the limits of exploration. In 1956, a group of French cavers climbed 1,000 meters (3,280.8 feet) into the Earth. In 2004, Ukrainian Yuri Kasjan led a team of cavers more than 2 kilometers (1.2 miles) into the Arabika Massif in the former Soviet state of Georgia, the farthest anyone had ever gone into the Earth. The cavern was only 10 meters wide by 10 meters high (33 by 33 feet). This accomplishment has been compared to reaching the North and South Poles or climbing Mount Everest (Bethge 2005).

Other cavers experience an adrenaline rush during the unexpected moments, perhaps when a dark, cramped tunnel leads to a cavernous area. Here is one description:

We entered by wading against a waist-high current of cold water pouring from the wide cavern mouth. Where the stream angled away, we scrambled single file up a mud-slick rock, then duckwalked through a low corridor. The kids preceded me and their chorus of "ooohs" and "ahhhs" floated back as, one by one, they dropped into a large room decorated with flowstones, stalactites, and stalagmites. (Mizejewski 1996, 4)

When exploring caves, people sometimes find items of historical significance, such as aquatic fossils preserved in limestone that can be anywhere from 300 to 500 million years old. They may also find items left behind many centuries ago, when humankind commonly used caves as shelter from enemies and as places to store food and treasures. One of the most amazing finds occurred in Lascaux, France, on September 12, 1940, when teenagers found the first of nearly 2,000 realistic prehistoric paintings, mostly of animals, geometric shapes, and a few human beings, that date back to somewhere between 15,000 and 13,000 BCE.

Cavers, in general, do not attempt to retrieve items found in caves, believing that caves are valuable resources in need of protection. They are among the most environmentally conscious of all extreme sports participants. Their motto is "take nothing but pictures; leave nothing but footprints; kill nothing but time."

Some cavers even keep the location of caves a secret, so that others do not pollute, destroy historic evidence found in caves, create graffiti, or damage the stone inside the caves. U.S. cavers in particular have a reputation, worldwide, of keeping this type of information secret from noncavers. Some cavers refer to this type of secretiveness as "recycling," because the joy that they had in discovering a cave can happen, over and over again, by others who find that same "unknown" cave.

In the United Kingdom, the location of caves is much more publicized; popular caves to explore include the vertical caves of the Dales, and the caves in South Wales. Caving organizations in the United Kingdom include the British Cave Research Association, the National Caving Association, and the Speleological Union of Ireland.

CHILDREN AND EXTREME SPORTS

Extreme sports are becoming increasingly popular with youth in the United States, as well as in other places worldwide, and the children are learning about extreme sports at increasingly younger ages. Although many of today's extreme athletes learned how to play their sports either by themselves or with friends, the upcoming generation of athletes will be much savvier. Besides watching the **X Games**, he or she may have grown up watching cartoons featuring extreme sports characters; received extreme sports toys as gifts; played **video games** with extreme sports themes and protagonists; and perhaps even attended an extreme sports camp.

CARTOONS AND EXTREME SPORTS
The following cartoons feature extreme sports:

- *SpongeBob SquarePants*, wherein a character named Sandy Cheeks participates in a variety of extreme sports; in one episode, SpongeBob and another character, Patrick Star, go sandboarding with Sandy
- *Goofy's Extreme Sports*, wherein the Disney character is seen rock climbing, paracycling, **wakeboarding**, participating in stunt rollerblading, and more

- *George of the Jungle*, wherein one episode featured two extreme sports characters who are trying to videotape themselves participating in dangerous stunts
- *Teenage Mutant Ninja Turtles*, wherein Michelangelo is run down by a bank robber using a **skateboard**
- *Gumby*, wherein he and his band perform at a skateboarding rally; Gumby's skateboard is stolen, but is recovered in time for Gumby to set a world record
- *Super Mario Brothers Super Show*, wherein a **snowboard** plays a key role in the Christmas episode
- *Simpsons*, wherein Bart Simpson skateboards sans clothing

Cartoons that have frequently featured extreme sports include *Action Man* on Kids WB and *Max Steel* on Fox Kids.

The television channel Nickelodeon created "Nickelodeon GAS: Games and Sports for Kids" programming during the summer of 1999. Extreme athletes **Ryan Nyquist** and Jen O'Brien covered skateboarding and **BMX (bicycle motocross)** racing news from PointXCamp, located in California. This programming continued through 2007.

Toys and Extreme Sports

Toy companies Hasbro and Mattel have created foot-tall action dolls based on the *Action Man* and *Max Steel* cartoon series. Hasbro's "The Greatest Hero of Them All" toys, based on Action Man, brought in $300 million from European sales. In 2000, Mattel's Max Steel toys brought in $100 million worldwide. As a result, the company added the MX99 Heli-Jet Vehicle and the Jet-Skater Radio Control Figure to its repertoire.

McDonald's has capitalized on the popularity of extreme sports by putting figurines of cartoon characters in their kids' meals; in one promotion, Smurf figurines are involved in snowboarding, rollerblading, and skateboarding. In 2004, McDonald's gave away eight other toys featuring skateboarding, BMX biking, and **motocross** as a tie-in to **Tony Hawk's** Boom Boom HuckJam Tour.

Burger King provided five extreme sports toys in 2004 in their children's meal offerings. In this promotion, characters from the Teenage Mutant Ninja Turtles participated in **street luge**, skateboarding, motocross, and snowboarding.

Taco Bell and Wendy's have put extreme sports figures into kids' meal offerings, as well.

JAKKS Pacific Road Champs has marketed its toys, including action figures, vehicles, and accessories, with the X Games label. Featured sports include street luge, snowboarding, and freestyle motocross, with more than 70 athletes represented in this toy line. X Concepts has created miniature extreme sports collectibles; and Spin Master was making 300,000 replicas of BMX bikes per week in 2000.

Video Games and Extreme Sports

Both Sound Source Interactive, Inc. and Disney Interactive have created video games for young children that have involved extreme sports. Sound Source Interactive created a game wherein the Berenstain Bears participated in six extreme sporting events: sledding, dirt biking, freestyle kayaking, dirt boarding, team tobogganing, and team rafting. The Berenstain Bears are characters from a popular book series for young children that were also turned into a cartoon series. Disney Interactive designed video games that featured Mickey Mouse, Minnie Mouse, Donald Duck, Daisy Duck, Goofy, Max, and Big Bad Pete participating in snowboarding, skateboarding, and motocross.

EXTREME SPORTS CAMPS FOR CHILDREN

Extreme sports camps for children can include the following activities: skateboarding, **bungee jumping**, paintball, **inline skating**, downhill **mountain biking**, BMX, freefall giant swing, rock climbing, helicopter rappelling, bungee trampoline, flying trapeze, **windsurfing**, **canoeing and kayaking**, horse jumping, mountain cycling, parasailing, glider flights, surfing, go-karting, Hollywood stunt training, hot air ballooning, and more.

One example of a successful extreme sports camp for children is Camp Woodward, which is a 70-acre (28.3-hectare) camp located in University Park, Pennsylvania. Young athletes from every state in the country and from at least 21 countries have attended sessions of this camp. Initially, 1,400 youth spent the summer at Camp Woodward, learning gymnastics. By 2003, the attendance had increased to 10,000, and the children were participating in BMX freestyle, skateboarding, and inline skating with such pros as Dave Mirra, Ryan Nyquist, Jay Miron, and others. The cost was $845 per week.

In 2000, Disney.com partnered with Camp Woodward, billing the camp as a training facility for future X-Gamers; through this collaboration, families could watch the extreme action going on at the camp from their computers. That same year, JAKKS Pacific signed an agreement with Camp Woodward to provide bike playsets for camp participants.

The Extreme Sports Camp of Aspen is an extreme sports camp for children with an autism spectrum disorder. This camp began as a two-session program in 2004; the 2008 summer camp will be a seven-session program with more than 70 children attending. Some of the more extreme sports include rock climbing and whitewater rafting.

EXTREME SPORTS AND FAMILY GUIDE

A book called *Extreme Kids: How to Connect With Your Children Through Today's Extreme (and Not So Extreme) Outdoor Sports* by Scott Graham shares how to introduce children to mountain biking, rock climbing, kayaking, kiteboarding, back-country skiing, and more. This book provides information about family-friendly parks and trails, and the author encourages parents to banish video game systems, such as Xbox, Nintendo, and Game Boy, and then replace them with real-life extreme sporting adventures. This book won the 2006 National Outdoor Book Award in the instructional category.

See also Children and Sports Injuries

CHILDREN AND SPORTS INJURIES

According to information provided by the National SAFE KIDS Campaign and the American Academy of Pediatrics (AAP), approximately 30 million youth participate in organized sports across the United States and more than 3.5 million children up to age 14 receive injuries while participating in sports and physical recreation. Included in the list of these sports are some that are often considered extreme: **inline skating**, **skateboarding**, and **snowboarding**.

Nearly one-third of childhood injuries are sports related, with sprains and strains being the most common. Although deaths are rare, the leading cause is a brain injury; sports are the cause of about 21 percent of brain injuries in children in the United States. Sports that are most likely to cause head injuries are bicycling, skateboarding, and skating.

More than 775,000 children go to hospital emergency rooms for treatment for sports injuries. The most common causes are falls, being hit by an object, collisions, and overexertion.

Following are the number of annual cases of hospital emergency room visits for children ages 5 to 14, by sport:

- Basketball: more than 205,400
- Baseball and Softball: nearly 108,300; highest fatality rate, with three to four children dying from baseball injuries each year.
- Bicycling: nearly 285,000
- Football: almost 185,700
- Ice Skating: nearly 10,600
- Inline Skating: nearly 27,200
- Skateboarding: more than 50,000
- Sledding: more than 15,000
- Snow Skiing/Snowboarding: more than 35,000
- Soccer: about 75,000
- Trampolines: nearly 80,000
- Ice Hockey: more than 18,000 young people under the age of 18

Protective gear is recommended for youth participating in sports. It is estimated that, for example, wrist and elbow protection for inline skaters and helmets for cyclists each prevent 85 percent of injuries from occurring.

See also Children and Extreme Sports

CLOTHING FOR EXTREME SPORTS
At least four types of clothing are associated with extreme sports:

- Extreme sports protective gear
- Extreme sports competitive gear
- Branded clothing for consumers
- Alternative and subculture clothing

EXTREME SPORTS PROTECTIVE GEAR
The purpose of this protective gear is to protect the athlete and help prevent injury; it also can be used to shield a previously injured area of the body. Protective gear includes helmets (full-faced and regular), pads for knees, elbows, hips, buttocks, and more; guards for knees, shins, wrists, and more; padded shorts and pants; and upper-body protection for the chest, ribs, shoulders, and neck. Although there is some cross-over in gear usage from sport to sport, each sport tends to have specific protection needs and, therefore, unique protection gear.

Gear that shields joints is especially useful during falls. Wrist guards protect wrists from injury when an athlete reaches out to break a fall. Knee guards and pads reduce the impact of falls on the knees, while elbow pads and guards protect that body part during falls and crashes. Mouth guards are used in **roller derby** to protect the skater's teeth.

In sports such as roller derby, **snowboarding**, street skate, and so forth, the athlete needs to protect himself or herself from injuries typically sustained by impact with concrete or asphalt. Head injuries are among the most serious of injuries, so each of these sports—and others—has specially designed helmets.

Protective gear is optional during practices and training, because its use cannot be enforced. During certain tournaments and sporting competitions, though, participants must wear appropriate protective gear to participate; one example is the bicycle and motorcycle events in the Olympics, wherein helmets are mandatory. As another example, any events organized by the U.S. Snowboard Association also require helmets. In extreme activities that do not fall under the auspices of any association or fit into any organized competitions—buildering, for example, wherein athletes climb skyscrapers—the use of protective gear is up to the individual. Some athletes shun the use of any protective gear.

Numerous companies manufacture and supply protective gear to retail stores, both online and brick and mortar. Popular companies include SixSixOne, ProTec, Burton, Giro, Bell, Fox, Pryme, Vans, ProDesigned, EVS, Crash Pads, Troy Lee Designs, and more.

Creators of extreme sports gear frequently sponsor extreme sports athletes or collaborate with these athletes to promote and sell their protective gear. ProTec, for example, sells helmets bearing the names of skateboarders Bucky Lasek, Omar Hassan, and Bob Burnquist. Bell collaborated with skateboarder **Tony Hawk** to promote a helmet bearing his name; and Burton RED did the same with snowboarding champion **Shaun White**.

EXTREME SPORTS COMPETITIVE GEAR

Competitive gear is intended to provide a comfortable fit for the extreme sports athlete, but it does not add an extra degree of protection. For example, some athletes wear nylon pants when riding **BMX (bicycle motocross)** that are easy to get into and out of and that do not get snagged on the bicycle during competition; the garments are flexible and move with the athlete.

As another example, snowboarding athletes may choose pants and jackets that keep them warm while competing. Although warm, without pads or guards or other protective elements to the gear, this is considered competitive gear rather than protective.

Retail stores and boutiques sometimes focus on a specific type of sporting gear. As one example, former competitive surfer Izzy Tihanyi and her sister, Coco Tihanyi, have opened a clothing boutique for surfers in La Jolla, California. This location is home base for one of their camps where they educate people about surfing and ocean preservation. This endeavor has been successful for the sisters. In 2008, they were quoted as saying that their sales have been increasing by about 15 percent each year (Chessman 2008).

BRANDED CLOTHING

Branded clothing is sold to consumers; when they wear the clothing, they are in effect advertising the name brand through the use of logos and branded text. Skateboarder

Tony Hawk has been especially successful in this endeavor. Hawk created a line of his branded clothing, selling it to a sportswear manufacturer, Quiksilver, in 2000. In 2005, Kohl's Corporation signed an agreement with Quiksilver to secure exclusive rights to Tony Hawk–branded clothes for boys and men. Under this agreement, Quiksilver continued to design the clothing, while Kohl's took over the distribution and marketing of the products. Kohl's goal was to offer alternative fashion for boys and young male adults. Some Tony Hawk clothing items are available for girls; in 2007, a shoe line was added at Kohl's Department Stores.

In the 1990s, Calvin Klein borrowed from snowboarders' style, creating parachute-nylon clothing; designer Ralph Lauren created a new fragrance: Extreme Polo Sport. The *New York Times* commented on these styles by saying that, "Being extreme has become so extremely chic" (Morris 1998). *Outside* magazine's editor in chief, Mark Bryant, shared his viewpoint, stating that, when "loaded down with that many logos, you aren't really alternative" (Morris 1998).

Freestyle **motocross** pro Carey Hart is another extreme sports athlete who expanded into the clothing business. Hart owns a tattoo shop and clothing line, with retail locations in Honolulu, Hawaii; Las Vegas, Nevada; Orlando, Florida; and Cabo San Lucas, Mexico.

ALTERNATIVE AND SUBCULTURE CLOTHING

Alternative and subculture clothing is worn to fit into the culture of extreme sports. Initially, the extreme sports "look" was perceived as that of a rugged backpacker who was wearing hiking boots. That evolved, however, into the baggy urban look of modern-day skateboarders and snowboarders. Tattoos and body piercings often accompany this look.

Some extreme athletes like to go against type, including freestyler Alison Gannett, who was known for wearing lipstick and fake fur during competitions. She has also been quoted as saying that she was "sick of techno stuff" and that she "liked faux-fur, satin, fun colors. When you're in these clothes 24 hours a day, it's like office clothes. You don't want them to be boring" (Morris 1998).

Kook Wear is an example of subculture action sports wear that is environmentally friendly. Clothing is made from 100 percent organic cotton, or a mix of cotton and hemp or bamboo. Ink is water based and packaging is minimal.

CRANDAL, LOUISE (1971–)

Louise Crandal has won the women's paragliding world championships twice, and she may be the first person to train a bird of prey to land on her hand while she was paragliding. From 2000 until 2003, Team Denmark sponsored her during paragliding tournaments.

Born in 1971 in Denmark, Crandal's grandmother was a horse jockey, so Louise grew up observing people train animals. By the time she was a young adult, she had begun paragliding in Switzerland. With her brother, Mads Crandal, and a few close friends, she brought the sport to Denmark in the 1990s. In paragliding, the athlete rests in a harness that is suspended from a fabric wing; he or she can take off via a foot launch from a cliff or other type of slope and glide through the air.

Crandal competed in an Italian tournament in 1995. In general, far more men than women participate in paragliding, but they can compete against one another in tournaments under equal conditions. The Italian tournament was to last 56 miles (90 kilometers), and Crandal had never paraglided more than 17.4 miles (28 kilometers) before that time. In this tournament, however, she traveled 28 miles (45 kilometers) in a three-hour time frame.

In 1998, Crandal won the Argentinean championship, beating out the men. In 2001, she won the world championship for women and set a distance record for women of 133.6 miles (215 kilometers). She came in third place in the 2003 world championships and, in 2005, she won back the world title.

Crandal took part in a documentary, *Flying With Eagles*, directed by Anton Gammelgaard, which told the story of Cossack, the eagle she had trained to fly with her and land on her hand. Crandal had found the Steppe Eagle in Scotland; initially, he refused to even eat from her hand. By the time they reached Denmark, though, Cossack was flying alongside Crandal; the documentary then records the rest of their journey, which ends at Lake Como in the Italian Alps. *Flying With Eagles* won first prize at the 2007 Coupe Icare Film Festival.

Crandal also began participating in a sport called parahawking; she first flew to Nepal to meet with falconer Scott Mason, who—along with Graham Saunders-Griffiths and Adam Hill—had merged paragliding with hawking to creating parahawking (Van Praagh 2005). Trained birds have even been taught to perform aerobatic moves with their human counterparts.

Crandal credits flying with the birds with improving her own paragliding abilities. Eagles, hawks, and other soaring birds have an ability to find thermals, which are warm pockets of air. When these birds "catch a thermal," they can glide across the sky without needing to flap their wings. With training, these birds can learn to help guide humans toward these thermals and, when paragliders are riding thermals, they can cover hundreds of kilometers in one day.

TIMEasia describes the experience of flying with soaring birds in this way:

[W]hen your whoop of exhilaration is answered by the shriek of an eagle or a falcon just ahead of you, well, all your cares melt away and the world is reduced to a cool rush of air, a dazzling view of glaciated peaks, and the sheer joy of being able to soar with birds of prey. (Baker 2004)

In an interview with *Cross Country Magazine* in December 2005, Crandal shared her own experiences with the birds and the thermals, saying that,

I left Nepal to fly the Worlds in Brazil and there was no doubt that I had learned from the birds. I flew better than ever before and out-thermalled most pilots. Flying that close with birds of prey definitely added another dimension to thermic flying. (Andrews 2005)

See also Gender and Extreme Sports; Hang Gliding

CSIZMAZIA, KIM (1960–)

Kim Csizmazia excels in Nordic **skiing** and rock climbing, but is best known for her **ice climbing** expertise. She earned three gold Winter **X Games** medals in ice climbing; won first place twice in the Ouray Ice Climbing Exhibition; and captured the first Ice Climbing World Cup title in 2000. She also placed first in the Courchevel Ice Festival in France.

Ice climbing, which has been called the "toughest winter sport," has been described in this way: "Try this. Fill a blender with ice. Hit the pulse button. Let the spray blast your face. Wait until the ice melts and drips into your clothes. At this point, if you're still smiling, you may be ready to take it outdoors and try waterfall ice climbing" (Christie 2004).

Csizmazia was raised in Whistler, British Columbia, and Sun Valley, Idaho, both mountainous regions. Her parents loved mountain sports and she learned how to ski by following them. At age 15, she was a nationally ranked Nordic ski racer.

In 1985, she was awarded a scholarship to the University of Utah. Csizmazia joined the Nordic ski team, and she learned the basics of rock climbing while at the university. After earning a degree in English, she dedicated more time to climbing and, by 1998, she was the top-ranked female ice climber in the United States. That year, she won the 1998 Winter X Games ice climbing competition, as well, in both the speed category and the difficulty category. Also in 1998, she won ESPN's "Survival of the Fittest" competition, which required significant strength and endurance.

The spring of 1998 was spent helping to make an ice climbing movie in Iceland, titled *Ice in Iceland*. This movie won the Best Film on Mountaineering Award at the Second Annual Vancouver International Mountain Film Festival.

After completing the filming of this movie, Csizmazia headed to Utah to learn how to climb solo. She was intrigued by solo climbing because it required constant motion, and significantly more physical and mental endurance than climbing with a partner; a solo climber covers about three times as much ground as a person climbing as part of a team.

Csizmazia has been sponsored by Black Diamond and she has attended festivals to promote their climbing gear.

In the 1999 Winter X Games, there was an extremely close competition between two Kims: Kim Csizmazia and Korea's Jum-Sook Kim. Both women reached the top of the course within the time limit, but Csizmazia completed her climb using seven fewer strokes than Kim, thereby winning her third X Games gold medal in ice climbing, this time in the difficulty category.

In 2000, she traveled to six different countries over a two-month period while successfully competing for the Ice Climbing World Cup; countries included Austria, France, Italy, Switzerland, the Russian Federation, and Sweden.

Csizmazia married another world-class ice climber, Will Gadd; the two of them had a daughter in June 2007. Csizmazia has said this about ice climbing: "I ice climb, in good part, for the beauty of the ice. It is always changing, and you have to get to know it very well, to learn its habits and tendencies, and always to respect it. You have to be very evolved with it to climb ice safely" (Levy 1998).

See also Gender and Extreme Sports

D

DA SILVA, FABIOLA (1979–)

Fabiola da Silva is perhaps one of the most successful women in extreme sports to date. She has won eight world championships in **inline skating**, which is the largest number of inline championships of any man or woman; she is accomplished in vert, park, and street skating. She was named as one of the Action Sports Alliance (ASA) top 10 skaters of all time, and she dominates the sport to the degree that the Aggressive Skaters Association Pro Tour created the "Fabiola Rule," which gives women the opportunity to qualify for men's inline vert competitions.

da Silva was born in São Paola, Brazil, on June 18, 1979. She was always interested in playing sports, whether that meant basketball, volleyball, football, soccer, or swimming. She became the best kickboxer in her class at age 12.

She received her first pair of skates at the age of 14; the following year, her mother bought her a pair of inline skates. Within a short amount of time, she was skating for Rollerblade; at the age of 16, she traveled to the United States to compete in the Pro Tour circuit. Her first pro tournament was the 1996 Extreme Games, where she came in first in the women's inline vert event. During that performance, she landed a backflip, the first time that an inline skater had done so in competition. *Sports Illustrated* has listed that moment as one of the most memorable in inline skating.

From 1996 through 2001, she nailed first place finishes in all competitions that she entered, except for one—when she placed second in the 1999 **X Games**. In the 2002 and 2003 Summer X Games, she also received a gold medal in inline skating, park. Although the X Games dropped inline skating competitions for women, da Silva kept competing, invoking the Fabiola Rule and qualifying to compete against men. In the Latin X Games in 2004, she took second place in a slate full of men; in the 2004 Summer X Games, she took sixth. That year, she also founded the Fabiola da Silva Circuit for amateur inline skaters. This tour's competition served to qualify Brazilian rollerbladers for the Latin X Games; although ESPN has since canceled the Latin Games, this tour kept going.

In 2005, she landed a double backflip on a vert ramp, the first woman to do so; few men can accomplish this trick. da Silva is, to date, the woman with the most X Games medals. She is also a four-time **Gravity Games** champion.

In 2005, ESPN dropped inline skating from the X Games. da Silva was not significantly affected by that move, as she and her boyfriend, a Brazilian **skateboarder** named Sandro Dias, picked up a **sponsorship** deal by LG Action Sports; they began competing on this company's world tour.

da Silva has appeared on an MTV show, *Switched*, and on *Jimmy Kimmel Live*. She was also signed to star in the movie *Slammin'*, which tells the story of a girl from Brazil who competes against men in inline skating. She has been sponsored by The Gap, Ignite, Solar Safe, and Mountain Dew, and she filmed commercials for Capri Sun and Mountain Dew.

She has this to say about females competing in sports: "I hope some little girl out there watches me and knows that you can be anything, even a pro in-line skater, if you are a girl" (Booth and Thorpe 2007, 80). Meanwhile, her official profile at EXPN.com notes that, "If rollerblading has a face, then it has olive skin and freckles, a shy smile and sparkling eyes. The face belongs to Fabiola da Silva, the Brazilian beauty who, in 2002, changed the rules of competitive rollerblading" (http://expn.go.com/athletes/bios/DASILVA_FABIOLA.html).

See also Gender and Extreme Sports

DE GAYARDON, PATRICK (1960–1998)

Patrick de Gayardon de Fenayl was perhaps the most well-known name in extreme sports in Europe. Although de Gayardon participated in a wide variety of extreme sports, what he excelled in was parachuting, winning two French national titles and a silver medal at the 1986 World Freefall Parachuting Championship.

He was a pioneer in the sport of **sky surfing**, creating many of the maneuvers used by sky surfers today, and in **BASE (Bridge/Antenna tower/Span/Earth) jumping**. In BASE jumping, athletes jump from distances much closer to the ground than in **sky diving** and sky surfing; therefore, their reflexes must be lightning fast so that they can open their parachutes in time.

de Gayardon was born on January 23, 1960, in Oullins, France, which is near Paris. He participated in **windsurfing**, lawn tennis, golf, and Alpine **skiing** when young. After studying law in Lyon, he turned his attention to parachuting, perfecting his freefall technique by jumping from high altitudes but not opening his parachute until he was near the ground.

In 1991, Reebok launched a new ad campaign with the slogan "Life Is Short. Play Hard." The company pledged to spend $20 million on their campaign, and the initial commercial—which aired during Monday Night Football—featured de Gayardon jumping from a plane wearing Reebok Pump Cross Trainers; he sky surfed on a surfboard, then opened his parachute to land in a lake.

In 1992, he joined the No Limit Sector Team, which was sponsored by Sector; he also received other **sponsorship** deals. In 1995, in Moscow, the Russian Federation, he jumped from a height of 12,700 meters (41,668 feet), without using oxygen; this was a world record. In 1996, he won the first World Sky Surfing Championships.

He also experimented with creating a "flying suit" or "bat suit" that allowed him to move horizontally through the air. During one test of the effectiveness of this suit, he jumped from a plane at 4,000 meters (13,123 feet) and then glided more than 5,000 meters (16,404 feet) before returning to the airplane. "It's the most incredible feeling," de Gayardon told the *Sunday Mirror*. "The fact that you are flying across the sky rather than falling through it takes your breath away" (Kelly 1998).

His passion for this project earned him the nickname of "Icarus" after the Greek mythological figure who created wax wings but flew too close to the sun, where the wings melted and he crashed to his death.

In retrospect, that nickname served as foreshadowing as to de Gayardon's own fate. On April 13, 1998, he was testing a wingsuit in Hawaii for a film. His modified parachute malfunctioned and then his reserve parachute got tangled up with the main canopy. At the age of 38, after successfully completing more than 11,000 jumps, he crashed to the ground and was killed. It is believed that a rigging error caused the fatal malfunction.

See also Baumgartner, Felix

E

ETHICS AND EXTREME SPORTS

In 2006, significant controversy surrounded the death of a British man who had been left to die near the top of Mount Everest. Approximately 40 people passed by him while he was still alive; this event came to the attention of media after other climbers blogged about the man's death and the circumstances under which it occurred.

Mount Everest is the highest mountain on Earth, when measuring its height above sea level, which is 29,029 feet (8,848 meters). The mountain is located in High Asia on the edge of the Tibetan Plateau (Qing Zang Gao Yuan) on the border of Sagarmatha Zone, Nepal, and Tibet, China; it is part of the Himalaya Range.

Although some have disputed that Mount Everest is the world's highest mountain, surveys conducted in the 1990s have confirmed that and, in fact, the mountain appears to be rising a few millimeters per year. To monitor this, Global Positioning System (GPS) technology is being used to detect changes in height caused by geological shifting.

MOUNT EVEREST AND THE "DEAD ZONE"

Sir Edmund Hillary and Sherpa Tenzing Norgay were the first people to successfully climb Mount Everest; since that event in 1953, more than 1,500 people have reached the summit, with some using supplemental oxygen, and some, not. Approximately 190 people have died while making the attempt to reach the peak, in large part because the human body does not function well at extremely high altitudes; somewhere around 26,000 feet (7,925 meters) above sea level, it becomes extraordinarily difficult for the body to function.

At this altitude, the digestive system starts to shut down, and oxygen levels plummet, which prevents as much oxygen from reaching the brain. People can hallucinate, which can prevent them from acting in their own best interests. Because of these factors and because of the deaths that have resulted at this altitude, the 26,000-foot (7,925-meter) mark at Mount Everest is known as the "dead zone."

This area of Mount Everest is also known as "Rainbow Valley" because, when a climber looks around, there are a significant number of bodies frozen in their brightly colored suits. Climbers need to physically step over a significant number of bodies to reach the summit.

Nepalese Sherpas with luggage make their way through the Khumbu Icefall to Everest base camp. (AP Photo/ Gurinder Osan)

On one especially lethal day, May 10, 1996, eight people died while climbing the mountain; these deaths were blamed on a fatal combination of bad weather, crowded routes, and the inexperience of some of the climbers. Five days later, a 34-year-old British man, David Sharp, died; weather was not a factor that day.

According to friends, Sharp was an experienced climber. In 2002, he reached the summit of a nearby mountain, Cho Oyu, which had a height of 26,750 feet (8,154 meters). He had almost reached the summit of Mount Everest twice, once in 2003 and once in 2004. Each time, he was about 1,000 feet (305 meters) shy of reaching the summit; the first time, he lost toes to frostbite. Friends say that the 2006 climb was going to be his last attempt, so he was especially determined to succeed. He was climbing solo and did not have a radio.

It is believed that Sharp reached the summit of Mount Everest on May 14, 2006, but, early in his descent, about 984.3 feet (300 meters) from the peak, he ran into trouble, becoming disoriented. He sat cross legged in a cave, still attached to a fixed line that other climbers were also using; he was only about 3 feet (0.9 meters) from the main route. Reports made after his death indicated that some people had stopped to comfort him, but they did not attempt to rescue him.

Witnesses also stated that a guide gave Sharp oxygen but, because the only movement made was in his eyes, it was determined that Sharp was too far gone to be saved. One witness, who used to work on mountain rescue teams, said that Sharp was already nearly frozen alive, adding that the temperatures that day were −38° Celsius (−36.4° Fahrenheit).

Conflicting information has been presented as to when the oxygen was administered to Sharp. Plus, some evidence and testimony suggested that a group of people saw him on their way up the mountain, but they did not try to help Sharp until they had reached the summit and were on their way back down. Others have testified that they did not see him until they were on their descent.

Some climbers have claimed that they contacted a rescue team farther down the mountain, named the Himalayan Experience (Himex). This rescue team had the resources to potentially rescue Sharp, but it was said that the rescue team did not respond. In response to that criticism, the representative of Himex stated that they did not receive a call about Sharp until 9:30 A.M. on May 15; by that time, his rescue teams were engaged in rescue attempts elsewhere on Mount Everest. At least one guide—not from Himex—admitted that, had Sharp been a client of his, a rescue attempt by his company would have taken place. He also added, though, that his company does not permit solo climbs (Heil 2006).

This death raised many questions as to how ethical climbers should act and respond in emergency situations. Some climbers said that, in order to survive themselves, it would be necessary to leave behind someone who was near death. Others believe that Sharp was left to die for purely selfish reasons; because climbing Mount Everest is so costly in terms of time and money invested, the climbers who saw Sharp were focusing on their own goals, they believe, and not on the needs of anyone else.

Sir Edmund Hillary criticized those who left Sharp behind. Hillary said that he never would have left behind another living person, as human life is far more important than successfully completing a climb.

Some climbers believe that mountaineering ethics are changing. In the past, these climbers claim, a dying climber would not have been abandoned—not unless the rescue would threaten more lives. They also believe that true mountaineers, the elite, are totally disgusted by what is now happening at Mount Everest.

Thomas Sjogren, a Swedish mountaineer, was quoted as saying that top mountaineers help one another and they would not leave another person unless he or she was confirmed as dead. Mount Everest has turned commercial, according to Sjogren, with people paying tens of thousands of dollars to guides. This situation puts pressure on guides to complete the climb, no matter the human cost, and it also means that some of the climbers are those who can afford to pay a guide, but do not necessarily have skills to help other climbers (Associated Press 2006). They are not necessarily prepared to help themselves in emergency situations, either.

Lydia Bradey from New Zealand became the first woman to reach the summit of Mount Everest without using supplemental oxygen in 1988. She believes that, because of the factors listed above, people who now climb Mount Everest should prepare themselves for situations in which they will make some decisions that are "not very ethically nice" (Associated Press 2006).

Mount Everest was named for Sir George Everest, the military engineer who was the surveyor general of India from 1829 to 1843; he was the first to record the location and height of the mountain, which the British had previously called Peak XV. Most Nepali call the mountain Sagarmatha (Forehead in the Sky) and Tibetans call it Chomolungma (Goddess Mother of the World).

See also Alpine Scrambling; Mountain Climbing

F

FREE RUNNING

In free running, participants move throughout often-crowded areas, running and perhaps performing gymnastic moves. Their goal is not speed; rather, they embrace the freedom inherent in their movements and they use their body to express themselves and to creatively show the beauty of the human form. British journalist Thomas Sutcliffe described free running as "essentially cat-burglary without the larceny" (Sutcliffe 2003).

The founder of free running is Sébastien Foucan, who was born on May 24, 1974, in Paris, France. As a child, Foucan befriended David Belle and participated in **parkour** with him. In fact, Foucan has suggested that free running is one way to do parkour, and he encourages each person to "follow the way" and adopt free running as a form of individual personal expression.

The following movements are used in free running:

- "360 Wallrun": athletes run up a wall by using their feet to propel themselves; after kicking off the wall, they turn a full 360 degrees and then grab the top of the wall
- "Reverse Vault": the athlete adds a 360-degree spin as he or she vaults over a railing
- "Superman Front Flip": the runner flips over an obstacle that has a large drop on the other side

Free running has been included in movies, including in *Live Free or Die Hard* (2007) with Bruce Willis, wherein Cyril Rafaelli is shown demonstrating both free running and parkour. Foucan himself is shown in the James Bond movie *Casino Royale* (2006), and the 2005 movie *Jump Britain* also showcased free running.

Debates sometimes ensue as to how parkour and free running are different and how they are alike. Although competitions are not part of parkour, free running contests have been held. In October 2007, Red Bull sponsored the World's First Freerunning Competition in Vienna, Austria.

See also Robert, Alain; Urban Climbing

G

GENDER AND EXTREME SPORTS

Traditionally, men have participated in sporting activities to a much greater degree than women. In some sports, participation has been almost exclusively male throughout its history, up to and including now. In the world of extreme sports, men's participation numbers once again trump those of women, but women are making inroads more quickly in these sports than they did in traditional sports.

Perhaps this is because, in the United States and other western civilizations, women have never been totally banned from modern extreme sports participation, either from literal bans or by cultural norms that did not permit women to participate in the sports and still be an accepted member of society. Perhaps women have more quickly found inroads into extreme sports participation because, by the time that modern-day extreme sports became part of mainstream awareness, women in most western nations already were actively participating in most segments of society. At the present time in the United States, approximately 35 percent of high school athletes and 34 percent of college athletes are female, so the notion of a successful female athlete is more easily accepted now than in previous generations.

It is fair to say that women are part of the extreme sports culture, but to a significantly lesser degree than males. It is also fair to say that, in many sports, women still face obstacles in reaching full and equal participation, but progress is being made toward parity.

The following extreme sports have a moderate to significant amount of female participation:

- **Inline skating**: 51 percent
- Alpine **skiing**: 46 percent
- Mountain climbing and rock climbing: 40 percent
- **Windsurfing**: 40 percent
- **Snowboarding**: 34 percent
- Surfing: 33 percent
- **Mountain biking**: 30 percent
- **Skateboarding**: 26 percent
- **Sky diving**: 15 percent

Sports that have little female participation include **motocross**, **BMX (bicycle motocross)**, and drag racing. Sports that are experiencing a significant increase in female participation include snowboarding, kayaking, paintball, and skateboarding. Women have increased their participation in surfing by 280 percent from 1999 and 2003 (Booth and Thorpe 2007, 109).

Other matters should be considered besides the percentage of women participating in a particular extreme sport, including the depth of the opportunities; here, women are clearly lacking. When women do participate in extreme sports, they typically are offered fewer opportunities to compete than their male counterparts. For example, in the 2002 Summer **X Games**, women were able to compete in only three of the six competitive categories: speed climbing, **wakeboarding**, and inline skating (freestyle motocross and skateboarding, both street and vert, were only exhibition sports in 2002).

Moreover, pay scales for competition winners are seldom equal and the disparity is generally significant. For example, at the Xbox World Championship of Skateboarding, male medal winners won a total of $34,000, while the female medal winners collectively won only $3,600 (Dirksen 2002). As another example, professional BMX racer Arielle Martin was rated fourth in the world in 2002, according to the National Bicycle League. A successful BMX weekend for her meant prize money of $200 to $300, whereas a male winner of a comparable race would win from $1,000 to $2,000.

The word **sponsorship** often has different meanings, too, depending on the gender of the athlete. Sponsored males often receive a salary and lucrative prizes, whereas sponsored females often receive free clothing and sporting gear and equipment.

EXTREME SPORTS AND GENDER STEREOTYPES

People who participate in extreme sports are often described as courageous; strong, both physically and mentally; and willing to engage in risky behavior. Although these traits are praiseworthy, these characteristics are among those that are stereotypically said to belong to males; looked at from their inverse, they can be used to exclude females. For example, someone who participated in extreme sports can be described as "daring," and that would most likely be perceived as a positive trait. If that is reworded, however, as "one must be daring in order to participate in extreme sports," then that sentence is exclusionary—and could be used by those who believe in traditional gender stereotypes to exclude females.

According to sports sociologist Helen Lenskyj, "the clearest way that ... sport is consolidated as male territory is through the exclusion of women from sport on the basis that it is too risky" (Booth and Thorpe 2007, 103). Surfer Buzzy Trent reinforced this notion when he claimed that "girls" were weaker than men and that they faced a lesser chance of survival in dangerous wipeouts.

There is also a widespread perception that men are physically more capable than women because of the biological natures of the genders. In reality, infant females are more healthy, overall, and less likely to die as an infant than boys. Nevertheless, the notion persists that men are physically more capable than women—and, some would even say, biologically superior to women—despite the lack of solid evidence for this assertion.

If the makeup of the people who believed that women were biologically inferior was entirely male, perhaps women could more easily overcome these prejudices through the achievement of sporting successes. What sports sociologist Lois Bryson discovered, though, makes things all the more complicated; she has determined that many women also accept that their gender is biologically inferior. To a large degree, what a person believes to be true becomes his or her reality. Thus, as long as a percentage of women believe they are the weaker sex, this image of inferiority will persist in modern-day society.

Women may be told that they cannot participate in extreme sports because they need to protect their bodies. Mountain climber Alison Hargreaves faced this criticism when she was the subject of significant controversy in 1988. That year, she climbed Mount Eiger in Switzerland while five months pregnant. This was labeled as "me-first mountaineering" by British journalist Nigella Lawson. Hargreaves, who in 1995 became the second person, male or female, to climb Mount Everest without needing oxygen, died in 1998 as she was descending from her second successful climb of Mount Everest. Posthumously, she was labeled by the media as an "errant, unthinking mother" who had "effectively abandoned her children by taking such extraordinary risks" (Booth and Thorpe 2007, 103–4).

EXTREME SPORTS AND ALTERNATIVE CULTURE GROUPS

Belinda Wheaton, who spent two years studying a group of skateboarders, came to the conclusion that the skateboarding participants appreciated their status as counterculture "outsiders"; "challenged adult authority; and expressed disdain for extrinsic rewards and standards." They mocked people who intended to be or even wanted to be a professional skater, as skating for money was deemed inferior to skating for the love of the sport and for the opportunity to be part of its alternative subculture.

Oftentimes, when a group considers themselves as part of an alternative subculture, they band together in an "us versus them" mind-set. Within the skater culture, Wheaton determined, the "us" group was divided into two tiers of social order: the males, who hold the dominate roles, and the females, who have subservient positions within the group. A female in the skater culture would fit into one of the following three categories:

- A "skate betty": an attractive female who hangs around with less attractive males because she is impressed with their talent and daring
- A skate groupie: a female who wants to be considered part of the skateboarding group
- An exception to the rule: a female whose talents—which are as good as and, in some instances, perhaps better than the males' in their social group—are explained away by the skater subculture (Wheaton 2004).

When Wheaton studied windsurfers, she came up with similar results. A windsurfing sales person, for example, described an especially powerful and superior sail as a "man's sail." Television commercials depicted men actively participating in water sports, while the beautiful, tanned women rested on the beach in tiny bikinis. The women were presented as passive, while the men were active. Meanwhile, the attitude of male windsurfers was described in this manner:

It wasn't anti-female exactly, and it was more complex than that. But it put girls and women in their place, and that place in that "naturalised order of being" was not out on the waves. Naturally, that was a place for boys to act out being real men. To conquer their fears. To conquer nature. To conquer each other. And, as a sort of afterthought, to not be a female. (Wheaton 2004, 134)

EXTREME SPORTS AND BEHAVIOR PATTERNS

Although the number of females participating in extreme sports is increasing, at least in some areas, social beliefs—and the corresponding behavior patterns—may take longer to change. The notion of female inferiority in the world of sports is deeply ingrained and may not always operate in people's brains at a conscious level. A significant number of parents and a significant percentage of society as a whole therefore still may treat and respond to young boys and girls differently. As infants, we may perceive a baby girl as pretty and sweet, and a baby boy as strong, Under these circumstances, babies of different genders are still being treated differently.

Because of these beliefs, boys continue to be taught to bounce balls, run, and otherwise engage in physical activities to a larger degree than girls. Meanwhile, girls continue to be encouraged to be involved with more sedentary behaviors. If these cultural norms continue to be reinforced and passed along from generation to generation, then boys will continue to have a head start in sports participation (Oglesby et al. 1998). and common sense dictates that an early start would continue to put those athletes at a distinct advantage.

FEMALE EXTREME SPORTS ATHLETES AND FEMININITY

Some female extreme sports athletes wish to distance themselves from the stereotypical image of femininity, eschewing makeup, manicures, and the like, and recreating roles for themselves that are not part of traditional gender roles. Extreme sports, then, "provide some women with an 'alternative' identity and thus have the potential to empower core female participants via both their physical and culture experiences" (Booth and Thorpe 2007, 108). Women who create these alternative identities for themselves tend to be athletes who are committed to their sports and their participation in them.

Committed athletes, though, are not the only females who are associated with the extreme sports world. There are, in addition, those who participate in a sport because a partner or spouse is involved, and even those who participate because of a desire to meet members of the opposite gender. These women are the type, according to one extreme sports instructor, who would "use their snowboards purely as a fashion statement" (Booth and Thorpe 2007, 108).

Women choose to be involved with the extreme sports arena for a variety of reasons; there can be discord among those who do not agree with the reasons behind others' involvement. There can also be dissonance between those athletes who believe traditional femininity must be discarded to achieve extreme sporting goals and those who believe that the two qualities—femininity in the traditional sense and intense competitiveness—can coexist.

FEAR, EGOS, AND GENDER

Several successful female extreme sports athletes have stated that women have more fear than men when participating in their sports, but some see this fear and innate caution as a strength for females, rather than a weakness. It can be a strength, these female athletes believe, as long as they use this fear to make quality choices and to effectively estimate risk factors when participating in their sports.

Meanwhile, mountaineer Kristen Lignell and rock climber Lynn Hill believe that, overall, women have fewer ego issues to overcome than men, which allows them to more easily tune in to their intuition and make more successful choices in their sports. It is not just female athletes who have made assertions about females having advantages when making decisions about sports. **Boomerang** champion Gary Broadbent, who teaches school-age **children** about the sport of boomerangs, notes that females often catch on more quickly than males; moreover, they tend to have more finesse. He attributes that to the common urge in male students to overpower the boomerang, which, in effect, reduces its accuracy and lowers its likelihood to return.

GENDER AND EXTREME SPORTS INJURIES

In the United States, approximately 40 percent of sports injuries are sustained by women; 37 percent of sports injuries that require emergency rescue involve females, as well. When considering the number of college sports athletes who are female—34 percent—these figures do not seem significantly out of line.

That said, female skiers sustain three times as many knee fractures as males; and female mountain bikers are 1.94 times as likely as males to sustain injuries, and 4.17 times as likely to sustain a fracture.

EXTREME SPORTS AND WHITE MALES

Michael A. Messner brings up an interesting point in his book, *Taking the Field: Women, Men, and Sports* (2002). Extreme sports have been, by their very nature, on the margins of the sporting world; even if these sports become mainstreamed, their creation still sprung from outside the world of traditional sports. It would seem natural, then, that disenfranchised or marginalized groups would have created and served as early participants in these sports; however, in fact, the typical extreme sports athlete is—and has been—a white male. How did this happen? Messner suggests that, when traditional sports began to have increasing numbers of females and black males as participants, the white males began to carve out a new arena for themselves in the area of extreme sports (Messner 2002).

Two other pieces of information bolster Messner's contention, the first of which is the passage of Title IX of the Education Amendments of 1972. The pertinent section of this law reads that, "No person in the United States shall, on the basis of sex, be excluded from participation in, or denied the benefits of, or be subjected to discrimination under any educational program or activity receiving federal assistance."

Title IX did in fact change the experience of women and sports. By comparing the athletic participation of females under the age of 10 before the law was passed to girls who reached that age after the law was passed, an increase of 19 percent in participation figures is seen. This act clearly was a boon to women wishing to participate in sports—and it also fits in with the timing of the early growth of extreme sports participation by white males in the United States—the 1970s. This supports Messner's contention that the increase in female athletes in part served as the impetus for white males to begin creating new alternative sports.

The second thing that bolstered women's place in the traditional sports was known as the "Battle of the Sexes," which occurred when tennis player Bobby Riggs challenged a professional female tennis player—Billie Jean King, the "women's lib leader"—to a match that would be broadcast on television. Riggs stirred much ire when he announced that women would never—and could never—beat men in sporting competitions.

Riggs had already won 20 Wimbledon titles, while King had won the Associated Press's Woman Athlete of the Year award in 1967 and 1973 and the *Sports Illustrated* Sportswoman of the Year in 1972.

King agreed to the match, in part because she believed this would draw attention to the lower pay for female athletes. Riggs further aggravated some viewers by wearing shirts asking for "Men's Liberation" and served as the hero to other viewers. In his interviews, he would boast that, if he was going to symbolize a male chauvinist pig, he would be the biggest one ever.

Approximately 50 million people watched this match on September 20, 1973. Riggs arrived in a carriage pulled by women, while University of Houston football players carried King onto the court. The match was not close, with Billie Jean King beating Bobby Riggs in three straight sets (6-4, 6-3, and 6-3). Riggs was gracious, crediting King's speed and overall excellence for the results.

Both Title IX and the Riggs-King match chipped away at the overwhelming dominance of males in the arena of traditional sports. Perhaps this lessening of control provided further impetus for increasing numbers of white males to find a new playing field in the world of extreme sports.

ORGANIZATIONS ADVOCATING FOR WOMEN IN EXTREME SPORTS

Action Sports Alliance (ASA, http://www.actionsportsalliance.com)

This organization, formed in 2005, "is constantly working to enhance action sports and increase opportunities for women" and is the "voice of female skateboarding professionals." ASA is the organization that in 2006 advocated for a larger percentage of the X Games prize money for female skateboarders, also pushing for and receiving increased media attention and television coverage for X Games events in which women participated. They also wanted input into the organization and management of skateboarding events for women. The increased coverage, ASA leadership reasoned, would help boost the popularity of women's skateboarding, which could boost sponsorship dollars and prize purses for competitors. If their demands for better prize money and more significant media coverage were not met, this group of female skateboarders had intended to boycott the 2006 X Games.

Before this discussion took place, women's vert skateboarders in 2006 were going to split a total purse of $14,000, with $5,000 going to the gold medalist. After this discussion, the gold medal prize was upped to $15,000, which was $13,000 more than the previous year's prize. The men's prize purse for vert skateboarding in 2006 was $108,000, with the gold medal winner receiving $50,000.

Another result of the talks was that Jen O'Brien, an ASA board member and 2003 X Games silver medalist, and **Cara-Beth Burnside**, ASA president, were added to the X Games selection committee, which to date had been exclusively male. Burnside had competed in the 1998 Winter Olympics in snowboarding half-pipe, finishing fourth. She has won numerous medals at the Summer X Games and the Winter X Games over the past 10 years, including a 2005 gold medal in skateboard vert; she also won a gold medal for skateboarding in the 2006 X Games. In part because of negotiations between ASA and ESPN, surfing was added as a women's sport at the 2007 Summer X Games. In the 2008 games, women will be competing in motocross for the first time.

Although this momentum was encouraging to the female athletes, the *New York Times* pointed out that, "Nothing resembling Title IX's federal legislation promoting gender equity in sports exists in network boardrooms, where the skateboarders face television executives who are focused on ratings" (Higgins 2006). Therefore, the struggle for parity in extreme sports likely will continue for some time.

To help people monitor the opportunities and challenges facing modern female athletes, the ASA Web site includes a page of links that leads to articles that discuss women and extreme sports, frequently focusing on pay disparities.

Skate Like a Girl (SLAG, http://www.skatelikeagirl.com)

This volunteer organization holds skateboarding events for women of all ages and skill levels. Their mission is to "build community among women, challenge oppression and teach confidence." Nancy Chang of SLAG shares why she is attracted to extreme sports: "When you're doing something that you normally see guys doing, that's like wow, I can do everything they're doing, or at least I can try to be a part of that. I think that's a very empowering thing, not to be scared to try" (http://www.wptv.com/content/segments/smartwomen/story.aspx?content_id=d345954d-9a17-4b0f-b580-9f0914f0a015).

Misty Blues All Female Skydiving Team (http://www.mistyblues.com)

This team has been performing globally for more than 20 years; five of the nine team members also hold a private pilot's license. By combining the records of all nine women, members of this team have set 35 world records and made 40,000 jumps. The professions of the Misty Blues include doctor, airport manager, accounting manager, engineer, business owner, and welder. In addition to performing throughout the United States, the team has performed in the following countries:

- Canada
- Indonesia
- Japan
- Malaysia
- Mexico
- Puerto Rico
- United Arab Emirates

Girls Learn to Ride (GLTR, http://www.girlslearntoride.com)

GLTR provides female-only action sports clinics and camps to help women master basic skills and increase confidence. Sports include skateboarding, surfing, snowboarding, wakeboarding, motocross, BMX, and mountain biking.

EXTREME SPORTS: FEMALE ROLE MODELS

Nancy Coulter-Parker, the editor of WomenOutdoors.com, believes that increasing numbers of females will participate in extreme sports in the future because they now have appropriate role models to follow. She lists snowboarders Shannon Dunn and Barrett Christy; surfers Lisa Andersen and Rochelle Ballard; and mountain bikers

Alison Sydor and Alison Dunlap as examples. Coulter-Parker believes that the increasing amount of extreme sports media coverage will also encourage more females to participate.

Coulter-Parker explains—

> I think women are drawn to sports that have fluidity and that require balance and coordination, not just a lot of "balls to the wall" attitude. For instance, women are attracted to surfing and snowboarding. Climbing is another sport in which women tend to excel, whereas skateboarding has not seen much growth in female participation. (Sutton n.d.)

She adds that alternative sports "empower women with independence, individuality, and confidence" in large part because these sports generally are self-directed and participants cannot rely on the encouragement of their team to achieve goals (Sutton n.d.).

EXTREME SPORTS ENTREPRENEURS

In January 2008, the online version of *Entrepreneur* published an article suggesting that catering to the female extreme athlete is a smart business move. They quoted the 2006 Surf Industry Manufacturers Association (SIMA) Retail Distribution Study; according to this study, the surfing industry grew from $6.52 billion in 2004 to $7.48 billion in 2006.

SIMA states that part of the growth came from the increasing purchasing power of women, adding that sales of women's surf apparel increased 32 percent: from $249 million in 2004 to $327 million in 2006 (Williams 2008).

EXTREME SPORTS AND ATTRACTIVENESS QUOTIENT

Richard Wiseman, author of *Quirkology: The Curious Science of Everyday Lives* (2008), provides results of quirky surveys on his Web site (http://www.quirkology.com/UK/index.shtml). One study surveyed 6,000 people as to which sport activities would make a person of the opposite sex more attractive. Fifty-six percent of the women stated that extreme sports participation would make a man more attractive to them; this was the second highest answer, beaten only by climbing at 57 percent. Aerobics was the answer that received the smallest number of votes (9 percent).

Conversely, 70 percent of men believed that aerobics participation made a woman more attractive, followed by yoga at 65 percent. Conclusions drawn from this study on the Web site were that women were attracted by bravery and a willingness to take on challenges, but "men are more shallow, looking for a woman who is physically fit but not challenging their ego by being overly strong" (http://www.quirkology.com/UK/index.shtml) It should be noted, however, that 32 percent of men found female extreme sports athletes attractive.

Questions raised—but not answered—by this survey include the following: To what degree do male and/or female athletes modify their behavior to conform to what pleases their friends, partners, and spouses of the opposite gender? Is their degree of extreme sports participation affected by these feelings?

PROFILES OF FEMALE EXTREME SPORTS ATHLETES

Christine Boskoff, is a 37-year-old woman who is one of two living females who have climbed six of the world's 26,246-foot (8,000-meter) mountains, including the tallest:

29,028-foot (8,848-meter) Mount Everest. She has also spent days living in tents flattened by 100 mile (161 kilometer) per hour winds. Her goal had been to climb 14 mountains but, when her husband committed suicide in 1999, she was forced to focus on running their company, Mountain Madness. Boskoff admitted that she has foregone a family to have enough time for her mountain climbing, but she added that mountain climbing enhances her self-confidence and helps her live for the moment (Stripling 2004).

Twenty-nine-year-old Lara Pazemenas calls herself a "ski streaker" because she has skied at least one day a month for 38 months in a row. She has faced significant illness and pain, surviving breast cancer at age 23, and she suffers from degenerative joint disease; when she skis, she's always in pain. She has also had more than one knee surgery. To support her skiing, she works as the Alaska operations manager for Wildland Adventures in the daytime, and she spends her evenings working as a house supervisor for the Seattle Children's Home.

She has been in risky situations while skiing in the past. "I've been caught in some avalanches," Pazemenas said, "and I've released avalanches on people, and it's not fun to watch somebody tumble and scream. There's always a risk, but I usually err on the side of caution because I want to go out there and do it again. Education is huge" (Stripling 2004).

Fifty-seven-year-old C.J. Sturtevant participated in the U.S. Paragliding Nationals, unofficially winning the "golden geezer" award. Sturtevant explained that she's "not into extreme danger, and I don't like extreme hardship, but I do like extreme freedom" (Stripling 2004).

She recalled being overweight and nearsighted as a child, always the last kid picked to be on a sports team. She began participating in rock climbing and **hang gliding** as an adult, and then she tried the sport that turned into her passion: paragliding. Besides participating in the sport, she is now the editor of *Hang Gliding & Paragliding* magazine (Stripling 2004).

See also Crandal, Louise; Csizmazia, Kim; da Silva, Fabiola; Roller Derby; Shaw, Brooke

GOLF, EXTREME

In traditional golf, the player with the lowest score wins the tournament. In extreme golf, the goal is to complete an entire standard 18-hole golf course with the lowest combination of strokes and time. A player makes a shot, and then must run to the next hole carrying anywhere from one to six clubs. Unlike in traditional golf, where caddies carry necessary equipment, in extreme golf, caddies and carts are not allowed. Speedgolf International recommends that competitors carry four to six clubs in a small bag; some players carry only one club and a putter.

Whenever a competitor needs to pass a slower competitor, the faster one has the right of way. The faster golfer should call "fore," which tells the slower player to temporarily stop to let the quicker competitor play through.

Scoring in extreme golf is straightforward. A speedgolfer's score is added to his or her time to compute the final score; the person with the lowest score wins. In other words, a person who shot 85 in 45 minutes (130) would beat the person who shot 75 in 57 minutes (132). In 1997, Jay Larson completed a course in less than 40 minutes, which is the amount of time that a traditional golfer uses to play three holes (Cavanaugh 1997). Extreme golf is also known as speedgolf, fitness golf, or hit-and-run golf. There is an entire television channel dedicated to this sport: Extreme Golf TV.

HISTORY OF EXTREME GOLF

The first game of speed golf was played by Steve Scott, the runner who set the U.S. record for 1 mile at 3:47:69 in 1982 and who won the silver medal at the 1,500-meter race at the first International Association of Athletics Federations (IAAF) World Outdoor Championships in Helsinki in 1983. In 1979, Scott wondered how quickly he could play 18 holes of golf; he discovered that it took him 29 minutes, 33.05 seconds at the 6,025-yard Miller Golf Course in Anaheim, California. Although his score—at 92—was too high to be successful in extreme golf, Scott took a golf shot every 19.27 seconds.

In 1997, Larson and other speedgolfers formed the International Speed Golf Association, basing it on the premise established by Scott. Larson, also a runner, has competed in the **Ironman Triathlon** in Hawaii, finishing as high as 11th place in the grueling competition.

By 1999, there were approximately 4,000 extreme golfers registered, worldwide (Garcia 1999). As an example of how far the influence of extreme golf has reached, in 2001, the Malaysia Speed Golf tournament was held at Kelab Golf Perkhidmatan Awam in Kuala Lumpur. Sponsors of the tournament included Cross Creek, Wilson, Coppertone, Pharmaton, Perskindol, Clark Hatch International, and RGT Sports.

EXTREME GOLF COMPETITION RESULTS

Following are the winners from several U.S. tournaments over the past several years:

2002 Chicago Speedgolf Class
Winner: Tim Scott
  Golf Score: 70
  Time: 42:07
  Total Score: 112:07

2003 Bandon Dunes Speedgolf Classic
Winner: Tim Scott
  Golf Score: 79
  Time: 55:15
  Total Score: 134:15

2003 Chicago Speedgolf Class
Winner: Tim Scott
  Golf Score: 71
  Time: 43:47
  Total Score: 114:47

2004 Chicago Speedgolf Class
Winner: Christopher Smith
  Golf Score: 72
  Time: 45:38
  Total Score: 117:38

2005 Bandon Dunes Speedgolf Classic
Winner: Tim Scott
    Golf Score: 76
    Time: 53:58
    Total Score: 129:58

2005 Chicago Speedgolf Classic
Winner: Christopher Smith
    Golf Score: 65
    Time: 44:06
    Total Score: 109:06

2006 Bandon Dunes Speedgolf Classic
Winner: Christopher Smith
    Golf Score: 72
    Time: 53:22
    Total Score: 125:22

2006 Chicago Speedgolf Class
Winner: Brad Walker
    Golf Score: 73
    Time: 52:12
    Total Score: 125:12

2007 Bandon Dunes Speedgolf Classic
Winner: Tim Scott
    Golf Score: 74
    Time: 53:58
    Total Score: 127:58

2008 Bandon Dunes Speedgolf Classic
Winner: Tim Scott
    Golf Score: 76
    Time: 55:12
    Total Score: 131:12

EXTREME GOLF EQUIPMENT
Competitors use the same equipment that they would in traditional golf, except they must lighten their load to maintain the speed and endurance needed for extreme golf. Competitors are expected to adhere to the traditional golf dress code.

GRAVITY GAMES
Gravity Games are a competition of high adrenaline extreme sporting events. Initially, the games were set up to occur twice a year, with one event featuring summer sports and the other featuring winter sports. As the games evolved, competitions became quarterly events, with one of the new competitions focusing on water sports and the other focusing on mountain sports.

The first summer Gravity Games were held in Providence, Rhode Island, in September 1999, with the 2000 and 2001 summer games also scheduled to occur in that venue. More than 200,000 fans watched as 230 athletes from around the globe competed for 51 medals and for the prize purse that totaled $800,000. More than 500 volunteers were needed to organize and run these games. Congressman Patrick Kennedy stated that he expected the Gravity Games to boost the state's economy by $75 to $100 million over a three-year period.

Events in the summer Gravity Games included biking races, **inline skating**, downhill skateboarding, **skateboarding**, **street luge**, **wakeboarding**, and freestyle **motocross** on various courses, which included downhill, water, vertical, dirt, and street.

The Gravity Games were created and financed by NBC Sports and EMAP Petersen, Inc. The latter is a specialty publishing house that publishes more than 160 niche magazines, including *Sport, Slam, Box, Skateboarder, Surfer, BMX Rider, MX Racer, Inline Hockey News, Snowboarder, Powder, Bike, Dirt Rider, Trail Rider,* and *Gravity Magazine*. Although the Gravity Games were not aired live, NBC aired the games over a period of five Sundays, starting in October. According to Business Wire, NBC anticipated that 200 million viewers in more than 100 countries would watch these broadcasts (Business Wire 1999).

Gravity Games organizers focused as much on the lifestyle of the athletes as the specific competitions at hand; perhaps this was intended to differentiate these games from the already established and financially lucrative **X Games**. In at least one way, though, the Gravity Games and the X Games were remarkably alike: each relied heavily on corporate sponsors. This reliance is evident in the list of activities available for spectators, which included the opportunity to—

- Test their skills on the U.S. Marine Corps obstacle course
- Sample Atari Action titles at the Hasbro Interactive tent
- Try free samples of Speed Stick Ultimate
- Play the Toyota wheel of fortune
- See the talents of graffiti, painting, photography, and video artists at the Unionbay booth
- Visit the Mountain Dew & Doritos Loud Lounge (Business Wire 1999)

Mountain Dew was the exclusive beverage sponsor; Toyota was the exclusive automotive sponsor; the U.S. Marine Corps was the exclusive armed services sponsor; and Unionbay was the exclusive apparel sponsor. GAS Entertainment Company provided all of the **music** and entertainment.

The inaugural winter Gravity Games took place on Mammoth Mountain in California in January 2000; the games were televised in February. Events included the following:

- Freeskiing big mountain
- Men's big mountain skiing
- Men's **snowboarding**
- Women's snowboarding
- Boardercross
- Women's skiercross
- Women's superpipe
- Skiercross (snowboarder **Shaun Palmer** challenging nine Olympic skiers)
- Women's big mountain skiing
- Women's skiing, freestyle
- **Snowmobiling**

- Men's superpipe
- Men's big air skiing
- Men's skiercross

After the first three summer Gravity Games were held in Providence, Rhode Island, the venue switched to Cleveland, Ohio, for the next three summers. Attendance at the Gravity Games held in Cleveland was 153,000 spectators (2002), 163,000 spectators (2003), and 76,819 (2004)—it is suspected that rain kept some spectators away in 2004.

Television viewership of these games continued to rise—in particular, teenage and young adult male viewership (the target market) was monitored. In 2001, 200,000 male teenagers watched the 2001 Gravity Games, which was an increase over the 2000 figures. When adding in viewership numbers from men in their early 20s, results indicate that nearly 320,000 males ages 12 to 24 watched the 2001 Gravity Games.

By analyzing the sponsors, though, a shift can be noted. Originally, the sponsors of the Gravity Games were manufacturers of products that younger fans of skateboarding and **BMX (bicycle motocross)** would buy: snack foods and soda pop. Skating and biking gear and clothing were also available. By the time the games switched to Cleveland, though, the sponsors were targeting the young adults, with Saturn being the primary sponsor, and Kohl's department stores serving as an apparel sponsor.

In 2003, announcers used Activision's **Tony Hawk's** Underground **video games** to illustrate the moves that the street and vert skateboarding athletes were using in the Gravity Games competitions. Activision already was a key sponsor of the Gravity Games, and the company used the Gravity Games to promote the newest version of Tony Hawk's Underground video game. Also providing promotional support for the launch were AT&T Wireless, Nestlé's Butterfinger and Tombstone Pizza, DC Shoes, Hawk Clothing, Vans, Transworld SKATEboarding, and Quiksilver.

In July 2003, Don Meek, the Gravity Games president, announced the first live broadcast of the games. The format of the games, overall, would change somewhat, with a competition occurring every quarter throughout the year. The new format would feature the following events:

- Gravity Games, winter, which would include snowboarding, and skiing superpipe, slopestyle, and big mountain; these games would take place over the Super Bowl weekend
- Gravity Games, summer, which would include biking, inline skating, wakeboarding, freestyle motocross, and skateboarding, with the games taking place in May
- Gravity Games, mountain, which would include street luge, downhill skateboarding, downhill mountain biking, and BMX, over the Labor Day weekend
- Gravity Games, water, which would include wakeboarding, **kite surfing**, and tow-in surfing, with the games to be held over the Thanksgiving holiday

In 2004, Cleveland hosted the first medal competition for women's skateboarding in the Gravity Games; more than 6,000 spectators watched the competition, which had these results:

- Gold medal: Elissa Steamer of Fort Myers, Florida
- Silver medal: Lauren Perkins of Newport Beach, California
- Bronze medal: Lyn-Z Adams Hawkins of San Diego, California

Steamer who, at age 29, was the oldest person in the competition, was awarded $3,500. The total purse for women's street skate was $12,500, which was nearly $3,000 more than the amount awarded for this event at the X Games.

The prize purse for the 2004 Summer Gravity Games overall was $602,000; approximately 225 athletes competed for those dollars. The athletes ranged in age from 14 (skateboard gold medalist Ryan Sheckler) to 37 (Jim Burgess, BMX vert, and Dennis McCoy, bike street and bike vert).

In 2004, Perth, Australia, served as the venue for water sports (wakeboarding, kite surfing, and tow-in surfing), and the accompanying festival featured a BMX course, a skate park, a rock climbing wall, and more. The Gravity Games H2O, as these came to be called, were shown in more than 60 countries, with an estimated viewership of more than 300 million people, including viewers in China, Japan, Singapore, Malaysia, Germany, the United Kingdom, New Zealand, South Africa, Scandinavia, and the Middle East. Hosts of these games expected to see $1.15 million in direct revenue.

Aspen, Colorado, has hosted the winter Gravity Games since 2002, with the Aspen Skiing Company serving as a key sponsor. The Outdoor Life Network, owned by Comcast Corporation, televises the games. The president of the Outdoor Life Network has identified the target audience as 18 to 25 year olds, and has sponsored the games in the hopes of attracting this demographic to the Aspen Skiing Company resort. The number of spectators for these games has increased from 36,000 spectators in 2002, to more than 48,000 in 2003, to 66,500 in 2004, to 69,700 spectators in 2005.

Steve "Maverick" Hass walks up the outdoor vert ramp for the Gravity Games. (AP Photo/Carolyn Kaster)

GRAVITY GAMES: 1999 MEDALISTS
Aggressive Inline Skating
Men's Vert

First: Taig Khris, Paris, France $18,000
Second: Shane Yost, Melbourne, Australia $10,000
Third: Cesar Mora, Sydney, Australia $7,000

Women's Vert

First: Fabiola da Silva, São Paolo, Brazil $10,000
Second: Merce Borrull, Barcelona, Spain $5,500
Third: Maki Komori, Fukouka, Japan $4,000

Men's Street

First: Sven Boekhorst, Den Bosch, Holland $18,000

Second: Louie Zamora, San Diego, California $10,000
Third: Mike Budnik, Irvine, California $7,000

Women's Street

First: Fabiola da Silva, São Paolo, Brazil $10,000
Second: Anneke Winter, Weil am Rhein, Germany $5,500
Third: Kelly Matthews, Hoboken, New Jersey $4,000

Bike
Street

First: Dave Mirra, Wilmington, North Carolina $18,000
Second: Ryan Nyquist, Gilroy, California $10,000
Third: Jay Miron, Thunder Bay, Canada $7,000

Dirt

First: Ryan Nyquist, Gilroy, California $18,000
Second: Tony Walkowiak, Pittsburgh, Pennsylvania $10,000
Third: T. J. Lavin, Las Vegas, Nevada $7,000

Vert

First: Jamie Bestwick, Heanor, England $18,000
Second: Jay Miron, Thunder Bay, Canada $10,000
Third: John Parker, Mesa, Arizona $7,000

Downhill Skateboarding
2-Man

First: Lee Dansie, Reigate, England $6,000
Second: Biker Sherlock, San Diego, California $4,500
Third: Dane von Bommel, San Diego, California $3,000

4-Man

First: Biker Sherlock, San Diego, California $6,000
Second: Dane von Bommel, San Diego, California $4,500
Third: Emanuel Antuna, Carros, France $3,000

Freestyle Motocross
First: Travis Pastrana, Annapolis, Maryland $18,000
Second: Brian Deegan, Canyon Lake, California $10,000
Third: Carey Hart, Corona, California $7,000

Team Freestyle
First: Travis Pastrana, Annapolis, Maryland $18,000
Kenny Bartram, Stillwater, Oklahoma
Second: Kris Rourke, Santee, California $10,000

Ronnie Faisst, Corona, California
Third: Adam Pierce, Bakersfield, California $7,000
Brian Ferrell, Bakersfield, California

Skateboarding
Vert

First: Bob Burnquist, Rio de Janeiro, Brazil $18,000
  Second: Bucky Lasek, Baltimore, Maryland $10,000
  Third: Andy Macdonald, San Diego, California $7,000

Street

First: Brian Anderson, Groton, Connecticut $18,000
  Second: Rodil Araujo, Jr., Wenceskau, Brazil $10,000
  Third: Eric Koston, Los Angeles, California $7,000

Street Luge
6-Man

First: Biker Sherlock, San Diego, California $15,000
  Second: Sean Slate, Cardiff, California $10,000
  Third: Wade Sokol, Huntington Beach, California $7,500

4-Man

First: Sean Mallard, Fullerton, California $15,000
  Second: Biker Sherlock, San Diego, California $10,000
  Third: George Orton, Huntington Beach, California $7,500

Wakeboarding
Men's

First: Shaun Murray, Orlando, Florida $18,000
  Second: Parks Bonifay, Lake Alfred, Florida $10,000
  Third: Rob Struharik, Boardman, Ohio $7,500

Women's

First: Andrea Gaytan, Mexico City, Mexico $13,000
  Second: Tara Hamilton, Lantana, Florida $7,000
  Third: Christy Lee Smith, N. Little Rock, Arkansas $4,500

H

HANG GLIDING

In Greek mythology, Icarus flew on artificial wings, dying after flying too close to the sun. The heat melted the wax holding his wings together and he plunged to his death—a bitter end to what was a mythological story of a human trying to fly. Many centuries later, Italian artist and inventor Leonardo da Vinci imagined the power of flight, sketching out his ideas—and some of these drawings resembled modern-day hang gliders (MacCurdy 1938).

In the early 1890s, German inventor Otto "Glider King" Lilienthal created the early form of a hang glider using research that he and his brother Gustav conducted (and that Gustav published in a book, *Bird Flight as a Basis for Aviation*). After creating 18 models of gliders, Otto tried to create flight using a carbonic acid gas motor on August 9, 1896, but he crashed from a distance of 56 feet (17 meters), breaking his spine. The next day, he died of his injuries after saying, "[s]acrifices must be made" (Day and Mcneil 1998, 436).

Sir George Cayley of England and John Montgomery of the United States also created nonmotorized flying machines in the nineteenth century. The research of the Lilienthal brothers, Cayley, and Montgomery then inspired the Wright brothers to study flight. Both Orville and Wilbur were experienced hang gliders before they took their historic flight in Kitty Hawk, North Carolina, in 1903.

The modern hang glider is based on a NASA design from the 1960s when the agency was researching ways to return the Gemini two-man orbital spacecraft to Earth. The lightweight, flexible wing that they created for this purpose—known as the Rogallo wing after inventors Francis and Gertrude Rogallo—is the basis of contemporary hang gliding and of the invention of the sport hang glider. Technology has continued to improve upon this invention, leading to hang gliders that are safer and less likely to crash. They are also more comfortable and easier to fly. By the 1970s, hang gliders could be launched by foot; this innovation caused the sport to spread throughout the United States and England.

The U.S. Hang Gliding Association was formed in 1971. This organization, now known as U.S. Hang Gliding and Paragliding Association, Inc. (USHPA), conducts trainings, promotes the sport, and sanctions competitions. Competitions sponsored by USHPA include the Hang On Hang Gliding Nationals, which is described as an "out

Jason Otto, a hang glider from Tucson, Arizona, jumps from the launch ramp at the top of Dry Canyon during a Memorial Day fly-in. (AP Photo/*Alamogordo Daily*)

and return, triangles and cross country race to goal" (www.ushpa.aero/calendar.asp). A helmet, a Global Positioning System (GPS) device, and a radio that can receive and transmit signals are required for all those who enter the competition.

In extreme hang gliding, experienced pilots perform full barrel rolls, inverted maneuvers, and other stunt flying moves. It is no longer unusual for an experienced hang glider to travel 200 miles (320 kilometers) or reach altitudes higher than 10,000 feet (3,000 meters). In 1979, five Americans flew across the country in hang gliders with auxiliary motors. In 1985, American hang glider Larry Tudor set a height record of 14,250.69 feet (4,343.61 meters) as he flew above Horseshoe Meadows, California. In 2001, Manfred Ruhmer of Austria flew the longest distance—431.14 miles (700.6 kilometers) over Zapata, Texas.

Those who pilot hang gliders can become quite poetic about their sport. "In a hang glider," says one such aficionado, "you feel the sound of the wind going past you. You're not falling; you're gliding through the air" (*Washington Times* 2005). According to another testimonial, "[y]ou can get so high that you can see the curvature of the Earth. You can soar with hawks and eagles off your wing tips. You can dive and swoop in the sky on a good day. You can drive like a race car in the sky" (*Washington Times* 2005).

In hang gliding, the pilot is suspended from a strap, generally in a prone position, that hangs from a nonmotorized aluminum wing covered by nylon or Mylar. The pilot makes a running start from a hill or other high elevation and then uses his or her foot to push off. The hang glider then moves up, rather than down. The goal of the hang gliding pilot is to reach enough elevation that he or she can "ride" the thermals, which are warm pockets of air. A powerful thermal can pull a hang glider up 3,000 feet (914.4 meters)—and then it is possible to reach another level of thermals and then another. With experience, pilots can stay in the air for hours.

It is estimated that 5 to 10 percent of hang glider pilots in the United States are female. With the development of lighter gliders and more advanced instruction techniques, the sport is becoming better adapted to lighter-weight pilots, which should advance the percentage of females participating in hang gliding.

Kari Castle of the United States holds the distance world record for women; in 2001, she flew 217.5 miles (350 kilometers) from Zapata, Texas. Judy Leden of England holds the altitude record of all hang gliders, male or female: on October 25, 1994, she launched at 38,898 feet (11,856 meters) from a balloon over Wadi Rum, Jordan. Except for the Women's World Meet held every other year, men and women compete together in competitions. The three types of competitions are as follows:

- Aerobatics/Freestyle: Aesthetics are the goal and participants are judged on precision, technique, and elegance.
- Speed Gliding: This short race is held close on the ground.
- Cross Country: This is the most common type of competition, and races usually last between one and two weeks and the course is charted for participants. Each day, the racers are assigned a different task that may take 2 to 6 hours and may involve 80 to 240 kilometers in distance. Participants must take photos of their turn points or document their flight with a GPS device. The goal is to complete all of these tasks accurately and in the shortest amount of time.

The hang glider is steered by the shifting of the pilot's weight, which shifts the center of gravity of the glider. When the pilot moves forward or back or from side to side, the glider rolls in the same direction. People new to hang gliding can be trained in larger tandem hang gliders, wherein an experienced instructor demonstrates moves before the pilot-in-training tries by himself or herself. Training on a tandem glider can shorten the learning curve by up to 30 percent (Tomlinson and Leigh 2004).

Rather than pushing off from a hill or cliff, hang gliding students generally practice on level ground. During early lessons, the instructor tends to handle the launching and landing phases of the flight, gradually allowing the student to do more and more on his or her own. In some instances, the students are taught through truck towing or aerotowing. With truck towing, the glider is attached to a winch in the truck and is released as the truck accelerates; in aerotowing, the glider is towed by another aircraft.

Individual maneuvers are taught through trial and error, until the student has learned enough to fly solo—or when he or she is no longer a beginner or a "wuffo." Students may need as many as 60 to 80 lessons before being certified as novices by the USHPA. It is typical to spend about $750 for these lessons; choosing to learn by aerotowing can cost anywhere from $1,200 to $1,500. Some instructors charge fees based on the altitude reached during a lesson.

To save money on the sport, some students take lessons in the winter, when they often get a discount. Plus, as relatively more experienced gliders are looking to buy new equipment in the spring, they sell off their old gliders at a reduced price during the winter. Moreover, learning to hang glide in the cooler, denser air of winter makes it easier to launch and land the glider.

Hang Gliding Risks and Injuries

The USHPA monitors the number of hang gliding accidents and publishes annual reports. In 2006, six nonmotorized paragliding deaths occurred in the United States, which is twice the average (this figure was higher than usual in 2006 because of rare tandem accidents occurring). Forty-nine accidents were recorded, which includes the fatalities. In the "2006 Paragliding Accidents" report, writer Mike Steed puts the fatality figure into context, stating that, in 2006, 22 people died in the U.S. from human stampedes (Steed 2006).

Tree landings are uncommon, and they are seldom problematic; however, one injury in 2006 did occur because of a tree landing. USHPA offers insurance plans to cover expenses if a hang glider pilot hits another person, animal, or tree while landing. More problematic are sudden thunderstorms because of the dangerous combination of lightning and metal parts in hang gliders.

Hang Gliding Equipment

Hang gliders cost between $3,600 and $5,000, plus another $500 or more if a two-way radio and a variometer (a device that tells you if you are going up or down and at what speed) are purchased. The typical life span of a regularly used hang glider is four years. Harnesses cost anywhere from $200 to $800, and an emergency parachute can cost anywhere from $300 to $600. Helmets cost approximately $150. Pilots need to wear helmets and should take along hook knives to cut harness lines or straps when needed; light ropes to lower themselves after landing on a tree or to haul up tools; and first aid equipment. If hang gliding in the winter, participants wear long underwear and ski-like attire, including gloves, snow boots, and goggles.

Technology used to create hang gliders continues to improve as lighter and stronger materials are being employed. Hang gliders are now being built with aircraft aluminum and stainless steel with a polyester fiber sail; these sails generally can lift 1 ton without breaking. These hang gliders also contain full instrumentation, radios, and rocket-deployed emergency parachutes.

See also Crandal, Louise; Gender and Extreme Sports

Ultralite Triking

In the sport of ultralite triking, an athlete rides in a motorized hang glider, sitting in the aluminum trike frame. He or she steers the device by shifting his or her weight, which is also the method of controlling speed. The trike wing is crafted of strong nylon or Mylar. Trikes can climb up to an elevation of 15,000 feet (4,572 meters); remain in the air for an average of 3 hours; and travel significant distances. If the motor stops working, the trike can still safely glide to the ground.

New ultralite trikes cost anywhere between $8,000 and $30,000. A trike typically lasts four years, after which the exposure to ultraviolet light may damage the wing. Accessories for the trike—including two-way radios, instruments, and safety helmets—generally cost between $1,000 and $1,500. Used trikes are often for sale at reduced prices. Although a license is not required to fly a trike, flying lessons are recommended. Pilots do not need to push off to start flight, as the motor will lift the pilot without any outside aid.

A video, *Monumental Triking: Ultralight Powered Hang Gliding in Monument Valley*, was filmed on the border of Arizona and Utah, along with a few scenes from Hawaii. This video captured scenic views as seen from the ultralite triking athlete.

HAWK, TONY (BIRDMAN) (1968–)

Anthony "Tony" Hawk is perhaps the most well-known skateboarder in the world today, both because of his accomplishments in **skateboarding** and because of his commercial products: fashion apparel, videos, **video games**, skateboards, helmets, and more. He has successfully combined the rebel image of skateboarding with commercial concerns and *Sporting News* has named him as one of the top 100 most influential athletes in the world today (Hawk is number 72).

Hawk was born on May 12, 1968, in San Diego, California, to World War II and Korean War veteran and decorated Navy pilot Frank Hawk and his wife, Nancy. He has three siblings: Steve, Patricia, and Lenore, who were 12 to 21 years older. In his autobiography, *Hawk: Occupation: Skateboarder*, Hawk describes himself as a "hyper, rail thin geek on a sugar buzz," adding that his mother found him "challenging." As a young child, he was kicked out of preschool for bad behavior; tipped over game boards if he was going to lose; and threw frequent tantrums.

Hawk shared how his parents took him to see a psychologist when he was 8 years old, in large part because of the frustration he would feel when he could not accomplish a physical task. The psychologist described him as having a 12-year-old mind in an 8-year-old body, and it was not until his brother Steve gifted 9-year-old Tony

Tony Hawk takes part in skateboard vert practice for the X Games in Los Angeles, August 15, 2003. (AP Photo/Chris Polk)

Hawk with his old skateboard—known as a "banana board"—that the youngster found a way to channel his energy and his desire to achieve outstanding physical feats.

At first, he just sped down alleyways on his skateboard. Then he learned how to turn so that he could stay on the board without having to jump off and turn the board around manually. When he was in the fourth grade, his father built a ramp for him to practice his jumps and turns. The following year, he was permitted to go to the Oasis Skate Park, where youth skated in two empty swimming pools and a U-shaped half-pipe ramp.

Hawk practiced "rock 'n' rolls," which were 180-degree turns; "airs," where he allowed himself to go into the air at the top of the ramps; and "fakies," where he returned down the ramp by skating backward. At age 11, Hawk competed in his first competition, finishing near last for his age-group. To combat that, he learned how to perform a "frontside rock 'n' roll," a difficult trick that caused him to be moved up above his age bracket in future competitions. Within a year, he was finishing at or near the top in competitions.

His father supported his love of skating, drove him to skateboarding competitions throughout southern California, and invited visiting competitors to stay at their house when the competition took place at Oasis. One guest was the manager of the Dogtown Skateboard team, Denise Barter, who invited Hawk to join their team, giving him the opportunity to skate with some of the finest skate athletes of the day and with better equipment—and to have expenses paid for him.

Overall, though, skateboarding was fading as an activity, and the Association of Skatepark Owners folded. In response, Frank Hawk founded the California Amateur Skateboard League (CASL) and then, in 1983, the National Skateboard Association (NSA). Right about when Hawk was finishing seventh grade, the Dogtown team disbanded; fortunately, Stacy Peralta, a skateboarding champion, offered Hawk a spot on the Power Peralta Skateboards team, better known as the Bones Brigade. In 1981, Hawk competed in his first national tournament in Jacksonville, Florida, where he placed poorly. Nevertheless, he stayed with the Bones Brigade and continued to compete in amateur competitions, both regional and national, in both vert (skateboard park) skating and street skating. Right around his 14th birthday, he turned pro. "When I told my parents I had turned pro," he reminisces, "they said, 'That's nice'" (Miller 2004).

To compensate for his relatively small size (as a child, he was so thin that he had to wear elbow pads on his knees), Hawk became the first skater to start his tricks with an "ollie," which meant that he made himself airborne by tapping the skateboard's tail; he then held onto the board with his feet while performing his trick. Although other skaters at first mocked him for this move, it became the standard. Hawk placed first in his second pro competition, with his photo displayed on *Thrasher*, a popular skateboarding magazine.

Over the next 17 years, he won 73 out of the 103 pro contests that he entered, achieving second place in 19 more of them. The Bones Brigade traveled to Australia, Canada, Europe, and throughout the United States. He had his first skateboard named after him, a Powell professional model, with 25,000 boards being sold monthly throughout the late 1980s and early 1990s. Powell also produced posters, T-shirts and more with Hawk's name and image. By 1983, he was earning $500 to $1,000 monthly from these products. In 1984, he appeared in the Bones Brigade Video Show, receiving $3,000 a month from this venture, and, in 1985, he earned $100,000. That year, he also taped the sequel to the Bones Brigade video, *Future Primitive*. By this point, Hawk was performing 540s (one and a half rotations, with a mid-flip) and 720s (involving another half flip). His first attempt at a 900, though, with two and a half rotations, caused him to break a rib.

In 1986, he filmed a Mountain Dew commercial; advertisers were beginning to see this former "rebel" sport as a marketable "extreme" one. He also filmed a third video, *The Search for Animal Chin*. The following year, he played a role in a skateboarding movie, *Gleaming the Cube*, and, in 1988, he was hired as a stunt double for actor David Spade in *Police Academy 4*. He was quickly fired, however, when they realized that Hawk was nearly a foot taller than Spade.

Shortly before his 20th birthday, he temporarily retired from skateboarding, in part because of the criticism he often received for his stiff style while skateboarding and in part because of the criticism he received whenever he did not garner a first place finish. He bought a house and built a private skate ramp for himself; within three months, though, he was ready to tackle skateboarding again; after winning titles in Denmark and Germany, he was ranked the number one skater in the world.

In April 1990, at the age of 21, Hawk married Cindy Dunbar. In 1992, the couple had a son, Hudson Riley. Times became tough, however, when the public interest in skateboarding began to wane again. Hawk took a risk and mortgaged his home to start Birdhouse Projects along with skater Per Welinder, a company that sold Tony Hawk skateboards and apparel, and sponsored a skate team. The company struggled financially and, in 1994, he and Cindy divorced, making that year a low point in his life.

In September 1996, Hawk married Erin Lee, an **inline skater** who was performing in a show along with him. On March 26, 1999, Hawk and Erin had a son, Spencer; on July 18, 2001, they had their next son, Keegan.

To promote Birdhouse Projects and boost its success, Hawk agreed to compete in the first ESPN Extreme Games, later renamed the **X Games**. Winning first in the vert competition and second in the street competition, Hawk took home a gold and silver medal and, because of this, he became a household name outside of the skate community.

Because of this national exposure, Birdhouse Projects became a lucrative business, and he began receiving top-level **sponsorship** deals from Adio shoes, Jeep, and Sirius Satellite Radio; Airwalk created a Tony Hawk shoe that became a bestseller. While on a tour with the Birdhouse team, though, his father died from cancer, a tough loss for Hawk and for the skateboarding community as a whole.

After his father's death, Hawk poured his energies into skateboarding, even more. In 1996, he performed in the closing ceremonies of the Olympics held in Atlanta, Georgia. Television executives estimated that 3 billion people saw his performance.

For the 1996 X Games, ESPN used Hawk's performance from 1995 to promote the games. Although Hawk won a silver medal in vert, he placed seventh in street; in the 1997 X Games, though, he won double gold. In the 1999 competition, in front of 50,000 people, Hawk finally perfected the 900, known as the "Holy Grail" of skateboarding, spinning two and a half times in midair, and landing on his board; this caused him to win the vert best tricks gold. He repeated that trick later that year in an MTV tournament and sponsorship deals flooded in for him.

In 1998, he founded a line of children's skateboarding clothing, Hawk Clothing, and he filmed a video called *The End*, parts of which were used in the Disney movie *Tarzan*. In 1999, he partnered with Activision to create a Playstation skateboarding game called Tony Hawk's Pro Skater, which became one of the most popular video games ever made. The following year, Activision released a second version of the game, which became the top game sold for a solid month, and subsequent versions have come out nearly annually. Overall, more than $1 billion worth of these games have sold.

In 2002, he created the Tony Hawk Gigantic Skateboard Tour for ESPN; its ratings are the second highest for ESPN, behind the X Games. He also started the Boom Boom HuckJam, a tour that meshes punk and hip-hop **music** with skateboarding, **motocross**, and **BMX (bicycle motocross)**—plus pyrotechnics and light shows. He has appeared in commercials for Pepsi, Schick, Coca-Cola, Levi's, and more. In 2004, Bell Helmets began featuring Tony Hawk helmets. Hawk has also created the Tony Hawk Foundation to build skateboarding parks in low-income cities across the country; he has given out more than $1.7 million to date to fund 336 new skate parks.

From 1995 through 2005, Hawk won 10 gold X Games medals and 18 X Games medals, overall, and he was chosen as the best vert skateboarder in the world for 12 years by the National Skateboard Association. To put Tony Hawk into perspective, in 2003, he made more money than Michael Jordan.

While traveling around the globe during his skateboarding career—including trips to Asia, Africa, Europe, and Central and South America—he created dozens upon dozens of skateboarding moves, transforming the sport. Hawk was creating one such move while teaching skateboarding in Sweden and simultaneously complaining about the food he had been eating—which was stale fish. A student asked him if he was creating a move called the "stalefish" and Hawk responded, "yes." This move is still popular with skaters today. In a "stalefish," Hawk twists around in the air and grabs the board with his back hand.

Although Hawk has avoided serious injury throughout his career, he has broken an elbow, sprained ankles, and broken his front teeth.

He divorced his second wife, Erin, in 2004; in January 2006, he married Lhotse Merriam.

See also Burnside, Cara-Beth; Mullen, Rodney

HIGH-WIRE ACT/TIGHTROPE WALKING (FUNAMBULISM)
In tightrope acts, trained performers walk across thin tensioned wires that are placed between two points. If the wire is 20 feet (6.1 meters) or more above the ground, the performance is often called a "high-wire act." If the wire is placed exceptionally high above the ground, it could be considered "skywalking." Some performers place a net below the wire to save themselves in the event of a fall; others do not. This extreme sport is often connected to a circus act or is performed by someone wishing to break a record in height or distance, or based on other parameters. Few people are tightrope walkers; the potential dangers for the athletes, especially those involved in high-wire acts, are quite high, and include paralysis and death.

Tightrope acrobats move across the ropes by shifting most of their body weight to the part of their bodies holding them up, usually the arms or legs. Shifting their body mass in this way is what allows them to maintain their balance on thin wires. They also keep their feet parallel to one another, with one foot positioned in front of the other, and they use a balancing pole or hold their arms out straight to create additional balance.

Tightrope walkers often wear extremely thin, leather-soled slippers that allow them to curve their feet around the wire. Some less experienced performers walk barefooted so that they can place the wire between their big toes and their second toes. Beginners practice by walking on a wire that is only a couple of feet off the ground, learning how to keep their body straight and their eyes focused straight ahead.

Some tightrope performers walk across a wire wherein the tension is provided only by the weight of the athlete; this is known as slackwire. These ropes are generally 15 to 30 feet (4.5 to 9 meters) in length and are placed only a couple of feet off the ground at the center points. Performers use these ropes or webs to swing back and forth, adding another dimension to their acts.

In any of these tightrope specialties, performers may ride a unicycle, juggle, or perform other tricky maneuvers while crossing the wire. One performer is known to juggle across a slackwire while blindfolded; it is said, though, that he knows how to shift the blindfold to clear his vision in one eye. In this manner, the slackwire performer can also incorporate magic into his routine. Some people refer to slackwire acts as "freestyle slacklining" or "rodeo slacklining."

EARLY TIGHTROPE WALKERS

In June 1859, French acrobat Charles Blondin (real name: Jean Francois Gravelet; nickname: the "Daredevil Wirewalker") strung a rope across the Niagara River Gorge located below the falls—and then walked across the wire. His tightrope was 1,100 feet (335 meters) in length, placed 160 feet (50 meters) above the water. Throughout that summer, he continued to perform tightrope walking over the gorge, adding degrees of difficulty each time. A theatrical man, it is said that he crossed the wire while blindfolded; while in a sack; and while pushing a wheelbarrow, walking on stilts, or carrying his manager, Harry Colcord. He is also credited with stopping at midpoint to cook and eat an omelet. After Blondin succeeded, other thrill seekers attempted to duplicate his experiences. In 1897, a ban was placed on tightrope walking across Niagara Falls.

A book published in 1849, *Memoirs of the Life of William Wirt: Attorney General of the United States*, shares the story of a slackwire artist who performed his act in a dancing room by candlelight. While swinging on the wire, he played the drum, balanced hoops and swords, and danced, the spangling of his shoes glittering in the candlelight (Kennedy 1849). As an even earlier example of the activity is noted in *The Diary of Thomas Turner, 1754–1765*. The diary includes the anecdote of paying one penny to watch the slackwire performance at the Uckfield Fair (Turner 1984).

HIGH-WIRE PERFORMERS: FLYING WALLENDA FAMILY

Worldwide, there are only a few high-wire performers; perhaps the most well known is the Flying Wallenda family, a group that has performed a significant number of high-wire feats over the past several decades.

This family has seen its share of tragedies while pursuing their vocation. In a circus performance on January 30, 1962, the Wallenda clan formed a seven-person high-wire human pyramid; this was one of their specialties. News reports state that during this performance, Dieter Schepp, the nephew of Karl Wallenda, lost his footing, causing at least three family members to fall; Schepp and Karl Wallenda's son-in-law died, and Wallenda's adopted son, Mario, became paralyzed from the waist down at the age of 21.

Karl then incorporated Mario's injuries into the family act, pushing Mario and his wheelchair across the high wire; at one point, Karl suggested that he perform a handstand off of Mario's shoulders while the two were high in the air. Mario did not want to pursue this kind of high-wire lifestyle, and he retired from the high-wire act altogether.

On July 18, 1970, Karl Wallenda, who was now 65 years old, walked across a wire stretched one quarter of a mile across the Tallulah Gorge in Georgia. He performed two successful handstands during this feat.

In 1978, Karl Wallenda attempted to cross a wire stretched between two towers of the Condado Plaza Hotel in San Juan, Puerto Rico. The wire was 121 feet (37 meters) above the ground. Winds exceeded 29 miles (48 kilometers) per hour that day and Wallenda plunged to his death, a fatal accident witnessed by the millions of people who were viewing the event on television.

In 2001, 42 years after retiring from the family high-wire act, Mario Wallenda crossed the high wire once again in a wheelchair for a television program associated with the *Guinness Book of World Records*. In 2005, 64-year-old Mario made his second successful attempt to cross a wire; this one was 40 feet (12.2 meters) above the ground. Mario used his motorized two-wheeled "sky cycle" and a button-operated balancing pole to cross the wire.

Another of the Wallenda performers, Karl's grandson Tino, planned to walk across a 400-foot (122-meter) high wire stretched across Shea Stadium on opening day in 1981; the wire was to slope down so that Tino would reach the pitcher's mound, where he would throw out the first pitch of the season. Tino practiced and was prepared, but the game was rained out and he did not have the opportunity to perform. Nine years earlier, on August 13, 1972, Karl Wallenda successfully walked 600 feet (183 meters) across a high wire stretched between the foul poles in Veterans Stadium.

In 2004, a mother-daughter Wallenda act took place during the Moscow State Circus; Rietta and Lyric Wallenda performed the high-wire act, and Yetty Wallenda performed aerial ballet.

OTHER HIGH-WIRE PERFORMERS

Other high-wire athletes include the Russian father-and-son team Gusein and Vaguif Khamdulaev; Gusein has been performing high-wire acts for more than 40 years. In 2006, the duo crossed a high wire placed 45 feet (13.7 meters) from the ground, the world's highest indoor tightrope, for the Moscow State Circus act being performed in Birmingham, England. Whenever Vaguif is not performing his high-wire act, he is starring in a soap opera, *Life Is Life*, which is taped in South America.

Still another high-wire performer is Canadian Jay Cochrane, nicknamed the "Prince of the Air." He set a record for the longest tightrope act when he spent 21 days and nights on the high wire, performing six shows a day in San Juan, Puerto Rico. In October 1995, Cochrane also set a record for height and distance when he crossed the Qutang Gorge in China on a 1.125-inch (2.9-centimeter) wire; he walked the wire for 2,098 feet (640 meters), with the Yangtze River 1,350 feet (412 meters) below. The performance took Cochrane 53 minutes to complete. Estimates of people who witnessed this act live range from 100,000 to 200,000, while Cochrane himself estimates that 200 million more watched it on television. In 2005, Cochrane crossed Niagara Falls, traveling 1,800 feet (548.6 meters) while 400 to 600 feet (122 to 183 meters) above the water. In his act, he does not use a safety net; his pole is 40 feet (12 meters) in length and it weighs 60 pounds (27 kilograms).

Cochrane's accomplishments are all the more amazing when factoring in his 1965 accident; a tower collapsed during a performance, and Cochrane fell 90 feet (27.4 meters). Doctors told him that the most he could hope for was to walk again using two canes. Cochrane used his recovery time to obtain a master's degree in bridge and structural engineering from Toronto University.

Other notable high-wire artists include Fredi Nock and Zhang Sheng-Ling.

HOFFMAN, MAT (1972–)

By the time he retired from freestyle **BMX (bicycle motocross)** and bicycle stunt riding, Mat "Condor" Hoffman had won 10 bicycle freestyle world championships and earned two Summer **X Games** gold medals. In the year 2000 alone, he was the reigning Bicycle Stunt Series champion, the Crazy Freakin' Bikers (CFB) Series champion, and the 2000 European champion. He created more than 100 bicycle tricks, and he is also well known for his business acumen. He has broken 50 bones, had 17 operations, and sustained several concussions.

Mathew T. Hoffman was born on January 9, 1972, in Edmond, Oklahoma, the fourth child of Matthew and Joni Hoffman. Even as a young child, he played intently; at the age of 6, he broke his left leg while chasing a Frisbee and, two days later, he slid down a 15-foot (4.6-meter) slide, breaking his wrist. He already knew how to do backflips on a trampoline, and once took his bicycle onto the roof of his house and then jumped on the bike from the roof into the family pool.

Hoffman got his first BMX bike at the age of 11, and he began entering the bicycle freestyle competition scene at the age of 13, quickly becoming a top amateur competitor. At the age of 15, he was invited to join a BMX traveling team sponsored by Skyway bikes. He did so, but then he switched to a freestyle team sponsored by Bob Haro.

At the age of 17, he turned pro, becoming the youngest BMX pro to date. He won the King of Vert contest in California by performing a new trick, one he called the "nothing fakie." In this move, he was airborne, about 5 feet (1.5 meters) above the half-pipe, when he completely got off his bike. He was able to get back to his bike in time to land on the ramp—backward.

By this time, he had already gotten the attention and respect of riders throughout the country, and was creating a large segment of the vert tricks that are used by riders today. As *Ride* magazine put it, "What's left to say about a guy who ignored all established limits and redefined vert riding—at age fifteen?" (EXPN n.d.).

In 1989, while he had a broken thumb, Hoffman attempted a 900—two and a half rotations—in a Waterloo, Ontario, competition; he landed the move. The following year, he tried a backflip at a competition in Paris, France. After he succeeded, the magazine *Go* put a photo of Hoffman performing this move on the cover; the text read: "Sickest Trick Ever."

That same year, his mother died of cancer; shortly thereafter, he was competing in England, where he met a young fan who was dying of cancer. To cheer the boy up, Hoffman attempted a backflip with a 180-degree twist. The first time, he failed, but the second time, he landed the new move. This trick is now called a "flair." Hoffman created another trick, wherein the rider does a backflip, but then lands backward on the ramp; this is known as a "flip fakie."

In 1991, Hoffman left the Haro team to create his own promotion company: Hoffman Promotions. He then gathered together a group of elite freestyle riders, including Jay Miron (who went on to win the first X Games gold medal for Dirt Bike) and Dave Mirra (who, by 2007, had earned 32 X Games medals), and they created a traveling show called the Sprocket Jockey Bicycle Stunt Team. They built a portable half-pipe ramp and traveled the country, performing on this half-pipe. The Sprocket Jockey team is still considered to be among the best on the circuit.

Hoffman decided to modify his bike to withstand the rigors of freestyle bicycle riding and, after creating one that satisfied him, he created a second business—Hoffman Bikes—and began selling the bikes in 1991. This bicycle company sponsors its own team of riders; as of 2007, some of the team members included Seth Kimbrough, Ryan Barrett, Kevin Robinson, Bruce Crisman, and Baz Keep.

Hoffman developed the BS (Bicycle Stunts) Series to allow riders to showcase their skills; this event became successful, to the degree that ESPN asked to televise this annual series. It now serves as the prequalifying series for the X Games, and is seen by more than 35 million viewers in more than 177 countries. Hoffman also created the Hoffman Sports Association (HSA), which organizes the bicycle stunt events for ESPN and the X Games. He and his team took part in the closing ceremonies of the Summer Olympics in 1996 in Atlanta, Georgia.

In 1994, Hoffman set a world record by flying 23 feet (6 meters) off of a quarter-pipe that was 21 feet (5.8 meters) tall. In 2001, he built a quarter-pipe with a 400-foot (121-meter) runway. Hoffman's partner, Steve Swope, pulled Hoffman and his bike with his motorcycle, traveling up to 50 miles (80 kilometers) an hour. Going up the ramp, he went 26.5 feet (8 meters) off the ramp, which meant that he was more than 50 feet (15.24 meters) off the ground.

He also traveled to Norway to fly off of a 3,200-foot (975-meter) cliff, going at a speed of 150 miles (241 kilometers) per hour. While he was making a flip, his pants got caught in the bike chain, so he disconnected himself from his bike, activated his parachute, and landed safely.

In 1999, the HSA created the CFB Series, which is a competition for both amateur and professional riders; winners can advance to the next level of competition. These competitions also air on television. Other bicycle stunt events organized by HSA include the Soul Bowl in Hermosa Beach, California; the Alp Challenge in Innsbruck, Austria; and the Freestyle.ch.00, hosted in Zurich, Switzerland.

In 2001, Activision released a **video game** called the Mat Hoffman's Pro BMX video game. Hoffman has produced, directed, and hosted ESPN programs, including the *Kids in the Way* series; the CFB Series; and *Mat's World*, which shares information about alternative sports and the people who compete in them. In 2002, he won the EXPN Action Sports and Music Awards, Lifetime Achievement.

In 2003, he and Mark Lewman wrote his autobiography, titled *The Ride of My Life*. To promote the Kids' Choice Awards in 2004, Hoffman paired up with Nickelodeon to jump out of an airplane, on his bike, at 14,000 feet (4,267 meters) above ground. When he landed, he landed in a bunch of green slime.

Hoffman is married to Jaci, and they have two children.

X GAMES

Hoffman has competed in the Summer X Games since their inception in 1995. He placed 1st in bicycle stunt, vert, in both 1995 and 1996. He has also placed 3rd in 1997, 7th in 1999, 3rd in 2000, 3rd in 2001, and 2nd in 2002. In the 2002 games, he performed a no-handed 900.

See also Carmichael, Ricky; Motocross; Nyquist, Ryan

HOLMENKOLLEN SKI FESTIVAL: HOME OF THE HOLMENKOLLDAGEN (SKI JUMP)

At the annual Holmenkollen Ski Festival held in Oslo, Norway, winter athletes continue a tradition that began regionally in 1866 and moved to the Holmenkollen hill on January 31, 1892: a **ski jumping** competition. This day is so important in Norway that it has been called "Norway's Second National Day." The Norwegian Royal Family always attends the festival, as do thousands of other people; the venue now seats 50,000 people.

During the festival, athletes also compete in downhill skiing, slalom, giant slalom, and cross-country skiing. In 1976, a **children's** cross-country race was added to expand the festivities, and a new closing event—a cross-country ski marathon (26 miles/42 kilometers) for men, women and children, regardless of expertise—was also added.

Before 1903, only athletes from Norway could compete in festival events. Even when the events were opened up to people of other nationalities, it took until 1939 for a nonnative to win an event—when a Swedish man won the ski jumping contest.

Holmenkollen has been the site of the world championships for ski jumping in 1930, 1952, 1966, and 1982. It was the host site for the Winter Olympics in 1952, when more than 100,000 people paid to watch the competition and another 40,000 watched from nearby places.

The first ski jump ramp at Holmenkollen was constructed out of tree branches; the longest jump from that set up was 70 feet (21.5 meters), achieved by Arne Ustvedt. The jump structure has been improved more than 15 times since. The current site record is a jump of 446 feet (136 meters), made by Tommy Ingebrigtsen in 2006. The current ski tower is 196 feet (60 meters) above the ground and 1,368 feet (417 meters) above sea level.

The Ski Museum, founded in 1923, shares information about the 4,000-year history of skiing, and displays skis used by the ancient Vikings, modern athletes, and more. Ski equipment used by polar explorers Fridtjof Nansen and Roald Amundsen and those of the late King Olav V and other royalty are also on display. At the base of the ski jump is a virtual entertainment device that allows visitors to vicariously experience a 100-meter (328.1-foot) jump.

This venue will be modernized again to host the *Fédération Internationale de Ski* (FIS, International Ski Federation) Nordic World Ski Championships in 2011.

See also Skiing, Extreme and Freeride

HOTTER 'N HELL HUNDRED: CENTURY BICYCLE RACING

The Hotter 'N Hell Hundred (HHH) is an annual cycling event held in Wichita Falls, Texas. Bicyclists from across the country and around the world compete in a race in the blazing August sun. The heat of the day is usually above 85° Fahrenheit (30° Celsius), which is the temperature at which people are advised to curtail their outdoor activities. Participants generally come from 40 to 44 different states and from five foreign countries. This race is believed to be the largest "century" race, meaning the largest one with a 100-mile (161-kilometer) course.

The race began in 1982 to celebrate the centennial of Wichita Falls; the event is always scheduled nine days before Labor Day. The best riders can complete 100 miles in approximately 5 hours. The race currently consists of endurance rides, plus an off-road race/trail run; the longer routes include long inclines and race days often experience significant wind.

Beginners can choose a 10-kilometer route, while more experienced cyclists can select from a 25 mile-, 50 mile-, 100 kilometer-, or 100-mile route. Riders choosing the 100-mile race must reach Hell's Gate (found at the 60.3-mile mark) by 12:30 P.M., which is 5.5 hours after the race begins; if riders do not reach Hell's Gate by that time, then those riders are routed a way that is only 84 miles in length.

At this event, there is also a 10-mile off-road route; this includes a single track with short climbs and drops. Riders are cautioned about natural hazards such as trees, water, wild animals, and poison ivy.

The first HHH had 1,100 participants, but the numbers have climbed to an annual participation figure of 8,000 to 10,000 bicyclists. The following supplies are needed to put on this event:

- More than 20,000 bananas
- 9,000 oranges
- More than 5,000 gallons (18,927 liters) of sports drinks containing electrolytes
- 10,000 gallons (37,854 liters) of water
- 70,000 pounds (31,751.5 kilograms) of ice

HHH RISKS AND INJURIES

Larry Magruder, who has served as medical director for the event, estimated that, in the first 22 years of the HHH, 120,000 people participated, with five deaths occurring. One fatality included a rider who suffered from severe cardiomyopathy, a disease wherein the heart becomes inflamed and cannot work to its full capacity. According to Magruder, the HHH was also the first major cycling event that required all riders to wear helmets, a rule that was instituted in 1988; most major cycling events have since followed suit.

The most common injuries are heat related, although collisions and accidents also happen each year. Magruder states that the collisions and accidents tend to occur early on in the event, with heat-related injuries increasing in frequency throughout the day. On race days when the winds are stronger than 20 miles (32 kilometers) per hour, more heat-related injuries are reported. Other medical issues include road rash (abrasions sustained in crashes), insect bites, snakebites, and dog bites.

FIRST-TIME HHH RIDING EXPERIENCE

Don Mecoy, a staff writer for the *Sunday Oklahoman*, signed up for the 50-mile course in 2006, and then wrote about his experiences. According to Mecoy, "With 15 miles to go in my inaugural Hotter 'N Hell ride, I was hurting and humbled and nearly hopeless. And my bike was moving slower than sales of the T-shirts congratulating disgraced Tour de France champ Floyd Landis" (Mecoy 2006).

Mecoy credits large doses of water, pickles, pickle juice, oranges, and bananas for his ability to complete the race, stating that, "The physical discomfort and inconveniences of the massive crowds were far surpassed by the thrill of finishing and the camaraderie shared by fellow riders and volunteers" (Mecoy 2006).

OTHER CENTURY BICYCLING RACES

There are three categories of century races: self-planned, brevet, and organized. In a self-planned ride, the bicyclist has the freedom to chart the course and to stay close to home or go far away, depending on personal preference and budget. Challenges of the self-planned rides include the need to plan around construction and poor-quality roads; the lack of mechanical support; the cost of meals, which is usually more expensive in a solo ride; and the risks associated with riding alone, including medical and safety issues.

In a brevet race, riders pay a minimal fee to get a map to an already laid-out course; supply stops usually are available for the riders. Another advantage of brevet races is the company and companionship of other riders. Disadvantages include the lack of mechanical support and provision of food.

In an organized race, all food is included in the fee and both mechanical and medical assistance are available. Disadvantages of organized races include the potential need to travel to the race site and the unpredictability of the weather on the chosen race date.

ULTRAMARATHON RIDING

Ultramarathon riders tackle courses that are beyond 100 miles in length; they average a speed of 25 miles (40 kilometers) per hour. The UltraMarathon Cycle Association (UMCA) organizes and sponsors races, certifies racing records, and publishes the *UltraCycle Magazine* six times a year to provide information to riders.

One Ultramarathon race of note is the Great American Bike Race, which was founded in 1982. Riders travel from the Santa Monica Pier in California to the Empire State Building in New York. In 2006, nearly 180 athletes participated, with racers from Austria, Australia, Brazil, Canada, France, Germany, Great Britain, Hungary, Italy, Liechtenstein, the Netherlands, Portugal, Slovenia, Switzerland, and the United States.

See also Adventure Racing; Ironman Triathlon; Stamstad, John

I

ICE CLIMBING

In the sport of ice climbing, athletes ascend ice-covered rocks or mountains; frozen waterfalls; ice shelves, which are the floating portions of huge ice sheets found in locales where the ice never melts; and man-made vertical climbing walls that are artificially covered with ice.

In some instances, the ice climbing sites have ice screws and nylon ladders securely in place for climbers to latch on to them as they ascend; other locales require that the climber carry an ice ax to create footholds, to stop a fall, and to secure 8- to 10-inch (20.3- to 25.4-centimeter) protective ice screws into the ice during the climb upward. It can take a couple of minutes to place one set of these screws, a period of time in which the climber has only one arm to prevent himself or herself from falling. This increases the risk of the sport significantly.

Most climbers use a rope as a climbing aid; free ice climbers, though, use ropes for safety, but not to assist in climbing; and those who climb free solo do not use ropes, harnesses, or any protective gear at all. Enthusiasts of free soloing speak of the adrenaline rush they experience when climbing without a backup safety system.

A related sport is bouldering, where an athlete might climb 20-foot (6-meter) boulders without a rope as a guide or safety net. Other climbers prefer mixed climbing in an area in which they can go from rock climbing to ice climbing and then back again.

DEVELOPMENT OF THE COMPETITIVE SPORT

According to the International Mountaineering and Climbing Federation (*Union Internationale Des Associations D'Alpinisme*), ice climbing competitions have existed since 1912, when athletes climbed in Courmayeur on the Brenva glacier, located on Mont Blanc in the Italian Alps.

Starting in 1970, competitions have been held each winter in the Russian Federation (the former Soviet Union), with athletes being judged on the difficulty of the climb, and the speed of climbing, as well as the speed of climbing more than 100 meters (328 feet) in a roped group, wherein the leader must change every 40 meters (131 feet). In the late 1980s, ice climbing became a national sport in Russia; during the winter of 1996–97, Russian athletes competed in France and, ever since, the Russian ice climbers have followed the French competition rules.

French competitions have been held in Courchevel since 1995; the goal is to climb as high as possible with as few ax hits as possible in a time span ranging from 8 to 14 minutes. Shortly before the 2000 competition was set to begin, an enormous piece of ice dislodged and fell.

In the United States, the most well-known ice climbing competition took place in the Winter **X Games** through 1999, with events for speed and difficulty. In the X Games, climbers were required to wear harnesses and the ice was man-made, which posed fewer risks than ice found in nature. Attention was given to the technical aspects of the game, including how a climber used the ice ax and their crampons. Participants were judged on the height that they reached before falling off, and there was also a speed competition.

In Ouray, Colorado, a park devoted entirely to ice climbing was created. There is no fee for climbing in the Ouray Ice Park. Funds to support the ice park are raised at the annual Ouray Ice Festival, a world-famous ice competition first held in 1996. Attendees can also participate in climbing clinics (beginning to advanced); see the latest climbing gear displayed by manufacturers; and try their luck at ax throwing contests, tightrope walks, and other similar events. There is also a Kids Climbing Wall so that **children** can learn the sport.

Eric Siefer, climbing guide for the International Climbing School, leads a route on Dracula, a 150-foot (45.7-meter), grade 4+ wall of ice in Crawford Notch, New Hampshire. (AP Photo/*Conway Daily Sun*, Jamie Gemmiti)

Canadian events include the International World Cup competition held in Quebec, and the Canmore Ice Climbing Festival in Canmore, Alberta. In the latter event, climbing techniques are taught and demonstrations given.

From 1994 until 1999, duel speed competitions took place in the Bohinj in Slovenia; since 2000, Solcava has served as the venue for difficulty and speed races. Because of climate changes, ice climbing competitions are becoming more challenging to hold in Slovenia.

International competitions began in 2000, following the generally accepted rules established in 1998. The man credited with gathering these rules together, ice climber Michael Boos-Diehl, died in an avalanche while ice climbing on July 29, 2005.

EQUIPMENT AND EXPERIENCE

Climbers wear crampons, which are shoes with cleats made especially for climbers, along with a helmet. Most climbers carry an ice ax, ice screws, ropes, and harnesses. If climbing where there is a risk of snow avalanche, climbers should carry beacons and a shovel; have skiing abilities and survival training; and understand rescue techniques and first aid. Climbers, besides being good skiers, should have rock climbing experience, as well.

CHALLENGES

There are a myriad of environmental risk factors inherent in ice climbing, including flash floods, mud slides, snakes and predatory animals, falling rock, lightning and high winds, avalanches, extreme temperatures, and more. Climbers run a risk of falling, drowning, getting lost, being separated from the group, having equipment malfunctions, and suffering from high altitude sickness. Injuries range from cuts and bruises to strains, sprains, and broken bones—and from paralysis to death. Another significant risk in ice climbing is fatigue.

In an article entitled "Is This the Craziest Sport in the World," the writer describes how an ice athlete may be climbing a slippery slope with someone who speaks no English, while a breakdown in communication could lead to a fatal fall. Ice climber Dean Jones explains that the inability to understand one another's words does not really matter that much, as ice climbers tend to be 50 meters (164 feet) apart on a rope. Any type of significant communication, he explained, takes place through a series of tugs on the rope (Western Mail 2006, 20). Jones recently attended the European International Ice Climbing Festival held in Argentiere La Besse in the French Alps where two climbers were killed—not from falling, but because of avalanches.

According to Jones, "Climbing is absolutely about self-control. 99% of climbers are fairly hardened emotionally, and are fairly robust. They're able to control their emotions, and not panic—that's the biggest thing. We all have moments, but being able to control yourself at those moments is massively important" (Western Mail 2006, 20).

See also Alpine Scrambling; Csizmazia, Kim; Mountain Climbing

ICE YACHTING (ICE BOATING)

As early as the 1600s, the Dutch were attaching both sails and runners to boats, to let the wind power the vehicle across the ice. Painter Hendrick Avercamp, who often created winter scenes in his art, allows us a glimpse at those long-ago ice boats that were probably intended for practical transportation purposes rather than sport. Starting around 1820, the Canadians used ice yachts on the Toronto Bay; although ice boats were first seen in the United States in 1790 on the Hudson River in New York, they were basic squares with three runners and a sail. In 1853, more advanced designs were introduced in the United States and, at about that time, ice sailing began to be seen as a recreational activity as well as something done for pragmatic reasons.

By 1866, Poughkeepsie, along the Hudson River, was the center of ice yachting in the United States; this area was known as Millionaire's Row and these wealthy residents enjoyed ice yachting as a sport, building elaborate boats with sails even larger than 600 square feet (183 square meters). The fastest ice yacht of that era was the "Icicle" designed by Franklin Delano Roosevelt's uncle, J. A. Roosevelt; it was 69 feet (21 meters) in length with 1,070 square feet (326 square meters) of sail. It seated seven to nine passengers, but not always entirely safely as crashes were frequent, in large part because of the ruddered steering that preceded the safer bow steering

Bob Cook shoots across the ice on March 8, 2008, during the Gull Lake Ice Yacht Club races on Gull Lake, Michigan. Conditions were right for racing for the first time in eight years. (AP Photo/*Kalamazoo Gazette*, Jill McLane Baker)

invented in 1933; with an inexact steering system, the boat could all too easily hit an ice crack or encounter a hole in the ice, leading to damage and injuries.

In January 1866, three ice boats—the Minnehaha, Snow Flake, and Haze—raced 89.5 miles (144 kilometers) on the Hudson, a race that lasted three days. The winds were heavy and a few mishaps occurred, including when the Snow Flake broke through some loose ice and when the steering stopped working on the Haze. Although all three ice yachts completed the race, the Minnehaha, the only yacht not encountering troubles of significance on the journey, finished first.

Hudson residents enjoyed climbing into their ice yachts to race the trains that chugged along tracks parallel to the river; given a good wind, the yachts traveled between 60 and 70 miles (96 and 112 kilometers) per hour, beating the trains and therefore serving as the country's fastest vehicles.

The first known ice yachting fatality in the United States occurred in 1871 when two ice yachts collided and the bowsprit of one boat stabbed Jacob Best, who was on the other boat, in the heart. Jacob "cried 'Oh, dear!' once, a newspaper reported, 'gasped twice, and was a corpse'" (DeLoca 2007, 127). Although other ice yachting deaths later occurred, usually by drowning or concussions, that did not stop other communities in the United States from creating their own ice yacht clubs.

In 1881, the American Challenge Pennant was held on the Hudson River; this race continues to this day and is generally considered the most prestigious of the races. In 2003, the Poughkeepsie ice yachters staged a racing reenactment (using the larger boats of the nineteenth century, powered by canvas sails) with their fiercest rivals

The fastest recorded racing speed has been 68 miles (109.4 kilometers) per hour; this was accomplished by Switzerland's Yvon Labarthe in 1999. The fastest assisted speed has been 190 miles (305.8 kilometers) per hour, achieved by Switzerland's Jörg Schläfli as he was being towed by a motorcycle.

Top skaters participate in the **X Games**, the Aggressive Skaters Association (ASA) tours, and the **Gravity Games**. Most competitive events are timed events, with skating runs that last about one minute each. Competitors are also awarded points on style, creativity, difficulty of moves, and so forth. In the IMYTA (the I Match Your Trick Association) events, skaters must duplicate other skaters' moves or face elimination.

Aggressive Skating: Vert and Street Skating

There are two main forms of aggressive skating: vert and street. Both forms of aggressive skating require significantly more creativity than recreational or speed skating.

Vert skaters use the large bowl-shaped half-pipe construct originally created for skateboarders as their playing field. They gain speed while skating on the half-pipe and perform stunts, including a 180-degree turn; grabs, which involve grabbing a skate while in the air; flips; and more.

Initially, there were hard feelings between skateboarders and aggressive inline skaters as the latter moved onto **skateboarding** territory, but that has since calmed down. Australian Matt Salerno is named as a strong influence in the vert skate movement.

Street skaters use the urban landscape, including steps, rails, curbs, and so forth as their skating venue. Street skaters sometimes upset local residents and security or police forces if they cross over into private property. These skaters also incorporate tricks, including flips, jumps, and twists, into their skate routines.

This sport is included in the X Games, and other aggressive skating events are often televised as well.

Governing Bodies

The U.S. Olympic Committee (USOC) recognizes USA Roller Sports (USARS) as the official governing body for all competitive roller sports in the United States. USARS had requested that the *Federation Internationale de Roller Skating* (FIRS) allow inline skating in international competitions, which was granted in 1992. A current goal is to get inline skating accepted as an Olympic sport in 2016.

Inline Skating Risks and Injuries

Typical injuries occur to the wrists, arms, and head when skaters fall. Broken bones are not unusual, but injuries are less likely to occur when the skater wears a helmet, plus elbow, wrist, and knee protection.

Some reports suggest, though, that only about half of the inline skaters wear protective gear. Because of this, approximately 40 percent of all inline skating accidents result in broken bones. Skaters who participate in "skitching," or grabbing onto a moving vehicle while skating, have had fatal accidents.

Inline Skating Equipment

Inline skates can cost anywhere from $20 to $500 a pair; some even have built-in speedometers. It is important that the skates fit well. Most people start with four-wheeled skates and perhaps work up to the five wheels preferred by many racers. Five-wheeled boots allow for a faster stride and a bigger surface for pushing out; racing skates are lighter in weight than nonracing ones, and the boots are cut lower to allow for more movement. Four-wheeled skates typically have a heel stop, while five-wheeled racing versions generally do not.

Three-wheeled skates are available for freestyle skating. These skates usually have a kick stop to use in tricks.

To keep skates in excellent shape, skaters need to change the bearings (cylinders inside each wheel that contain small steel balls) regularly and rotate the wheels monthly, moving the front wheels to the back, the back to the middle, and the middle to the front, so that wheels wear down evenly.

Wheels are rated on the A scale, with numbers ranging from 77 to 93. Recreational wheels have a hardness of 77A to 80A; if rated above that figure, the wheels are harder, which makes them longer lasting and allows the skater to skate more quickly. Softer wheels, however, absorb shocks better.

Skaters should carry a small repair tool kit that includes spare wheels and brake pads. If planning to skate when it is dark, skaters should include night lights, as well, that can be clipped onto clothes or helmets. Some skaters carry two-way radios and even Global Positioning System (GPS) devices in case they get lost.

SLANG
Inline skaters have created interesting slang, including the following:

- Black ice: smooth asphalt
- Bonk: what happens when you run out of energy, mid-skating
- Face plant: when your nose is the first body part to hit the ground in a fall
- Poser: a person who looks like an inline skater, but is not adept at the sport
- Cheese grater asphalt: rough surface conditions
- Bail to fall: intentional fall to avoid major wipeout
- Slam tan: tan lines caused by protective gear

See also da Silva, Fabiola; Roller Derby

IRONMAN TRIATHLON
Triathlon athletes participate in races wherein three different activities take place: bicycling, swimming, and running. This is not a team event; athletes need to individually participate in all three facets of the triathlon in consecutive order. The Ironman Triathlon requires a significant amount of both physical and mental toughness. It is estimated that Ironman athletes train for seven months for the event, training 18 to 22 hours per week. The current participation fee is $500 and athletes from 75 countries are expected to travel to Hawaii to compete for the next Ironman title.

Weather conditions often serve as an additional challenge to race participants. Temperatures average 88° Fahrenheit (31° Celsius); humidity ranges from 40 to 85 percent; and winds can reach 60 miles (97 kilometers) per hour.

The Ironman competition came to be as a method of settling a debate. In 1977, at an awards ceremony for a running race, people began to debate the fitness of swimmers, runners, and other athletes, when compared and contrasted against one

Heather Wurtele of Victoria, British Columbia, Canada, wipes tears from her face as she talks to her husband on the phone after winning the 2008 Ironman Coeur d'Alene, Idaho, women's title June 22, 2008, with a time of 9 hours, 38 minutes, 58 seconds. (AP Photo/*Coeur d'Alene Press*, Shawn Gust)

another. One of the race participants, Navy Commander John Collins, and his wife, Judy, decided to create a race that would settle the debate once and for all. They did so by combining three already existing races:

- The Waikiki Rough Water Swim (2.4 miles/3.9 kilometers)
- Around Oahu Bike Race (112 miles/180 kilometers)
- Honolulu Marathon (26.2 miles/42.2 kilometers)

Thus, the Ironman Triathlon was created. Fifteen men competed on February 18, 1978; 12 of them finished the race, and the first Ironman, Gordon Haller, finished with a time of 11 hours, 46 minutes, and 58 seconds.

A larger crowd was anticipated for 1979, but bad weather delayed the race for a day and seemed to dilute some of the momentum. Once again, 15 people participated; this time, though, a woman—Lyn Lemaire from Boston, Massachusetts—participated, and finished fifth. Coincidentally, Barry McDermott from *Sports Illustrated* was in the area to cover a golf tournament; while in Hawaii, he learned about the Ironman competition, and it intrigued him so much that he wrote a 10-page story about the triathlon.

In 1980, ABC's *Wide World of Sports* covered the event, which had 106 men and two women compete. Because of this attention, other triathlon events were organized. In 1981, the event was moved to Kona in Hawaii; a much more barren locale, this move added the human-against-nature element that has since been promoted by event organizers. That year, 73-year-old Walt Stack competed, finishing at 26 hours and

20 minutes. In 1982, Bud Light became the sponsor of the Ironman, serving as fore-shadowing of the extreme sports **sponsorship** deals during the 1990s and beyond.

Also in 1982, competitor Julie Moss became severely dehydrated and collapsed shortly before completing the race; just yards away from the finish line, she was passed up by Kathleen McCartney. Moss then crawled to the finish line, disoriented and struggling, and she has since served as the Ironman symbol of determination. Other highlights of Ironman competitions include the following:

- In 1984, the first representative of the Eastern Bloc countries, a Czechoslovakian named Vaclav Vitovec, participated.
- In 1985, participants from 34 countries raced in the triathlon; two years later, people from 44 countries participated.
- In 1994, Paula Newby-Fraser won her fourth consecutive women's title—her seventh, overall—with a time of 9 hours, 20 minutes, and 14 seconds.
- In 1996, the first European—Luc Van Lierde of Belgium—won the event, breaking the Ironman record with a time of 8 hours, 4 minutes, and 8 seconds.
- In 1998, race founder John Collins returned to participate in the 20th Annual Ironman Competition, finishing in 16 hours, 30 minutes, and 2 seconds; he had not participated since the original race.
- In 2001, Tim DeBoom became the first American to win the title since 1995; he won just three weeks after September 11, as the crowd shouted, "USA … USA … USA."

The 1996 Ironman record set by Luc Van Lierde still stands as the course record.

Race Sponsorships

The 1982 sponsorship by Bud Light was a precursor of the numerous corporate sponsors that would partner with the Ironman Triathlon over the years. Currently, Ford Motor Company is the overall race sponsor. The official drink for the bike course is orange-flavored Gatorade; lemon-lime Gatorade is the official drink on the running course. PowerBar Harvest bars are the official energy bars.

Other sponsors include Timex, Foster Grant, Anthony Travel, Ultimax, Cannondale, Florida Sports, VISA, Janus, Spenco, Michelin, Endless Pools, CompuTrainer, the Kona Beach Hotel, Blue Seventy, BOB Strollers, Wear-Dated Carpets, Headsweats, Aqua Sphere, Keys Fitness, Profile Design, the City of Clearwater, Look, the St. Petersburg/Clearwater Area Convention and Visitors Bureau, Zephyrhills, Inside Out Sports, Tanita, Meyer & Meyer Sport, Morton Plant Mease Health Care, American Interbanc, Zorrel. Philadelphia Insurance Companies, Michelob Ultra, PODS, and Kinesys.

See also Adventure Racing; Hotter 'N Hell Hundred; Stamstad, John

KITE SURFING (KITEBOARDING OR FLYSURFING)

In kite surfing, participants use special equipment to harness the power of the wind to propel themselves across a body of water, either a relatively still body or one with waves. The athlete may use the momentum of the wind to perform tricks and maneuvers.

Kite surfers attach their feet to a board that is similar to a surfboard—but called a kiteboard. A kite is attached to the board with a set of kite lines, and the surfer is connected to the kite lines by a harness, with a release button available for emergencies. Also attached to the kite lines is a bar, which allows the rider to control the direction of the kite.

This sport combines elements of kite flying with those of **windsurfing** and water surfing—plus elements of **skateboarding**, **snowboarding**, and paragliding. Proponents of the sport often share how close kite surfing can make them feel to nature, as they commune with the water, air, wind, and sky, and some have described this type of surfing as a joyful spiritual experience. By 2006, it was estimated that 150,000 to 200,000 people were participating in the sport, worldwide.

DEVELOPMENT OF THE SPORT

People have known how to harness the power of wind with kites for centuries, with Indonesian and Polynesian fishermen powering their canoes with kites as far back as the twelfth century. In 1826, British inventor George Pocock received a patent for his four-line kite system that powered boats across water, and carts and carriages on land. People have used similar kite systems as propulsion on ice and snow, as well. In 1903, Samuel Cody crossed the English Channel in a canvas boat fueled by a kite that he had invented; another kite design of his was used by the British military to test lifting human beings into the air. In 1948, Francis Rogallo created the wing used in modern-day **hang gliding**.

Technology improved in the 1970s, with materials such as Kevlar and Spectra being created. This gave inventors more options when creating or improving upon kites.

In 1977, Gijsbertus Adrianus Panhuise of the Netherlands received the first patent for a kite system that was specifically intended for a sport. The following year, Dave Culp of the United States improved upon the kite designs by adding an inflated leading edge. Then, in 1987, two French brothers, Dominique and Bruno Legaignoux, patented their kite sail design, called a "wipika." Meanwhile, American Cory Roeseler and his father Bill (a Boeing aerodynamicist) were experimenting with sailing upwind with a "kiteski"; in 1994, they were awarded a patent for their design.

In 1997, the Legaignoux brothers came up with an innovative way to use inflatable tubes to streamline the process of relaunching the kites when surfing. Their design forms the basis of a significant portion of the kite systems used in kite surfing today.

Hawaii quickly became a center for kite surfing, with California and Florida also being excellent locations for the sport. A kite surfing competition was held in Maui, Hawaii, in September 1998; the winner was Marcus "Flash" Austin.

Kite surfers are now found around most of the globe, with people kite surfing in Europe, Africa, North and South America, the Caribbean, Australia, and Asia. In 2004, the Democratic presidential candidate for the United States, John Kerry, was seen enjoying the sport.

There are a variety of styles used in kite surfing, including freestyle, wherein the athlete chooses which jumps, twists, and

A man kite surfs off the coast of Condado, San Juan, Puerto Rico, December 15, 2006. Regular strong winds have made kite surfing a growing sport in Puerto Rico. (AP Photo/ Brennan Linsley)

spins to perform; many competitions focus on freestyle events. In wave riding, the athlete surfs much like a water surfer would, with the kite providing the power. In big air riding, the athlete tries to stay in the air as long as possible. More advanced kite surfers may participate in "kickers and sliders," wherein they slide up a ramp and then perform tricks and maneuvers. These well-trained surfers may also compete in speed events.

As the sport develops, more specialties are being created, including kite snowboarding, kite skiing, kite snow blading, kite skating on snow and ice, kite skateboarding, and kite buggying on land.

KITE SURFING EQUIPMENT

There are two types of kites used in kite surfing; one is roughly the shape of a "C" and it is between 20 and 65 feet (6 and 20 meters) in length. This style, which comes with a fifth line, is better for more experienced kite surfers. For those starting out, the bow kite may be a better choice. It is flatter than the C-shaped kites and it is easier to learn how to operate this style. When not in use, kites can be packed down into a backpack-size container, which helps in transporting the kite. When ready to be used, the kites are reinflated.

Kite surfers need to choose among a variety of styles of kiteboards and between a seat harness and a waist harness. Some athletes like to wear a wetsuit to stay in the water longer. Helmets and impact suits are recommended; participants should choose one specifically made for water sports.

Equipment for this sport generally costs $1,500 or more. Because the price of equipment is so high, beginners should consider renting the equipment while learning the sport.

KITE SURFING INJURIES

In an article published in the *Taipei Times* in 2004, "More of a High Than Sex," one kite surfer shares his experience when a strong wind caused him to crash in South Africa (Reuters 2004). He broke his legs and bones in his feet, and he compressed the bones in his spinal cord. He counted himself as fortunate, however, as he missed crashing into 10-centimeter (4-inch) metal nails by a matter of inches.

Kite surfing can be a dangerous sport, as the wind, water, and waves are all unpredictable. A sudden gust of wind could cause the athlete to go hurtling through the air, and this experience has been described as feeling as if shot from a cannon. Riders may find themselves trapped under the surface of the water or injured by the equipment itself.

During a six-month study, 235 kite surfers self-reported seven injuries for every 1,000 hours of practice. The most common injuries were to the foot and ankle (28 percent); skull (14 percent); chest (13 percent); and knee (13 percent). Fifty-six percent of these injuries occurred when the rider could not detach from the harness.

Florida kite surfer Rick Iossi tries to keep track of all significant kite surfing injuries, and his records indicate that about 20 people have died participating in this sport from 2001 to 2004 alone. One fatality occurred in northern Germany when an athlete crashed against a rock; another German kite surfer, Silke Gorldt, died when she became caught up in another surfer's line and was smashed against a fence on the shore. Because of these accidents—and because of some lawsuits filed—there is a push for kite surfers to become certified before participating in the sport. This is already required for hang gliding and diving.

EXTREME KITE SURFING

As in many other sports, a group of athletes have decided to push the limits of what can be accomplished, and many athletes can now achieve speeds of 25 to 30 miles (40 to 50 kilometers) per hour while kite surfing; in 2005, the world record was 77.4 kilometers (approximately 48 miles) per hour. The record was set by Olaf Marting of South Africa on October 12, 2005. The women's speed record was set on the same day by Aurelia Herpin of France, with a speed of 65.19 kilometers (approximately 40 miles) per hour.

In 2007, the men's record was broken by Alexandre Caizergues, when he traveled at 88.7 kilometers (approximately 55 miles) per hour. Also in 2007, Sjoukje Bredenkamp from South Africa established the new female record at 42.35 knots, which is approximately 48 miles (approximately 77 kilometers) per hour.

It is not uncommon for kite surfers to reach air time of 5 to 10 seconds. In 2006, Erik Eck established a world record of 39 seconds after reaching a height of approximately 164 feet (50 meters) in Hawaii. This feat, however, was not intentional; rather it was accomplished during a "kitemare" or a nightmarish situation while kite surfing. Eck was unintentionally caught in an updraft that launched him high into the air; he was caught in a thermal and was fortunate to survive. Eck did not even break any bones.

ORGANIZATIONS AND COMPETITIONS

The International Kiteboarding Organization (IKO) was formed in 2001 to communicate safety practices, develop standards, provide insurance, and promote the sport. The Kiteboard Pro World Tour (KPWT) began in 1999 with freestyle events; in 2003, wave master events were added. The Professional Kite Rider's Association (PKRA) formed in 2002 to provide overall direction to the sport's professional athletes; this organization also sanctions the Kite Speed World Championships, where four events are held in the high wind areas of Namibia, France, and the Canary Islands.

See also Barefoot Water Skiing; Wakeboarding

L

LAND YACHTING (LAND SAILING)

Many centuries ago, the Chinese discovered how to capture the power of the wind to provide transportation; perhaps the Egyptians did the same. Then, in 1600, Flemish engineer Simon Stevin of Bruges, Flanders, created a massive land yacht with two masts. In that yacht, 28 passengers could travel on the beach at a speed of 20-plus miles per hour. During the nineteenth century, the Baltimore and Ohio railroad created a sailing-type car for the Russian czar and, in 1849, during the California Gold Rush, prospectors attached sails to their wagons for faster travel. That same principle is what powers the land yachts of today, with the modern-day sport generally considered to have started in the 1960s.

Modern-day land yachts are generally three-wheeled boat-shaped vehicles with a sail that can achieve speeds of more than 100 miles (160 kilometers) per hour. Many of these yachts have wheels that can be replaced with ice blades for wintertime use; these ice yachts have reached speeds of nearly 150 miles (240 kilometers) per hour. The vehicles used on land are sometimes called land sailers, land yachts, sand boats, or even dirt boats. Vehicles used for urban land sailing, which occurs in parking lots, are smaller and more flexible than those crafted for other venues.

Land Yachting Equipment

A single-seater Manta Landsailer can cost $1,500 to $2,000, with a twin-seater going for $2500 and up, depending upon the upgrades desired.

Yacht technology continues to improve, and the newest yachts are lighter than previous models, often crafted with epoxy resins and glass fiber materials, and better able to withstand crashes. Softer sails are being replaced with hard, adjustable wings that are lighter and more efficient, and that produce more speed. Because of the speed of the yachts and the hardness of the surfaces beneath the vehicles, crashes can lead to significant injuries and even death. That said, according to the North American Land Sailing Association (NALSA), there are a "few hundred people landsailing in North America" with only one known fatality over a 15-year span (1988–2003) (Dill 2003).

NALSA was formed in 1972, with one of their main goals being to promote exciting yet safe, nonpolluting recreation. The group provides its members with safety information, racing regulations, land operating rules, and more. As of December 2007, NALSA listed 11 official land yachting clubs.

There is also a global organization, the International Land and Sandyachting Federation, as well as clubs located in Argentina, Australia, Belgium, Brazil, Chile, France, Germany, Italy, Mexico, New Zealand, Sweden, the United Kingdom, and the United States. There is a European Championship and world championships; the 2008 international event will be held in Patagonia, Argentina.

The organization's Web site provides information about speed and distance records, including a distance world record of covering 1,522 kilometers (948 miles) within 24 hours, which broke a previous record of 20 years' standing of 1,244 kilometers (773 miles). The current speed record is 116.7 miles (187.8 kilometers) per hour, set on March 20, 1999, just outside of Las Vegas; a British team is determined to beat that record.

Land sailing is featured in *Sahara* (1995), a novel written by Clive Cussler.

See also Ice Yachting

LAVA SLEDDING

In lava sledding, also known as Hawaiian sledding, mountain sledding, and he'e holua, participants race on large wooden sleds down grassy slopes or sledding tracks built on rock.

This type of sledding took place in Hawaii 2,000 years ago, when the ali'i, which was the ruling class of Hawaii, participated in holua. This sport also existed on other islands in the Pacific, including Tahiti and New Zealand. In ancient times, these sleds were between 7 and 18 feet (2.1 and 5.5 meters) in length, with matting on the cross bars to raise up the sledders' chests. The sleds were lashed together with coconut fiber and were extremely durable. The Bishop Museum in Hawaii displays an 800-year-old sled that is still intact.

The traditional sled track—or kakua holua—was created by building a rocky foundation and then covering it with soil; the track was then covered with leaves and grass before a race to create a smoother surface; only one sled could fit on this track at a time so there could be no side-by-side racing. Some tracks were set up so that the sledder would slide into the ocean at the end of the race.

Ancient Hawaiians believed that they were honoring their gods though this sport, especially Pele, the goddess of fire—and, by extension, of volcanoes. Hawaiians for the most part

Tom "Pohaku" Stone positions himself aboard a new Hawaiian sled. For Stone, what began as childhood fun on a natural roller coaster ride has evolved into a journey aimed at reviving the 2,000-year Hawaiian tradition of he'e holua, or Hawaiian lava sledding. (AP Photo/ Ronen Zilberman)

stopped participating in this activity in 1825, though, when Christian missionaries disapproved of the practice, considering it a wasteful use of time.

Native Hawaiian Tom "Pohaku" Stone remembered his grandfather telling him stories about holua and, as an adult, he became curious about the ancient sport. So, in 1993, while attending the University of Hawaii at Manoa, Stone wrote a college paper on this 2,000-year activity that combined sport with religious beliefs. After receiving a bachelor's degree in Hawaiian Studies in 1998, Stone earned a master's degree in Pacific Island Studies in 2001 and a master's in American Studies in 2004. He currently is teaching at Kapi'olani Community College while working on his doctorate—and he has been credited for single-handedly reviving the practice of holua.

Stone is believed to be the first person to have ridden the traditional Hawaiian sled in more than 100 years. He has since taught more than 250 people how to sled in the traditional manner. According to Stone, speeds of up to 50 miles (80.5 kilometers) per hour are achievable, although the risks are high in a crash. In 2001, he sliced open 18 inches (45.6 centimeters) of his thigh after sledding over a buried fence post. He has also broken his neck in pursuit of holua.

Stone crafts sleds in the ancient tradition, creating 50-pound (22.7-kilogram) sleds that are 12 feet (3.7 meters) in length. The runners are carved out of hard woods found in Hawaii, such as ohia. Stone spends about two weeks crafting each sled, which he sells for $3,000 or more. He has also restored a long-neglected 700-foot (213.4-meter) sledding run, and discovered more than 50 other traditional runs, including one that was 60 feet (18.3 meters) wide by 5,200 feet (1,585 meters) long.

Stone would like to revive a traditional contest wherein a sledder races down a mountain at the same time that a surfer tackles a large wave. When asked about participation figures, he measures the number of regular sledders in Hawaii in the dozens; when asked about serious injuries, he had none to report, although his broken neck seems to qualify.

In 2007, Stone organized the He'enalu/He/eholua Surfing Series. In this series, athletes used traditional wooden surfboards that weighed more than 100 pounds (45.4 kilograms) each and also rode on traditional holua sleds.

See also Noll, Greg

MANAGING RISK FACTORS OF EXTREME SPORTS

People who engage in extreme sports often take significant risks during practices and competitions and when trying to set records. In many instances, however, these athletes are in fact effectively managing their levels of risk through calculated strategies.

STRATEGY

Perhaps the best example of an athlete accomplishing extraordinary feats through well thought out strategies is **BASE (Building/Antenna tower/Span/Earth) jumper Felix Baumgartner**. He practices for several months to several years before attempting to break a particular record or accomplish a specific feat. Before diving head first into the Mamet Cave, for example, he prepared for 10 months by jumping from a hot air balloon that hovered at a height that exactly duplicated the distance of his cave jump; he also relied upon a 40-person support team to identify potential dangers and to target the best strategy for jumping into the cave. Overall, Baumgartner prepares by understanding the task being undertaken in minute detail, and by precisely pinpointing his abilities and limitations, thereby reducing risk to the smallest level possible.

Although few extreme athletes prepare themselves to a degree comparable to Baumgartner, many do survey a venue (race course, half-pipe, mountain, and so forth) before attempting to participate in an extreme sport. In some competitions, however, such as **artificial wall climbing**, athletes may be forbidden from seeing the course before competing.

Another preparation method involves increasing the level of difficulty of a jump, trick, and so forth with each attempt during practices. In this way, the athletes learn more about the precise actions required—and what to avoid—as they prepare for an event.

EQUIPMENT

Experienced extreme sports athletes know the importance of using the correct equipment and checking it carefully before participating in an activity. Sky divers need their parachutes, rock climbers need their ropes, and scuba divers need their oxygen tanks all to be in prime form. Moreover, experienced athletes avoid ramps, rails, race courses, and other structures and venues that have been pieced together or are otherwise unsafe.

Each sport has its own specialized protective gear, with helmets being a common denominator among multiple sports, ranging from **skateboarding** and **snowboarding** to **BMX (bicycle motocross)** and **motocross**. Some helmets are full face, which means that protection exists over part of the face as well as over the head; open face or "regular" helmets provide protection to the head, but not the face. Other common forms of extreme sport protective gear include wrist guards; gloves; pads and guards for knees, elbows, and shins; padded undershorts or pants; goggles; and boots.

Information released by the University of Alabama–Birmingham (UAB), states that almost 75 percent of injuries that occur during extreme sports practices happen because the athlete was not wearing protective gear. Katherine Terry from the UAB Injury Control Research Center references another reason for injuries. "Participants also often overestimate their ability to perform high risk maneuvers" (University of Alabama–Birmingham 2001).

TRAINING
Physical training is also important to effectively manage risk. Although some extreme athletes resist the idea, participating in athletic training by lifting weights and exercising on cardio equipment is useful as a strategy to increase fitness and thereby avoid injuries. Besides that training, athletes in board sports (skateboarding, snowboarding, **wakeboarding**, and so forth) also may participate in balance training; athletes across a broad spectrum benefit from flexibility training, which extends and stretches the muscles.

COMMON SENSE
Groups
In sports for which athletes will travel to unpopulated or sparsely populated venues, such as caving and mountain climbing, they are encouraged to travel in groups and to back up one another, whenever necessary. Another safety tactic is to inform others who are not participating in the activity where the athletes will be climbing or exploring, and when they are expected to return. Another advantage of participating in groups is that the more experienced athletes can mentor and serve as role models to the up-and-coming athletes. If alone or in a secluded location when practicing or training, athletes should be conservative and not try any jumps, tricks, or other activities that are new to them.

Weather
Extreme sport athletes should also listen carefully to weather reports and learn how to recognize the signs of impending storms. Extreme skiers must learn how to avert potential avalanches, while kite surfers must be able to decipher ocean waves and extreme downhill mountain bikers must understand their environment and the wildlife that inhabits the area. Experienced athletes also create back up safety plans in case of poor weather conditions or the occurrence of other unexpected factors.

Sobriety
Sobriety is key. Participants of some extreme sports, fairly or unfairly, have earned the reputation as drinkers and drug users; snowboarding is one such example. When drunk

or high, athletes cannot realistically judge their limits or the hazards surrounding them, and they may in fact encourage others to attempt feats that are unsafe or unwise.

PROTECTIVE GEAR

In 2005, the American College of Sports Medicine (ACSM) released information about teenage athletes, ages 13 to 18, who were underusing protective gear when participating in extreme sports; sports reviewed were **inline skating**, skateboarding, and snowboarding. Approximately two-thirds of the teens surveyed were male. Teens self-reported using significantly less protective gear than that recommended by the American Academy of Pediatrics and American Academy of Orthopedic Surgeons; inline skaters wore the most, followed by skateboarders, and then snowboarders. Nearly half of the teens in each sport group said that nothing would persuade them to wear protective gear, with younger teens more willing to wear the gear than older ones.

More specifically, 60 percent of inline skaters, 65 percent of skateboarders, and 72 percent of snowboarders "never" or "rarely" used helmets or only wore them when required (Reuters India 2008).

Teens who did use protective gear listed parental influence, peer influence, and venue requirements as the reasons for compliance; teens from ages 13 to 15 listed parental influence more frequently than those ages 16 to 18. Reasons cited for not using protective gear included discomfort and a lack of need, according to the teen's perception. Being part of or witnessing an accident was a factor that influenced these teens to wear more protective gear.

The Consumer Product Safety Commission estimates that nearly half of the 16,000 head injuries that occur during a snowboarding or **skiing** season could be prevented or reduced in severity just by participants wearing helmets.

Teenagers are not the only people unwilling to take safety precautions that would reduce their levels of risk. In fact, there are adults who also fight against this strategy. Free soloists, for example, deliberately choose to climb rocks and mountains without the use of climbing aids and without companion athletes. Athletes who share this mind-set participate in other extreme sports, as well.

At organized extreme sports events, medical personnel are generally on site, and some medical teams now specialize in extreme sports medicine. In some instances, such as the extreme snow sporting events that take place on Mount Verbier in Switzerland, medical personnel ride in helicopters that circle above the sporting venue. That said, extreme sporting events that result in a significant amount of injuries can overburden the medical personnel. In one particular event, the Fort William Mountain Bike World Championship held in Scotland, 30 percent of the participants (52 out of 173) were injured, with two of them requiring hospitalization (Coris 2008).

In spite of this potential for serious injury, Dr. Eric E. Coris, associate professor of Family Medicine and Orthopedics and Sports Medicine, and director of the Division of Primary Care Sports Medicine at the University of South Florida, believes that extreme sports participation is a positive activity, given that safety precautions are followed. Coris is quoted as saying, "So, to all extreme sports enthusiasts, I say, 'Shred away, dude. But wear a helmet!'"

See also Psychology of Risk

MOTOCROSS (EXTREME MOTOX)

In motocross sports, participants race motorcycles over a predetermined course, either at an indoor arena or on an outdoor track. Initially, motocross athletes raced motorcycles on flat tracks. As the sport developed, the tracks became more complex and were no longer level, so participants needed to jump over broad ranges of obstacles. In modern-day competitions, several jumps may be included on the course with varying degrees of difficulty. In a single jump, the athlete jumps 20 to 60 feet (6 to 18 meters) onto a flat landing. In a double jump, the athlete jumps off of one object or ramp and must land on the far side of another obstacle; in double jumps, athletes generally cover 20 to 70 feet (6 to 21 meters) of area. Athletes attempt triple jumps, as well.

Starting in the 1980s, riders began incorporating trick moves into their competitions; this style of riding is often called freestyle motocross. As the sport continued to develop, freestyle skills used by **skiers**, **snowboarders**, and **BMX (bicycle motocross) riders** increasingly became integral elements of the sport.

DEVELOPMENT OF MOTOCROSS

In 1924, the American Motorcyclist Association (AMA) formed to represent the interests of motorcycle riders across the country, and to oversee competitions.

Doug Parsons, of Riverside, California, pulls off a "Superman" freestyle motocross trick, July 24, 2004. (AP Photo/*Las Cruces Sun-News*, Norm Dettlaff)

Although organized competitions ceased during World War II, the sport resumed again after the war ended, with European countries also joining in. Races usually took place on flat ovals, often on horse race tracks, with some road racing occurring as well.

AMA became the U.S. affiliate to the *Fédération Internationale de Motocyclisme* (FIM). In 1947, the FIM created the *Motocross des Nations* to annually determine the World Team Motocross Champions. In 1957, the World Motocross Championship Series was formed. The motorcycles used to compete were heavy compared with today's models, with basic suspension systems that did not do much to ease the roughness of the ride. During the 1960s, the AMA held amateur and professional motocross races.

In 1971, the AMA took motocross out of the rural areas where most races had occurred, holding a pivotal event at a track created at the Daytona International Speedway; there, significantly larger numbers of people could gather to watch the action. The following year, the National Championship Motocross Series began. Events were held in large stadiums, starting with the Los Angeles Coliseum. These events were sometimes referred to as "Supercross," which combined the terms "Super Bowl" and "Motocross." At this time, the Europeans, such as Belgium's Roger DeCoster, were more accomplished than Americans in the sport; however, by the 1980s, the Americans once again began to dominate.

DEVELOPMENT OF EXTREME MOTOCROSS/FREESTYLE MOTOCROSS

As the racing portion of the sport continued to develop, so did a more extreme version of motocross, in which riders maneuvered extreme obstacles; at one point, the notion of a 40-foot jump (12 meters) was considered the ultimate goal. Today, much more significant jumps must be achieved by competitive riders.

One of the earlier pioneers of the extreme version of motocross was Evel Knievel, who was also the most well known of the motocross daredevils of the era. From the late 1960s through the early 1980s, his extreme motorcycle jumps were televised by ABC's *Wide World of Sports*. Perhaps his most famous event was when he jumped across the Snake River Canyon in Twin Falls, Idaho, in 1974. Although he sustained only minor injuries in that jump, in which more than one equipment malfunction occurred, it is said that Knievel broke 40 bones during his motocross career.

It was in the 1980s that riders began incorporating freestyle acrobatic moves into their motocross racing. Daredevil riders began removing their hands from their handlebars while in midair; the AMA initially disapproved of this element of racing, but eventually came to accept the "no-hander" as part of the sport. Riders claimed this added an additional element of thrill to their performances.

The no-handed move became a standard part of AMA-sanctioned races held indoors and out, and this encouraged riders to develop other innovative ways to add excitement to motocross. This, in turn, caught the attention of television producers who began to televise extreme and freestyle motocross events. In freestyle motocross, judges award points to riders based on amplitude, transitions, degree of difficulty, originality, and overall performance.

European riders did not begin freestyle motocross as early as riders in the United States; the 2001 Night of Jumps event, though, held in Germany, brought significant attention to the sport in European countries. That same year, the World Freestyle Association (WFA) received sponsorship from television networks to create a world championship event. In 2002, United States rider Heidi Henry performed well in the **X Games** and that performance is considered the official entry of women into freestyle motocross.

Jeremy McGrath is an excellent example of what a modern-day motocross athlete, using newer technology and a lighter-weight bike, can do as he maneuvers the bumps, ruts, obstacles, and jumps found in an AMA Supercross Series. Other athletes of note are Jeff Emig, Kenny Bartram, and Kevin Windham.

Daredevil athletes continue to push the parameters of motocross venues, performing in the snow, in hilly areas, and over obstacles as large as trucks and airplanes. Sometimes, several riders attempt synchronized jumps.

RACE COURSES

In a typical course, racers line up behind a gate; a set of aluminum tubes prevents them from starting early and, when the tubes fall down, the race begins. The racers then must ride through a tunnel that narrows from 80 to 20 feet (24 meters to 6 meters) across. This 200- to 400-foot (60- to 120-meter) tunnel forces riders to jockey for position. The first turn after exiting the tunnel is always a left, and a significant number of crashes occur at this turn; crashes nearly always eliminate a rider from placing in a race.

Those who are still in the race then begin to navigate a series of obstacles that require them to make single, double, and triple jumps; there are also "whoops," which are short, steep bumps that jolt the rider. Whenever the riders are in the air, they have the opportunity to perform trick maneuvers, including the "cancan," wherein they move one leg to the opposite side of the motorcycle and back again, before landing. McGrath is well known for the "nac nac," where he moves one leg off the motorcycle, swinging it backward—and then turning his trunk toward the back of the bike, and getting back into position before landing. In Windham's "hell clicker" move, he lifts his feet to the front of the bike, clicking his heels together before landing.

Flags of different colors are used to communicate with racers; the track is far too noisy for spoken communications to be heard. If a racer's motorcycle becomes disabled during a race—but he or she has completed 50 percent of the required laps—the rider can push his vehicle (unassisted by mechanical aids or the help of other people) to the finish line to receive the checkered finish flag.

Amateur motocross riders often practice using obstacles found in the natural terrain.

MOTOCROSS INJURIES

Common injuries include shoulder injuries, including rotator cuff tears, and wrist injuries. More significant injuries, up to and including fatal ones, also occur in motocross; a Web site sponsored by Dyno Port (http://www.motocrossjumps.com) records specifics about motocross injuries and deaths. Often times, families provide site visitors with e-mail addresses and Web site addresses to monitor riders' recoveries. One comment, referring to the risks taken during motocross, notes that, instead of having one Evel Knievel, there are now 300 of them.

The National Institutes of Health published results of motocross injuries studied in medical facilities in southern California, where the sport is popular, during a predetermined time; the injuries occurred from January 2000 through December 2001. Out of the 270 patients studied, five were females; the average age was 26.

In 52 percent of the cases, trauma to the extremities was noted, including closed-head injuries (33 percent); blunt chest trauma (23 percent); abdominal injuries (15 percent); spinal injuries (14 percent); and pelvic injuries (8 percent). Surgery was required for 96 patients, which was 36 percent of the total, usually for orthopedic injuries. One hundred and seventy-nine patients were admitted to the hospital (66 percent of the total); 60 (22 percent) were discharged; 29 (11 percent) were transferred elsewhere for more intensive care; and two (1 percent) died. The average hospital stay was 2.3 days.

Surprisingly, the more extreme the jump, as far as distance goes, the more likely a rider is to land safely, as he or she has more time to coordinate the landing.

MOTOCROSS EQUIPMENT

Modern-day motocross machines are generally 125- to 250-cubic centimeter bikes, with most professionals preferring 250 cubic centimeters. Most engines are two-stroke models, although Yamaha makes a popular four-stroke engine model that provides more stability on slippery surfaces. Riders often modify their bikes, adding grips to the seats, lowering front wheels, and making other adjustments. Helmets are necessary to help prevent the worst of injuries.

MEDIA

Television coverage of motocross has occurred for nearly 40 years or so, in large part because of the self-promotional abilities of Evel Knievel and the daredevil athletes who followed in his footsteps. As trick elements became increasingly used during the competitions of the 1980s, television coverage also burgeoned.

In 1993, a television film, *Crusty Demons of Dirt*, brought freestyle motocross to the attention of a significant number of Americans; modern-day athletes also produce videos of themselves as promotional tools. All Clear Channel began filming competitions during the 1990s and, in 1997, Four Leaf Entertainment created the first U.S. freestyle motocross competition and also played a role in the formation of the International Freestyle Motocross Association (IFMA). In 1999, freestyle motocross competitions were first televised for the X Games and the **Gravity Games**.

See also Carmichael, Ricky

MOUNTAIN BIKING

On October 21, 1976, 10 people gathered together just west of Fairfax, California, located in Marin County. They arrived with their modified bicycles originally built in the 1930s and 1940s, and they planned to race down Repack Road, a dirt road that plummets 1,300 feet (396 meters) in less than 2.1 miles (3.4 kilometers). The road was so named because bikes descending the twisting path down Mount Tamalpais would often overheat and the grease on the bikes' brakes would vaporize and need to be reapplied—or repacked.

The winner of this race was Alan Bonds—the only man who did not crash—and so ended the first officially organized downhill mountain biking race. During a series of subsequent races held on Repack Road, Gary Fisher clocked the fastest time at 4 minutes and 22 seconds. Fisher was probably the first racer to modify a mountain bike to have several different gears; although this made riding the bike easier, it also added 25 pounds (11.35 kilograms) to the bike's weight.

To get to the Repack Road starting line for downhill mountain racing, racers often loaded their bikes onto trucks, which could wind up a paved road for the first 1,000 feet (304.8 meters). After that, racers would ride or push their bikes up a dirt road for two more miles, and then climb the final 500 feet (152.4 meters)—and that was the warm up before the race. From this vantage point, the racers could see the San Francisco Bay in the distance.

Racers took off, one by one, with 2-minute intervals in between. Whoever had the best time in the previous race went last in the next race, to help build suspense—although it is hard to imagine this type of racing needing any help to be suspenseful.

DEVELOPMENT OF THE SPORT

Because of these Repack Road races, Marin County has been called the spiritual home of mountain biking. Even before World War II, locals had modified their balloon-tired Schwinn Excelsior bicycles (created by Ignaz and Frank S. Schwinn in the 1930s) to use them on the mountainous roads, including Mount Tamalpais, the highest peak in Marin County, measuring 2,571 feet (783.6 meters); that this endeavor evolved into downhill racing seems a natural progression. These bikes were easy to locate in the 1970s; they were also relatively inexpensive and sturdy enough to be nicknamed "clunkers."

Although this Marin County group deserves credit for developing the sport of downhill racing, other athletes—members of the Velo Cross Club Parisien—had modified bikes in a similar fashion as early as the 1950s in France. During the 1970s, in Cupertino, California, yet another biking group—the Morrow Dirt Riders—had been meeting regularly to ride on similarly modified bicycles. Some of these riders brought their bikes to race in the 1974 California State Cyclocross Championships, and several racers who witnessed the Morrow Dirt Riders in action went on to become early pioneers of mountain bike racing, including Joe Breeze, Charlie Kelly, and Gary Fisher.

Another small group of California riders—the Velo Club Tamalpas—were taught how to ride these modified bikes by Marco Vendetti from the Larkspur Canyon Gang. They also held an informal downhill race, with the winner said to have received a bag of marijuana.

THE MODERN MOUNTAIN BIKE

In 1977, Joe Breeze built the first modern mountain bike from lighter-weight chrome. In 1980, Gary Fisher and Charlie Kelly formed a company, MountainBikes, and they sold 150 bikes, which was about half of the bikes sold in the United States at that time. In 1983, Specialized Bikes introduced the rugged StumpJumper, the first mass-produced mountain bike and, in 1986, the sales of mountain bikes surpassed those of traditional bicycles.

The mountain bike went through several incarnations, with mountain bike frames now being made smaller than those of traditional bicycles. Originally, bikes had balloon tires, which were replaced by "fat" tires that resembled those used in motocross;

mountain bikes now had stronger rims on the tires. Sweeping handlebars straightened out as the bikes evolved and seats became broader with more padding. An added bar allowed riders to lean forward and upward. In modern-day mountain bikes, special pedal clips allow a rider to detach himself or herself from his or her bike in a fall. Bikes are now made from aluminum, titanium, space-age ceramic, and other composite materials.

Originally, these bikes had one front and one back sprocket (gear); mountain bikes then went from one gear to three—and then to 10, 15, 18, 21, and then 24. Frames went from rigid construction to a suspension system.

Mountain Bike Equipment

The most important piece of mountain biking safety equipment is a helmet to prevent head injuries during crashes or falls; full-face helmets are recommended for the more aggressive style of mountain biking, such as downhill racing. Other safety equipment includes sturdy gloves, as it is natural to reach out to break a fall, which could lead to cuts, bruises, and other abrasions on a rider's hands. Mountain bike riders who ride aggressively sometimes wear padded body protection. Some riders strap on a hydration system that allows them to drink water without needing to reach for a water bottle or to balance while riding and drinking. Riding glasses or goggles keep dust from flying into the rider's eyes and can shield eyes from bright sunlight. Riders usually take along a bike pump and other tools to repair flat tires or to fix other mechanical problems.

Governing Bodies

Mountain bikers are expected to follow the USA Cycling Code. The code requires helmet use, using caution when overtaking another, staying on designated trails, not disturbing wildlife or littering, respecting private property, and biking in pairs or in groups.

Clashes can occur between mountain hikers and mountain bike racers, with the hikers sometimes complaining about the erosion caused by mountain biking or about mountain bikers interfering with their hiking. Both the International Mountain Biking Association (IMBA) and National Off-Road Bicycle Association (NORBA) are working to decrease the impact that mountain biking has on the environment.

NORBA was formed in 1983 to oversee the multitude of mountain biking races, including the first world championship, held in Purgatory, Colorado, in 1990. By that time, the sport was evolving from the more laid-back, tight community-like atmosphere of the 1970s and 1980s into the intense international sport of the 1990s and beyond. Although early racers were American or Canadian, by this point, European teams had joined in the sport.

Until fairly recently, mountain bikers needed to make all repairs during races themselves. Because of an adjustment to the international rules of the *Union Cycliste Internationale* (UCI), riders can have teams to provide aid.

Mountain Bike Racing

Although many people ride mountain bikes for exercise and for pleasure, in the extreme version of the sport, it is all about racing and stunt riding. One current event is cross-country (XC) racing, wherein competitors race for the best time on a closed course over difficult, often twisting terrain. In a typical cross-country race, men race anywhere between 40 and 50 kilometers (25 and 31 miles), while women cover 30 to 40 kilometers (18 to 25 miles). In marathon races, the course may be 97 kilometers (60 miles) long. The terrain may have climbs and descents and endurance is a key asset.

In downhill racing, racers attempt to get the best time on a descending closed course; racers may need to ride a ski lift to reach the starting line. Downhill racers use mountain bikes with larger brakes and dual suspension systems as they may travel down extremely steep terrain; some courses may include jump-off spots of up to 40 feet (12 meters) or drops of 10 feet (3 meters) or more. In short-course races, generally held in the United States, courses are only 1 to 2 miles (1.6 to 3.2 kilometers) in length and this sport is far more fan- and television-friendly. No matter the length of the course, skilled racers can achieve speeds of 60 miles (97 kilometers) per hour or more; when crashes occur, they can be quite dramatic.

In an elimination race, two riders are pitted against one another to see who can receive the best score out of two runs. In the dual slalom, the closed course has tight turns, and each of the two riders must tackle both of the two courses; the four-cross was accepted by the UCI in 2002, to allow for quicker eliminations.

In observed trials, the course contains obstacles and hazards, and "dabbing" or putting a foot down for balance purposes is penalized. In this event, the lowest score wins. Uphill racing consists of timed competitions of sustained climbing, often in remote terrains.

In freeride, which is freestyle racing that may including jumps and stunts, overcoming obstacles, and so forth, riders often custom build their bikes to accomplish individually determined extreme goals. Style, originality, and technique are important in freeride. In slopestyle riding, **BMX (bicycle motocross)** tricks are incorporated into the event, and riders highlight their individual skills in hopes of getting higher rankings from the judges. In the 24-hour event, teams and individual riders compete to see who can go the farthest in that time period; teams must ride throughout the night, using lighted helmets.

When a mountain biker ascends over jumps, he or she is "catching big air"; if a crash occurs, it is known as "stacking."

Even more extreme events include the Iditasport Extreme, a 300-mile course in Alaska, and the La Ruta de Los Conquistadores, which lasts for three days and also has a 300-mile course; this race takes place in Costa Rica. Still other "extremists" return to the earlier days of the sport by only using one gear in their races.

In 1990, world championships were held for mountain biking, and in 1996, the sport became an Olympic event in Atlanta, Georgia. In that first Olympic competition, Bart Brentjens of the Netherlands won the gold medal after racing approximately 30 miles and then crossing the finish line in 2 hours, 17 minutes, and 38 seconds; his average speed was 13 miles (21 kilometers) per hour. Thomas Frischknecht of Switzerland won the silver medal (2 hours, 20 minutes, and 14 seconds) and Miguel Martinez from France secured the bronze (2 hours, 20 minutes, and 36 seconds). Although the sport's beginnings were credited to male Americans, the top American men racers finished in 19th and 20th place: David Juarez, Sugarloaf, California (2 hours, 35 minutes, and 15 seconds), and Don Myrah, Saratoga, California (2 hours, 35 minutes, and 50 seconds).

For the women, the medals went to Paola Pezzo from Italy (1 hour, 50 minutes, and 51 seconds); Alison Sydor from Canada (1 hour, 51 minutes, and 58 seconds); and Susan DeMattei from the United States (1 hour, 52 minutes, and 36 seconds).

In the second Olympics for mountain bike athletes (2004), the course in Australia was about 7 kilometers (4.3 miles), and it featured steep drops and areas of the course that were only 50 centimeters (20 inches) wide. Medal winners in the men's competition were Miguel Martinez from France; Filip Meirhaeghe from Belgium; and Christoph Sauser from Switzerland. Female champions were Paola Pezzo from Italy, Barbara Blatter from Switzerland, and Margarita Fullana from Spain.

In the 2004 Olympics, held in Athens, Greece, at the Parnitha Olympic Mountain Bike Venue, the men's cross-country winners were Julien Absalon from France, José Antonio Hermida from Spain, and Bart Brentiens from the Netherlands. Women's medals went to Gunn-Rita Dahle Flesjå from Norway; Marie-Hélène Premont from Canada; and Sabine Spitz from Germany.

Mountain biking, as the Olympic athletes could attest, can be physically grueling; but that is not the only challenge. According to Pamela Fickenscher, in her article "Off-Road Ministry: What I Learned from Mountain Biking,"

> [W]hat most surprised me was the mental discipline it took to make it through a course in one piece. I quickly learned that most of mountain biking is in the eyes. The bike will follow you where you look. If you watch fellow bikers crash, you're likely to end up as part of the crash. If you obsess about that rock or tree you don't want to hit, you will run into it. (Fickenscher 2007)

MOUNTAINBOARDING

Mountainboarders plummet down slopes of rock, dirt, grass, and sand on a wheeled board that is a hybrid between a skateboard and a snowboard, with a suspension system and bindings to attach the riders' feet to the boards. These boards are called mountainboards, dirtboards, or all-terrain boards.

On their way down the slope, mountainboarders need to avoid crashing into rocks, trees, thistles, and other dangerous obstacles. Some athletes ride up ski lifts at resorts during the summer months to reach their starting point, while others scout out mountain biking trails and similar venues to go mountainboarding.

Two different branches of mountainboarding—speed boarding and freestyle boarding—are developing in this relatively new sport. In freestyle events, athletes use elements of the natural habitat to jump, spin, and perform tricks and stunts while in "big air," perhaps 40 feet (12 meters) above the ground. These tricks include 180- and 360-degree rotations; back and front flips; grabbing the board from the back (tail) or from the front (nose); and variations of these tricks using only one foot. Performing a double backflip while traveling at speeds of approximately 30 miles (48 kilometers) per hour is a feat only the most experienced mountainboarders have accomplished (Moore 2007).

In speed boarding (also known as "boardercross" or "dirt boarder X"), athletes participate in downhill races, while avoiding obstacles. This is similar to the slalom event in skiing. Other names for mountainboarding include dirtboarding, grassboarding, or all-terrain boarding (ATB).

Development of the Sport

A snowboarding duo from the United States and a surfer from Australia are credited with inventing a board specifically for mountain riding at about the same time in 1992. Patrick McConnell and Jason Lee formed a U.S. company, MountainBoard Sports, LLC, in 1993 to sell their four-wheeled board as a tool for snowboarders to cross terrain; these boards now come in multiple lengths, with shorter boards more suitable for freestylists and longer boards providing better stability for speed boarding. The wheels range from 9 to 12 inches (23 to 30.5 centimeters) in diameter so that they can roll over obstacles; riders can change the air pressure in the wheels to modify the board's capabilities.

Meanwhile, an Australian surfer named John Milne created a three-wheeled board in Australia that has two wheels in front, plus one wheel in back, and a brake; this has been marketed as the Outback Mountainboard. Both the American and the Australian systems are steered like a skateboard, with the athlete using his or her body to direct the board. It seems that the four-wheeled version is becoming more popular with boarders.

Mountainboarding quickly spread to the United Kingdom, where riders Dave and Pete Tatham created their own mountainboard company, noSno, in 1992. The All Terrain Boarding Association of the United Kingdom (ATBA-UK) formed in 1997 with the purpose of looking after the interests of the mountainboarders. In 2000, the first mountainboarding track opened in North Wales; three years later, the first mountainboarding track was opened in Ireland. Other mountainboarding organizations formed around the world include the Japanese ATBA and the Australian ATBA.

Currently, the United States does not have a governing body for mountainboarders, so competitions are run independently. The largest of them, the U.S. Mountain Boarding Championship, is held annually at Snowmass Village in Aspen, Colorado. Competitions began in the United States in 1994 and in the United Kingdom in 1997.

In 2006, ex-pro mountainboarder Justin Rhodes estimated that there were 5,000 hard-core mountainboarders, worldwide, with a majority of them living in the United Kingdom. He also estimates that approximately 100,000 people around the world may mountainboard as recreation; a great number of boarders are teenagers, especially those who enjoy **skateboarding**, **snowboarding**, surfing, and **mountain biking** (Smith 2006). Another source of information, *Defying Gravity: Land Divers, Roller Coasters, Gravity Bums and the Human Obsession with Falling*, puts the number of mountainboarders at about 500,000 (Soden 2005).

The adrenaline rush experienced by boarders seems to be a large part of the sport's appeal. One mountainboard athlete summed up his experience in this way: "Every rider has his or her reasons for their commitment to what may appear as insanity, but I believe there is one that sums them all up. One way or another we are all in it for the ride" (http://www.mountainboard.net/index.php/category/features).

Here is another viewpoint: "The sport tends to attract thrill-seeking, type-A adrenaline junkies who thrive on snowboarding and surfing. And just about every mountainboarder has a harrowing list of injuries to brag about" (Engelson 2002).

MOUNTAINBOARDING RISKS AND INJURIES

Scratches, cuts, and abrasions occur because of regular contact with rocks, trees, and uneven ground, as well as collisions with riders and other objects. Dislocated joints and broken bones can result from rough rides and falls, even in the most experienced of athletes. In 2005, boarder Milly Wallace won first place in the freestyle competition at the U.S. championship; shortly after that, she attempted a jump that left her with a broken back. All boarders should ride with others.

MOUNTAINBOARDING EQUIPMENT

The main piece of equipment is a mountainboard, which can cost from $150 to $600. Lighter-weight riders need a softer deck on their board, while heavier riders need a stiffer one. Mountainboard companies generally provide information so that a rider can match his or her weight to the most suitable board.

Protective gear to prevent injuries includes a helmet; some people use a basic helmet while others use a **BMX**-style helmet that also covers the face. Knee and elbow pads, wrist guards, and gloves are also recommended.

If interested in freestyle riding, a smaller and lighter board with a stiffer deck is best. Freeride boards are suitable for riders who want to ride the entire mountain. Freeride boards must be stiff enough to handle cliff drops; some companies make boards with larger, 9-inch (23-centimeter) wheels that give a rider more clearance from the ground while others have a brake. Boardercross requires a lighter, maneuverable board.

POP CULTURE

A made for television movie, *Johnny Kapahala: Back on Board*, premiered on the Disney Channel in June 2007. Johnny is a teenage snowboarding champion who ends up competing in a mountainboarding competition as the climax to the movie.

MOUNTAIN CLIMBING

Mountain climbers ascend mountains, either by hiking up them (nontechnical climbing) or by using specialized equipment (which protects climbers from falling if they lose their grip) to scale up difficult areas, including sheer mountain walls (technical climbing). This information focuses on technical climbing. In some instances, parts of the mountain are covered with ice, which adds additional challenges when climbing. Some of the most daring mountain climbers scale up difficult rock "solo" without using any equipment other than chalk on their hands to maintain a grip on the mountain.

One estimate states that there are between 250,000 and 300,000 mountain climbers in the United States alone. The *Union Internationale des Associations D'Alpinisme* (UIAA, International Mountaineering and Climbing Federation), which has organizations in about 60 countries, states that nearly 3 million people, worldwide, share a "passion for mountains." This figure, though, encompasses more than just mountain climbers.

This sport requires its participants to be physically and mentally fit. In general, people climb mountains in pairs or in small groups. Each person must be aware of the

Jeremy Haas climbs Creation of the World on Moss Cliff, a rock climbing trail in the high peaks area of the Adirondack Mountains. (AP Photo/Photo provided by Jim Lawyer)

actions of the other climbers and each person must look out for the safety of the entire group. Each member of the team should be skilled in first aid and emergency aid procedures.

Mount Everest represents the kind of extreme challenge that some mountain climbers undertake. This type of climb requires climbers to be at the peak of fitness and requires several months and sometimes years of planning.

EARLY MOUNTAIN CLIMBING

The earliest record of people climbing mountains is in 1786, when Michel Gabriel Paccard and Jacques Balmat climbed Mont Blanc. Located on the borders of France, Italy, and Switzerland, this mountain has a peak of 15,770 feet (4,807 meters).

MODERN CATEGORIZATION OF CLIMBS

Mountain climbs are ranked by their degree of difficulty. In France, mountains are assigned a series of numbers and letters, while climbers in the United States follow the Yosemite Scale:

- Class 1: hiking on trails, bike paths, walking uphill or along a clear path or walkway
- Class 2: cross country, with map skills needed and hands needed for balance; more difficult cross-country travel, perhaps with fallen trees; uneven or intermittent trails
- Class 3: scrambling on rocks; may use a rope for climbing, but not a necessity
- Class 4: a fall could be deadly, so a rope or belayer system is required
- Class 5: climbing requires technical moves and significant protective equipment

Some climbers include a Class 6 for climbs more difficult than those in Class 5, but that is not part of the Yosemite Scale. For Class 5 climbs, a decimal system further breaks down levels of difficulty:

- A0: preexisting climbing aids available
- A1: requires chocks (devices anchored into openings); easy to place
- A2: requires difficult chocks
- A3: requires installation of hooks because chock placement is not possible
- A4: aids used, but they may not hold; very risky climb
- A5: extremely sketchy
- A6: being climbable is debatable

In some situations, a group of mountain climbers rope themselves together, with the most experienced and knowledgeable climber in the lead.

Mountain Climbing Equipment

For nontechnical climbing, the most important piece of equipment is a pair of properly fitting, quality hiking shoes or boots. For technical climbing, it is important to choose the right ropes, harnesses, and belay devices (the metal piece of equipment that secures the climbing rope and provides the friction needed to brake a fall). Quality shoes, clothes, and helmets are also important. Climbers should maintain their equipment carefully, as this literally could make the difference between life and death.

Climbers must carefully choose what items to place in their back packs. Some important items include a first aid kit, a compass, and radio transmitters. Those who will climb for more than one day must bring along camping supplies, including a tent and food. If snow is anticipated, then shovels and snow and ice gear are required.

Mountain Climbing Risks and Injuries

It is vital that climbers are alert when climbing and that they use good judgment about when, where, and how to climb. Risks encountered by climbers are numerous and any one of them could lead to serious injury and even death. Risks include falling rock and other falling objects, equipment failure, avalanches, lightning and other storms, and more. To stay safe, a climber must make realistic assessments about his or her strength and abilities, as well as those of other climbers in the group.

The most common injuries are pulled muscles, sprains and strains of the foot, sprained knees and ankles, and injuries causing hip and back pain. In a presentation given at the annual meeting of the Wilderness Medical Society at Aspen, Colorado, in August 1986 and at Leavenworth, Washington, in November 1987, information about 220 injured rock climbers was shared. Eighty-eight percent of the climbers in this survey were male and the average amount of mountain climbing experience was 5.9 years; in 66 percent of the cases, these injured men fell while leading climbs. Twenty-seven percent of climbers were rescued by the National Park Service.

Climbers in this survey reported 451 injuries, with 50 percent of them involving the skin; 28 percent were lower extremity injuries, mostly fractures. When asked to focus on their most significant injury, 45 percent of the people listed lower extremity injuries, with 30 percent of them being ankle injuries.

Thirteen head injuries were sustained, with 12 of them fatal; this fatality rate of 6 percent is low compared with some other studies of mountain climbing injuries. People requiring surgery or blood transfusions usually died before rescue and aid could be given.

A British study puts the overall mortality rate of mountain climbing at 4.6 percent. Falls, rock falls, and avalanches accounted for 69.6 percent of the deaths; cerebral and pulmonary edema accounted for 17.4 percent; and a lack of a specific cause accounted for the other 13 percent (UIAA Mountain Medicine Centre n.d.).

Mount Everest Controversy

Sir Edmund Hillary and Sherpa Tenzing Norgay were the first mountain climbers to successfully scale the summit of Mount Everest (29,035 feet/8,850 meters), doing so on May 29, 1953. Norgay died in 1986; Hillary lived until January 10, 2008.

Approximately 200 climbers have died making the attempt to climb Mount Everest, with 19 of them dying in 1996 alone (by June 2006, 10 had died). Factors that make climbing Mount Everest so difficult include the low concentration of oxygen at higher altitudes and its frigid temperatures.

In 2006, a mountain climbing controversy erupted when about 40 climbers passed by a nearly frozen hiker, leaving him behind to die. Those defending that decision say that it is nearly impossible to request help by phone or radio at such extreme altitudes and, even if help could be summoned, it is nearly impossible for helicopters to reach the height of Mount Everest to effect a rescue. They also stated that time and energy, and oxygen and food are all at a premium on this climb; expending some of these resources on a person who is likely to die may lead to other deaths.

Critics of these climbers say that, because an average person spends $10,000 to $40,000 to attempt to scale Mount Everest, they are focusing more on achieving their own (expensive) dreams rather than on the safe return of all climbers.

ORGANIZATIONS

The UIAA was formed in 1932 and currently represents about 80 associations worldwide. The UIAA advocates for mountain climbing safety and education, and addresses issues of environmental concern. In the United States, the American Alpine Club, the Appalachian Mountain Club, the Colorado Mountain Club, and the Sierra Club also focus on these issues.

See also Alpine Scrambling; Ethics and Extreme Sports; Ice Climbing

MULLEN, RODNEY (1966–)

In 2003, viewers of the Extreme Sports Channel chose freestyle and street **skateboarder** John Rodney Mullen, known as "Mutt" or "King," as the greatest extreme sports athlete ever. Mullen has been credited with creating or at least popularizing many of skateboarding's standard tricks, largely during the 1980s, but also beyond that decade. These tricks include the following:

- "Flatground ollie," which became the basis for all flatground tricks: in this trick, the skater bends his or her knees, using body force to pop down the tail end of the skateboard; then, the skater slides his or her front foot up the board and lifts the back foot off the board to gain height.
- "Ollie impossible," in which the skater causes the skateboard to flip, end over end, and then he or she lands in his or her original position.
- "Kickflip": this trick is similar to the "ollie" but, after performing the "ollie," the skater gives the board a kick to make it spin beneath him or her; this is considered one of the hardest of the basic skateboarding tricks to learn. Skateboard champion **Tony Hawk** once said that this trick seemed impossible to perform and it took him a year to learn how.
- "Heelflip": after performing an "ollie," the skater kicks the board in a way that makes it flip around, rather than spin.
- "360 flip": the skater and the board turn a full 360 degrees in the air; when he or she lands, the board is traveling in the original direction.
- "Helipops (360 nollie)": a "nollie" occurs when a skater puts pressure on the front of the skateboard, rather than the back, to gain air.

Other extreme athletes who received a significant number of votes in the Extreme Sports Channel competition included skateboarder Tony Hawk, motorcyclist Evel Knievel, **Mat "Condor" Hoffman**, and Kelly Slater.

Mullen was born on August 17, 1966, in Gainesville, Florida. At the age of 10, he persuaded his father, a doctor, to allow him to skateboard; his father agreed, given that Rodney always wore protective gear and that, if he were injured, he would give up the sport. On January 1, 1977, Mullen bought his first skateboard; he had a significant disadvantage, being severely pigeon-toed, but he did not allow his inwardly pointing toes to stop him.

Within one year, he found sponsors, starting with the Inland Surf Shop, where he originally skated. In his first competition, he placed third in boys' freestyle, garnering the attention of skateboard manufacturer Bruce Walker; Walker Skateboards then became his sponsor. For three years, he won all amateur contests that he entered (nearly 30) and then, after winning the Oceanside Nationals in California, he won first place at the Oasis Pro in San Diego, turning professional at age 13.

Skating for the Powell Peralta Bones Brigade team, Mullen won 34 more competitions over a 10-year period, losing only once, when he was ill (to Per Welinder). Mullen still won second place.

Mullen skated freestyle, which means that he performed on flat ground, without ramps or rails, stopping frequently to perform stationary tricks. A competitor would usually get 2 minutes to perform to music and his performance would then be rated.

In 1990, the popularity of street skating surpassed freestyle and so Mullen used his freestyle skills to revolutionize street skate. In 1987, Mullen left Powell Peralta to skate for World Industries; he also invested in that company, which was transformed into Kubic, the world's leading marketer of skateboarding hard goods. In 2002, Globe International (from Australia) bought out Kubic for $45.9 million. After Kubic was sold, Mullen formed a new company, Almost Skateboards, which is still in business.

Mullen has contributed to pop culture, appearing in The Bones Brigade Videos, 1–4, among other videos; these videos showcase the prowess of Bones Brigade skateboarding team members. Mullen also appeared in the movie Gleaming the Cube (1989) and wrote The Mutt: How to Skateboard and Not Kill Yourself (2004). He also appeared on the Extreme Sports Channel in "Hanging Happy with Rodney Mullen."

He became well known for his natural, relaxed, and comfortable style of skating. In an interview with About.com's Steve Cave, Mullen shared what first attracted him to the sport: the kind of people who enjoyed the sport, the fact that there was no perfect way to compete, and that no one ever told him that he was not doing something right.

In addition to tricks already described, Mullen invented an incredible number of tricks:

- 50/50 saran wrap
- 50/50 sidewinders
- 360 pressure flip
- 540 double kickflip
- 540 shove-it
- Airwalks
- Backside 180 flip
- Casper 360 flip
- Casper slides
- Caballerial impossible
- Double heelflips
- Frontside heelflip shove-its
- Gazelles

- Godzilla rail flip
- Half-cab kickflip underflip
- Half flip darkslide
- Handstand flips
- Helipop heelflips
- Kickflip underflip
- No handed 50-50 kickflip
- Ollie fingerflip
- Ollie nosebones
- One footed ollie
- Rusty slides
- Sidewinders
- Switchstance 360 flips

Mullen stresses the importance of originality in skateboarding and has said that a skater must relate the skateboard to his or her body in a variety of categories, including—

[R]olling forward, backward rail, stationary, 50/50 or aerial ... I kick my board around sometimes and watch its motions as it twirls around ... I get an idea of what I want to do, then I think over it a lot, like where my feet have to be to press the board back. I think about the mechanics of it after the fact. (Borden 2001)

See also Burnside, Cara-Beth

MUSIC AND EXTREME SPORTS

Extreme sporting events are often packaged with musical entertainment, with organizers planning events that combine extreme sports competitions with live musical performances or music played by DJs. Musicians at these dual events range from well-known to up-and-coming bands that play music suitable for the audiences at extreme competitions. Examples of extreme sporting events that incorporate music include the **X Games**, the **Gravity Games**, **Tony Hawk's** Boom Boom HuckJam, and more.

Music played at these events is sometimes packaged and sold as its own product long after the competitions have ended—for example, *ESPN Presents X Games, Volume 1, Music From the Edge*, which includes alternative rock and heavy metal songs; and *Gravity Games 2000: Summer Sounds, Volume 1*, which includes music described as third-wave ska, hardcore hip-hop, and latter-day punk pop. Clips of action sports uploaded to the Internet as YouTube videos nearly always include adrenaline-producing music in the background.

Extreme sports athletes—such as those in **roller derby**, **skateboarding**, and **snowboarding**, among others—also use music to set the mood before practices or competitions. Some songs are chosen because of the beat and tempo, while others are written specifically for or about a sport. An example of the latter is *Roller Derby Saved My Soul* by Uncle Leon and the Alibis; this song has been called the unofficial anthem of the sport. Songs written about extreme sporting events are frequently rock and roll songs, and often of the punk rock subgenre.

Other songs specifically associated with an extreme sport include the following:

- *Roller Derby Queen* by Jim Croce, wherein the singer shares when he first saw and fell in love with a large, mean roller derby queen

- *Skateboarding Saves Me Twice* by Grandaddy, a band described as one performing psyche-delic pop
- *Skateboard Love Song* by General Direction, in which a skater laments the breaking of his skateboard deck
- *Snowboard Song* by NU Funk Mafia
- *My BMX* by Brian Keegan, in which, in a dream, the singer jumps over the Grand Can-yon on his **BMX (bicycle motocross)** bike; subsequently, in the dream, all the girls want his autograph
- *I Love Racing Motocross* sung to the tune of *Electric Eye* by Judas Priest
- *They Call It Motocross*, sung to the tune of *Rodeo* by Garth Brook

Long before skateboarding and snowboarding were sports earning the attention of youth, surfing songs were popular and played on mainstream radio stations. This atten-tion to surfing occurred, in large part, because of songs sung by the Beach Boys, but they are not the only musical group that performed surf songs in the 1960s and beyond. In fact, because so many pop songs focus on surfing, Web sites have set up top 100 lists for this niche subgenre of music.

Some of the many surfing songs include the following:

- *Surf City*, sung by Jan & Dean, along with Brian Wilson of the Beach Boys
- *Surfer Girl*, sung by the Beach Boys
- *Wipeout*, sung by the Surfaris
- *Surfing USA*, sung by the Beach Boys
- *Surfin' Safari*, sung by the Beach Boys

Research conducted by Dr. Daniel Levitin suggests that, at the young age of 5, people can already recognize and respond to numerous songs, making most of us "musical experts" by the time we reach kindergarten. He has determined that listening to music causes the release of dopamine, which triggers the perception of reward (Thompson 2006). It follows logically, then, that music prized by a particular niche group, such as those involved in extreme sports, can trigger feelings of excitement as well as a sense of bonding with those who share a positive reaction to similar music.

N

NOLL, GREG (1937–)

Greg Noll was one of the initial group of athletes who rode the big waves north of Oahu, Hawaii; because of the way he charged at waves, he became known as "Da Bull." Besides being a professional surfer, Noll worked as a lifeguard, surfboard maker, and cinematographer for surfing moves. On December 4, 1969, Noll rode a nearly 25-foot (7.6-meter) wave at Makaha, Hawaii; this ride, which was believed to be impossible to master, was immortalized in *Makaha 1969*, a serigraph by Ken Auster. Although it was impossible to quantify, it is believed that this was the largest wave ever ridden on a surfboard.

Noll was born on February 11, 1937, in San Diego, California. He spent his childhood in Manhattan Beach, California where, in 1948, he learned how to surf at the age of 11 on a solid redwood surfboard that weighed 110 pounds (50 kilograms). He began to regularly visit Hawaii and, in 1954, he moved there, living in a Quonset hut, and going surfing, diving, and fishing. In retrospect, Noll described that experience as living "like rats in a hut on O'ahu on two bucks a day eating peanut butter sandwiches" (Bradley 2007).

When he returned to California, he dropped out of school and began to work as a lifeguard; he also began making surfboards. He opened and operated a business from his garage, and he then opened up a shop at Manhattan Beach; his next move was to open a surfboard factory and shop in Hermosa, operating that from 1965 until 1971.

During that time, he tackled the nearly 25-foot wave that was, as Noll described it, higher than if you had "stacked two eighteen-wheel semis on top of each other" (Reed 1999). Although this was a huge endeavor, this was not an easy time in Noll's life. That time frame coincided with the death of his stepfather. Noll sold off his shop, which was struggling financially, and he stopped going to Hawaii. He briefly worked as a lifeguard, and then he left for Alaska where he spent several years working as a commercial fisherman. He returned to California, where he began reproducing copies of original Hawaiian surfboards.

In 2004, famous skateboarder Stacy Peralta filmed a documentary, *Riding Giants*, which focused on the early surfers, including Noll. This documentary won the 2004 American Cinema Editors Eddie Award for Best Edited Documentary.

In 2007, when Noll was 70, *National Geographic* interviewed him and provided a retrospective of his work. The interview coincided with the publication of the new book, titled *Greg Noll—The Art of the Surfboard*, which was compiled by Noll, his wife Laura, and surfing journalist Drew Kampion. Noll talked about replicating the solid wood boards used by ancient Hawaiians, by measuring those now housed in the Bishop Museum that were buried in graves 200 years ago. His son Jed, who is 38 years younger than Noll, helps him shape the boards.

When Noll visits Hawaii now, the waters are crowded and he thinks back to the time when there were only a few people who surfed; at that time, they were happy to have some company. He still surfs, when he can without drawing attention to himself, saying that

> My heart is so much with the ocean. I fish and dive. Every once in a while, if I can find a place where nobody will laugh at me, I'll get out and fall off a surfboard. But the shaping of these boards and honoring the tradition is my way of being a part of it. It's a way of keeping myself focused on a really special time of my life. (Bradley 2007)

See also Lava Sledding; Yoga Surfing

NYQUIST, RYAN (1979–)

Ryan Nyquist is a professional **BMX (bicycle motocross)** rider who rides dirt, street, and park, and who has won multiple gold medals and BMX awards throughout his career, including medals in the **X Games**, **Gravity Games**, Vans Triple Crown competitions, Dew Action Sports Tour (AST), and more. By 2003, Nyquist had won every major BMX dirt competition; in 2007, EXPN listed Nyquist as the "winning-est dirt jumper of all time" (Seligman 2007). His awards include the following:

- 2003 NORA Cup Dirt Jumper of the Year
- 2004 ESPY Best Action Sports Athlete
- 2004 BMX Plus! Dirt Jumper of the Year
- 2007 AST Dew Tour BMX Dirt Dew Cup Champion
- 2007 Freestyler of the Year, BMX Plus!
- 2008 Dirt Jumper of the Year, BMX Plus!

Nyquist was born on March 3, 1979, in Los Gatos, California. He began riding at the age of 3 and entered his first freestyle BMX competition at the age of 16. He became an X Games regular, winning numerous medals in both dirt and park, including the following:

- Summer 1997: bronze in dirt
- Summer 1998: silver in dirt
- Summer 1999: bronze in dirt
- Summer 2000: bronze in park
- Summer 2000: gold in dirt
- Summer 2001: silver in dirt
- Summer 2002: gold in park
- Summer 2002: silver in dirt
- Summer 2003: gold in park
- Summer 2003: gold in dirt
- Summer 2004: silver in park

- Summer 2005: bronze in park
- Summer 2006: silver in dirt

Nyquist has had multiple sponsors, including Haro Bikes, Thor, Rockstar Energy Drink, Bell Helmets, Ogio, Schick Quattro, and Jiffy Mart of Los Gatos, among others. He has a signature shoe with Adidas, and a signature bike series with Haro Bikes; his likeness appears in both trading cards and action figures.

NYQUIST AND POP CULTURE

Nyquist has been featured frequently in the media, from magazines and online sites, to television shows (including cartoons and news programs), a movie, and a **video game**: Dave Mirra Freestyle BMX 2.

He has appeared on the television show *MTV Cribs*, and he made a guest voice over appearance on the *Kim Possible* cartoon show. Other media appearances include *Ride BMX*; *Transworld BMX*; *Men's Health*; *Sports Illustrated for Kids*; *ESPN the Magazine*; ESPN and Touchtone Pictures' IMAX movie, *Ultimate X*; and *Fox News Live*. He also made a guest star appearance on Disney's *The Jersey* and hosted *Nickelodeon's Game and Sports Show* and *Slime Time Live*.

MORE COMPETITION WINS

In 2002, Nyquist was named the top CFB (Crazy Freakin' Bikers) athlete in dirt BMX riding. He was also named the second best of the year by CFB in park riding. The 2002 wins that contributed to Nyquist being so named include the following:

- The gold medal in the EXPN Invitational, held in Grand Prairie, Texas, in the park event
- First place finish in the Freestyle Worlds, held in Cologne, Germany, in dirt, mini ramp, and street
- Winning the King of Dirt, Huntington Beach, California, competition
- Winning the Nokia FISE (*le Festival International des Sports Extremes à Montpellier*) competition, held in Palavas, France, in dirt
- Receiving year-end standings (first place in dirt and second in park) by Vans Triple Crown; in the Cleveland competition and the Denver competition, he earned gold medals in both park and dirt
- Placing first in Nokia FISE, dirt, and second in park

In 2003, Nyquist was named the world champion in BMX park by LG Action Sports. Other 2003 wins included a gold medal at Bike 2003 in Birmingham, the United Kingdom, and in the 2003 Core Tour/King of Dirt competition (in both the Jones Beach, New York, and Venice, California, events). Other first place wins in 2003 included the Vans Triple Crown event, held in Denver, Colorado (dirt); and the X Air, held in Hamilton, New Zealand (street).

In 2004, he was the Triple Crown champ, overall, in park, winning first in both park and dirt at the Denver, Colorado, meet and the Salt Lake City, Utah, competition. He was the LG Action Sports world champion in park; he also medaled at the Gravity Games, winning the gold in park and the silver in dirt, and was the winner of the Mobile Skatepark Series.

In 2005, he ranked first in dirt and second in park at the AST Dew Tour, held in Orlando, Florida, and first in park at the Portland, Oregon, stop of the tour. Nyquist earned a first place finish in the Bike 2005 in the park event.

In 2006, he rode the AST Dew Tour with a torn ACL (anterior cruciate ligament), but he still placed first in dirt and third in park. He won first in park at the Portland stop; at the Denver stop, he placed first in dirt and second in park. In 2007, he had more first place finishes in the AST Dew Tour in Cleveland and in Baltimore, and he won the Red Bull Elevation 2007, against 31 of the world's top ranked BMX riders. In the Red Bull Competition, Nyquist beat reigning champion Corey Bohan by just one-tenth of a point to secure the title after injuring his wrist and crashing a bike. In 2008, Nyquist won the first AST Dew Tour race of the season, performing a "double barspin 720," a trick never before done in a competition.

See also Carmichael, Ricky; Hoffman, Mat; Motocross

P

PALMER, SHAUN (1968–)

Shaun Palmer is a multidisciplinary extreme athlete, winning **X Games** events in **snowboarding**, **mountain biking**, **extreme skiing**, and boardercross. He has competed in several other sports, as well, including **motocross** and **BMX (bicycle motocross)**. Nicknames for Palmer include "The World's Greatest Natural Athlete," "Palm," and "MiniShred"; he has also been labeled as the undisputed king of extreme athletes.

Although Palmer found success in numerous extreme sports at a relatively young age, he did not have an easy childhood; rather, he seems to have used his challenging experiences as fuel for his daring exploits. According to a *USA Today* interview from November 2005, "Winning at the highest levels of snowboarding, mountain biking and motocross blasted the angry, punked-out, tattooed bad boy out of the gritty trailer parks on the wrong side of this resort town" (Ruibal 2006).

A feature article on Palmer in *Outside Magazine* in 1997 sums up his attitude in this way:

> He's helped define the delinquent ethos of alternative sports, mostly through his off-the-course style: flamingly rude and crude, with a devotion to the black arts of partying … Palmer was a true sports punk, hyperactive, substance-abusing, mocking toward what he perceived as the shiny, neon, one-piece-suit conformity of the ski world, and derisive toward the dignity of sports in general. (Buchanan 1997)

Palmer was born in November 1968 in San Diego, California, to Tim and Jana Palmer. His father, a construction worker, left the family when Palmer was young, and Palmer did not get along with his mother's boyfriends. When he was seven, he and his mother moved in with his maternal grandmother, Perky Neely, in South Lake Tahoe on the California-Nevada border. Neely was a waitress at Harrah's casino and Palmer credits her for raising him, teaching him to be tough, and helping him learn to take care of himself. He quickly earned a reputation as someone who settled matters with his fists, and he and his friends drank and smoked pot. In his official biography, he stresses that there are no limits and that seems to sum up his attitude from a young age, onward.

Palmer played All-Star baseball as a young child and he got into **skateboarding**, as well. In a 1997 interview, he stated that, once he got into skateboarding, he also got involved in the drug world, both using and selling. He also participated in motorcycle riding and BMX riding.

He showed an aptitude for skiing at a young age, but his interest veered toward snowboarding. In 1980, he made his own snowboard; he was a natural at the sport, and he would go out with his friends, partying late into the night, and then ride his snowboard in the day. He already played to the camera, chugging down booze while looking straight at the cameraman or purposely covering the camera crew with sprays of snow.

In 1985, he entered the junior snowboard race in the world championships; he won the gold in half-pipe, slalom, and downhill. At the age of 17, he left school to follow the junior snowboarding tour. In 1989 and 1990, he won the snowboarding world championship against the polished and experienced Craig Kelly; some call these two competitions the greatest in snowboarding history. Palmer discovered that he also excelled in boardercross (also known as boarder-X, BX, or snowboardcross), wherein four to six athletes ride downhill simultaneously on courses full of challenging turns, gaps, and jumps. It is common for racers to crash into one another as they each attempt to be the first to cross the finish line.

When Palmer was about 21 years old, his father tried to reenter his life, but Palmer was not interested in creating a relationship with him. In 1992, his grandmother was diagnosed with cancer, and Palmer struggled with her illness and rapid death. He drank even more heavily and became the leader of a punk band called Fungus that played in squalid bars.

In 1995, he partnered with Swiss investor Jurg Kunz to create his own company: Palmer Snowboards. The manufacturing facility was set up near Bischofshofen, Austria, an area where top ski and snowboard equipment is manufactured. Palmer remains the chief executive officer of this successful company to this day.

Also in 1995, he began expanding his athletic horizons by adding **mountain biking** to his repertoire. He spent $60,000 to learn the sport and to equip himself for championship riding. In 1996, he competed in the World Cup held in Nevegal, Italy, placing seventh in downhill. He won the National Off-Road Bicycling Association (NORBA) Championships in California. People were shocked that a fledgling rider had won NORBA; Palmer's quote after that win has become part of mountain biking lore. "Oh shit," he said, bending over at the waist and breathing hard. "I gotta get in shape" (Buchanan 1997). One month later, he nearly won the World Cup downhill race in France, losing to Frenchman Nicolas Vouilloz, the reigning champion, by only 0.15 of a second.

Overall, he was ranked number five in the World Cup standings in 1997 and seventh overall in the NORBA National Championship Series. This attracted the attention of the Mountain Dew mountain biking team and, in 1997, they signed him to a three-year contract for $900,000; he traveled in a custom-built touring bus. Palmer also signed a $300,000 **sponsorship** deal with Specialized Bicycles and an endorsement deal with Swatch Watches; the latter company developed a Shaun Palmer watch, and more than 150,000 watches sold.

Meanwhile, Fox Racing provided Palmer with his motocross racing gear. An ad from 1997 showed him wearing orange sunglasses and standing in front of a bright green limo; he had crossed his arms in a way that highlighted his tattoos and his expression was intimidating. The text of the ad read, "Just Wait 'Til I'm Clipped In and Sober."

Other accomplishments of Palmer's include the following:

- In 1997, he placed first in the Winter X Games for downhill mountain biking, and in boardercross.
- He received the gold in snowboarding and boardercross in 1998; *Details Magazine* named him Athlete of the Year.
- Between snowboarding and mountain biking seasons in 1998, Palmer competed in the Toyota Celebrity Grand Prix, winning the event.
- In 1999, he placed 14th in motocross; first in boardercross and snowboarding; 15th in snocross **snowmobiling**; and sixth in extreme skiing; he also won the NORBA National dual slalom biking event.
- In 2000, he placed first in extreme skiing and fourth in boardercross.
- In 2001, he placed first in ultracross and 12th in boardercross; that year, he was named the Action Sports Athlete of the Year by ESPN.
- In 2002, he placed sixth in boardercross in the X Games and he won the skiercross event at the **Gravity Games**.

Also in 2002, Palmer signed a promotional deal with Honda's Motorcycle Division, wherein he competed in the American Motorcyclist Association (AMA) Chevy Trucks U.S. Motocross Championships with a Honda CR motocross bike specially created for the competition. However, he crashed in the first run. In 2003, Palmer competed in motorcycle racing in the Supercross Tour, qualifying for the AMA 125-cubic-centimeter Supercross main event. Palmer also partnered with Activision, Inc. to release *Shaun Palmer's Pro Snowboarder* **video game**.

Although he became a millionaire at age 28, Palmer was living near an area of trailer parks in his old neighborhood, a neighborhood that was full of bars and casinos. His house stood out somewhat, as Palmer owned an acre of wooded land and surrounded his one-bedroom home with a security fence and electric security gate. His pit bull Vinny prowled around outside. Although his home had heated granite floors, it had no interior doors, as Palmer thought navigating his house was easier without them.

Palmer continued to struggle with his addictions as they became even more challenging. On May 30, 2005, Palmer overdosed on a combination of alcohol, cocaine, and prescription medicines after an opportunity to ride for a professional motocross team did not materialize; he was airlifted to a hospital in Reno, Nevada. While he was hospitalized, his home was burglarized; he lost $60,000 worth of possessions. For some reason, though, the thieves did not take his X Games medals.

After this experience, Palmer announced that he needed to turn himself around, so he set a goal of Olympic participation in 2006 as an incentive. The sport he chose was snowboardcross, an event that Palmer "practically invented and dominated in the X Games from 1997 to 2000" (Ruibal 2005). His training strategy included competing in every event on the World Cup circuit; he needed to secure a top-four spot in the World Cup and place first for the United States to guarantee his place in the Olympics. Palmer also competed in the Winter X Games.

During Palmer's attempted comeback, post overdose, he could not get the attention of previous sponsors and so he had to pay his own expenses; concerns expressed by former sponsors included his age—now 37—and his lack of recent training. One of the founders of the X Games, Ron Semiao, welcomed his return, though, saying,

> Shaun Palmer has been a snowboarding pioneer, a hero and an anti-hero to many. His gold medal-winning performances in the Winter X Games are legendary due to the dominant way in which he won. We're thrilled the (boardercross) discipline has been added to the Winter Olympics, and we are rooting for the Palm to be on the U.S. team. (Snowboard Revolution 2005)

Although it seemed likely that Palmer would clinch the third of three spots on the Olympic snowboardcross team, he tore an Achilles' tendon during practice and required surgery. Palmer has since stated that he remained sober during these difficult times.

In 2007, Palmer won the Jeep King of the Mountain snowboardcross meet. In 2008, he won the event again, and he earned a second place finish at the *Fédération Internationale de Ski* (FIS, International Ski Federation) World Cup in Switzerland. "Everybody roots for the Palm," X Games general manager Chris Stiepock said. "You want the Palm doing well and in a great frame of mind, so it's great to see him back on track and healthy" (Associated Press 2008).

Palmer has since retired; on his company's Web site (www.palmersnowboards.com), it states that the action sports hero has "died. Not in the physical form but the mental." He also shares that

> Though you may act like a gangster, walk with a lean so mean you embarrass the entire scene, be tattooed from head to toe, have too many piercings to count with your fingers and toes, wear your clothes half-on, half-off your body, or laugh at fear, whatever your attributes may be, you can be the next action sports athlete to rise above the rest. If you believe in yourself, there's no second guessing what you can do.

See also White, Shaun

PARKOUR

Adherents of parkour attempt to move from one location to another as smoothly and efficiently as possible, overcoming whatever obstacles may be in their path. These obstacles could be part of the natural environment—downed trees, sharply jutting rocks, and so forth—or man-made, ranging from a metal fence to a concrete wall to a brick building.

In parkour, the participant uses his or her body plus what already exists in the environment to achieve the goal of efficient mastery of objects in the world; this can involve running, jumping, climbing, and crawling—or whatever else is needed. There are no rules to parkour, per se, and there are no competitions, records, or rankings.

The philosophy behind parkour teaches that humans should become as agile and fluid as possible in both mind and body, and should be in complete control of themselves, so that they can overcome whatever obstacles they encounter in life. Creativity, harmony, and personal expression are valued and there can be a mystic, meditative feel to the activity. At least one parkour adherent believes that participants are in fact duplicating the movements that our long-ago ancestors used to hunt or to hide from predators, with parkour devotees resurrecting these movements in an instinctual manner (American Parkour 2004).

Sebastien Foucan of France negotiates a symmetrical landing on scaffolding during the first Italian Parkour gathering. (AP Photo/Corrado Giambalvo)

Males who participate in parkour are called "traceurs" and women are called "traceuses," and a significant number of adherents would reject the notion that parkour is a sport, as they consider it more of an art or a discipline.

PARKOUR MOVEMENTS

When a traceur or traceuse performs a series of motions that seem to be effortless and that occur without any discernable breaks between the motions, it is known as a "run." Other parkour moves include the following:

- "Cat leap": mostly used to clear space between two buildings, the athlete makes a running leap and then crouches shortly before landing; the hands end up on the ledge of the second roof, while the legs are pressed against the wall, requiring traceurs and traceuses to then propel themselves onto the roof
- "Precision jump": standing on the edge of a wall or roof, the athlete leans toward the destination point; bending his or her knees, the athlete then jumps, straightening out the body while in motion
- "Roll": when landing after a jump, the athlete rolls onto one shoulder to lessen the impact of the landing, protecting his head with his hands; the goal is to land, roll, and then get back up to a standing position in one smooth, fluid movement
- "Tic-tac": after taking one or several steps along a ledge, the athlete then leaps
- "Underbar": this move involves diving feet first through a gap between fence rails, then using a higher rail to right oneself
- "Vaults": the athlete flips over an object (a gate, a railing, and so forth); different types include the lazy vault, reverse vault, turn vault, speed vault, dash vault, and kong or monkey vault, among others

HISTORY OF SPORT

This activity was founded by David Belle, who was born on April 29, 1973, in Fécamp, France. His father, Raymond, was a firefighter known for his heroic feats. In 1969, Raymond was photographed hanging from a cable that was attached to a helicopter; the helicopter was hovering over Notre Dame, where someone had attached a Vietcong flag to the cathedral's tower. Raymond removed the flag while dangling in midair and a photo of this feat appeared in newspapers.

David spent much of his childhood living with his mother's father. Nevertheless, his father was an important influence on his life; David was often told stories about his father's feats and he wanted to duplicate them.

Another influence was his brother, Jeff, who exposed him to the beliefs of sports theorist Georges Hébert. Hébert did not believe in using elevators and other modern conveniences; instead, he believed that people needed to focus on developing inner strength, courage, and self-discipline without these conveniences. Jeff believes that this philosophy was crucial to the formation of parkour. "David took Hébert's ideas," Jeff Belle told *The New Yorker* writer Alec Wilkinson, "and said, 'I will adapt it to what I need.' Instead of stopping at a reasonable point, he just kept going" (Wilkinson 2007).

David Belle explored a career as a firefighter, but that did not pan out; he became a Marine, and then left the military to move to India for a few months. In 1997, Jeff Belle arranged to have David Belle and his friends demonstrate parkour at an annual firefighting ceremony, dressed as Ninjas and calling themselves the Yamakasi—or the "strong spirit." In this demo, David Belle climbed a tower and completed a handstand at its peak; after climbing a fire ladder, he did a backflip.

PARKOUR AND POP CULTURE

After this demonstration, people began inviting Belle to demonstrate his parkour, which he does without wearing gloves or using any form of hand protection. As an adult, he has demonstrated parkour for commercials, including one in which he returned home from work by crossing rooftops rather than walking in or driving on the crowded streets below. He also traveled to the Czech Republic where he played the role of an Internet parkour gang leader in the movie *Babylon AD* (2008), which starred Van Diesel.

"It's just intuitive," he said about parkour.

> My body just knows if I can do something or not. It's sort of an animal thing. In athletics, they have rules—you have to take your distance and stop and jump, everything has a procedure—but I never did it that way. I don't take a risk, though, that I know I can't do. I like life too much. (Wilkinson 2007)

Belle discussed a potential role in *Spider-Man* with director Sam Raimi, but he decided he would rather perform under his own name than to create another character. A French director, Luc Besson, paid him to perform in Madagascar; he has also performed in Italy, Germany, and Portugal. Other movies featuring Belle include the following:

- *Yamakasi* (2001)
- *District B13* (2004)
- *The Great Challenge* (2004)
- *Casino Royale* (2006)
- *Breaking and Entering* (2006)

- *Live Free or Die Hard* (*Die Hard 4*) (2007)
- *Rush Hour 3* (2007)

PARKOUR AND THE UNITED STATES

Parkour spread to the United States after Mark Toorock from Washington, D.C., traveled to England on a business trip; Toorock tried to track down the "nutter" he had heard about who leapt from rooftop to rooftop on television. Although he found a French Internet parkour forum, they were protective of their sport and did not provide him with information about Belle or parkour. While in England, though, Toorock discovered an "Urban Freeflow" parkour group and he joined them as they climbed walls; two years later, when he returned to the United States, he started the American Parkour Web site (http://www.americanparkour.com).

Toorock practices parkour by gradually increasing the difficulty of the moves he attempts. He reports that at least one park sign (in Bethesda, Maryland) prohibits "parkour type exercises," which is concrete evidence of the sport's presence in the United States.

In 2002, Belle and Sébastien Foucan, a childhood friend of Belle's and the founder of **free running**, an extreme sport that has features in common with parkour, starred in a Nike ad campaign that promoted parkour shoes. Ironically, Belle likes going barefoot.

In 2008, the *Washington Post* covered a parkour event; some attendees intended to participate in a parkour boot camp to be held shortly thereafter (Bane 2008). Attendees would include police officers, military personnel, Department of Defense contractors, Special Weapons and Tactics (SWAT) team members, and other people who needed the agility attained by the practice of parkour.

Although no official body oversees or sanctions parkour, people interested in the sport can find information and make contacts with parkour enthusiasts at the following sites:

- American Parkour: www.americanparkour.com
- Urban Freeflow–Parkour (London, England): http://urbanfreeflow.parkour.us
- Bristol Parkour (Bristol, England): http://bristolparkour.org/home2.html
- Australian Parkour Association: http://www.parkour.asn.au/
- Parkour Philippines: http://pkph.multiply.com

Smaller regional parkour organizations also exist, such as the following:

- Texas Parkour: http://www.texasparkour.com/
- Pacific Northwest Parkour Association: http://pnwpa.com/
- Washington Parkour: www.washingtonparkour.com
- Oregon Parkour: www.oregonparkour.com

The parkour Meetup Group (http://parkour.meetup.com) is dedicated to matching up parkour enthusiasts from around the world.

See also Robert, Alain; Urban Climbing

PERFORMANCE ART AND IRONY IN EXTREME SPORTS

In their book *Post-Olympism? Questioning Sport in the Twenty-First Century* (2004), John Bale and Mette Krogh Christensen point out how, in extreme sports, athleticism and art can effectively blend together. As just one example, they mention how **sky**

surfers have referred to themselves as artists, rather than athletes, who are pioneering a new form of art. Another source focuses on **BASE (Building/Antenna tower/ Span/Earth) jumpers**, with one of them saying, "We see it as an art form or philosophy where we try to express freedom from restrictions of urban landscape" (Horton 2004).

Bale and Christensen discuss the satirical nature of some extreme sports, such as **sky jumping** from a plane while also riding a "water heater, wagon, golf cart or automobile through the air at 150 mph, lawn-mower racing, toe skiing, waterfall skiing or low altitude parachuting" (Bale and Christensen 2004).

EXTREME IRONING
Perhaps nowhere, though, has extreme sport, performance art, and irony merged together as seamlessly as in the sport of extreme ironing. According to the *Pittsburgh Post-Gazette*, extreme ironing was invented in 1997 in Leicester, England, by Phil Shaw (nickname "Steam"), a man who authored the book *Extreme Ironing* (2005). He was working in a knitwear factory and, when returning home, the last thing he felt like doing was his own ironing. Steam was therefore inspired to create the sport after he realized that, rather than having to choose between ironing (the activity he did not want to do) and rock climbing (the activity that he did want to do), he could in fact combine the two activities by taking necessary ironing supplies along on his climb. After testing out the feasibility of his newly invented sport, Steam then partnered with his roommate, Paul "Spray" Cartwright, to form the Extreme Ironing Bureau to promote the sport where its athletes often choose nicknames for themselves, such as "Starch."

In extreme ironing, participants (known as "ironists") transport an iron, an ironing board, and usually a power source and extension cord to a remote location (mountains or forests, for example) and perhaps combine ironing with another activity (**canoeing** or **skiing**, as just two examples); in some events, ironists compete solo, and in others, they compete on teams. In urban-style extreme ironing, the event takes place on the street in front of crowds and may include **skateboarding** and **inline skating** moves. In freestyle events, ironists may jump on trampolines or build human pyramids while ironing; in underground extreme ironing, the athletes may go deep into caves to perform. Some purist ironists insist, though, that rock climbing, the original inspiration for the sport, is the one true form of extreme ironing.

Because of the weight of the iron and the board, and because of the heat of the iron, it is recommended that novices first participate in this sport in less challenging locales and then work themselves up to pairing extreme ironing with an activity such as **snowboarding**. Because battery powered irons have not been accepted in the more mainstream extreme ironing competitions, it is important that a power source also be located nearby; note that, in competitions, the power source is provided for participants.

By 1999, the British Extreme Ironing Team (including Steam and another ironist named "Short Fuse") was encouraging other countries to form teams; in 2000, the German Extreme Ironing Section (GEIS) formed. German ironists are credited with creating eso, where extreme ironing merges with meditation, and with the creation of water ironing, which uses a nonpowered iron for obvious safety reasons. After the German team was established, the British team traveled around the world, sharing news of its sport; in response, more than 20 countries created teams, including the United States, Australia, Austria, Canada, Chile, Croatia, France, Iceland, Japan, Madagascar, New Zealand, South Africa, and Taiwan (China).

In 2002, the first world championship was held in Munich, Germany. Twelve teams from 10 countries participated, with each team competing in five different events using a variety of fabrics. Contestants moved from one station to another, where preheated irons awaited them. An international panel of judges rated the ironists on their style and ability to iron; judges also weighed in the difficulties of each move when rating performances.

A four-man British team won the world's first Extreme Ironing Photo Competition, for which judges saw only a photo of an event (this helps considerably with travel expenses). This first winning team had a photo taken after climbing the 5,500-foot (1,676-meter) Aiguillette d'Argentiere in the French Alps with an iron and ironing board. Iron Man Stumpy then ironed the team's towels at the peak. Honorable mentions include a German who pressed his linen while snorkeling in Malta, and two athletes from South Africa who combined ironing with **BMX (bicycle motocross)** racing.

In 2004, the Rowenta Tour was the first extreme ironing competition held in the United States, with events at Mount Rushmore, South Dakota; New York; Boston; and Devil's Tower in Wisconsin. Extreme ironists hope that their sport will be included in the Olympics in 2012, when the competition will be held at the home of extreme ironing: England.

In any discussion about extreme ironing, one question always arises: is this a serious sport or is it just a joke? According to participant Jeremy Irons (real name: Craig Simons), it is a bit of both, and it is a lighthearted sport best suited to exhibitionists because of the stares participants often receive from spectators.

Irons participates in extreme ironing events with Astroboy (Ben Campbell); as of 2004, they were the only two extreme ironing athletes living in Victoria, Australia. Irons first attempted extreme ironing when he attached an ironing board to his boat and pressed a shirt (the "classic garment," although a hankie is best for beginners and a woman's pleated shirt would be the ultimate) while leaning out on the yacht's trapeze. More recently, the duo ironed as they used a chairlift to ascend Mount Buller and then they continued to iron as they plunged downhill on mountain bikes, ironing with one hand and steering with the other. (An ironing board was specially attached to the handlebars for this purpose.)

The duo, neither of whose wives cares to do the ironing, discuss extreme ironing adventures of others around the globe, including scuba diving and deep sea ironing in Sydney, Australia, and extreme ironing combined with BASE jumping, done by Frinkle Wee. Irons and Astroboy would like to try extreme ironing in conjunction with snowboarding or surfing and they are looking forward to the next Extreme Ironing World Championship; they hope that an iron manufacturer or a producer of ironing sprays will sponsor them, cautioning that these sprays may be considered a performance-enhancing substance in the competitions. For safety, the pair always wear a full-face helmet, whenever competing.

On a final note about this sport, extreme ironing has already created some controversy, as witnessed by this newspaper quote: "The EI crowd disowns an alleged breakaway group, Urban Housework, which promotes Extreme Vacuuming" (Leo 2007).

PERFORMANCE ART AND IRONY

Other extreme sports with components of performance art or irony include the following:

- Extreme Cello Playing, in which musicians perform at places such as a 331-foot (100-meter) tower in the Anglican Cathedral in Liverpool
- Haggis Hurling, in which athletes toss haggis as far as possible from a platform or barrel
- Wife Carrying, in which Finnish men carry their wives around obstacles; in the world championships, men are penalized for dropping their wives, and if a woman weights less than 108 pounds (49 kilograms), her husband must carry extra weight to compensate
- Elephant Polo, which, according to the World Elephant Polo Association, originated in India
- Underwater Hockey, which was created in the United States; note that there are no goalies in underwater hockey
- Extreme Accounting, which was invented by a man who realized his taxes were due immediately; thus far, he is the only person to have proclaimed himself as an athlete in this new sport

POGO JUMPING, EXTREME

The sport of extreme pogo jumping is also known as aggressive freeride pogo sticking, stunt pogo, Xpogo, and high amplitude pogo sticking. Athletes use performance-boosted pogo sticks that allow the users to jump more than 6 feet (1.8 meters) in the air, perform flips, and jump over gaps and obstacles, as well, in creative fashions that could not happen with the old-fashioned spring-powered pogo sticks. One trick, "leap-frogging," involves an athlete jumping from one pogo stick to another.

It is extraordinarily unlikely that, in the 100-year-plus history of pogo sticking, only one person came up with the idea to perform tricks on a pogo stick. Almost certainly, numerous people have had that idea over the decades and then they practiced their tricks with friends, neighbors, and family. The use of the Internet—more specifically, the Web site located at www.Xpogo.com—has prompted this recreational activity to become an extreme sport on multiple continents. Through this online venue, an activity once sporadically enjoyed was given a name—Xpogo—and, therefore, legitimacy. The production of online videos—specifically YouTube—has initiated the spread of this sport even further.

HISTORY OF THE POGO STICK

According to one legend, the pogo stick was named when a German backpacker in 1918 saw a young Burmese girl using a hopping stick that her father had made for her; the girl's name was Pogo. This German man allegedly returned home, where he began making wooden jumping sticks that he named "pogo sticks." Another version of that story had American George Hansburg traveling through Burma, where he met an impoverished farmer and his daughter, Pogo. This young girl wanted to pray every day at the temple, but she had no shoes to wear as she walked over the rocks that were strewn about on the road. So, the farmer created a jumping stick for her; when Hansburg arrived back home, he was said to have copied the farmer's idea.

The reality is that, in 1919, wooden pogo sticks were imported to the United States from Germany; at least one source puts the invention of the first German pogo stick at 1820. By the time the sticks arrived from Germany in 1919, the wood was rotting. Gimbel Brothers Department Store had ordered these pogo sticks and, after seeing the poor condition of their imported merchandise, they asked Hansburg, who manufactured baby furniture and toys, to create his own version of the pogo stick. He did so, using painted metal with a spring inside the stick. He patented his design in 1919.

People enjoyed using the pogo stick in the 1920s; Hansburg was said to teach the members of the Ziegfield Follies how to bounce on them and

> [F]rom there on out, showmanship and the Pogo just sort of went hand in hand. The New York Hippodrome chorus girls performed entire shows on them, marriage vows were exchanged on them, jumping contests were held, and world records for most consecutive jumps were set, and then re-set again. (http://www.pogostickusa.com/history.htm)

These early pogo sticks were basically metal poles with footpads near but not at the bottom. The bottom of the stick was covered by rubber to provide traction. Powered by springs, the user could place his or her feet on the footpads, hold on to handlebars at the top of the pole, press down on the footpads, and then jump around on the pogo stick.

In 1947, Hansburg released a pogo stick with an improved design. These sticks had longer-lasting springs and were named the Master Pogo. In the 1960s, aeronautical engineers from Stanford University created a lunar pogo stick that came equipped with a seat for the astronaut, rockets for steering, and gyroscopes for stability. This stick was estimated to have the capability to jump 30 feet (9.1 meters) straight up while on the moon or to jump forward by 50 feet (15.2 meters).

In 1990, the pogo stick company founded by Hansburg (SBI) reported that sales over the past 10 years had gone up, adding that, during the five-month rush before Christmas, SBI manufactured 1,800 sticks every day. The company that claimed to be second in sales, behind SBI, stated that it was manufacturing 75,000 to 100,000 pogo sticks per year.

During peak production, SBI was employing approximately 30 people to bend steel foot plates, punch holes in poles, and attach rubber fittings. Pogo sticks were shipped to numerous countries, including Hong Kong (China), Canada, England, Singapore, and, before the Iraqi invasion, Kuwait.

HISTORY OF THE SPORT

By the 1990s, regular pogo jumping began to turn into a more extreme endeavor for some jumpers, but it took an Internet-savvy daredevil, Dave Armstrong, to provide the impetus for organized competitions. In the summer of 1999, Armstrong tried bouncing on a pogo stick in his friend's garage. He began to experiment, jumping with the stick behind him, and then jumping one handed, and then no handed. For his 16th birthday, he asked for a pogo stick; researching the Internet for a stunt pogo site to share his ideas and accomplishments with other like-minded people, he could not find one, and so he invented one.

Armstrong does not claim to be the first person to think of doing tricks on a pogo stick; he believes that countless people around the country and world may have done exactly what he did, but he went one step further when he created a Web site that averages more than 7,000 visitors per month and contains an Internet forum wherein more than 200 jumpers actively participate.

Dan Brown organized the first-known national pogo stick event, Pogopalooza, in 2004. Brown publicized the event, held in Lincoln, Nebraska, on Xpogo.com. The

2005 Pogopalooza was held in Chicago, Illinois, while the 2006 event was scheduled for Schodack, New York. Pogopalooza events took place in Huntington Beach, Florida, in 2007.

Four extreme pogo enthusiasts from England created a Web site to share information and to build enthusiasm for the sport. Enthusiasts have done something similar in Germany and Australia, as well.

EXTREME POGO STICK RECORDS

As far as pogo stick endurance goes, Gary Stewart from Cincinnati, Ohio, jumped 177,737 times in 20 hours and 20 minutes. SBI built a double-barreled pogo stick for this endeavor. In September 2007, James Roumeliotis beat this record, jumping 178,457 times. Another record was set when someone jumped all 1,899 steps of Toronto's CN Tower in 57 minutes and 51 seconds.

On June 22, 1997, Ashrita Furman of Jamaica, New York, set a pogo stick distance record after jumping 23.11 miles (937.18 kilometers), which was a Guinness World Record. Furman has more Guinness World Records than any other individual, setting them in sack racing, brick carrying, and underwater rope jumping, among others. On his Web site, Furman stated that he also was able to pogo jump 1 mile while in Antarctica in just 18 minutes, although the stick froze near the 0.75-mile marker. In Oxford, England, during the summer, he pogo jumped 1 mile in just 13 minutes. Yet another accomplishment recorded was jumping 11.5 miles (18.5 kilometers) up and down hills of Mount Fuji.

Furman also provided details about "aqua pogo," wherein the jumper dons a mask and snorkel, diving into 8 to 10 feet (2.4 to 3 meters) of water. After reaching the bottom, the athlete jumps back to the surface, gulps in air, and repeats the process. In a YMCA pool, Furman was able to continue this activity for 3 hours and 20 minutes. He then traveled to Peru, where he and some friends took a boat down the Amazon River and he attempted to perform aqua pogo in the wild. He tied a rope around his waist, in case he needed help getting away from piranhas, and then he descended. He discovered, though, that the bottom of the Amazon is clay; it was not until he found submerged tree roots that he could find purchase and jump back to the surface. At one point, a water snake wrapped around his leg, but the snake let go when Furman jumped.

POGO JUMPING EQUIPMENT

Extreme pogo sticks range in price from $200 to $400. To obtain significant height, these sticks may contain:

- Elastic band thrusters, crafted from rubber tubing that, after being compressed, provide an extra lift
- A leaf spring, which is a flexible bow that, after being bent, springs upward
- Pneumatic pressure, which, according to at least one video, enables a pogo user to jump as high as 12 feet (3.7 meters)

These high performance pogo sticks have names such as the Flybar, the Vurtego, and the Motostik.

EXTREME POGO STICKS AND ENGINEERING

Kimberly Clavin, an instructor at the Ohio State University, saw people with extreme pogo sticks at the **X Games**, and she shared what she learned with an associate professor at the university with a reputation as a daredevil; his name was Tony Luscher. Between the two of them, they integrated the study of pogo sticks into Luscher's mechanical engineering classes.

In those classes, students experimented with making innovative pogo sticks. Some of the ideas that worked included a pogo stick that could do the following:

- Light up each time it hit the ground
- Change into a scooter
- Collapse and be transported easily
- Fire Nerf darts from its handlebars

One idea that did not make it past the drawing board was a pogo stick that incorporated an iPod into its structure. Pogo clubs are forming at universities, including at the Ohio State University.

PSYCHOLOGY OF RISK

Risk: the probability of a negative event ensuing from an action, and the projected severity of the potentially negative event.

Determining the precise degree of risk in any particular situation is difficult. The physical and mental abilities of a person undertaking the action, as well as his or her levels of preparedness, all play a role. Plus, even if one could determine the precise statistical likelihood of a negative event, factoring in potential levels of severity complicates the assessment.

Although degrees of risk exist in all sports and in all physical activities, risks associated with extreme sports are higher than average, sometimes significantly so. People who study extreme sports—and people who know about them but do not participate—therefore often ask, "Why? Why do people choose to take unnecessary risks in pursuit of a sport?" Taking this question one step further, they may ask, "Why now? Why is there such an intense interest to participate in or watch extreme sports during the 1990s and 2000s in the United States? What makes this time ideal for its impetus and growth?"

RISK THEORY

An article in *Psychology Today* titled "Risk" points out this revealing irony: the interest and participation in extreme sports began rising during an era in which much of our lives was becoming ruled by increasingly strict seat belt laws, burgeoning numbers of guardrails, and an explosion of warning labels (Roberts 1994).

Psychologist Michael Aptor, author of *The Dangerous Edge: The Psychology of Excitement* (1992), believes that this is no coincidence. He suggests that, as life in industrial countries is becoming so much "safer," some people need to deliberately create risk to counteract life's predictability. Other experts question how this plethora of safety precautions has chipped away at the American cultural identity as a group of people who tackle difficult frontiers. Perhaps, these experts suggest, "courting uncertainty is the only way to protect the inner force America was founded on. Or to define the self" (Roberts 1994).

Over the past 125 years, psychologists have formulated a variety of theories about risk, with Sigmund Freud postulating one of the first that gained prominence. Since that time, other psychologists have formed theories either supporting the ideas of Freud or, as the twentieth century progressed, proposing alternate theories.

In Freudian psychology and psychoanalysis, mentally healthy human beings work to equalize or reduce the tension in their lives, moving toward situations that provide comfort, security, and pleasure, and away from risk. According to Freud and others who subscribe to his theories, people who deviate from that pattern and who move toward risk taking are demonstrating aberrance. It is safe to assume that Freud would have believed that extreme sports participants who push their activities to the point of injury, and sometimes death, must be dysfunctional, acting out an unconscious death wish.

Post-Freudian research and theory, though, suggests that the psychology behind risk is far more complex than what psychoanalysis purports. Some theories suggest a genetic component to risk, more prevalent in some people than in others, while other theories focus more on behavioral or cultural explanations—or, to use fairly well-known terms: some focus on nature (genetic causes), while others focus on nurture (environmental influences). One study that attempted to tease out the importance of nature and nurture in risk-taking behavior patterns studied identical twins who were raised in different households. This particular study recorded similar levels of risk taking, whether high or low, in 60 percent of the twins.

Here are two more demographic observations: (1) more men than women exhibit risk-taking tendencies; and (2) people who exhibit higher risk-taking behavior as young adults tend to decrease their level of risk taking as they age.

To review genetic explanations of risk taking, research indicates that the tendency toward risk may be hard wired into our brains. One in every five people, mostly males, shows high levels of a risk-taking pattern, and some experts suggest that this trait gave early members of the human race a distinct advantage when hunting and protecting their families. These people, then, and perhaps their families, lived longer lives and had the opportunity to reproduce more often.

If one is to accept the "high risk gene" theory, then perhaps those with this genetic makeup who live in contemporary societies wherein hunting, fighting, and other high-risk behavior is no longer routinely necessary, or sometimes even acceptable, funnel this energy into extreme sports participation. Because life is so structured and regulated, as Aptor has stated, thrills must be deliberately created and sought after. Perhaps the fact that the thrill-seeking gene is believed to be connected to the part of the brain that seeks pleasure explains why extreme sports participants generally report a "thrill" or "high" when taking risks.

PERSONALITY TYPES

Some researchers who study the brain's reaction to risk do not necessarily focus on the evolutionary advantages that high risk takers might have enjoyed. Another group of experts, who also disagree with Freud's theory of risk, believe that the human brain actually seeks arousal, with each person having an optimal amount.

Dr. Frank Farley believes that, in addition to Type A (more driven) and Type B (more relaxed) personalities, there is also a Type T: thrill seekers. Type T-positive personalities tend to become inventors, entrepreneurs, and explorers, while Type T-negative personalities may gamble compulsively, commit crimes, and engage in unsafe sexual practices. Farley also envisions an intellectual and physical type of thrill seeker, and he believes that all people fall somewhere on his quadrant with different levels of risk taking inherent in their personalities. He echoes what other experts think about risk taking and the founding beliefs of American culture when he says, "This nation was founded by risk takers. Ben Franklin didn't wear no freakin' helmet when he rode his horse" (Rouvalis 2006).

Psychologist Salvadore Maddi suggests that people who engage in high-risk behaviors are not necessarily cognizant of the degree of risk they are pursuing. They may, according to Maddi, actually feel a greater sense of control over their environment than what is typical and thus do not perceive the level of risk connected to activities in the same way as others do. Perhaps these individuals must seek out higher levels of arousal to find their optimal level.

Marvin Zuckerman, a psychologist at the University of Delaware, has created a profile of the high-sensation seeking (HSS) personality. According to Zuckerman, these individuals are more impulsive and uninhibited, overall; more sociable; and more liberal, politically speaking. They enjoy a high stimulus entertainment, whether that means loud **music** or pornographic movies. They tend to gamble more often and they may try a variety of illegal drugs. They tend to choose friends who have more offbeat interests and lives, often selecting other HSS personalities, and they are more likely to have more sexual partners than average.

Zuckerman points out that HSS individuals can handle higher levels of arousal before the physiologically based fight-or-flight response kicks in. As the human brain—or, more specifically, its amygdala—perceives and begins processing a risk factor, physical changes occur in the body to prepare the human being to protect himself or herself.

During this phase, the heart can beat three times as fast as normal and blood pressure therefore increases. Because the brain perceives this risk as something producing fear, the production of adrenaline and noradrenaline skyrockets. Another chain reaction also occurs: the brain's hypothalamus releases the corticotropin-releasing hormone (CRH), causing the pituitary gland to produce adrenocorticotropin (ACTH), and the adrenal glands release cortisol.

Pupils dilate to allow the person to better see the object of danger; this physiological change occurs even in darker circumstances than what is normally optimal for human eyes. Blood races into the muscles that need to be strengthened to either fight or take flight; the body pulls the blood away from the stomach area, causing a tummy sensation described as "butterflies." The body also releases glucose to give muscles the burst of energy needed to deal with the impeding threat. Moreover, the person begins breathing harder, sucking more oxygen into his or her lungs and, by extension, to the muscles.

Psychologically, this reaction has been dubbed the fight-or-flight syndrome. Physiologically, this bodily reaction is intended to warn the individual of impending danger and to prepare the body to fight or to flee, both of which require bursts of physical energy and strength. Although prehistoric threats nearly always required one of those two responses (fight or flight), modern-day stresses, which might include lack of access to the Internet on a busy work day, a long line at the bank when you really need to get home to cook dinner, or a mound of paperwork waiting for you at school, are not the types of problems easily solved by either of those two reactions.

Zuckerman states that HSS individuals need higher states of physical and mental arousal before the fight-or-flight reaction kicks in. It can be inferred, then, that extreme sports participants do not perceive the physiological reactions of risk until they are performing actions that are significantly more risky than what is typical for them.

Psychologist Randy Larsen, Ph.D., University of Michigan, takes Zuckerman's logic one step further, documenting that HSS personalities in fact crave high stimulus. He believes that these individuals do not mentally register the full intensity of incoming stimuli; he therefore calls these HSS individuals "reducers." Because they do not as easily perceive the level of arousal that they crave, they seek out more thrills. Conversely, Larsen shows that low-sensation seekers mentally add to or "augment" the actual intensity of incoming stimuli and thus try to reduce the amount of excitement in their lives.

PERCEPTION OF RISK

One study of brain chemicals potentially explains why people perceive risk differently. In 1974, researchers discovered that monoamine oxidase (MAO), a brain enzyme, regulates levels of both arousal and pleasure. When Zuckerman tested HSS individuals, they showed exceptionally low MAO levels.

Analyzing implications more closely, MAO regulates norepinephrine, dopamine, and serotonin, three key neurotransmitters. The first arouses the brain when detecting stimuli; the second helps create the level of pleasure associated with the stimuli; and the last limits or slows down the state of arousal.

One theory states that HSS individuals have low levels of norepinephrine, which means that the inhibiting effects of serotonin do not kick in as quickly with these individuals. So, to achieve the levels of pleasure that they seek, they must participate in activities that more significantly arouse the brain. Another theory suggests low levels of dopamine in the brains of HSS individuals, which also suggests lower levels of pleasure without intense arousal. Perhaps, in some people, sensory perceptions reach saturation levels, and so they need increased amounts of the stimuli to trigger a response of pleasure.

Many people who participate in extreme sports live stable lives, but a certain percentage struggle to maintain full-time jobs or healthy relationships, and others use drugs such as marijuana and LSD (lysergic acid diethylamide) to intensify their extreme sports experiences. According to studies, the way that these drugs interact with the brain mimics the thrill-seeking desire that pushes many people into extreme sports participation.

Belinda Wheaton, in her book *Understanding Lifestyle Sport: Consumption, Identity, and Difference* (2004), puts forth a culturally based theory. She suggests that extreme sports provide "everymen," specifically identifying American white males, with an opportunity to perform "supra-normal athletic feats," thus reviving the traditional American masculine values of "rugged individualism, conquering new frontiers, and achieving individual progress." She refers to an issue of *Time* that suggests that Americans connect extreme sports with "pushing boundaries, taking risks, and being innovative," values admired by Americans and considered part of the fabric of our culture (Wheaton 2004).

Wheaton sees the white American male as a demographic in need of ego bolstering after a combination of events and cultural changes, including the feminist movement; the civil rights movement, and governmental attempts to address historical inequities against the black population by affirmative action; lesbian and gay movements; the Vietnam War; and the economic decline that caused the income of working-class men to decrease. To recapture a sense of masculinity and power, some American men turned to extreme sports wherein they could—just as the American frontiersmen had centuries ago—express their "insatiable appetite for risk, a thirst for adventure" (Wheaton 2004, 204).

Conversely, Harvey Lauer, president of American Sports Data, Inc. (ASD), a group that surveys trends and demographics in extreme sports participation, believes that the interest in extreme sports is a rejection of traditional American values. Traditional values such as teamwork and character building are being discarded, Lauer says, in favor of defiance and alienation; individual efforts are being considered more important than group competition.

Whether Wheaton's or Lauer's reasoning resonates with you more soundly, how Americans perceive extreme sports and its participants may say as much about our culture as it does about extreme sports and risk psychology. As Farley points out, police officers put themselves in risky situations regularly, more so than many extreme sports participants do. And although the majority of Americans may see police work—or firefighting or emergency room work, for that matter—as examples of positive forms of risk taking, the same people may not feel the same way about rock climbers or **BASE (Building/Antenna tower/Span/Earth) jumpers**.

Why? In part, this may be because of the ultimate goal: saving a life is greater justification for risk-taking behavior than trying to jump higher, faster, or more elaborately than you previously have. Also, risk taking that is required for a job that provides people with their income and sustenance justifies risk taking in a way that **bungee jumping** or parasailing probably never will.

Why, then, if the distinguishing factor is professional risk taking versus amateur efforts, do we not question the Olympic skiers who suffered head trauma while not wearing a safety helmet (before it was a requirement in the Games)? Do we see Olympic athletes as well-trained machines who are prepared to take on a significant amount of risk and their actions are therefore not perceived as foolhardy? When an accident occurs in the Olympics, do we chalk that up as a dreadful accident of fate? If so, then why is this not the typical response to an extreme sporting event? Has the pursuit of an Olympic medal gained an aura of respectability that the chase after an extreme sports award has not yet achieved—and perhaps never will?

As another consideration, is it merely a coincidence that extreme sports have blossomed at a time wherein multiple forms of media exist to publicize individual accomplishments—and the wilder and more extreme, the better? Conversely, would fewer people participate in these sports if the potential for gaining attention and notoriety did not exist?

Is it possible that some extreme sports participants are addicts, addicted to the thrills connected to their sport and to the attention that they receive from friends and family? As just one example, consider **mountain climber** Jim Wickwire. He witnessed one climbing partner freeze to death, he saw another one plunge to her death, and he himself has lost toes to frostbite and half a lung to altitude sickness. Nevertheless, Jim Wickwire continues to climb. Is this commitment—or addiction? Who decides?

In general, scientists now believe that human beings experience positive brain chemical reactions to pleasure and that humans seek to repeat these pleasurable sensations. Although this is considered "normal" behavior, it can also serve as the first step toward an addiction. As a person repeats a behavior that brings pleasure, he or she can develop a tolerance, and a larger scope or amount of the activity will be needed for the pleasurable response to kick in. Furthermore, a psychological dependence can occur, along with physiological changes in the brain and alterations in behavioral patterns. As the steps toward addiction continue their path, the behavior in question begins taking up increasing amounts of a person's time and energy (Rodgers 1994). Components of the addiction process, then, clearly could explain some participants' dedication to extreme sports.

What about extreme sports participants themselves? What do they think? Although responses to that question would be as individual as the person giving them, at least some extreme sports participants discard all of the psychological, physiological, genetic, behavioral, and cultural theories described above. They say that their participation in extreme sports is a deliberate choice and nothing more.

Some say that they participate in their sport to increase self-esteem or to test their limits.

Others credit mentors for introducing them into a subculture in which they feel a sense of belonging. When these individuals achieve difficult feats, they receive admiration from peers and mentors, and this can give them a sense of power. Some speak of overcoming fears, even phobias, through tough extreme sports challenges. Other climbers and participants in other extreme sports speak of "getting into the zone" or "being in the zone," which is a meditative state or an endorphin-like high sometimes experienced by long-distance runners. Still other participants point out that, with training and appropriate equipment, risks are minimized and perhaps may be no greater than National Association for Stock Car Auto Racing (NASCAR) racing, boxing, or hunting, activities typically not included in the category of extreme sports.

Response to Risk

Steve Tooze, in his 1998 article "Daredevils Who Dice with Death," shares the stories of extreme sports participants and their perceptions of their participation. First is a BASE jumper, Gary Connery, who recognized his desire to do something higher, faster, better than anyone else from as far back as his childhood. Connery finds it difficult to fully explain the attraction he has to risk, still strong after several compressed vertebrae, "smashed" ribs, and a punctured lung; the night before a jump, he cannot sleep at all. He spends the night imagining every conceivable consequence of his jump, including a bloody death. Then—and only then—can he imagine the perfect jump, so perfect that he can once again face his fears and slow down the thumping of his heart. Connery knows that it is time to jump when a sense of all-encompassing calm arrives; after a safe landing, he feels a sense of high that lasts for days.

Interestingly, Connery says that his girlfriend never asks him to stop; in fact, she helps with his equipment checks. If he stopped, his girlfriend explains, he would become a different person entirely, and not the one that she loves.

A woman, Tanya St. Pierre, mountain climbs with her husband—and says that she learned to climb when she was 6 years old, and her parents took her with them on **caving** expeditions. St. Pierre believes that the intense concentration needed to successfully climb allows her to face her fears. Involved in the task, she forgets them until she reaches the top and allows herself to realize how far she has climbed; the fear, though, is quickly replaced by euphoria. St. Pierre adds that she loves the challenge of climbing alone, without support from anyone else. She says that, when climbing solo, the euphoria intensifies and heightens.

Chris Gauge, a psychology teacher and top British sky surfer, believes that he was born to take risks and that he inherited that trait from his father, a racer. Even after his mentor, **Patrick de Gayardon**, died in a fall, and even after he himself landed into a 158,000-volt power line that caused second- and third-degree burns over 35 percent of his body and created the need for a week on life support, Gauge continues to jump. Gauge also notes how the camaraderie of fellow jumpers adds to his love of the sport; his girlfriend also **sky surfs** and Gauge believes that only a sky surfer can truly love and understand another's mutual obsession.

Lembit Öpik, the Liberal Democrat Member of Parliament for Montgomeryshire, says that after his serious paragliding accident, he no longer is afraid of dying. He felt an "immense calm" in the hospital, realizing that his life was out of his hands. He now has a stronger belief in an afterlife and believes that he was given a second chance to live. He denies having a death wish and in fact has given up paragliding after realizing the fear that his girlfriend and parents had for him when he was hurt.

Skier Emily Cook is drawn to the fear factor and the feeling that follows a successful trick. She also enjoys doing something that she knows most other people would not do. Cook missed competing in the 2002 Olympics after breaking both feet shortly before the games; after a two-and-a-half-year recovery period, Cook admits to reducing the level of risk that she takes (Handwerk 2004).

Risk Levels

Writer Steve Tooze also lists the risk levels associated with extreme sports from an insurance company perspective. Category six (the riskiest) activities include bungee jumping and mountaineering higher than 4,500 meters (14,764 feet); interestingly enough, this is the same category for all professional sports and for "overland trips" to Africa, Asia, or South America.

Category five extreme sports include **hang gliding**, parachuting, paragliding, rock climbing, mountaineering up to 4,500 meters, and ski racing and **ski jumping**. Some examples of category four activities include scuba diving deeper than 30 meters (98.4 feet) and **snowboarding**, which are equivalent, risk-wise, to piloting air craft.

Category three includes scuba diving up to 30 meters, hot air ballooning, **skateboarding**, white water rafting, and **canoeing**. Category two includes **mountain biking**, jet skiing, high diving, as well as activities that generally are not considered to be extreme sports, such as hunting, fencing, boxing, martial arts, polo, rugby, and soccer. Category one does not include any sports normally considered "extreme."

See also Managing Risk

R

ROBERT, ALAIN (1962–)

Frenchman Alain Robert has a reputation for climbing what seems impossible to climb, including soaring skyscrapers and sheer cliffs in the French Alps, without using ropes or climbing bolts or safety nets of any kind. Because of this ability, he is known as "Spiderman" and the "Human Spider." Robert has completed seemingly impossible tasks in spite of being 60 percent disabled after two serious climbing accidents in 1982.

As of April 2008, he has successfully climbed more than 80 tall buildings around the world, including the National Bank of Abu Dhabi, where more than 100,000 people watched his performance; the Petronas Twin Towers in Kuala Lumpur, Malaysia; the Debis Tower in Berlin, Germany; Moscow's Federation Tower in Moscow, the Russian Federation; Centrepoint Tower in Sydney, Australia; and the Eiffel Tower in Paris, France, among others.

He has, however, called his climb up the Sears Tower in Chicago the "most exciting." When he was near the top of the 110-story building, the fog became so thick that he struggled to see the glass and metal walls; the fog also made the outside of the building moist and slick. He climbed approximately 20 stories under these conditions before reaching the top.

He wears special climbing shoes and sometimes carries chalk for his hands in a bag that he straps to his belt, but employs no other climbing aids. He uses the drainpipes, window ledges, air conditioning units and so forth to gain purchase to climb—or to use the term he prefers, to "ascend"—a building. When training, he exercises each of his fingers and he claims to be able to do pull-ups with just his pinkie finger (Thompson 2004). Robert has talked about feeling very much alive after one of his death-defying climbs, even feeling born again after successfully completing a climb.

Robert sometimes climbs for pay, sometimes to raise money for charity, and sometimes to raise awareness for a cause, including a protest against the war in Iraq and concerns about global warming, among others.

Born on August 7, 1962, in Digoin, Saône-et-Loire—Bourgogne, France, his birth name was Robert Alain Philippe. In interviews, he has alluded to oppressive rules in his household, and to a number of childhood fears and phobias. On his Web site,

Alain Robert, using only his bare hands and no ropes, climbs up the 180-meter (590-foot) Marriott Hotel in Warsaw on June 3, 1998. After he reached the top of the building, he was arrested by police. (AP Photo/Przemek Wierzchowski)

Robert shares that his childhood heroes were rock climbers with the names of Bonatti, Rébuffat, and Desmaison. His parents did not encourage his ambition to climb, but he learned the basics of climbing in Boy Scouts, nevertheless.

A life-altering event occurred for Robert when he was 12 years old. He forgot his keys while his parents were at work. He therefore climbed eight stories and entered his apartment by a window. Although Robert had been a shy child, he remembers that occasion as the moment when everything changed.

He worked in a sports shop as a teenager, but he also began training on cliffs in the French Alps by his home town of Valence. He aspired to climb bare-handed without ropes for backup, so he practiced on sheer cliffs with a rope and then tried climbing without one.

In 1982, he had two climbing accidents; in the worse of the two, he fell head-first, 49 feet (15 meters), when a rope failed to hold him; he was in a coma for five days and he suffered fractures in his cranium, nose, wrists, elbows, pelvis, and heels. He was told that he could never climb again. Because of injuries sustained during those two falls, he required nine operations. After he healed, he still had vertigo, and so the National Health Organization of France labeled him as disabled up to 60 percent.

The following year, he returned to climbing and spent the next decade perfecting his skills. In 1993, he received the International Olympic Committee (IOC) award for his performances; he also set a world record for the largest number of solo (bare-handed) climbs.

Robert was sponsored by Sector, and this company wanted to film a documentary of Robert climbing a skyscraper. So, in 1994, he climbed a skyscraper in Chicago—thereby becoming an **urban climber**. He began climbing other skyscrapers, sometimes being arrested for his actions. In 1997, he climbed the world's tallest skyscraper (1,483 feet/452 meters), located in Kuala Lumpur in Malaysia. After that, he was asked to climb the Sabah Foundation building on the island of Borneo; this climb, unlike many others, was sanctioned by the government. A crowd of approximately 15,000 watched him climb, and Robert raised more than $150,000 for charity by this endeavor.

In May 2007, he donned a Spiderman costume before climbing up—and then down—the 88-story (1,380-foot/420.6-meter) iron-and-glass Jim Mao Tower in Shanghai, China; it took him approximately 90 minutes. Police arrested Robert as soon as he landed. He had been warned that he would receive 15 days in custody plus a fine of up to 10,000 yuan ($1,300), although he was in fact released from jail after five days.

When asked why he went ahead with this climb, Robert explained that, after climbing the three tallest buildings in the world, it made sense for him to climb the fourth tallest, as well.

Robert was not the first person to climb this tower; credit for that goes to a 31-year-old shoe salesman from the Anhui province named Han Qizhi who completed the feat on "rash impulse" in 2001. He completed the climb wearing street clothes and shoes, and was arrested and detained for two weeks. Robert resented that Qizhi climbed the building shortly after Robert announced plans to attempt that climb. Qizhi, in a statement made after his arrest, expressed remorse for his action and promised not to repeat his actions.

In a 2008 interview, Robert said that he has fallen seven times, including the two times that led to his disability. In 1993, he fell 26 feet (8 meters) while demonstrating climbing techniques for people who wished to learn how. He had his hands behind his back when he lost his balance; he fell head first, shattering both wrists and going into another coma. He was hospitalized for two months while he recovered. Another time, he needed to be rescued by Parisian firefighters after he dehydrated and cramped up while climbing the 363-foot (110.6-meter) Grande Arche de la Defense. The heat of the sun was being reflected from the white slabs of the building and that led to his dehydration.

According to interviews with Robert, he has been arrested more than 100 times. In most instances, the police were friendly; in Lisbon, Portugal, Robert played poker at the police station, and in Russia he had shots of vodka with the police before leaving. In China, however, after he was released from jail, he was taken to the airport and banned from the country for five years. In at least one instance, he broke away from the police and then hurried up the first 10 stories of a building so that they could not catch up with him; he was arrested, however, by the police officers who were waiting for him on the roof.

During one arrest in the United States, where he had planned to climb the 678-foot-tall (206.6-meter) building known as One Houston Center, police also charged him with possession of a drug similar to Xanax. Although this drug is usually taken for symptoms of anxiety, Robert said he had the pills because he had experienced two epileptic seizures, a consequence of previous head injuries.

Robert is married to Nicole and they have three children, Julien, Hugo, and Lucas. After each climb, Robert calls home to talk to them; he has said that his children do not like to discuss their feelings about his climbing, and he and his wife have an unspoken agreement not to get emotional before he leaves for a climb.

He stands out in a crowd, even when not climbing, as "his attire—red leather trousers, orange shirt, necklace, earring, pointy snakeskin boots—suggest a streak of exhibitionism. He has long, carefully tended hair and a rock star persona which he cultivates—imagine a wiry, fleshless version of Jackson Browne" (*Guardian* 2003).

A 52-minute documentary, *The Wall Crawler* (1998), has been made about him, and a television series called *Cutting Edge* taped an episode about Robert called "The Human Spider." Robert has written an autobiography, titled *With Bare Hands* (2008) and has appeared in ads for the Hairgrafting Medical Centre, where he received hair transplants.

See also Free Running; Parkour; Urban Climbing

RODRIGUEZ, FRANCISCO FERRARAS (1962–)

Francisco Ferraras Rodriguez, known as Pipin by his fans in Europe, Latin America, and Japan, is well known for his "no limits" free diving accomplishments, setting a world record in 1996 by diving 367 feet (116 meters) into the sea. In free diving, athletes take one deep breath, and then submerge themselves hundreds of feet beneath the water with the aid of weighted sleds attached to cables; this takes about one minute. When the diver reaches his or her destination, a weight is then dropped. As a tank fills with air, the diver rushes to the surface, with no danger of getting the bends, as no air entered the submerged body. Other disciplines of the free diving sport include the following:

- Dynamic free diving competitions: the winner is the person who can swim the farthest using only one breath of air
- Distance free diving competitions: the winner is the person who can stay under water the longest

According to Carlos Serra, president of the International Association of Free Divers (IAFD), "Free diving is getting in touch with yourself. It's a very quiet and peaceful feeling, and you get to understand your body" (Sainz 2002).

Rodriguez was born on January 18, 1962, in Matanzas, Cuba, where he began swimming as an infant and free diving at the age of 5. He was ill as a young child, though, and he did not walk or talk until he was 3 years old. His family tried to get him to speak; when he tried to say "Papa," though, it came out as "Pipin," which became his nickname.

He immigrated to the United States in 1993; three years later, he set his no limits free diving world record. He began performing two-breath dives, as well, wherein he took one breath before diving and another one from a scuba tank to extend the depths of his dives. Not everyone, however, has accepted two-breath dives as a legitimate form of no limits diving.

He has heavily promoted both himself and the sport, to the degree that the U.S. representative to the *Confédération Mondiale des Activités Subaquatiques* (CMAS) has dubbed Rodriguez as a "freak show" (Charlston 2007, 91). CMAS has had long-standing issues with no limits diving; in 1970, CMAS had stopped sanctioning no limits free diving over safety concerns. To fill that gap, the *Association Internationale pour le Développement de l'Apnée* began overseeing no limits diving; Rodriguez broke away from that organization, though, helping to form the IAFD.

Rodriguez has been the subject of more than one controversy. In 1996, two of his safety divers—experts who were to maintain safety guidelines during his dives—died while serving as support staff during his training.

Also in 1996, Rodriguez met a marine biology student named Audrey Mestre; they wed and she became deeply involved in the sport, as well. On October 12, 2002, she attempted to set an IAFD record with a 531.5-foot (148-meter) dive near La Romana in the Dominican Republic; this dive was expected to take 3 minutes and she had already achieved this depth in practice. Mestre reached the desired depth but she did not resurface. After more than 8 minutes, she was rescued; she was unconscious and could not be revived.

Rodriguez was sharply criticized by fans of no limits free diving, and by other divers, as well. Critics pointed out a lack of enough safety staff for the dive, and they believed that he was covering up for other mistakes made. Demands were made for Rodriguez to release the video made of the dive (taken from a camera attached to Mestre's sled) and the information from the computerized depth gauges attached to her body. Carlos Serra did state that a sled malfunction occurred at the depth of approximately 530 feet (161.5 meters).

At his wife's funeral, Rodriguez pledged to reach the world record depth that Mestre had attempted to make on October 12; meanwhile, her mother had this to say about her daughter's death: "No one is at fault. The sea wanted her forever. If I had to lose my daughter, I preferred it be the sea that takes her than some traffic accident. She lived and breathed the ocean" (Sainz 2002).

After Mestre's death, the IAFD decided to recognize one of her practice dives, wherein she reached a depth of 482.3 feet (147 meters), as the new world record.

On the first anniversary of Mestre's death, Rodriguez free dived 170 meters (557.7 feet) into the Los Cabos Bay in Mexico, using just one breath; the dive took 2 minutes and 40 seconds. He had in fact broken his own record of 162 meters (531.5 feet), set in January 2000. When Rodriguez completed his dive on October 12, 2003, fans presented him with white flowers that he tossed into the water as a tribute to his wife.

In 2004, Rodriguez published a book, *The Dive: A Story of Love and Obsession*, which shared the story of the marriage of Rodriguez and Mestre, including details about their diving careers. Meanwhile, Rodriguez continued to be criticized for his wife's death by insiders in the free diving world, including Carlos Serra, who initially had supported him.

In his book, Rodriguez listed a few reasons why Mestre's dive was not successful; most important was that the gas cylinder that should have inflated the escape balloon was nearly empty. Moreover, too few safety divers were on hand to rescue her from that extreme depth; plus she was not wearing an inflatable jacket. After her death, these jackets were made mandatory for free diving competitions. In retrospect, he summed it up this way: "When I look back on it, I realize I was pushing her—pushing her as hard as I tend to push myself. It was blind ambition on my part, and blind devotion on hers" (Ecott 2004).

Publishers Weekly has this to say about the book: "With fluid writing and vivid descriptions, this compelling autobiography explores emotional depths while detailing the sport's beauty, technologies, drama and dangers" (http://www.amazon.com/Dive-Story-Love-Obsession/dp/0060564164). Oscar-winning director James Cameron expressed interest in making a film from this book. In 2008, it was announced that Cameron would be making a new film, called *The Dive*.

ROLLER DERBY

Roller derby is perhaps the only female-dominated extreme sport. Nearly all of the contemporary roller derby leagues are all female, although mixed-**gender** as well as all-male leagues do exist.

The majority of roller derby competitions take place indoors on a flat oval-shaped track, with a few leagues using a curved banked track. In a roller derby match, two teams of five skaters each compete against one another; each team has a "jammer"

Allison "Mel Ignant" Janssen and Dee "Big Diesel" Saunders go up against one another during a roller derby match at Fast Forward, in Madison, Wisconsin, January 30, 2005. (AP Photo/*Capital Times*, Michelle Stocker)

whose job it is to score points, while the rest of the players perform defensive roles. The jammer scores a point after successfully passing a skater on the other team. The defensive players are called "blockers" and they try to stop the jammer from scoring; one of the defenders is called the "pivot," as she is the last line of defense for her team. Meanwhile, the teammates do their best to support the jammer's efforts to score points.

Players' positions are identified by the covers on their helmets. A striped cover indicates that the players are pivots, while two-starred covers indicate that the players are jammers; blockers have no covers on their helmets.

A referee blows a whistle at the beginning of a jam, which is the two-minute time frame in which teams try to score points; at the end of each jam, players get back into formation and then the process starts all over. Players committing fouls may end up sitting in black metal cages with brass door handles; these cages are known as the "Skank Tanks." Penalties can be awarded to players who fight, illegally block another player, or break rules. Half-time entertainment can include punk **music**, pillow fights, or fun activities for the family, depending on the venue and the league organizers.

Roller derby participants create stage names for themselves, such as "Honey Homicide," "Savage Animal," "Joann Thraxx," "Divalicious," and more. They choose these names based on their perceived alter egos. In one ESPN interview, roller derby athletes shared how they felt like different people when dressed up in their derby gear— and yet, they believe, these characters allow them to be who they truly are: strong, confident, sexy women. Women in this ESPN show also shared their professions, which included a radio disc jockey, massage therapist, full-time student, mother of five daughters, business analyst, flight engineer for NASA, and more.

This sport is overseen in the United States by the Women's Flat Track Derby Association (WFTDA), which was founded in 2004. This organization "promotes and fosters the sport of women's flat track derby by facilitating the development of athletic ability, sportswomanship, and goodwill among member leagues" (www.wftda.com). Women primarily serve as the owners, managers, and operators of each league under the WFTDA's auspices.

In 2007, the WFTDA membership voted to become a member of USA Roller Sports, an organization recognized by the *Federation Internationale de Roller Skating*. USA Roller Sports is also recognized by "the U.S. Olympic Committee as the national governing body for competitive roller sports" (http://www.usarollersports.org).

History of Roller Derby

The *Chicago Tribune* is given credit for first using the term "roller derby" in print in 1922; the newspaper was referring to roller skating races taking place on a flat track. The sport evolved, however, into a different roller-skate-based competition because of a film publicist named Leo Seltzer.

In 1929, it was Seltzer's job to get people into movie houses in Oregon, but the Great Depression had just struck and attendance was low. He noted how people were flocking to dance marathons, so he created his own marathon with a $2,000 cash prize for the person who could dance the longest. Hundreds of unemployed people competed in Seltzer's dance marathons; celebrities such as Frankie Laine and Red Skelton served as master of ceremonies, and these marathons grossed $6 million in just three years. Because the finalists were always so exhausted near the end of the competitions that they shuffled rather than danced, these events earned the nickname of "walkathons."

Seltzer began developing other entertainment-type events, including "The Race of Nations" at the World's Fair in Chicago in 1933; racers from 33 countries participated. Seltzer was an interesting character. He admitted needing to pay off politicians to get permission to open his shows and events, calling these politicians "dignified gangsters." He served on the board of directors for the National Endurance Amusement Association, an organization formed to monitor the ethics of contests such as walkathons. Although this group received significant attention in *The Billboard*, a publication for which he wrote, Seltzer later denied the organization's existence.

By 1935, fewer people were interested in walkathons, but more people were roller skating again, so Seltzer created a roller skating contest that required great endurance. It seems obvious that, by combining roller skating with endurance, he was melding what the *Chicago Tribune* had called a "roller derby" with a marathon structure, but Seltzer denied any connection between the two events.

Seltzer called his skating event the Transcontinental Roller Derby, and he held it at the Chicago Coliseum. In this event, 25 pairs (composed of one male and one female) of competitors skated 11.5 hours daily; the winning team would be the one completing 3,000 miles (4,828 kilometers) of skating—which was the distance between Los Angeles, California, and New York City. According to the National Museum of Roller Skating, this was one of the first opportunities for women to compete directly against men in a sport, following the same rules.

The race began at noon on August 13, 1935, while 20,000 people watched. The winning team would be the one that finished the race in the shortest amount of time; a team would be automatically disqualified if, at any point in time, neither member of the team was skating during official race times. Seltzer provided the competitors with meals and free medical care. Still, only 9 of the 25 teams completed the race, with the other 16 dropping out because of injury or fatigue. Clarice Martin and Bernie McKay won the event on September 22, after holding the lead for the final 11 days of the race.

After the success of this event, Seltzer held tryouts for a traveling roller derby team; after forming the league and taking it on the road, attendance averaged 10,000 at these events. In 1937, sportswriter Damon Runyon suggested ways to increase the physical contact elements of the sport, increasing the level of excitement—and the amount of violence—at roller derby matches. Seltzer agreed with and incorporated Runyon's recommendations.

These pumped-up matches were met with enthusiasm. Roller derby fan clubs were formed and the *Roller Derby News* (changed to *RollRage* in the 1940s) was published, gaining thousands of subscribers. Seltzer's roller derby appeared in more than 50 cities in 1940, with more than 5 million spectators watching the competitions. Roller derby stars were professional athletes, receiving payment for their performances, and it seemed as though roller derbies were on their way to becoming a well-established sport. When World War II began, though, more than 50 percent of the athletes enlisted, effectively ending the first round of enthusiasm for roller derby.

The sport of roller derby was revived in the 1960s, at least in select cities and regions of the United States, most notably in parts of California; rather than using flat tracks, these roller derbies were generally held on curved banked tracks. During this era, movies such as *Kansas City Bomber* (starring Raquel Welch in 1972) brought attention to roller derbies. While making the movie, Welch—who did her own roller skating in the film—broke her wrist and needed six weeks to recuperate.

Once again, roller derbies were gaining popularity and momentum—but then, in 1973, high gas prices prevented teams from traveling and the sport once again waned. In 1977, a man named David Lipschultz revived the roller derby and the first game of the International Roller Skating League appeared on television on April 24, 1977; this league lasted for 10 years, ending on December 12, 1987 because of financial problems.

Critics of roller derby during this era claimed that skaters were simply putting on a choreographed show, including faking injuries and pain, and putting on staged fights. Under these circumstances, critics believed, the roller derby participants should not be considered athletes.

Shaun White, 19, participates in the Dew Action Sports Tour in Louisville, Kentucky, on June 24, 2006. White, an Olympic snowboarding medalist, embarked on a professional skateboarding career. (AP Photo/Garry Jones)

Windsurfers glide across the water at Leo Carrillo State Beach near Malibu, California, August 24, 1997. (AP Photo/Michael Caulfield)

Scott McCandless, 14, of Philadelphia, wears a painted "X" on his face as he attends the last day of the Summer X Games, August 19, 2002, in Philadelphia. (AP Photo/H. Rumph Jr.)

With the Manhattan skyline as a backdrop, professional skateboarder Rich Lopez of Bloomfield, New Jersey, is suspended above the vert ramp during practice for the Mountain Dew National Championships of Skateboarding. (AP Photo/*Home News Tribune*, Mark R. Sullivan)

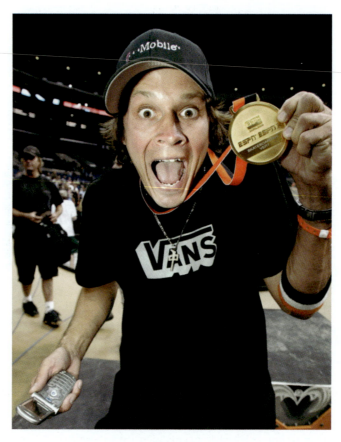

Bucky Lasek holds his gold medal after winning the X Games skateboard vert finals, August 15, 2003, in Los Angeles. (AP Photo/Chris Polk)

Kenny Bertram gets his motorcycle airborne as he performs in the Moto X Freestyle demonstration with a mural backdrop of former Los Angeles Lakers players during the kickoff event of X Games 11 in Los Angeles. (AP Photo/Kevork Djansezian)

Second at the half-pipe race, Espen Arvesen of Norway rides at the International Snowboard Federation (ISF) World Cup Race, in Leysin, Switzerland, January 23, 2000. (AP Photo/Fabrice Coffrini)

New Zealand's Martin Jillings of Wanaka flies upside down during the jib day of the Heli Bash extreme skiing in Wanaka, New Zealand, August 16, 2002. The Heli Bash is a three-day extreme skiing event of a half-pipe, Chinese downhill, and a slopestyle day. (AP Photo/Rob Griffith)

CONTEMPORARY ROLLER DERBY

According to *Cincinnati Enquirer* reporter Lauren Bishop, who was quoted during an episode of ESPN's *Outside the Lines*, the revitalization of roller derbies occurred in 2001, when women in Austin, Texas, single-handedly revived the sport. Bishop estimated that, worldwide, there were approximately 300 amateur roller derby leagues; in the United States, she stated that there were more than 200 all-female leagues.

In 2004, there were approximately 800 roller derby members; by 2008, there were nearly 6,000. In 2001, there was one only roller derby league (in Texas); by 2008, there were nearly 300—with 26 leagues in California and 14 in Florida. Leagues have since formed in Canada, Australia, Scotland, New Zealand, and Hong Kong (China).

In 2006, the A&E channel began broadcasting *The Rollergirls* on television, a show that shared the competitions taking place in the Austin Thunderdome; this coverage further boosted the roller derby revival.

Sponsorships are key to funding modern-day roller derby events and are a challenge for leagues and individual teams to tackle. As just one example, the Gotham Girls of New York City have garnered sponsorship dollars from Arnicare's pain relief product, Triple 8 protective gear, and the *Village Voice*, among others. Meanwhile, the Carolina Rollergirls have relied on sponsorships from the North Carolina Museum of Natural Sciences, Planned Parenthood, Larry's Beans: Coffee Artists on a Mission, and more. In Ottawa, Canada, Kelly McAlear needed to create a strategy in 2007 to find appropriate sponsors. Because she had selected a dominatrix theme for her team, she decided to pursue bars and tattoo shops for sponsorship dollars.

Modern-day roller derby is intricately intertwined with the punk music scene; it can also skirt the edges of the S&M (sadism and masochism) scene. *The Guardian* describes one such alternative scene that took place in the United Kingdom:

> [I]magine that the women who play this sport have names like Ivana S. Pankin, Sybil Disobedience and Gori Amos. And how about tiebreakers settled by a pillow fight between a punk mother in a skimpy sailor costume and a heavy metal librarian in a fluorescent orange porn-fantasy prison mini-dress? And how about—instead of red cards or sin bins—bad girls have to spin a "wheel of shame"? With punishments including being spanked with plastic flyswatters by the entire crowd? (Wells 2005)

PSYCHOLOGY OF ALTER EGOS

Roller derby competitors generally take on pseudonyms that are aggressive or sexual in nature, often involving double entendres. Moreover, they dress in ways that can only be referred to as costumes. According to the *Miami Herald*, most players "doll up to resemble '50s pinup queen Bettie Page—only with tattoos, fish-net stockings, hot pants and body piercings. And the sexy pseudonyms abound: Betty Knock-her, Surely MacPain, Nauti-Sea-Cups and Filthy Scar-Lit are just some of the Broward Derby Grrls *skate de plumes*" (Santiago 2008).

In an interview televised by ESPN, roller derby athletes spoke about how it feels to be in their personas while participating in roller derby action. They shared how hurting one another is part of the sport, how the players need to get over being nice, and how hitting friends is fun. They discussed their alter egos as if they were speaking about other people; they sometimes spoke of themselves in the third person, as well.

This raises the question as to whether these women need to separate themselves from their more mundane, everyday identities to play roller derby as aggressively as the sport requires for success. It also raises the question as to why women may feel this need while, in nearly every other sport, all of which are more male oriented, this alter ego is not necessary to act aggressively.

Some contemporary roller derby athletes have mocked the derby athletes in the 1960s and 1970s who probably did choreograph scenes and fake injuries, while insisting that today's action is real. Although there is no reason to doubt the veracity of their claims, the stagey pseudonyms, exaggerated costuming, and showy nature of the sport give the rough-and-tumble action a sense of unreality. In fact, some aspects of roller derby bring to mind World Wrestling Entertainment (WWE) events, wherein men create characters and pseudonyms, and then dress and act in a manner that allows them to stay in character while performing.

Shauna Cross, who wrote the screenplay for *Whip It* (2009), a roller derby movie, was quoted in *USA Today* on the subject of the dual personalities required of roller derby athletes: "I'm actually very sweet and girly off the track," Cross said, "but utterly relentless on the track—a bit of a bruiser, really. Jammers are pretty scared of me. But that's half the fun of derby: You get to be someone else. It's better than therapy" (Neale 2008).

ROLLER DERBY RISKS AND INJURIES

In 2007, the WFTDA conducted a study to determine the type and extent of injuries sustained in roller derby; here is a portion of what was discovered via the responses of 1,070 participants:

- 574 (54 percent) had an injury that kept them from participating in roller derby
- 262 of those 574 people (46 percent) had suffered a knee injury
- 36 of the 262 people (14 percent) mentioned the PCL (posterior cruciate ligaments) in the description of their knee injury

The most common injuries include bruises, fractures, strains, and sprains, as well as skin burns from sliding across the floor of the rink; these burns are known as "rinkrash" or "fishnet burn."

A league in Seattle, Washington, maintains an online "Hall of Pain," in which the Rat City Rollergirls display the injuries sustained in their competitions; the Gotham Girls have an Internet forum in which injuries are discussed; and other teams and leagues post information about injuries on their blogs and Web pages.

ROLLER DERBY EQUIPMENT

The WFTDA requires that competitors wear protective gear while on the rink; this includes wrist guards, elbow pads, knee pads, mouth guards, and helmets. Optional gear includes padded shorts, shin guards, knee and ankle supports, and tailbone protection.

See also Inline Skating

SANDBOARDING

In the sport of sandboarding, athletes strap their feet on to a laminated, waxed board and then ride down steep sand dunes at speeds between 30 and 50 miles (48.3 to 80.5 kilometers) per hour. The rider controls the direction of the board by turning or shifting his or her body. Winds continually alter the shapes of the dunes and the athletes must adjust to the changing conditions on an ongoing basis.

There are two main methods of strapping feet to sandboards. In one type of board, the athlete can slip into bindings while remaining barefooted or while wearing booties; other boards are set up so that riders wear sport boots that are buckled into the bindings.

Athletes maintain their balance by flexing their knees and leaning slightly forward. Although it is a less common method, some people sandboard while lying down on their boards, achieving speeds of up to 50 miles (80.5 kilometers) per hour. Some of the more extreme boarders may choose to stand but use a board with no bindings whatsoever.

Approximately 14,000 people in the United States participate in sandboarding, with Nevada, Colorado, and southern California serving as key locales for the sport, along with parts of Florida and North Carolina; other areas with rapidly increasing numbers of riders include South America, New Zealand, Tunisia, Chile, Peru, southern Africa, the Sahara, and Australia.

Namibia is a popular sandboarding spot in Africa, as it contains some of the world's tallest dunes, including one that is 396 feet (120 meters) in height with six different faces; this dune is located about 7 miles (10 kilometers) from the town of Swakopmund. People travel from Australia, New Zealand, Britain, South Africa, Botswana, and Zimbabwe, as well as from Canada and the United States, to ride this dune.

Like many other sand dunes frequented by sandboarders, the dune in Namibia does not have a chairlift, and so athletes need to climb back up the dune after each time they race down. Climbing up loose sand is challenging, even more so in hot climates with burning sand. While ascending, the sandboarder is lugging up a board and, most likely, a backpack with water and other necessities, which further increases the arduousness of the climb. Some climbs can take up to 20 minutes to complete.

Sand surfers make their way to the top of the tallest sand dunes, near Swakopmund, Namibia, August 2003. The dramatic red, rolling dunes make the southern African country the best spot in the world for sandboarding. (AP Photo/JoJo Walker)

Sandboarders also ride on dunes located in sand parks; in the parks, the venues contain rails and ramps and so forth, which causes the course to be similar to those in skateboarding parks. The Sand Master Park, located in Oregon and opened in 2000, is said to be the original sandboarding park. This park contains 40 acres of sculpted dunes, with the highest reaching nearly 300 feet (91.5 meters). Rails and jumps and so forth are available for beginning sandboarders, as well as intermediate and advanced sandboarders.

In the United States, spring is the best time for sandboarding, as the melting winter snow adds moisture to the sand and spring rains fall, making a slicker dune.

The U.S. National Sandboard League sanctions six yearly events; numerous international competitions are held, as well, including the annual world championships in Germany. Internationally, an organization called the Dune Riders International (DRI) oversees competitive sandboarding. Formed in 1995, this organization also advocates for the preservation of dunes.

Recently, sandboarders have appeared in commercials for Ford and Nissan.

History of the Sport

Lou Beale, the publisher of *Sandboard* magazine, has said that sandboarding has existed for more than 2,000 years; he was referring to evidence that suggests that ancient Egyptians rode on dunes using planks of hardened pottery and wood. Moreover, although the beginning of modern sandboarding is said to have occurred in the 1960s, text at *Sandboard* magazine's Web site mentions black-and-white photos of people sandboarding in an upright position from as early as World War II.

In the 1960s, sandboarding enthusiasts creatively found ways to ride down the dunes, attaching their feet to discarded car hoods, old surfboards, and even pieces of cardboard, among other recycled items. Surfers and snowboarders were especially interested in this new sport, and they usually found it easy to cross-train in sandboarding.

By the mid-1970s, sandboarding occasionally showed up in the media: in written publications, advertisements, and televised sports blurbs. Beale, who became the editor of *Sandboard*, tried sandboarding for the first time in 1973. Other early sandboard riders were Jack Smith and Gary Fluitt. These men were featured sandboarding in the movie *Adventures in Paradise* and in magazines, including *Action Now*. From 1980 through 1983, Smith and Fluitt sold sandboards commercially.

Sandboarding was introduced in numerous other countries throughout the 1980s, including in Chile in 1987. A particularly scenic sandboarding venue, the Cerro Dragon summit, is located by Iquique in Chile's Atacama Desert. By 2000, the sport was receiving a significant amount of attention in that country, even though Chilean sandboarders can be measured in the hundreds, rather than in the thousands. The majority of them—but not all—are male.

In the 1990s, Beale began hosting sandboard competitions in California. He was also looking for a centerpiece venue; after visiting Florence, Oregon, he leased 40 acres of dunes and he created the Sand Master Park. The park opened in 2000, and numerous competitions are held in that venue. The highest dune is about 600 feet (183 meters) and, from the top, people can see the Pacific Ocean, which is 2 miles (3.2 kilometers) away. In 2003, approximately 6,000 people visited Sand Master Park. In 2006, approximately 8,000 people visited and used his park; in 2007, approximately 10,000 people participated in the sport.

Beale's "headquarters" at his park is a metal hut wherein he keeps jars of sand that he has collected from dunes, worldwide, including from Egypt, Saudi Arabia, China, Brazil, and Peru. For about $100 an hour, beginners can use a simulator at the Sand Master Park that resembles a treadmill; this device allows novice sandboarders to practice their moves and jumps before trying them on the sand.

SANDBOARDING COMPETITIONS

In competitions, athletes try to capture the most air, complete a 360-degree spin with the most style and finesse, and race down the sand dune the quickest. Some competitions focus on just one element of sandboarding, which could be rail sliding, jumping, performing tricks, or slaloming, which is similar to the ski sport with the same name.

The largest competitions include the Sand Master Jam held in Florence, Oregon, at the Sand Master Park. Other competitions—the National Sandboarding League Rail Jam and the Xwest Huck Fest for Big Air and Jump—are also held at this sand park.

The Sandboarding World Championships are held each year in Hirschau, Germany, at Monte Kaolino; attendance figures as high as 50,000 have been reported. This locale has dunes reaching more than 300 feet (91.5 meters), and sandboarders land in water at the bottom of the dune. This site has a sand lift, similar to a ski lift, which negates the need for climbing back up the dunes. The area also has a large water park for people attending competitions to use.

The Pan-American Sandboarding Challenge is held at the Prainha Beach in Aquiraz, Ceará in Brazil. There, amateurs and professionals compete in freestyle and jumping events.

The Sand Sports Super Show is held every September in Costa Mesa, California, at the Orange County Fair and Expo Center. New equipment is often presented during the show, with well-known sandboarders performing new tricks for the attendees.

SANDBOARDING CHAMPIONS

Sandboarder Erik Johnson established a record for the Guinness Book of World Records, traveling 51 miles (82 kilometers) per hour on his sandboard. There have been reports of people riding up to 60 miles (96.6 kilometers) per hour, but they have not been verified.

Since 1999, snowboard instructor Josh Tenge has won more than 20 championships, including world championships, winning his first sandboarding competition less than two years after he began participating in the sport. His first win took place when he tied another champion, Marco Malaga from Peru, in the 1999 Sand Master Jam competition.

At the 2000 Xwest Huck Fest, located in Sand Mountain, Nevada, Tenge set a Guinness Book of World Records event for the longest backflip, measured at 44 feet, 10 inches (13.7 meters). This would be an extremely difficult record to beat because dunes much steeper than that would begin to collapse. Tenge's ability to snowboard has served him well, as he has been able to perform flips, spins, and even switch riding, by transferring what he learned in snowboarding and applying that to sandboarding. In 2005, he was named the DRI world champion.

Tenge's sponsors have included the following:

- Venomous Sandboards
- Zeal Optics
- Xwest
- Sand Master Park
- Ecko
- Dr. Dune Sandboard Wax
- Crash Pads

SANDBOARDING EQUIPMENT

Sandboards are generally between 3.3 to 5.2 feet (100 and 160 centimeters) in length, although they can be longer. Sandboard manufacturers have relied upon research conducted to craft and improve on **snowboards** to refine their boards; the main difference between sandboards and snowboards is that a slick substance needs to be applied to the bottom of the sandboards so that athletes can move more quickly downhill; snow provides a naturally slick venue that gritty sand cannot duplicate.

Some novice sandboarders use skis or other types of boards to learn how to sandboard, but experienced sandboarding athletes generally use boards made especially for their sport. The cost of sandboards ranges from $99 to $400, while bindings run from $20 to $120.

Sandboarding athletes use a variety of protective gear, including the following:

- Helmets
- Gloves and wrist guards
- Elbow and knee pads, and ankle supports
- Back supports
- Pair of sand socks, which prevents sand from sticking to the feet, and also wicks away moisture

- Boarding shorts, which are light-weight and comfortable, and have extra padding to protect the hips and buttocks in case of a fall
- Goggles, which protect the eyes from sand and from sun

Some athletes have worn snowshoes to help them climb up the sand dunes.

Wax for the boards usually costs $3 to $5, but one type of board wax does not suit all situations. Cold and wet sand requires a different kind of wax than hot and dry sand. Champion sandboarders will want a slicker wax than would suit novices' needs.

SANDBOARDING RISKS AND INJURIES
Although information about sandboarding injuries is sparse, typical, less serious injuries include bumps, bruises, and abrasions, as well as eye injuries from the sand and sunburn. Wrist injuries, including sprains and breaks, are common as people attempt to break falls with their hands.

POP CULTURE
The cartoon character SpongeBob SquarePants sustained a sandboarding injury in an episode of the show. SpongeBob had crashed, falling on his backside, so Sandy takes him to the hospital. It takes the doctor 20 hours to staple, tape, and glue SpongeBob back together; he is warned that, with another such injury, he'll need to get an iron butt. His friends are then put on "around-the-clock butt patrol."

SANDBOARDING AND ENVIRONMENTAL ISSUES
In some environments, sandboarders and environmentalists have clashed, with the latter expressing concern over damage done to the ecosystem. In the Death Valley National Park in California, the issue has been the damage done to endangered plants—more specifically, Eureka Valley dune grass and the Eureka Dunes evening primrose—neither of which grows anywhere else.

The dune grass is in many respects similar to North African vegetation and is believed to have grown in Death Valley for millions of years. The grass only reproduces once every 8 to 10 years during specific weather conditions, which makes new growth chancy; so, damage done by sandboarders could have long-lasting ramifications. Moreover, this grass grows in the higher slopes, which is also where sandboarders prefer to ride, which puts the two groups—the athletes and environmentalists—in direct conflict.

Another concern is the chemicals imparted to the ecosystem through the wax used by boarders; this concern is especially great near Great Sand Dunes National Monument in Colorado. Wax for the board must be chosen carefully, as residue collects in rivers and even the water tables; some sandboarders use furniture polish on their boards to accelerate their descent and the makeup of furniture polish is not environmentally friendly. The majority of people who visit the Great Sand Dunes are not sandboarders, however; a park ranger has estimated that only about 1 percent of annual visitors, which totals nearly 300,000, are sandboarders.

SHAW, BROOKE (1991–)
Brooke Shaw is a U.S. **snowboarder** who placed third in the snowboardcross discipline in the World Junior Championships in 2007; she was predicted to also do well in the

half-pipe event, but a lack of enough snow caused that event to be canceled. Shaw also won the following:

- Half-pipe and snowboardcross events in the 2007 Chevrolet Revolution Tour
- Boardercross and giant slalom events in the 2007 United States of America Snowboard Association (USASA) Nationals
- Fourth place in the 2007 U.S. Snowboarding Grand Prix half-pipe event
- In the 2008 World Junior Championships, she earned the bronze medal in snowboardcross, behind Callan Chythlook-Sifsof, also from the United States, and Marion Perez from France. She had also qualified for the Alpine event. In the 2008 USASA competitions, Shaw placed first in the giant slalom event; second in the super pipe, group 2; and second in the slalom event.

Shaw has told *SBX* magazine that her goals are to compete in both the Olympics and the **X Games**. In January 2008, she attempted to qualify for the Winter X Games, wherein the top 12 athletes compete for the medals; Shaw had the 17th fastest time, however, so she did not qualify on her first attempt. She missed a spot by 3.66 seconds. At the time of the X Games tryouts, Shaw was the third-highest-ranked female snowboarder in the United States, at the age of 16.

Shaw was born on May 12, 1991, in Danbury, Connecticut. She first skied at the age of 2, switching to snowboarding at age 6. She began to be homeschooled after the 8th grade; she travels with a tutor so that she can study and maintain a fulltime snowboarding schedule.

Shaw has been sponsored by O'Neill, Swix, Vitamin Water, Scott USA, and Stratton Mountain; on the USASA Web site, she also lists another sponsor: Team Mom and Dad. She enjoys playing soccer, **wakeboarding**, surfing, dirt biking, carve boarding, horseback riding, and going four-wheeling. She also trains in gymnastics several times a week to further develop her sense of balance and air awareness.

See also Gender and Extreme Sports; Palmer, Shaun; White, Shaun

---

Shaw's Siblings

Brooke's brother Spencer is two years younger, and he also competes in snowboarding. In 2008, he placed first in the Chevy Revolution Tour in the half-pipe event. He has placed first in the USASA Nationals in the giant slalom event and second in boardercross. He competed in an event in New Zealand where the majority of competitors were adult men, finishing eighth out of 52 competitors. Spencer has the same sponsors as his sister, Brooke. In April 2008, Shaw garnered a first place finish in the Burton Am Series at Mount Hood in the half-pipe event.

Spencer has been featured on Fuel TV; in *East Coast Snowboarding Magazine*, and *Sports Illustrated for Kids*; on the NBC *Sports Illustrated Next Snow All-Star Show* and the NBC *Today Show*; in *Stratton Magazine*; and on Groms TV.com and NBC Sports *Fruit by the Foot Jam*.

Brooke's sister Serena is a competitive gymnast, as well as a dancer and a snowboarder. She is in the Breaker group (12 to 13 year olds) in the USASA, wherein she has competed in numerous events. Serena Shaw won all four of the snowboarding events in the March 2007 National Championships for her age group.

The youngest in the family, Maverick, began snowboarding at the age of 2 and is especially skilled in jumps, gaining more height than boarders several years his senior. Maverick is currently in the Grommet division (8 to 9 year olds) in the USASA. He won the national championship for his age group in March 2007 and has placed first in dozens of events between December 2007 and March 2008.

SKATEBOARDING

In skateboarding, participants stand on—and gain momentum on—boards that have slightly curved fronts and backs, wheels, axles, and a suspension system. Skateboarders often perform tricks on their skateboards, ranging from fairly simple ones to elaborate—and sometimes risky—ones. Skateboarders often attempt to create original tricks and moves, and many skateboarders enjoy the rebellious subculture reputation that skateboarders have gotten. Skateboarding is an ideal sport for athletes who enjoy activities that require creativity but are without significant boundaries or time limits.

In general, there are two types of skateboarding: street and vert. In vert skateboarding, skaters ride in specially designed skateboarding parks with ramps, half-pipes (U-shaped ramps that allow a skater to go from side to side at great speed), bowls, and more. Street riders use railings and steps and ramps found naturally in architecture throughout the city. Empty pools are also a venue for skateboarding, as are parking garages.

Bigger wheels work better for ramps and parks, while smaller wheels are more suitable for street riding. Some riders prefer a "regular foot" stance, while others prefer a "goofy foot" one. With a regular stance, the left foot is forward, and in the goofy foot stance, the right foot is forward. Both work well, so it is a matter of preference. To stop, skaters can drag the back foot on the ground, jump off the skateboard, or drag a heel during a wheelie.

Sometimes, participants are called skateboarders; other times, they are called "skaters," although this can be used in a derogatory sense about the lifestyle of the participants, which includes their appearance, slang, attitude, and more. Skateboarders might refer to themselves as "thrashers" or "shredders."

According to a newspaper article, "Skateboarding Phenomenon Soaring Across America," the perception of skateboarding has been changing and most likely will continue to change:

> Once the underground province of bored disaffected urban youth, skateboarding has crawled out from its seedy subculture beginnings and exploded into the mainstream with the help of a hefty stamp of approval from corporate America. It has not only hit the big time with TV, movies and video games, but it also dares to dream of a day it might snare a spot in the Olympics. (Fussell 2004)

A study by the Sporting Goods Manufacturers Association (SGMA) showed that 13 million people skateboarded in the United

Zachary Hicks, of Blue Springs, Missouri, takes a break on his skateboard for a few minutes inside the Blue Springs Parks and Recreation Department shop in Pink Hill Park. (AP Photo/*The Examiner*, Paul Beaver)

States in 2002, up 4 percent from the previous year. Eighty-six percent of these skaters were between the ages of 6 and 17, with almost 97 percent of them under the age of 24. About 37 percent come from households with incomes more than $75,000 and more than 80 percent are males under the age of 18 (*Washington Times* 2004). The International Association of Skateboard Companies estimated that, in 2004, there were approximately 16 million skateboarders (Perez 2004). In 2004, Board-Trac shared annual sales figures of $5.2 billion for the industry.

History of the Sport

Skateboarding as a sport emerged in the 1950s and 1960s, in large part because of California surfers who were looking for ways to surf without needing the waves. Long before that, however, ingenious youth combined wheels and boards in creative ways and then performed tricks for their friends. At the beginning of the twentieth century, for example, skateboards were really wheels from roller skates that were attached to boards. "Often the wood had a milk crate nailed to it with handles sticking out for control.... Tens of thousands of roller-skates were dismantled and joyfully hammered on to planks of wood" (Warburton 2003).

Some of the quirkier commercialized versions of the modern-day skateboard were the KneKoster, created in Chicago in 1927, and the Skooter Skate, a three-wheeled contraption built in 1939. By the 1950s, skateboards looked much like shortened scooters, but the ride still was not smooth, as evidenced by this description:

> It was wobblier than hell, moved way too fast and vibrated on the asphalt enough to jar every bone in your body and loosen every tooth. It was more like getting electrocuted than anything else.... Sand and dirt had no problem getting in, and any time that did you were a gonner for sure. You'd lock up and go flying at the worst possible time, usually just when you were trying to avoid the handlebars of a bike or a parked car. (Borden 2001)

In 1959, the **Roller Derby** Skateboard began to be commercially produced. In 1964, Jan and Dean's hit "Sidewalk Surfing" brought this quirky sport to the attention of **music** lovers across the country. The first skateboarding magazine, *Surf Guide*, was published.

Early skateboarders include Torger Johnson, Woody Woodward, and Danny Berer. In this era, skateboarders mainly stayed on the ground, with a few twists and gymnastics moves incorporated into what was known as "freestyle" skateboarding.

On May 14, 1965, skateboarding received national media attention when Pat McGee, the national girl's champion, was spotlighted on the cover of *Life* magazine. Consider this: other covers in 1965 covered national politics, civil rights marches, the death of Winston Churchill, the Vietnam War, the Watts Riots, the space race and more; this was lofty territory for the lowly skateboard, indeed.

That year, more than 50 million skateboards had been manufactured, including the Hobie Skateboards, created in 1964 by surfer Hobie Alter. To promote the newer sport of skateboarding, Alter put on exhibitions for audiences gathered together to watch the surfing movie *The Endless Summer*. Also in 1965, Noel Black wrote and directed *Skaterdater*, the first widely released skateboarding movie.

Unfortunately, the early skateboards were not always of the highest quality and too many accidents—and even deaths—occurred, so many that skateboarding was called a "new medical menace." Skateboarding was restricted in many locales around the world; Norway banned the sport altogether. Popularity of skateboarding waned.

SKATEBOARDING IN THE 1970S

The decline of the sport did not last long. In the 1970s, newer skateboards with polyurethane wheels (first created by Frank Nasworthy in 1973), rather than ones of clay, maneuvered more easily. The second innovation was the addition of a kicktail (invented by Richard Stevenson). The kicktail is the upwardly bending part of the skateboard deck; the front kicktail is the nose and the back is the tail. The combined inventions of these two men—plus boards now being made out of fiberglass and aluminum—revolutionized the sport.

During this time, increasing numbers of skateboarding parks were also being built. Because of a drought in California in the early 1970s, skateboarders frequently used drained pools as their venues, as well.

During the sport's peak in the 1970s, more than 40 million skateboards were sold and the sport became increasingly associated with punk rock music and the overall punk movement. During this decade, teen idol Leif Garrett starred in a mainstream movie, *Skateboard* (1978), which added to its position in pop culture.

Women, including Ellen O'Neal, Peggy Oki, Vicki Vickers, and Ellen Berryman, become involved in competitive skateboarding, while Tony Alva, Jay Adams, and Stacy Peralta began demonstrating more aggressive skating techniques.

Companies began sponsoring skateboarders during this time but, just as it appeared as though skateboarding would become a well-established sport, it once again declined as the price of insurance at skateboarding parks skyrocketed. This caused skateboard park admission fees to rise, which kept many skateboarders away. This combination of challenges caused many skateboard parks to close down and forced skateboarding to once again become an underground sport.

INCORPORATION OF SKATEBOARDING TRICKS

Although the late 1970s were a declining time for skateboarding, overall, these were also the years that skateboarding took "air." In 1978, a Florida skater, Alan Gelfand, accidentally discovered how to become "airborne" by slamming down on the tail of his skateboard; this action caused him—and his skateboard—to be propelled into the air. Friends of Gelfand named this move the "ollie." Although it took about a year for another skater to duplicate Gelfand's move, as people attempted and then mastered the move, the "ollie" transformed the sport of skateboarding.

Other moves created by skaters in the 1970s include the following:

- "Invert aerial" by Bobby Valdez, 1978: with this move, a skater becomes airborne and also upside down
- "Layback," 1978: the skater leans back and puts his or her trailing hand on the lip of the board; with this trick, the athlete maintains a surfer-like pose
- "Rock 'n' roll," 1978: the skateboard rocks the top of a wall in a see-sawing motion
- "Alley oop aerial," 1978: a trick is performed in the direction that is opposite of the direction that the skateboarder is traveling
- "Layback air" by Kelly Lind, 1979: a frontside aerial
- "Miller flip" by Darryl Miller, 1979: a 360-degree frontside invert aerial

During the 1970s, "skateboarding skill quite literally keeps on rising: new unreal bio tricks, impossible variations and combinations of moves and perfection in style—all make past efforts look decidedly tame" (Borden 2001).

SKATEBOARDING IN THE 1980S

The National Skateboard Association (NSA) formed in 1981, with assistance from the Boy Scouts of America. The NSA began organizing and sanctioning competitions; some competitors began creating their own boards and apparel for sale.

During the latter part of the 1980s, skateboarders saw a revival of the sport's popularity and prominence in American pop culture. The revival of the sport in the 1980s has been credited, in large part, to the skateboarding Marty McFly character played by Michael J. Fox in the *Back to the Future* movies.

Although the "ollie" was invented in the 1970s, it was not until the 1980s that a significant number of skaters incorporated the move into their skating. The 1980s also saw the rise of street-style skateboarding, with Mark Gonzales and Natas Kaupas credited for much of this movement. Meanwhile, Christian Hosoi and **Tony Hawk** were creating significant interest for their accomplishments on the ramps and half-pipes.

Skateboarding magazines included *Thrasher* and *Transworld Skateboarding*, each with circulation of more than 150,000. Skateboarding also spawned its own music genre, with a similarly wild image. Meanwhile,

> [G]roups with names like Septic Death and Gang Green record their "speed metal" music on small labels devoted to "skate rock." One skate rock disc jockey, Skatemaster Tate, describes the music vividly: "It's punk rock and skating rolled up in a ball of confusion and screaming down the alley in a gutter." (Gianoulis 2000)

These trends are blamed for the reduction in female participation in the sport during this era.

Skateboarding videos became popular during this decade, with skateboarders being taped while demonstrating tricks and selling products. A group of skateboarders, known as the "Bones Brigade," were especially known for their videos; skaters such as **Rodney Mullen**, Tony Hawk, Steve Caballero, Lance Mountain, and Tommy Guerrero participated. Overall, the skateboarding industry was dominated in the 1980s by a few large companies, most notably Powell Peralta, started by George Powell and represented by noted skater Stacy Peralta.

European championships were established during the 1980s, as well as international competitions. Tensions were increasing, however, between those advocating corporate involvement and those skateboarders who felt that sponsorships were akin to selling out. Tensions also grew between punk skaters and those who were not involved in the punk movement.

SKATEBOARDING IN THE 1990S

In the 1990s, the International Association of Skateboard Companies worked with government entities to create quality legislation to govern the sport. In 1993, the NSA became World Cup Skateboarding (WCS), organizing events in the United States, Canada, England, Germany, the Czech Republic, France, Switzerland, Austria, and Brazil. In 1998, the United Skateboarding Association formed to focus solely on U.S. competitions.

Tony Hawk became a skateboarding superstar, the first skater well known to people who did not know much about the sport. Skateboarding moves also became common in advertising.

Skateboarding began serving as a core element of the **X Games** and as the theme of some of the most popular **video games** ever made, including Tony Hawk's entire series. Skateboarding was also featured in movies, including *Ultimate X*, which had the participation of several top skateboarders, including Hawk, Bucky Lasek, and more. In 1999, a cartoon called *Rocket Power* debuted on Nickelodeon; this cartoon featured four friends who enjoyed participating in extreme sports, including skateboarding. MTV used skateboarding in its show *Jackass* and in its two feature films based on that show's premise.

Skateboarding became intricately connected to pop culture and popular music, fashion and so forth—and was used to sell items as disparate as perfume and bed sheets.

During the 1990s, skateboarders were at a tipping point: Was skateboarding still the alternative, rebellious sport it once was? Or was it finding its way into the mainstream? *The Berkshire Encyclopedia of Extreme Sports* uses an excellent example to show this dichotomy. In the late 1990s, Nike created a commercial for their skateboarding shoes. In the commercial, athletes who played more traditional sports were chased by police officers and even harassed by them. The key message of the ads was—what if every athlete was treated like a skateboarder?

Skaters applauded the commercial—but did not buy the shoes. Perhaps, as the encyclopedia entry suggests, buying those shoes would mean that skaters were buying into the idea that skateboarding was, in fact, now mainstream—and the 1990s skaters were not willing to do that. Nike switched to having well-known skateboarders sell their shoes, and this campaign worked.

SKATEBOARDING IN THE 2000S

In the millennium, skaters are enjoying both street and park (ramp) styles of skateboarding and some are reviving the slalom version of skateboarding that made a brief appearance in the late 1960s and 1970s, but virtually disappeared after that. Slalom skaters race through a course set up with orange cones, skating around them; contestants go through the course one by one, and the person with the fastest time wins. Using a technique called "pumping," experienced skateboarders can accelerate through the course, even when on flat ground.

Slalom racing events are held in many locales throughout the United States and Europe, with an emerging interest in Japan and Australia. At the end of 2007, SlalomRanking.com listed the top five slalom skateboarders, basing these rankings on the slalom performances of these athletes from 2004 through December 31, 2007. They are, in order, as follows:

- Jason Mitchell, United States
- Luca Giammarco, Italy
- Ramón Königshausen, Switzerland
- Chris Barker, United States
- Richy Carrasco, United States

Slalom skateboarders use skateboards with tall, wide, and soft wheels; this allows them to pick up more speed and to have the grip necessary to make quick, hard turns. The skateboards themselves are usually made of titanium and an extra light board made of carbon wrapped foam core.

When racing on flat ground, slalom skateboarders average a speed of about 12 miles (20 kilometers) per hour, although some can pick up speeds of about 18 miles (30 kilometers) per hour. When racing downhill, skateboarders can go anywhere from 18 to 37 miles (30 to 60 kilometers) per hour.

Besides the revival of slalom, the 2000s have witnessed other skateboarding accomplishments. One of the most spectacular individual events was when Danny Way, a former member of the well-known Bones Brigade of the 1980s, used a huge ramp to jump the Great Wall of China.

Female athletes reemerged during the 2000s, including **Cara-Beth Burnside**, Holly Lyons, Mimi Koop, Elisa Steamer, Vanessa Torres, Amy Caron, and Karen Jonz. The women have created a skater tour, the Girls Skate Jam, which is similar to Tony Hawk's Boom Boom HuckJam.

To put the popularity of skateboarding and its stars in perspective, in 2003, Tony Hawk made more money than the basketball superstar Michael Jordan.

In 2007, Australian skateboarder Jake Brown was involved in an accident in which most people would not have survived; he was extremely fortunate, however, and is expected to resume participation in his sport. In a competition, Brown had gained momentum by traveling down an 80-foot (24.4-meter) ramp and, in the 70-foot (21.3-meter) gap between the two ramps, completed a trick known as the "540 McTwist." In this trick, the skater completes an entire 360-degree revolution—plus another 180-degree turn. Although Brown successfully completed this trick, he did not have enough control to land on the other ramp, and he fell approximately 45 feet (13 meters); upon landing, he did not move for an entire 2 minutes.

"I seriously thought he was dead, broke his back or broke both legs," said fellow skater Pierre-Luc Gagnon of Carlsbad. "That was the gnarliest slam I've ever seen in my life" (Norcross 2007).

In an astonishing turn of events, after 8 minutes, Brown got up and walked away on his own, weakly waving to the crowd. Taken to a hospital, he discovered that he had fractured a wrist and a couple of vertebrae, and had a lung contusion and liver laceration.

According to Brown's orthopedist, Dr. William Previte, 50 percent of people who fall 30 feet (9 meters) do not survive—and the odds for survival drop dramatically at 45 feet (13 meters), which was how far Brown had fallen. Other than the liver laceration, which healed, he sustained no life-threatening injuries.

SKATEBOARDING TRICKS

Since the late 1970s, skateboarders have continued to create tricks and to modify and improve upon them. Here are just a few:

- "Manual": a wheelie using the back wheels; when using the front wheels, it is known as a "nose manual"
- "Noseslide": sliding on the board nose; when sliding on the back of the board, it is known as a "tail slide"
- "Fakie": riding backward on the board

If a skater says, "ABD," that indicates that a trick has "already been done."

Tricks can be put into categories, with freestyle tricks being those that require fewer than four wheels to perform. These tricks were among the earliest and formed the basis of freestyle flatground skating.

Aerial tricks occur while the skateboarder is in the air (completely off the ground). In these tricks, the skater needs to use his or her hands or feet to hold on to the board. Tony Alva became well known for developing aerials using empty pools as his venue in the late 1970s.

Flip tricks are based on the "ollie," skateboarding's original trick. Boards are spun around in different fashions; flip tricks are often used in street skate. Slides and grinds involve using the edge of a rail or other object to perform a trick. When the board is in contact with the edge, the trick is a slide; when the axle is in contact, it is a grind. Lip tricks are performed on the coping of pools and ramps; coping is the coverage of a structure.

Still other tricks involve going from a regular foot stance to a goofy foot one, or visa versa, which has been compared to people switching between using their right and left hands to write.

SKATEBOARD APPAREL

According to one source, "For most young people of today, skateboarding is not a means of transport but a lifestyle in which a whole industry of fashion and other accessories complements the sport" (Forsman and Eriksson 2001).

In 2002, the skateboard apparel business had revenues of $2.6 billion, with $1.6 billion for shoes only. Skateboarding apparel is generally worn for one of two reasons: for its cool appearance and for protective reasons. Skateboarding apparel is often named after well known skateboard icons, such as Tony Hawk, Shaun Palmer, and Bucky Lasek.

SKATEBOARDING EQUIPMENT

The most important piece of safety equipment for skateboarders is a quality helmet. Skateboarders often purchase a pair of shoes specifically made for skateboarding, and pads are also important to protect knees and elbows. In the earlier days of skateboarding, when empty swimming pools were a frequent venue for skaters, plastic cap pads worked well because the rider could slide during a fall; these pads still work well for ramp and park riding.

SKATEBOARDING RISKS AND INJURIES

According to the National Electronic Injury Surveillance System (NEISS), which is part of the U.S. Consumer Product Safety Commission, 54,532 skateboarding injuries occurred in 1998.

For that year, NEISS recorded 20.2 injuries for every 100,000 participants. As comparison points, NEISS also recorded the following injuries per 100,000 participants: soccer, 62.0; baseball, 115.7; and basketball, 223.5.

Research conducted by the Consumer Protection Safety Council (CPSC) shows that new skateboarders receive about one-third of the injuries, with more than half of the total skateboarding injuries occurring on irregular riding surfaces. Experienced skateboarders receive injuries most often when they skate into rocks or irregular surfaces, or when they attempt particularly difficult stunts.

The University Hospital of Umea, located in the United Kingdom, monitored the skateboarding-related injuries that they treated from 1995 through 1998. They recorded 139 injuries, three of which were pedestrians being hit by a skater, and the rest, the skaters themselves. Injured people ranged in age from 7 to 47, with an average age of 16. All injuries were minor to moderate, with fractures being considered moderate.

Twenty-nine percent of the injuries were fractures, the majority of which were ankle or wrist breaks, and four were concussions. Older patients tended to ask for treatment for sprains or soft tissue injuries. The majority of **children** injured had been hurt while riding on ramps or in arenas. Only 12 people (9 percent) were injured while riding on the road. Thirty-seven percent lost their balance, while 26 percent were hurt while failing to complete a trick. The majority of falls occurred because of surface irregularities, and these falls caused most of the moderate injuries.

Slalom skaters tend to suffer most from road rash, which are skin abrasions caused by crashing and sliding across the ground; the estimated number of injuries for slalom skaters is similar to those sustained by athletes participating in skiing or snowboarding.

SKIING, EXTREME AND FREERIDE

Extreme skiing was a phrase first used in the 1970s and generally referred to skiing downhill on remote and difficult terrain at extreme downward angles. Helicopters and Sno-Cats are often needed to transport these skiers to starting points, and athletes face significant risks as a single fall could lead to serious injury, paralysis, or even death. Extreme skiing pioneer Chris Landry is credited with this saying, "You fall, you die" (Robinson 1987).

Although extreme skiing still exists as a sport today, the term itself is somewhat fading from use and more attention is being given to another sport known by these names: freeride skiing, freestyle skiing, or freeskiing.

By the mid-1990s, the sports of **snowboarding** and skiing had merged to create freeride skiing. In this hybrid sport, athletes use a wide stance while skiing and they incorporate **skateboarding** and snowboarding tricks into their movements; rather than wearing the sleekly fitting traditional skiing outfits, freeride skiers often wear baggy clothing more often seen on skateboarders and snowboarders.

Definitions of these terms—extreme skiing, freeride skiing, freeskiing, freestyle skiing, and even big mountain skiing—seem to take on different nuances based on the person or group pursuing the sport; these definitions continue to evolve.

DEVELOPMENT OF SPORT

At the dawn of the twentieth century, European mountain climbers sometimes skied down the mountainside, rather than climb down. That said, Sylvain Saudan of Switzerland is generally considered to be the founder of extreme skiing, in large part because he navigated the couloir Spencer (Blaitiere, France) in 1967 and the couloir Whymper (L'Aiguille Verte, France) after that; these slopes had inclines of more than 55 degrees. To put that in perspective, if Saudan were skiing sideways, the angle of the terrain would cause him to bump his elbow on the mountain. A modern skiing champion has likened extreme skiing to being a race car driver on skis (Lloyd 1997)

Saudan quickly realized that skiing at such an extreme angle and at such great speed prevented him from using the traditional jump turns; he therefore created the windscreen wiper turn, wherein he turned on the backs of his skis, and made other modifications as necessary. Two French skiers—Patrick Vallencant and Anselme Baud—furthered the sport.

Because of his accomplishments, Saudan has been called the "skier of the impossible" (Quinodoz 1997). He also stirred up controversy by traveling to the top of a slope by helicopter. By placing more value on the descent versus the ascension, Saudan broke a cardinal rule of Alpinism. Despite the controversy, other skiers began tackling extreme locales around the globe, including in Europe, the Middle East, and South America.

Modern-day extreme skiers place special value on venues that have not been skied before or "marked." These skiers often pursue their sport in the European Alps, North American Rockies, the South American Andes, the Southern Alps of New Zealand, and the Chugach in Alaska.

Austria's Oliver Andorfer does a "360 safety grab" during the jib day of the Heli Bash extreme skiing in Wanaka, New Zealand, August 16, 2002. (AP Photo/Rob Griffith)

By the 1990s, when the popularity of snowboarding and skateboarding was rising, ski manufacturers began producing parabolic skis that made turns easier and the ski learning curve shorter—which gave rise to freeride skiing. Although freeride skiing has its own inherent risks, it is safer than extreme skiing; in the extreme version, athletes are choosing to ski locales with up to 60-degree inclinations, where death is a real possibility.

EXTREME SKIING RISKS AND INJURIES

The first confirmed extreme skiing death happened in 1993, when Paul Ruff crashed against rocks while skiing at a high velocity near the Kirkwood Ski Resort in California. In 2006, a double tragedy occurred when American extreme skier Chad Vander-Ham died after falling 1,500 feet (457.2 meters) off a cliff in the French Alps; when former world champion Doug Coombs tried to rescue VanderHam using a rope, Coombs plunged off the same cliff to his death.

Freeriders focus less on extreme terrain and more on using "big" maneuvers. When a skier is said to be "going big," this might mean tackling steep terrain, but it also may mean flying through the air and making a controlled landing or achieving a new maneuver.

Nevertheless, risks also exist in freeskiing; on January 22, 2008, the 29-year-old athlete and ski film actor Billy Poole died while freeskiing in Utah's backcountry for a ski video. In response, the chief executive office of Black Diamond, a manufacturer of ski equipment, said that "in this sport, death is part of life" (Frank 2008).

COMPETITIVE EXTREME SKIING/FREERIDING

The World Extreme Skiing Championship (WESC) began in 1991 in Valdez, Alaska, and turned into an annual event. The following year, the U.S. Extreme Free Skiing Championship was held in Colorado. In 1996, the International Free Skiers Association (IFSA) formed, setting standards for competition judging; scoring standards encompass the difficulty of the route, including its steepness and current weather conditions; aggressiveness; technique, including style and turns; fluidity; and control. Freestyle skiing is also featured in the Winter **X Games** and the **Gravity Games**.

Freestyle skiers often mimic skateboarding and snowboarding tricks, including grabbing their skis while in midair and incorporating hand rails and other urban venues into their sport.

EXTREME SKIING EQUIPMENT

Extreme skiers need snowshoes, ice picks, crampons, and avalanche safety equipment when skiing. Freestyle skiers use twin-tips skis that perform well when skiing in either direction, plus more flexible boots that allow the athletes to maneuver more easily. They also use larger "fat boy" skis that allow them to incorporate snowboarding moves more easily and to tackle backcountry skiing. Beginning skiers can use snow blades to learn the sport, but these blades cannot be used in landing big jumps. Some freeskiers choose not to use ski poles as they push the limits of their sport

POP CULTURE

Filmmakers Warren Miller and Greg Stump began producing extreme skiing films in the late 1980s and early 1990s, including *The Blizzard of AAHHHs*. Skiers Glen Plake, Scot Schmidt, and Mike Hattrup starred in the films, increasing their name recognition. These films glamorized the sport, expanding skiing into a personal challenge for many athletes. Moreover, as many as a dozen extreme skiing videos are released each year.

See also Holmenkollen Ski Festival; Ski Jumping

SKI JUMPING

In the sport of ski jumping, athletes initially position themselves high above the jump-off point, crouching down at their starting points to optimize their aerodynamic potential. The athlete then skis downhill at speeds of 55 miles (90 kilometers) per hour or more, gaining momentum before performing a predetermined jump off of a large ramp.

Typically, the skier is in flight for a range of 3 to 5 seconds before needing to make a controlled landing. Judges rate the jumpers on the style of the jump from the moment of takeoff until the landing, along with the solidity of the landing and the distance achieved.

A more extreme version of ski jumping is known as "ski flying." In ski flying, jumpers aim for a distance of at least 606 feet (185 meters) in their jumps; this gives an impression that the skiers are temporarily flying.

Countries with accomplished ski jumpers include Austria, Finland, France, the Czech Republic, Germany, Japan, Norway, Poland, Slovenia, Switzerland, and the Russian Federation.

Although ski jumping was considered a sport for men only during its first century of competitions, in 2004, the *Fédération Internationale de Ski* (FIS, International Ski Federation) started holding competitions for women. However, an attempt to include women's ski jumping in the 2010 Olympics was rejected by the International Olympic Committee (IOC).

DEVELOPMENT OF THE SPORT

Throughout the centuries, the ability to ski downhill and avoid obstacles while doing so was an ordinary part of life in mountainous Norway and surrounding countries. It is therefore logical that an 1861 invention of Sondre Norheim of Telemark, Norway, provided the impetus for the sport of ski jumping. Norheim developed a loose heel binding for cross-country skiing (also known as Nordic skiing). Because the heel of the ski boot is not attached to the skis, the skiers have the freedom to experiment with jumping. The first Nordic skiing and jumping contest took place in 1892 in Oslo, where the annual **Holmenkollen Ski Festival** takes place to this day.

As Norwegians emigrated to the United States and Canada, they brought along their ability to Nordic ski. During the late nineteenth and early twentieth centuries, the sport was also introduced to some European countries. Some of the earlier ski jumping athletes were accomplished gymnasts, with Birger Ruud from Kongsberg, Norway, and Alf Engen of the United States being two of the most notable. They attempted to incorporate multiple somersaults into their jumps, an extreme skiing technique that did not become part of the mainstream sport.

In 1924, ski jumping was an event in the first Winter Olympics, held in Chamonix, France. Today, the Nordic Combined medals are given to the athletes with the best combined scores for cross-country racing and ski jumping events. Meanwhile, the scoring system has evolved to consider both distance and style during the jumps.

In the earlier Olympic events, athletes were achieving jumps of approximately 230 feet (70 meters) and, by the 1930s, non-Olympic daredevils began showing numbers of 295 feet (90 meters) and more. The first person confirmed with a jump of more than 328 feet (100 meters) was the Austrian skier Sepp Bradl, who achieved a jump of 331 feet (101 meters) at Planica, Slovenia, in 1936. In 1994, Toni Nieminen of Finland broke the 200-meter (656-foot) mark with a jump of 666 feet (203 meters); this accomplishment also occurred on the hills of Planica. Just nine years later, Daniela Iraschko of Austria also achieved a 200-meter (656-foot) jump, the first woman to accomplish this feat.

As the athletes' desire to maximize the distance covered with their jumps increased, they learned how to make their bodies more aerodynamic for that purpose. One of the earlier techniques used to achieve this goal was the windmilling of arms while in flight. Athletes then began stretching their arms forward until they landed or leaning over their skis in a jack-knife position. Finally, they began creating a "V" with the skis, where the backs of the skis nearly touch and the front parts are spread wide open in a "V" shape. This innovation was introduced by Jan Boklöv from Sweden in 1986; although this technique was originally criticized and sometimes caused judges to score an athlete poorly, it became the standard and is still used today.

Olympic ski jump hills initially ranged between 300 and 395 feet (90 and 120 meters), meaning that this was the distance from the takeoff point to the part of the hill that begins to flatten out. As jumpers' skills have increased, so too have the distances of the Olympic jump hills (to 459 feet, 140 meters).

Skiers are required to land in the traditional Telemark style, with one foot placed in front of the other. The front foot should be flat with a bent knee, the back heel is somewhat elevated, and the back knee is bent.

OLYMPIC JUDGING

Five judges award points, and each judge can award up to 20 points for style. The highest and the lowest scores are tossed out, which makes 60 a perfect style score for a ski jumper. The same logic applies to distance; if a skier reaches the K-point, which would be 140 meters (460 feet) from the takeoff point, he or she earns 60 points. If a skier misses or surpasses the K-point, his or her score is adjusted accordingly.

SKI JUMPING EQUIPMENT

As jumping styles and judging philosophies evolved, so did the skis themselves. Modern-day skis for jumping are between 8 feet, 2 inches and 8 feet, 10 inches (2.5 and 2.65 meters) in length, which is about twice as long as the original skis. This increased length adds lift to the skis, which allows for longer jumps. In the past, skiers hovered 20 feet (6 meters) or more above the ground but, with today's techniques and equipment, skiers typically fly about 10 feet (3 meters) above the ground.

EXTREME SKI FLYING

Once the K-point of a hill—that is, the distance between the takeoff point and the point where the hill flattens—reaches 606 feet (185 meters), then the athletes are participating in sky flying, rather than ski jumping. Norwegian Bjørn Einar Romøren set the world record of 784 feet (239 meters) in 2006. Janne Ahonen of Finland jumped—or flew—further at that competition, but his 787 feet (240 meters) was not counted, because he fell upon landing.

Some skiers prefer galondee jumping; in this style, skiers wear the traditional Alpine skiing equipment. Because their ski boots are fixed to the skies, they cannot generate as much lift and their jumping distances are therefore shorter. Galondee skiers often use natural venues for the sport rather than man-made hills.

GOVERNANCE AND ORGANIZATIONS

The National Ski Association was founded in 1905 at Ishpeming, Michigan; in 1922, the U.S. Eastern Amateur Ski Association formed. In 1924, the FIS was created to oversee ski jumping and to create regulations for the competitions, hills, and equipment, including the length of skis and their materials. Initially, FIS was against skiers attempting to break world records in jumping distances. The world record philosophy of ski jumping was part of the North American ideology from the start, but it was not popular in other parts of the world. When it became clear that distance records were a popular element of the sport for spectators, FIS began to acknowledge them while still trying to temper this facet of ski jumping.

Ski Jumping Risks and Injuries

The *American Journal of Sports Medicine* has stated that few data are available on Nordic ski jumping injuries. A survey from the early 1990s received 133 responses (out of 286 surveys sent). Eighty-one of the respondents (60.9 percent) stated that they had required a physician's care at least once because of a jumping injury. The risk of injury, according to this small survey, was about 9.4 percent, which is lower than the rate reported for most high school or college intramural sports.

A 1985 survey of Norwegian ski jumpers was also reported in the *American Journal of Sports Medicine*, with more serious findings for a small percentage of the athletes. Out of 2,200 licensed jumpers, at least 12 had suffered an injury associated with a permanent medical disability. Four injuries involved the central nervous system; two were leg amputations; one was blindness in one eye; and the other five involved fractures.

See also Skiing, Extreme and Freeride

SKY DIVING

Sky divers jump out of an aircraft, which is usually an airplane, but could be a helicopter or a hot air balloon. People who sky dive for sport do so for recreational or competitive purposes. The divers usually jump from an altitude of 13,000 to 15,000 feet (4,000 to 4,600 meters), and they freefall for approximately 50 seconds before opening a parachute to slow down and to control their direction and then their landing.

Generally, the parachute is operational at about 2,500 feet (762 meters) above the ground. At that point, the jumper can use the steering lines attached to the parachute to choose the best landing spot. A skilled parachutist can travel horizontally at a speed of 10 miles (16 kilometers) per hour, but the length of time between deploying a parachute and landing is generally between 10 and 12 seconds.

In competitive sky diving, participants earn points for style during the freefall and for their ability to land at a prespecified point. Some sky divers may choose to explore related sports, such as **sky surfing** and **BASE (Building/Antenna tower/Span/Earth) jumping**. The Fédération Aéronautique International was founded in 1905, and this organization is the governing body for most aeronautic sports.

Participants in this sport talk about the beauty of the experience, when—

[T]he instructor gives you the signal to jump, you take a deep breath, then you jump into a world of heart-racing freefalling adventure and rely on nothing but your parachute to land you safely on the ground.
Once you start falling at a constant speed (about ten seconds after jumping), you'll experience a sense of relaxation as you take in all the beautiful colors circling on the ground beneath you. You could almost reach out and touch the clouds, and this is probably as close to heaven as you are going to get. (Press Digital 2007)

Sky diving is sometimes called recreational parachuting or sport parachuting.

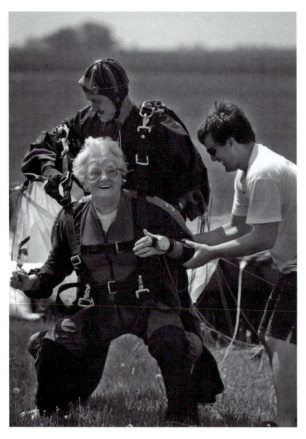

Sylvia DeVries, from Kalamazoo, Michigan, turned 80 on May 22, 2007. DeVries decided that skydiving would be a unique way to celebrate Mother's Day with her children. (AP Photo/*Journal and Courier*, John Terhune)

DEVELOPMENT OF THE SPORT

Chinese legend states that Emperor Shun (2258–2208 BCE) performed the first parachuting act in history. This legend was recorded in the Chinese Historical Records known as Shi Ji; this record was completed around 90 BCE. The writer, Sima Qian, shares the story of how Shun's father, Gu Sou, wanted to kill his son. When he found him on top of a tall granary tower, he had his opportunity and so he set the tower on fire. Shun cleverly attached several large conical hats together and then floated down to safety. In the eighth century CE, a Chinese writer named Sima Zhen recorded his belief that the hats acted like giant bird wings, keeping Shun's body light enough to land safely on the ground.

Other sources say that parachutes were developed as early as the twelfth century in China and in the sixteenth century in Venice, Italy. Both Leonardo da Vinci and Fausto Veranzio, a well-educated inventor and author from a family of minor nobility, have been credited with sketching out a parachute, the latter doing so in 1595 and calling it "Homo Volans" or "flying man."

The first-known living creature to descend from high in the air to the ground using a parachute was not, however, a human being; rather, it was a dog. In August 1785, the French balloonist Blanchard went on a 300-mile (483-kilometer) trip and, during that trip, he released a basket containing a dog; a parachute was attached to the basket and the dog landed safely. Little is known about the dog, although some sources suggest it was a stray snatched from the streets.

In 1797, André-Jacques Garnerin stood in a basket that was attached to a parachute, which in turn was attached to a hydrogen balloon. Garnerin cut the cord leading to the balloon at about 3,280 feet (1,000 meters) above the ground and, to the cheers of a sizable crowd, landed safely. In 1808, Jodaki Kuparento from Warsaw had a much closer call when he needed to jump from a burning balloon with his parachute, but he did survive.

MODERN PARACHUTE USE

Although some aviators have shunned parachutes, believing that they imply a lack of confidence in the plane or pilot, parachutes became a part of military operations during World War I.

In 1930, the first-known parachuting competition took place in Russia; contestants received points for accurately landing on a ground target. Shortly before World War II, parachuting for sport became an attraction at some fairs. In 1948, the Frenchman Leo Valentin used stabilized freefall when descending (in a stabilized freefall, the sky diver gets into a position that allows him or her to make controlled, planned movements).

Sky diving received a significant amount of attention after the end of World War II. This excitement was fueled, in part, by the news of famous airborne combat units, including the 82nd (All American) Airborne Division and the Screaming Eagles of the 101st Airborne Division. In 1951, the Parachuting World Championships were held in the former Yugoslavia, and in 1957, the U.S. Parachute Association (USPA) was founded; this organization sponsors an annual national championship.

On August 16, 1960, Captain Joseph Kittinger jumped from a height of 102,800 feet (31,334 meters), making that the first "supersonic" jump. His ascent took an hour and a half to a place where temperatures were at −94° Fahrenheit (−34.4° Celsius). Between 90,000 and 70,000 feet (27,000 to 21,000 meters), breathing was difficult, but he survived. After falling for 4 minutes and 37 seconds, his freefall ended when his parachute opened. It took him approximately 8 minutes from that point to land on solid ground. Kittinger set a record for the highest parachute jump, the longest freefall, and the fastest speed of a human through the air at 614 miles (988 kilometers) per hour. A Russian named Roger Eugene Andreyev set the world's freefall record on November 1, 1962, at 80,325 feet (24,483 meters).

In the 1970s, some U.S. jumpers began tandem jumping, in which two people shared a special parachute; this subdiscipline became popular during the 1980s and now is used as a method to train new sky divers.

ADVANCED SKY DIVING

Some modern-day jumpers create canopy formations as they descend. In these formations, two or more sky divers intentionally maneuver their canopies—or the fabric portions of the parachutes—so they are close to each another. They perform this maneuver either while in freefall mode or shortly after deploying their chutes. As one example of a canopy formation, the sky divers hook their legs into the lines of the canopies of the jumpers directly below them or they hold hands. When jumpers perform geometrically patterned maneuvers that involve hooking onto canopies of other jumpers, everyone must carry secondary canopies; if someone becomes entangled in another person's primary canopy, he must quickly cut himself out, which damages the other jumper's primary canopy.

Significant sky diving accomplishments include that of Linger Abdurakhamov of Russia who accurately landed on a 20-inch (500-millimeter) target 50 consecutive times. In Eloy, Arizona, in 2002, 300 sky divers linked themselves together while still in freefall mode; in February 2004, 357 divers successfully linked together; and on February 8, 2006, 400 sky divers created a freefall formation that lasted 4.5 seconds.

In 2003, 64 deployed jumpers linked themselves together over Lake Wales in Florida. In 2007, 100 parachutists formed the largest diamond pattern to date, also over Lake Wales.

Other sky divers perform acrobatic maneuvers during freefall; this aerial ballet is filmed and then judged for style and artistic presence. A group of divers known as the

Freefly Clowns started to experiment with creative, nontraditional freefall positions in the mid-1980s. Typically, sky divers use a belly-toward-Earth position as they descend; the Freefly Clowns and subsequent freefall groups also fall feet first or head first. Using these positions, the sky divers can make new formations and routines, creating three-dimensional art with their bodies and parachutes.

SKY DIVER DEMOGRAPHICS

A *Washington Times* article quotes Chris Needels, the executive director of the USPA, as estimating that approximately 300,000 people per year go sky diving for the first time. Only 3 percent of those people, though, ever make a second jump. Needels also estimates that 15 percent of sky divers are women.

Divers tend to be between 30 and 49 years old, with an upper-middle-class income and level of education. Approximately 40 percent of sky divers live in the United States, with the overwhelming majority of non-U.S. sky divers residing in other industrial countries. According to a 2003 report by the International Parachuting Commission (IPC), from 1989 to 2002, between 285,000 and 417,000 people performed between 4.59 million and 6.87 million jumps during each of those years.

SKY DIVING TRAINING

Beginners can take their first jump as a tandem jump, wherein they are attached to an instructor with whom they share a harness. Another option is to use a static line—a heavy cord that is attached to the airplane on one end and the parachute canopy bag on the other. When the static line is straightened to its entirety, the parachute opens. When using a static line, the diver usually jumps between 4,000 and 5,000 feet (1,200 and 1,500 meters) above ground.

The other choice is the accelerated freefall, wherein instructors jump with the beginning jumper, but they are not physically attached. This is the most expensive option, but also the fastest way to become a certified jumper. The first jumper to learn with this method may have been Johnny Carson in the 1970s, when he demonstrated his first lesson for his television show. In 1981, this method began to be used in some sky diving training schools, rendering the static line method somewhat obsolete.

SKY DIVING EQUIPMENT

Sky diving equipment costs between $2,000 and $6,000, depending on the quality of equipment purchased, and whether it is new or used. The main piece of equipment is the rig, which contains a main parachute and a backup one.

In the 1960s, the development of the square "Ram Air" parachute gave jumpers more flexibility than the older round parachutes did. With Ram Air chutes, jumpers can steer more easily and they enjoy additional lift, which helps with a gentler landing. Therefore, jumpers using Ram Air parachutes are to some degree pilots, rather than just people falling at the dictates of the wind. The shapes of parachutes have gone from round to rectangular to elliptical.

The parachute industry has developed a safeguard called the Automatic Activation Device (AAD); this barometrically controlled device monitors whether a jumper is falling too quickly, and if so, the parachute automatically opens. This device was first invented in the 1950s, but tended to malfunction; as the years have passed, the technology has greatly improved.

Lessons also range in cost, with a tandem jump costing between $220 and $235. A static line jump is generally a bit less expensive, perhaps $205; and the accelerated freefall costs approximately $350 for two instructors.

The cost for jumps may decrease as a student gains expertise, and it generally takes a person about eight jumps to gain the ability to jump solo. Completing a training program may consist of ten to fifteen jumps and will probably cost between $1,000 and $1,200. To earn an "A" license, a person must complete twenty-five jumps and pass a performance test.

Sky Diving Risks and Injuries

In 2002, the USPA stated that there are 33 sky diving deaths for every 2.15 million jumps taken by USPA members. The IPC estimates that for every 4,500 divers making 76,000 jumps, there is one fatality. Injuries are believed to be grossly underreported and therefore no quality data are available. More experienced divers tend to suffer more fatalities, according to the IPC data, and this trend is accelerating. In 1990, sky divers with 250 or more freefalls accounted for 33 percent of the fatalities; in 2002, expert divers accounted for 60 percent of all fatalities. Also in 2002, 52 percent of these fatalities were attributed to landing errors.

Experienced divers who participate in multiple-person formation freefalls face danger when holding onto another person, including the possibility of a high-speed collision.

See also de Gayardon, Patrick; Sky Surfing

SKY SURFING

Sky surfing is a relatively new sport, developed in France, that combines freestyle **sky diving** with the type of board used in **snowboarding** or surfing the waves. In sky surfing, two athletes jump from a plane and then, one of them, the sky surfer, performs stunts on a surfboard, while the other athlete, the camera flyer, videotapes the action from a helmet camcorder as the two descend, separately parachuted, from 13,123 feet (4,000 meters) in the sky.

This action can include gymnastic or ballet-like spinning and twisting, as well as actual surfing motions. In sky surfing, an athlete can move from left to right and vice versa; and up and down, as well as forward and backward. To capture the performance, the camera operator also needs to flip, spin, and roll, synchronizing his or her movements with that of the sky surfer.

History of the Sport

The origins of sky surfing began around 1980, when sky divers in California started doing freefalls while lying flat on boogie boards, which added speed and directional control to their descents. It was Frenchman Joel Cruciani, however, who, in 1987, jumped from a plane with a small surfboard bound to his feet using snowboard bindings. He repeated this traditional surfing stance—but in the sky—for the movie *Hibernator*.

In 1988, Frenchman Laurent Bouquet used a skateboard-size board, strapped to his feet, which was more easily controlled than the type used by Cruciani. Shortly thereafter, the French **BASE (Building/Antenna tower/Span/Earth) jumper** and parachutist **Patrick de Gayardon** created a system that allowed the athlete to release the board

Spectacular sky surfing over the Swiss mountains near Samedan in the St. Moritz area on September 16, 1995. The ski resort St. Moritz is located on the right; the lakes, from foreground to background, are Lake St. Moritz, Lake Sils, and Lake Silvaplana. (AP Photo)

during freefall, to gain control over his or her fall. de Gayardon also played the character "Silver Surfer" in the movie *Pushing the Limits 2.*

The sport spread quickly; by 1990, several European jumpers became involved with sky surfing, as did Jerry Loftis, the first American to tackle this sport. In the fall of 1990, the World Freestyle Championships were held in Texas. This competition was the first time that judges considered the quality of the video shot during the performance to determine the winners.

Photographer Pete McKeeman was the pioneer who captured many of the initial competitive surfs for posterity. With video serving as a required portion of a competition, sky surfing quickly became a sport ideally suited for television clips. In 1991, the athletic shoe company Reebok released a sky surfing commercial featuring de Gayardon with the theme of "Life Is Short. Play Hard." In the commercial, de Gayardon was wearing Reebok Pump Cross Trainers.

It is difficult to know exactly how many people are sky surfing. ESPN notes that, worldwide, there are approximately two dozen top-class sky surfing pairs. A study in the United Kingdom reveals that, in 1999, approximately 189,000 sky surfing descents took place in the country; in 2000, that figure jumped to approximately 220,250.

From 1995 through 2000, sky surfing was part of the **X Games**. When it was included, it was the most expensive event of those games because of the cost of being transported to the "starting line" that was so high in the sky (Sapiee 2000).

For the U.S. sky surfing team to compete in five events, including the X Games, it cost between $40,000 and $45,000 for equipment, training, and travel. Teams traveling from foreign countries also needed to add in the costs for traveling to the United States for the X Games.

Prize money does exist, but sky surfing is not a lucrative sport. ESPN estimated that, in 1996, if a sky surfing athlete took all the prize money available (as Bob Greiner and Cliff Burch, gold medal winners of the 1996 X Games, nearly did), the most they could have earned that year was $22,000.

Top sky surfers make an average of 500 jumps per year. Assuming that each jump allows for 1 minute of intense training, jumpers get, at most, 10 minutes of training time, spaced out over an 8- to 10-hour day. This adds up to slightly more than 8 hours of training time—per year.

Sky surfing athletes have created numerous intriguing slang words, such as "chicken soup" for a jump that does not go as planned; "burble" for the rough air found above the freefalling athlete; and "chop" (to jettison a sky board in an emergency), among others. One sky surfing move is known as a "helicopter," wherein the athlete spins his or her body, so that the board appears like chopper blades.

Sky Surfing Equipment

Recommended equipment for sky surfing includes a hard helmet and shoes with foot bindings on the board, plus a jumpsuit that fits tightly on the legs. The board should be lightweight and smooth, with rubber edges; the recommended width is 11 inches (28 centimeters).

Costs to participate in the sport can be prohibitive. According to ESPN, each jump costs about $18 in the United States and $20–$34 in Europe; this generally covers each person's portion of the plane rental fees. Camera helmets cost between $300–$700; parachute rigs, $4,000–$5,000; the skyboard, $600–$700; jump suits, $300; and the digital camcorder, $2,000–$3,000. Sky surfers also should have a cutaway cable so that they can quickly disconnect the board in case of emergency.

Sky Surfing Risks and Injuries

Not surprisingly, sky surfing has significant risk factors, including a potential collision of the two jumpers. Surfers can be moving at speeds more than 120 miles (193 kilometers) per hour and collisions can be fatal.

In August 1998, America's first sky surfer, Jerry Loftis, died when his chute failed to open during the World Free Fall Convention in Illinois. In February 2000, British sky surfing champion Chris Gauge died in a jump when his parachute failed to open. He had won the British championship in August 1999 and was ranked eighth in the world in a match held in Australia in October 1999. In January 2004, Australia's number-one-ranked female sky surfer, Pauline Richards, died during a heavy landing; her equipment was said to have been properly functioning. On December 14, 1996, while sky surfing for a Mountain Dew commercial, Rob Harris (the 1995 X Games gold medal winner) was killed in an accident.

SNOWBOARDING

In the sport of snowboarding, an athlete binds his or her feet to a board that resembles a wide ski or perhaps a cross between a surfboard and a ski. Snowboarding

Ross Rebagliati of Canada skis to victory in the first-ever Men's Giant Slalom snowboarding competition, February 8, 1998, in Yamanouchi, Japan. (AP Photo/Robert F. Bukaty)

athletes do not use poles to navigate down the slopes; instead, they learn to balance themselves as they accelerate downhill by centering their weight on the board and holding their arms out to their sides.

As the athlete—sometimes called a "boarder"—travels down a snowy incline, he or she may perform tricks that resemble ones used in skateboarding. Snowboarding tricks are numerous and include the following:

- "Ollie": a jump into the air; snowboarders often combine this with other tricks
- "Grab": while in the air, snowboarders bend their knees and then grab the snowboard with one or two hands; a "tail grab" occurs when the boarder grabs the back end of the board.
- "Fakie": snowboarders ride backward and often combine this feat with other tricks
- "Aerial Spins": a half spin in the air is a 180; a complete spin is 360; a Norwegian snowboarder named Terje Haakonsen performs "1080s," spinning completely around three times
- "Shifty": the rider rotates the snowboard by 90 degrees by shifting his or her hip; the athlete then returns the board to the original position
- "Soup": the rider starts out with an "ollie," then lands on the nose—or the front—of the board

A popular snowboarding technique is known as jibbing. In urban jibbing, boarders use man-made objects, such as ledges and handrails, to perform maneuvers in nonhilly venues; jibbing can also take place using natural elements such as stumps and fallen trees.

A variety of more extreme subdisciplines of snowboarding have arisen over the past two decades, more extreme because of the speed involved, the venues chosen, the tricks performed, and so forth. In large part because of extreme snowboarders, people who snowboard have earned a reputation as daredevils, adrenaline junkies, and rebellious outcasts who identify with the counterculture.

Although there is some truth to that assertion for many snowboarders, conflicting information exists about the risk levels of snowboarding. On the one hand, the National Ski Areas Association, after reviewing fatality statistics, stated that snowboarding is significantly safer than bicycling or swimming. That said, another study labels snowboarding as the third most dangerous sport, behind boxing and tackle football.

Perhaps the reason for the conflicting results is this: risks taken by snowboarders vary significantly and, as one would expect, the more risks taken and the more extreme the subdiscipline of snowboarding followed, the more potential dangers exist. Perhaps each of these studies reflects segments of the snowboarding population in different proportions and therefore shows different conclusions.

Without question, snowboarding is a popular sport. According to the National Sporting Goods Association, there are approximately 6.6 million snowboarders in the United States, with half of them between the ages of 7 and 17, and 75 percent of them under the age of 24. Globally, it is estimated that 18.5 million people snowboard. It is also estimated that 70 percent of snowboarders are male, making teenage boys and young adult males the largest boarding demographic. Snowboarding is also one of the world's fastest growing sports; participation increased by 385 percent from 1988 through 2003.

Some snowboarders board in terrain parks because these parks contain ready-made snowboarding jumps, as well as rail slides, which are objects on which snowboarders can learn to slide their boards and still maintain a sense of balance. These parks usually contain half-pipes, as well, which are snow formations with rounded sides; snowboarders gain momentum on the half-pipe, and then they ride up one side, go into the air and then perform tricks. Parks designate snowboarding areas as easy (marked by a green circle); intermediate (marked by a blue square); or difficult (marked by a black diamond), so that boarders can choose the best levels for their abilities and avoid areas they are not yet prepared to tackle.

Snowboarding is an unusual sport in that, in less than 40 years, it evolved from a new and unstructured cutting-edge activity to an Olympic sport.

PHILOSOPHY OF SNOWBOARDING
Although many snowboard fanatics enthuse about the thrill and the rush of snowboarding, the feeling that snowboarding provides has also been described as "soulful" and a way to connect with nature. "Just as **skateboarding** and surfing have a Zen-like quality to them, snowboarding, especially in deep, fresh powder, delivers a sensation that is about as close to pure harmony as any extreme sport offers" (Tomlinson 2004, 112).

The belief system of the now-defunct International Snowboard Federation (ISF) also sheds light on the values of snowboarders; the ISF stated that it was "not just a sports federation, but a lifestyle/peace movement and philosophy." When snowboarding, members of the ISF would hope to "race hard, maybe earn a few bucks, then party afterward" (http://www.natives.co.uk/news/2002/0702/05fed.htm).

HISTORY OF THE SPORT

Snurfing

Although people had attempted to surf on the snow for decades before the 1960s, the beginning of snowboarding as a sport is usually said to be 1965. That year, Sherman Poppen, an engineer in Michigan, wanted his daughter Wendy to be able to surf down a snowy slope; to achieve that end, he screwed together a pair of **children's** skis to create what he called a "snow surfer" or a "snurfer."

Other children saw Wendy's snurfer and they wanted one, as well; Poppen contacted the Brunswick Corporation, and that company, which normally manufactures bowling equipment, began manufacturing and selling snurfers. To provide some stability, ropes were attached to the snurfer's front so that the people could ride the boards sideways and hold on to the ropes. Snurfing tournaments began to be held and, largely because of a young teen named Jake Burton Carpenter, snurfing evolved into the modern-day sport of snowboarding.

Burton Carpenter skied and surfed, and was a natural at snurfing. He even won $250 in a snurfing tournament, but he felt confined by the limitations of the sport and by the lack of venues for snurfing. Overwhelmingly, ski resorts did not allow snurfers to share space with them; the derogatory term of "shredder" for a snowboarder came from a common skier belief that snowboarders were damaging or "shredding" the slopes. When snowboarding was a newer sport, most people, according to a sales manager for snowboarding equipment, "visualize[d] snowboarders as a bunch of skate rats who are going to terrorize the mountain" (Booth and Thorpe 2007, 288).

The clash between skiers and snowboarders is somewhat predictable. Skiing is a more expensive sport, with expected rules of conduct on the slopes and a focus on disciplined technique. Snowboarding appeals more to creative and individualistic people, often those with small budgets and a desire for free and open experimentation. Overall, when compared with skiers, snowboarders are younger and less educated, and usually are single males with lower incomes who often identify with the counterculture.

Snurfing Evolves

An uneasy to a sometimes hostile relationship between boarders and skiers still existed when Jake Burton Carpenter decided to experiment with his snurf board. To that end, he hiked up Stratton Mountain in Vermont to a ski resort that had closed for the night. He then tested various moves and techniques. He envisioned a board that had more potential; to accomplish that goal, he widened and modified the snurfing board so that the riders' feet were attached to the board, which increased the boarders' balance. Although his invention was initially greeted with some suspicion—and although it was banned from use in snurfing tournaments—Burton snowboards are now one of the most respected brand names in the snowboarding market.

During that same era, Tom Sims also created his own version of a snowboard and formed his own company; another early innovator was Dimitrije Milovich from the eastern coast of the United States, who created a more advanced board but one too costly for the average boarder. Then, a man named Jeff Grell created practical and effective snowboard bindings. These innovations allowed the sport to gain more momentum, with surfers and skateboarders easily adapting to the new sport and others eager to try it out.

Beginning of Competitions

Also aiding snowboarding's momentum was the recession in the 1980s in the United States. Because of the sluggish economic conditions, ski resorts saw a drop in revenues; to combat this, many resorts began allowing snowboarders to use their slopes and, by the mid-1980s, 80 to 90 percent of the ski resorts did so. (However, even today, a few holdout ski resorts will not allow snowboarders to use their runs.)

The 1980s also saw the start of organized competition, including the U.S. Open, wherein athletes from around the world competed. In 1983, the United States hosted the first world championships and, in 1987, a world tour was formed, with two stops in the United States and two in Europe.

By 1988, however, snowboarding still accounted for only 6 percent of the overall usage of ski slopes and, that year, *Time* magazine dubbed snowboarding as the worst new sport. Perhaps some of *Time* magazine's negativity arose from the outlandish behavior demonstrated by some of the snowboarders. Damien Sanders and **Shaun Palmer**, for example, were well known for their wild antics; the latter was credited with jumping out of a hotel room window; tossing a snowboard into a Japanese bath that was considered sacred; and throwing a hot dog at an event organizer.

Positive press also appeared in the late 1980s, as mainstream media began reporting on snowboarding. Moreover, snowboarding magazines began to appear, including *Transworld Snowboarding* and *Snowboarder*, and films such as *Snowboarders in Exile* (1990) were released. Perhaps even more important was the attention given to snowboarders by corporate sponsors who saw an opportunity to reach the young male market through the lure of snowboarding. It was to the sponsors' advantage to cultivate the aggressive and daring image of snowboarders in the media, so that the ads appealed to the target market.

Meanwhile, snowboarding continued to grow, worldwide, with the ISF forming in 1990. By the mid-1990s, snowboarders were located on at least three continents and in 33 countries, with more than $1 million available in prize money for professional snowboarders.

Other opportunities were expanding for boarders. In 1996, big air tricks were first permitted in the U.S. Open and, in 1997, snowboarders competed in the **X Games**, with Peter Line winning for the men and Tina Dixon for the women. In 1998, the X Games were televised in 198 countries with audio available in 21 languages. Corporate sponsors of professional snowboarders included Target, Visa, Nike, Mountain Dew, Campbell's Soup, and Boost Mobile, among others.

The Olympics

In 1998, the sport of the counterculture—snowboarding—was added to the Winter Olympics, held in Nagano, Japan; specific events held included the giant slalom and half-pipe. The giant slalom event is considered a snowboarding Alpine event and the half-pipe event is considered a snowboarding freestyle event.

Snowboarding had its share of controversies in the 1998 Olympics. The first one occurred when the International Olympic Committee (IOC) gave the jurisdiction of Olympic snowboarding to the *Fédération Internationale de Ski* (FIS, International Ski Federation) rather than to the ISF, the organization that oversaw snowboarding competitions, including the U.S. Open. One of the world's best snowboarders, Terje Haakonsen from Norway, refused to attend the Olympics for that reason.

Snowboarding events went on as planned, however, accompanied by **music** by Metallica, Pearl Jam, and Cyprus Hill's *Hits from the Bong*. Ross Rebagliati from Canada won a gold medal for the men's slalom event, which he dedicated to a friend who had recently died in an avalanche.

Three days later, however, Rebagliati had his medal taken away because of a positive postrace test for marijuana; he tested at 17.8 nanograms per milliliter, exceeding the 15.0 limit. This decision was challenged with Rebagliati's supporters stating that he tested positive after inhaling secondhand smoke at a party and with rumors circulating that, if Rebagliati was not allowed to keep his medal, none of the other snowboarders would, either. Ultimately, the Court of Arbitration in Sport determined that the medal was taken away because of an FIS drug policy; under the IOC rules, however, marijuana was considered restricted rather than banned, and so the medal was returned to Rebagliati.

In an interview, Rebagliati said that,

> It would be hard to deny the fact that I probably got 300% more exposure from it [the medal controversy] than without it ... I didn't really want it to happen that way, but you roll with the punches and hopefully you can come out on top. (Love and Brookler 1999)

This controversy highlighted the culture clashes occurring between the more traditional elements of the Olympics and the renegade lifestyle embraced by some snowboarders. "Within some of the sport's core circles," a writer from *Time* magazine pointed out, "pot has been a common part of the life-style. Along with freedom, travel and the pursuit of that perfect powder day, marijuana is regarded by certain riders as traditional ritual" (Galbraith n.d.).

Unlike the men's slalom, the men's half-pipe competition in 1998 transpired without a hitch. Gian Simmen from Switzerland captured the gold medal; Daniel Franck of Norway took the silver; and Ross Powers from the United States won the bronze. In the women's event, Nicola Thost from Germany won gold; Stine Brun Kjeldaas from Norway won the silver; and Shannon Dunn-Downing from the United States held on to win the bronze.

In the men's slalom, Thomas Prugger from Italy won the silver medal, with Ueli Kestenholz from Switzerland capturing the bronze. In the women's event, Karine Ruby from France won the gold medal; Heidi Renoth from Germany won the silver; and Brigitte Köck from Austria won the bronze.

In the 2002 Winter Olympics, held in Salt Lake City, Utah, in the United States, the parallel giant slalom event replaced the giant slalom event. In parallel slalom, two athletes compete directly against one another on a side-by-side course, making the event more exciting for spectators to watch; the winner advances to the next round. Also in 2002, the half-pipe course was increased in size, to make it a superpipe course.

In 2002, members of the United States team swept the men's superpipe event, the first sweep in the Winter Olympics for the United States since 1956. Medals went to Ross Powers, Danny Kass, and Jarret Thomas. In the parallel giant slalom, Philipp Schoch from Switzerland won the gold medal; Richard Richardsson from Sweden won the silver; and Chris Klug from the United States secured the bronze. Two years earlier, Klug had undergone a liver transplant to combat a rare liver disease.

For the women, Kelly Clark from the United States won the gold medal in the superpipe event; Doriane Vidal from France won the silver; and Fabienne Reuteler from Switzerland won the bronze. In the parallel giant slalom, Isabelle Blanc from France clinched the gold; Karine Ruby from France won the silver; and Lidia Trettel from Italy earned the bronze.

It is estimated that 32 percent of the people in the United States (nearly 92 million) watched the snowboarding competitions in which the three American males swept the superpipe medals and Kelly Clark won the women's superpipe gold. More than 18 million viewers said they wanted to try snowboarding.

In the 2006 Winter Olympics, which were held in Torino, Italy, snowboard cross was added as an event. In snowboard cross, four riders compete at the same time on a course that contains jumps and obstacles. The best two athletes in each round proceed to the next one, until the final round when winners are determined.

The U.S. teams performed well in the superpipe events. In the men's superpipe, **Shaun White** won the gold, and Danny Kass won the silver. Markku Koski from Finland secured the bronze. In the women's superpipe, Hannah Teter won the gold, and Gretchen Bleiler won the silver. Kjersti Buaas from Norway earned the bronze.

In the men's snocross, Seth Wescott won the gold. Radoslav Zidek from Slovenia won silver, and Paul-Henri Delerue from France won the bronze. In the women's event, Tanja Frieden from Switzerland won gold; Lindsey Jacobellis from the United States won silver; and Dominique Maltais from Canada won the bronze.

In the men's parallel giant slalom, Philipp Schoch from Switzerland won gold; Simon Schoch from Switzerland won silver; and Siegfried Grabner from Austria won bronze. In the women's event, Daniela Meuli from Switzerland won gold; Amelie Kober from Germany won the silver; and Rosey Fletcher from the United States won the bronze.

EXTREME SNOWBOARDING

In extreme snowboarding, slopes generally exceed 40 degrees in pitch, which increases the likelihood of falls and the consequences of them, should they occur; in some locales, boarders face the constant danger of falling off of steep cliffs. Athletes need to be well aware of the potential for avalanches and slough, the latter term referring to the small avalanches that can occur when a rider turns sharply on a steep angle, releasing the top layer of snow and possibly creating the conditions for a dangerous mini-avalanche.

One form of extreme snowboarding is the big air style, wherein boarders jump off of natural or man-made ramps and then perform tricks while in midair. Artificial ski ramps can be 100 feet (30 meters) high; although natural drop offs are not generally that high, with them, boarders must also contend with the unpredictability of natural terrain. In competitions, big air snowboarders receive points for height achieved, tricks performed, and solid landings attained.

Another form of extreme snowboarding is big mountain riding, in which boarders tackle especially challenging mountainous terrain, complete with cliffs and extreme weather conditions. According to Susanna Howe, big mountain riding is "downright dangerous: avalanches, sluffs, helicopter crashes, crevasses, rocks, and exposure to the elements" which "take their toll on those who aren't prepared or aren't lucky"

(Booth and Thorpe 2007, 292). Big mountain boarders need to be experienced in rock climbing, and knowledgeable about snow and weather conditions, emergency rescue techniques, and more before attempting this snowboarding subdiscipline.

Big mountain boarders meet annually in Switzerland for the Xtreme Verbier competition at the Bec des Rosses; this mountain is jagged and 10,570 feet (3,222 meters) in height. Competitors use binoculars to find the most advantageous starting points and then they hike to their chosen spots. Performances are judged on the "steepness, exposure, snow conditions, difficulty of terrain, obstacles, jumps, control, falls, continuity, pace, smooth transitions, style, technical ability, and energy" as they descend 1,640 feet (500 meters) (www2.thenorthface.com).

In 2008, 37 big mountain snowboarders competed in the 13th annual Xtreme Verbier, with Kaj Zackrisson from Sweden winning the competition after landing three "massive cliff drops" (First Tracks 2008). Although big mountain boarding participants are usually men, Julie Zell, Victoria Jealouse, and Tina Basich compete, as well.

Other forms of extreme snowboarding include boardercross, extreme downhill, and backcountry boarding. In boardercross, several athletes race against one another on courses with sharp burms or turns, which increase their speed. Jumps and moguls are scattered throughout the course and athletes must maintain control of themselves while achieving significant speed.

In extreme downhill, athletes race down steep courses, sometimes slalom style. Boarders can achieve speeds of up to 70 miles (112 kilometers) per hour. In wind snowboarding, athletes attach sails to their boards and the wind propels them downhill—and, sometimes, uphill, as well. In backcountry boarding, athletes tackle rough and isolated terrain, sometimes after being dropped off in a mountainous area by a helicopter.

Extreme competitions of note include the X Games, the **Gravity Games**, the U.S. Extreme Snowboarding Championships, and the World Extreme Championship.

In the U.S. Extreme Snowboarding Championships, which are held in Crested Butte, Colorado, boarders compete on courses with drop offs of 30 to 40 feet (9 to 12 meters), with significantly rocky areas; winners of this competition move on to the World Extreme Championships.

In freestyle competitions, the events held are usually half-pipe and slopestyle; race events include slalom, parallel slalom, giant slalom, and the super G. In the half-pipe, the curved course is between 250 and 350 feet (76 to 106 meters) long, with walls that are 7 to 14 feet (2 to 4 meters) high on either side. Athletes garner speed by riding the half-pipe and then they "catch air" and perform tricks; typically, a boarder performs 5 to 10 times in a single competitive performance.

In the slopestyle event, boarders tackle obstacles placed in random order. They perform tricks on rail slides or downed trees or whatever else suits their style. In extreme competitions, boarders are generally judged on their style; their aggressiveness; the execution of maneuvers; the degree of difficulty of the chosen tricks; the originality and variety of those maneuvers; and the number of falls, as well as how they occurred and how they affected the athlete's performance.

In the extreme competitions, the slalom courses are generally between 260 and 500 feet (79 to 152 meters) long; giant slalom courses are between 300 and 900 feet (91 to 274 meters) long; and super G courses are between 500 and 1,300 feet (152 to 396 meters) long.

SNOWBOARDING EQUIPMENT

Most boards are made from wood laminates. Snowboards range from 40 to 71 inches (100 to 181 centimeters) in length; shorter boards are usually chosen for big air. The width of the snowboard is usually between 7 and 10 inches (18 and 25 centimeters) in the center. Freestyle boards are more flexible than freeride boards, with flexible boards being more suitable for big air riding.

The best length for a snowboard also depends on a person's height and weight. Most people do best with a board that reaches their chins or mouths when the board is stood up, end to end. Heavier snowboarders can add a bit of length when choosing a board to compensate for their added weight. Boarders can expect to pay between $200 and $600 for their snowboard.

Snowboard boots can be soft or hard; snowboarders who attempt tricks usually prefer the flexibility of the softer boot. Bindings can be of the strap-on or step-in variety. Snowboarders often wear helmets, goggles, and gloves for protection, as well as padding. They also should wear sunblock as snow can reflect up to 90 percent of the sun's rays.

SNOWBOARDING RISK AND INJURIES

Hazards include rocks covered with snow, unexpected or dangerous drop offs or cliffs, and extreme cold. Falls lead to the most injuries, with one-quarter of injuries occurring on a snowboarder's first experience; nearly one-half of injuries occur to people who are in their first snowboarding season. The injuries tend to be relatively minor, with sprains and fractures being the most likely. The likelihood of a fatal accident is 0.000000231 per day, which is lower than the rate for skiers.

Snowboarders must be alert to signs of hypothermia and react quickly if they are noted; signs can include chills, then sleepiness and confusion. To prevent hypothermia, boarders should eat well before boarding and should wear layers of warm clothing, including head protection. Dehydration is another concern, as is frostbite.

Boarders who choose remote mountainous locales face the danger of avalanches and should listen to avalanche reports to avoid the danger spots. All snowboarders should listen to weather reports, board with others, and carry two-way radios to contact one another, if necessary. Boarders who snowboard in remote locales should also carry small shovels, probes to seek out others covered in snow, first aid equipment, and food and water.

One study shows that snowboarders are twice as likely as skiers to suffer certain injuries, including serious fractures, such as concussion, and dislocated joints. Snowboarders are twice as likely as skiers to have teeth knocked out and to lose consciousness.

Injuries can be significant after a hard-fought competition. In the 2002 X Games, one participant said that, with his four cracked ribs and twisted knee, he was the least injured person there, adding that others had fractured skulls and gotten "massive" back injuries.

Snowboarding injuries may appear in the news, as the accidents that cause the injuries can be quite dramatic. In 2004, professional snowboarder Tara Dakides intended to demonstrate a big air snowboarding performance live on *The Late Show with David Letterman*. Because of melting snow, Dakides did not get the take off she needed and she fell 25 feet (7.6 meters) to the asphalt below, knocking herself unconscious as her head split open.

In February 2005, a 16-year-old male snowboarder collided into—and killed—a 29-year-old female skier. This accidental death also received attention in the press, causing some to once again suggest that snowboarding was a risky, radical sport.

As snowboarders continue to push their limits, the risks also increase. A number of top snowboarders have died in their pursuit of the sport, including Craig Kelly, Jeff Anderson, Tristan Picot, Line Ostvold, Josh Malay, and Tommy Brunner.

POP CULTURE

Snowboarders became part of the **video game** world, with the release of Playstation's *Cool Boarders* and Shaun Palmer's *Pro-Snowboarder*. Other snowboarding video games include *1080 (degrees) Snowboarding*; *1080 (degrees) Avalanche*; *Amped: Freestyle Snowboarding*; *Amped 2*; *Amped 3*; *Massive Snowboarding*; *Snowboard Super Cross Series*; *Snowboard Kids*; *ESPN's Winter X Games Snowboarding*; and more.

Jumping the Mount Baker Highway Gap

The Mount Baker Ski Area is located in Bellingham, Washington. Snowboarders—professional and amateur alike—attempt to jump across a two-lane highway while riding their snowboards to repeat the feat first performed by snowboarder Shawn Farmer in 1989.

After Farmer successfully completed the jump, he stripped from the waist up and repeated the jump; his second jump was recorded for *Totally Board* (2002), a snowboard film created by Standard Films of Tahoe.

Snowboarders interested in duplicating this jump must first board their way through a winding woods. Upon reaching the clearing, they need to make their jump as high as 60 feet (18 meters) above the highway to complete the crossing; some add spins and flips to their journey across the highway.

Locals say they do not remember any major injuries occurring from these jumps, although one of them points out that a faulty jump would be like falling off a 40-foot (12-meter) building and then landing on the concrete below.

Mount Baker has another claim to fame; it receives the highest amount of annual snowfall, worldwide, for a ski and snowboard locale. Mount Baker also holds the world record for the largest amount of verified snowfall in one season, with 1,140 inches (2,895 centimeters) during the 1998–1999 ski and snowboard season.

The Rebagliati Controversy

In April 2008, snowboarder Ross Rebagliati, who had won an Olympic gold medal—and then had it temporarily removed when he tested positively for marijuana following the race—settled a defamation lawsuit against CTV Television and the producer of the syndicated television show *Whistler*.

Rebagliati had objected to a character named Beck MacKaye who was a former Olympic snowboarder whose death was connected to alcoholism, blackmail, and womanizing. This character lived in the Whistler ski resort, which is where Rebagliati lived when he won the gold medal. He also claimed that the MacKaye character bore a striking similarity to him in appearance.

The show's producers denied any connection; the terms of the settlement were not disclosed.

A snowboarding movie called *First Descent* was released on December 2, 2005. Its producers wanted to document the history of snowboarding and its fast ascent to a major sport. Other snowboarding movies include *Chulksmack*; *Pulse*; *Shakedown*; *Video Gangs*; *The Resistance*; *True Life*; *Critical Conditions*; *Decade*; *Technical Difficulties*; *Back in Black*; *Notice to Appear*; *Return of the Wildcats*; *The Haakonsen Faktor*; *White Balance*; *Full Metal Edge*; and *Nine Lives*.

See also Shaw, Brooke

SNOWMOBILING, EXTREME (SNOCROSS)

Snocross athletes race against one another on an obstacle-filled course, using specially crafted snowmobiles. Racers achieve speeds of up to 60 miles (96 kilometers) per hour, jump up to 30 feet (9 meters) to circumvent obstacles, and navigate sharp turns. The name "snocross" is a combination of the words **"motocross"** and "snowmobile," and the sport resembles a motocross event taking place on snow. Elimination rounds are used to narrow down the playing field, and the person with the fastest time in the final race wins.

Although snocross is an extreme sport, the average snowmobiler is not participating in extreme activities. In 2006, the average user was 42 years old, as compared with 37 years old in 1997; 92 percent of them are men. Most participants are married, and 80 percent of them use snowmobiles on established trails; some also use the snowmobile to go ice fishing.

Snowmobiles somewhat resemble motor-cycles, with the back wheel being replaced with a rubber tread with paddles; different lengths of paddles can handle snow in different conditions. Two steering skis replace the front wheel. Snowmobilers use the handlebars to steer; a thumb throttle plus a lever on the tread both act as brakes. For snocross—the more extreme version of snowmobiling—the snow-mobiles have better suspension systems and more powerful engines.

Snocross racing is practiced in places with colder winters, with Wisconsin, Minnesota, and Michigan serving as popular places in the United States for snocross events. Participants are usually teenagers and adults in their 20s and 30s. Professional snocross athletes often have budgets of at least half a million dollars to transport their equipment—and their mechanics team—to races.

This sport became an event in the **X Games** in 1998. One of the most exciting X Games

Jimmy Fejes from Anchorage, Alaska, performs a back-flip 12 feet (3.6 meters) in the air with his 550-pound (250-kilogram), 600 cc Yamaha snowmobile during the Freestyle Snowmobile demo during the X Games. (AP Photo/Nathan Bilow)

races occurred in snocross in 2006, when Blair "Superman" Morgan won his fifth gold medal after lagging behind three other competitors; that year, the riders needed to complete 15 rounds, rather than the six previously required. By the end of the 2006–2007 season, Morgan had won 84 out of 200 national events. In 2007, snocross freestyle became the second snocross discipline to be included in the Winter X Games. A **video game** called *Snocross 2* features Morgan. Another snocross video game is titled *SnoCross Extreme*.

HISTORY OF THE SPORT

Without a snowmobile, the sport of snocross would not exist. In 1927, Carl J. Eliason of Sayner, Wisconsin, was issued a patent for a snow machine, a predecessor of the modern snowmobile. Thirteen more patents for similar items were approved between Eliason's invention and the year 1962.

It was a man named Joseph-Armand Bombardier, though, who successfully invented a vehicle for travel over the snow. Born in 1907, Bombardier seemed born to tinker; it was said that, by the age of 10, he was able to create a model of a tractor using just a cigar box and a broken alarm clock. Growing up in snowy Quebec, he decided to craft a vehicle to drive in the snow. At the age of 15, in an early attempt, he attached a motor to what was really a large sleigh; it was so noisy that his father insisted that he stop using the vehicle.

In the 1930s, he developed a much more workable model; in 1937, he sold 12 of his "B7" machines and, in 1942, he formed his company, *l'Auto-Neige Bombardier Limitée*. He then spent years streamlining a motorized sled intended for 12 passengers, one that was used for postal services, police, and the military in snowy conditions. In 1958, Bombardier invented the "Ski-Doo," which is considered the first modern-day snowmobile. He began producing them in 1959; he received a Canadian patent in 1960 and a United States patent in 1962. They sold especially well in the United States, Canada, and Scandinavia.

In 1970, the U.S. Snowmobile Association was formed, sanctioning more than 250 races that winter that took place over frozen lakes; increasingly larger engines were used on the vehicles, which gave them more power but also made them more difficult to handle.

For about 20 years, racing was the only competitive snowmobiling event. In the 1990s, though, American and Canadian snowmobilers began to go freeriding in remote areas that could be accessed only by helicopters—which was an expensive proposition—or by sled. Many adventurous snowmobilers began incorporating jumping and dropping off cliffs into the overall extreme sporting experience.

In 2001, professional snowboarder Jim Rippey performed a snowmobile backflip, which was recorded and used in the video titled *Slednecks 4*.

By 2006, the snowmobile industry was a $2.2 billion business. Although that sounds significant, only 164,860 snowmobiles were sold worldwide in 2006, compared with the 239,000 sold in 2000. Meanwhile, the age of the average snowmobiler was continuing to rise. Therefore, from the perspective of people who make money in the snowmobile industry, the figures were somewhat alarming. The average cost of a snowmobile, which was $8,269, partially explained why more young people were not purchasing them; this is not an amount of expendable income readily available to the average man in his 20s. To entice more people to purchase snowmobiles, especially those in a younger demographic, Bombardier Recreational Products began offering a freestyle snowmobile for $4,000.

The debut of snocross freestyle in 2007 in the Winter X Games portends well for those who want to attract the young demographic, as teenagers and people in their 20s make up a significant portion of the X Games audience. During the snocross freestyle event in the X Games, with "a few thousand frozen fans looking on, 400-pound snowmobiles hurtled several 100-foot jumps as riders did aerial stunts on a snowy course on Buttermilk Mountain" (Higgins 2007). Competitors were scored on the difficulty of tricks performed and the amount of time it took to complete the track, which had multiple jumps and obstacles.

Tucker Hibbert from the United States won gold in the 2007 X Games with a time of 186.226 seconds. Hibbert is the second most successful snocross athlete, behind Blair Morgan, with 34 wins. Hibbert stopped participating in snocross for about three years to compete in motocross full time, but he returned to snocross in the 2006–2007 season. The silver medal went to Canadian Ryan Simons, with a time of 186.543 seconds. Simons was named Racer of the Year in 2007. T. J. Gulla won the bronze with a time of 192.684 seconds. This event replaced a freestyle motocross event that took place in the snow; plans are to keep motocross as an event in the Summer X Games.

EXPN.com named some of the sport's other stellar athletes in May 2007, including the following:

- Chris Burandt, who EXPN believes may be the world's best snowmobile freestyler
- Jimmy Fejes, known as "Jimmy Blaze," who is the only freestyler who works full time as a snowmobiler, spending 300 days on the road; he participated as the token snowmobiler on the Crusty Demons of Dirt tour, was the third person to successfully flip a snowmobile, and is working on a double flip
- Heath Frisby, who broke his back in 2006 after a 200-foot (61-meter) jump and who spent five months in a cast
- Justin Hoyer, the only person to flip both dirt bikes and snowmobiles
- Kourtney Hungerford, who built the first snowmobile freestyle ramps

SNOWMOBILING RISKS AND INJURIES

In deep snow, snowmobiles can be difficult to handle and the sled can set off avalanches. More typically, a snowmobile can become bogged down or stuck in the snow; the snowmobile can start to sink and will need to be pulled out of the snow by another snowmobile. For this reason, it is never advisable to snowmobile alone.

Crashing into windshields has cost some snowmobilers their teeth and at least one person significantly damaged his voice box by this type of impact; for that reason, windshields are seldom part of snowmobiles.

A certified snocross trainer, Mike Pilato, gathered data from the 2004–2005 season to determine the most common snocross injuries and potential ways to reduce them. The most common injuries were bruises, fractures, strains, and sprains, with forearm fractures in the wrist especially common. Of these snocross injuries, 15.5 percent were fractures, with 30 percent more injuries sustained on the riders' left side of the body than the right.

If the rider sustained a bloody wound, there was a 53 percent chance that the face was bleeding and a 66 percent chance that the head was bloodied. Chin cuts occurred when the helmet buckle hit the handlebars. Seventy-two percent of the injuries in Pilato's study occurred during Saturday races.

Pilato predicts that the number of spinal injuries sustained through snocross will increase, and he anticipates that snocross athletes will suffer from degenerative arthritis more often than the average person.

SNOWMOBILING EQUIPMENT

Pilato recommends that riders wear helmets, and use elbow protection, kidney belts, and chest protection. If a rider already has a knee injury, he recommends a knee brace, but he does not believe that knee braces have a preventative value.

SPONSORSHIPS AND ADVERTISING, EXTREME SPORTS

In 2002, *Demographics* magazine indicated that 58 million Americans were between the ages of 10 and 24, with a collective annual buying power of $250 billion. This demographic group not only has enormous financial clout, but also has far fewer financial responsibilities than Americans who are older than 24, thereby making their income truly more disposable. It is not surprising, then, that corporations and their marketing teams are actively searching for ways to target this segment of the American population.

As CNN had already noted, four years earlier, "'X,' whether for extreme sports or Generation X, has come to symbolize a romantic image of youth in America today—edgy individualism, a hint of danger, a cool and casual style. The image has struck a chord not just in the neighborhoods of America, but on Madison Avenue" (Hattori 1998).

At approximately the same time as when the *Demographics* data was collected, more than 200,000 male teens were watching the 2001 **Gravity Games**, which was an increase in viewership numbers over the 2000 figures. When adding in viewership numbers from men in their early 20s, results indicate that nearly 320,000 males ages 12 to 24 watched the 2001 Gravity Games. During the 2000 Summer **X Games**, the number of 12- to 17-year-old viewers increased to about 219,000 viewers (an 86 percent increase compared with the previous games). For the 18 to 34 male demographic, the ratings increased by about 40 percent to about 330,000 viewers.

Considering that a key demographic—people between the ages of 10 and 24—had a substantial amount of buying power, and considering that teenagers and young adults were watching extreme sports in ever increasing numbers, it is not surprising that corporations began targeting the extreme sports fan base through their marketing efforts. These corporations began to use extreme sports activities in their advertising or they began sponsoring extreme sports athletes or extreme sporting events—and some companies even purchased and began managing extreme sports teams.

This partnership between corporate sponsors and extreme athletes is somewhat ironic, as many extreme sports participants have cited the opportunity to perform as an individual as one of the reasons that they were initially drawn to their sport, in particular, and to the extreme sporting arena, in general. Nevertheless, these corporations saw an opportunity to market their products and services to a key demographic: teenagers and young adults—and the teenagers and young adults responded to the advertising messages that they received. Through this interaction, numerous extreme sports athletes became marketable commodities, and extreme sports, overall, became a multimillion dollar industry in the United States and in other places around the world.

Following are just some of the dollar figures associated with extreme sporting events:

- Skateboarding is a $2.3 million industry
- Surfing, worldwide, is a $5.7 billion industry
- The 2002 Gravity Games generated approximately $25 million for the host city of Cleveland, Ohio
- Sponsorship dollars for extreme sports overall skyrocketed from a respectable $23 million in 1993 to an astounding $135 million just five years later
- In 1999, corporate sponsors paid $3 million for premium packages in the Gravity Games
- Also in 1999, the X Games raised $22 million in sponsorship deals

One extreme sports writer summed up the situation in this way: "Whether it is young people **kite surfing** while drinking Coca-Cola or **mountain biking** while drinking Mountain Dew, the media and the market economy have certainly found their product niche in extreme sports" (Bach 2007, 74).

EXTREME GAMES—OR THE X GAMES

In the early 1990s, Ron Semiao, the program director for ESNP2, noticed how some companies were using extreme sports activities in their marketing. He therefore decided to further explore the connection between extreme sports and media. Semiao searched for magazines that focused solely on extreme sports, but had little luck; because of this void, he sensed a tremendous opportunity. In 1993, Semiao presented the idea of hosting an action sports competition with athletes from around the globe. ESPN management agreed and so, on April 12, 1994, station representatives announced that the first annual Extreme Games would be held in June 1995 in Rhode Island.

Approximately 198,000 spectators attended the Extreme Games, wherein athletes competed in 27 events. The seven sponsors for these events were Advil, Mountain Dew, Taco Bell, Chevy Trucks, AT&T, Nike, and Miller Lite; although this was not the first pairing of extreme sports and advertising/sponsorship, the success of the first Extreme Games provided the momentum that explains how the two became so intricately entwined. Because of the large amount of attention paid to the Extreme Games, it was decided to hold the event annually, rather than every other year, as initially planned.

In 1996, the name of the event was changed to "X Games." ESPN decided to create a competition that focused on winter extreme sports, which opened up even more sponsorship opportunities. Thus, the name of the original event changed from "Extreme Games" to the "Summer X Games."

The X Games continued to expand in scope and in viewership. In 1998, the games were held in San Diego, drawing a quarter of a million spectators, and the television audience was estimated to reach 74 million. San Diego also benefited as $35 million was funneled into the city. In 1999, the games were held in San Francisco and the prize money totaled more than $1 million. The more attention that the X Games received, the more attractive they became to corporate sponsors that were wishing to target the teenage and young adult demographic.

Moreover, the benefits of becoming host cities were growing increasingly large. The economic windfall for host cities increased from $5 million in 1996 to $30 million in 1998; San Diego benefited from $14 million directly and an additional $18 million indirectly.

EFFECTIVENESS OF SPONSORSHIPS

How effective are extreme sports and sponsorship relationships? A 2005 survey by Performance Research tested the effectiveness of extreme sports sponsorship, with this level of awareness of individual sponsors:

- Mountain Dew (92 percent)
- Taco Bell (85 percent)
- Nike (80 percent)
- Coors Light (75 percent)
- AT&T (62 percent)
- Chevy Trucks (55 percent)

Approximately 46 percent of the viewers expressed cynicism about the sponsor's motives, however, stating they were "only trying to sell me something." Fifty-two percent stated that sponsorships of extreme sports events did not change their impression of the sponsoring companies, with 57 percent saying that they were not more likely to buy a product from one of these companies. Thirty-two percent said that they would "almost always" or "frequently" buy one of these products. This level of loyalty is less than that found with auto racing, professional tennis, golf, cycling, basketball, football, baseball, and the America's Cup, but higher than Olympic and World Cup sponsors.

GRAVITY GAMES

Sponsorships have been a component of another extreme sports competition: the Gravity Games. These games, which began in Providence, Rhode Island, in 1999, also feature multiple extreme sports from various countries. Initially, the sponsors of the Gravity Games were manufacturers of products that would appeal to young **skateboarders** and **BMX (bicycle motocross)** riders. Manufacturers of skating and biking clothes and gear also set up shop to sell their wares to athletes and spectators.

Three years later, though, when the Gravity Games were held in Cleveland, Ohio, the sponsors were targeting young adults rather than the skateboarding or bike riding teenager. The main sponsor was Saturn, which was giving away a custom skateboard deck and other prizes. Other sponsors included Kohl's department stores, which was promoting its Urban Pipeline clothing; and Lego, which featured skateboard street and vert building blog sets. Someone once built a skateboarding venue with these Legos, and a toy skateboarder could be run through the course.

MAJOR SPONSORS OF EXTREME SPORTING EVENTS

Key corporate players in extreme sports advertising include the following:

- Mountain Dew: This soft drink company created edgy commercials featuring extreme sports activities as part of their "Do the Dew" campaign. This campaign began in 1992.

Mountain Dew has been a sponsor for the X Games and they organized and manage the Dew Action Sports Tour.

- Red Bull: This energy drink company sponsors a significant number of extreme sports athletes and events, and also owns action sports teams. Plus, Red Bull has created new extreme sporting events.
- Vans: The manufacturer of extreme sports footwear creates and financially backs the Vans Warped Tour, which is a combination extreme sports and alternative **music** tour, plus the Vans Triple Crown, which is composed of three annual events for seven different extreme sports.
- Fox Racing: This extreme sports clothing company manufactures extreme sports gear, footwear, and apparel for **motocross**, BMX racing, mountain biking, and various snow sports.
- Schwinn: This bicycle company played a key role in the creation and development of the sport of BMX.
- Sony: Their **video game** system, PlayStation, sponsors a significant number of extreme sporting events, and the company produces video games that feature extreme sports.

Other companies that have sponsored extreme sporting events include Motorola, Ford Motor Company, Morningstar Foods, Adidas, Heineken, The Gap, Volkswagen, and Disney. Some of the more memorable ad slogans include Bell helmets ("Courage for your head") and Reebok ("Life Is Short. Play Hard."), the latter of which featured **sky surfing** in its commercials. Plus, as far back as 1997, the U.S. Marine Corps recognized a value in advertising during extreme sports games. According to one general, the goal was not to recruit the athletes—many of whom already sported piercings and tattoos—but the youth watching the games.

The general's comment brings up an interesting point: that the goal of the advertising is not to reach the athletes, but to reach the viewers. We can assume that advertising on extreme sports programming has been lucrative for the companies involved, as the advertising figures continue to increase—and so we can also assume that viewers who are watching extreme sports competitions are buying products and services from these advertisers.

Josie Appleton, in her article titled "What's So Extreme About Extreme Sports?" offers this explanation as to why:

> Deep down, we all feel that we should be pushing ourselves a bit more; the extreme sports industry sells the image of aspiration. Wear a "Just do it" cap; drink a can of "Live life to the max" Pepsi; talk on an X-Games mobile phone. This is about the appearance of living on the edge, posing at taking risks while actually doing nothing at all. In the passive act of buying a consumer good, you are offered thrills and spills. It's not the real act of grappling with a challenge, but the image of "pushing it to the MAX." This is why extreme sports are so hyped up: the adrenaline factor is sold in concentrated form. (Appleton 2005)

Even though the commercials need to appeal to the masses for the marketers' return on investment to be worthwhile to corporations, many commercials with extreme sports themes appear to be appealing to the elite extreme athlete. For example, the Hydra Fuel sports drink commercial states that "we didn't make them for the masses. We didn't make them for the average jock. We didn't make them for athletes who settle for second best," thus implying that their product is only for the extreme athlete who pushes beyond the normal limits of speed, height, or daring. Perhaps Appleton's contention that these commercials make us feels as though we are living on the edge—when in fact all we have done is purchase a product—provides a credible explanation as to why these commercials are effective.

EXTREME SPORTS VIDEOS AND OTHER MEDIA

Extreme athletes in numerous sports, including skiing and snowboarding, skateboarding, motocross, and more, have created videos of themselves and others performing extreme maneuvers. Prior to the invention of the VCR, spectators needed to either travel to attend an extreme sporting event—given that they knew about the event in the first place—or be at the mercy of television producers who would decide what events would be televised and when they would appear.

Once the VCR—and then the DVD players—debuted, though, increasing numbers of extreme athletes began creating, marketing, and selling videos. When Internet use became widespread, and YouTube became a viable way of sharing smaller clips of video, the number of extreme sports videos available for the average person to watch exploded. Type "YouTube Extreme Sports" into the Google search engine and you will literally get hundreds of thousands of results.

In the summer of 2001, ESPN used broadband and streaming media capabilities to allow people to watch the Summer X Games on their computers. Fifty thousand people in the Philadelphia area were the test market.

EXTREME SPORTS AND YOUNG CHILDREN

Toy manufacturers are marketing extreme sports concepts through the action figures and accessories that they sell. ESPN, for example, licensed JAKKS Pacific's Road Champs to use the name X Games while marketing their toys. Another company, X Concepts, creates extreme sports collectibles, while Spin Master was making 300,000 replicas of BMX bikes each week in 2000. Meanwhile, Taco Bell was putting extreme sports figures in their kids' meals.

Cartoons began to feature increasing numbers of extreme sports activities; examples include the Action Man and Max Steel cartoons. Extreme sports activities are also incorporated into numerous music videos, which generally appeal to older children and teenagers.

EXTREME SPORTS AND THE OLYMPICS

Sports that were once considered extreme are making their way into the Olympics; as two examples, snowboarding debuted in the 1998 Olympic Games and BMX events were included in the 2008 Summer Olympics.

Furthermore, marketers of the Olympic Games have decided to use the extreme concept in their advertising; this first occurred in ads for the 2002 Winter Olympics in Salt Lake City, Utah. Ratings for the previous winter games, held in Australia, were the worst ever, and organizers knew they needed to make a change; they also recognized the marketability of extreme sports, and so this is the promotional path they chose to take.

Vince Manze, co-president of the NBC Agency, had this to say about that decision:

> We are going to focus on the fact that the Winter Olympics are a littler wilder, a little more extreme. The popularity of Extreme Sports is not just with snow, but skateboarding,

street luge, inline skating, and all of the rest, which have just taken off over the last several years. (Gutman and Frederick 2002, 255)

Extreme sports that were not yet part of the Olympics sometimes showed up in advertisements for the 2002 Winter Games. Aerial photographer Tom Sanders, for example, photographed a **BASE (Building/Antenna tower/Span/Earth) jumping** commercial for Nike that was to run during the Olympic Games; he also photographed a man jumping out of an airplane while wearing skis for an NBC advertisement and promotional clip. Moreover, shortly before the Olympics began, NBC created and showed 20 different spots that focused on extreme sports, including aerial skiing and snowboarding.

POSITIVES AND NEGATIVES OF EXTREME SPORTS SPONSORSHIPS

Some observers believe that, once extreme sports athletes began accepting sponsorship dollars or even when they began participating in organized events sponsored by corporations, they had begun the process of "selling out" by refuting the alternative cultural values that they embraced when they first participated in extreme sports. Rather than focusing solely on individual achievement or embracing the freedoms inherent in bucking the mainstream sports world, the focus turned to the following:

- Breaking records of other extreme athletes
- Having spectators watch their achievements and performances
- Winning the sporting event
- Becoming a star athlete

Some of the more marketable extreme sports athletes have also used their accomplishments to brand and sell products, including apparel, sports gear, and the like.

Because of sponsorships, many extreme sporting events now have lucrative prize purses, some of them totaling in the millions. These prizes allow the elite in extreme sports—or at least the elite in some extreme sports—to earn a living by pursuing perfection in their chosen athletic endeavor. It stands to reason that, given the opportunity to pursue their particular sport full time, these athletes will continue to push the envelope and to stretch the physical boundaries of human endeavor.

Because of the attention provided by sponsors, today's extreme athletes receive more attention than ever before. Some extreme athletes have taken advantage of this name recognition by becoming public speakers and giving motivational speeches.

Sky diver Jim McCormick, as just one example, has provided motivational talks about calculating risks when making decisions, and the importance of self-confidence in all that a person does. McCormick says that, wherever he goes, people will approach him to share an extreme sports experience that has given them more confidence in other areas of their lives. McCormick also wrote the book *The Power of Risk: How Intelligent Choices Will Make You More Successful, A Step-by-Step Guide* (2008). He has completed more than 2,700 sky dives, and he has set five world records in sky diving. He was the U.S. delegate to the World Team 2006; he was also part of an international group that sky dived to the North Pole.

Mountain climber Sharon Wood, who had a fear of public speaking, also gives presentations. Through the act of presenting her seminars, she overcame that fear; it is her belief that fewer fears mean greater freedoms. In her seminars, she talks of ordinary people achieving great things, and she encourages people to look for their own untapped potential. Wood was the first North American woman to successfully climb the challenging west ridge–north face of Mount Everest.

On the positive side, extreme sports sponsorships can free up athletes to more fully pursue their chosen sports; extreme activities can also inspire others and provide a basis to share life's lessons.

Negative effects, however, also are associated with the lucrative prize purses that usually are funded through sponsorship dollars. Some athletes push their bodies too far in hopes of capturing an extreme sporting event title. Bill Gutman, author of *Being Extreme: Thrills and Dangers in the World of High-Risk Sports*, suggests that "Injuries and fatalities have undoubtedly risen because the numbers of participants are increasing, many of them taking excessive risks with a percentage not fully prepared for what they are attempting to do" (Gutman and Frederick 2002, 251).

Moreover, it is possible that the commercialism of extreme sports is in effect mainstreaming extreme sports by making them part of American culture. Extreme sports athletes initially were outside the usual boundaries, refusing to create or follow rules, and perhaps dressing and acting in an atypical manner; they created a subculture that was not part of the majority norm. Now, as extreme sports athletes become well known, children, teenagers, and young adults are wearing the same styles of clothing as their extreme sports heroes and wearing clothing lines that are sponsored by those heroes.

In what ways, then, are these extreme athletes different from those participating in more traditional sports? Has the partnership between extreme sports athletes and event organizers with corporate sponsors ruined what originally made extreme competitions unique? The answers to these questions are not clear cut.

See also Children and Extreme Sports; Sponsorship, Extreme Sports: Mountain Dew; Sponsorship, Extreme Sports: Red Bull; Sponsorship, Extreme Sports: Vans

SPONSORSHIPS, EXTREME SPORTS: MOUNTAIN DEW

Mountain Dew is a carbonated and caffeinated soft drink that is yellow in color and has a citrus flavor. Currently owned by PepsiCo, Inc., Mountain Dew was first marketed in 1948 in Tennessee, and then in North Carolina; by 1964, Mountain Dew was being marketed across the United States. In 2006, *Beverage Digest* reported that Mountain Dew was the fourth most popular soft drink in the country, behind Coke Classic, Pepsi Cola, and Diet Coke. In 2006, Mountain Dew had 6.6 percent of the soft drink market share.

The name of Mountain Dew was taken from a euphemism for "moonshine" and was originally marketed as zero-proof moonshine. Dave DeCecco, spokesman for PepsiCo, acknowledged that Mountain Dew initially had a reputation as a "hillbilly drink," something hard to deny as early Mountain Dew advertisements often featured "guns, outhouses and corny copy like, 'It'll tickle yore innards.'"

This reputation began to change when a significant part of Mountain Dew's marketing strategy involved creating edgy commercials that featured exciting and energetic extreme sports athletes and activities as part of their "Do the Dew" campaign. This ad campaign began in 1992, which PepsiCo credits for making Mountain Dew the fastest-growing soft drink in the 1990s. By featuring extreme sports in their ads, Mountain Dew was targeting teens and young adults; it appears as though they were successful in the endeavor, as the number of teens who agreed with this statement— "Mountain Dew is a brand for someone like me"—increased by 10 percentage points between 1998 and 2001 (Raymond 2002).

Mountain Dew became a sponsor for the **X Games** and, in June 2005, the company debuted the annual Dew Action Sports Tour (Dew AST). This tour lasts five months, June through October, featuring the following sports:

- **Skateboarding**, both park and vert
- **BMX (bicycle motocross)**, including park, vert, and dirt
- Freestyle **motocross**

Athletes compete in five locales each year, and winners in each of the six events receive the Dew Cup, based on their cumulative scores; prize money is $2.5 million, which Mountain Dew lists as the highest purse in extreme sports. The company also offers a $1 million bonus contingent on the athletes' standings at the end of the year.

The Dew AST is broadcast in the United States on NBC and USA Network; televised events are also shown in more than 100 other countries. Other events that take place at competition sites include the following:

- Outdoor festivals with video gaming
- BMX and skate interactive courses
- A two-story, 3,200-square-foot House of Dew that features a DJ
- Airbrush tattoo parlors
- Movie theaters
- PlayStation 2 gaming lounges

Winners of the 2007 Dew Cup were:

- Nate Adams (freestyle motocross)
- Jamie Bestwick (BMX vert)
- Daniel Dhers (BMX park)
- **Ryan Nyquist** (BMX dirt)
- **Shaun White** (skateboard vert)
- Ryan Sheckler (skateboard park)

In December 2, 2005, a film financed and edited by PepsiCo was released; called *First Descent*, the film focused on the history of snowboarding, featuring five accomplished snowboarders of varying ages: Shawn Farmer, Terje Haakonsen, Nick Peralta, Hannah Teter, and Shaun White. The snowboarders went in search of mountains upon which no one had ever snowboarded; they would be the first to do so, which meant that they would be participating in that mountain's "first descent."

Press material released by PepsiCo stated that "The documentary *First Descent* chronicles the rebellious, inspiring and sometimes controversial rise of snowboarding— as seen through the eyes of the snowboarders setting the standards and breaking the boundaries of this worldwide phenomenon" (PepsiCo 2005). Had this film been successful, Mountain Dew and PepsiCo intended to continue with this film-making venture, but *First Descent* met with poor reviews and ticket sales, overall.

In October 2006, Mountain Dew representatives spoke to *BrandWeek* about replacing their "Do the Dew" strategy with one focusing on "fueling the core," which, according to PepsiCo, meant "satisfying people's need for excitement or fulfillment in whatever they do" (http://www.allbusiness.com/retail-trade/food-stores/4490276-1. html). This decision was made because many companies were now marketing to the extreme sports niche, to the degree that, according to PepsiCo, "extreme is no longer extreme." That said, Mountain Dew, which was the only PepsiCo product to gain market share in 2005, intended for its commercials and marketing to continue to focus on "exhilaration, energy and the enjoyment of finding new passions" (http://www. allbusiness.com/retail-trade/food-stores/4490276-1.html).

In 2005, PepsiCo spent $58 million for Mountain Dew media expenses and $15 million more for the first eight months of 2006. The diet version of the drink received $25 million in marketing funds for the first six months of 2006.

CRITICISM OF MOUNTAIN DEW ADVERTISING CAMPAIGNS

Mountain Dew faced significant criticism in the 1990s, when its commercials asked youth to register for the "Mountain Dew Extreme Network." Once registered, members could send in 10 Mountain Dew proofs of purchase plus $29.99 for a beeper and six months worth of air time. Mountain Dew had created a multimillion dollar advertising campaign to promote the promotional beeper deal, advertising on promotional packaging, and in magazines and on MTV commercials, with this message: "Do the Dew … Get the Beeper … Join the Network."

Once a week for six months, Mountain Dew would send promotional information to the registered teens through their beepers in an attempt to learn more about their purchasing habits; the company promised not to send these advertisements during school hours. Teens enrolled in this program would receive prizes and discounts from Frito-Lay, Sony Music, Universal Studios, and other companies, and they could call a toll-free number to hear Lou Piniella and Ken Griffey, Jr., of the Seattle Mariners tout promotional offers and prizes. Other partners in this venture included Footaction, Burton Snowboards, Killer Loop sunglasses, and K-2 In-Line Skates.

Critics spoke out against this form of one-on-one marketing to minors; one vocal critic was Kathryn Montgomery, president of the Center for Media Education in Washington, who said that "Technology is unleashing new creativity on the part of marketers who will stop at nothing to reach children. You may as well just wire them up to the advertiser so they can get a stream of ads" (Barboza 1996).

Business Week labeled this promotion as part of the "new hucksterism," pointing out that the combination of beepers and teenagers has the connotation of drug dealing (Kuntz, Weber, and Dawley 1996).

See also Sponsorship and Advertising: Extreme Sports; Sponsorship, Extreme Sports: Red Bull; Sponsorship, Extreme Sports: Vans

SPONSORSHIPS, EXTREME SPORTS: RED BULL

Red Bull is a highly caffeinated drink that is marketed as a product that can combat mental and physical fatigue, provide energy, help with concentration and focus, and give the person who drinks Red Bull "wings." The company that manufactures, distributes, and markets this product sponsors numerous extreme athletes and sporting events, and this has been a tremendously successful marketing strategy. The company spends approximately $300 million on sports sponsorships, which is one-third of Red Bull's entire marketing budget.

A unique facet of Red Bull's strategy is that the company also owns extreme sports teams, which gives the company more control over the promotional appearances and performances of the extreme athletes on those teams. This includes the ownership of two Formula One racing teams and the New York MetroStars of Major League Soccer; the latter was renamed the New York Red Bulls.

Red Bull has also sponsored events in **snowboarding,** cliff diving, Alpine skiing, buildering, **BASE (Building/Antenna tower/Span/Earth) jumping**, kayaking, sailing, **BMX (bicycle motocross)** freestyle dirt, motorcycle racing, surfing, **inline skating** and speed skating, beach volleyball, free climbing, **mountain biking**, paragliding, triathlons, and **skateboarding** vert, among others.

Red Bull has also created events for the following sports: BMX biking, kiteboarding, extreme snowboarding, **windsurfing**, freeskiing, paragliding, and **sky diving**. Some of those events include the Red Bull King of the Air kiteboarding event in Maui, and the Big Wave Africa Surf Competition. Athletes sponsored by Red Bull include BASE jumper Felix Baumgartner, **kite surfer** Robby Naish, kayaker Shaun Baker, and skateboarder Ali Cairns.

Other events created by the company itself have included the Red Bull Ultracross; the Red Bull Huckfest (wherein skiers and snowboarders compete in freestyle events); and the Red Bull Flugtag, which is German for "flying day," and wherein amateur pilots try to soar off the San Francisco/Santa Monica pier in unusual handmade flying machines.

The founder of Red Bull, Dietrich Mateschitz of Austria, allegedly came up with the idea of a high energy drink after drinking a health tonic in a Hong Kong, China, bar in 1982. Two years later, he and Chaleo Yoovidhya, a businessman from Thailand, modified the health tonic's recipe by adding more carbonation and reducing the drink's syrupy taste. Mateschitz was quoted as saying that people have a thirst for "antiauthoritarian" products; he himself is a snowboarder and a climber, and he claims to drink 10 cans of Red Bull daily. *Forbes* magazine reported that Mateschitz became a billionaire in 2003.

Publications that have written about Red Bull's comprehensive marketing strategy include *Time* magazine, the *Washington Post*, and *Business Week*, among others; it has also been covered by CNN. This drink reached the United States in 1997 and it is now sold in more than 100 countries.

In November 2007, *Time* magazine reported that Red Bull had captured 70 percent of the global market for energy drinks, with sales of $1.5 billion in 2006. Also in November 2007 was Red Bull's sponsorship of the Giants of Rio Challenge in Rio de Janeiro, where competitors swam through "pounding surf" and also ran 20 kilometers (12.4 miles). For those fans who could not make the event, the company provided a live webcast, with Red Bull banner ads also shown to further market the Red Bull product; in fact, in the live feed, more than "2 million video ad impressions were delivered, with full view rates as high as 66 percent and click-thrus as high as 2.07 percent!" (Scheidt 2005).

In an interview with the *Bangkok Post*, Mateschitz said that "It is essential that one develops a unique communication and advertising strategy ... a campaign that combines body and mind in a very nonconformist way."

There has been backlash against this overwhelmingly successful marketing strategy. As one example, Steven Wells, while writing "To sponsorship hell in a homemade go-kart" for *The Guardian*, had this to say: "Then there's December's Red Bull Soapbox Race—a corporate whorefest that's just one tiny part of the soft drink leviathan's wholesale global co-opting of so-called grassroots and 'xtreme' sports. In some cases they've even invented sports, just so they can sponsor them." Later on, he refers to Red Bull as "arty-farty kamikazes crashing into the wreck-pitted deck of the aircraft carrier of corporate homogenization" (Wells 2008).

See also Sponsorship and Advertising: Extreme Sports; Sponsorship, Extreme Sports: Mountain Dew; Sponsorship, Extreme Sports: Vans; X Games

SPONSORSHIPS, EXTREME SPORTS: VANS

Vans sells namebrand extreme sports footwear, selling shoes for **skateboarders**, **BMX (bicycle motocross)** riders, surfers, **snowboarders**, and **motocross** racers, among others. Annual sales are generally around $350 million, with the company's key market being teenagers and young adults; 65 percent of their teenage customers are male and 35 percent are female. The company also sponsors extreme sporting events and has created two of them: the Vans Warped Tour and the Vans Triple Crown.

Vans tends to advertise at skateboarding parks, in skate magazines, at alternative **music** tours, and during extreme sports programming. In 2000, Vans took what *BrandWeek* calls a "guerrilla approach" to its advertisements, which featured extreme sports participation from the viewpoint of the athletes involved in them.

In 2002, the company filmed a documentary called *DogTown and Z-Boys*. This film focused on the 1970s skate scene in and around Venice, California; these were the first people to use drained swimming pools as their skating venues. The film was directed by Stacy Peralta, who was part of the Z-Boy group in the 1970s; Sony Pictures Classics distributed the documentary. Although the documentary received some criticism for marketing Vans, it was well received on the festival circuit and can be credited with spreading awareness of skateboarding and its early proponents and participants.

Also in 2002, Vans purchased Mosa Extreme Sports, a company that owned Pro-Tec, which is a manufacturer of helmets for BMX racing, snowboarding, and skateboarding. The cash and stock deal was between $10 and $15 million.

Vans was founded by Paul Van Doren, who, according to the Vans Web site, dropped out of school in the eighth grade and began spending time at the race track; his nickname was "Dutch the Clutch" and he charged $1 to give someone the race's odds. His mother disapproved, so she got him a job making shoes and sweeping the factory's floor. Twenty years later, Van Doren was the executive vice president of Randy's, a Boston-based shoe manufacturer; this is where Bob Cousy of the Boston Celtics bought his canvas shoes.

Although Randy's was successful, becoming the third-largest U.S. shoe manufacturer, the California factory associated with Randy's was losing $1 million a month.

Van Doren, his brother Jim, and his friend Gordon Lee were assigned the job of turning around the factory, and they did so in eight months.

The trio then left Randy's to form the Van Doren Rubber Company; a Belgian named Serge D'Elia also invested in this company. Vans was set up somewhat differently from the other three shoe manufacturers in the United States, in that the company also had a retail branch; both opened up in March 1966. After a year and a half of being in business, Vans had 50 stores.

In the Santa Monica store, skateboarders such as Tony Alva and Stacy Peralta wanted shoes that suited their purpose; this is how Vans became involved in the skateboarding shoe industry. Vans then paid Peralta $300 to wear their shoes as he traveled around the world, skateboarding. In the late 1970s, the company hired a team manager, whose job was to drive to the skateboarders and demonstrate the company's shoes. The company also provided the cast of the movie *Fast Times at Ridgemont High* with checkerboard slip-on shoes, and these shoes ended up on the cover of the soundtrack album.

The company suffered financially throughout the 1980s and it was questionable whether or not Vans would survive. Because of two ideas—the Vans Warped Tour and the Vans Triple Crown—the company not only survived, but also became one of the key companies involved in extreme sporting events.

Vans Warped Tour

In the 1990s, Vans partnered with Kevin Lyman, a man who had worked on creating skateboarding shows that included skateboarding contests and music. From that collaboration arose an annual tour that, starting in 1995, combined alternative music with extreme sports. Although at first the tour traveled only across the United States, in 1998 the tour also traveled to Australia, Japan, Europe, and Canada. Spectators can listen to the music, watch the skateboarding competition, and shop for music, magazines, and skate products.

In the 2000s, as many as 100 bands performed in a single touring stop; each band plays approximately 30 minutes on one of the 10 stages. Fans get to vote as to which band gets an extra 10 minutes of performing time, and each year one band is designed as the BBQ Band, which means that they need to prepare the food for tour participants.

Vans Triple Crown

Because of the Warped Tour, Vans became even more entrenched in the extreme sports world, creating and financially backing the Vans Triple Crown, which consists of three championship events in each of these seven sports: skateboarding, wakeboarding, surfing, snowboarding, BMX racing, freestyle motocross, and Supercross. Cosponsors have included Mountain Dew, PlayStation, *Rolling Stone* magazine, and more. Prize purses, which are funded by Vans, can reach up to $2 million annually.

This sponsorship deal has benefited the company, with the Vice President of Marketing Chris Strain saying that, "The Triple Crown Series has been a fantastic vehicle in the growth and development of these sports. As these sports become more successful, so do our brands" (Kelly 2001).

See also Sponsorship and Advertising: Extreme Sports; Sponsorship, Extreme Sports: Mountain Dew; Sponsorship, Extreme Sports: Red Bull; X Games

STAMSTAD, JOHN (1966–)

John Stamstad is a professional Ultramarathon **mountain biker**. Besides being an exceptionally skilled endurance mountain biker with multiple titles and world records, he was the force that shaped a solo version of this challenging sport.

Stamstad was born in 1966 and he grew up in Madison, Wisconsin. As a young adult, he worked at his father's business and, rather than driving to work, he ran both ways, until he fractured his femur bone. To recover from his injury, he began cycling; he quickly became intrigued by mountain biking, and he would ride up to 199 miles (320 kilometers) per day. In 1986, he entered a 550-mile (885-kilometer) race across the state of Missouri, in which he placed third.

In 1987, he dropped out of the University of Wisconsin, just a few credits away from earning a degree in psychology. He moved to Cincinnati, Ohio, where he pursued a career in photojournalism and continued to ride his mountain bike. He again entered the Bicycle Across Missouri race, this time dropping out at midpoint with severe mononucleosis symptoms. Although it took another two years before he raced in earnest again, his philosophy was that he should "Do the hardest races in the world and try to find the one that breaks me" (Balf 1996). His accomplishments have included the following:

- Winning the 24-hour Montezuma's Revenge wilderness mountain biking race, which includes a 2,703-mile (4,350-kilometer) climb up Gray's Peak in Colorado
- Winning the Alaskan Iditasport race along the Iditarod Trail during each of the eight times in which he entered the race; the first time that he attempted this 160-mile (257.5-kilometer) winter race, he placed third, despite five flat tires and temperatures that dipped to −35° Fahrenheit (−37.2° Celsius)
- Setting the world record of 357.7 miles (566 kilometers) in the Ultra-Marathon Cycling Association 24-hour off-road race

Shortly after he had competed in the first Alaskan Iditasport race, he entered the Trans-Australia Off-Road Challenges, but he was disqualified after arguing with the race organizer. He kept riding, however, persuading some tourists to be his support crew; under those circumstances, he rode the remaining 1,500 miles (2,414 kilometers) to Byron Bay. He did not compete in that race again, but this incident earned Stamstad a reputation as a "puritanical curmudgeon" (Balf 1996).

He has expressed his opinion in other races, as well, including one year's Iditasport, wherein he did not believe that certain other top racers were carrying their required 15 pounds (6.8 kilograms) of gear. He believes that headphones should be banned in long-distance races, and during one race in Maine, he thought that his win should be removed from the record books because the course was too easy; he also criticized the women's record holder, Amy Regan, for exaggerating the level of difficulty of the course.

In 1995, he was sponsored by Ritchey Design; this company paid him $12,000 a year, plus bonuses, which included a health club membership. Stamstad, who used to ride long distances with only a quarter in his pocket for an emergency phone call, talked about the luxury of having a "ten spot" to take with him on his races.

In 1996, he entered the 24 Hours of Canaan race, which required a team; Stamstad planned to ride alone, so he entered four versions of his own name and participated in the race, beating about half of the 380 five-person teams. The following year, a solo category was created.

In 1999, he rode alone along the 2,385.5-mile (4,000-kilometer) Great Divide mountain bike trail. He traveled nearly 200,131 feet (61,000 meters) of vertical climbing in 18 days. To keep up his energy in between stops at rural gas stations, it was said that he drank pure canola oil; he would then purchase Spam, Little Debbie snack cakes, and cheese.

In 2000, Stamstad was inducted into the Mountain Bike Hall of Fame. He moved to Seattle, Washington, where he opened the Singletrack Ranch, which is a camp for mountain bikers. In 2001, *Outside Magazine* picked him as the "best of the best." In 1996, that magazine had stated that Stamstad was his "own weird science project, a 135-pound, mountain-bike-based experiment in the limits of human endurance" (Balf 1996). In 2005, he went on a solo ride along the 210.6-mile (339-kilometer) John Muir Trail in California.

Stamstad has taken a dual approach to nutrition and in his strategies to keep himself fueled during races. On the one hand, he would read medical textbooks and journal articles on such topics as creatine loading and branch-chain amino acids. He would buy complex carbohydrates in bulk and make his own energy drinks. On the other hand, he has advocated Twinkies and Pop-Tarts, as well, as they did not freeze while he was riding and provided him with plenty of needed calories at a good price. He would buy bubble wrap for his toes to keep them warm on long wintry rides, he covered his drinking tube with weather stripping to keep his water in a liquid state, and he once said that he could buy all the clothing he needed for a major race at Wal-Mart.

See also Adventure Racing

STREET LUGE

Street luge is a gravity-based sport also known as "land luge" or "road luge" or "downhill **skateboarding**." The sport involves riding, while in a supine position, on a street luge board down a concrete or asphalt road or course. Street luge should not be confused with "luge," in which people ride down mountains and hills (or artificial tracks) of ice and snow while on a special sled.

Athletes lie face up on their street luge boards, riding feet first to maintain the best possible aerodynamics. Street luge boards do not have brakes or steering devices, so athletes direct their boards by slightly shifting their weight and stopping the street luge board by using their feet. The street luge board is typically 16 inches by 8.5 feet (41 centimeters by 2.6 meters) long, with four to six small wheels about the size of skateboarding wheels; the board itself resembles a longer skateboard and is made of steel or aluminum. The bottom of the board has foot pegs, and the board's handlebars extend the rider's arms straight, with hands pointing toward the feet. A quality board costs up to approximately $1,000.

Riders typically go at speeds of 40 to 70 miles (64 to 112.7 kilometers) per hour, and sometimes faster, while lying 2 inches (5.1 centimeters) or less away from the asphalt or concrete. Street luge is technically illegal, as the riders usually exceed the speed limits on streets, and some athletes have been stopped by the police.

Scooting along at more than 45 miles per hour, Jarryd Collyer, 13, hangs on and lies low on a land luge as he negotiates a street corner. (AP Photo/*Las Cruces Sun-News*, Norm Dettlaff)

Participants of street luge live in numerous places, including the United States, the United Kingdom, Australia, Canada, South Africa, Switzerland, Germany, and Sweden.

Street luge athlete Mike "Biker" Sherlock explained the thrill of the sport in this way: "the drive to experience intensity, in terms of both athletics and danger—is widespread. The body and the mind are taken to the edges of the human envelope, into realms that are unforgiving of the slightest mistake" (Kannapell 1998).

History of the Sport

It seems likely that street luge evolved from skateboarding, although the precise evolution is not clear. Several groups lay claim to inventing the sport of street luge, in Oregon, in Oklahoma, in California—and even as far away as Austria—during the 1970s. All that is certain is that someone discovered that high speeds could be achieved by lying down on a skateboard, and then people began racing one another.

Competitions were held in Signal Hill, California, during the 1970s, sponsored by the U.S. Skateboard Association; the goal was to finish a race first, so speed was paramount. Some people used skateboards in the race, while others used an enclosed cart. This race was not referred to as "luge," but racers could choose how to ride their boards, and "luge" was used to describe the supine position chosen by some racers. So many injuries occurred at Signal Hill, to participants and spectators alike, that the race was canceled in 1978 and not revived.

People who wanted to ride street luge continued to do so, but without the support of the U.S. Skateboard Association. Groups that organized luge races, included the following:

- Underground Racers Association (URA): organized races that were publicized by *Skateboarder* magazine and local television channels
- Road Racers Association for International Luge (RAIL): organized in 1990, the group began to hold races in 1993; by 1999, they had 180 members
- Federation of International Gravity Racing (FIGR): formed in 1996
- National Street Luge Association (NSLA): the eastern RAIL organization reformed and renamed itself in 1997
- International Gravity Sports Association (IGSA): this organization worked to bring luge to the **X Games** and served as the official contact for the games

These groups—and others—each developed their own rules for street luge competitions, with minor differences among them.

The first professional race is believed to be the one organized by RAIL and its founder, Bob Pereyra, in 1993. Held at the Laguna Seca Raceway in Monterey, California, 22 racers competed. The following year, Pereyra appeared in a commercial in which he was racing down steep hills in Hawaii.

Street Luge and Extreme Competitions

Some people credit Ron Semiao, the founder of the X Games, with creating the term "street luge." Whether he did or not, the appearance of street luge at the 1995 Extreme Games brought significant attention to the sport. Thirty-two men competed in that race.

The street luge competition was one of the highlights of the 1999 X Games because of Dennis Derammelaere, who had won the bronze medal in street luge dual in the Extreme Games in 1996. He captured the silver in the 1997 X Games, but an injury—a badly broken lower right leg—prevented him from competing in 1998; he required a plate and eight screws for his ankle to mend. He came back in 1999, though, to win the gold.

Street luge continued to be a part of the X Games until 2001, when it was determined that too many accidents occurred with this sport; street luge was also featured as part of the **Gravity Games**.

Some athletes have not been content with riding 60, 70, or even 80 miles (95.6, 112.7, or 128.7 kilometers) per hour on their street luge boards. To boost the speed, some riders have ridden jet-powered luge boards; the world record had been 98.5 miles (158.5 kilometers) per hour, until Joel King from Bognor Regis, United Kingdom, used a jet-powered luge to set a speed record of 112.7 miles (181.4 kilometers) per hour. This accomplishment earned him the nickname of "The Gravity King."

King describes the thrill of street luge in this manner:

> As I lie down, the eerie silence is broken only by the sound of my heavy breathing reverberating around the inside of my crash helmet. I can feel my heart thumping for all it's worth. Suddenly, just four inches behind my helmet, the jet engine's electric motor hums into life and builds to a peculiarly anxious whine. Then, as the propane gas ignites, the whine builds inexorably to a scream that, as the kerosene fuel kicks in and the turbines start to whir, turns to a bone-juddering roar of terrifying intensity. (Hernu 2007)

Street Luge Equipment

Athletes should wear helmets and goggles to protect their heads and faces because they are so close to the pavement. The racers also should wear a body suit made of strong material, perhaps Kevlar or thick leather. Padding—including elbow pads, knee pads, shoulder pads, and wrist pads and guards—and sturdy gloves also help protect the racers. It is important to wear sturdy footwear, as well, as the rider's feet are the only brakes a street luge has; it is not unheard of for lugers to burn the rubber soles off their shoes.

STREET LUGE EVENTS

The following are some of the popular types of street luge events:

- Super Mass: Thirty racers take two qualifying runs, and the top 24 racers compete in groups of six. Racers speed down streets lined by hay bales, with the top three moving on to the next category. The winner is the person who finishes the race with the final six athletes in the shortest amount of time.
- Dual: Qualifying rounds reduce the playing field to the fastest 16 athletes; the races are then head-to-head competitions.
- Endurance: Some athletes also compete in endurance races that cover several miles.
- King of the Hill: First tried in the 2000 X Games, the gold medalists from the previous five X Games raced against one another to determine who was truly "King of the Hill."

The competitors in the King of the Hill event were Biker Sherlock (1996, 1997, 1998); Rat Sult (1998); Bob Pereyra (1995); David Rogers (1999 Super Mass); Dennis Derammelaere (1999 Dual); and Chris Ponseti (1997 Super Mass). Among them, they had won 11 gold medals, and 21 medals, overall. The winner of King of the Hill was Derammelaere, who said that "[t]he monetary reward for this is a lot less, but the prize, the title, was worth more than any money I could have. I beat the best in the history of Street Luge, and I'm on top of the world" (Castellanos 2000).

STREET LUGE SLANG

Street luge athletes have created some interesting slang, including the following:

- Bacon: rough and hazardous roads
- Banana: rider who often wipes out
- Flesh wing: extending an arm during a race to create better balance
- Puke a wheel: to either blow up or melt a wheel; a wheel melts when the urethane literally catches fire at high speeds
- Screaming mimis: worrisome sounds from a street luge board during the race
- Wad: to crash as a large group

STREET LUGE RISKS AND INJURIES

Because there are no street luge courses, athletes often practice on regular streets, making traffic accidents a major danger for riders. While riding, injuries often occur to fingers, elbows, and ankles; concussions are a concern and broken legs are a possibility. Fatalities also have occurred, spurring friends and family to create Internet pages for people to leave messages of condolence.

Riders must maintain their equipment, which includes replacing the wheels often. Wheels can soften with use, and wheels that are too soft make it difficult for the athlete to steer. Another danger occurs when the foot pegs at the bottom of the street luge board connect—or hook—with the pegs on another board.

U

URBAN CLIMBING

In urban climbing, athletes climb the outside of structures built by humans, including skyscrapers and other tall buildings. This activity is generally illegal because of trespassing laws. Some climbers use ropes to climb, while others do not; some use protective gear, including pads and helmets, while others refuse to do so. Most climbers use special climbing shoes and apply chalk to their hands for a firm grip. Some climbers do not feel they are successful unless they reach the top of the building; others focus on the experience itself, rather than on an ultimate goal.

Extreme climbers attempt feats that are especially challenging, perhaps because of the height of the building or the level of difficulty involved in ascending the structure—or getting past security to attempt the climb in the first place. The most well-known urban climber is Frenchman **Alain "Spiderman" Robert** who has climbed more than 80 skyscrapers, including the four tallest in the world, without using ropes, climbing bolts, or safety nets.

This sport is also known as buildering (a combination of "building" and "bouldering"), roof climbing, and structuring. Another term is stegophily, which is the Greek word for "roof climbing."

History of the Sport

Although urban climbing shares many characteristics with rock climbing and **mountain climbing**, including the need for the strength and mastery to climb up steep inclines without losing one's balance, they are not the same activity and they developed independently from one another.

The roots of urban climbing may be traced back to Cambridge, England, where Geoffrey Winthrop Young published a book with W. P. Spalding called *The Roof Climber's Guide to Trinity* in 1899. A second edition was published in the 1930s and a third in 1960; the third edition was significantly rewritten, with many Greek quotes removed from the text.

In 1905, Winthrop Young published a second book on the subject, called *Wall and Roof Climbing*, which was published by Spottiswode, Eton College. This book took a "theoretical approach, with chapters on building styles, drainpipes etc. Also a large number of literary references and an extremely useful appendage on haystack climbing." (Cambridge Underground 1983, 31–32).

In October 1937, *The Night Climbers of Cambridge* was published by Chatto and Windus. The author, Noel Howard Symington, used the pseudonym of "Whipplesnaith," perhaps keeping his real name a secret because of the illicit nature of the activities suggested. To quote the book itself, "outlaws keep no histories" (Symington 1937).

This book has since been called "The Bible, with all the classic routes" (Cambridge Underground 1983, 31–32). The edition was reprinted a month later to add a diagram showing how to escape from the Marks and Spencer building, which was missing in the original. This book was reprinted in 1952 and 1953 and, in 2007, it was reissued by Oleander.

Interestingly enough, *The Night Climbers of Cambridge* warns against damaging the building during a climb, much as a modern-day mountain climber might caution someone against hurting the environment. Moreover, many of today's urban climbers operate under the same sense of secrecy as those climbing Cambridge roofs more than a century ago, often climbing under the cover of darkness. This is due, in large part, to trespassing laws that make buildering an illegal activity. To quote *The Night Climbers of Cambridge*, "When one man goes, there is no one to take up the thread where he left off. The blanket of the dark hides each group of climbers from its neighbours, muffles up a thousand deeds of valour, and almost entirely prevents the existence of dangerous rivalry" (Symington 1937).

In the earlier part of the twentieth century, though, at least one urban climber was open about his activities and even publicly lauded for his accomplishments. Harry Gardiner, dubbed the "Human Fly" by President Grover Cleveland, would climb tall buildings while wearing sneakers and using his bare hands for purchase. On October 7, 1916, a crowd of approximately 150,000 gathered in downtown Detroit to see Gardiner scale the building that would house the ad department of the *Detroit News*. He had been hired by the newspaper to draw attention to their want ads that could now be transmitted by "private phone wires."

The *Detroit News* published a promotional story the day before this event, in which they shared that Gardiner would cross himself and then refuse to speak a word until he completed his quest. "It is his way," the reporter explained, "of giving himself into the care of his Creator before he ventures forth on his walk between heaven and earth" (Baulch 1996).

Other urban climbers include—

- George "Human Fly" Polley, who participated in the sport in the 1910s; it was said that he first attempted this activity because of a bet in which he won a suit of clothing
- Harry and Simon Westaway, who climbed Big Ben in London, England
- George Willig, a mountain climber who climbed the World Trade Center in 1977; he signed his name on the observation deck on the South Tower
- Dan "Spidey Dan" Goodwin, who climbed the Sears Tower and John Hancock building, both in Chicago, in 1981; in 1986, he climbed the CN Towers in Ontario, Canada, twice in one day
- Allen Roberts who, when questioned about the similarity of his name to Alain Robert, called himself the "thinking man's Alain" (http://www.buildering.net/interviews/allen)

The main challenge faced by urban climbers, technically speaking, is to find the best holds in a structure that may be smooth. It has been described as a puzzle that can only be "solved through ingenuity, persistence and foolhardiness. Buildering is both a lifestyle and a philosophy of taming the modern landscape" (http://urbanclimbingxx.blogspot.com/).

See also Free Running; Parkour

VALERUZ, TONI (1951–)

Toni Valeruz is probably the most well-known Italian extreme sports athlete, known for his expertise in **extreme skiing**; he has skied more than 50 of the most challenging slopes found around the world. Valeruz helped spread that sport in Europe and in South America.

Valeruz was born in Alba, situated between Italy and Austria, in 1951. He grew up in the Val di Fassa, where he learned how to ski at a young age. His first notable experience in extreme skiing occurred in 1968, when he skied the Marmolada, mountains with peaks reaching 10,964.6 feet (3,342 meters), with 55-degree slopes. In 1975, he skied the eastern face of Cervino; in 1978, Mont Blanc; and, in 1983, the Eiger. Each of these mountains was more than 13,123 feet (4,000 meters) high.

Other accomplishments include the following:

- Skiing the Lyscamm, a 3,937-foot (1,200-meter) mountain with 57-degree slopes, in 5 minutes' time
- Descending the western face of Makālu, which is an 26,575-foot (8,100-meter) peak in the Himalayas
- In 1997, he skied down the northern side of Vernel Mount in the Alps at 2 A.M., using the light of the moon to guide him

Valeruz now works as a skiing instructor and a guide for mountain excursions. He stresses that extreme skiers must learn how to ski Alpine style, **snowboard**, and mountaineer.

VIDEO GAMES

Companies that produce video and computer games have partnered with numerous extreme sports athletes to produce games that appeal to the primary demographic for both extreme sports events and video games: male teenagers and young male adults.

By 1993, each of the two parties—video game producers and extreme sports organizers—recognized the opportunities inherent in targeting that demographic. In the late 1980s and early 1990s, both Nintendo and Sega were quite clear that their gaming systems and games were intended for boys and young men. Attempting to market to females, according to their logic, would threaten the success of their true market: males.

Meanwhile, in 1993, Ron Semiao, the program director for ESPN2 (the Entertainment and Sports Programming Network), recognized that corporations wishing to target the teenage and young adult male audience should sponsor an Olympic-like event featuring extreme sports. From this line of thinking arose the Extreme Games or, as they became known in 1996, the **X Games**. In the late 1990s, video game producers began to collaborate with individual extreme athletes and with the extreme sports industry, overall, in what became a successful venture.

By 2006, the gaming industry was worth $27.5 billion, with some extreme sports video games among the most popular.

HISTORY OF VIDEO GAMES

Video games as commercial entertainment started in 1971, when Nolan Bushnell created *Computer Space*. The following year, Magnavox introduced a home gaming system called the Odyssey, which allowed people to play 12 games in the privacy of their own homes. In 1975, Atari released "Pong," a game sold through Sears and Roebuck; in 1977, Atari began selling home gaming systems that separated the games from the gaming systems themselves. Previously, gamers could only play the games already programmed into a particular system. Starting in 1977, they could purchase a gaming system along with the specific games—stored on individual cartridges—that they wanted to play. This innovation meant that the variety of games played was limited only by the ability of the video game industry to produce them.

Although there were ebbs and flows in the profitability of the video game industry, overall, the dollar signs continued to increase; by 2002, the video and computer game industry was worth $11.4 billion and was estimated to reach $21.1 billion by 2005. In 2006, MSNBC stated that video gaming was now a $27.5 billion industry; in March 2008, that same news channel reported that "video games defied the otherwise discouraging retail sales figures of December 2007" (CNBC 2006). In February 2008, CNET news predicted that, soon, no one would be left out of video gaming.

From the inception of the industry, video game producers were targeting teenagers, particularly males, as the prime audience for their products. By 2001, those teenagers were spending $155 billion a year on entertainment, clothes, and food alone. Video and computer games were clearly included in that mix, with as many males playing video games as those watching movies, reading books, or studying. These figures were provided by Teenage Research Unlimited, a company that conducts market research for Coca-Cola, Levi Strauss, and Nike, among other companies.

By the late 1990s, video game companies realized the potentially profitable partnership that could exist between video game producers and the extreme athletes who have captured the attention of male preteens, teenagers, and young adults.

Extreme sports used in video games have included **skateboarding**, **snowboarding**, **BMX (bicycle motocross)**, demolition derby, river rafting, surfing, **wakeboarding**, **motocross**, **extreme skiing**, **street luge**, paintball, and more. Athletes featured in these games are numerous, including Dave Mirra (BMX); **Mat Hoffman** (BMX); Kelly Slater (surfing); Andy Macdonald (skateboarding); Shaun Murray (wakeboarding); and more.

After snowboarder **Shaun White** won Olympic gold in 2006, Ubisoft quickly announced plans to develop a line of video and computer games based on White's snowboarding style; the red-headed star had, by this point, become well known as the "Flying Tomato."

As gaming technology continued to improve, game systems began allowing gamers to compete against anonymous players via the Internet. Codes called "cheats" are also provided online; gamers in possession of cheats learn how to add more elements to their gaming experience, usually in ways to help them more easily "defeat" the game or their opponents.

VIDEO GAME SERIES: TONY HAWK

Another relatively recent trend is the extreme sports video and computer game series, wherein a new version of a previously established game is released, sometimes on a regular basis. The most popular extreme sports series to date is the **Tony Hawk** skateboarding series.

In 1999, Activision released *Tony Hawk's Pro Skater* for the PlayStation game system; this game was later modified for use on the Nintendo 64, Dreamcast, N-Gage, and Game Boy Color systems. Within a year, *Tony Hawk's Pro Skater* was a best-selling game. This game was so successful that a new version has been released annually, with the 2000 version named *Tony Hawk's Pro Skate 2*; the 2002 version, *Tony Hawk's Pro Skate 3*, and so forth. As the game systems evolved and changed, versions of the Tony Hawk series were adapted to suit.

In 2003, the name of the newest release changed to *Tony Hawk's Underground* (or *THUG*); in 2004, *Tony Hawk's Underground 2* was released. In 2005, the title of the new release was *Tony Hawk's American Wasteland*, with *Tony Hawk's American Sk8land* created for the Game Boy Advance system. In 2006, games released include *Tony Hawk's Project 8* and *Tony Hawk's Downhill Jam*. In 2007, *Tony Hawk's Proving Ground* was released; gamers had the choice of playing four different levels: hardcore, rigger, pro, and street. It seems likely that this annual release of Hawk games will continue, as Activision has a contract with Tony Hawk through 2015.

In Hawk's skateboarding games, animations and names of real-life skaters are used, along with other fictional characters. Hawk has insisted on realism in his games, "down to the paint jobs on the decks." As the games progressed, plot lines began to be developed, with gamers being part of the unfolding story line.

According to an article published by *USA Today* in 2008, 30 million Tony Hawk games have sold over the past nine years; these games have been in the top 10 in the United States, based on sales, since their inception. Tony Hawk games alone have generated more than $1 billion in sales, in large part because this series is popular among skateboarders and nonskaters alike—only 25 percent of the players of these games own a skateboard.

Top Ten Reviews created a list of the top 50 extreme sports videos and the top four positions go to the Hawk series in this order:

- *Tony Hawk's Pro Skater 3*
- *Tony Hawk's Underground 2*
- *Tony Hawk's Pro Skater 2*
- *Tony Hawk's Pro Skater 4*

Game number 13 in the list is *Tony Hawk's American Wasteland*.

Video Games and Females: Lara Croft in Tomb Raider

The majority of video and computer extreme sports games feature male athletes, heroes, and protagonists. However, one extreme action video game series starring a female—albeit a fictional character—has been successful: *Tomb Raider*. This video game series was based on movies with the same name, produced by Paramount Pictures; Angelina Jolie played the role of Lara Croft in the series of *Tomb Raider* films. In 2006, the Guinness Book of World Records listed Lara Croft, the lead character in the movie and game, as the "Most Successful Human Videogame Heroine."

This poses the question as to whether or not the gaming industry was changing—or at least broadening—its target markets. According to Helen W. Kennedy, in her article "Lara Croft: Feminist Icon or Cyberbimbo: On the Limits of Textual Analysis," the character of Lara Croft was a "significant departure from the typical role of women within popular computer games. Although a number of fighting games offer the option of a female character, the hero is traditionally male with females largely cast in a supporting role." Kennedy believes that Paramount Pictures wanted to at least "potentially" appeal to women; however, she points out that Croft was a provocatively sexual fantasy female figure who clearly would appeal to males as an "object of sexual desire, a factor which the marketing/advertising of *Tomb Raider* was keen to reinforce" (Kennedy 2002).

Therefore, although Tomb *Raider* is clearly revolutionary in that a female character is at the center of a highly popular video gaming series, the perspectives provided by Kennedy suggest that the target audience was largely the same as it had been in the past. "Nude raider" Web sites bolstered the notion that the Lara Croft character was praiseworthy in large part because of her physical sexual attributes, rather than because she was a strong and independent woman. On "nude raider" sites, webmasters showed the character performing video game actions without wearing any clothes. BBC also noted the rumored existence of a *Tomb Raider* patch; if a gamer obtained this piece of computer coding, it was reported, Lara Croft would appear nude during game play.

Video Games and Young Children

Although the majority of extreme sports video and computer games target the teenage and young adult males, and perhaps the preteen group, video games containing cartoon characters and story book characters participating in extreme sports began to be released; this targeted an audience as young as five.

In 2000, Sound Source Interactive, Inc. announced that the Berenstain Bears would be participating in six different extreme sporting events in a new video game; this game could be played on the Game Boy Color gaming system. In promotional material, the announcement read that "Brother and Sister Bear flip, spin, slide and fly as they do battle against gravity and the terrain in some adrenalin-pumping individual time trials. Mama and Papa Bear join the siblings for equally exciting and fun team events" (Business Wire 2000). The events included sledding, dirt biking, freestyle kayaking, dirt boarding, team tobogganing, and team rafting.

In 2002, Disney Interactive announced that Disney characters, including Mickey Mouse, Minnie Mouse, Donald Duck, Daisy Duck, Goofy, Max, and Big Bad Pete would participate in snowboarding, skateboarding, and motocross in a video game; game systems that would support this action were Nintendo and Game Boy Advance.

See also Children and Extreme Sports; Gender and Extreme Sports

217

W

WAKEBOARDING

In wakeboarding, a participant attaches his or her feet to a wakeboard, which is a single board that resembles a thicker snowboard or a shorter surfboard. A rope is attached to the tower of a power boat and the wakeboarder holds on to a handle located at the other end of the rope. While in a standing position, wakeboarders then ride on their boards across bodies of water, usually rivers and lakes, while the boat pulls them across the water. The boat, if driven at the correct speed, creates v-shaped "wakes," which are the waves that the wakeboarders use to perform tricks, jumps, and maneuvers.

The sport of wakeboarding combines features of several sports. In some ways, it resembles water skiing, wherein athletes ski on water while being pulled by a boat. Wakeboarding is also similar to **snowboarding** because of the way in which the boarders attach their feet to their boards and then perform tricks without needing to worry about losing their boards; and it is also similar to surfing, as athletes attempt to maintain their balance while standing on boards and performing maneuvers.

Boarders must learn how to land safely after their maneuvers, bending their knees to absorb the impact of the landing and holding onto the ropes; if the athletes allow the ropes to go slack during their jumping and maneuvering, they may not land well.

For each rider, two other people are needed for wakeboarding: the boat driver and a spotter who watches and interprets hand signals of the rider and who lets the driver know if the rider falls down. Having an expert driver is important while wakeboarding, but so is having a qualified spotter. Hand signals from the wakeboarder include the following:

- Thumb up in the air: go faster
- Thumb down toward the water: slow down
- Wave after a fall: I'm okay
- Bend an arm over the head and make an "O" out of fingers: I'm okay, but pick me up
- Cut across throat with a hand: I'm dropping the rope
- Pat head: I'm done

In 2004, an estimated 3.1 million people were participating in wakeboarding. Newer riders usually travel between 16 and 20 miles (25.7 and 32.2 kilometers) per hour, while more experienced riders will go up to 24 miles (38.6 kilometers) per hour. If a driver goes more quickly than 24 miles per hour, then the wake—or the waves generated by the boat—flattens out, preventing the rider from being able to take advantage of those waves.

HISTORY OF WAKEBOARDING

The sport of wakeboarding evolved from water surfing, as surfers attempted to find ways to enjoy the water when there were not significant waves. Some surfers tethered themselves to a boat and rode on their surfboards in that way; others even tried attaching their boards to a rope on a truck that drove close to the shoreline. Neither were especially satisfying methods.

In 1985, a surfer from San Diego, California named Tony Finn invented the "Skurfer," a board that was more suitable for the activity. The Skurfer was shorter than a surfboard and was therefore more manageable for more people. That summer, Finn also experimented with bindings to keep the boarder more stabilized and to allow more maneuvers to occur. An Austin, Texas, man named Jimmy Redmon was also experimenting with technologies, creating a "skiboard" and working on suitable bindings.

John Wirtz of Blue Springs does a flip while wakeboarding at Blue Springs Lake in Blue Springs, Missouri, August 13, 2004. (AP Photo/*The Examiner*, Jeff Stead)

The importance of foot bindings in wakeboarding is paramount. This advance gave riders the opportunity to try tricks on their boards, and to "go aerial" as they attempted new ones in the air, without having to worry about losing the wakeboard.

ESPN televised the first skiboarding championship in 1990, which increased the interest in the sport. However, people still struggled to balance themselves on the skiboards and so the sport did not grow significantly until the technology for wakeboarding improved even further.

In 1990, another skiboarder, Herb O'Brien, decided to improve on the design of the boards. As the owner of a successful water skiing company named H.O., he had the connections to consult with manufacturers and, using what he learned, he invented the Hyperlite, a board that was neutral-buoyant. This means that the board did not sink, but it also did not float on the surface. This allowed riders to push the board below the water's surface to more easily get on the boards. The Hyperlite also had phasers, which were large dimples on the bottom of the board that smoothed out the ride. O'Brien then worked to thin out the board so that it cut through the water in a manner similar to a slalom ski. Increasing numbers of people then began skiboarding—or wakeboarding, as the sport began to be called.

In 1993, Jimmy Redmon created a twin-tipped board that had fins under the fronts and backs of the boards, which allowed the boarders to move forward and backward. Plus, the boarder could ride with either the left or right foot forward and could switch stances. As in skateboarding, a rider who puts his or her left foot in front is using a "regular" stance, whereas those who put the right foot first are using the "goofy" stance. As the technology of wakeboards continued to develop, people could choose from a variety of fin options, including removable ones.

WAKEBOARDING COMPETITIONS

Redmon also contributed to wakeboarding in another important way, forming the World Wakeboard Association (WWA) in 1989; this organization began setting standards for competitions and for wakeboarding equipment. Competitions now over-seen by the WWA include the U.S. Pro Tour, the Masters, **X Games**, Wakeboard U.S. Nationals, and the Wakeboard World Cup. Competition courses include ramps and other obstacles for the wakeboarder to overcome.

In 1992, the first extreme wakeboarding competition was held in Orlando, Florida; competitors from around the globe participated, and ESPN and ESPN2 televised these competitions, increasing the popularity of wakeboarding.

In 1996, men competed in wakeboarding during the X Games, with Parks Bonifay winning the gold. The following year, a women's event was added, with Tara Hamilton becoming the champion. Both amateurs and professionals compete in the X Games wakeboarding events

In 1998, the first Wakeboard World Cup was held. Competitors from around the world traveled to North America, where they competed in 15 different cities. Competitors received points for each competition, and the person with the most points after all competitions were completed was named the winner. Also in 1998, the Vans Triple Crown of Wakeboarding was held for the first time; these competitions continue to this day.

In many competitions, athletes must turn in their list of planned tricks to the judges before competing; lists should contain 11 tricks. Judges award points based on the difficulty of the tricks and on the wakeboarder's style. Each competitor takes two passes of 26 seconds each; during each pass, the athlete must perform five tricks. If a competitor is able to add in additional tricks not found on the list, these maneuvers are called "wild card" tricks, for which they receive extra points.

WAKEBOARDING MANEUVERS

The majority of wakeboarding tricks take place in the air; to achieve this, the boarders must propel their entire board out of the water. Basic tricks include the following:

- "Grabbing the rail": while in midair, boarders grab onto the wakeboard with one hand while holding onto the ropes with the other hand
- "Flips and spins": wakeboarders turn themselves upside down or spin completely around; to achieve this, they often need to transfer the ropes from one hand to the other
- "Inverts": the rider is upside down while performing a trick; "handle-pass inverts" also include a spin that requires the rope handle to switch from one hand to the other

Other tricks are surface tricks, which are generally easier to accomplish than aerial ones. One trick is the "butter slide," wherein the boarders slide their boards sideways across the water. Other tricks involve spins, with a half spin being called a "180," a full spin a "360," and a double spin a "720." More complex wakeboarding tricks often have colorful names, such as the "hoochie glide-to-fakie," the "scarecrow mobius," the "bunny hop heli," and more.

Wakeboarding Equipment

A beginner may use a 60- to 65-foot (18.3- to 19.8-meter) rope, while a more experienced athlete might choose an 80-foot (24.4-meter) rope. There are rubber handles on the ropes for gripping and the rope material is generally polyurethane. Wakeboards are usually between 3.9 feet to 4.8 feet (1.2 to 1.5 meters) in length, and approximately 1.5 feet (0.5 meter) in width. They are concave in shape and often crafted from fiberglass, aluminum, and carbon graphite. Fins on the board range from 1 to 3 inches (2.5 to 7.6 centimeters) in length. Wakeboards typically weigh between 6 and 7 pounds (2.72 to 3.17 kilograms). Prices for wakeboards range significantly. It is possible to purchase one for $100, but a better model may cost $700 or more.

Most extreme wakeboarders wear high-wrap boots, which are rubber boots on metal plates that are attached to the boards; these boots protect the wakeboarders' feet and ankles. Some boarders, though, prefer bungee-strap bindings. These stretch more easily and can release during falls, which reduces the likelihood of injuries. Wet suits are recommended in cold weather, and these can cost up to $300. Helmets specifically made for wakeboarders and goggles protect the riders.

Wakeboarding Risks and Injuries

In 2004, the *American Journal of Sports Medicine* conducted a study of wakeboarding injuries, "Wakeboarding Injuries," based on data provided by 156 orthopedic surgeons and 86 wakeboarders. Study results indicate that the most common injuries are ACL (anterior cruciate ligament) tears, shoulder dislocations, and ankle sprains, often sustained when a wakeboarder falls and slams into the water. Because wakeboard bindings do not automatically release as do water skis, the athletes could collide with the wakeboard during a fall. Injuries seldom happen, though, because of a collision with a dock or other fixed object. This study also found that 21 percent of all wakeboarding injuries involve a fracture.

A second study, "Characteristics of Water Skiing-Related and Wakeboarding-Related Injuries Treated in Emergency Departments in the United States, 2001–2003," was also published by the *American Journal of Sports Medicine* in 2005. This study noted that wakeboarders were 6.7 times more likely than water skiers to be treated in the emergency department for a head injury. Lacerations were the most common injury, and the head and face were the most commonly injured part of the body. Males sustained the great majority of wakeboarding injuries, and wakeboarding accidents were most likely to happen to adolescents.

Wakeboarding Safety

Injury prevention suggestions from these studies include professional instruction and strength training before wakeboarding. Helmets and other protective gear should be investigated, the study suggested, along with the benefits of plastic or foam coating on ropes to reduce risk of lacerations and abrasions. Bindings that release easily during falls are recommended.

Other recommendations that were not included in these particular studies include the following:

- Wakeboarders must be proficient swimmers.
- Wakeboarders should wear life jackets, even if they are excellent swimmers.
- If boarding in cold water, wet suits are recommended.
- Wakeboarders should avoid shallow water and wakeboarding in bad weather conditions.
- Only board with an experienced driver.
- Before each ride, boards and ropes must be inspected.
- Sobriety is key to injury prevention.

See also Barefoot Water Skiing; Kite Surfing; Windsurfing

WEEKEND WARRIORS

The term "weekend warrior" refers to a person who does not regularly exercise during the work week, but then actively participates in vigorous physical activities during the weekend. Some have suggested that this term originated in the United States during the 1970s.

According to information culled from the Behavioral Risk Factor Surveillance System and the National Health and Nutrition Examination Survey, 1 to 3 percent of adults are in fact weekend warriors. This information was published in a report in the May 2007 issue of the *Medicine and Science in Sports and Exercise* journal (Stenson 2007).

Many adult extreme sports participants are characterized as weekend warriors, in large part because the overwhelming majority of extreme sports enthusiasts do not make a living by participating in the sport(s) they love. If they are lucky, they will work a full-time job to support themselves and then make enough money from their weekend competitions to cover the costs of their extreme sports participation; if they are not that lucky, then the costs of participating in their sport is just that: an expense.

Because of this situation, many athletes are not able to practice or engage in their preferred sport during the week or do the strengthening and flexibility exercises that are needed to prevent injuries. This creates a downwardly spiraling situation: because of job responsibilities, these adults do not have the time to exercise sufficiently during the week, which increases the likelihood that they will sustain injuries when they do participate in sporting activities. And, if they do sustain injuries, they may need to miss work, which may affect their finances negatively—which means that they would become less able to afford participating in extreme sports.

Weekend warriors are facing increasing challenges when trying to fit in more exercise time during the work week, in large part because people in the United States on average are working far more hours than those from a generation or so ago. Some estimates indicate that the average amount of time spent at work increased by 163 hours per year between 1969 and 1987. Therefore, it is increasingly difficult to schedule time to exercise regularly during the work week.

CHARACTERISTICS OF WEEKEND WARRIORS

Two studies—the 2003 Behavioral Risk Factor Surveillance System (BRFSS) and the 1999–2004 National Health and Nutrition Examination Survey (NHANES)—found that more men than women were weekend warriors. In the BRFSS study, 64.7 percent of weekend warriors were non-Hispanic whites; in the NHANES study, 74.7 percent were non-Hispanic whites.

Eighty-one percent of weekend warriors tended to overdo physical exertion by participating in household or transportation activities, while 65 percent of them did so by participating in sports and exercise activities.

SPORTING INJURIES

According to a 2003 study conducted by American Sports Data, Inc., between 3.5 and 4 million emergency room visits per year are sports related. A study conducted in 1997 focused more specifically on injuries caused by extreme sports participation. This study by the U.S. Consumer Product Safety Commission showed that 48,000 Americans arrived at hospital emergency rooms because of **skateboarding** injuries; this was an increase of 33 percent when compared with the previous year. Emergency room visits because of **snowboarding** injures rose 31 percent, while **mountain climbing** injuries rose by 20 percent. The report concludes that, "[b]y every statistical measure available, Americans are participating in and injuring themselves through adventure sports at an unprecedented rate" (Greenfeld 1999).

The question arises, then, as to why people are willing to risk injury to participate in extreme sports. *Time* magazine addresses that question, writing that,

> The rising popularity of extreme sports bespeaks an eagerness on the part of millions of Americans to participate in activities closer to the metaphorical edge, where danger, skill and fear combine to give weekend warriors and professional athletes alike a sense of pushing out personal boundaries ... you name the adventure sport—the growth curves reveal a nation that loves to play with danger. (Greenfeld 1999)

Tips to Avoid Sports-Related Injuries

The U.S. Department of Health and Human Services provides a series of tips to avoid sports-related injuries, many of which apply to extreme sports:

- Maintain a reasonable level of activity throughout the week, rather than segregating all exercise to the weekend
- Learn the proper way to participate in your sport
- Wear safety gear, as needed, including helmets, knee, elbow, and wrist pads and guards
- Gradually increase your level of exercise
- Include cardiovascular exercise, strength training, and flexibility exercises into your routine

---

WHEELCHAIR EXTREME SPORTS

People who use wheelchairs have adapted a number of extreme sports to suit their physical abilities and levels of mobility. Examples include power wheelchair racing; extreme chairing; sit ski; four cross (4X); chair bungee; body surfing; quad rugby; **sky diving**; scuba diving; **wakeboarding**; paragliding; and more. In some instances, the athletes had participated in extreme sports before their injuries and have since modified how they participate; in other cases, the athletes have only experienced extreme sport participation postdisability.

WHEELCHAIR SPORTS HISTORY

As early as the late 1940s, competitive wheelchair sporting events were held, when war veterans who were disabled during World War II began playing basketball in hospitals. General Omar N. Bradley is credited with leading this initiative.

Sports organization was also occurring in England. In 1948, 26 World War II veterans with spinal cord injuries competed in a sports competition in Stoke-Mandeville, England. This event was organized by noted neurosurgeon Dr. Ludwig Guttmann and included shot put, javelin, club throw, and archery events. In 1952, athletes from the Netherlands competed in those events, as well, which was the beginning of the International Stoke-Mandeville Games. The following year, athletes from Canada, Finland, France, and Israel joined in the competition.

In 1956, in the United States, the National Wheelchair Athletic Association formed (renamed Wheelchair Sports, USA in 1994) and, in 1957, the first National Wheelchair Games were held in New York City. In Rome, in 1960, approximately 400 athletes participated in a competition with Olympic-style flair. An expanded version of that event was held in Toronto in 1976 and, during that same year, the Paralympic Winter Games took place in Sweden. These games continue in different host cities to this day.

Aaron Fotheringham, 15, Vegas AMJam Team Member, tightens the bolts on his wheelchair before competing in the Vegas Valley Amateur Skatepark Series at Bunker Skatepark in North Las Vegas, February 10, 2007. (AP Photo/Jane Kalinowsky)

In the 1984 Summer Olympic Games, held in Los Angeles, California, wheelchair athletes performed exhibition track events, the first time that wheelchair athletes had competed during the Olympic Games.

WHEELCHAIR SPORTS

Wheelchair Rugby

One of the earliest extreme sports is quad rugby, also known as wheelchair rugby; the sport can be so rough that it has also been called murderball. Created by three Canadians, a Winnipeg quad rugby team coordinated an exhibition meet in Minnesota in 1979, the same year that a national tournament was first held in Canada.

In 1981, Brad Mikkelsen formed the first U.S. team, the Wallbangers, at the University of North Dakota. In 1982, quad rugby was played at the Southwest State University in Minnesota, when the North Dakota Wallbangers challenged the Minnesota Rolling Gophers. That same year, teams from Canada and the United States participated in the first international quad rugby tournament held at the University of South Dakota.

The U.S. Quad Rugby Association (USQRA) formed in 1988; the organization promotes the sport, worldwide; its existence arose during the first U.S. National Championships for quad rugby.

The International Wheelchair Rugby Federation (IWRF) formed in 1993, the year that seven countries met at Stoke-Mandeville, England, for the World Wheelchair Games. According to estimates, more than 45 quad rugby teams exist in the United States today, with at least 20 international teams.

In 1996, wheelchair rugby was an exhibition sport at the Summer Paralympic Games, with the gold medal going to the United States; the silver to Canada; and the bronze to New Zealand. After that, it became a full medal sport for the Paralympics. The 2000 Paralympics gold medal match was watched by more than 10,000 fans; the United States took the gold; Australia, the silver; and New Zealand, the bronze.

In 2005, a movie called *Murderball* was released, receiving excellent reviews, and highlighting the sport.

Wheelchair Racing

Power wheelchair racing was first organized as a sport in 2006, under the auspices of the Power Wheelchair Racing Association. In this sport, participants race against one another while in their wheelchairs; the fastest speed achieved so far is approximately 10 miles (16 kilometers) per hour. The association is trying to raise funds to develop a chair that can go 25 miles (40 kilometers) per hour or more that also has excellent suspension. The Power Wheelchair Racing Association welcomes everyone who wants to participate in this sport, creating racing levels that factor in an athlete's speed, abilities, and experience.

A wheelchair athlete named John "J2" Mryczko will travel 200 miles over a seven-day period in 2008 to raise funds for spinal cord research and a sport vehicle for his personal use.

Chairing

In chairing—also known as extreme chairing, depending upon the intensity and difficulty of the maneuvers—athletes gain momentum by going down ramps, and then they perform twists and spins and other **skateboard**-like moves while in their wheelchairs.

Four-Cross

In four-cross events, which are held in lift-assisted mountain biking locales, participants race in four-wheeled bikes. These bikes do not have pedals and can reach up to 30 miles (48 kilometers) per hour; because of their low center of gravity, they are significantly more stable than the average mountain bike.

Athletes in the United States and Canada have been participating in four-cross events for the past couple of years. In the United Kingdom, a group called the Rough Riderz is actively promoting the sport and pushing for venues for their wheelchair athletes.

Sit Ski

Sit ski athletes use a ski-like apparatus that includes a seat to ride down snowy slopes, using short ski poles to maneuver themselves. Rather than using a sit ski, athletes of certain abilities can use a mono ski or a bi-ski. In a mono ski, a molded seat is attached to the frame of the ski and shock absorbers remove some of the jolting; to use a mono ski, the athlete needs significant upper body strength and balance and, given the ability, the skier can independently use a chair lift. The bi-skis are better choices for beginners, as the two skis below the seat provide a wider base, which in turn offers more stability to the athlete.

Water Sports

In body surfing, athletes lie on their surfboards and use their arms and overall body motion to ride the waves. A program called "They Will Surf Again" occurs annually; former surfers who have sustained spinal cord injuries and nonsurfers with limited mobility gather to spend a day body surfing.

The International Water Ski Federation (IWSF) organizes slalom, trick, and jump tournaments for water skiers with limited mobility; the British Disabled Water Ski Association helps disabled individuals learn to water ski. Other organizations who provide support to these endeavors are the National Ability Center in Utah and Disabled Sports USA Far West.

Bungee Jumping

Some athletes **bungee jump** while in their wheelchairs; their bodies are attached to a bungee cord apparatus and their wheelchair is, as well.

WHEELCHAIR ATHLETES

One of the most well-known wheelchair athlete is Aaron Fotheringham who, as a teenager, learned to perform a full 360-degree flip while in his wheelchair; he has also performed the first wheelchair backflip. Some people call what he does "wheelchair skateboarding," but Aaron prefers the term "hard core sitting," and he uses that term to include—but not limit himself to—skateboarding moves. He observes skateboarders and **BMX (bicycle motocross)** riders and incorporates those moves into his own athleticism, using a wheelchair with suspension to soften the shock of his landings. Aaron has broken his elbow while performing his maneuvers and has knocked himself unconscious more than once.

Another athlete of renown is Mark Wellman, the first paraplegic to climb El Capitan and Half Dome in Yosemite National Park. He is also the first paraplegic to sit-ski across the Sierra Nevada mountain range without outside assistance. Wellman was chosen to carry the flame for the opening ceremonies of the Paralympic Games, held in Atlanta, Georgia, in 1996, and he needed to climb up a 120-foot (36.6-meter) rope to light the cauldron. Wellman has appeared on national television, and he has received congressional commendations; he has written about his experiences in his autobiography, *Climbing Back* (Wellman and Flinn 1996).

NATIONAL VETERANS WHEELCHAIR GAMES

The National Veterans Wheelchair Games are a combination sporting event and rehabilitation program for military veterans who use wheelchairs because of spinal cord injuries, amputations, and neurological challenges. More than 500 athletes participate in these games. Sports played at these events include swimming, table tennis, weightlifting, archery, air guns, basketball, nine-ball, softball, quad rugby, bowling, hand cycling, wheelchair slalom, power soccer, a motorized wheelchair rally, and track and field.

PARALYMPIC GAMES

Modern-day Paralympic Games feature accomplished athletes with six varieties of disabilities, with an emphasis on the athletes' outstanding abilities rather than their disabilities. Summer and Winter Paralympics are held during the same years as the corresponding Olympic Games and, since the 1988 Olympics in Seoul, Korea, and the 1992 Olympics in Albertville, Canada, the venues for the Olympics and Paralympics are the same.

In 2002, the International Paralympic Committee recognized several athletes for outstanding accomplishments in their chosen sports. These athletes included Mustapha Badid of France, Heinz Frei of Switzerland, Baruch Hagai of Israel, and Mike Dempsey of the United States.

In 2004, in the Summer Paralympic Games in Athens, Greece, 3,806 athletes from 136 countries participated in 19 sports. The 2006 Paralympics in Torino, Italy, featured 58 events, with wheelchair curling added for the first time; 139 nations sent athletes. The 2008 Paralympics in Beijing, China, offered 20 sports for more than 4,000 athletes from 148 countries. The 2010 Winter Paralympics will be held in Vancouver, Canada; the 2012 Paralympics will be held in London, England; and the 2014 Winter Paralympic Games will be held in Sochi, Russia.

Twenty-seven sports are played at these games, which are overseen by one of several organizations. The International Paralympic Committee (IPC) oversees the following events:

- Alpine Skiing
- Athletics
- Biathlon
- Cross-Country Skiing
- Ice Sledge Hockey
- Power Lifting
- Shooting

- Swimming
- Wheelchair Dance Sport (a non-Paralympic sport)

The Cerebral Palsy International Sports and Recreation Association (CPISRA) oversees boccia and football seven-a-side. The International Blind Sports Federation (IBSA) manages the football five-a-side, goal ball, and judo; the International Wheelchair and Amputee Sports Federation (IWAS) oversees wheelchair fencing and wheelchair rugby. Finally, international federations manage these events:

- Archery (International Archery Federation)
- Bowls (International Bowls for the Disabled)
- Cycling (International Cycling Federation)
- Equestrian (International Equestrian Federation)
- Rowing (International Rowing Federation)
- Sailing (International Foundation for Disabled Sailing)
- Table Tennis (International Table Tennis Federation)
- Volleyball (Sitting) (World Organization for Volleyball for the Disabled)
- Wheelchair Basketball (International Wheelchair Basketball Federation)
- Wheelchair Curling (World Curling Federation)
- Wheelchair Tennis (International Tennis Federation)

WHITE, SHAUN (1986–)

Shaun Roger White is a professional **snowboarder** from the United States who has won numerous gold medals in the Winter **X Games** and an Olympic gold medal in 2006. White began competing on an amateur level at the age of 7 and turned professional six years later. He is known for crossing over to the sport of **skateboarding** and successfully competing at two sports on a professional level, as well as for his effortless style, his shaggy red hair, and his quirky sense of humor.

Early in his career, he was called "Future Boy" because snowboarders believed that he was the face of the future of their sport. Because of his vivid red hair, he is perhaps better known as the "Flying Tomato"; for a while, White wore headbands featuring flying tomatoes, but he eventually tired of wearing them. Other nicknames for White have been "The Egg" (describing how he looks with a helmet) and "Señor Blanco." In a post-Olympics interview with *Rolling Stone* titled "Shaun White: Attack of the Flying Tomato," White said that if he were allowed to create his own nicknames, they would be "Incredibly Handsome Man" and "Sir Shaun of Shaunalot" (Edwards 2006). He also expressed hope that his Olympic gold medal would help him out with the ladies.

White was born on September 3, 1986, in Carlsbad, California (near San Diego) to Roger and Cathy; his older brother is named Jesse and his sister, Kerri. White was born with a heart condition that affected the flow of oxygen in his blood, but a pair of surgeries corrected the problem. Even as a young child, Shaun White looked for new adventures, learning to surf, ski, play soccer, skateboard, and jump on trampolines.

At age 6, White went on a skiing trip near Big Bear Lake with his family; there, he enviously watched snowboarders, but he could not take lessons because he was too young (the required age was 12). So, his father took lessons and then shared what he learned with his son. White quickly caught on; his brother Jesse has been quoted as saying that, just as "Mozart was supposed to play piano," snowboarding was "that kind of deal for Shaun" (Booth and Thorpe 2007, 356).

White entered—and won—his first snowboarding competition when he was 7 years old. This win allowed him to compete in the U.S. Amateur Snowboard Association (USASA) national championships, where he placed 11th in the 12 and under division. He continued to compete, winning five national titles in that division. His decision to turn pro in 2000 was fueled in part by the rising costs of travel and equipment; his family was spending up to $20,000 annually on his snowboarding ventures, but money troubles were quickly eased when Burton Snowboards contracted with White to endorse their products.

In 2002, White competed for a spot on the snowboarding Olympic team for the United States, but he missed qualifying by 0.3 points. Competing in the Winter X Games, he won the silver medal in both events: half-pipe and slopestyle. That summer, White toured with **Tony Hawk's** Gigantic Skatepark Tour, and Hawk proposed that White become a professional skateboarder. Although White enjoyed skateboarding and was intrigued by the offer, he was not yet ready to reduce his level of focus on snowboarding.

During the 2003 winter season, White demonstrated his 1080 (360 degrees times three) snowboarding moves, wherein he would rotate three complete times before landing. He once again competed in the Winter X Games, where he captured two gold medals (half-pipe and slopestyle). That same year, White became the youngest boarder to win the U.S. Open Slopestyle Championship, and he was subsequently ranked as the number one snowboarder worldwide. Another accomplishment was a first place finish in the Global X Games in the half-pipe event.

White achieved all these successes even though he cut his 2003 snowboarding season short to turn professional in the sport of skateboarding. He competed in the 2003 Slam City Jam North American Skateboarding Championships, held in Vancouver, Canada; he finished fourth in the vert competition. White also competed in skate in the Summer X Games, where he finished sixth in vert. That year, he received the ESPN ESPY Award for the Best Action Sports Athlete.

In the 2004 Winter X Games, White won the gold in the slopestyle event but, after qualifying for the superpipe event, he had to drop out of the competition because of a knee injury. After having surgery, he returned too soon to competition and reinjured his knee. Because of the heart surgeries performed when White was a child, he was unable to get the MRI (magnetic resonance imaging) tests needed to track the progress of his recovery.

White recovered in time to compete in the 2005 Winter X Games, where he garnered his third gold medal in the slopestyle event. Later that year, White won the skateboarding vert event in the Dew Action Sports Tour, following that up with a silver medal in skate in the Summer X games. This dual accomplishment made White the first athlete to win medals at both the Summer and Winter X Games.

In 2006, White won both snowboarding gold medals in the X Games, and he came in first place in five U.S. Snowboarding Grand Prix Series events. Other accomplishments include a first place finish in the Dew Action Sports Tour and in the U.S. Open in both half-pipe and slopestyle.

White then became focused on the upcoming Olympics. To train for the 2006 Winter Olympics, to be held in Torino, Italy, White spent half a year in New Zealand to take advantage of the winter weather. At the Olympics, on his first qualifying run for the half-pipe event, White lost his balance, something that he rarely did; after the first run, he was in 7th place and only the top six advanced to finals. On his second run, though, he was back on track as the song *Back in Black* by AC/DC blared. He earned a score of 45.3, the highest of the day, and qualified for the U.S. Olympic snowboarding team.

In the final run of the Olympics, White went all out for the medal, starting with a "McTwist," which meant that he combined a one and a half spin with a front flip. He then completed a "frontside 1080," which was composed of three full 360-degree turns, counterclockwise, followed by a "fakie 1080," which is a snowboarding trick performed in reverse. He ended with a "backside 900," which has a clockwise spin. This performance earned White his Olympic gold medal; his tears at the ceremony brought him significant media attention.

Rolling Stone proclaimed him as the "coolest kid in America," while skateboarder Tony Hawk called White "one of the most amazing athletes on the planet. He's got his own style—plus he can do tricks five feet higher than everyone else." In the *Rolling Stone* interview after his win, White simply said, "I got a gold medal; I guess I'm an athlete now. I gotta start going to the gym" (Booth and Thorpe 2007, 356).

In 2007, White won the Burton Global Open Championship and the TTR Tour Championship, both in snowboarding. He won the gold in the Winter X Games, as well, with *Transworld Snowboarding* naming him Rider of the Year. He was also the 2007 AST Skate Vert champion.

In 2008, White scored 96.66 out of a possible 100 in the Winter X Games, super-pipe event, after completing both "front and backside 1080s" and a "frontside 1260"—and he clinched the gold medal. White also won the 2008 X Games bronze for slopestyle snowboarding. With these performances, White tied Tanner Hall for the most X Games medals awarded to a single athlete. In the Burton European Open, he won first in slopestyle and second in superpipe, and he was named the overall champion for the Burton Open. White was also given the Laureus World Sports Award for "World Action Sportsperson of the Year" in skateboarding.

White has appeared in a full-length snowboarding DVD called *The Shaun White Album* (2004), plus the documentary *First Descent* (2005). In 2006, he signed with Ubisoft to create a snowboarding video game. Shortly before the 2008 Winter X Games, White signed a 10-year sponsorship deal with Burton Snowboards, the longest snowboarding deal made to date. Other sponsorship deals have included ones with Oakley, Volcom, Mountain Dew, Sony PlayStation, and Target.

See also Palmer, Shaun; Shaw, Brooke

WINDSURFING

Windsurfing is a sport in which participants use a combination board and sail to navigate the water while standing on the board. The board—called a sailboard—resembles a wide surfboard with an attached sail, mast, and boom; a universal joint is used to connect the board and sail, which creates a mobile sail that can be controlled by the surfer. Using the power of winds and waves, and steering with his or her feet, the windsurfer glides across the water, making this sport a combination of surfing and sailing. There are various disciplines of windsurfing, including the following:

- Racing
- Freestyle (performing tricks, stunts, and maneuvers)
- Slalom (racing with the wind)
- Course racing (racing against the wind)
- Wave sailing (sailing in and performing maneuvers on the waves)

Basic tricks include jumps, sailing backward, going from a standing to a sitting position, and so forth. More advanced tricks use more complicated spins and turns. Windsurfing has been called "sailboarding" and "boardsailing."

The majority of participants are white, middle-class males who have enough disposable income to purchase the necessary equipment and travel to locations where they can windsurf. The majority of top class windsurfers are males in their 20s, but more casual windsurfers range in age from their teens through their 60s. Studies indicate that between 13 and 30 percent of windsurfers are female; however, some women participate only in the sense that their male partners are part of the windsurfing subculture.

Modern-day sailboards range from 8 to 12 feet (2 to 4 meters) in length and they weigh between 15 and 40 pounds (7 to 18 kilograms). Some athletes have exceeded speeds of 40 knots (46.1 miles/74.2 kilometers per hour). Beginning sailboards cost between $1,000 and $1,800, with high-end sailboards often costing more than $5,000.

CONTROVERSIAL ORIGINS OF THE SPORT

It is possible that ancient peoples living along the Amazon River in South America used a combination of a raft and movable sail to navigate the river, which would make them the predecessors of modern-day windsurfers.

In the 1930s, a man from the United States named Tom Blake wanted to find an easier way to surf, as he was tired of having to paddle with his arms to get out to the waves. He experimented with using his umbrella as a sail, and then he added a mast and sail to his surfboard. Later, he added a rudder, and he then tried to sell his invention. Although he had created a workable sailboard, he met with no commercial success. Moreover, his name is seldom included in the history of windsurfing.

The traditional history of windsurfing states that two Californians, an aeronautics engineer and surfer named Jim Drake and a businessman and surfer named Hoyle Schweitzer, invented the windsurfing sailboard in 1968. The two men called their invention a "freesailing system." Their invention was 12 feet (3.65 meters) in length, and crafted from molded plastic. It took them a couple of years to get an approved patent—and this patent met with controversy almost immediately in England, and then in the United States, decades later.

The first controversy arose when the men, who had obtained patents in several places internationally, tried to patent their invention in England. This patent was contested by Peter Chilvers, who claimed to have been using a sailboard since 1958, when he launched off of Hayling Island in Hampshire, England. A judge agreed with Chilvers and so, in England, Chilvers is considered the father of this sport.

In 1985, in the English lawsuit *Windsurfing International Inc. v Tabur Marine*, Drake and Schweitzer's company sued another company for manufacturing a product similar to their sailboard. Tabur Marine presented a defense based on the fact that Chilvers, in fact, had invented the sailboard, not Drake and Schweitzer. The judge sided with the defense and Drake and Schweitzer's English patent was declared invalid. These became definitive cases in the United Kingdom and frequently are cited by attorneys and judges in patent-related legal matters.

The second controversy took place in 1996, when *American Windsurfer* published an article, "Origins of Windsurfing," that focused on the accomplishments of Drake and Schweitzer. An archivist for the Smithsonian Institution, who had previously done research on the beginnings of windsurfing, asked that *American Windsurfer* forward a copy of this issue to a retired sign painter named S. Newman Darby. The publisher did so, and Darby responded by sending the magazine a three-hour video of his contributions to the sport of windsurfing.

Darby claims to have invented and tested a sailboard in 1964, sailing around Chesapeake Bay with it in 1965. He published an article about these experiences in a small newspaper, the *Pittston Gazette*, in July 1965. The following month, he published an article about his invention in *Popular Science* and advertised his invention in the back of the magazine. He was offering to sell do-it-yourself plans and kits, as well as pre-built sailboards. At that time, *Popular Science* had a circulation of about 6 million, but the article did not garner significant attention.

Darby did not file a patent on his invention, citing a shortage of cash during the years that he was raising his family. He and his brothers, Ronald and Ken, manufactured approximately 160 boards and sold about half of them at a price of $295 each; Darby's wife, Naomi, sewed the sails. Darby kept careful notes during this time frame, as well as early versions of his boards and sails. He also kept photographs and a home movie that his wife shot in 1965.

American Windsurfer found the evidence gripping, stating that, "The photographs and the film footage were so complete and so compelling that we were stunned that such evidence existed and we didn't know about it. What we prided as the definitive article on the 'Origins of Windsurfing' became embarrassingly incomplete" (Riordan 1998).

In response, the magazine published two articles in 1997 about Darby's accomplishments, and neither Drake nor Schweitzer responded to the articles. It should be noted that, in the "Origins of Windsurfing" article, Drake called himself the "re-inventor" of the sailboard, not the inventor. This statement, however, raised another question because, in a patent application, the applicants need to list "prior art," which is information about related inventions; Drake and Schweitzer did not list Darby's work. If they were in fact aware of Darby's invention, why did they not list it in their patent application? Shortly after the interviews with Darby appeared, the Smithsonian Institution gained possession of some of Darby's artifacts, which further cemented Darby's role in the creation of windsurfing.

Returning to the traditional timeline of windsurfing's origins, Schweitzer and Drake had trademarked their patented invention as a "windsurfer" in 1970. That same year, these sailing boards began to be mass produced. In 1972, Schweitzer bought out his partner's rights to the patent for a sum of $36,000. Hundreds of thousands of these windsurfers have since been sold and, by the 1990s, more than 1.5 million people were windsurfing in the United States alone.

DEVELOPMENT OF THE SPORT

As early as 1975, windsurfing freestyle competitions were held in New York City and San Diego, California. In 1977, slalom events were held in Sardinia, Italy; in 1980, speed trials took place in Maalaea, Maui, with a speed of 21.8 knots (slightly more than 25 miles/40 kilometers per hour) achieved by competitors.

During the 1980s, a "fun board" was developed, and this evolution of the sailboard caused increasing numbers of people to begin windsurfing. The fun board was shorter than a typical sailboard, lighter, and more maneuverable. In this decade, windsurfing was the fastest-growing sport in Europe, with more than half a million sailboards being sold globally. By the 1990s, boards weighed as little as 5 kilograms (11 pounds) and surveys suggest that 640,000 people were "regularly" windsurfing in the United Kingdom.

Windsurfers embraced a philosophy that included having fun and living life as an individual; perhaps this is why so few windsurfers belong to clubs, preferring to loosely associate with informal windsurfing groups. Rather than compete against one another, many windsurfers believe that true competition comes from facing the elements of nature. Many windsurfers reject the label of "extreme" and even of "sport," as they consider windsurfing more of a lifestyle choice than an organized sport.

There is, however, a national association, the Professional Windsurfing Association (PWA), that oversees the fun board events; PWA competitions include wave sailing, freestyle, racing, speed sailing, and even indoor windsurfing.

One of the most recognized windsurfers is Robby Naish, who won his first title in 1976 as a young teenager and who continued to compete for more than 20 years. Another athlete, Dutch Björn Dunkerbeck from the Canary Islands, won 12 PWA Championships from 1988 to 1999. Two women who have dominated the sport are twins: Iballa and Diada Ruano Moreno from Spain.

Companies have capitalized on the windsurfing subculture, creating and selling sunglasses, T-shirts, jewelry, and so forth that are specifically targeted to windsurfers.

Windsurfing is currently popular in Europe, Australia, and North America, with Hawaii—where windsurfing foot straps were invented—serving as a center of activity. Other places in the United States where windsurfing is popular include northern California and Oregon. In Europe, the Atlantic Coasts of the United Kingdom, Ireland, and France, and parts of Holland, Denmark, Germany, Austria, Italy, and Switzerland are popular spots for windsurfers. Other places include South Africa, South America, and the Caribbean and Pacific Islands.

WINDSURFING AND THE OLYMPICS

Windsurfing took another significant step forward as an officially recognized sport when it became part of the Olympics in Los Angeles, California, in 1984. Initially, only men competed but, in 1992, a women's event was added.

In 1984, medal winners were Stephan Vandenburg from Holland, Scott Steele from the United States, and Bruce Kendall from New Zealand. In 1988, Bruce Kendall from New Zealand won the gold, Jan Boresma from the Netherlands Antilles won silver, and Mike Gebhart from the United States captured the bronze medal.

In 1992, women competed in Barcelona, Spain, with Barbara Kendall from New Zealand, Zhang Xiaodong from China, and Doreen De Vries from Holland winning the gold, silver, and bronze medals, respectively. In the men's event, the medal winners were Frank David from France (gold), Mike Gebhart from the United States (silver), and Lars Kleppich from Australia (bronze).

In 1996, the women's winners were Lai Shan Lee from Hong Kong (gold), Barbara Kendall from New Zealand (silver), and Alessandra Sensini from Italy (bronze). Men's winners were Nikos Kalaminakis from Greece (gold), Carlos Espinola from Argentina (silver), and Gal Friedman from Israel (bronze).

In 2000, Alessandra Sensini from Italy won gold; Amelie Lux from Germany, the silver; and Barbara Kendall from New Zealand, the bronze. For the men, Austria's Christoph Sieber, Argentina's Carlos Espinola, and New Zealand's Aaron McIntosh received the medals.

EXTREME WINDSURFING

In 1979, an adventurer named Baron Arnaud de Rosnay windsurfed across the Bering Strait, which is the narrowest point between the United States and Russia. This strait is frozen for nine months out of the year, but de Rosnay successfully traveled the 85 miles (136.8 kilometers) on his sailboard, making him the first person to cross the Bering Strait without the help of a motor.

In 1980, the baron traveled 750 miles (1,207 kilometers) in 11 days, traveling from the island of Nuku Hiva in French Polynesia to the Ahe atoll, near Tahiti. In doing so, he windsurfed four times longer than anyone has to date; he suffered from both severe sunburn and shark attacks during this adventure.

In 1982, he windsurfed across the English Channel in 1 hour and 39 minutes, which shaved almost 3 hours off the previous record. On November 24, 1984, he was windsurfing the Formosa Strait, which is located between mainland China and Taiwan. He did not complete this journey and both he and his sailboard vanished.

Another adventurous windsurfer was Christian Marty, a French pilot who windsurfed 100 miles (161 kilometers) from Guadeloupe to Martinique, both in the Caribbean. In 1980, he windsurfed from Nice, France, to Corsica, Spain, which is a distance of 105 miles (169 kilometers). In 1982, he crossed the Atlantic Ocean, a 2,400-mile (3,219-kilometer) journey from Africa to South America; his sailboard tipped over several times as he slept, but he survived to complete his quest.

In 1980, Anne Gardner and Jack Wood windsurfed across Lake Titicaca in South America, which is the highest lake in the world.

Other notable windsurfing adventurers include Ken Winner from the United States, who windsurfed 100 miles (161 kilometers) along the coast of Florida in less than 7 hours in 1979. Meanwhile, the Italian Sergio Ferrero traveled 150 miles (241.4 kilometers) from the island of Ibiza to Barcelona, Spain. Stephane Peyron windsurfed from New York to France, and he attempted to windsurf to the North Pole, although he turned around before reaching his destination.

On April 10, 2005, Irishman Finian Maynard set an average speed world record of 48.70 knots (56.05 miles/90.2 kilometers per hour), while surfing a 500-meter (1,640.4-foot) course at Saintes-Maries-da-la-Mer in France. On March 5, 2008, at the same location, Frenchman Antoine Albeau broke Maynard's world record when he sailed at an average speed of 49.09 knots (56.49 miles/90.9 kilometers per hour).

WINDSURFING RISKS AND INJURIES

Although some deaths have been reported because of collisions or drownings, serious injuries are relatively rare in windsurfing. That said, one form of windsurfing, called wave sailing, causes more injuries when surfers "loop"—or somersault high in the air—and the sailboard lands on top of the athlete.

Windsurfers are warned against surfing alone; however, if a person is windsurfing alone and is in distress, he or she should make alternating X and V movements with hands held high over head.

Windsurfers should check weather reports before heading out into the water. Hypothermia is a concern, as lowered body temperatures make it more difficult to paddle to shore; dehydration is another condition to avoid. Depending on the venue, other risk factors include jellyfish, such as the Portuguese man-of-war, whose sting can cause shortness of breath and pain at the site of the sting; sharks; and sharp coral.

More typical injuries in windsurfing include cuts and bruises; sunburn; back strains; ankle and foot sprains or fractures, which often occur during falls when the feet are still hooked to straps on the board; and dislocated shoulders. Factors that increase the likelihood of injuries include an overall lack of fitness; inexperience; faulty technique; lack of protective gear; and high-risk maneuvers, such as jumping.

WINDSURFING EQUIPMENT

Windsurfers should wear life jackets in case of an emergency, and helmets, especially when racing. Harnesses can be purchased and hooked up to the boom; this way, surfers do not need to solely rely on their arm strength to hold on to the boom. Windsurfing booties make it easier to maintain a grip on the sailboards, and gloves protect the surfers' hands while holding on to the boom. Wet suits keep the body warm. Other important items for windsurfers include sunglasses and sunscreen, and flares, whistles, and fluorescent flags to signal for help.

See also Barefoot Water Skiing; Kite Surfing; Wakeboarding

X GAMES

Before 1993, the average American probably did not have too much knowledge about extreme sports. Only a handful of extreme athletes—most notably **Tony Hawk**—had become anything close to a household name. Although a few corporate advertisements contained snippets of extreme sports participation—most prominently the Mountain Dew commercials—these sports did not receive much media coverage. Niche magazines did exist, but they focused on a single extreme sport, and they were not available on grocery store and drug store magazine racks where a browser could pick up a copy.

All of that began to change in 1993 after Ron Semiao, the program director for ESPN2 (Entertainment and Sports Programming Network), noticed how some companies were using extreme sports activities in their marketing. He researched the subject, but could not find any source that provided information about extreme sports as a whole. He quickly recognized that extreme sports would appeal to a key demographic—teenage boys and young adult males with a substantial amount of buying power—and he realized that an extreme sports competition could be a significant moneymaker for ESPN.

Semiao presented the idea of hosting an action sports competition with athletes from around the globe. Winners would receive medals—gold, silver, and bronze—just as they would at the Olympics. ESPN management agreed and so, on April 12, 1994, at a press conference held at Planet Hollywood in New York City, station representatives announced that the first annual Extreme Games would be held in June 1995 in Rhode Island. Although ESPN was the subject of derisive comments by those who did not think **skateboarding**, **snowboarding**, and the like were "real" sports, they moved ahead with organizing this sports festival. In the meantime, ESPN also searched for corporate sponsorships to provide a tantalizing prize purse and to allow the Extreme Games to become a lucrative proposition.

ESPN was successful in securing sponsors; the seven **sponsors** for the initial games were Advil, Mountain Dew, Taco Bell, Chevy Trucks, AT&T, Nike, and Miller Lite. The sponsors were well pleased with their return on investment and the 1995 Extreme Games provided the impetus for future sponsorships of extreme sports athletes and events.

HISTORY OF THE GAMES

The 1995 Extreme Games

The first Extreme Games were held from June 24 to July 1, 1995, in Newport, Providence, and Middletown, Rhode Island, and Mount Snow, Vermont.

Approximately 198,000 spectators attended these games, watching athletes compete in 27 events. The average daily television viewership was 307,138 households.

Competitive events included aggressive **inline skating**, bicycle stunt riding, **bungee jumping**, extreme **adventure racing**, skateboarding, **sky surfing**, snowboarding, sport climbing, **street luge racing**, and **wakeboarding**.

Because of the large amount of attention paid to the Extreme Games, it was decided to hold the event annually, rather than every other year, as was initially planned.

The 1996 Summer X Games II

In 1996, the name of the event was changed to "X Games," in part because of the marketability of the letter "X," and in part because "X Games" could more easily be branded in international markets. ESPN decided to also create a competition that focused on winter extreme sports, which opened up even more sponsorship opportunities and more opportunities for American viewers to learn about extreme sports athletes and events. Because of these two changes, the name of the event changed from "Extreme Games" to the "Summer X Games."

Newport, Rhode Island, served as the venue for the X Games in 1996. Three sports—**kite skiing, windsurfing**, and **mountain biking**—were removed from the roster. Approximately 200,000 spectators watched the competition, which brought the host city $5 million.

On June 30, it was announced that the first Winter X Games would be held at the Snow Summit Mountain Resort, which was located in Big Bear Lake in California. Events would include trick skiing contests, snowboarding, **ice climbing**, snow mountain bike racing, super-modified shovel racing, **motocross**, and a multisport event.

The 1997 Winter X Games I and Summer X Games III

The first Winter X Games were held from January 30 to February 2, 1997; these games were televised in 198 countries, and translated into 21 languages. ABC Sports broadcast the events and more than 38,000 spectators attended.

In March, ESPN held qualifying events in Providence, Rhode Island, to determine who could participate in the X Games; this practice continued through 2002 in various cities across the United States.

The Summer X Games were held from June 20 through June 28 in San Diego and Oceanside, California; approximately 221,000 people attended the games. Although it was summer, one event was called "snowboard big air," in which athletes performed a 10-story jump off of "hundreds of tons of manmade snow" (EXPN 2007). It was estimated that 74 million people watched the televised X Games.

In September, the X Games created their first-ever road show, named Xperience. This show traveled to Disneyland in Paris, France, where the X Game athletes performed with Eurosport athletes.

The 1998 Winter X Games II/Summer X Games IV

In 1998, an international qualifying event was held in Phuket, Thailand, featuring 200 athletes; the most elite of these athletes would be assured of a place at the Summer X Games to be held in San Diego, California, in June.

That year's Winter X Games were held at the Crested Butte Mountain Resort in Colorado, where three new sports were added: freeskiing, **snowmobile snocross**, and skiboarding. Approximately 25,000 fans attended the games.

Attendance at the summer games continued to rise, as more than 233,000 people traveled to Mariner's Point to watch the games. Sponsorship dollars also continued to be attractive, with a prize purse of more than $1 million, while the city benefited by an influx of $30 million.

The 1999 Winter X Games III/Summer X Games V

The 1999 Winter X Games were again held at Crested Butte, with women's freeskiing added to the mix. More than 30,000 fans attended the games.

The 1999 Summer X Games were held in San Francisco, where nearly 275,000 people attended. Tony Hawk successfully performed his first skateboarding "900," which involved two full rotations, plus another half twist. At these games, ESPN announced that future summer games would be held in August.

The 2000 Winter X Games IV/Summer X Games VI

From February 3–6, the Winter X Games were held in Mount Snow, Vermont, with the largest crowd ever: 83,500; the snowboard superpipe was added.

The 6th Summer X Games were held from August 17–22 in San Francisco. Motocross step-up was added as a new event; Tommy Clowers was the winner, reaching a record-breaking height of 35 feet (10.7 meters) on his motorcycle.

The 2001 Winter X Games V/Summer X Games VII

The Winter X Games were held from February 1–4, again in Mount Snow. Motocross big air was added. Approximately 85,000 fans attended the games.

The 7th Summer X Games were held from August 17–22 in Philadelphia, Pennsylvania, with downhill **BMX (bicycle motocross)** added to the roster of events. There were 234,950 attendees. At the games, ESPN and the Mills Corporation jointly announce that they would build public X Games skateparks in several locations around the country, where people could skateboard, inline skate, and practice bicycle stunt riding.

Several highlights mark these games. Bob Burnquist scored 98 points in the skateboard vert event, the highest point average awarded to a skateboarder to date. Taig Kris won the inline vert event, performing the first double backflip in the X Games. Danny Harf completed a 900 spin in wakeboarding.

The 2002 Winter X Games VI/Summer X Games VIII

The Winter X Games were held in Aspen, Colorado, at Buttermilk Mountain; new events included ski slopestyle and ski superpipe. The entire 2002 U.S. Olympic snowboard freestyle team competed in the snowboard superpipe event; there were 36,300 spectators at these games.

During the Asian X Games qualifying round held in January, more than 100,000 spectators watched the competitions. The Latin X Games qualifier was held in Rio de Janeiro, Brazil, on March 21–24; more than 200 athletes competed in skateboarding, bike stunt, aggressive inline skating, and wakeboard events. More than 37,500 spectators watched the live events and more than 30 million households watched the televised games. The European qualifying rounds were held in July, wherein athletes from 20 different countries competed in Barcelona, Spain. Approximately 35,500 attendees watched 10 athletes win a spot to the X Games; these athletes were from Spain, the United Kingdom, Germany, France, and Sweden.

The 8th Summer X Games were held in Philadelphia on August 15–19. New events included women's skateboarding and motocross. The average daily attendance was the highest yet at 40,210, with a total of 221,352 in attendance. Nearly 63 million people watched the televised games on ESPN, ESPN2, and ABC Sports.

These games were highlighted by two firsts. **Mat Hoffman** landed a no-handed 900-spin in BMX. Mike Metzer completed the first backflip in motocross freestyle over an 80-foot (24.4-meter) gap.

The 2003 Winter X Games VII/Summer X Games IX

The 7th Winter X Games were held in Aspen, Colorado, from January 30 to February 5; featured sports were motocross, skiing, snowboarding, and snowmobiling. Attendance reached 48,700, and television viewership hit an all-time high for winter games, with 412,673 viewers (a 33 percent increase from the previous year).

ESPN also introduced the X Games Global Championship to be held on May 15–18. In these games, athletes from six regions around the globe competed in summer and winter extreme sports simultaneously at two locations: San Antonio, Texas, and Whistler Blackcomb, British Columbia. Nearly 70,000 spectators watched as Team USA scored a total of 196 points and Team Europe scored 167 points.

The Summer X Games were held at Los Angeles, California, on August 14–17; total attendance was 187,141, with a record-breaking one-day attendance on August 16 of 67,500. Surfing was added to the roster of events, and women's skateboarding (park and vert) was included in the official competitions, rather than as an exhibition. The bike stunt vert competition was aired live, with record viewership numbers for the 12- to 17-year-old demographic. Overall, television viewership increased by 10 percent from the previous year. The highlight of the games occurred when Brian Deegan landed an off-axis backflip in motocross freestyle.

The 2004 Winter X Games VIII/Summer X Games X

The 8th Winter X Games were held in January at Buttermilk Mountain in Aspen, Colorado. These games, which included motocross, skiing, snowboarding, and snowmobiling, were the first to be broadcast live in the X Games.

The 10th annual Summer X Games were held in Los Angeles from August 5–8. This year's games featured a new finals-only format that was broadcast live; 150 athletes competed in aggressive inline skating, bike stunt, motocross, skateboarding, surfing, and wakeboarding. The television viewership was the highest ever, with a 47 percent increase from the last year's totals. Attendance was 170,471, with a record-breaking Saturday attendance of 79,380.

Highlights of the 2004 summer games included Tanner Hall's performance in ski slopestyle, in which he earned his third consecutive gold medal. Additionally, Nate Adams defeated the previously undefeated Travis Pastrana in motocross freestyle; and Danny Way won the gold in a new event: skateboard big air.

The 2005 Winter X Games IX/Summer X Games XI

The winter games were held in Aspen, Colorado, from January 29 to February 1, with ESPN's telecasts reaching 33 percent more households than last year, with an average of 677,000 households. On-site attendance was a record high at 69,750. Held in Los Angeles from August 4–7, ESPN broadcast the summer games to more than 75 countries. ESPN signed a contract with event organizers to keep the Summer Games in Los Angeles through 2009.

At these games, snowboarder **Shaun White** won the slopestyle event for the third year in a row. Highlights of the summer games included when White attempted to land the 1080 in skateboarding 29 times, but failed to complete the trick; and Jamie Bestwick landed the first "double tailwhip flare" in BMX vert.

The 2006 Winter X Games X/Summer X Games XII

The winter games were held in Aspen, Colorado, from January 28–31. That year, ESPN signed a contract with the Aspen Skiing Company to locate the Winter X Games in Colorado through 2010. These games generated $3.9 million for Aspen's economy; daily, local businesses collectively benefited by approximately $435,500. There were 69,650 spectators at the games, the second-highest attendance in its history; this is a 92 percent increase over the first time the events were held in Aspen. Prime time television viewership tied the Winter X Games record; the average viewership figures during prime time were 676,895 households, an increase of 8 percent over 2005. The afternoon viewing figures were 520,772 households, an increase of 45 percent over 2005 figures. Across all three networks carrying coverage—ABC Sports, ESPN, and ESPN2—these Winter X Games set an all-time coverage record with 747,130 households. This exceeded the previous year's figures by 45 percent, according to Nielsen Media Research.

A new event at these games was the sport of snowmobile freestyle. The X Games added mono skier X for disabled athletes; this event featured 16 men and women in individual sit-skis, competing in heats of four. Other changes included adding a best trick showdown to the snowboarding lineup, and eliminating motocross, which would remain in summer and international competitions.

During the 2006 games snowboarder Jeaux Hall landed a 1080 in the half-pipe contest. Tanner Hall returned after breaking both ankles and heels in 2005. After having been told he would never ski again, Tanner captured the gold medal in ski pipe. Additionally, snowboarder Shaun White won the slopestyle event for the fourth year in a row, becoming the only male extreme sports athlete to four-peat in a single X Games event.

The summer games were held in Los Angeles from August 3–6. New sports included rally car racing and BMX big air. More than 138,000 fans attended, which is nearly 13 percent more than 2005. More men in the 18–34, 18–49, and 25–54 age groups watched these games than any other X Games. Round-the-clock coverage was provided via ESPN and its affiliates, and ABC; pay-per-view was available for the first time, featuring BMX big air and moto-madness. Game highlights included when Travis Pastrana landed the double backflip in motocross.

The 2007 Winter X Games XI/Summer Games XIII

The winter games were held in Aspen, Colorado, from January 25–28. Attendance records were broken with 76,150 spectators. Fans could follow the games through the Internet or through their iPods. Some 734,000 households watched the games during prime time, the highest viewership to date. Sixty-four percent more men from ages 18 to 24 watched the games; the final day of the games 925,377 households watched, making it the highest-rated telecast since 1997. More than 2 million people viewed online content, including game videos, interviews, and more. This more than doubled 2005 usage; more than 3 million pages on EXPN.com were viewed, as well.

The summer games were held in Los Angeles from August 2–5. During these games, Australian skateboarder Jake Brown, while landing after a big air move, fell more than 40 feet (12.2 meters) to the ground below. Although he did not move for about 8 minutes, he was able to walk out of the venue with assistance. Injuries included a fractured wrist, bruised lung and liver, ruptured spleen, and a concussion. Other notable highlights of these games include Ricky Carmichael's medal in a new event (the motocross racing circuit); Mat Hoffman returned to compete in BMX big air; and Simon Tabron completed back-to-back 900s in BMX vert.

X GAMES CONTROVERSIES

Initial critics of the games felt that there was not enough interest in the United States for the Extreme Games to be sustainable, and others questioned whether the events planned for the games were in fact sports. Richard Sandomir of the *New York Times* called the Extreme Games the "Psycho Olympics."

Conversely, others claimed that, although the events included in the games could be considered sports, their value rested in the athletes' individuality and rebellion from the strictures of rules and scoring systems. These critics claimed that, when extreme sporting events became funded by corporate sponsors, the athletes were selling out. Thus, in their view, the meaning of the extreme sports had been degraded and the sports were turning mainstream.

The founder of the X Games, Ron Semiao, has been quoted as saying that, "When we launched the X Games, the reaction from mainstream sports media was, 'These aren't real athletes. These aren't real sports.' Now, in terms of the X Games sports turning mainstream, to me it's a sign of greater acceptance of the sports and greater acceptance of the athletes" (Simpson 2003).

Another criticism is that the courses set by ESPN are dangerous. To this charge, Semiao has responded this way: "I think if the athletes told us something was dangerous, we wouldn't do it. It's never been anything where we've pushed athletes to do something that they were against doing or unsure of doing" (Simpson 2003).

In 1997, the National Audubon Society and other environmental groups attempted to get a restraining order to prevent the athletes from competing where the California Least Tern and the Western Snowy Plover lived.

Environmentalists also criticized when freestyle motocross athlete Travis Patrana jumped his motorcycle so that he could land in the San Francisco Bay. Because he did so, ESPN determined that, even if he won the competition, he would need to forfeit. This caused some to ask why extreme and nonconforming behavior caused an athlete to be banned at a sporting competition that was billed as extreme and innovative. It seemed to these critics that ESPN was trying to soothe corporate sponsors who did not want to be associated with behavior that upset potential customers.

See also Gravity Games

YOGA SURFING

In this sport, participants use yoga movements and positions to strengthen their body and focus the mind, with the overall goal being to improve their ability to surf. Yoga surfers practice stretches to strengthen the shoulder muscles needed for paddling and perform certain movements to bolster the power in their core muscles so that they may more quickly position themselves on their surfboards. During relaxation exercises, participants imagine being on their favorite beach.

Proponents of this sport say that targeting yoga moves for their surfing activities lowers their risk of injury, increases their sense of flexibility and balance, and boosts their lung capacity.

DEVELOPMENT OF THE SPORT

The creation of yoga surfing is credited to swimmer Peggy Hall of Laguna Beach, California. In the 1990s, she tried surfing while vacationing in Hawaii; at about that time, she also started practicing yoga, hoping to prevent shoulder surgery for the chronic tendonitis that she suffered because of her swimming. Hall then noticed that her yoga moves allowed her to feel stronger and more balanced while surfing, and so she began teaching yoga specifically for surfers. Hall has since created yoga programs for **snowboarders**, **wakeboarders**, and **skateboarders**.

Bibliography

"Acrobats Strut Stuff at Moscow State Circus." *Sarasota Herald Tribune*, September 24, 2004.

"Action Man, Hasbro's Extreme New Action Figure, Is Introduced to American Kids." Business Network, August 23, 2000. www.bnet.com (accessed July 24, 2008).

AMA Motocross. www.amaproracing.com (accessed July 24, 2008).

American Parkour. "Extended: What Is Parkour?" May 12, 2004. www.americanparkour.com (accessed October 13, 2008).

Anders, Mark. "Lava Sledding Erupts Again." *Outside*, September 2003. http://outside.away.com (accessed July 26, 2008).

Andrews, Julian. "From 9 to 5 to Feeling Alive." *Cross Country Magazine*, December 2005. Louise Crandal www.crandal.dk (accessed July 26, 2008).

Appleton, Josie. "What's So Extreme about Extreme Sports?" Spiked Online, August 30, 2005. www.spiked-online.com (accessed July 26, 2008).

Arrington, Debbie. "They're Happily Hitting the Wall: Ricky Carmichael, a Six-Time Hangtown Winner, Is Turning His Attention to NASCAR." *Sacramento Bee*, May 18, 2007. HighBeam www.highbeam.com (accessed July 26, 2008).

Associated Press. "As Others Pass, Climber Dies Alone on Mount Everest." May 27, 2006. ESPN http://sports.espn.go.com (accessed July 26, 2008).

———. "Veteran Palmer Still King of Hill." *The Record*, January 26, 2008. HighBeam www.highbeam.com (accessed October 13, 2008).

"Back on the High Wire: Paralyzed 42 Years Ago, a Wallenda Wants to Show Off New Act." *Sarasota Herald Tribune*, January 3, 2005.

Baker, Aryn. "Best Tonic for a Tired Brain: Parahawking." *Time*, November 15, 2004. www.time.com (accessed July 26, 2008).

Bale, John, and Mette Krogh Christensen, eds. *Post-Olympism? Questioning Sport in the Twenty-First Century*. Oxford: Berg, 2004.

Balf, Todd. "That Which Does Not Kill Me Makes Me Stranger." *Outside*, September 1996. http://outside.away.com (accessed July 26, 2008).

Bane, Colin. "Jump First, Ask Questions Later." *Washington Post*, January 13, 2008.

Baulch, Vivian M. "The Adventures of the Human Fly." *Detroit News*, February 4, 1996. www.detroitnews.com (accessed July 26, 2008).

Beavers, Michael. "About USAWildwater.com." USAWildwater.com. www.usawildwater.com/about.htm (accessed October 13, 2008).

Bethge, Phillip. "The Search for the Basement of the World." Spiegel Online International, May 2, 2005. www.spiegel.de/international (accessed July 23, 2008).

"Bicycle Racing." *The Columbia Encyclopedia*, 6th edition. New York: Columbia University Press, 2007.

Blevins, Jason. "ESPN to Announce Winter X Games Will Remain in Aspen, Colo." *Denver Post*, January 21, 2004. HighBeam www.highbeam.com (accessed July 26, 2008).

Bleyer, Jennifer. "Barefoot Water Skiing. Putting Your Wet Foot Forward." *New York Times,* July 28, 2006. http://travel.nytimes.com (accessed July 24, 2008).

Boer, Martin. "Nambia: Sandboarding on a Sand Dune." *AP Worldstream,* August 19, 2004. HighBeam www.highbeam.com (accessed July 26, 2008).

"Boing! Boing! As Tricked-Out Pogo Sticks Become Part of the Curriculum, Mechanical Engineering Classes at Ohio State Get Whimsical." Ohio State University, June 15, 2007. http://oncampus.osu.edu (accessed July 26, 2008).

Booth, Douglas, and Holly Thorpe, eds. *Berkshire Encyclopedia of Extreme Sports.* Great Barrington, MA: Berkshire Publishing Group, 2007.

Borden, Iain. *Skateboarding, Space and the City: Architecture and the Body.* New York: Berg, 2001.

Bradley, Ryan. "Q+A: Greg Noll on Surfing as Art, Life." *National Geographic,* May 17, 2007. www.nationalgeographic.com (accessed July 26, 2008).

"British Is Easily Best after Those Austrians Send Me Snowblind: Alan Fraser's Screen Test." *Daily Mail,* February 21, 2005.

Buchanan, Rob. "Poser." *Outside,* June 1997. http://outside.away.com (accessed July 26, 2008).

Burnham, William. "Calm in Dark Places." *World and I,* January 1, 2004. Goliath http://goliath.ecnext.com (accessed October 13, 2008).

Burnside, Anna. "Racers Lead Charge of Women to Extreme Sport." *Sunday Times,* May 25, 2008. www.timesonline.co.uk (accessed July 26, 2008).

Calabria, Frank M. *Dance of the Sleepwalkers: The Dance Marathon Fad.* Bowling Green, OH: Bowling Green State University Press, 1993.

Castellanos, Vince. "Luge Vets Rule Seal Rock Run." EXPN.com, August 14, 2000. www.expn.go.com (accessed July 26, 2008).

———. "Sled NeX." EXPN.com, May 11, 2007. www.expn.go.com (accessed July 26, 2008).

Cavanaugh, Jack. "Speeding Up Play: Rounds on the Run." *New York Times,* October 2, 1997. www.nytimes.com (accessed July 26, 2008).

"Cellists' Tour Scales the Height of Achievement: Musicians Have Dreamt Up an Extreme Sport." *Daily Post,* August 3, 2006.

Chase, Ron. "Up a 'Steep Creek.'" *Sun Journal,* June 4, 2006. HighBeam www.highbeam.com (accessed October 13, 2008).

Chessman, Kristin Edelhauser. "Still Riding the Wave of Success." *Entrepreneur,* January 15, 2008. www.entrepreneur.com (accessed July 25, 2008).

———. "Tricks, Tats, and a Comeback." *Entrepreneur,* January 15, 2008. www.entrepreneur.com (accessed July 26, 2008).

Christie, Jack. "Hard-Core Ice Climbers Clamber Over Frozen Falls." Straight.com, February 18, 2004. www.straight.com (accessed July 26, 2008).

Clarey, Christopher. "A Free-Diver's Death: Tragic Plunge to the Limits." *International Herald Tribune,* October 19, 2002. www.iht.com (accessed July 26, 2008).

Coris, Eric E. "Are Extreme Sports a Good Thing?" *Tampa Bay Online,* May 9, 2008. www.2.tbo.com (accessed July 26, 2008).

Cox, Ralph. "United Kingdom: An Early Route to Market for Genetics, Confidentiality at a Price, and Other Recent Developments." Mondaq, March 5, 2008. www.mondaq.com (accessed July 26, 2008).

Cronin, Mike, and Wray Vamplew. *Sport and Physical Education: The Key Concepts.* London: Routledge, 2002.

Crookshanks, Ben. "Cavers and Spelunkers." ACE Adventure Center. www.aceraft.com/mediapg/medapg40.html (accessed October 13, 2008).

David, Leonard. "Space Diver Prepares for Big Jump." Space.com, July 13, 2006. www.space.com (accessed July 26, 2008).

Day, Lance, and Ian Mcneil, eds. *Biographical Dictionary of the History of Technology.* London: Routledge, 1998.

"Death of Skysurfer." *Sunday Mail,* August 16, 1998. HighBeam www.highbeam.com (accessed July 26, 2008).

Dill, Bob. "Frequently Asked Questions." North American Land Sailing Association, 2003. www.nalsa.org (accessed October 13, 2008).

Dirksen, Erica. "Young Women in Extreme Sports." *Wire Tap Magazine*, November 5, 2002. www.wiretapmag.com (accessed July 26, 2008).

Ebert, Karl. "The Lore of Iceboating: Pure Speed, Slick Boats—Low-Profile Sport Has Its Devotees, No Matter That Taking Vessels out on the Ice Is a Rare Event." *Wisconsin State Journal,* January 26, 2003. HighBeam www.highbeam.com (accessed July 26, 2008).

Ecott, Tim. "From Fantasy to Fatal Ambition." DiversNet, September 2004. www.diversnet.com (accessed July 26, 2008).

Edwards, Cristobal. "Sandboarding the Dragon: Iquique, Chile, Nestled Between the Pacific and the Atacama Desert, Is the Birthplace of Dune Surfing." *The Advocate*, November 8, 2005. HighBeam www.highbeam.com (accessed July 27, 2008).

Edwards, Gavin. "Shaun White: Attack of the Flying Tomato." *Rolling Stone*, February 24, 2006. www.rollingstone.com (accessed July 26, 2008).

Engelson, Andrew. "Where There's a Hill There's a Way to Enjoy the Thrill of Mountainboarding." *Seattle Post Intelligencer*, September 26, 2002. www.seattlepi.nwsource.com (accessed July 26, 2008).

"Everest's Cold Hard Fact." *Sydney Morning Herald,* May 25, 2006. www.smh.com.au (accessed July 26, 2008).

EXPN. "This History of X Games." About.com, July 30, 2007. http://skateboard.about.com/cs/events/a/XGamesHistory.htm (accessed October 13, 2008).

EXPN. "Mat Hoffman." EXPN.com. http://expn.go.com/bmx/hoffman/s/aboutmat.html (accessed October 13, 2008).

"Extreme Ironing: How Iron Men Let Off Steam." *Daily Record*, January 19, 2005.

"Fans Feel the Force of Gravity after the Inaugural Gravity Games: Over 200,000 Spectators Descend upon Providence." *Business Wire*, September 23, 1999. HighBeam www.highbeam.com (accessed July 26, 2008).

Farrow, Damian, and Justin Kemp. *Run Like You Stole Something.* Crows Nest, Australia: Allen & Unwin, 2004.

"FED: Champion Skysurfer Dies." *AAP General News*, January 23, 2004. HighBeam www.highbeam.com (accessed July 26, 2008).

"Felix Baumgartner Conquers the 'Seating of the Spirits.'" *Middle East*, February 26, 2007. HighBeam www.highbeam.com (accessed July 26, 2008).

Fenton, Mary. "W Skate Vert: CB Burns 'Em." EXPN.com, August 6, 2005. www.expn.go.com (accessed October 13, 2008).

"Ferraras Breaks Own Free Diving Record." *Sydney Morning Herald*, October 13, 2003. www.smh.com.au (accessed July 26, 2008).

Fickenscher, Pamela. "Off-Road Ministry: What I Learned From Mountain Biking." *Christian Century*, March 6, 2007.

Fiore, D. C. "Injuries Associated with Whitewater Rafting and Kayaking." *Wilderness and Environmental Medicine* 14 (2003): 255–60.

First Tracks. "Shaun White Wins X Games Snowboard SuperPipe Final." Online Ski Magazine, January 27, 2008. www.firsttracksonline.com (accessed July 26, 2008).

———. "Nissan O'Neill Xtreme Verbier Concludes Freeride World Tour." Online Ski Magazine, March 16, 2008. www.firsttracksonline.com (accessed July 26, 2008).

Fitzgerald, Toni. "Hip and Hipper: Winter X Games." *Media Life*, February 6, 2006. www.medialifemagazine.com (accessed July 26, 2008).

"Flights of Fancy: Hang Gliding Called the 'Purest' Way to Fly." *Washington Times*, June 20, 2005.

Forsman, L., and A. Eriksson. "Skateboarding Injuries of Today." *British Journal of Sports Medicine* 35 (2001): 325–28.

Frank, Matthew. "Pro Extreme Skier Billy Poole Dies after Cliff Jump." NewWest.Net, January 22, 2008. www.newwest.net (accessed October 13, 2008).

Fussell, James. "Skateboarding Phenomenon Soaring across America." *Knight Ridder Newspapers/Tribune News Service*, September 24, 2004. HighBeam www.highbeam.com (accessed December 29, 2007).

Galbraith, Jeff. "Dazed and Confused." *Time*, February 23, 1998. www.time.com (accessed July 26, 2008).

Garcia, Jose Esteban, Jr. "Speed Golf Can Be a Rush: Are You a Runner and a Golfer, But Don't Have Time to Do Both?" *Star Tribune*, August 20, 1999. HighBeam www.highbeam.com (accessed July 26, 2008).

Gianoulis, Tina. "Skateboarding." *St. James Encyclopedia of Pop Culture*, 2000. Find Articles www.findarticles.com (accessed December 31, 2007).

Gibbs-Smith, C. H. *A History of Flying*. New York: Praeger, 1954.

"Glider." *The Columbia Encyclopedia*. New York: Columbia University Press, 2004.

Godino, John, and John Bartholomew. "Rogaine Beginner's Guide—Top Ten Tips." Columbia River Orienteering Club. www.croc.org (accessed July 24, 2008).

Gorski, T. F., Y. C. Gorski, G. McLeod, D. Suh, R. Cordero, F. Essien, D. Berry, and F. Dada. "Patterns of Injury and Outcomes Associated with Motocross Accidents." *American Surgeon* 69 (2003): 895–98.

Graham, Matthew. "Free Flight Fans Warm to Winter." *Washington Times*, February 10, 2000.

Graves, Helen. "On Frozen Lakes: Iceboaters Satisfy Their Need for Speed." *Boston Globe*, March 26, 2000. HighBeam www.highbeam.com (accessed July 26, 2008).

Greenfeld, Karl Taro. "Life on the Edge." *Time*, August 29, 1999. www.time.com (accessed July 26, 2008).

Griffin, Drew, and James Polk. "Whitewater Deaths Surge in U.S." Cable News Network, September 6, 2006. www.cnn.com (accessed July 24, 2008).

Grose, Thomas K. "Depths of Passion: Did Francisco 'Pipin' Ferreras Murder Audrey Mestre?" Cyber Divers News Network. www.cdnn.info (accessed July 26, 2008).

Gutman, Bill, and Shawn Frederick. *Being Extreme: Thrills and Dangers in the World of High-Risk Sports*. New York: Kensington Publishing, 2002.

Handwerk, Brian. "Fear Factor: Success and Risk in Extreme Sports." National Geographic News, July 9, 2004. http://news.nationalgeographic.com (accessed January 28, 2007).

Harris, Julia. "XTreme Engineering." Ohio State University, May 16, 2007. http://oncampus.osu.edu (accessed July 26, 2008).

Harryman, Elizabeth. "Going to Extremes: Extreme Skiers Risk Life and Limb to Experience a Thrill Like None Other." *American Fitness*, February 3, 2008. HighBeam www.highbeam.com (accessed July 26, 2008).

Hattori, James. "Extreme Sports Diving into Mainstream." Cable News Network, November 30, 1998. www.cnn.com (accessed July 26, 2008).

Heil, Nick. "Left to Die on Everest." *Men's Journal*, August 2006. http://climb.mountainzone.com/2006/david_sharp/index.html (accessed October 13, 2008).

Hernu, Piers. "Thrilled to the Bone: Thought Rock Climbing Was a Challenge? It's a Stroll in the Park Compared to the Blood-Chilling Adventure of Indoor Ice Climbing." *The Mail on Sunday*, November 6, 2005. HighBeam www.highbeam.com (accessed February 3, 2008).

———. "Luge Control: Race Downhill at Extreme Speeds." *Daily Mail*, October 2007. *Daily Mail* www.dailymail.co.uk (accessed July 26, 2008).

Higgins, Matt. "On a Mission, and Rolling." *New York Times*, July 26, 2006. www.nytimes.com (accessed July 26, 2008).

———. "Winter Sports: Hoping That Winter X Games Can Turn White Into Green." *New York Times*, January 28, 2007. www.nytimes.com (accessed July 26, 2008).

Hill, Craig. "Look, Ma—No Skis! Experts Offer Their Advice and Warnings for Those Wanting to Learn How to Ski on Water Barefoot." *News Tribune*, September 14, 2006. www.thenewstribune.com (accessed July 24, 2008).

Hill, Silvie. "Welcome to the Terrordome." *Ottawa Xpress*, May 17, 2007. www.ottawaxpress.ca (accessed July 26, 2008).

Ho, Melanie. "For Red Bull, It's Here, There, and Everywhere: Energy Drink Maker Corners the Marketing." *Washington Post*, August 23, 2006.

Horton, Julia. "Freefall Freedom Extremists with Fighters or Just a Death Wish?" *Evening News—Scotland*, October 6, 2004. HighBeam www.highbeam.com (accessed July 26, 2008).

"How Tony Hawk Stays Aloft." *Business Week*, November 13, 2006. www.businessweek.com (accessed July 26, 2008).

"Iceboating." *The Columbia Encyclopedia*, 6th edition. New York: Columbia University Press, 2007.

"I'm Spiderman." *The Guardian*, May 14, 2003. http:film.guardian.co.uk (accessed July 24, 2008).

"Is This the Craziest Sport in the World?" *Western Mail*, March 24, 2006.

"It All Began with the First Pitch." *Sarasota Herald Tribune*, April 4, 2005.

Iwata, Edward. "Executive Suite: Tony Hawk Leaps to Top of Financial Empire." *USA Today*, March 10, 2008. www.usatoday.com (accessed July 26, 2008).

Jackson, Lorne. "Living on the Edge: At Work with Father and Son High Wire Daredevils." *Sunday Mercury*, January 1, 2006.

Jeffries, Stuart. "Anyone for Kitesurfing?" *The Guardian*, July 23, 2004. www.guardian.co.uk (accessed July 26, 2008).

Kalning, Kristin. "Is the Video Game Industry Recession-Proof?" MSNBC, March 7, 2008. www.msnbc.msn.com (accessed July 26, 2008).

Kannapell, Andrea. "Taking Sports to the Limit." *New York Times*, October 11, 1998. www.nytimes.com (accessed July 26, 2008).

Keillor, Lynn. "Safe SX: The Study of Snocross Injuries (injuries occurring from snowmobiling)." *Snow Week*, January 23, 2006. HighBeam www.highbeam.com (accessed July 26, 2008).

Kelly, Amanda. "Now Arriving on Board … at 6,000 Feet." *Sunday Mirror*, March 8, 1998. HighBeam www.highbeam.com (accessed October 13, 2008).

Kelly, Donna. "Rollins Mourns Loss of Hall of Fame Skier Dick Pope, Jr." *Lakeland Ledger*, November 12, 2007. Rollins Sports http://rollinssports.athleticsite.com (accessed July 24, 2008).

Kennedy, Helen W. "Lara Croft: Feminist Icon or Cyberbimbo? On the Limits of Textual Analysis." Game Studies, December 2002. www.gamestudies.org (accessed July 26, 2008).

Kennedy, John P. *Memoirs of the Life of William Wirt: Attorney General of the United States*, vol. 2. Philadelphia: Lea & Blanchard, 1849.

Kim, Anne. "Barefoot Water Skier Finds No Skis a Breeze." *Seattle Times*, September 2, 2006. http://seattletimes.nwsource.com (accessed July 24, 2008).

Kinmonth, John. "Jumping the Gap at Mount Baker: Dangerous, Thrilling, Legend." *Seattle Times*, February 28, 2008. www.seattletimes.nwsource.com (accessed July 26, 2008).

"Kitesurfing: The Basics." MagXZine, July 15, 2007. www.magxzine.com (accessed July 26, 2008).

Koeppel, Dan. *Extreme Sports Almanac*. Los Angeles: Lowell House Juvenile, 1998.

"Kohl's Signs Tony Hawk Clothing License." *Retail Merchandiser*, May 12, 2005. All Business www.allbusiness.com (accessed July 26, 2008).

Kuntz, Mary, Joseph Weber, and Heidi Dawley. "The New Hucksterism: Stealth Ads Creep into a Culture Saturated with Logos and Pitches." *Business Week*, 1996. www.businessweek.com (accessed July 26, 2008).

"Learning to Sky Dive Takes a Leap of Faith: Leaving a Perfectly Good Airplane at 15,000 Feet." *Washington Times*, July 13, 2006.

Lee, I. M., H. D. Sesso, Y. Oguma, and R. S. Paffenbarger, Jr. "The 'Weekend Warrior' and Risk of Mortality." *American Journal of Epidemiology* 160 (2004): 636–41.

Leo, Peter. "Poetry in Motion, Wildlife Transportation News, NFL SATs and Extreme Ironing." *Pittsburgh Post Gazette*. www.post-gazette.com (accessed, December 2007).

Levy, Buddy. "Adventure Athletes High Atlas Mountains—Morocco (Discovery Channel Eco-Challenge)." Buddy Levy, October 10, 1998. www.buddylevy.com (accessed July 26, 2008).

Lloyd, Barbara. "Speed, Jumping, Danger in Extreme." *New York Times*, February 20, 1997. www.nytimes.com (accessed July 26, 2008).

Love, Sarah, and Brent Brookler. "Ross Rebagliati: The Mountain Zone Interview." Mountain Zone, 1999. http://classic.mountainzone.com/snowboarding/99/features/rebagliati (accessed July 26, 2008).

"Lynnfield Student Claims Pogo Stick World Record." WBZ-TV, September 23, 2007. http://wbztv.com (accessed July 26, 2008).

MacCurdy, Edward. *The Notebooks of Leonardo Da Vinci*, vol. 1. New York: Reynal & Hitchcock, 1938.

Mageria, Marcie. "Media for a New World: Extreme Sport, Mainstream Marketing." *Media Post*, June 2002. http://publications.mediapost.com (accessed July 26, 2008).

Magruder, Larry. "Medical Aspects of the Hotter 'N Hell Hundred Bicycle Ride." *Wichita Falls Medicine Magazine*, 1998. www.medmag.org (accessed July 26, 2008).

Markels, Alex. "Going to Extremes: In Skiing, It Can Mean Death." *New York Times*, February 3, 2008. www.nytimes.com (accessed July 26, 2008).

Martin, Hugo. "Sandboarding Oregon: You, a Plank, a Heap of Dunes." *Los Angeles Times*, September 7, 2007. www.travel.latimes.com (accessed July 26, 2008).

Mecoy, Don. "Hotter 'N Hell Proves a Challenging Ride." *Sunday Oklahoman*, August 2006. http://68.12.132.110:8080/HotterNHell/HHH.htm (accessed July 26, 2008).

Messner, Michael A. *Taking the Field: Women, Men, and Sports*. Minneapolis: University of Minnesota Press, 2002.

"Mexico City Fines Company That Sponsored Austrian Stuntman's Skyscraper Jump." *AP Worldstream*, February 3, 2006. HighBeam www.highbeam.com (accessed July 26, 2008).

Miller, Raymond H. *Tony Hawk: Stars of Sport*. Farmington Hills, MI: KidHaven Press, 2004.

Miner, Lisa Friedman. "Sports You Won't See in the Olympics Any Time Soon." *Daily Herald*, August 19, 2004.

Mittelstaedt, Robin. "Indoor Climbing Walls: The Sport of the Nineties." *Journal of Physical Education, Recreation and Dance*, November 1, 1997. HighBeam www.highbeam.com (accessed February 3, 2008).

Mizejewski, Gerald. "Exploring Subterranean Wonders: Caving Clubs Provide Novice Spelunkers with the Lowdown." *Washington Times*, July 11, 1996.

Montgomery, Tiffany. "Nike Re-Enters Skateboard Shoe Market." *Orange County Register*, August 14, 2002. HighBeam www.highbeam.com (accessed July 26, 2008).

Moore, Tim. "Out to Grass." *The Guardian*, September 29, 2007. www.guardian.co.uk (accessed July 26, 2008).

"More of a High than Sex?" *Taipei Times*, April 20, 2004. www.taipeitimes.com (accessed July 26, 2008).

Morris, Bob. "Extreme Sports, Extreme Chic, Extreme Hype." *New York Times*, February 8, 1998. www.nytimes.com (accessed July 26, 2008).

"Most Wakeboarding Injuries Caused by Contact with Water." Smart Risk, August 11, 2005. www.smartrisk.ca (accessed July 26, 2008).

MSNBC. "CNBC Special: A History of Video Game Industry." November 30, 2006. www.msnbc.msn.com (accessed July 26, 2008).

Neale, Rick. "All-Female Roller Derby Elbows Its Way in as a Legitimate Sport." *USA Today*, June 24, 2008. www.usatoday.com (accessed July 26, 2008).

Needham, Joseph, and Colin Alistair Ronan. *The Shorter Science and Civilisation in China*. New York: Cambridge University Press, 1994.

Norcross, Don. "Brown Can't Recall McTwist's Landing." *Union Tribune*, August 3, 2007. Sign On San Diego www.signonsandiego.com (accessed July 26, 2008).

"'Nude Raiders' Face Legal Action." BBC, March 18, 1999. http://news.bbc.co.uk (accessed July 26, 2008).

"Oddball Corner: Extreme Skiing." *Evening Standard*, December 15, 2006. HighBeam www.highbeam.com (accessed July 26, 2008).

Oglesby, Carole A., Doreen L. Greensburg, Ruth Louise Hall, Karen L. Hill, Frances Johnston, and Sheila Easterby, eds. *Encyclopedia of Women and Sport in America*. Phoenix: Oryx Press, 1998.

Olsen, Marilyn. *Profiles of Women in Extreme Sports: Women Who Risk*. New York: Hatherleigh Press, 2001.

"On Deck." *Sarasota Herald Tribune*, January 1, 2005.

Overfelt, Maggie. "Surf and Turf." Cable News Network, February 1, 2005. www.money.cnn. com (accessed July 26, 2008).

Paul, Jill. "One Giant Leap as a Base Jumper Hurtles Himself off the World's Tallest Building." *Daily Mail*, December 13, 2007. www.dailymail.co.uk (accessed July 26, 2008).

"People." *International Herald Tribune*, August 1, 2003. HighBeam www.highbeam.com (accessed July 26, 2008).

PepsiCo. "Mountain Dew Films Teams with Universal Pictures for Theatrical Release of *First Descent*." News release, December 2, 2005. http://phx.corporate-ir.net/phoenix.zhtml?c= 78265&p=irol-newsArticle&ID=755351& (accessed October 13, 2008).

Perez, Henry. "Land, Air and Snow Extreme Sports Attracting Enthusiasts of All Ages." *Daily Herald*, July 28, 2004.

Peters, Glen. "Speed Golf Makes Its Debut Here." *New Straits Times*, March 30, 2001. High-Beam www.highbeam.com (accessed July 26, 2008).

Press Digital. "Experience the Thrill of Adventure Skydiving." November 23, 2007. http:// pressdigital.wordpress.com (accessed October 13, 2008).

Prior, Molly. "Extreme Toys Take Market by Storm." *DSN Retailing Today*, June 4, 2001. Find Articles http://findarticles.com (accessed July 24, 2008).

Purvis, Andrew. "Red Bull Energy." *Time*, November 14, 2007. www.time.com (accessed July 26, 2008).

Quinodoz, Danielle. *Emotional Vertigo: Between Anxiety and Pleasure*. London: Routledge, 1997.

Radford, Edwin. *Unusual Words and How They Came About*. New York: Philosophical Library, 1946.

Raymond, Joan. "Going to Extremes." *American Demographics*, June 1, 2002. Find Articles www.findarticles.com (accessed February 11, 2007).

"Red Bull Founder Rides Wave of Success." Cable News Network, 2004. CNN.com www.cnn.com (accessed July 26, 2008).

"Red Bull Takes Extreme Sports by the Horns: Market Winter Sports." *Brandweek*, January 22, 2001. Find Articles www.findarticles.com (accessed July 26, 2008).

Reeves, Hope. "Salient Facts: Pogo Sticks, Bouncing Back." *New York Times*, August 26, 2001. www.nytimes.com (accessed July 26, 2008).

Reuters India. "Many Skaters, Snowboarders Shun Protective Gear." February 4, 2008. www.in. reuters.com (accessed July 26, 2008).

Revkin, Andrew C. "Freeing the Icicle." *New York Times*, June 6, 1995. www.nytimes.com (accessed July 26, 2008).

Riordan, Teresa. "Patents: A Blow by Blow of How the Inventor of Windsurfing Found His Place in the Sun." *New York Times*, September 28, 1998. www.nytimes.com (accessed July 26, 2008).

Roberts, Charles C., Jr. "A Review of Water-Skiing Safety in the USA." Paper presented at the Tenth International Symposium on Skiing Trauma and Safety, Zell am See, Austria, May 17–21, 1993.

Roberts, Paul. "Risk." *Psychology Today*, November/December 1994. http://psychologytoday.com (accessed January 28, 2007).

Robinson, Ruth. "In Extreme Skiing, Risk Is Joy." *New York Times*, February 22, 1987. www. nytimes.com (accessed July 26, 2008).

Rodgers, Joann Ellison. "Addiction: Whole New View." *Psychology Today*, September/October 1994. www.psychologytoday.com/articles/pto-19940901-000020.html (accessed October 13, 2008).

Rouvalis, Cristina. "Risk-Taking Can Be a Two-Faced Monster." *Pittsburgh Post-Gazette*, June 14, 2006. www.post-gazette.com (accessed February 11, 2007).

Ruibal, Sal. "Going Downhill Fast and Sober." *USA Today*, January 18, 2006. www.usatoday. com (accessed July 26, 2008).

Sagert, Kelly Boyer. *'Bout Boomerangs: America's Silent Sport*. North Ridgeville, OH: PlantSpeak Publications, 1996.

Sainz, Adrian. "Carlos Serra, Francisco 'Pipin' Ferreras." Cyber Divers News Network, November 9, 2002. www.cdnn.info (accessed July 26, 2008).

"Sand Sport Threatens Plants: Environmental Aspects of Sandboarding." *National Parks*, May 1, 1999. HighBeam www.highbeam.com (accessed July 26, 2008).

Santiago, Roberto. "Derby Craze Rolls Full Force into Florida." *Miami Herald*, May 10, 2008. www.miamiherald.com (accessed July 26, 2008).

Sapiee, Radzi. "Sky Is the Limit for Air Surfers." *New Straits Times*, November 9, 2000. HighBeam www.highbeam.com (accessed October 8, 2008).

Saslow, Eli. "Just Dew It: With Great Reward Comes Greater Risk." *Washington Post*, June 19, 2007.

Schaben, Susan. "Hawk Line Ready to Take Wing for Quiksilver." *Orange County Business Journal*, November 13, 2000. All Business www.allbusiness.com (accessed July 26, 2008).

Scheidt, Jason. "Charging the Full Video Banner: Campaign Insight." iMedia Connection, January 4, 2005. www.imediaconnection.com/content/4847.asp (accessed October 13, 2008).

Seff, M. A., V. Gecas, and J. H. Frey. "Birth Order, Self-Concept, and Participation in Dangerous Sports." *Journal of Psychology* 127 (1993): 221–32.

Seligman, Todd. "New School Is in Session." EXPN.com, May 14, 2007. www.expn.go.com (accessed October 13, 2008).

Shafran, Michael. *Skate! Your Guide to Inline, Aggressive, Vert, Street, Roller Hockey, Speed Skating, Dance, Fitness, Training, and More*. Washington, DC: National Geographic Society, 2003.

Shemanski, Frances. *A Guide to World Fairs and Festivals*. Westport, CT: Greenwood Press, 1985.

Simpson, Kamon. "When Events Become Mainstream, X Games Cuts Bait." *The Gazette*, February 3, 2003. HighBeam www.highbeam.com (accessed July 26, 2008).

Sink, Mindy. "Adventurer: Sandboarding." *New York Times*, April 9, 2004. www.nytimes.com (accessed July 26, 2008).

"Skateboard Whiz Kids Are Always on a Roll: Sport Has Its Own Clothing and Slang." *Washington Times*, June 3, 2004.

"Ski Jumping: Norwegians 2nd and 3rd at Holmenkollen." *Norway Post*, March 10, 2008. www.norwaypost.no (accessed July 26, 2008).

"Skysurf Hero Dies in Plunge." *The Mirror*, February 12, 2000. HighBeam www.highbeam.com (accessed July 26, 2008).

Smith, Melissa C. "Board Games." Mountain XPress, July 26, 2006. www.mountainx.com (accessed July 26, 2008).

Soden, Garrett. *Defying Gravity: Land Divers, Roller Coasters, Gravity Bums, and the Human Obsession with Falling*. New York: W. W. Norton, 2005.

"Sound Source Interactive Brings the Berenstain Bears and Extreme Sports to the Game Boy Color." *Business Wire*, June 27, 2000. HighBeam www.highbeam.com (accessed July 26, 2008).

Spice, Byron. "BowGo! CMU Robotics Researchers Develop a Pogo Stick That Aims High." *Post-Gazette*, May 28, 2001. www.post-gazette.com (accessed July 26, 2008).

Spice, Ron. "This Pogo Stick's on Steroids." *Cincinnati Post*, June 1, 2001. HighBeam www.highbeam.com (accessed July 26, 2008).

"Spiderman Busted in Texas—Frenchman Alain Robert Goes to Court Tuesday." Mount Everest.net, November 28, 2005. www.mounteverest.net (accessed July 24, 2008).

"'Spiderman' Seeks Vengeance for China Climb." *Independent Online*, March 2, 2001. Independent Online www.iol.co.za (accessed July 23, 2008).

"Sports Active: Check This." *The Independent on Sunday*, November 9, 2003. HighBeam www.highbeam.com (accessed July 26, 2008).

"Sports Active: Rock Follies—It's Steeper than Hillwalking But Not as Technical as Rock-Climbing." *The Independent on Sunday*, September 2, 2001. HighBeam www.highbeam.com (accessed July 24, 2008).

Steed, Mike. "2006 Paragliding Accidents." U.S. Hang Gliding and Paragliding Association, 2006. www.ushpa.aero/safety/PG2006AccidentSummary.pdf (accessed October 13, 2008).

Steinberg, Dan. "Carmichael Hits Racing Milestone." *Washington Post*, June 21, 2004. High-Beam www.highbeam.com (accessed July 26, 2008).

Stenson, Jacqueline. "The Myth of the Weekend Warrior." MSNBC, June 26, 2007. www.msnbc.msn.com (accessed July 26, 2008).

Stiglich, Joe. "Supercross Star Rides to NASCAR." *Oakland Tribune*, January 26, 2007. High-Beam www.highbeam.com (accessed July 26, 2008).

Strange, Maura, and Joan Scruton. "Wheelchair Sport Celebrates 50 Years." Paralympic, 2002. www.paralympic.org (accessed July 26, 2008).

"Street Luging." *The Guardian*, September 29, 2007. www.guardian.co.uk (accessed July 26, 2008).

Stripling, Sherry. "Extreme Sports Are Not about Risk But Freedom for These Women." *Seattle Times*, September 19, 2004. http://seattletimes.nwsource.com (accessed October 13, 2008).

Sutcliffe, Thomas. "Last Night's Television." *The Independent*, September 10, 2003. Find Articles http://findarticles.com/p/articles/mi_qn4158/is_/ai_n12714209 (accessed October 27, 2008).

Sutton, Kyanna. "Girls in Extreme Sports." Family Education, http://life.familyeducation.com (accessed July 26, 2008).

Swanson, Mirjam. "New X Games Event Just for the Girls." *The Press-Enterprise*, June 4, 2008. www.pe.com (accessed July 26, 2008).

Symington, Noel Howard. *The Night Climbers of Cambridge*. London: Chatto and Windus, 1937.

Tedeschi, Mark. "Reebok Readies 'Play Hard' Drive." *Footwear News*, August 5, 1991. High-Beam www.highbeam.com (accessed January 7, 2008).

Thompson, Jonathan. "Sports Active: The Antisocial Climber Alain Robert Is Spider-Man Made Flesh." *The Independent on Sunday*, November 21, 2004. HighBeam www.highbeam.com (accessed July 24, 2008).

Thompson, Kelly. "Show Time: X-Brands Are Taking Their Product off the Air and into the Action." *Footwear News*, July 23, 2001. HighBeam www.highbeam.com (accessed July 26, 2008).

"Thrill-Seeking Enthusiasts of BASE Jumping Craze Risk Life and Limb as They Leap Between Buildings and Rooftops." *Daily Record*, October 13, 2004.

Todhunter, Andrew. *Dangerous Games*. New York: Doubleday, 2000.

Tomlinson, Joe, and Ed Leigh. *Extreme Sports: In Search of the Ultimate Thrill*. Buffalo, NY: Firefly Books, 2004.

Tooze, Steve. "Daredevils Who Dice with Death." *The Mirror*, June 27, 1998.

Turner, Thomas. *The Diary of Thomas Turner, 1754–1765*. Oxford: Oxford University Press, 1984.

University of Alabama–Birmingham. "Extreme Sports Injuries Rising." Press release, October 31, 2001. http://main.uab.edu/show.asp?durki=45514 (accessed October 13, 2008).

Van Praagh, Anna. "Fly Like a Bird." *The Mail on Sunday*, May 15, 2005. HighBeam www.highbeam.com (accessed October 13, 2008).

"Vans, Inc. Acquires Mosa Extreme Sports, the Owner of Pro-Tec Helmets and Accessories." *Business Wire*, April 16, 2002. Find Articles www.findarticles.com (accessed July 26, 2008).

"Video-Game Makers on the Hunt for Young Customers." *San Jose Mercury News*, May 16, 2001. HighBeam www.highbeam.com (accessed July 26, 2008).

"WA: Gravity Games to Come to Perth." *AAP General News*, May 11, 2004. HighBeam www.highbeam.com (accessed July 26, 2008).

"Wakeboarding Injuries." *American Journal of Sports Medicine*, January 1, 2004. Goliath http://goliath.ecnext.com (accessed July 26, 2008).

Warburton, Nicole. "Hitting the Concrete Wave." *Deseret News*, August 29, 2003. HighBeam www.highbeam.com (accessed December 28, 2007).

Wellman, Mark, and John Flinn. *Climbing Back*. Truckee, CA: ICS Books, 1996.

Wells, Steven. "Roller Derby Gets a Good Punking." *The Guardian*, May 23, 2005. www. guardian.co.uk (accessed July 26, 2008).

———. "To Sponsorship Hell in a Homemade Go-Kart." *The Guardian*, May 26, 2008. www.guardian.co.uk (accessed July 26, 2008).

Wester, Knut. "Serious Ski Jumping Injuries in Norway." *American Journal of Sports Medicine*, 1985. http://ajs.sagepub.com (accessed July 26, 2008).

Wheaton, Belinda. *Understanding Lifestyle Sport: Consumption, Identity, and Difference*. London: Routledge, 2004.

Wilkinson, Alec. "No Obstacles: Navigating the World by Leaps and Bounds." *New Yorker*, April 16, 2007. www.newyorker.com (accessed July 26, 2008).

Williams, Geoff. "Crash Course on Extreme Sports." *Entrepreneur*, January 15, 2008. www. entrepreneur.com (accessed July 26, 2008).

"Winter X Games Athletes Always Walk Fine Line: Danger, Entertainment Go Hand-in-Hand." *Telegraph-Herald*, February 2, 2005. HighBeam www.highbeam.com (accessed July 26, 2008).

"Women and Extreme Sports." WPTV, December 4, 2007. www.wptv.com (accessed July 26, 2008).

Wright, J. R., Jr., L. McIntyre, J. J. Rand, and E. G. Hixson. "Nordic Ski Jumping Injuries: A Survey of Active American Jumpers." *American Journal of Sports Medicine* 19 (1991): 615–19.

Youngblut, Shelly, ed. *Way Inside ESPN's X Games*. New York: Hyperion/ESPN Books, 1998.

"Young 'Extreme'Athletes Underuse Protective Equipment: Injuries, High-Risk Behaviors Linked to Infrequent Use." American College of Sports Medicine, June 1, 2005. www.acsm.org (accessed July 26, 2008).

Index

About the Author

KELLY BOYER SAGERT is a freelance writer who has published biographical material with Gale, Scribner, Oxford, and Harvard University, focusing on athletes and historical figures. She is the author of *Joe Jackson: A Biography* (Greenwood, 2004) and *The 1970s* (Greenwood, 2007).

120

D0022791

CORALS
AND CORAL REEFS
OF THE
GALÁPAGOS ISLANDS

CORALS
AND CORAL REEFS
OF THE
GALÁPAGOS ISLANDS

by
PETER W. GLYNN
and
GERARD M. WELLINGTON

with an
ANNOTATED LIST OF THE
SCLERACTINIAN CORALS OF THE GALÁPAGOS
by
JOHN W. WELLS

UNIVERSITY OF CALIFORNIA PRESS

Berkeley/Los Angeles/London

University of California Press
Berkeley and Los Angeles, California
University of California Press, Ltd.
London, England
Copyright © 1983 by The Regents of the University of California

Library of Congress Cataloging in Publication Data

Glynn, Peter W., 1933–
  Corals and Coral reefs of the Galápagos Islands.

  Bibliography: p. 297
  Includes index.
  1. Coral reef ecology—Galápagos Islands.
2. Scleractinia. 3. Corals—Galápagos Islands.
I. Wellington, Gerard M. II. Title.
QL377.C7G58   1983   593.6   82-25161
ISBN 0-520-04713-3

Printed in the United States of America

1 2 3 4 5 6 7 8 9

In memory of Robert E. Silberglied,
a dedicated and spirited student of Galápagos natural history.

CONTENTS

PREFACE

Perhaps no other area of comparable size has stirred man's imagination and creativity more than the Galápagos Archipelago. Herman Melville's tales of intrigue and exploit in these islands have excited readers far and wide. And, of course, one of the greatest impacts on the western world's thinking—the elucidation of the mechanism of organic evolution by means of natural selection—had its beginnings in the Galápagos Islands when Charles Darwin visited the area aboard HMS *Beagle* in 1835 (Darwin, 1839).

Fray Tomás de Berlanga, the Bishop of Panamá, is credited with the discovery of the Galápagos in 1535. More than a century later, the islands served as a base of operations for such English buccaneers as Clipperton, Cowley, Dampier, Davis, and Wafer, who preyed on the ships moving valuable cargoes from the Americas and the Philippines to Spain. For nearly a hundred years, from the latter half of the eighteenth century, Enderby and Nantucket whalers reaped a bountiful harvest in Galápagos waters. This marine oasis also attracted sealers and American and Japanese tuna fishermen until recent years. (The Ecuadorian government now claims political and economic jurisdiction to 200 miles offshore, thus limiting foreign commercial exploitation of fisheries resources in Galápagos waters.)

Since the *Beagle*'s visit, the Galápagos have continued to serve as an important center for empirical studies in the natural sciences, especially in the fields of biology, oceanography, and geology. The Galápagos Islands and surrounding waters are unique, and were recognized as such by their earliest visitors. A remarkable biological pattern, which inspired Darwin to formulate the theory of speciation, was the consistent differences observed in the morphology, behavior, and ecology of closely related species from island to island. The twenty known species and subspecies of tortoises and the fourteen species of Darwin's finches are noteworthy examples of the effects of evolution in isolation. The extreme tameness of the lizards and birds of the Galápagos is another example of the results of evolution in isolation. In this case, the insular fauna was not subject to the selective pressures of the diverse array of predators present on the South American mainland.

The unlikely mélange of life found in the archipelago is also remarkable. The abundance of endemic tortoises, snakes, lizards, and iguanas that inhabited the islands evoked Melville's astute observation: "No voice, no low, no howl is heard; the chief sound of life here is a hiss." Lamentably, lowing, howling, grunting, snorting, and many other new sounds are now commonplace following the introduction of cattle, dogs, pigs, goats, horses, cats, and rats.

The marine environment harbors a novel temperate/subtropical/tropical biotic mix, including coral reefs, fur seals, sea lions, penguins, marine iguanas, and lush beds of seaweed. It is possible to see penguins swimming over reef-building corals and sea lions scratching their bellies against the live coral bottom. This curious blend of marine life is due in large part to the unique location of the archipelago, which lies astride the paths of the major marine currents in the tropical eastern Pacific region. From the west, the islands are bathed by the cool, nutrient-rich, upwelled waters of the Equatorial Undercurrent; from the south and east, the cool and highly saline waters of the Peru Oceanic Current sweep by the islands; and from the north, warm, nutrient-poor waters of low salinity reach the islands seasonally (during the warm-wet season from about January through April). The flow from the north has its origin in the Panamá Bight and in certain years this tropical influence intensifies and penetrates along the mainland coast of South America as far south as Peru. Such extreme southerly incursions of a tropical water mass are referred to as "El Niño" years and they bring about a major derangement of the local ecology. A Niño event, in fact, can unleash a chain of disturbances producing the greatest natural marine perturbation known.

The dynamic nature of the oceanic circulation does not overshadow that of the Galápagos landmass and the surrounding seafloor that together comprise one of the most geologically active areas in the world. The Galápagos Islands are the summits of gigantic shield volcanoes that rise 2,000–3,000 m above the seafloor. At present there are seven volcanoes with historic activity (over forty known eruptions) and at least three that have had unrecognized eruptions in the last few hundred years. Vertical earth movements associated with volcanism, notably uplifts, have been witnessed recently. One such uplift in 1954 resulted in the sudden elevation of a stretch of the subtidal shelf and its inhabitants above sea level. To the north of the archipelago, new oceanic crust is being formed along the 2.5-km-deep rift of the Galápagos spreading center. Associated with these areas are newly discovered hydrothermal springs that harbor extraordinary communities of organisms, including notably large clams, mussels, limpets, and tube worms (vestimentiferan pogonophorans) at remarkably high population densities (Ballard, 1977; Corliss et al., 1979; Enright et al., 1981). The presence of these animals at such depths is especially interesting for they appear to receive their nourishment not from organic production originating in the photic zone at the sea surface, but from nonphotosynthetic carbon issuing from hot spring vents on the seafloor (Williams et al., 1981) and from high concentrations of sulfur-oxidizing, chemosynthetic bacteria. Some of the bacteria are consumed directly, while others function symbiotically in the tissues of metazoans such as the vestimentiferans (Cavanaugh et al., 1981; Felbeck, 1981).

The novel, deep-sea ecosystem, while illustrating another dimension of interest and discovery connected with the Galápagos, is the ecological antithesis of the subject matter of the present study. The communities of organisms dealt with here are confined to sunlit depths and are dependent on the photosynthetic fixation of carbon for their sustenance. The endosymbionts of reef-building coral polyps are algae and, as plants, utilize radiant energy.

During the past century the Galápagos have been visited by numerous, prominent expeditions. The list of institutions, vessels, and personalities connected with the scientific study of Galapagan waters contains many notable names in the annals of oceanography and marine biology. While it is tempting to discuss the various efforts that have contributed to the lore and scientific tradition of the Galápagos, it will suffice here to deal with studies relating to the marine environment and to reef-building corals in particular.

Possibly the first coral collected from the Galápagos for scientific study was a specimen found by Darwin during the *Beagle*'s sojourn in the islands in 1835. Compared with Darwin's incisive contribution to evolutionary biology, which resulted in large part from the Galápagos visit, he did not mention the presence of corals and had nothing to say about coral reefs in the islands. This is perhaps not surprising considering the small size of reefs in the Galápagos, their scattered distribution, and largely subtidal disposition. Darwin's insightful concept of the origin of atolls, through subsidence and involving a sequence of developmental stages from fringing to barrier reef morphologies, was conceived in South America and verified from observations made far west of the Galápagos—at the Society Islands in the South Pacific and at Cocos (Keeling) and Mauritius Islands in the Indian Ocean.

The R/V *Hassler*, a steamer serving the United States Coast and Geodetic Survey, visited the Galápagos in 1873 with Louis Agassiz in charge of the scientific program. The U.S. Fisheries Service R/V *Albatross*, with Alexander Agassiz serving as chief scientist, visited the islands in 1888, 1891, and again in 1904–1905. Our knowledge of coral biology did not benefit greatly from these earliest expeditions because their chief missions were connected with surveys, terrestrial studies, or the collection of deep-sea organisms. The combined efforts of the *Beagle*, *Hassler*, and *Albatross* resulted in the collection of some corals (about fifteen species) and the discovery that many of the Galápagos beaches contained large amounts of coral debris.

In 1924 the HMS *St. George*, serving a British expedition directed by James Howell, surveyed the extent of coral development in the islands. Cyril Crossland, a distinguished student of corals and coral reefs, was unable to substantiate the earlier claims of the significant contribution of corals to beach sediments. He concluded that reef corals were but meagerly present in the Galápagos Islands. The voyages of the research vessels *Noma* and *Arcturus*, in 1923 and 1925 respectively, with the inimitable William Beebe in charge, did much to stir further interest in the islands but reported little relating to coral biology. Beebe was, however, the first investigator to descend into Galapagan waters with a diving helmet (in Darwin Bay, Genovesa Island) to observe subtidal life in its natural surroundings. From 1927 to 1935, Allan Hancock financed a series of expeditions, served by the research vessels *Oaxaca*, *Velero III*, and *Velero IV*, that contributed significantly to our knowledge of Galápagos marine life. Many corals were collected by the various Hancock expeditions to the Galápagos. These collections and others formed the basis of a comprehensive systematic treatment of the corals of the tropical eastern Pacific region by J. Wyatt Durham and J. Laurens Barnard, which appeared in 1952. Durham published additional information on Galápagos corals in the 1960s and, as a result of field work there in 1964 under the auspices of the Galápagos International Scientific Project, surmised that modest coral buildups eventually would be discovered in the islands. By the 1960s, spanning a period of more than 100 years, our understanding of coral biology in the Galápagos was essentially at the alpha level of systematics (with thirty-two known living coral species). There was also the claim that coral reefs, loosely defined, probably occurred somewhere in the archipelago.

Our interest in the Galápagos has been motivated in part by the absence of information on the character and extent of reef-coral community development in this area, which approaches the southernmost limit of tropical conditions in the eastern Pacific. A general picture has emerged on the nature and distribution of coral communities in the Gulf of California, the northernmost area supporting coral growth. The unexpected extent of reef growth and the complexity of biotic interactions in coral communities in Central America have also been revealed recently. One of the chief objectives of the present study is to provide an introduction to the ecology of reef-building corals in the Galápagos Islands. It is our hope that this effort will help to dispel the vague and conflicting impressions that have surrounded this area for so many years.

ACKNOWLEDGMENTS

The field studies on which this book is based benefited greatly from the cooperation and assistance of many individuals. At the international level, we wish to extend our appreciation to the government of the Republic of Ecuador (especially to the Ministerio de Agricultura y Ganadería and to the Departamento de Parques Nacionales y Vida Silvestre), and to the Charles Darwin Foundation for the Galápagos Isles.

Our work in the Galápagos received the full support of Craig MacFarland, director of the Charles Darwin Research Station (1974–1977). We also thank Rolf D. Sievers, the station manager, and Bernhard Schreyer, master of the M/Y *Beagle III.* José R. Cañon, assistant director (1977), made the necessary arrangements to collect and export a shipment of corals to Panamá. Hendrik N. Hoeck, succeeding director of the Charles Darwin Research Station (1978–1980), supplied meteorological records and in other ways facilitated completion of the field work. Chantal De Ridder and Guy Coppois operated a thermograph for us during our absence from the islands and supplied a collection of *Eucidaris* for laboratory study. The A. DeRoy family of Academy Bay supplied useful information on the local marine setting. We are especially indebted to Charles Birkeland, who offered extensive help in the field, excellent photographic coverage of the study areas, and an important contribution toward the development of many of the ideas presented here.

An opportunity to continue and extend our field work in the Galápagos Islands was provided by Thomas J. Watson, Jr., and company who allowed us to join their interisland cruise aboard the M/Y *Palawan.* Master Paul Wolter and mate David Flanagan were very helpful during this phase of the study. Andy Hooten and John Fitter also helped with various aspects of the field work.

Technical assistance in the laboratory and during the data analysis was offered by many. We identify below those individuals who were particularly generous with their time and talents. The X-ray photographs of corals were supplied by Gorgas Army Hospital (formerly Gorgas Hospital of the Panama Canal Zone Government) through the cooperation and aid of Marjorie S.

ACKNOWLEDGMENTS

Adams, Michael Eisenberg, Frank A. Raila, and Jeanne Wagner. Aníbal Velarde and Guadalupe Scott measured cloud cover over the Galápagos Islands from satellite imagery loaned by the 5th Weather Wing (Detachment 25), Howard Air Force Base (United States Air Force), Panamá. Susan Sneed provided information on the feeding habits of the sea urchin *Eucidaris* in Panamá. We also wish to acknowledge the help offered by Donald Windsor when we required the use of a computer.

Information and help with the interpretation of local conditions and events were offered by the following who we believe greatly improved the accuracy of our conclusions. Thomas E. Simkin, Department of Mineral Sciences, Smithsonian Institution, provided detailed information on seismological and volcanic activity in the Galápagos. Robert L. Pyle, Satellite Field Services Station (NOAA), Honolulu, and James C. Sadler, Department of Meteorology, University of Hawaii, offered assistance in the interpretation of meteorological data. C. S. Ramage, Department of Meteorology, University of Hawaii, supplied sea surface temperature data. Aerial photographs of key study sites in the Galápagos were located and acquired by Marsha S. Cox, Smithsonian Institution.

H. William Johansen, Clark University, identified an articulate coralline alga, and Lawrence G. Abele, Florida State University, identified the crustacean symbionts associated with corals.

Various parts of this study benefited from the critical reviews offered by Charles Birkeland, Robert I. Bowman, Richard C. Brusca, Peter Castro, Richard Dodge, Ellen M. Druffel, Robert B. Dunbar, Richard W. Grigg, Joel W. Hedgpeth, Raymond C. Highsmith, Gail V. Irvine, Harilaos Lessios, Ian G. Macintyre, William A. Newman, D. Ross Robertson, James C. Sadler, David R. Stoddart, John W. Wells, and Hendrick Wolda. Editorial assistance offered by Arilla H. Kourany greatly facilitated final manuscript preparation; María Luz Jimenez and Arcadio Rodaniche assisted in the preparation of illustrations. Thanks are also due to R. K. Trench and The Royal Society (London) for permission to reproduce the photomicrograph in figure 2-E.

Funding for travel and facility support in the Galápagos Islands was provided by the Smithsonian Institution. The United States Peace Corps Program supported G. M. Wellington's residence at the Charles Darwin Research Station. We are grateful for the interest and constant encouragement offered by S. Dillon Ripley, secretary, and David Challinor, assistant secretary for science, Smithsonian Institution, and by Ira Rubinoff, director, Smithsonian Tropical Research Institute, throughout the course of this study.

Contribution No. 236 from the Charles Darwin Foundation.

CHAPTER ONE

INTRODUCTION

A REGIONAL PERSPECTIVE

It is becoming increasingly clear that the tropical waters of the eastern Pacific region are not without flourishing, reef-building coral populations, and coral reefs as was formerly claimed (e.g., Yonge, 1940; Rosenblatt, 1963). With the continuing exploration and study of coral communities along the west American coast, it is now recognized that coral reefs, notwithstanding (a) their small size (one to a few hectares or less in area), (b) their discontinuous occurrence (absence from sand/mud coastal stretches), and (c) their meager development in areas experiencing upwelling and high river drainage, are actually quite abundant in this region. In the recent literature, coral communities and reefs have been described from the Gulf of California (Squires, 1959; Dana and Wolfson, 1970; Barham et al., 1973; Brusca and Thomson, 1977), further south along the Mexican coast (Greenfield et al., 1970), from El Salvador (Gierloff-Emden, 1976) from Costa Rica through Panamá (Glynn, 1974a), in Colombia (Prahl et al., 1979) and on nearly all offshore islands (Clipperton Island, Sachet, 1962; Cocos Island, Bakus, 1975; Malpelo Island, Birkeland et al., 1975; Galápagos Islands, Durham, 1966). Additional unpublished observations indicate that coral reef formations are also present in southern Mexico (W. Gladfelter and W. A. Newman, personal communication), Costa Rica, Colombia, and mainland Ecuador (Glynn, unpublished data).

In Panamá, coral reefs are more numerous, larger in size, exhibit a higher growth rate, and have a greater variety of associated species in nonupwelling as contrasted with upwelling environments (Glynn et al., 1972; Rosenblatt et al., 1972; Dana, 1975; Glynn, 1977; Glynn and Macintyre, 1977). The sudden lowering of seawater temperatures during upwelling events in the Pearl Islands (Gulf of Panamá) causes a significant decline in coral growth and some death to corals on shores exposed to shoaling, cool water flow (Glynn and Stewart, 1973). Colony branchtips that succumb are quickly invaded and overgrown by epibenthic algae and a variety of animal species.

Birkeland (1977) demonstrated that the survival of juvenile corals during cool, nutrient-rich episodes in the Gulf of Panamá is low compared with fouling organisms. Under suitable conditions, however, coral growth is vigorous and reef development substantial even in upwelling environments (Glynn and Stewart, 1973; Glynn, 1977).

As the Gulf of California represents the northernmost extant outpost for reef corals (Durham, 1947; Squires, 1959), the Galápagos Islands similarly comprise the southernmost limit of hermatypic corals in the eastern Pacific.* El Pulmo reef (23° 26′N), located in the Gulf near the tip of Baja California, probably represents the northernmost incipient coral reef in the eastern Pacific (Brusca and Thomson, 1977). Squires (1959) noted the importance of temperature in limiting coral growth and showed that the number of coral species in the Gulf of California declined with increasing latitude and decreasing sea surface temperature. He also noted an apparent intense competition between algae and corals and a latitudinal replacement of corals by "kelps" (macroalgae) in the upper (northerly) gulf waters. Finally, Squires (1959) concluded that reef development in the Gulf in general is restricted, due to the absence of a more diversified reef coral fauna in this region. This may be true, in part, but it is now known from studies in Panamá that paucispecific reefs can attain significant dimensions at rapid rates of accumulation. More recently, the geologic and systematic basis of Squires's work has been broadened to include predator-prey interactions at the community level. The effects of *Acanthaster* on coral communities have now been investigated in the Gulf by Dana and Wolfson (1970) and Barham et al. (1973). Prior to the present study (see Glynn et al., 1979), virtually nothing was known of the ecology of Galápagos reef corals except that they are abundant at some localities (Durham, 1966).

The studies discussed here represent an attempt to determine the extent and nature of coral reef development and, as far as possible, the conditions limiting reef distribution in Galápagos waters. The Galápagos marine environment is highly varied, ranging from warm temperate conditions brought on by vigorous upwelling (Equatorial Undercurrent) and a moderately cool, warm temperate-subtropical influence (Peru Current), to seasonally tropical conditions (Panamá Flow). Consequently, the Galapagan biota contains a significant nontropical element (Abbott, 1966; Briggs, 1974) and lacks (or supports low numbers of) certain species that are abundant in coral communities on the mainland. For example, some eastern Pacific corallivores that can have significant effects on reef corals are absent or uncommon in the Galápagos. These include a coral-eating mollusk (*Jenneria*), the crown-of-thorns sea star (*Acanthaster*), and a pufferfish (*Arothron*). A sea urchin, however (*Eucidaris*) that has little effect on corals along the eastern Pacific mainland is locally abundant in the Galápagos where it grazes directly on live

---

*We have also observed a coral reef at Machalilla, mainland Ecuador (1°28′S; 80°47′W), which is located only slightly south (ca. 3 minutes south of Española Island) of the Galápagos Islands.

corals. In order to shed some light on the ecology of reef-building coral communities within the islands and provide a basis for comparisons elsewhere in the eastern Pacific and beyond, we examine the following areas: (a) reef structure (nature of framework, extent of vertical buildup, biotic composition, and zonation), (b) certain conditions of the physical environment (currents, temperature, light, salinity, cloud cover, volcanic events, including lava flows, and tectonism, rock falls, etc.), (c) distributions and extent of development of coral communities in relation to b above, (d) comparative growth rates of corals and estimates of reef growth, and (e) some species interactions (predation, symbiosis, competition, and biotic disturbance).

Early students of corals and coral reefs, from Darwin (1842) to Crossland (1927) and Chubb (1933), who visited the Galápagos Islands agreed that coral reefs were absent from this area. Joubin's (1912) chart indicates the presence of coral reefs in the Galápagos—and along the mainland coast of South America to Lima, Peru, and slightly farther south—but it will become clear later that most of the reef formations identified in the Galápagos were not correctly located. Wells's (1957a) revision of Joubin's chart, based in part on Crossland's (1927) survey, does not show coral reefs present in the Galápagos. The presence of coral reefs off Peru (indicated by both Joubin and Wells) is suspect and in need of verification. None of Joubin's reef sites in Peru was noted to support coral populations by Murphy (1936) or Hutchinson (1950).

Dana (1843) postulated that the influence of the cool, eastern boundary currents was generally responsible for the absence of reef formations along the western coasts of the Americas and the Galápagos Islands. Agassiz (1892) laid more stress on sedimentation as a factor limiting reef growth in this region. The distant location of the Galápagos Islands from continental influences, however, and their generally clear waters prompted Crossland (1927) to support Dana's earlier contention on the importance of temperature. Davis (1928) also favored a more important role for temperature, rather than siltation, in limiting reef growth in the Galápagos. A more recent assessment of thermal conditions in the Galápagos indicates that the archipelago is not subject to uniformly cool conditions (Abbott, 1966). Some parts of the islands rarely, if ever, experience sea surface temperatures below 18°C, the approximate boundary below which reef corals are stressed. Durham (1966) concluded, from an extensive diving survey, that coral reefs (broadly defined) do occur in the Galápagos.

Durham's concept of a coral reef follows that of Squires (1959, p. 377), who offered a biological definition describing small coral formations in the Gulf of California as: ". . . a community dominated by corals in which there is a degree of interdependence between members of the constituent flora and fauna" and ". . . an appreciable areal dimension and definable continuity." Wainwright (1965, see also Stoddart, 1969a) proposed that coral formations further be distinguished in terms of their ability or inability to produce the substratum on which they continue to grow. If coral populations continue to build on the products of their own making, they are termed structural reefs (true coral reefs); and, if not, they are defined as coral communities. This is a significant distinction because it allows one to assess (a) the contribution of extant corals toward construction of topographic features, and (b) the vitality of a coral assemblage through time. We will attempt to demonstrate that structural coral reefs, sensu Wainwright, do occur in the Galápagos Islands and that the potential for reef growth in Galápagos waters, in terms of the present-day physical environment, is very favorable over many parts of the archipelago.

The results of this study are divided into two sections: one systematic, arranged as an annotated list of Galápagos scleractinian corals by John W. Wells and forming the appendix; and one ecological, comprising the main body of the contribution. The ecological section is divided into seven chapters. The physical environment, following the introduction, is largely concerned with the oceanography, climatology, and volcanic and tectonic events. Nine aspects of the physical environment are examined, ranging from the major current systems that bathe the islands, to the patterns of cloud cover over island shores and the effects of volcanism on coral communities. The interplay of a dynamic physical environment and biotic response is particularly in evidence in the Galápagos and will emerge frequently throughout the study. This is followed by a descriptive treatment of the coral communities and provides information on the abundance of corals and their associated epibenthic species, the nature and extent of coral buildups, and an overview of the distribution of corals and coral reefs in the archipelago. The distribution of macrophytic algal communities is also considered because their presence can be used as an index of conditions generally unsuitable for abundant coral development. Coral growth, including growth rates of stained branching species and the analysis of density banding in massive species, is examined to establish a point of reference for an assessment of the effects of the physical environment on coral distribution and abundance. Various biological interactions, for example, predation, competition, symbiosis, and biotic disturbance, are explored at the community level. The significance of species interactions is dramatically underlined by a sea urchin that grazes on live coral to such an extent that reef growth appears to be limited by the urchin in certain areas. Additionally, our perception of Galápagos coral community ecology will be compared with other areas in the eastern Pacific. The absence or uncommonness of certain species, such as the crown-of-thorns sea star and an ovulid snail, in the Galápagos, which prey heavily on coral in many mainland communities, is possibly causally related to some of the differences evident in coral community structure on a regional scale. Finally, Galápagos coral reefs will be compared with the quintessence of coral reef development in the Indo-Pacific realm. This comparison, which will largely focus on the central Pacific (Polynesian) region, should reveal some of the differences and similarities between species-poor and species-rich coral reef assemblages on a global scale.

STUDY AREAS

The major islands and smaller islets and rocks identified in figure 1 were visited on two field excursions, the first by Charles Birkeland (CB), Peter W. Glynn (PWG), Gerard M. Wellington (GMW), and John W. Wells (JWW) in 1975 (10–26 January, solid circles); and the second by PWG and GMW in 1976 (31 January–14 February, asterisks). Several of the study sites were also visited periodically by GMW from November 1973 to November 1975. All of the thirteen large and intermediate-size islands listed below, in order of decreasing size (except for the islets and rocks), were surveyed. Our survey also encompassed four of the six small islands, and eighteen of the sixty-eight islets and rocks comprising the Galápagos Archipelago.

The Spanish island names referred to in this study are listed below along with their English equivalents (after Bowman, 1966 and Black, 1973). We employ the Spanish names preferentially because these are in most common usage among the inhabitants of the Galápagos Islands. Information on the sizes and elevations of the islands is given below under *Nature and Distribution of Coral Communities and Coral Reefs*.

Group	Spanish name	English name
Five large islands, each greater than 500 km²	Isabela	Albemarle
	Santa Cruz	Indefatigable
	Fernandina	Narborough
	Santiago (San Salvador)	James
	San Cristóbal	Chatham
Eight intermediate islands, each between 14–173 km²	Floreana (Santa María)	Charles
	Marchena	Bindloe
	Española	Hood
	Pinta	Abingdon
	Baltra	South Seymour
	Santa Fe	Barrington
	Pinzón	Duncan
	Genovesa	Tower
Four of six small islands 1–5 km²	Rábida	Jervis
	Wolf	Wenman
	Bartolomé	Bartholomew
	Darwin	Culpepper
Eighteen of sixty-eight islets and rocks less than 1 km²	Gardner (at Española)	Gardner
	Champion	Champion
	Corona del Diablo (Onslow)	Onslow (Devil's Crown)
	— —	Cousin's Rock
	Daphne Mayor	Daphne Major

Spanish name	English name
Daphne Menor	Daphne Minor
León Durmiente	Kicker Rock
Cowley (Isabela)	Cowley
Rocas Bainbridge	Bainbridge Rocks
Gardner (Floreana)	Gardner
Sombrero Chino	Sombrero Chino
Plaza Sur, Plaza	South Plaza, North
Norte (two islets)	Plaza
Albany	Albany
Enderby	Enderby
Guy Fawkes (two islets)	Guy Fawkes

GENERAL BIOLOGY OF CORALS

Corals, and their reef-forming skeletal accretions, are often the major constituents of tropical, shallow-water benthic communities. They belong to the Phylum Cnidaria (Class Anthozoa; Order Scleractinia) and are represented by well over 1,000 species. Most scleractinians are restricted in distribution to tropical latitudes, but many are also found in temperate waters and a few species occur in the deep sea.

Anatomically, corals are simple in design and nearly identical to sea anemones; the single major difference being that corals secrete a calcium carbonate exoskeleton (fig. 2). Many coral species are colonial, that is, composed of hundreds to thousands of individual fleshy *polyps* that are housed in rigid cuplike *corallites*. The sum of these genetically identical, interconnected entities is referred to as the colony. Each polyp is essentially a sac, capable of expanding by turgid (hydrostatic) pressure and contracting by columnar muscle contractions. Externally, the polyp body is composed of a muscularized column with a ring of tentacles surrounding an oral disk. *Nematocysts* (stinging capsules) and *spirocysts* (sticky capsules) reside within the epidermis over all parts of the polyp body, but are especially concentrated in the tentacles and along the edges of mesenteries (see below). Both kinds of stinging capsules discharge by the eversion of a tube or thread to the exterior. The everted tube of nematocysts is armed with spines or thorns; the thread of spirocysts is unarmed. Discharging nematocysts also release a toxin. These capsules function in capturing prey and are sometimes used to deter competitors and potential predators. The mouth, or *stomodaeum*, is a simple slit at the center of the oral disk which invaginates to form the pharynx. Captured food is passed down through the pharynx into the body cavity or *coelenteron*. Among colonial corals, the interconnected individual polyps essentially

FIGURE 1. Principal study sites in the Galápagos Archipelago. Solid circles indicate 1975 study sites, asterisks indicate 1976 study sites. From chart N. O. 22000, 14th ed., revised April 16, 1973, Oceanographic Office, Department of the United States Navy.

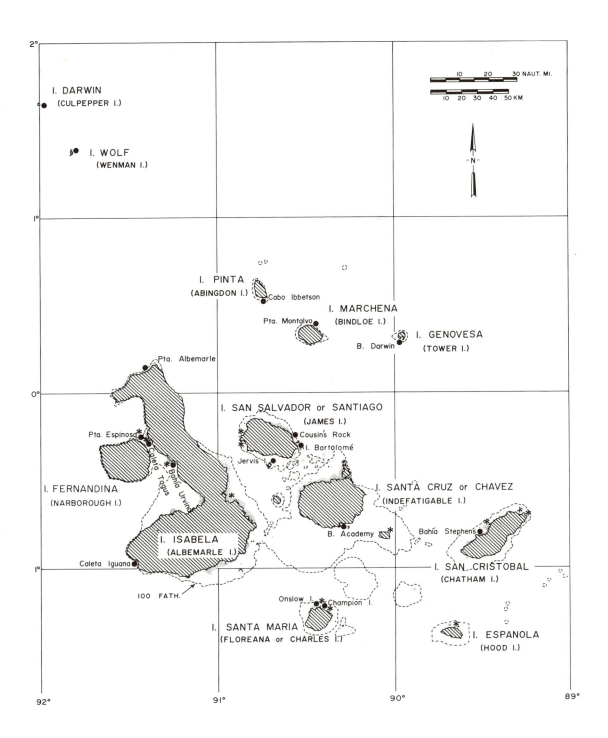

I. DARWIN
(CULPEPPER I.)

I. WOLF
(WENMAN I.)

10   20   30 NAUT. MI.

10 20 30 40 50 KM

-N-

I. PINTA
(ABINGDON I.)

Cabo Ibbetson

Pta. Montalvo

I. MARCHENA
(BINDLOE I.)

B. Darwin

I. GENOVESA
(TOWER I.)

Pta. Albemarle

I. SAN SALVADOR or SANTIAGO
(JAMES I.)

Cousin's Rock

I. Bartolomé

Jervis

Pta. Espinosa

Caleta Tagus

Bahía Urvina

I. FERNANDINA
(NARBOROUGH I.)

I. SANTA CRUZ or CHAVEZ
(INDEFATIGABLE I.)

I. ISABELA
(ALBEMARLE I.)

B. Academy

Bahía Stephens

I. SAN CRISTOBAL
(CHATHAM I.)

Caleta Iguana

100 FATH.

Onslow I.

Champion I.

I. SANTA MARIA
(FLOREANA or CHARLES I.)

I. ESPANOLA
(HOOD I.)

92°   91°   90°   89°

·7·

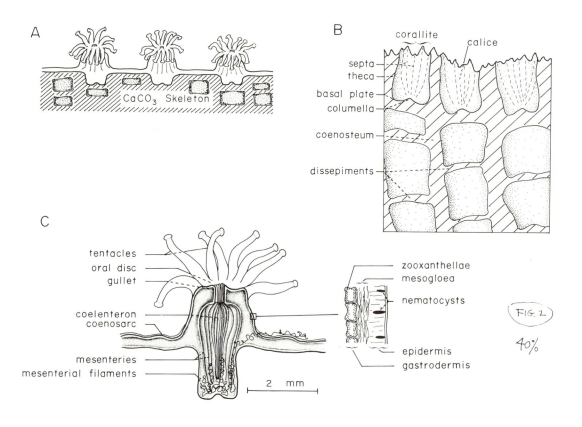

A

B

corallite   calice

septa
theca
basal plate
columella

coenosteum

dissepiments

C

tentacles
oral disc
gullet

coelenteron
coenosarc

mesenteries
mesenterial filaments

zooxanthellae
mesogloea

nematocysts

epidermis
gastrodermis

FIG. 2

40%

2   mm

CaCO₃ Skeleton

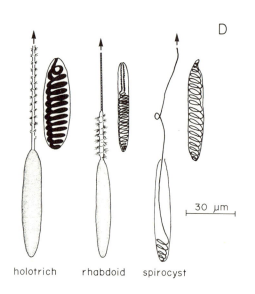

D

holotrich   rhabdoid   spirocyst

30 μm

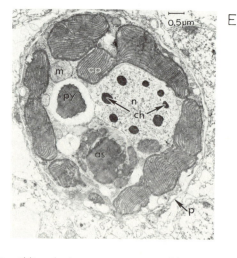

E

0,5μm

cp – chloroplast   py – pyrenoid
 n – nucleus   as – assimilation product
ch – chromosomes   p – periplast membrane
 m – mitochondrion

share a common coelenteron, and there is some evidence to suggest that nutrients gained from captured food may be distributed throughout the colony (Taylor, 1977).

Internally, the coelenteron is longitudinally partitioned by a series of radially-posed fleshy *mesenteries* and rigid calcareous *septa*, which are extensions of the corallite. Filaments are borne on the free edges of the mesenteries (mesenterial filaments), and possess numerous glands and nematocysts. These filaments can be extended out into the surrounding environment either through the polyp body wall or via the stomodaeum. They function in intra- and extracoelenteric digestion and, secondarily, in offensive and defensive interactions. The skeleton is secreted externally (by the epidermis) at the base of the coral polyps. The structural elements of the *calice* (pl. calices, the upper or open end of the corallite), that is, septa, columella, and horizontal interconnections called *dissepiments*, reflect the internal arrangement of the mesenteries.

The success of reef-building corals in the tropics is largely attributable to the presence of endosymbiotic algae, *zooxanthellae* (the vegetative stage of the dinoflagellate *Symbiodinium* [=*Gymnodinium*] *microadriaticum* Freudenthal), residing intracellularly within the gastrodermis of the coral. This association is mutualistic. For the animal, zooxanthellae provide energy through the translocation of photosynthetically fixed products such as glycerol, alanine, etc. (Smith et al., 1969; Muscatine and Cernichiari, 1969; Trench, 1971; and others). Algae also saturate the cell environment with oxygen for respiration and remove potentially toxic metabolic wastes such as carbon dioxide, phosphates, and nitrates. Also, zooxanthellae are thought to mediate the calcification process. If the corals are induced to expel their zooxanthellae, the rate of skeletal formation (*skeletogenesis*) is reduced to almost zero (Goreau and Goreau, 1959, 1960). For the plant, corals provide a predictable environment relatively free from predation and, through metabolic processes, supply the algae with a continuous source of otherwise scarce nutrients.

Aside from the zooxanthellae-derived food source, corals are capable of capturing zooplankton with their nematocyst-, spirocyst-laden tentacles. Other described mechanisms for food capture include suspension-feeding through extension of mesenterial filaments onto adjacent substrata (Muscatine, 1973). There is some evidence to suggest that corals may also feed on bacteria as well as assimilate dissolved organic compounds directly from sea-

FIGURE 2. Essential features of the body plan of a reef-building coral. A—relation of polyps to calcareous exoskeleton (vertical section); B—corallum (exoskeleton) showing the skeletal elements associated with three corallites (vertical section); C—coral polyp and enlargement of body wall showing three tissue layers (vertical section), modified after Goreau et al. (1979); D—cnidae or stinging capsules, holotrich and rhabdoid nematocysts after Schmidt (1974), spirocyst after Hyman (1940); E—electron micrograph of a zooxanthella in a gastrodermal cell of a sea anemone (after Trench, 1971). A–C, diagrammatic sketches based on the ramose coral *Pocillopora damicornis*.

water (Sorokin, 1973; cf. Wellington, 1982*a*). Corals are mainly phototrophic organisms, however, they also appear to be highly adaptable and opportunistic organisms capable of using a variety of methods for acquiring food resources (Muscatine and Porter, 1977).

Reproduction is quite varied among corals in both timing and mode. Breeding can be continuous throughout the year in some species or occur on an annual cycle (Stimson, 1978). Gametes are produced and borne on the mesenteries. In some species, fertilization is external; eggs and sperm are liberated into the milieu where they unite to form a free-swimming pelagic *planula* larva. In other species, fertilization is internal and planulae are brooded for a time prior to release. It is not known how long the planulae remain in the plankton; but, for some species, settlement is suspected to take place within hours or days after release (Connell, 1973). In others, there is some evidence to suggest adaptation for long-distance dispersal (Harrigan, 1972*a*; Richmond, 1983).

Sexes can be separate; that is, entire colonies are either male or female. In others, colonies may be hermaphroditic with male and female gametes maturing at the same time (simultaneous) or sequentially; the former favoring the potential for selfing and the latter promoting outcrossing. Detailed studies on the modes of sexual reproduction and their possible evolutionary significance to life history characteristics are just beginning to appear in the literature (Stimson, 1978; Rinkevich and Loya, 1979*a, b*).

The growth of a colony by polyp division is often considered a mode of asexual increase in mass. Another mode, although uncommon, involves the formation of polyp-clusters that are free of skeleton. These clusters form "polyp balls" that detach and independently develop separate colonies (Rosen and Taylor, 1969). Propagation by breakage and fragmentation of larger colonies is analogous to this. For some corals, this appears to be the most frequent method of reproduction (see Highsmith, 1982, for a review).

Growth in many corals is indeterminate, that is, growth rates are consistent from year to year and do not diminish with age (Barnes, 1973; Buddemeier and Kinzie, 1975*a*). Many corals appear to be long-lived; barring mortality by predation or some physical catastrophe, most colonies persist with no evidence of senescence (Hughes and Jackson, 1980). Large, massive colonies reaching 3–4 m in height, growing one cm/year, are at least three to four hundred years old.

The distribution of corals is constrained by extremes in such physical factors as light, temperature, sedimentation, tidal exposures, and wave stress. Due to their dependency on symbiotic algae, reef-building corals are restricted to the photic zone. Under conditions of optimum water clarity, corals can extend to depths of 100–150 m (Goreau and Goreau, 1973; Wells, 1957). The range of temperatures in which corals can flourish is generally between 18°–32°C. Outside of this range, prolonged exposures result in decreased calcification and metabolic dysfunction (Clausen and Roth, 1975). Where major drainage occurs, sedimentation can be a problem for most corals. Colonies must continually expend energy to keep surfaces clear in order to maintain proper gas exchange and to keep tentacles from fouling (Marshall and Orr, 1931). Additionally, desiccation from extreme tidal exposures poses a limit to the vertical extent of reef growth (Fishelson, 1973; Glynn, 1976; Loya, 1976). Lastly, where wave stress is severe, only the most robust corals (or encrusting colonies) will escape damage by mechanical breakage (Roberts, 1974; Adey, 1978).

Terms that will be used frequently herein include *hermatypic, ahermatypic, framework,* and *buildup*. The first two terms refer to a coral's ability or inability, respectively, to produce reef structures. On one hand, hermatypic (from the Greek *herma,* a reef) corals typically contain zooxanthellae and are of the reef-building type (Wells, 1933). This generally excludes solitary species; although, on some reefs, unattached, single-polyped corals such as *Fungia* can contribute substantially to overall carbonate deposition. On the other hand, ahermatypes are usually nonreef builders. They generally lack zooxanthellae and are solitary or weakly colonial (that is, with few polyps). Interestingly, some supposedly ahermatypic corals lacking zooxanthellae do form impressive thickets in relatively deep water (100–900 m) that may qualify as bona fide coral reef structures (Teichert, 1958). Banks of *Oculina* (without algal endosymbionts) off the east Florida coast have been described recently as ranging from 17–24 m in relief (Reed, 1980). Individual colonies attain 2 m in height and form the massive, intermeshing thickets that build the banks. The term framework refers to the condition whereby colonies have coalesced to form a structural unit that is resistant to physical abrasion. An *Oculina* bank is a coral framework. With reference to reefs in the eastern Pacific, framework indicates the vertical extent of a coral buildup above an underlying, often noncalcareous, substratum.

CHAPTER TWO

PHYSICAL ENVIRONMENT

In this section some physical environmental factors known to affect corals—both hermatypic and ahermatypic species—are examined in detail. Special attention will be given to surface currents, light penetration (shelf depth and turbidity), salinity, sea temperature, cloud cover, and emersion events (tidal and tectonic). This information, while limited in scope, will provide a preliminary description of certain factors that are later related to coral distributions and abundance, and growth rates in an attempt to elucidate patterns of coral development in the Galápagos Islands.

METHODS

Light penetration was measured with a LI-COR (Lambda Instruments Corporation) Model LI-185 Quantum/Radiometer/Photometer coupled with a LI-212S underwater photometric sensor. The sensor was held in a vertical upright position in the center of a bronze ring. In order to eliminate shadows, the ring was suspended from monofilament nylon line and the sensor cable was looped loosely (1 m above) over the sensor element. Readings were made at 1 m intervals from a skiff as close as possible to coral formations (when present) along the shore. Subsurface readings were multiplied by the constant 1.34 to correct for the immersion effect. Measurements were obtained at six different localities, under clear skies between 0900–1400, from 3–14 February 1976. Extinction coefficients (ϵ m^{-1}) were calculated for all sites with L = 8 meters depth.

Surface seawater temperatures were measured with hand-held, calibrated thermometers at all localities visited in 1975 and 1976, and with the thermograph on the M/Y *Palawan* between islands while underway in 1976. The shipboard thermograph was calibrated against our field thermometers and the necessary corrections were made. Bottom temperatures were measured with calibrated Peabody Ryan thermographs (model F) at various localities in order to obtain continuous, long-term (up to forty-five days) records (see

Glynn and Stewart, 1973).

Satellite imagery (Defense Meteorological Satellite Program, DMSP) was utilized to determine the distribution of cloud cover over the five largest islands (Isabela, Santa Cruz, Fernandina, Santiago, and San Cristóbal). The imagery was transmitted about 1200 ± 30 minutes to Panamá or 1100 ± 30 minutes Galápagos time. The imagery was recorded on positive photographic transparencies (high-resolution visual data with high contrast for low cloud cover), from which black-and-white positive enlargements were made of the Galápagos region. The surface area of all clouds present around the shoreline of each island, in a 2-km-wide belt, was measured with a planimeter. Data were analyzed over a period of eighteen months, from April 1977 to September 1978. Due to technical difficulties, complete monthly records were never obtained. The number of observations per month ranged from twelve to twenty-three days except for April 1977 during which only six days were recorded. Each of the five largest islands (Isabela, Santa Cruz, Fernandina, Santiago, and San Cristóbal) was partitioned into coral and noncoral shores as indicated in figure 3-D. On Isabela Island, for example, coral and noncoral shores dominated mainly the eastern and western sides of the island respectively. Coral shores on the remaining four islands were partitioned as follows: Santa Cruz, north and east sides; Fernandina, northeast corner at Espinosa Point; Santiago, east sector at Bartolomé Island and west sector in the Boquerizo Point area; and San Cristóbal, north and northwest coast. Although some minor exceptions to this classification are discussed later (see *Nature and Distribution of Coral Communities and Coral Reefs*, especially fig. 44), reef-coral development, as presently known on the five large islands, generally conforms to this scheme.

GENERAL CLIMATOLOGIC AND OCEANOGRAPHIC CONDITIONS

The Galápagos lie astride a transition zone and thus experience variable climatologic and oceanographic conditions. There exist two distinct seasons in the Galápagos: a wet season, from January to April, and a dry season with persistent fog drip (garua), for the remainder of the year (Palmer and Pyle, 1966). Factors influencing these seasonal events are examined below in relation to the major current systems in this region.

Peru and South Equatorial Currents: The Peru Current is not a single current but a complex system of coastal currents, countercurrents, and undercurrents. Two currents in this system that have a marked influence on the Galápagos are the Peru Oceanic Current and the Peru Coastal Current (Humboldt Current). The Peru Oceanic Current is located west of 82°W longitude and carries the relatively cool (20°–24°C), subtropical, saline (35°/$_{oo}$),

PLATE 1. *Porites lobata* colonies in growth position that were elevated suddenly above sea level in 1954 at Urvina, Isabela Island (photograph taken 9 February 1976).

PLATE 2. Tunicates overgrowing ahermatypic corals, ceiling of rock ledge, Cousin's Rock (off Santiago Island), 21 meters depth (22 January 1975).

offshore waters of Peru and Chile in a northwesterly direction (fig. 3-A). As it reaches the equator at approximately 83°W, it turns westward and joins the South Equatorial Current (SEC). The Peru Coastal Current extends only about 700 km offshore from the Peruvian mainland. This relatively narrow strip of cool (as low as 15°C) water also moves northwesterly and leaves the coast at approximately 5°S where it flows west and joins the SEC.

Both of these currents are driven by the almost constant southeast tradewinds in this region. These winds move surface water away from the continental landmass, thus causing a replacement by cool, saline, subsurface waters that upwell near the shore. Along the coast of Peru, local temperatures may reach as low as 14°–15°C. As this water mass moves northward, it experiences some horizontal and vertical mixing with warmer water masses; but, by the time it reaches the Galápagos, it is still relatively cool, 18°–22°C (Enfield, 1975).

The seasonality of these currents is governed by the changing intensity of the southeast tradewinds. Generally, these winds blow strongest during the months of August and September and weaken in February and March, corresponding respectively to the dry-cool and wet-warm seasons in the Galápagos.

The South Equatorial Current, a massive current that sweeps the entire length of the Pacific from east to west, originates just east of the Galápagos. The Peru Current, as it crosses the Equator from the south, provides the initial impetus of the flow. Additionally, some water is added to the SEC from the north via a southerly deflection of the North Equatorial Countercurrent (NECC) in the Panamá Bight. The NECC marks the northern boundary of the SEC near 4°N. The intensity of the SEC is directly related to the Peruvian system, which is strongest in August and September and weakest in February and March.

Equatorial Undercurrent (Cromwell Current):   As the name implies, this is a subsurface current (Wooster and Hedgpeth, 1966; Wyrtki, 1966). It flows beneath and counter (west to east) to the westward flowing South Equatorial Current (fig. 3–A), and is well developed as far west as the Line Islands (150–160°W) (Taft et al., 1974). The Equatorial Undercurrent (EUC) is confined to the area between 2°N and 3°S and has an average thickness of approximately 200 m. Its core is generally found at a depth of 100 m, but it tends to shoal as it approaches the Galápagos Islands. As the EUC approaches the island pedestals of Fernandina and western Isabela, it is deflected upward. This causes cool, nutrient-rich water to upwell, thus accounting for the high productivity evident in this area much of the year. Pak and Zaneveld (1973) traced the approach of the EUC to the Galápagos in October of 1971. As the islands were encountered, the 14°, 15°, and 16°C isotherms moved toward the surface. After the EUC made its way through the islands to the east, the cool water isotherms were again restricted to depth (between 50–100 m). The presence of the EUC east of the Galápagos at depth simply represents a convergence of the current streams that passed around and between the islands. As is generally the rule with countercurrents, their velocity and duration are proportional to the main current, which is the SEC in this case. Therefore, the undercurrent is most evident during the months of August and September.

Throughout the islands, the cool waters of the SEC and EUC combine with warm tropical air, and form a low-level inversion resulting in extensive cloud cover (stratus clouds are prevalent) with little or no precipitation. At this time of year the Intertropical Convergence Zone (ITCZ) is located between 8° to 17°N (Forsbergh, 1969, table 1).

Panamá Current: Every year tropical surface waters (warm and low in salinity and nutrient levels) flow south from the Panamá Bight and arrive in the Galápagos area in about January (fig. 3–A). This is the time of year the southeasterly tradewinds slacken and the southern currents decrease in intensity, thus allowing the ITCZ and warm (25°–28°C) northern waters to shift south. We call this tropical water mass the Panamá Current.

Periodically, a complex chain of events, related to the intensity of the Southeast Trades, results in an increased strength of the eastward-flowing countercurrents (North Equatorial Countercurrent and Equatorial Undercurrent) and a weakening of the westward-flowing currents (Quinn, 1974; Enfield, 1975; Wyrtki, 1975). This results in the accumulation of warm water in the area off Peru. The Panamá Current also flows south along the northwestern coast of South America at such times. When the Panamá Current penetrates far south and is of long duration, this set of circumstances gives rise to El Niño events (Wyrtki et al., 1976), which have a devastating effect on the marine ecosystem in this region. Unusually warm water years occur periodically in the Galápagos; and while these are often referred to as Niño years locally, their effects may not extend to the mainland. Henceforth, the periodic occurrence of a strong tropical water influence in the Galápagos will be referred to as PCI (Panamá Current Influence), so as not to confuse this local effect with the widespread El Niño phenomenon.

INSHORE CURRENTS

Surface currents within the Galápagos commonly flow in a northwesterly or southwesterly direction, which is a result of the influence of the South Equatorial Current (Cromwell and Bennett, 1959). A westerly component is present year-round, but is less pronounced during the wet-warm season (January–February) when the southeast tradewinds slacken at this latitude. Interisland current drift observed in December (Garth, 1946a) indicates significant southerly (Wolf to Santiago islands) and easterly (Isabela to Santa Cruz islands) movements as well.

Near-shore currents over coral reefs and coral patches were generally vigorous. Current flow was so strong at times that it was difficult to maintain

TABLE 1. Current Speed over the Onslow Island Coral Reef, Floreana Island.

Date	Time	Tidal State	Time and Height (cm) of Tide	Current Speed (cm/sec.)
4 Feb 1976	1735–1740	Low to high	1911 (128)	35.0
5 Feb 1976	1640–1644	Low to high	1950 (128)	61.5
	1610–1613	Low to high	1950 (128)	58.3

one's position on the bottom (2–5 m depth). Current speed was measured on the Onslow coral reef by introducing wood chips upstream (southeast passage; see fig. 18) and timing their movement to the downstream westerly exit. Data in table 1 indicate that current speeds ranged from 35.0–61.5 cm/sec during two flooding tides in February. At low water, current direction was similar, but current speed was somewhat less. Similar current regimes were observed over coral reefs on the northeastern sectors of San Cristóbal and Española islands.

WATER TURBULENCE

Wave action is generally strong on the south and southeastern island shores. Due to the steep bathymetry of the islands, wave trains strike the shoreline full force, unimpeded by the frictional drag of a shallow coastline. During the greater part of the year, sea and swell direction is from the south-southeast, and is generated by the prevailing Trades, which are strongest in August and September. In these months, water turbulence is greatest, and waves 2–3 m in height buffet the exposed southern and southeastern island shores. Most of the interisland channels, bays, and adjacent shores, however, are protected to some extent, and wave height only occasionally exceeds 0.5 m in these areas.

Since the Galápagos Islands lie outside tropical storm tracts, meteorological disturbances of great magnitude are probably rarely experienced here. However, it was apparent, from the condition of a coral community observed along the east shore of Floreana Island (directly across from Champion Island) on 6 February 1976, that the intensity of the prevailing southeasterly seas sometimes reaches destructive proportions. Between 3–6 m depth, we observed numerous large colonies of *Pavona clavus*, up to 3 m in diameter, that were recently tilted, fallen sidewise, and overturned. Most affected colonies still had extensive live surface areas, even in positions of altered exposure to light and water flow. This disturbance probably occurred in the high seas period of July–September 1975 since the same area was unaffected in prior surveys by GMW.

Coral reef areas that are subject to infrequent storms, or infrequent high swells (or abnormal swell directions), seem to experience the greatest damage. On one hand, hurricanes in the Caribbean Sea that may have local visitation rates measured in decades typically result in catastrophic reef damage (Stoddart, 1969b; Woodley et al., 1981). On the other hand, reefs located on a main typhoon corridor, such as the Caroline-Mariana-Philippine region, have formed in adjustment to severe and frequent storms and are accordingly only slightly affected by major disturbances (Ogg and Koslow, 1978). Considering the loose structure of Galapagan reefs (see chapter 3), unusually high waves, or a change in swell direction, would be expected to have severe effects in this area.

LIGHT PENETRATION

Shelf Depth: Factors associated with light penetration, such as depth and transparency, have important limiting effects on hermatypic coral growth. Under conditions of high water transparency, some reef-building corals are present at 100 m depth and slightly deeper (Stoddart, 1969a). The extent of the Galápagos insular shelf is indicated generally in figure 1 by the locations of the 100 fathoms (183 m) and 10 fathoms (18 m) contours. The 10-fathom contour is denoted by stippling. Additional comments on near-shore shelf depth are noted in the following section (*Nature and Distribution of Coral Communities and Coral Reefs*). Most of the larger islands, comprising the central island mass, are surrounded by a relatively broad (100–200 m) gently sloping shelf that is well illuminated to 20–30 m depth. The shallow shelves surrounding Pinta, Marchena, Wenman, and Culpepper, all islands relatively isolated bathymetrically (Houvenaghel, 1977), are very narrow (especially at Wenman) but are still of sufficient area to support abundant coral growth. The limited shoal bathymetry of these northernmost islands is similar to that at Malpelo Island (Stead, 1975) and Cocos Island (Bakus, 1975) in the extreme eastern Pacific.

Turbidity: In most areas where hermatypic corals were abundant, lateral water clarity throughout the year was usually $\geq$ 15 m. Two notable exceptions were Cartago Bay (Isabela) and the east side of Darwin Bay (Genovesa) where lateral visibility was no greater than 3–4 m. Relative light levels at 8 m depth (fig. 4) were 36–43 percent at stations in the southeast sector of the archipelago (Española, Floreana, Santa Fe) and 18–29 percent at Punta Espinosa (Fernandina), Tagus Cove, and Cartago Bay (Isabela) toward the west. Extinction coefficients (ϵ) increased from 0.11–0.13 m^{-1} in the southwest to 0.16–0.22 m^{-1} in the west.

Our limited data on light penetration are in agreement with the east-west difference in water transparency reported by Maxwell (1974). Mean annual (excluding three months that were not sampled) Secchi disc measure-

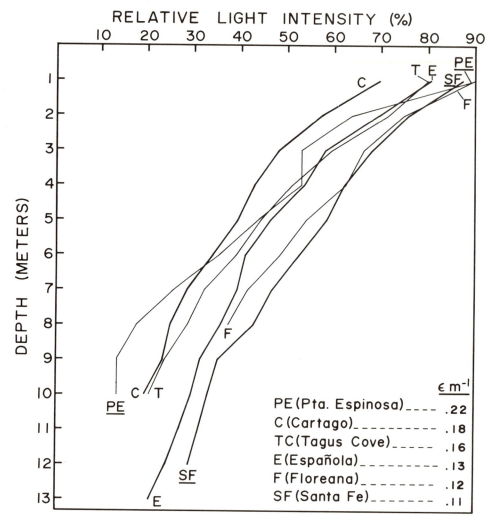

FIGURE 4. Relative light intensity as a function of depth at six localities in the south-eastern to western sectors of the islands. Extinction coefficients (ε) are also noted for each locality.

ments east of Isabela Island ranged between 16–18 m (fig. 3–B). Mean annual values on the west side of Isabela Island ranged from 7–13 m. Upwelling west of Isabela, due to the shoaling of the Equatorial Undercurrent, supports high levels of plankton productivity that reduce water clarity in that sector.

Compared with continental shelf waters off Panamá, it appears that water transparency, at least in the eastern Galápagos, is less variable seasonally. At offshore islands (Contreras and Secas islands) in the Gulf of Chiriquí,

Panamá, relative light at 3–5 m fluctuated widely over the wet (14–32 percent) and dry (58–80 percent) seasons (Glynn, 1977). Dana's (1975) modified Secchi disc measurements in the Gulf of Chiriquí, although observed during a particularly turbid-water period, also showed a pronounced seasonal difference. His Panamá data ranged between 3.5 m–14 m, and 3.5 m was the mean datum estimate for the water column over the Cavada Island (Secas Islands) reef. Mean ϵ of 0.18 m^{-1} in the Pearl Islands following the upwelling influence (Glynn and Stewart, 1973) is similar to ϵ values observed in the western Galápagos. As a first approximation, water transparency in the western Galápagos is similar to that in the Pearl Islands, Panamá, during the upwelling (dry) and nonupwelling (wet) seasons (Glynn, 1977). Water transparency in the southeastern Galápagos is similar to the nonupwelling Gulf of Chiriquí area in Panamá in both the dry and wet seasons. In the latter area, however, turbid conditions (comparable with the Gulf of Panamá) are sometimes experienced in the wet season, for example, < 5 percent surface irradiance at 8 m (Dana, 1975), primarily due to suspended sediments from river runoff and plankton blooms.

Turbidity caused by river runoff is negligible in the Galápagos compared with mainland areas. The Galápagos Islands are situated near the eastern end of the Central Pacific Dry Zone; the mean annual rainfall in this zone is 760 mm (30 inches) or less (Palmer and Pyle, 1966). The low rainfall (the annual range at Academy Bay from 1965 to 1976 was 84.3–928.8 mm) and high evaporation ($\sim 1,000$ mm per year), combined with the small drainage area and virtual absence of topsoil, dictate an absence of rivers and minor sediment input from runoff. Along the coasts of Colombia, Panamá, and southern Costa Rica, river runoff can drastically reduce water clarity.

SALINITY

Due to high rates of freshwater discharge, salinities are greatly reduced along certain sectors of the mainland Central and South American coasts; and, in combination with reduced light levels and increased sediment load, probably have caused a depressant effect on coral growth. Along the northwestern coast of Colombia, adjacent to the Chocó rain forest drainage system, surface salinities of $20°/_{oo}$ to $29°/_{oo}$ are reported in the rainy season (Forsbergh, 1969). The minimum tolerance limit for reef-building corals has been set at $27°/_{oo}$ (Wells, 1957b; Kinsman, 1964); however, some adult coral species in the eastern Pacific can tolerate salinities below $26°/_{oo}$ (and daily as low as $19°/_{oo}$) for three-month periods (Glynn, 1974a). The lowest surface salinities in the Galápagos occur when the Panamá Current moves south and reaches the islands. At such times, particularly during strong Panamá Current Influence or in El Niño years, surface salinities range from $31.5°/_{oo}$ to $32.5°/_{oo}$ (Wyrtki et al., 1976).

SEA TEMPERATURE

Harris (1969) identified five sea surface temperature (SST) zones in the Galá-pagos Islands (fig. 3–C). With reference to zone 1, which is centered around Santa Cruz Island, zone 3 (northern sector) is warmer, zone 2 (southern sector) is cooler, and zone 5 (western sector) is the coolest area in the archipelago. Zone 4 is similar to zone 3 in the warm season and slightly cooler than zone 1 in the cool season. We offer additional SST data plus some bottom temperatures—twelve years of SST observations from Academy Bay (Santa Cruz Island), continuous bottom records from five localities (in zones 1, 2, 4, and 5), and SST observations from all localities visited in this study (zones 1–5)—and examine these in relation to Harris's scheme.

Mean monthly sea temperatures at Academy Bay for the period 1965–1976 are shown in figure 5. The annual mean range in temperature is considerable, often amounting to 5°–6°C. A fairly consistent annual pattern is evident in zone 1 with high SSTs from January to April and thereafter a rapid decline with minimum values occurring from August to September. This is due to the southerly migration of the tropical Panamá Current (PCI) and an increasing influence of the South Equatorial Current later in the year. Relatively warm years, when the PCI was strong and monthly means were above 22°C, occurred in 1965, 1969, 1972, and 1976. Lowest mean SSTs were observed in 1967 (20.1°C, September) and 1970 (19.7°C, August). Daily measurements over a nine-year period showed a minimum temperature of 17.8°C in 1970 (July). In five different years the lowest surface temperature recorded was never below 20°C. The extreme annual range at Academy Bay was 8.4°C (1970).

Shallow bottom sea temperatures were also recorded continuously over four periods in Academy Bay in 1975 and 1976. Three of these records are from the warm season (fig. 6, Academy Bay, trace *a*, table 2) and show mean temperatures ranging between about 24.5°C–26.0°C. The minimum warm season temperature recorded was 20.7°C. A transition cool-warm period is shown in figure 6 (Academy Bay, trace *b*). The temperature dropped slightly below 20°C briefly on four days during that time.

While Onslow Island belongs to Harris's cool zone 2, the warm and cool season records shown in figure 5 do not differ appreciably from those in Academy Bay. Additional warm season temperature data from Onslow (table 2), although lacking contemporaneity, are rather similar to those at Academy Bay. While the mean temperature at Academy Bay was 1.4°C higher than at Onslow, the minimum temperature at Academy Bay was 1°C lower than at Onslow. Two cool season records at Onslow showed minimum temperatures of only 18.7°C and 19.5°C. Abbott (1966) and Harris (1969) have demonstrated that Wreck Bay, San Cristóbal Island, is considerably cooler in all seasons than most other areas in the Galápagos outside of zone 5 (west side of Isabela Island). Temperatures we observed along the northwest and east sides of San

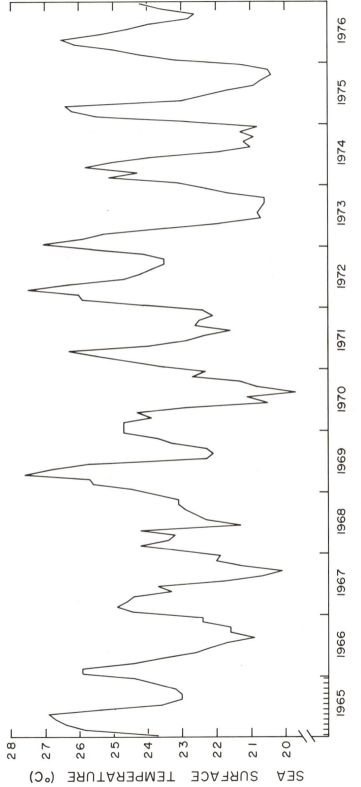

FIGURE 5. Monthly mean sea surface temperatures (°C) observed at the Charles Darwin Research Station, Academy Bay, Santa Cruz Island. Readings were made on the shore at 0700 hours at approximately 0.3 m depth.

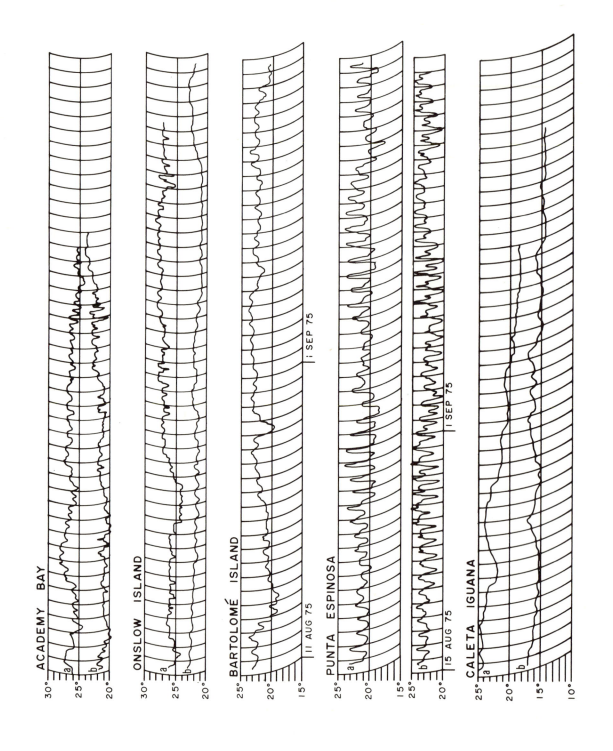

ACADEMY BAY

ONSLOW ISLAND

BARTOLOMÉ ISLAND

PUNTA ESPINOSA

CALETA IGUANA

i SEP 75

I SEP 75

II AUG 75

15 AUG 75

TABLE 2. Continuous Bottom Seawater Temperature Records at Four Different Localities in the Galápagos Islands. Data obtained with Peabody Ryan Thermographs (model F). Mean temperatures were calculated from the areas under the curves with a digitizer.

Locality	Period	Temperature °C		
		Mean	Minimum	Maximum
Academy Bay	3 January–9 February 1976	24.46	20.7	26.8
Santa Cruz Island	9 February–7 March 1976	25.76	21.3	28.4
Onslow Island	12 January–10 February 1975	23.13	21.7	24.8
Floreana Island	23 March–29 April 1975	25.71	20.6	27.8
	20 July–1 August 1975	19.96	18.7	20.5
	20 August–4 September 1975	21.07	19.5	22.2
Caleta Iguana	9 July–21 July 1975	16.91	15.1	18.1
Isabela Island				
Punta Espinosa	15 October–4 November 1975	20.10	17.2	24.3
Fernandina Island[a]				

[a]Offshore (1 m depth) outside lava rock pools.

Cristóbal, over a two-day period in 1976, indicate that Wreck Bay may at times be abnormally cool and subject to rapid temperature changes (upwelling ?). From 31 January to 2 February, SSTs recorded at various localities and times outside of Wreck Bay, from 1.3 km southwest of Wreck Bay to Punta Pitt, ranged from 23.0°C to 26.0°C (n = 8). In Wreck Bay the SST was 21.1°C on 31 January (1825 hrs.). On 2 February (1855 hrs.) the SST in Wreck Bay had risen to 27.0°C. These observations and those at Onslow Island suggest that zone 2 may experience warmer conditions than those recorded at the tide station in Wreck Bay which have served to characterize this zone (see also Houvenaghel, 1978).

The warmest temperature zone (zone 3) encompasses five islands north of the equator. Three SSTs observed at Wolf and Darwin, 18–19 January 1975, ranged from 26.0°C–26.4°C. Waters surrounding Pinta, Marchena, and Genovesa Islands were lower and ranged from 22.0°C–24.9°C (n = 5) on 20–22

FIGURE 6. Bottom seawater temperature records at five localities in the Galápagos Archipelago. Each panel represents a twenty-four-hour period. Academy Bay: 2 m depth, west side of bay near European settlement; trace *a*, 2–31 March 1975; trace *b*, 3 December 1975–2 January 1976. Onslow Island: 2 m depth, *Pocillopora* reef; trace *a*, 11 February–21 March 1975; trace *b*, 1 June–13 July 1975. Bartolomé Island: 2 m depth, south side, *Porites* reef. Punta Espinosa: trace *a* offshore, 1 m depth; trace *b Pocillopora* reef in lava pool, 1 m depth; traces *a* and *b* were recorded synchronously. Caleta Iguana: 2 m depth; trace *a*, 16 April–5 May, 1975; trace *b*, 17 August–23 September 1975.

January. The mean SST in Academy Bay in January 1975 (22.9°C) was 3.2°C and 0.9°C below the mean SSTs observed at Wolf and Darwin (26.1°C) and Pinta, Marchena, and Genovesa (23.8°C), respectively.

Vertical temperature differences were often pronounced in the Galápagos, and observations at Wolf Island deserve note in this connection. While diving on the east side of Wolf, we descended through a thermocline at 21 m depth (1,358 hrs., 19 January 1975) with an estimated temperature gradient of 1°C (25°–26°C). Within a period of thirty minutes, the thermocline had shoaled to 11 m depth.

Our SST observations in zones 3 and 4 agree with Harris's statement that these zones are similar in the warm season. Waters surrounding Santiago Island (zone 4) showed the following mean SSTs: 23.2°C on the east side of the island at Bartolomé Island (n = 3, 22 January 1975) and 27.2°C on the west side at James Bay (n = 3, 7 February 1976). The 1975 data agree with the readings made in the southern sector of zone 3 (at Pinta, Marchena, and Genovesa). The 1976 SSTs at Santiago Island were relatively high, probably because of the stronger influence of the Panamá current later in the year. Our continuous temperature record in zone 4 (Bartolomé Island), however, was not lower than temperatures observed in zone 1 (Academy Bay) in the cool season, as predicted by Harris. The mean temperature at Bartolomé was 21.9°C (fig. 6), and at Academy Bay monthly mean SSTs in August and September were 20.9°C and 20.7°C respectively. Temperatures dropped below 20°C at Bartolomé on three days during the forty-three-day period of record with a minimum temperature of 18.7°C.

Zone 5 west of Isabela Island is the coolest sector year-round in the Galápagos. During our cruise in 1975, the mean SST observed in zone 5 (14–17 January) was 20.7°C (n = 12), compared with zones 1–4 (10–13 January and 18–25 January) where the mean SST was 23.6°C (n = 16). In 1976 the mean SST observed in zone 5 (8–9 February) was 23.8°C (n = 5) and in zones 1–4 (31 January–7 February and 10–14 February), 25.2°C (n = 40). These records are indicative of conditions in the early warm season. In the cool season, SSTs dropped markedly in zone 5. This is evident at Punta Espinosa where continuous temperature records showed means of 20.8°C (fig. 6, trace *a*) and 20.1°C (table 2). Temperature trace *b* at Punta Espinosa is discussed below. The cooling trend was particularly noticeable at Caleta Iguana. At the end of the warm season, the temperature dropped from 24.6°C (16 April 1975) to 17.8°C (5 May 1975) (fig. 6, trace *a*). By July the mean temperature was 16.9°C (table 2) and in August–September it was 15.4°C (fig. 6, trace *b*). The minimum temperatures recorded over these periods were 15.1°C and 14.3°C, respectively. A similar trend was observed during a cruise from Fernandina to Cape Marshall (east side of Isabela) from 18 to 19 May 1975. Sea surface temperatures at Cape Hammond and Espinosa Point were 18.0°C and 21.0°C respectively. At Albemarle Point (north end of Isabela) the SST was 21.5°C and had increased to 27.8°C at Cape Marshall.

While it is fairly obvious that waters west of Isabela Island are significantly cooler than elsewhere in the Galápagos, there do exist some habitats in zone 5 which experience relatively high thermal regimes. One such habitat is represented by lava rock basins (1–2 m depth), which are partly isolated from the sea, at Punta Espinosa. These basins contain abundant live corals. A series of SSTs observed in one semi-enclosed basin and adjacent areas up to 100 meters offshore show a significant difference in temperatures, up to 4°C, among these stations (table 3). Thermal regimens observed simultaneously at Punta Espinosa immediately offshore (trace *a*) and in a rock basin (trace *b*) are shown in figure 6. The mean temperature in the rock basin was 22.7°C, or 1.9°C higher than the mean outside the basin. In addition, sea temperatures below 20°C occurred frequently outside the basin with a minimum of 17.7°C. Inside the basin, the minimum temperature was 19.9°C. Note the daily variations in temperature, especially those in the basin, which track the semidiurnal tidal oscillations. This thermal-tidal synchrony is probably due to intense, midday heating at ebb tide followed by flushing with cool water during the flooding tide, a phenomenon observed on fringing coral reefs in the Gulf of Panamá (Glynn and Stewart, 1973).

Although no temperature data are available for Urvina Bay, which is southeast of Punta Espinosa on Isabela Island, we suspect that this area is partly sheltered and not fully subject to the cool upwelling regime that generally occurs in zone 5. Our evidence for this supposition derives from the variety and abundance of hermatypic corals found on the raised shelf at Urvina (see chapter 3, *Nature and Distribution of Coral Communities and Coral Reefs*).

CLOUD COVER

Seasonal Differences: Mean monthly cloud cover observed at Academy Bay, Santa Cruz Island, over a twelve-year period demonstrates a consistent annual pattern of relatively clear skies in the warm season and high cover during the remainder of the year (fig. 7). Cloud cover and SSTs compared over the same period (fig. 8) show a significant inverse relation ($r = -0.688$, $0.02 > P > 0.01$, Kendall rank correlation). Note the generally reduced cloudiness in 1965, 1969, 1972, and 1976, which were especially warm-water years in the Galápagos (fig. 5). The reason for these seasonal differences is that warm sea surface waters, due to the influence of the Panamá Current, are correlated with convective clouds that produce significant rainfall but are intermittent in duration. Cooler sea conditions, brought on by a greater influence of the SEC and EUC water masses (currents), are correlated with stratiform clouds that cover the area persistently for days at a time, but which produce only a drizzle.

TABLE 3. Sea Surface Temperatures at Punta Espinosa, Fernandina Island, 24 April 1975.

Habitat	Low Water (0738 hours)	High Water (1410 hours)
Lava rock basin	24.0°C	23.5°C
Adjacent outer basin (10 m seaward)	24.0°C	22.0°C
Outer protected (SE) side (50 m seaward)	22.8°C	21.0°C
Outer exposed (NW) side (25 m seaward)	21.5°C	20.0°C
Offshore (100 m seaward)	20.0°C	19.5°C

Intra-Island Cloud Cover: A strong relationship between the penetration of radiant energy in the water column and the depth distribution of reef-building corals has long been recognized (Wells, 1957a; Stoddart, 1969a; Buddemeier and Kinzie, 1975a). Photosynthetically active light is required by the symbiotic algae of corals that enhance coral skeletogenesis. The amount of light reaching corals is affected by many factors, such as sea surface conditions, suspended sediments, plankton abundance, nature of the bottom (its reflectivity), and cloud cover. Cloud cover and coral growth have been shown to be significantly inversely correlated (Goreau and Goreau, 1959; Bak, 1974; Glynn, 1977).

In order to test for a possible relationship between cloud cover density and abundance of reef corals on a given island, all daily observations within a particular month were pooled. Each month was then analyzed by the X^2 test (applying Yates's correction for continuity) with clouds/no clouds and coral/noncoral shores comprising the 2 X 2 contingency table. Except for Fernandina Island, this analysis was limited to central island shores in the lee of strong upwelling, thus excluding possible effects due to differences in sea temperature. The heterogeneity X^2 statistic was calculated on the pooled data (a 2 X 2 contingency table of all data over the eighteen-month period) for each of the five large islands and was found to be highly significant ($P < < 0.001$ for four islands; $0.005 > P > 0.001$ for Fernandina Island). Thus, monthly samples were not pooled but treated separately. The results are summarized in table 4. Significantly high ($+$) and low ($-$) cloud densities over coral shores were determined from the observed deviations from expectation.

Significant trends in cloud cover were evident over Isabela and Santa Cruz islands and, to a lesser degree, over Santiago Island (table 4). The coral shores of Isabela experienced relatively high cloud densities for thirteen months or 72 percent of the eighteen-month record. Santa Cruz Island was subject to a relatively high cloud density over noncoral shores; this pattern was observed for fourteen months or for 78 percent of the record. Santiago

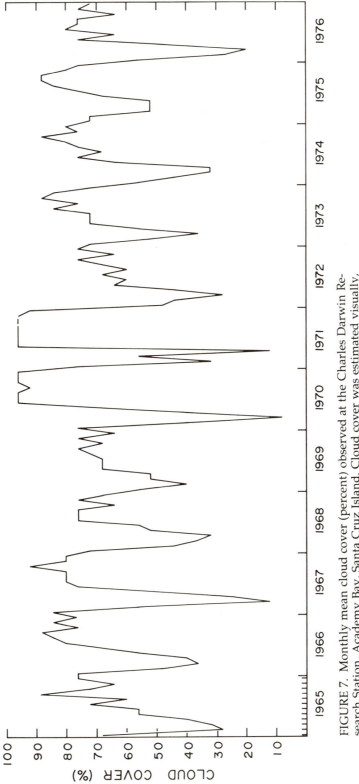

FIGURE 7. Monthly mean cloud cover (percent) observed at the Charles Darwin Research Station, Academy Bay, Santa Cruz Island. Cloud cover was estimated visually, on a scale of eighths, three times daily (0700, 1300, 1900 hr).

EMERSION EVENTS

Tidal Emersion: Tidal predictions in the Galápagos are based on the reference station at Salina Cruz, Mexico, and are available at seven localities (subordinate stations) from Caleta Tagus, Isabela Island (91°22'W) eastward to Wreck Bay, San Cristóbal Island (89°37'W) (NOAA, 1975 and 1976). The tidal oscillations are semidiurnal to unequal diurnal with slight irregularities occurring between successive highs and lows (Hedgpeth, 1969; Houvenaghel and Houvenaghel, 1974). The range of spring tides varies from west to east between islands, from 1.5 m at Elizabeth Bay (Isabela Island) to 2.0 m at Darwin Bay (Genovesa Island). These tidal differences may be due to the influence of upwelling by the Equatorial Undercurrent. Houvenaghel (1978) has suggested that upwelling along the western sides of Isabela and Fernandina stalls westerly flowing surface waters along the eastern side of Isabela Island, thus causing slightly elevated tides to occur in the eastern sector.

Tide-related mass mortalities have now been documented for several reef areas throughout the world. Many shallow coral reef habitats have been affected by extreme and prolonged unpredictable low-water stands caused by anomalous meteorologic or oceanographic conditions. Such cases have been reported on Caribbean reefs (Glynn, 1968; Hendler, 1977), in the Red Sea (Fishelson, 1973), and in Guam (Yamaguchi, 1975). The sea level drops and mass mortalities observed at Guam are possibly related to El Niño events and Wyrtki's (1973) "teleconnections" hypothesis (Yamaguchi, 1975). Extensive reef flat mortalities have also occurred during predictable but extreme low-water exposures coincident with unusual meteorologic conditions such as cool weather, intense solar insolation, and heavy downpours (Endean, 1976; Glynn, 1976).

Over a three-day period, 2–4 February 1976, an 8–10 cm vertical section of the reef crest (with some live pocilloporid corals) at Onslow Island was exposed briefly during a 0.0 low-water stand. Tidal predictions for 1975 and 1976 indicate that extreme low-water exposures at midday were not uncommon and could have reached as low as −18 cm. Crustose coralline algae and low algal turfs predominate at the highest levels of the reef crest, suggesting that the vertical buildup of reef-forming corals at these points has reached an equilibratory state with respect to present sea level. Dead reef crest corals in growth position at or near observed spring low tide levels (including species of *Pocillopora* and *Porites*) were observed elsewhere in the islands, such as at Santa Fe, Bartolomé, and Punta Espinosa. A mass mortality of pocilloporid corals observed in lava rock pools at Punta Espinosa is, in part, attributed to low-water exposures but, in this case, may be largely the result of very recent tectonic activity (see below). Unfortunately, to our knowledge, there are no established and monitored tidal stations in the islands. Thus, for some circumstances it may be difficult to identify the direct influences of tidal exposures and tectonic events on coral mortality.

Tectonic Uplift: In September 1974 a patch reef of *Pocillopora elegans* Dana was discovered by one of us (GMW) in a shallow, protected embayment approximately 150–200 m southeast of the landing pier at Punta Espinosa (see chapter 3, *Nature and Distribution of Coral Communities and Coral Reefs: Fernandina Island*). At that time it was observed that the uppermost (approximately 10 cm) portion of the reef crest, covering an area of about 0.5 ha, had been killed. Concomitant observations of intertidal sessile invertebrates on surrounding mangrove roots and along adjacent rocky shores suggested a slight vertical displacement upward when compared with the same species' populations elsewhere in the islands.

Subsequent visits to the area revealed extensive coral mortality; the reef crest had risen to approximately 40 cm above the minimum low water mark of 3 cm on 16 January 1975 (see figs. 39 and 40) and 30 cm above the minimum low watermark of 12 cm on 8 February 1976. If these reef exposures are normalized to the 0.0 tidal level, it is seen that the Punta Espinosa reef crest (42–43 cm) is 32–35 cm higher than that at Onslow Island (8–10 cm). We suggest that the coral mortality observed at Punta Espinosa in late 1974 and early 1975 resulted from tectonic uplifting. Our observations indicate that the uplift probably began just prior to September 1974 and continued until January 1975. By February 1976 the uplift appeared to have stabilized. Evidence supporting the magnitude and timing of this event comes from the vertical displacement of conspicuous intertidal organisms. By January 1975 dead barnacle tests of the mid-intertidal species *Tetraclita squamosa milleporosa* Pilsbry were centered close to the high tide mark and *Megabalanus galapaganus* (Pilsbry), which is generally restricted to the lowest intertidal levels (Hedgpeth, 1969) and subtidally, was present along the lower boundary of the mid-intertidal level. These anomalous species distributions indicated a vertical displacement of the order of 0.3–0.5 m, concordant with the observed shift on the reef crest. In addition, the Flightless Cormorant *Nannopterum harrisi* Rothschild, which constructs nest sites close to the water, moved their nests about 0.5 m vertically downshore during this same period (Harris, 1979). It is interesting to note that this uplift event preceded a major crater eruption in February 1977 and may have represented a movement of lava toward the surface (T. Simkin, personal communication).

A pronounced tectonic uplift elevated a large section of the subtidal shelf (< 5.5 m) in Urvina Bay, Isabela Island, probably early in 1954 (Richards, 1957). This event followed the eruption of Volcán Alcedo, located near the center of Isabela Island, in November 1953 and is believed to have resulted from the tumescence of rising lava.* The uplifted area was visited in March 1954 and the condition of dead marine animals (their state of decay

---

*The date of eruption noted in Richards (1957, p. 28) is 9 November 1954. We believe that the year 1954 is a typographical error and that the eruption occurred in late 1953 according to the sequence of events described in this account.

FIGURE 9. Aerial views of the tectonically uplifted shoreline in Urvina Bay, Isabela Island (4 July 1968, courtesy of T. Simkin). A - view toward the east of uplifted shelf; B - near-vertical view of shelf and narrow uplifted shoreline to the south (see arrow).

and death postures) indicated that the elevation occurred suddenly and probably shortly before March. The greatest area affected was the shallow shelf just west of the head of the bay (91° 10′ W; 0° 17′ S); this was uplifted evenly (without tilting) to a maximum distance of 1.2 km seaward of the old shoreline (figs. 9A and B). The uplift also embraces a narrow zone along the shore for a distance of about 6 km to the south.

In 1975 and 1976, we observed numerous reef corals in growth position and a variety of associated organisms on the broad, elevated shelf at the head of the bay (pl. 1). Massive corals, but no coral reefs (contrary to Richards's 1954 claim), were abundant on certain parts of the old submarine shelf. Colonies of *Pavona clavus* Dana and *Porites lobata* Dana, up to 2 and 3 m in diameter respectively, were observed. *Pavona gigantea* Verrill was smaller than the above species with no colony exceeding about 0.5 m in diameter. One 10 × 20m patch of pocilloporid coral [probably *Pocillopora damicornis* (Linnaeus)] formed an incipient framework about 0.5 m in thickness.

Thus, tectonic uplift was possibly responsible for the presumed vertical displacement of reef crest corals at Punta Espinosa and was certainly the cause of the emergence and mass mortality of coral populations on the Urvina Bay shelf. Crossland (1927) noted the occurrence of dead mangrove roots in the low intertidal zone at Conway Bay, Santa Cruz Island, and attributed this to recent, local subsidence. Since the Galápagos Islands comprise one of the most active volcanic fields known (McBirney and Aoki, 1966; Williams, 1966a), one must not lose sight of the effects of tectonic disturbances in this area.

SHORELINE STABILITY AND VOLCANISM

From the discussion above, it is evident that substrate stability is important for long-term coral growth and the formation of framework features. Other physical events that can interfere with the establishment of coral communities are slides and slumping (Goreau and Hartman, 1963), and volcanic activity. Volcanism may lead to coral mortality through the release of noxious gases (Wood-Jones, 1912 in Endean, 1976) and by direct contact or the heating of surrounding waters from lava flows that pour into the sea.

Some coral communities we examined were present on steeply sloping, near-vertical rock substrates (talus slopes) adjacent to steep island cliffs. It was apparent that coral mortality at these sites had resulted from the physical impact of falling rock debris and from the downslope movement of corals, individually or en masse, into deep water below the required light levels. The effects of rock slides and volcanism will be examined later with regard to particular sites (see chapter 5, *Physical Correlates of Coral Distribution, Abundance, and Growth*).

NATURE AND DISTRIBUTION OF CORAL COMMUNITIES AND CORAL REEFS

In the following account of coral community structure (species composition and abundances) and extent of reef frame development, with reference to local geographic and hydrographic settings, we will consider in order:

1. Southern islands (San Cristóbal, Española, and Floreana)
2. Central islands (Santa Fe, Santa Cruz, Pinzón, Rábida, east side of Isabela, and Santiago)
3. Western sector (west side of Isabela, and Fernandina)
4. Northern islands (Genovesa, Marchena, Pinta, Wolf, and Darwin).

This classification corresponds closely with the thermal zones discussed previously (see *Physical Environment)*, that is, the southeastern islands are bathed by relatively cool water (warm temperate-subtropical), the central islands are thermally intermediate or seasonally cool and warm (subtropical), the western sector is very cool (warm-temperate), and the northern islands are generally the warmest in the archipelago (subtropical-tropical).

Reference is also made in this section to corallivores and other species (potential competitors) that may have an influence on coral community structure. Vertical wall communities, with a greatly reduced light regime, were examined in the central, western, and northern sectors of the Galápagos. Areas harboring rich macrophytic algal floras, indicative of upwelling and consequent high nutrient levels, are also examined briefly here as such environments are the antithesis of those favoring coral community development.

METHODS

Ordinal-level measures (sparse, common, and abundant) of coral abundance were determined by snorkeling or scuba diving at frequent intervals along the shore, usually between 2–10 m depth. According to the scale adopted herein, sparse denotes few or < ten individual coral colonies observed by one diver in a fifteen-minute swim; similarly, common denotes many corals (> fifty colonies), and abundant denotes numerous corals growing in close contact and often forming an incipient reef frame. At times, under conditions of high water transparency and slight wind movement, surveying was carried out from a boat with frequent spot checks from the surface or by free-diving.

More exact measures of coral abundance and of other macroscopic epibenthos (as well as rock and sand) were determined with chain transects (Porter, 1972). The chain transects were 10 m and 11 m in length and consisted of 1.3-cm and 1.4-cm links respectively. The chain was laid out parallel to depth contours and positioned to conform to bottom irregularities. All items below each link were enumerated. Sampling sites were usually selected after a preliminary reconnaissance of the bottom in order to delimit particular areas of interest (e.g., different depth zones and species assemblages). These areas were then subdivided into particular transect sites at arbitrary and equal (often 10 m distant) intervals. Nearly all species and higher taxa were identified in situ; occasionally voucher specimens were removed for laboratory study. A total of thirty-two transects was analyzed: eighteen (transects I–XVIII) were sampled in 1975, and fourteen (transects XIV–XXXII) in 1976.

Photographic transects were carried out when time was limited, that is, when a particular locality was visited only briefly or when sampling in relatively deep water (> 20 m). These transects were laid out to sample coral abundances either horizontally (parallel to depth contours) or vertically (perpendicular to depth contours). Quadrats 0.25 m² and 1.0 m² were spaced at equal intervals (3–5 m distant) along the transect and photographed with color film and a strobe light source. Replicate sampling, with usually three quadrats, was carried out in the vertical transects. Notes were taken in situ of the organisms present, and sometimes specimens were collected, in order to facilitate identifications from the photographic transparencies. The transparencies were projected onto white paper on which the outlines of organisms were traced. A planimeter was used to determine the surface coverage of the projected images of each species.

Reef frame relief features were recorded with a portable Raytheon Explorer II (DE-725B) recording fathometer. Fathograms were obtained by traversing reefs on a straight line course from the shoreline seaward.

A probe consisting of 1.2-m-long sections of black-iron pipe was hammered into pocilloporid reefs to determine the thickness of the reef framework. Core samples were also obtained from the probe holes, thus providing material to determine the character of internal reef features. Further details on the design and operation of the probe are given in Glynn and Macintyre (1977).

SOUTHERN ISLANDS (SAN CRISTÓBAL, ESPAÑOLA, AND FLOREANA)

San Cristóbal Island: San Cristóbal is one of the five largest islands in the Galápagos group with an area of 55,809 ha. The southwestern half of the island is formed by a single large volcano, with a few parasitic cones on its flanks, that is, ⌣ 730 m high; the northeastern half of the island contains numerous small cones and is less than 152 m in elevation. San Cristóbal appears to be one of the oldest islands of the archipelago; its youngest lava flows were judged to be of Pleistocene age (McBirney and Williams, 1969; further information on the geology of the various islands is mainly from this source). The northwest-facing coast has a relatively broad shelf, indicated by the position of the 6 m depth contour; the shelf along the southeast coast is narrow (fig. 10). All areas surveyed were on the northwest coast and included Wreck Bay, Bassa Point, Finger Point, Hobbs Bay, and Pitt Point.

The Wreck Bay area is characterized by a series of shallow, rock terraces with intervening sand patches. The predominant benthic plant cover included encrusting calcareous algae with some stands of macrophytic algae (*Sargassum* spp., *Blossevillea galapagensis* Piccone and Grunow, and other species). Hermatypic corals were sparse and the echinoid *Eucidaris thouarsii* (Valenciennes) ranged from common to abundant.

Transect sampling in the Bassa Point area indicated that hermatypic corals were relatively sparse with *Pocillopora elegans* comprising less than 20 percent of the surface cover (fig. 10). The mean percent cover of *Pocillopora* in the four transects was 16.0 percent. Massive corals observed sparingly in this area, but not sampled in the transects, were *Porites lobata*, *Pavona clavus*, and *Pavona gigantea*. *Eucidaris thouarsii* was relatively abundant; it ranged between about 5 percent and 10 percent of the surface coverage. Some echinoids were observed grazing on the live branchtips of *Pocillopora*, but the majority were more commonly grazing on the abundant crustose coralline algae that exceeded 20 percent cover in all transects and in one (transect IV) made up more than 70 percent of the epibenthos. An algal turf was also abundant and ranged from near 40 percent to more than 50 percent cover in three transects.

Quadrat sampling (n = 24) adjacent to transects I and II, on rock rubble overgrown with crustose coralline algae and an algal turf, was carried out to determine the general level of echinoid abundances. The median density of *Eucidaris* was 32 individuals/m^2 (24–44 individuals/m^2, 0.95 confidence limits of median) and ranged from 0 to 100 individuals/m^2.* In the same quadrats, *Lytechinus semituberculatus* (Valenciennes) had a median density of four individuals/m^2 (0–12 individuals/m^2) and ranged from 0–144 individuals/m^2.

---

*Confidence limits of median calculated from K = 0.5 (n + 1) – $\sqrt{n}$ where K is used to set the limits by counting from the ends of the data array toward the median.

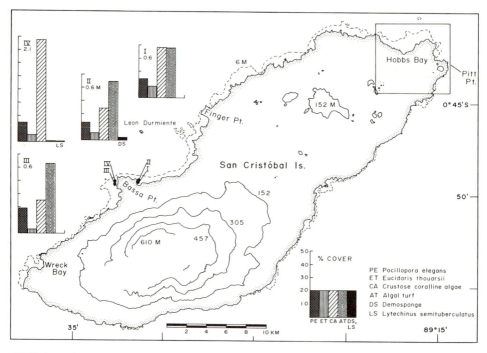

FIGURE 10. San Cristóbal Island showing location of study sites and results of transect sampling in the vicinity of Bassa Point (10 January 1975). The Hobbs Bay and Pitt Point areas are illustrated in greater detail in figure 11. Base map from U. S. Navy Hydrographic Chart No. 5943, 1st ed., March, 1947, corrected edition June, 1962.

Brief surveys at Finger Point and Hobbs Bay disclosed a general paucity of corals in these areas. The predominant cover consisted of algae, that is, algal turf, fleshy algae, and crustose coralline algae. The latter was particularly prominent in Hobbs Bay with large numbers of the echinoids, especially *Lytechinus semituberculatus* and, to a lesser extent, *Eucidaris thouarsii*, grazing on the coralline pavement. Asteroids were also abundant in Hobbs Bay, particularly *Heliaster cumingii* (Gray), *Nidorellia armata* (Gray), and *Oreaster occidentalis* Verrill.

The Pitt Point area on the northeast end of San Cristóbal Island disclosed abundant reef-coral populations and incipient reef development adjacent to a small offshore islet (fig. 11). Pocilloporid corals, namely, *Pocillopora elegans* and *P. damicornis*, exceeded 20 percent cover in three transects, and when combined with massive corals (*Porites lobata* and *Pavona clavus*) contributed a mean total cover of 25.0 percent. This is not significantly higher (P ⁓ 0.09, Mann-Whitney U-test), however, than the 16.0 percent mean coral cover observed in the Bassa Point area. Of the pocilloporid corals sampled at Pitt Point, *P. damicornis* was the most abundant, comprising 72.3 percent of the two species. The only reef framework observed in this area was located on the north and lee side of a small islet approximately 2 km offshore (fig. 11). Here live pocilloporid corals had constructed an interlocking frame that was close to 1 m in thickness. Massive coral cover was predominantly the species *Porites lobata*, which made up 97.0 percent of this category. The largest share of the *Porites* sampled (87.2 percent, denoted by arrow in transect XXIII), however, had recently died and the cause of death is unknown. Enormous colonies of *Porites lobata*, some 3 m in diameter, were present along the south side of a small rock point in the southern half of the bay near Pitt Point (see occluded circle, fig. 11). Other hermatypic corals observed in this area outside of the transect sampling sites were *Pocillopora capitata* Verrill, *Pavona gigantea, Pavona varians* Verrill, and *Psammocora stellata* Verrill.

Eucidaris was encountered in transect XIX only. This echinoid occurred commonly in the Pitt Point area, however, and was observed grazing on live pocilloporid corals. Crustose coralline algae covered a large portion of the substratum as it did in the Bassa area. Unlike Bassa Point, an algal turf was not well developed at Pitt Point.

Other corallivores observed at Pitt Point, in addition to *Eucidaris,* were the hermit crab *Trizopagurus magnificus* (Bouvier) and the gastropod *Latiaxis (Babelomurex) hindsii* Carpenter. The hermit crab occurred commonly among the live branches of *Pocillopora.* Two individuals of *Latiaxis* had stripped the tissues from a portion of a pocilloporid colony. *Arothron meleagris* (Lacépède), a pufferfish, was present and was observed feeding on the branchtips of *Pocillopora.* Parrotfishes were abundant, namely, *Scarus ghobban* Forskål, *Scarus perrico* Jordan and Gilbert, and *Scarus rubroviolaceus* Bleeker. *Porites lobata* colonies were heavily nicked, and it is believed that the parrotfishes produced these scars.

Española Island: The southernmost of the Galápagos Islands, Española is a relatively small, (6,048 ha in area) low island with a maximum elevation near 206 m. This island is an uplifted block of submarine lavas. A relatively broad, shallow shelf is present along the north coast with the 37 m contour extending 1–2 km offshore. The south coast has high cliffs, rising to 92 m, and a steep shelf with 31 to 49 m depths less than 1 km offshore (see inset in fig. 12). Our survey was confined to the Gardner Bay and Suarez Point areas.

The northeastern sector of Española, in the vicinity of Gardner Bay, revealed high coral cover on hard substrates in certain areas, with incipient reef development at one site, and extensive patches of loosely attached calcareous algae on soft substrates. Compared with massive corals, pocilloporid corals predominated in three transect samples; the mean percent coverages of *Pocillopora damicornis* and *Pavona clavus* respectively in four transects were 32.0 percent and 5.4 percent (fig. 12). In the eastern Pacific, massive corals often occur more frequently at the reef base in slightly deeper water than on slopes or reef flats (Glynn et al., 1972; Glynn, 1976; Porter, 1972, 1974) and the

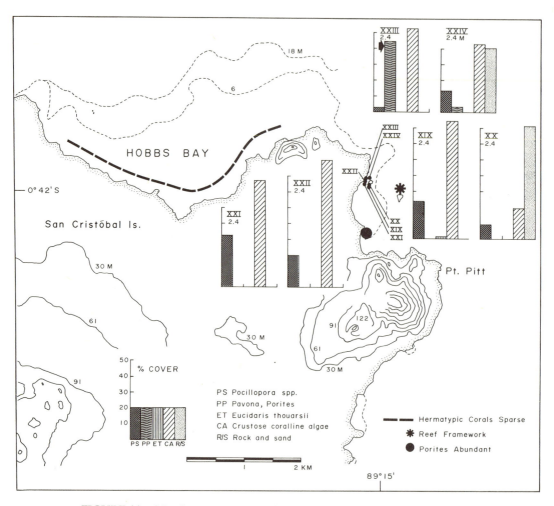

FIGURE 11. Northeastern sector of San Cristóbal Island (see fig. 10 for orientation) showing location of transect sampling sites and the relative abundances of the predominant epibenthic organisms. *Pocillopora* spp. (PS) denotes the presence of *P. damicornis* and *P. elegans*. Massive corals (PP) were represented by *Porites lobata* and *Pavona clavus*. Also indicated are areas of pocilloporid reef framework and abundant large colonies of *Porites lobata*.

high incidence of *Pavona* in transect XXV, which is the deepest transect in this series at 3.7 m depth, is in keeping with this trend. *Porites lobata* was also observed at the reef base, but no colonies were included in the transects. *Eucidaris* was present, for example, in transect XXVII, but was not abundant. Crustose coralline algae predominated in all transects but one (transect XXVI), where these algae had a mean cover of 46.8 percent.

Pocilloporid corals (*Pocillopora elegans* and *P. damicornis*) formed a nearly

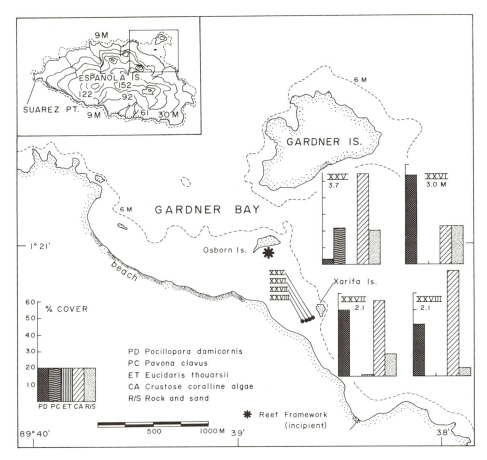

FIGURE 12. Northeastern sector of Española Island showing location of transect sampling sites and relative abundances of the predominant epibenthic organisms. Also indicated is an area of pocilloporid reef framework. Island names Osborn and Xarifa from Durham (1962). Base map from U. S. Navy Hydrographic Chart No. 22524 (formerly H.O. 5944), 1st edition 1942, corrected edition 23 February 1974.

continuous patch between 1–2 ha in area along the south side of Osborn Island (figs. 12 and 13-A, arrow 1). While no reef frame per se was observed during this brief reconnaissance, the abundance and continuity of corals here indicate that a structural reef is probably now forming at this site. A subsequent visit in 1977 showed that pocilloporid corals were abundant farther along the shore of Osborn and extended along most of the southwestern sector of the island. A similar site off the southwestern end of Gardner Island was likewise veneered with *Pocillopora* (fig. 13-B, arrow 3).

Other hermatypic coral species were observed at various sites in relation to Xarifa Island (named after the "Xarifa Expedition," Durham, 1962), notably

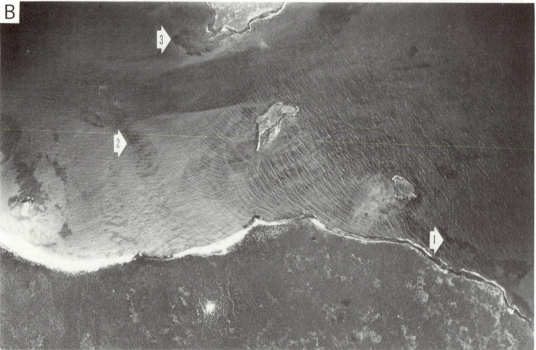

FIGURE 13. Aerial views of Gardner Bay, NE sector of Española Island (13 March 1959, 6,000 ft.), courtesy U. S. Defense Intelligence Agency. A - arrow number 1 identifies an incipient pocilloporid reef that possibly extends to the southwest as indicated by arrow 2; dark patches similar to that identified by arrow 3 consisted of carpets of loosely attached calcareous algae. B - arrows 1 and 2 denote additional calcareous algal patches; arrow 3 indicates the location of a possible incipient pocilloporid reef off the southwest corner of Gardner Island.

small monospecific patches of *Psammocora stellata* at < 1 m depth on the west side, isolated individuals of *Cycloseris elegans* (Verrill) at 8 m depth and 50 m northwest, and *Pavona gigantea* at 8 m on the east side and along the shore of Española about 1 km southeast of Xarifa.

Loosely attached calcareous algae, chiefly *Amphiroa compressa* Lemoine and other species of melobesioids in lesser abundance, formed 10–20-cm-thick carpets over much of the sandy bottom in Gardner Bay. The extent and location of these algal mats can be seen in figure 13 (A, arrow 3; B, arrows 1 and 2). The white sand beaches contained chiefly the calcareous remains of these algae. Taylor (1945) lists other algae found in Gardner Bay and provides additional information on collections made at several islands in the Galápagos.

Two individuals of *Arothron meleagris* were observed in this area. Parrotfishes *(Scarus ghobban* and *S. rubroviolaceus)* were also present. The distribution of parrotfishes associated with corals at Española, reported by Rosenblatt and Hobson (1969), suggests a marked difference in the kinds of communities developed on the north and south sides of this island. Their observations in February 1967 revealed the presence of four species of *Scarus* (including the two above) on the north coast where the sea temperature was 26.7°C (at 5 m depth). No *Scarus* were seen on the south coast, but another parrotfish *(Nicholsina)* that is closely associated with *Sargassum* was seen there. *Sargassum* was abundant on the south coast, and the sea temperature at that time was 21.7°C.

Floreana Island: Intermediate in area (17,253 ha) and altitude (640 m), Floreana Island, with its numerous parasitic cones, probably formed from an earlier shield volcano. Volcanic activity has occurred recently on the island, perhaps with significant discharges within historical times. The shallow shelf (10–15 m depth) and satellite islands of Floreana were surveyed in detail from the Black Beach anchorage on the west (fig. 1), around the north coast to Champion Island, and along the main shore just opposite Champion (fig. 14). From Black Beach to Point Cormorant, comprising virtually the entire northwestern sector of Floreana, reef corals were absent or rare. This sector has a relatively broad, shallow shelf (37 m deep from 1–3 km offshore) compared with the northeastern sector and particularly the steep, south coast exposures. Large macrophytic algal communities [composed dominantly of *Chondrus* (?) *albemarlensis* Taylor, *Gelidium* sp., *Kallymenia latiloba* Taylor, *Sebdenia* sp. and *Ahnfeltia durvillei* (Bory) J. Agardh] were well developed on a large rock boulder bottom off Black Beach, however, and their presence there is correlated with periodic cool water conditions. As noted earlier, it is probable that the western side of Floreana Island is periodically influenced by an eastward-moving stream of the Equatorial Undercurrent. Coral communities and reefs were generally best developed at the northeastern end of Floreana, in the Cormorant Bay area, which we examine in detail below.

Reef framework was observed at four sites: inside the basalt-ringed la-

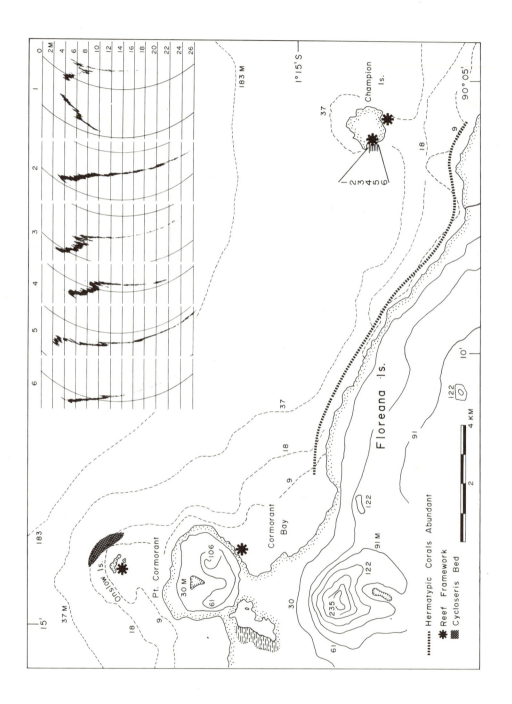

0
2 M
4
6
8
10
12
14
16
18
20
22
24
26

183 M

1

2

3

4

5

6

1° 15' S

Champion Is.

37

2
3
4
5
6

18

9

90° 05'

183

37 M

Onslow Is.

Pt. Cormorant

18

9

37

18

9

30 M

106

61

30

0

122

Cormorant Bay

Floreana Is.

91

122

235

91 M

122

61

15'

10'

4 KM

2

······ Hermatypic Corals Abundant

✳ Reef Framework

▨ Cycloseris Bed

goon of Onslow Island (Devil's Crown), on the north shore of Cormorant Bay, and along the west and south shores of Champion Island (fig. 14). Massive corals were generally abundant south of Cormorant Bay, along ⌒ 13 km of the coastline (figs. 15 and 16). Figure 17 is an aerial view of the reefs at Onslow Island and in Cormorant Bay (arrow 1) and shows algal mats (arrow 2). These mats consisted mostly of the brown alga *Padina durvillaei* Bory but in some cases also contained large quantities of melobesioid calcareous algae similar to those observed at Española Island.

The location of seven transects (V to XI, table 5) at Onslow Island is indicated in figure 18. Six of the seven transects sampled abundant coral populations, which comprised the reef frame. The total live coral cover ranged from 16.5 percent to 73.5 percent. *Pocillopora elegans* and *Porites lobata* predominated at shallow depth from 0.5–1.8 m (fig. 19). A moderately high proportion of these corals, from 7.4 percent to 20.0 percent, were dead, most probably a result of low water exposures. *Pavona clavus* was the predominant coral at 3.0–4.6 m depth (fig. 20). Transect IX, outside the reef frame proper, contained only the coral *Psammocora stellata*. *Megabalanus* and *Eucidaris* contributed, overall, 1.0 percent and 7.8 percent of the surface cover respectively. Barnacles were attached to basalt, dead corals, and frequently to live pocilloporid colonies. The attachment to live corals was presumably to damaged areas initially, with subsequent overgrowth of live coral surfaces. *Eucidaris* was abundant in some shallow transects (VI and VII) with a high abundance of *Pocillopora* and in some deep transects (X and XI) where *Pavona clavus* predominated. More detailed sampling of the echinoid, considered below, will demonstrate a significant live coral–sea urchin abundance trend. Crustose coralline algae contributed 7.0 percent to the mean surface cover. Algal turf was sampled in three transects and was associated with massive corals in every case. While some other invertebrates were observed, these accounted for only 1.8 percent, overall, of the surface cover. Rock and sand substrates were prominent, amounting to 33.0 percent of bottom surfaces.

Because of the high abundance of *Eucidaris* (fig. 21) and its frequent grazing on live coral (fig. 22), we directed our attention to certain aspects of its ecology relative to coral and reef growth. Some relevant data have already been published (Glynn et al., 1979). Here (and below, see chapter 6, *Biological Interactions: Predation*) we offer additional data and some details not presented in the earlier study.

FIGURE 14. Northeastern sector of Floreana Island showing fathograms and their location at Champion Island, areas with abundant massive corals along the Floreana coast and reef framework construction on Floreana and at Onslow and Champion Islands. Fathograms (lengths of transects exaggerated, see below) were obtained along the west shore of Champion and are numbered consecutively from north to south (13 January 1975). Each trace is approximately perpendicular to the shoreline and follows the bottom seaward from left to right. The average transect lengths or horizontal distances traced are about 70 m. Elevations above sea level in contour intervals of ∼30 m. Base map from U. S. Navy Hydrographic Chart No. 5940, corrected June 1972.

FIGURE 15. View of low-lying and nearly continuous cover of *Pavona clavus* on Flor-eana Island opposite Champion Island (see fig. 14), ~ 6 m, 6 February 1976.

FIGURE 16. View of incipient *Pavona clavus* buildup on Floreana Island opposite Champion Island (see fig. 14), ~ 6 m, 6 February 1976. Maximum vertical height of colonies was 1 to 1.5 m.

FIGURE 17. Aerial view of Cormorant Bay - Onslow Island area, Floreana Island, 12 March 1960, ∼ 1800 m (6000 ft.). Arrow 1 identifies location of live pocilloporid fringing reef along north shore of Cormorant Bay; arrow 2 identifies a calcareous algal mat.

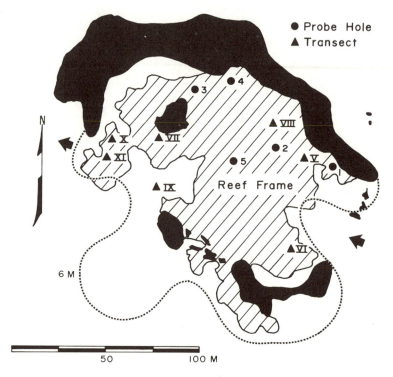

FIGURE 18. Planar view of Onslow Island showing location of transects (triangles) and probe-hole sites (solid circles). Arrows denote the eastern and western points of entry and exit respectively of prevailing currents over the reef. Current velocities were measured along this course. Also indicated are the 6-m depth contour and location of the reef frame.

Figure 23 indicates that the urchins were most abundant along the reef edge, at ⌣ 5 m depth, where pocilloporid corals were relatively abundant but not growing contiguously as a reef framework. On the reef edge, the median density was 34 individuals/m². On the shallow reef flat, where *Pocillopora* was most abundant, the median densities of *Eucidaris* in two surveys were 2 and 8 individuals/m². These data indicate that the inverse correlation between *Eucidaris* abundance and live pocilloporid cover reported in Glynn *et al.* (1979) is related to the depth gradient with urchins on open surfaces increasing in abundance toward the deep reef edge. Where *Psammocora* was abundant, slightly seaward of the reef edge, the median density was 0 (no urchins were found in 12 of 20 quadrats), but ranged as high as 32 individuals/m² in one quadrat. The majority of the urchins sampled in association with *Psammocora* occurred in two large aggregations in this habitat. The frequent absence of *Eucidaris* from quadrats and from transect IX (table 5) in large part was due to sampling outside the aggregations. Because adult ur-

FIGURE 19. Onslow Island reef flat with continuous cover of pocilloporid corals, predominantly *Pocillopora elegans*, ∼ 1 m, late August, 1976 (courtesy D. R. Robertson).

chins graze on open surfaces during the day and night, we consider these census data to be accurate measures of adult densities. Juveniles and sub-adults, however, were secretive; and since we did not break apart attached corals on the reef flat, it is certain that urchin abundances, particularly on the reef flat, are even greater than these data indicate.

A marked difference in urchin test diameters was found between the reef flat and *Psammocora* habitats (12 January 1975). Thirty-six *Eucidaris* from the reef flat had a median test diameter of 4.4 cm (4.3–4.6 cm, 0.95 confidence limits), whereas 21 urchins from the *Psammocora* patch had a median test diameter of 6.2 cm (5.8–6.5 cm). It seems reasonable to assume that juvenile urchins are sheltering within the interstices of the rigid coral frame and later move onto open surfaces when they are larger and less vulnerable to predation. (Predation experiments with different sized sea urchins in the Galápagos and Panamá are considered later in chapter 6, *Biological Interactions*.)

Sea urchins grazing on live pocilloporids were most pronounced along the reef edge with 60.9 percent of forty individuals feeding on live coral (from reef edge sample at 4.6 m depth in fig. 23). Of the sixty urchins sampled at 0.6 m on the reef flat, 25.0 percent were feeding on live coral. Live pocillo-

FIGURE 20. Onslow Island reef edge with mixture of pocilloporid corals and the massive species *Pavona clavus*, ∼ 4 m, 12 January 1975. *Pavona* colony in foreground ∼ 80 cm across.

porids were grazed chiefly on the branchtips, which often caused the release of mucus strands. For mechanical reasons, larger urchins normally could not gain access to the basal branches of pocilloporid corals unless they were broken, or the outer branches sufficiently grazed down to allow entry to the central areas of colonies. *Eucidaris* was also infrequently observed grazing on the live, smooth surfaces of the massive coral *Pavona clavus*, but was not observed feeding on *Porites lobata*. Large numbers of the urchins grazed on dead coral surfaces that were encrusted with a variety of species, including coralline and filamentous algae, polychaetous annelids, bryozoans, and barnacles. Numerous urchins were observed grazing on the encrusted plates of

TABLE 5. Abundance of Macroepibenthos at Onslow Island Expressed as Number and Percent (Top and Bottom Lines Respectively for Each Quadrat) of Chain Links Touching the Various Categories noted (11–13 January 1975).

Quadrat No. & Depths (m)	Coral Species[a]				Other Invertebrates[a]		Algae[a]		MIS	Rock/Sand
	PE	PL	PC	PS	MG	ET	CCA	AT		R/S
V 0.5	441(127)[b]	25	0	0	0	10	9	0	0	22
	69.6(20.0)	3.9	0	0	0	1.6	1.4	0	0	3.5
VI 0.9	115(74)	0	0	0	17	89	27	0	0	375
	16.5(10.6)	0	0	0	2.4	12.8	3.9	0	0	53.8
VII 1.8	267(55)	0	0	0	0	88	0	0	0	248
	40.6(8.4)	0	0	0	0	13.4	0	0	0	37.7
VIII 0.9	99	231(51)	0	0	0	5	112	41	0	149
	14.4	33.6(7.4)	0	0	0	0.7	16.3	6.0	0	21.7
IX 3.0	0	0	0	86(7)	25(20)[b]	0	11	0	11H 56B 11S	410
	0	0	0	13.5(1.1)	3.9(3.1)	0	1.7	0	1.7 8.8B 1.7S	64.4
X 3.0	87	18	192	0	0	79	149	76	5T	95
	12.4	2.6	27.4	0	0	11.3	21.3	10.8	0.7	13.6
XI 4.6	22	0	150(121)	0	5	95	22	11	0	251
	3.2	0	22.2(17.9)	0	0.7	14.0	3.2	1.6	0	37.1
Mean %	22.0(5.5)	5.8(1.1)	7.3(2.6)	1.8(0.2)	1.0(0.4)	7.8	7.0	2.7	1.8	33.0

[a]PE = *Pocillopora elegans* Dana; PL = *Porites lobata* Dana; PC = *Pavona clavus* Dana; PS = *Psammocora stellata* Verrill; MG = *Megabalanus galapaganus* (Pilsbry); ET = *Eucidaris thouarsii* (Val.); CCA = crustose coralline algae; AT = algal turf; MIS = miscellaneous, H = holothurian, B = bryozoans, S = *Salmacina*, T = *Tubastraea coccinea* Lesson.
[b]Dead coral and other invertebrates in parentheses.

FIGURE 21. Onslow Island reef edge with numerous sea urchins, *Eucidaris thouarsii*, grazing on live coral and coralline algae, ∼ 4 m, 5 February 1976. Test diameters of urchins in foreground were about 5 cm.

barnacles *(Megabalanus galapaganus)* attached to corals, but in no case did *Eucidaris* ever attack a large barnacle directly through the operculum.

In order to determine the extent of vertical reef development at Onslow, five drilling sites were located on the summits of the pocilloporid frame (fig. 18). These sites were probed, and cores examined periodically, until the basement basalt was reached. The probe holes indicate a median reef thickness, composed entirely of pocilloporid corals, of 0.61 m (table 6).

A synoptic view of the distributions of major communities at Onslow is given in figure 24. Pocilloporid corals predominated in shallow, relatively protected areas with good circulation. Massive corals, especially *Pavona clavus*, tended to occur at greater depths and exposure to sea conditions. Patches of *Porites lobata*, however, were common on the shallow margins of the reef proper. Some of these colonies assumed the form of microatolls, most likely a result of coral death at the summits due to low water exposures. A *Psammocora* community, ∼ 2,000 m², was present on the sand plain adjacent to the reef base. Hard substrates, predominantly around the margins of the basaltic crown and subject to relatively strong wave action and currents, supported dense populations of *Megabalanus*. Reef flanking sediments were chiefly coarse, calcareous sands made up of barnacle remains (43.8 percent to 54.5

FIGURE 22. *Eucidaris* grazing on live pocilloporid coral near reef edge, Onslow Island, ∼ 4 m, 5 February 1976. The white branchtips of the coral have been grazed (and abraded) by the sea urchins. Test diameters of urchins between 4 and 5 cm.

percent) and pocilloporid and coralline algal fragments (25.8 percent to 43.2 percent) (Glynn et al., 1979). These bioclastic sediments are generated probably at a high rate by the abundant populations of asteroids *(Heliaster cumingii)* and thaidid gastropods [*Thais planospira* (Lamarck)] that feed on barnacles, and by *Eucidaris* that grazes on corals and coralline algae.

Slightly east of Onslow Island, 0.5 km east-northeast and at 15–20 m depth (fig. 14), a dense bed of the fungiid coral *Cycloseris mexicana* Durham was found. The bottom in this area was composed of clean, coarse sand and was subject to a relatively strong (ca. 0.25 to 0.50 knot) northward-moving current. Associated with *C. mexicana* were, in order of decreasing abundance, *Psammocora stellata, Cycloseris elegans,* and the ahermatypic coral *Balanophyllia galapagensis* Vaughan. In some areas, up to ∼ 100 m² of bottom, *C. mexicana* was exceedingly dense with live individuals actually piled on top of one another (fig. 25). *Cycloseris elegans* also occurred in these dense populations, but only at a frequency of about 1 individual per 500 of *C. mexicana*. While many fungiid species in the Central and Indo-West Pacific normally cohabit reef-coral communities, eastern Pacific *Cycloseris,* like their counterparts in the Indo-Pacific (Goreau and Yonge, 1968; Scheer, 1971; Thomassin, 1971), tend not to occur where most reef-building corals flourish. We examined live

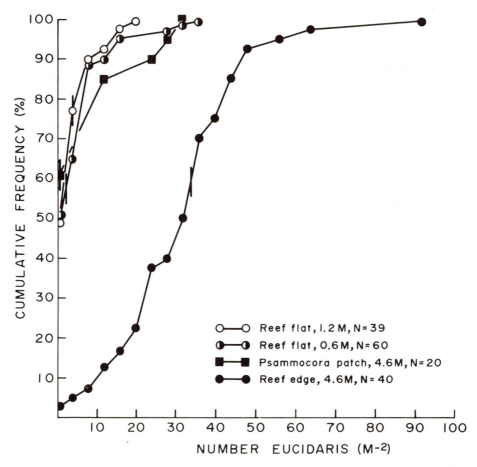

FIGURE 23. Cumulative frequencies of number of *Eucidaris* encountered in 0.25 m^2 quadrats in three different habitats at Onslow Island (11 and 12 January 1975). The median number of urchins for each habitat is indicated by a vertical line.

specimens of *C. mexicana* and *C. elegans* and found that they contained numerous zooxanthellae. The expanded polyps were pale brown and the stomodaeum green.

A fringing pocilloporid reef, about 0.5 km long, was present along the northwest shore inside Cormorant Bay (figs. 14 and 17). This reef was smaller in areal extent than that at Onslow, but appeared to have undergone slightly greater vertical development. In places, large coral blocks stood somewhat separated (possibly due to erosion) from the main reef formation, and here it is possible to view sections of coral growth (the lattice work of pocilloporid branches) that comprise the reef frame. Our eight estimates of the vertical buildup of this reef, based on horizontal sightings from the reef base to the

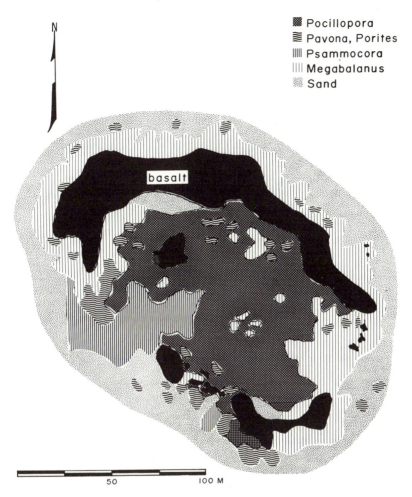

FIGURE 24. Planar view of Onslow Island showing distributions of major reef coral and barnacle communities and surrounding, largely bioclastic, calcareous sand deposits.

summits of isolated coral blocks (the reef crest), are: 1.11, 1.11, 1.22, 1.24, 1.54, 1.54, and 2.73 m. Median reef thickness was 1.24 m (51 percent greater than at Onslow) with a maximum accumulation of 2.73 m (72 percent greater than at Onslow).

Massive corals occurred abundantly along the Floreana coast southeast of Cormorant Bay to opposite Champion Island where our survey ended (fig. 14). Present in this area were *Porites lobata, Pavona gigantea,* and *Pavona clavus;* the latter was by far the predominant species (figs. 15 and 16). Relatively few pocilloporid corals were present. Several large (≤ 1 m diameter) massive colonies were found overturned. In some cases the sides of such colonies were

FIGURE 25. Close-up of *Cycloseris/Psammocora* bed at 15 m depth east of Onslow Island (13 January 1975). The most abundant species is *Cycloseris mexicana*. Also visible are *Cycloseris elegans* (right center), *Psammocora stellata* (left center) and rhodoliths (left upper corner). Virtually all *Cycloseris* polyps are expanded. *Cycloseris elegans* is about 6 cm in diameter.

still alive and showed a reoriented growth form. It would appear from these observations that this area is at times buffeted by high seas. While *Pavona clavus* was clearly the major species at several sites, with colonies often growing in juxtaposition and forming nearly continuous live coral cover (see fig. 15), we did not observe any coherent and continuous reef frame development.

A significant reef buildup, about 0.5 km long, fringes the west side of Champion Island (fig. 14). The principal coral forming this reef was *Pavona clavus*, but *Pavona gigantea* (often growing in a platelike or unifacial habit) and *Porites lobata* (2–3-m-diameter colonies) were also abundant. *Pocillopora elegans* and *Pocillopora capitata* were common in shallow water but did not form a framework. *Pavona clavus* predominated on the reef crest and upper slopes (fig. 26) whereas *Pavona gigantea* was most abundant on the lower slopes. *Pavona varians* was present as a minor element. The fathogram traces in figure 14 indicate the extent of vertical buildup. The spurs shown in panels 1, 3, and 4 represent a *Pavona clavus* ridge (4–5 m high) that borders the steep fore-reef face with live coral extending to 23 m depth. The reef base gave way to a gently sloping calcareous sand plain. Figure 27 is a view of the columnar growth habit of *Pavona clavus* looking down the lower fore-reef face at about 12 m depth. The reef base and sand plain are barely visible in the upper left

FIGURE 26. Champion Island *Pavona* reef, view of crest and two large mounds of massive corals, ∼ 6 m, 13 January 1975. A large school of surgeon fish, *Prionurus laticlavius* with other species is visible in the foreground.

FIGURE 27. Champion Island *Pavona* reef, view of lower forereef face, ∼ 12 m, 6 February 1976.

TABLE 6. Onslow Island Reef Probe Holes (see also fig. 18).

Number	Description of Site	Reef Thickness (m)
1	Upper reef slope, live *Pocillopora elegans*	0.56
2	Upper reef slope, live *Pocillopora elegans*	0.56
3	Reef flat, mostly dead pocilloporid frame overgrown with crustose coralline algae	0.76
4	Reef flat, mostly dead pocilloporid frame overgrown with crustose coralline algae	0.64
5	Upper reef slope, live *Pocillopora elegans*	0.61

corner of the picture. We estimate that the greatest overall vertical reef growth here is on the order of 10 m.

On the south side of Champion (fig. 14), a pocilloporid patch reef is present. This is an incipient reef formation, similar to that present at Onslow, both in areal extent and vertical buildup ($\leq$ 1 m).

CENTRAL ISLANDS (SANTA FE, SANTA CRUZ, PINZÓN, RÁBIDA, ISABELA EAST, AND SANTIAGO)

Santa Fe Island: Southernmost of the central islands, Santa Fe is a relatively small (2,413 ha), low-lying (maximum elevation slightly greater than 244 m) horst with steep cliffs along the coast except for the extreme northeastern and southeastern corners (fig. 28). The north coast shelf is broad, $\leq$ 9 m deep from 200–400 m offshore; the south coast shelf is narrow and ends abruptly nearshore. Our survey encompassed the anchorage on the northeastern corner of the island.

A synoptic view of coral abundance at the northeastern anchorage is presented in figure 28. The most significant coral development within this area was found on the lee side of two rock reefs between which flowed a strong tidal current. The corals flanking this channel are pocilloporids exclusively, and together form patch reefs of about 1,500 m² in area. Maximum reef frame thickness appeared to be about 0.5 m. In four transects, the mean live cover of pocilloporid corals was 47.9 percent and ranged between 22.3 percent and 70.6 percent. The shallowest transect (2 m depth) with 22.3 percent live coral cover also contained 32.3 percent dead pocilloporids, which appeared to have died from a low tidal exposure not long before our visit. The

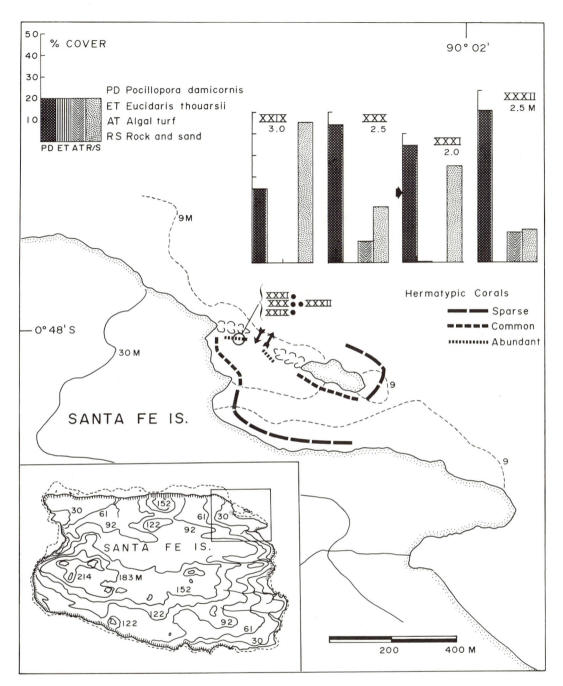

FIGURE 28. Northeastern sector of Sante Fe Island showing coral abundance observed 13 and 14 February 1976. Height of arrow on percent cover plot for transect XXXI denotes proportion of dead coral. Relative positions of transects are shown within brackets. Arrows indicate a strong tidal current flow through a rock-reef passage. Base map from U. S. Navy Hydrographic Chart No. 22528, corrected February 1974.

remainder of the substratum was comprised of largely sand, rock, and algal turf.

Only a single individual of *Eucidaris* was encountered in the chain transects (comprising 0.6 percent cover), and this occurred in the shallow transect (XXXI). We also censused *Eucidaris* by broadening each of the four transects to 0.6 m (total sampling areas 6.1 and 6.6 m²). This sampling also indicated that the urchin was not abundant at this site. Transects XXIX through XXXII respectively contained 1.1, 1.2, 1.8, and 1.1 individual *Eucidaris*/m². Territorial damselfishes [*Eupomacentrus arcifrons* (Heller and Snodgrass) and *Eupomacentrus beebei* (Nichols)] were especially numerous on this patch reef and quickly removed *Eucidaris* introduced by us. Some experiments that involved introducing potential trophic competitors to damselfish territories and the possible role of these fishes in regulating herbivore abundances are considered below (chapter 6, *Biological Interactions: Corallivore Interference*).

Pocilloporid corals were common along a small stretch of the inner western margin of the anchorage. Here, too, an incipient reef frame of 0.5 m thickness was observed. The southern shore of the embayment contained a few *Porites lobata* colonies up to 1 m in diameter. Massive corals, including *P. lobata* (up to 3 and 4 m in diameter), *Pavona gigantea* and *Pavona clavus* were found commonly on the lee side of the small island marking the entrance to the anchorage. Corals were sparse or absent on the seaward side of the anchorage and along the north coast as far as 3 km west.

Santa Cruz Island: While Santa Cruz is the second largest of the Galápagos Islands, comprising 98,555 ha, it is only moderately high, reaching a maximum elevation of ⁓ 864 m. Geologically, the island can be divided into two parts: (a) old uplifted submarine lava flows and tuffs interbedded with fossiliferous limestones, and (b) a young broad shield of basaltic lavas surmounted by a cluster of youthful scoria cones. The older part is present as a narrow strip along the northeast coast and possibly at the northwest corner of the island; the younger part is by far the larger, covering the highlands and the remainder of the island. Compared with the islands already considered, Santa Cruz has an extensive shallow shelf and numerous protected bays (fig. 29). Only the northeast corner of the island, from Plaza Islands to Baltra Island, is steep with deep water near shore.

Our knowledge of the shoal marine communities of Santa Cruz and surrounding islands is still relatively fragmentary. It is clear, however, that reef-building corals are present around much of the island, which has been determined from the early and brief surveys of Agassiz (1892) and Crossland (1927) in the vicinity of Conway Bay, from the survey of the Xarifa (Durham, 1962) at the north end of Santa Cruz (including Seymour and Baltra islands), from one of us (GMW) who examined sites at different island exposures, and from information supplied by the A. DeRoy family of Academy Bay.

A species-rich coral community is present near the harbor entrance of

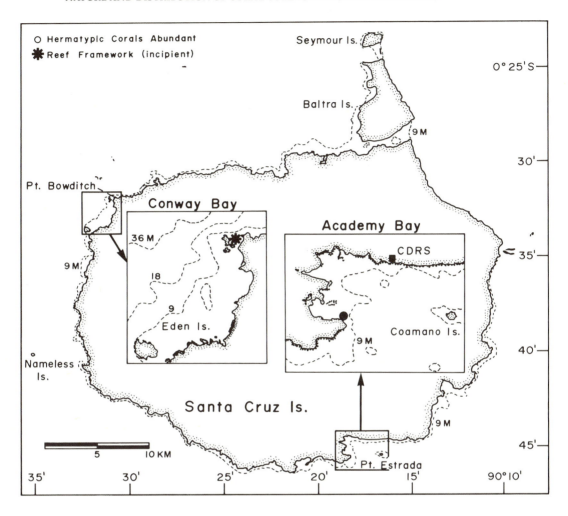

FIGURE 29. Santa Cruz Island showing the locations of Conway Bay and the alleged pocilloporid patch reef at Point Bowditch, and Academy Bay with the species-rich coral community inside Point Estrada. Base map from U. S. Navy Hydrographic Chart No. 22528, corrected 23 February 1974. Island topographic details not printed.

Academy Bay on the south side of Santa Cruz (fig. 29). Immediately inside Estrada Point, eight hermatypic and three ahermatypic species respectively were present as follows: *Pavona varians, P. clavus, P. gigantea, Gardineroseris planulata* (Dana), *Pocillopora damicornis, P. elegans, Psammocora stellata, Porites lobata, Tubastraea coccinea* Lesson, *Balanophyllia galapagensis,* and *Culicia rubeola* (Quoy and Gaimard). The massive species *Gardineroseris* was observed only at this site in the Galápagos Archipelago. Both small and large (≤ 1 m diameter) colonies were present, and the entire population numbered slightly more than twenty-five colonies. The massive corals formed dense, single and mixed species aggregations on the open bottom, but no reef-building had occurred. One interspecific contact suggested that *Gardineroseris* had over-grown a colony of *Pavona clavus*. The ahermatypic corals were prevalent in shaded habitats such as rock walls and the ceilings of overhangs.

Elsewhere in Academy Bay, *Pocillopora elegans* is the only common her-matypic coral. Crustose coralline algae and the brown fucoid alga *Blossevillea galapagensis* form the predominant cover on hard substrates to a depth of 5–6 m. In general, we believe that the low water visibility and frequent exposure to southern swells from June to December make Academy Bay a marginal environment for reef-building corals.

The occurrence of subtidal coral formations at Conway Bay was inferred from beach material (Agassiz, 1892; Crossland, 1927). Hornell (in Crossland) noted that "just beyond the north end of Conway Bay is a high bank of dead coral, of reef-forming facies." The DeRoy family informed us of a pocilloporid patch reef (with some massive corals) that is present near Bowditch Point at the north end of Conway Bay, presumably very near the shore area explored by Hornell. This coral formation is situated between some offshore rocks and the point (fig. 29). A vigorous current flows through this channel.

Pinzón and Rábida Islands: Pinzón Island is 1,815 ha in area and 458 m high. It was formed from a single volcano and consists almost wholly of lava flows. Marine erosion and down-faulting have produced steep cliffs along the western and southern coasts. The shelf is very narrow or virtually nonexistent. This island was examined at one site on the northeast coast (fig. 1).

According to A. DeRoy, pocilloporid corals were common to abundant at shallow depth during the early 1970s. At that time, a small pocilloporid patch reef was observed at this site. When one of us (GMW) visited the same area in 1977, pocilloporid corals were sparse and the patch reef appeared to have been inundated with sand. During the later visit, however, *Pavona clavus* and *Pavona gigantea* were observed to form an incipient reef frame on a rock ledge perpendicular to the shoreline. These species were also present at 20 m depth. We suspect that other substantial *Pavona* frameworks may exist along this shoreline.

Rábida Island, with an area of 495 ha and 367 m in elevation, like Pinzón, contains abundant lava flows. This island is also relatively steep with deep water near shore. Our survey was confined to the beach landing and anchorage on the north end of the island (fig. 1).

In general, coral communities were well developed on the north end of Rábida. *Pavona clavus* was the predominant species along the rock promon-tory to the east of the anchorage where colonies often occurred side by side. Many of the colonies at this site formed erect, cylindrical columns 1.0–1.5 m high. Coral biomass was highest between 3–5 m depth. Other massive corals observed here, though at lower abundances and smaller in size, were *Pavona gigantea* and *Porites lobata*. *Pocillopora* spp. were also present and the aherma-type *Oulangia bradleyi* Verrill was abundant on the undersides of coral rubble. *Pavona varians* was present at 15 m, but at this depth live coral cover was very low.

Isabela Island East: Isabela Island with 458,812 ha, almost five times the size of Santa Cruz Island, is by far the largest island in the Galápagos group. All five of its active shield volcanoes exceed 1,000 m in elevation and two are approximately 1,700 m high. These volcanoes have produced lava flows that have reached the sea in recent years. At least fifteen eruptions (as of February 1979, T. Simkin, personal communication) have occurred on Isabela since 1911.

The eastern sector of Isabela Island has the greatest area of shallow shelf of all the Galápagos Islands (fig. 1). The major shoal areas, where the 9 m contour extends between 1–2 km offshore, are found in the southeastern coastal stretch between Point Alfaro south to Villamil (fig. 30). Our survey included site visits at Point Albemarle, Cape Marshall, and a more thorough reconnaissance of the south end of Cartago Bay.

In the Cartago Bay area, reef-building corals were confined largely to shallow, near-shore depths, usually within the 5 m contour (fig. 30). Very few corals were observed on rock outcrops in the southwestern sector of the bay. About 2 km southwest of Cape Barrington, coral abundance increased markedly. Here, colonies of *Pocillopora damicornis*, *Porites lobata*, and *Pavona gigantea* were found. No massive corals (*Porites* and *Pavona*) were seen that exceeded 1 m in diameter. Large colonies of *Pavona gigantea* were quite common in some areas, with as many as six to eight visible at any one time, but they usually did not occur in actual contact. From Cape Barrington south (to 0° 37′ 10″ S), corals were abundant. A modest reef formation was found at 2 m depth about 100 m off Cape Barrington. The chief framebuilder here was *Pavona clavus* that, on superficial examination, had built vertically to at least 1 m. Also present in this formation were *Pocillopora damicornis*, *Porites lobata*, and *Pavona gigantea*. Poor water clarity (~ 1 m lateral visibility) prevented our mapping this structure, but we estimate that it extends a minimum of 100 m along the coast.

The single mangrove canal surveyed contained a dense population of *Psammocora stellata* (fig. 30). This coral was most abundant in the inner reaches of the canal where in some areas it covered the bottom completely.

Observations made elsewhere along the east coast of Isabela Island have disclosed abundant populations of pocilloporid and massive corals in Cartago Bay, immediately north of the area surveyed in figure 30, and south of Albemarle Point. In addition, sparse to common population densities of herma-

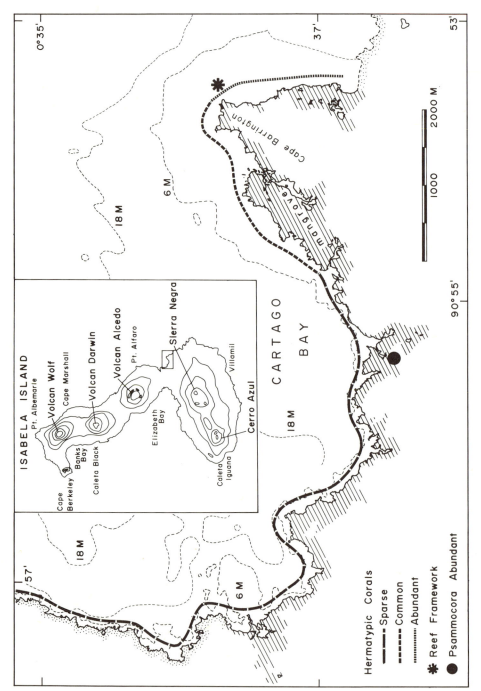

FIGURE 30. Cartago Bay showing relative abundance of hermatypic corals in a near-shore, survey transect (10 February 1976). Base map from U. S. Navy Hydrographic Chart No. 5925, 1st ed., August, 1943. Inset of Isabela Island from Admiralty chart 1375, 4 September 1953; contour intervals 305 m (1000 ft.).

typic corals, similar to those noted in Academy Bay, were observed south of Cape Marshall.

Santiago Island: Santiago Island, like Santa Cruz, is a large (58,465 ha), high island (907 m) located on the east side of Isabela, in the lee of the Equatorial Undercurrent. Its high relief in the northwestern sector is due to a major volcano. Numerous minor cones are also present on Santiago. These small volcanoes have undergone frequent eruptions; the discharge of copious lava flows have reached the sea, during Holocene and more recent (early 20th century) times. A shallow shelf is best developed along the northeast coast. Only a small portion of the island was examined. The west side of Santiago, an area southeast of Boquerizo Point, was surveyed briefly in 1976; and on the east coast, the Bartolomé Island area was examined in rather more detail in 1975 (fig. 31).

The white sandy beaches in the area surveyed southeast of Boquerizo Point contained large amounts of hermatypic coral sediment. Immediately offshore, in 2–10 m depth, live massive and branching corals were abundant. At most sites *Porites lobata* was predominant with some colonies nearly 4 m in diameter and 2–3 m high. Occasionally we observed large colonies growing side by side and thus forming isolated patches of incipient reef structures. *Pavona clavus* was common, as were *Pocillopora damicornis* and *P. elegans*. *Pavona gigantea* was uncommon. Areas that exhibited especially well developed coral communities are indicated in the inset sketch in figure 31.

Associated corallivores included the echinoid *Eucidaris* and the puffer-fish *Arothron meleagris*. Several individuals of these species were observed feeding on the live branchtips of pocilloporid corals. The parrotfishes *Scarus rubroviolaceus* and *S. perrico* were also abundant in the Boquerizo Point area.

At Bartolomé Island, reef-building corals were abundant along the south and southwest shores only (figs. 32 and 33). Elsewhere, to a depth of ~ 10 m, sand and rock (basalt) substrates predominated, with the latter supporting an algal turf and melobesioid crusts. Calcareous sediments flanked bottom areas with abundant coral and also continued around the island to the east and northeast. Brownish-black tuffaceous sands were especially common along the north to northwest shore.

Transects XVI through XVIII cut across a *Porites lobata* patch reef (fig. 34). Near shore, at 0.9 m depth, live pocilloporid corals predominated (34.4 percent cover versus 12.6 percent for *Porites*); these were growing from basalt and dead *Porites* rock. Massive *Porites* colonies, 1–2 m in diameter, predominated abruptly in slightly deeper water (1.5 m) and continued as the chief hermatypic element (24 percent to 55 percent cover) to 6–7 m depth where the patch reef ended on a gently sloping calcareous sand bottom. *Pavona clavus* was occasionally locally abundant; for example, it contributed 25.1

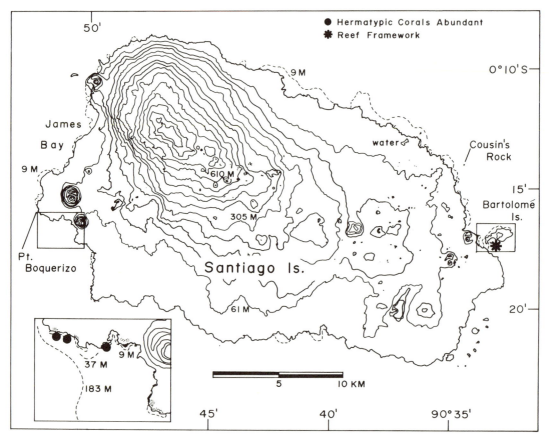

FIGURE 31. Santiago Island showing extent of hermatypic coral development in the areas surveyed at Point Boquerizo and Bartolomé Island. Contour intervals are 61 m (200 ft.). Base maps from U. S. Navy Hydrographic Charts No. 22549 (corrected 6 May 1972) and No. 22545 (corrected 23 October 1971).

percent to the surface cover in transect XVII. In the reef core, the *Porites* colonies were either abutting or located close together and separated by narrow channels and sand patches.

The majority of the colonies at shallow depth (0.9–2.1 m) had horizontally flattened summits that were largely dead, suggesting upper colony death at extreme low water exposures. Fish nicks (probably due in part to *Scarus ghobban*) were noted commonly on the summits of *Porites* colonies and *Eucidaris,* which made up between 1 percent and 2 percent of the reef cover, was observed rasping the dead basal areas of *Porites* colonies. The feeding activities of these species, however, probably are not responsible for most of the dead bare patches that are virtually confined to the extreme low tidal level.

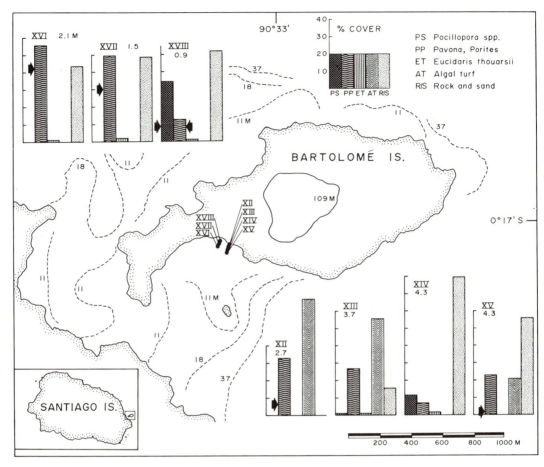

FIGURE 32. Bartolomé Island, east side of Santiago Island, showing location of transect sampling sites and the relative abundances of the predominant epibenthic organisms (23 January 1975). Height of arrows on percent cover plots denotes proportion of dead branching and massive corals. Base map enlarged from U. S. Navy Hydrographic Chart No. 5921, corrected June 1974.

Judging from the fathogram profiles (fig. 33, traces 5–7), it appears that this *Porites* reef has built vertically between 4–5 m. The long spikes in the fathogram traces represent individual colonies that had reached 3 m in height. The significant erosion due to corallivores, and presumably boring sponges and bivalves, is probably generating calcareous sediments at a very high rate on this patch reef. It would appear that lateral, seaward reef growth is being facilitated by the deposition and shoaling effect of autochthonous bioclastic sediments.

A short distance to the east of the *Porites* patch reef, reef coral populations were less prominent with reef rock, rubble, calcareous sand, and algal

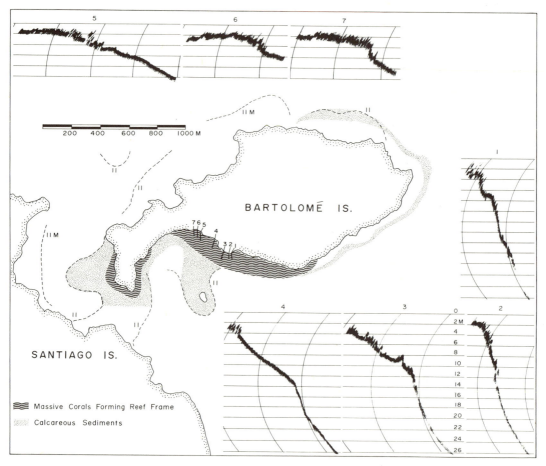

FIGURE 33. Bartolomé Island, east of Santiago Island, showing location of fathogram transects (not to scale, see below) on south shore in area of abundant massive corals (*Porites* and *Pavona*). Each fathogram is approximately perpendicular to the shoreline and traces the bottom seaward from left to right (23 and 24 January 1975). Transects 1 and 2 are about 50 m in length; 3, 4, 6, and 7 are about 90 m in length; and transect 5 is about 140 m in length. Base map from U. S. Navy Hydrographic Chart No. 5940, corrected June 1972.

turf predominating (transects XII through XV, fig. 32). Fathogram trace 4 (fig. 33) indicates the narrow band of coral development nearshore (2–4 m depth) and the extensive sand slope present between 4–14 m depth. Farther east, in the vicinity of fathogram transects 1 through 3 (fig. 33), reef-coral development again assumed significant proportions. Nearshore, between the extreme low tide datum and ~ 5 m depth, pocilloporid corals (*Pocillopora elegans* and *P. damicornis*) and *Porites lobata* were especially abundant (fig. 35). *Pavona*

FIGURE 34. View of massive *Porites* reef (dark patch indicated by arrow) present on south shore of Bartolomé Island (June 1974). This view faces east and is the same area traversed by fathogram transects 5, 6, and 7 in figure 33.

clavus and *P. gigantea* were also present, but the latter species was usually small, platy, and secretive, found in recesses or under other massive corals. Many large *Porites* colonies were present here as evidenced by the 2 and 3 m spikes in trace 1. While the population densities of branching and massive corals were high, as at Boquerizo Point on the west side of the island, no reef frame construction was observed. Calcareous sand deposits with occasional colonies of *Porites, Pavona clavus, Pavona varians,* and *Pavona gigantea* predominated from ~ 5 to 8 m depth. Unmistakable reef-building was observed at 7 m, 9–11 m, and 8–12 m respectively at fathogram transects 1, 2, and 3 (fig. 33). The chief frame-builders were *Pavona clavus* and *P. gigantea*, the latter occurring more on open surfaces compared to its secretive habit at shallow depth. Colony growth form was generally erect and usually ~ 1 m high. The disposition of the reef frame indicates that it formed a more or less continuous ridge between 7–12 m depth. The nature of the underlying substratum could not be discerned; no basaltic rock exposures were observed in this area. On

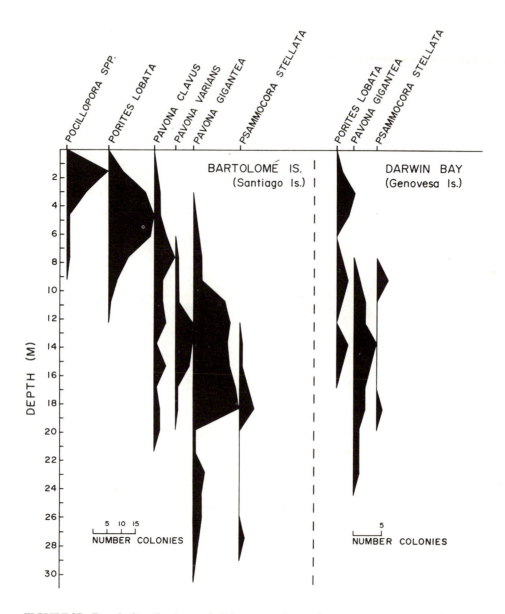

FIGURE 35. Depth distributions of all hermatypic coral species encountered from the surface to 32 m depth at Bartolomé Island (fig. 33, south side, parallel to fathogram transect 1) and in Darwin Bay (fig. 41, east side, transect site). Numbers of colonies observed are indicated by respective scales and refer to all corals present in two ~4-m-wide transects censused simultaneously by two divers.

TABLE 7. Relative Abundance (Percent Cover) of Epibenthos on Primary Substrates of Vertical and Near-Vertical Rock Walls at Three Island Sites (15–22 January 1975).

Area	Caleta Tagus		Cousin's Rock	Bahía Darwin
Surface	Vertical Wall or Undersurface of a Shelf	Upper Surface of Sloping Rock	Vertical Wall	Vertical Wall
Depth range (m)	12–20	12–25	12–22	12–22
No. of quadrats[a]	31	32	10	32
"Open space"				
Bare rock or sediment[b]	1.2	16.0	0	0
Crustose coralline algae	6.8	3.8	19.4	0.9
"Occupied space"				
Algal turf	0	4.3	0	8.1
Articulate branching coralline algae	0.9	10.1	0	0
Porifera	2.7	9.1	20.8	68.4
Ascidiacea (colonial)	59.4	29.8	34.6	13.5
Scleractinia				
Ahermatypic	18.1	3.1	12.8	0
Hermatypic	0	0	0	9.1
Salmacina[c]	7.1	13.3	0	0
Other sessile benthos[d]	3.8	10.5	12.4	0

[a]Each quadrat consisted of a color photograph (35-mm transparency) approximately 0.2 m². Data were obtained as counts from contact of five sets of ten random points on each projected photograph. Each quadrat thus provided 50 count data.

[b]Most of the "unoccupied space" on the upward-facing substrate was actually covered rather thickly with sediments. Therefore, it was still not "open" for coral recruitment.

[c]A genus of colonial serpulid polychaete annelid.

[d]This category includes anemones, zoanthids, bryozoans, and barnacles.

the basis of the fathogram traces, we estimate that this ridge has undergone a maximum vertical growth of about 6 m. A second minor *Pavona clavus* build-up, estimated to be 2–3 m in vertical thickness, was observed at 16–18 m depth in fathogram transect 1 (fig. 33).

A vertical, south-facing, rock wall community was examined at Cousin's Rock (fig. 31). Slightly more than one-third of the primary substrate was covered by colonial ascidians and, in less abundance, by sponges, crustose coralline algae, ahermatypic corals, and other epibenthic species (table 7). Ahermatypic corals [*Culicia rubeola, Phyllangia consagensis* (Durham and Barnard), †*Balanophyllia eguchi,* Wells *Dendrophyllia gracilis* Milne Edwards and Haime, *Tubastraea coccinea,* and †₂*Tubastraea tagusensis* Wells] were common, yet they were presumably being overgrown by colonial ascidians and, less frequently, by sponges (pl. 2)*. *Eucidaris* was abundant both in holes and crevices and in ledges that cut across the rock wall face. Opposite the vertical wall, the bottom slope was more gentle. Here widely dispersed colonies of *Porites* and *Pavona* were present, probably in part because the gentle slope is less often in the shade.

WESTERN SECTOR (ISABELA WEST AND FERNANDINA)

Isabela Island West: The northwestern and southwestern sectors of Isabela generally are exposed to the open sea and flank deep water, to 200–400 m, within 2 km of the shoreline. The west central area is relatively protected in the lee of Fernandina Island and contains large to small areas of shallow bottom, namely, Elizabeth Bay, Urvina Bay, and Tagus Cove (figs. 1 and 36).

At least three volcanic events have affected the west central area of Isabela Island in recent years. Eruptions of Sierra Negra in 1953 and 1963 produced lava flows that reached the sea along the south side of Elizabeth Bay. The eruption of Alcedo Volcano in 1954 was apparently responsible for the considerable submarine upheaval in Urvina Bay (see chapter 2, *Physical Environment: Tectonic Uplift*.)

On the open coast, we examined sites in the Iguana Cove area, at Black Cove and at Cape Berkeley, and east along the north side of Banks Bay. The protected sites surveyed included the innermost reaches of Elizabeth Bay, the coastal stretch to the northwest, to and including the Urvina uplift, and Tagus Cove.

Along the southwestern sector of Isabela, where upwelling is pronounced, benthic algal communities are found. These communities are characterized by large, foliacious and some warm-temperate or cool-water species. (Typically cool water genera are identified below by asterisks.) At Iguana Cove, two red algae, *Ahnfeltia durvillei* and *Chondrus albemarlensis* Taylor, occurred abundantly in the mid-intertidal zone. In the low intertidal zone, another red alga, *Dendrymenia flabellifolia* (Bory) Skottsberg, was abundant. In contrast to the southern and central island regions, the subtidal algal communities were more diverse and luxuriant here. At shallow subtidal depths, *Sargassum* was abundant. *Sargassum ecuadoreanum* Taylor was found at Iguana Cove, while at Espinosa Point, *Sargassum setifolium* (Grunow) Setchell and *Sargassum albemarlense* Taylor were prevalent. Also co-occurring with *Sargassum* at Iguana Cove were large, brown algae, mainly *Spatoglossum velerone* Taylor, *Glossophora galapagensis* Farlow, and *Padina durvillaei*. Below the brown algae were a variety of red algae, in order of abundance: *Asparagopsis*

*The descriptions of the new coral species resulting from this study (identified by †) were published in *Pacific Science*, vol. 36, no. 2, 1982, pp. 211–219.

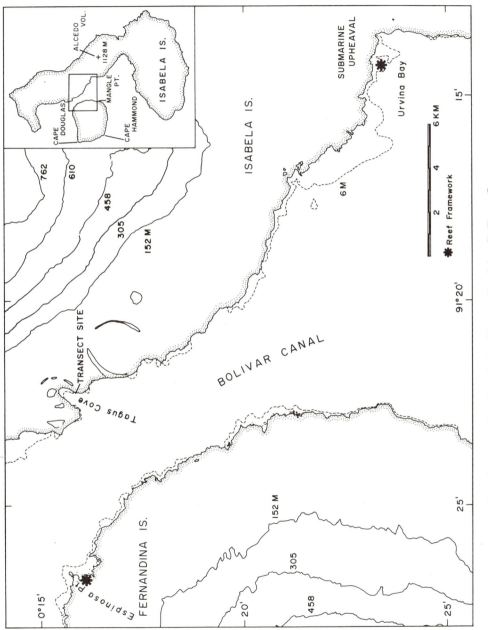

FIGURE 36. Location of study sites at Espinosa Point (Fernandina Island), Tagus Cove, and area of upheaval in Urvina Bay (Isabela Island). Base map from U. S. Navy Hydrographic Chart No. 22541, 1st ed., February 1945.

stanfordi Setchell and Gardner, *Laurencia oppositoclada* Taylor, *Gelidium fili-cinum* Bory, *Ochtodes crockeri* Setchell and Gardner, and *Gracilaria johnstonii* Setchell and Gardner. A large, warm temperate, leafy, red alga, **Kallymenia latiloba*, was observed abundantly below 5 m to a depth of 20 m or more. Several additional warm-temperate species were common to abundant to 5 m and deeper: **Phycodrys elegans* Setchell and Gardner, **Desmarestia munda* Setchell and Gardner, **Eisenia galapagensis* Taylor, and *Dictyopteris cokeri* (Howe) Taylor.

No hermatypic corals were seen at Iguana Cove. *Lytechinus semituberculatus*, which commonly feeds on algal drift, was often very abundant ($\geq$ 70 individuals/m²) on flat or gently sloping rock surfaces.

Proceeding to the north, in the innermost reaches of Elizabeth Bay (to the north of a group of small islands and rocks near Perry Isthmus), large fleshy algae were absent and tropical floral elements predominated. Some reef-building corals were present at this locality, mainly large colonies of *Porites* and *Pavona* in shoal areas. This sudden displacement of cool and warm floras over short distances is similar to that reported by Dawson (1952) for an upwelling area off Baja California, except that in the Galápagos corals often co-occur with warm water algal assemblages.

Our reconnaissance of the former (uplifted in 1954) shallow, broad shelf at Urvina Bay (fig. 36), in the lee of Fernandina Island, demonstrated that reef-building corals were present and occasionally locally abundant at this site. Two aggregations of massive, subfossil corals, each consisting of several large colonies, were found about 1.5 km west-northwest of the landing beach. One group was made up exclusively of *Porites lobata*, up to 3 m in diameter, and the other group of *Pavona clavus* with some colonies up to 2 m in diameter. *Pavona gigantea* was relatively uncommon with most colonies small ($\leq$0.5 m diameter) and highly eroded. Three small patches of pocilloporid framework (probably chiefly *Pocillopora damicornis*), approximately 0.5 m thick and 300 m² in area, were also found in the same general area. Finally, *Psammocora stellata* was present as were some ahermatypic corals (*Astrangia equatorialis* Durham and Barnard, *Oulangia bradleyi*, and *Phyllangia consagensis*), the latter often on the undersides of rocks and eroded, massive corals.

Tagus Cove (fig. 36) was formed by the breaching of one of four nested craters of the Tagus Cone (McBirney and Williams, 1969). The steep-sided bay is composed of tuff that dips toward the south along the southeastern shore. Differential erosion of the bedding has produced ledges that continue below sea level. Some of the submarine ledges have been undercut extensively and have 3-m-wide ceilings. The subtidal habitat here is similar to that at Cousin's Rock with a predominantly near-vertical rock substrate and only small bottom areas that are well exposed to sunlight.

FIGURE 37. Vertical distribution of ahermatypic corals in Tagus Cove, Isabela Island (9 February 1976). Data pooled from two photographic transects along the same rock wall (see fig. 36) from the surface to about 21 m depth. N signifies the number of 0.25 m² quadrats sampled at each depth. The location of shallow and deep ledges is indicated along the depth axis.

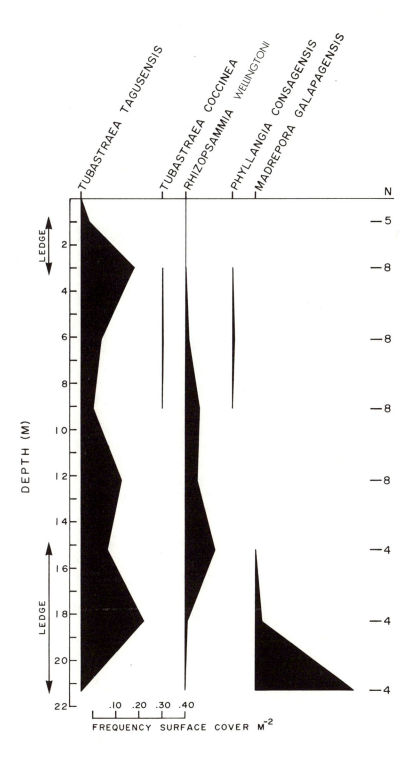

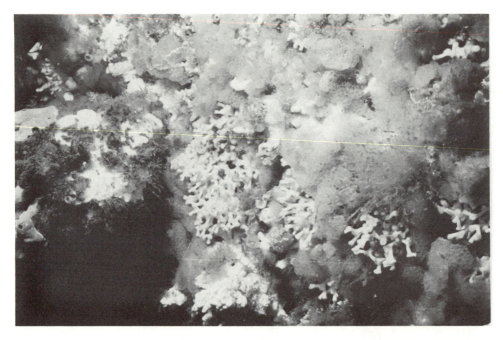

FIGURE 38. Ahermatypic coral *Madrepora galapagensis* in competition with colonial tunicates, ceiling of ledge, Tagus Cove, ∼ 18 m, 15 January 1975. *Madrepora* colonies are 6 to 8 cm high.

While no scleractinian hermatypes were observed at Tagus Cove, ahermatypic corals were abundant. Figure 37 shows the mean abundances of five species, expressed as colony surface coverage, that were censused in 1976. †*Tubastraea tagusensis* was the most abundant ahermatype, usually ranging from a mean coverage of about 10 percent to almost 30 percent of the total sessile epibenthos (pl. 3). *Tubastraea coccinea* and *Phyllangia consagensis* occurred only rarely between 3–9 m depth. †*Rhizopsammia wellingtoni* Wells and *Madrepora galapagensis* Vaughan were most abundant at 15 m and 21 m, respectively. *Madrepora* was not present shallower than about 16 m and in this survey was largely confined to the ceilings of a ledge (pl. 4, fig. 38). This was the most abundant ahermatype with mean surface coverage equal to 42.8 percent at 21 m. While the deepest we observed *Madrepora* at this transect site was only 24 m, the depth record of 550 m reported by Vaughan (1906) indicates that this is a relatively deepwater species. The cool and dark conditions at Tagus probably favor the shallow occurrence of *Madrepora* at this site.

The abundance of other sessile benthos, determined from a transect sampled in January 1975, is summarized in table 7. Algae (*Ulva* and *Sargassum*) were common only in the intertidal zone and at shallow subtidal depths (to about 4 m depth). Large clusters of *Salmacina* (a serpulid polychaetous annelid) and sea anemones extended into the intertidal zone. Colonial ascidians were prevalent subtidally, on upper rock slopes, in grottoes, and on the undersurfaces of overhanging ledges (fig. 38) to depths of 25 m. The five species of ahermatypic corals present here were frequently overgrown by colonial tunicates (fig. 38). Presumably healthy *Salmacina* colonies frequently had been overgrown by any of several species of colonial tunicates or by articulate coralline algae. In addition, *Salmacina* was observed being preyed upon by the asteroids *Nidorellia armata, Oreaster occidentalis,* and *Heliaster cumingii* (pl. 3). How *Salmacina* remains abundant under these pressures of competition and predation is as yet unknown.

Fernandina Island: This volcanically active and steep-sided island is the third largest in the archipelago, comprising 64,248 ha. It is the second highest island and is completely dominated by Fernandina Volcano, which reaches an elevation of about 1,500 m. Eighteen eruptions have been recorded since 1813, and five of these have resulted in lava flows that have reached the sea (Meredith, 1939; Slevin, 1959; T. Simkin, personal communication). The western, northern, and southern shorelines of Fernandina generally are exposed to the sea and flank very deep water. Only the east coast is protected and contains relatively shallow embayments.

This island was examined briefly just south of Mangle Point, at Cape Hammond, Cape Douglas, and about halfway between the two capes (fig 1). Espinosa Point, due west of Tagus Cove (fig. 36), was examined more thoroughly in 1975, 1976, and on other occasions.

The predominant algal assemblages along the southern and western sectors of Fernandina consisted of a mixture of large, warm- and cool-water species similar to those described earlier at Iguana Cove. Echinoids *[Lytechinus semituberculatus, Caenocentrotus gibbosus* (A. Agassiz & Desor), and *Echinometra vanbrunti* A. Agassiz] were also abundant. No reef-building corals were observed.

Only at Espinosa Point, in lava rock pools partially separated from the sea, were corals found in abundance. The predominant species were *Pocillopora damicornis* and *Pocillopora capitata,* brownish and pinkish-brown in color respectively. These species occurred as continuous patches and in their upward and lateral expansion nearly completely filled two pools south of Espinosa Point (fig. 39). While both species contributed significantly to the reef frame, each tended to occupy a relatively large, several meters square, monospecific patch rather than occurring as intermingled colonies (fig. 40). The maximum pool depth was about 2 m and co-occurring with the pocilloporids were occasional large colonies (1–2 m in diameter and 1 m high) of *Porites lobata.* Most of each pool's volume, however, appeared to have been filled by the horizontal and vertical growth of pocilloporid corals. Frequently the reef frame stood higher than the water level in the pools at low tide (figs. 39 and 40). At these levels virtually all of the coral was dead, but still remained in growth position (see chapter 2, *Physical Environment: Emersion Events*). The combined area of coral framework in the two rock pools was probably close to 0.5 ha, although this is a rough approximation as no accurate topographic maps are available for this region.

In order to determine the maximum thickness of the pocilloporid reef

FIGURE 39. Lava rock basins near Espinosa Point nearly filled with pocilloporid corals, 16 January 1975. Summits of coral mounds were exposed (~30 cm maximum) and dead. Two persons are visible in background (left) and also base of cloud-enshrouded Fernandina Volcano.

frame, five different sites (at the highest elevations relative to sea level) were probed in the southernmost rock pool. Pocilloporid coral fragments were recovered from the core barrel to depths of 0.98, 1.04, 1.22, 1.22, and 1.52 m. Penetration below these depths was virtually impossible; since volcanic rock fragments were recovered, it is highly likely that basement rock had been reached. Thus, the above thicknesses indicate a median reef-frame buildup of 1.22 m.

Along the exposed coast immediately south of Espinosa Point, a shallow, gently sloping platform ($\leq$ 10 m depth) extends to a distance of 200 to 300 m offshore. The bottom is composed of several rock types (pebbles and boulders) and the most common substrate (~ 50 percent of the surface area) is flat plates of pahoehoe lava. Reef-building corals are absent here. Upwelling occurs frequently in this area and the cool, nutrient-laden waters support lush algal turf communities and several kinds of herbivore populations. Two species of *Sargassum* (*S. setifolium* and *S. albemarlense*) were the prevalent algae at shallow depth (to about 1.5 m). Leafy *Ulva* sp., which was often present

FIGURE 40. Close-up view of pocilloporid mounds illustrating their compactness and rigidity, lava rock basin, Espinosa Point, 16 January 1975.

with *Amphiroa galapagensis* Taylor and *Codium* sp., formed a turf on open, horizontal substrates between 1.5 and about 7 m depth, but was still present down to 13 m. Herbivores frequenting this area included the marine iguana (*Amblyrhynchus cristatus* Bell), green turtles (*Chelonia mydas agassizii* Bocourt), and the fishes *Girella fremenvillei* (Valenciennes), *Scarus ghobban*, *Prionurus laticlavius* (Valenciennes), and several species of pomacentrids. Relatively few *Lytechinus* were present in the area. Their near absence could be explained by (a) the relatively strong wave action here (*Lytechinus* cannot adhere effectively to surfaces under turbulent conditions), and (b) the presence of large populations of carnivorous fishes [*Bodianus eclancheri* (Valenciennes) and

Oplegnathus insigne (Kner)] that are known to feed on echinoids, or the above effects operating in combination.

NORTHERN ISLANDS (GENOVESA, MARCHENA, PINTA, WOLF, AND DARWIN)

Genovesa Island: One of the most distinctive features of Genovesa, a relatively small (1,411 ha), low-lying (64 m) island possibly derived from a single shield volcano, is its steep-sided bay (Darwin Bay) on the south side of the island (fig. 41). Darwin Bay is deep with its center exceeding 200 m in depth. The north and south sides of the bay are shallow, and a sill is present across the south bay entrance. Our survey was restricted to the Darwin Bay area.

Reef framework was present on the west side of Darwin Bay and outside the bay near the southeastern entrance (fig. 41). Inside the bay, between 2–5 m depth, the framework consisted of pocilloporid corals. The vertical buildup was of the order of 1 m, and this extended along the shore for about 150 m as an incipient but discontinuous fringing reef. *Ulva* sp. and filamentous red algae formed a conspicuous turf on the tops and sides of rocks. Because of the narrow but shallow shelf here and the not-so-steep cliffs, this side of the bay is well illuminated.

On the outside of the bay, *Pavona clavus* formed a framework between 8 and 10 m depth. This buildup, 2–3 m in vertical thickness, had formed parallel to the depth contour and was about 20 m in length. Also present at this site were *Pavona varians, Porites lobata,* and *Pocillopora* spp. A gently sloping, sand bottom was present below the coral framework, between 10 and 15 m depth.

The east side of Darwin Bay is a steep, vertical escarpment like that at Tagus Cove and Cousin's Rock, but the epibenthic assemblages differed in that hermatypic corals were present (table 7, fig. 35). *Porites lobata* occurred as hemispherical colonies from near the surface to 17 m depth (see transect site, fig. 41). One colony at 11 m was 1.5 m high. *Pavona gigantea* was found between 8 and 24 m and exhibited a shinglelike (unifacial) growth habit in the lower range of its depth distribution (18–24 m). A few colonies of *Psammocora stellata* were also present. Encrusting sponges were more abundant than ascidians at this site, but the latter were more frequently overgrown by hermatypic corals.

Marchena and Pinta Islands: Marchena and Pinta are moderately large islands, approximately 13,000 and 5,940 ha in area respectively. The land forms of both islands are due chiefly to single, young volcanoes; in addition, the west coast of Pinta has cliffs, representing the remains of an old downfaulted volcano. The summit of Marchena is 343 m and that of Pinta is 777 m. Although the records of volcanic activity are very poor for these

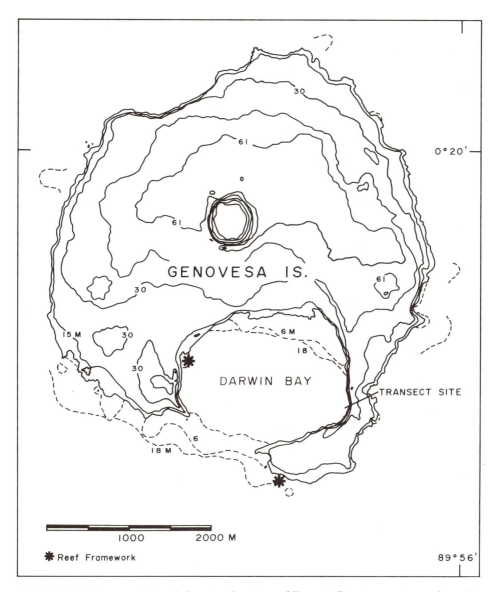

FIGURE 41. Genovesa Island showing location of Darwin Bay, transect sampling site and reef framework inside and outside of the bay. Base map from U. S. Navy Hydrographic Chart No. 5945, 1st ed., March 1947, corrected ed., June 1974.

islands, the youthful appearance of lava flows indicates eruptive events within the past few centuries. Except for the southeastern sector, Marchena has a rather extensive subtidal shelf. Pinta is surrounded by deep water, reflective of its relatively small and high aspect.

We visited the north coast anchorage of Marchena at Montalvo Point and the southeastern coast in the vicinity of Espejo Point (fig. 1). The rocks that were observed subtidally at the Montalvo site had a barren aspect and showed little signs of erosion. Hermatypic corals were sparse. The species that were observed were small colonies of *Pavona clavus, Pavona gigantea,* and *Porites lobata,* all present on vertical rock surfaces. No pocilloporid corals were seen. Ahermatypic corals that were observed here were *Tubastraea coccinea* and *Dendrophyllia gracilis.*

Three small rocky islets lie just offshore of Espejo Point at the southeastern corner of Marchena. On the west side of the middle and most seaward islet, *Pocillopora* spp. and *Pavona* spp. form a moderately dense assemblage amid large boulders. No framework was evident, however.

We examined Pinta Island at a protected site, along a small indentation of the coastline, immediately west of Cape Ibbetson (fig. 1). A relatively rich reef-coral community was observed here at shallow depth ($\leq$ 10 m). All three species of *Pocillopora* were present, as were *Pavona clavus, Psammocora stellata,* and *Porites lobata.* In some places *Pocillopora* spp. formed a nearly continuous cover over the bottom. Interspersed among the pocilloporid stands were crustose coralline algae, filamentous red algae, and *Hipponix* sp. Large, massive corals were also present with some *Porites* colonies that measured 2 m in diameter. In spite of the abundance of hermatypic corals at this site, we could find no evidence that framework construction had occurred.

As in the southern and some of the central islands, large *Eucidaris* present on open surfaces were exceedingly abundant in this coral community. And their densities, as a function of live coral cover, paralleled the pattern observed at Onslow Island (fig. 23). Along the edge of a pocilloporid patch, where crustose coralline algae predominated, the median density of *Eucidaris* (n = 40 quadrats) was 34.0 individuals/m^2 (32–36 individuals/m^2, 0.95 confidence limits of median). Within the pocilloporid patch, where the median surface cover of coral was 30 percent, *Eucidaris* had a median density (n = 20 quadrats) of 8 individuals/m^2 (4–16 individuals/m^2). During our stay here (0930–1200, 20 January 1975), relatively few *Eucidaris* were feeding on live *Pocillopora*; 0.3 percent of the urchins were grazing on live coral where this food source was sparse, and 2.7 percent were grazing on pocilloporids in the thick coral patches. This grazing pressure is an order of magnitude less than that observed at Onslow Island, where 61 percent and 25 percent of *Eucidaris* grazed on live coral along the reef edge and on the reef flat respectively. It is not presently known whether this difference is consistent over the long term.

Among a group of about twenty *Eucidaris* on and beside a colony of *Pavona clavus,* two were grazing on (and eroding) the live coral and twelve were grazing on crustose coralline algae at the base of the coral colony. Although *Porites* was abundant in this area and several urchins were grazing on coralline algae from the dead basal areas of these colonies, urchins were never observed feeding on the live surfaces of this species.

Wolf and Darwin Islands: Both Wolf and Darwin, the northernmost islands in the Galápagos Archipelago, are eroded tops of two very large volcanoes that rise from depths of more than 1,800 m (McBirney and Williams, 1969). The two islands are small and low. Wolf is 134 ha in area with an elevation of 253 m, and Darwin encompasses 106 ha and is 168 m high. These islands have steep cliffs and are subject to frequent rock slides during the wet season*. The insular shelves generally have steep slopes with no suitable anchorages.

Our survey of the northern half of the main island of Wolf indicated that reef-building corals were most abundant along the east side (fig. 42). In this area the shelf slope was not so abrupt, ranging between 15° and 25° from the horizontal. Corals were present on rocks (boulder and block talus), which formed the underlying substratum between 5–20 m depth. Some coral colonies were found on coarse, calcareous sediment that was usually encountered deeper (25–35 m).

The centers of distribution of hermatypic corals were relatively deep at Wolf (fig. 43). Four of the most common corals had peak abundances (numbers of colonies/m^2) at 11 m (*Pocillopora*) and 18 m (*Porites, Pavona clavus,* and *Pavona gigantea*). The surface cover of three species showed a parallel trend except that one (*Pavona clavus*) covered the most area at 24 m. It is evident that the surface cover plot, based on photographic coverage, includes only three of the seven species observed at this site. We believe that this discrepancy is largely due to (a) the poor resolution of smaller coral species in photographs, (b) the tendency for some corals (especially *P. gigantea*) to grow on the sides and undersurfaces of substrates, and (c) perhaps to a lesser extent, sampling error (the total bottom area sampled by counting was 50 m^2, whereas only 30 m^2 was sampled photographically).

Because of the limited time at this site, we decided to sample quantitatively at five depth levels only. We also surveyed the bottom here qualitatively from 7 m to the surface and from 31–38 m. Fewer corals were present at shallow depth (surface to 6 m) than at 7 m and deeper; the subtidal zone was dominated by what appeared to be relatively fresh rock debris. We also conclude that the depth limit for hermatypic corals is at about 30 m. Only a single colony of *Psammocora superficialis* (Gardiner) was encountered between 31–38 m.

In comparing the depth distributions of hermatypic corals at Wolf (fig.

---

*One such massive rock slide, which occurred on 29 January 1963, nearly claimed the lives of Peter Kramer and Eberhard Curio who were carrying out field work from a minuscule camp site on the west side of Wolf Island (E. Curio, personal communication). On this occasion the talus included chiefly small boulders, not exceeding 0.5 m in diameter. In the same area in early February, a large boulder, $\sim$ 4 m in diameter, fell to the shoreline.

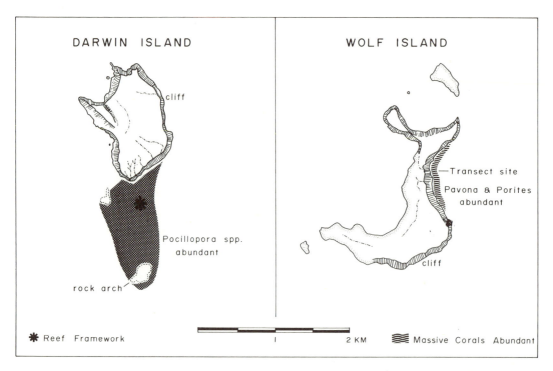

FIGURE 42. Northernmost islands of Darwin and Wolf illustrating areas with high coral abundance, reef framework construction at Darwin, and location of transect site on Wolf. Base maps from D. Weber (12 and 15 March 1970); courtesy of D. Weber and Charles Darwin Research Station.

43) and Bartolomé (fig. 35), it is evident that the Wolf coral community is displaced somewhat deeper than that at Bartolomé. The results of a species-by-species comparison of the most common species at the two sites are presented in table 8. For statistical testing, we apportioned each species into two depth levels (shallow and deep) according to their overall depth range. Three species of *Porites* and *Pavona* showed their centers of distribution to be significantly deeper at Wolf than at Bartolomé. *Pocillopora* spp. showed a similar, but slightly nonsignificant, trend in the same direction.

At least two factors are probably responsible for this difference. First, judging from the numerous talus deposits observed on shore and subtidally at Wolf, corals at shallow depth are subject to greater disturbance than those deeper. Another index of disturbance is the maximum size attained by corals. On one hand, at Wolf no massive corals present shallower than 15 m exceeded 1 m in diameter; most colonies were ≤ 0.6 m. On the other hand, at Bartolomé massive corals at shallow depth often were 1–2 m in diameter, and some colonies of *Porites* had attained 4 m. We would not expect the realization of such large colony dimensions in an area with frequent rock slides.

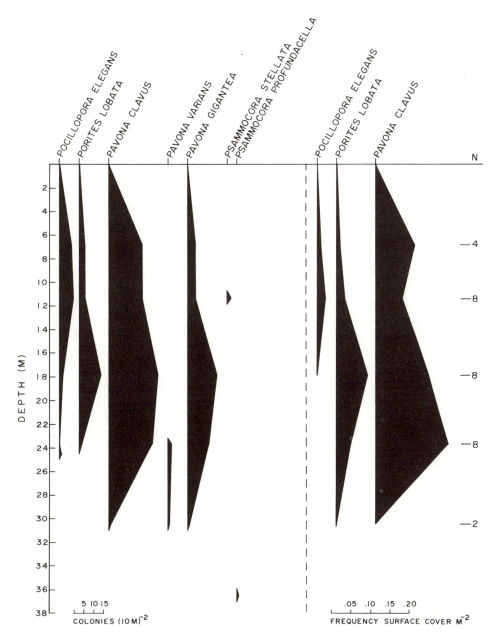

FIGURE 43. Reef-building coral abundance as a function of depth at Wolf Island. Left side, number of colonies counted in 1 X 10 m strip parallel to depth contour. Right side, frequency of live coral surface cover per m² as determined from approximately 1 m² photographs; number of photographs at each depth is indicated along right-hand margin.

· 87 ·

TABLE 8. Comparison of Depth Distributions of Hermatypic Corals at Bartolomé (fig. 35) and Wolf (fig. 43) Islands. These data indicate a greater depth extension of corals at the northern island of Wolf than at the central island of Bartolomé.

| Species | Depth (m) | | Number | Test and Associated P^a |
	Shallow	Deep		
Pocillopora spp.	0–11	12–25	41	FEP,[b] $P = 0.052$
Porites lobata	0–11	12–25	78	FEP, $P \ll 0.001$
Pavona clavus	0–15	16–31	116	$X^2_{(1)} = 20.21$,[c] $P \ll 0.001$
Pavona gigantea	0–15	16–31	138	$X^2_{(1)} = 9.42, 0.01 > P > 0.001$

[a]All probability levels are for one-tailed tests.
[b]Fisher exact probability test employed when one or more cells contained less than five colonies.
[c]Chi-square tests corrected for continuity.

Second, it is our impression that water transparency is higher in the northern than the central islands, and therefore we might expect corals to extend somewhat deeper in the northern island areas. While sea surface temperatures are higher in the northern compared with the southern islands, the shoaling thermocline observed at Wolf (see chapter 2, *Physical Environment: Sea Temperature*) indicates that corals here do experience sudden cooling spells. While several species of reef-building corals cohabited some bottom areas, no significant framework development was observed at Wolf.

We examined only the south side of Darwin Island, from the shore of the main island south to a large rock arch (fig. 42). Compared to Wolf Island, the area surveyed at Darwin was shoal (< 30 m deep) over a broad expanse and appeared less affected by rock slides. Nearshore *Pocillopora elegans* and *Pavona clavus* were most common. At 8–10 m depth, a pocilloporid buildup (*P. elegans*) was found (fig. 42). This had a maximum thickness of 1 m and had formed on eroded colonies of *Pavona clavus*. Other hermatypic corals observed in the vicinity of abundant *Pocillopora* denoted in figure 42 were *Pocillopora damicornis*, *Pavona gigantea*, *Pavona varians*, and *Porites lobata*. Along the eastern edge of the shelf, at ~ 20 m depth, coral was gradually replaced by a gently sloping, coarse calcareous sand bottom.

SUMMARY AND OVERVIEW

Among the southern islands (San Cristóbal, Española, and Floreana), coral communities were most prevalent on the northern coasts. Framework construction, in particular, was observed only on the northeastern corners of these islands (fig. 44). Coral development on Santa Fe Island, the southernmost member of the central islands group, also conformed to this pattern. The remainder of the central islands (Santa Cruz, Rábida, Pinzón, Isabela east, and

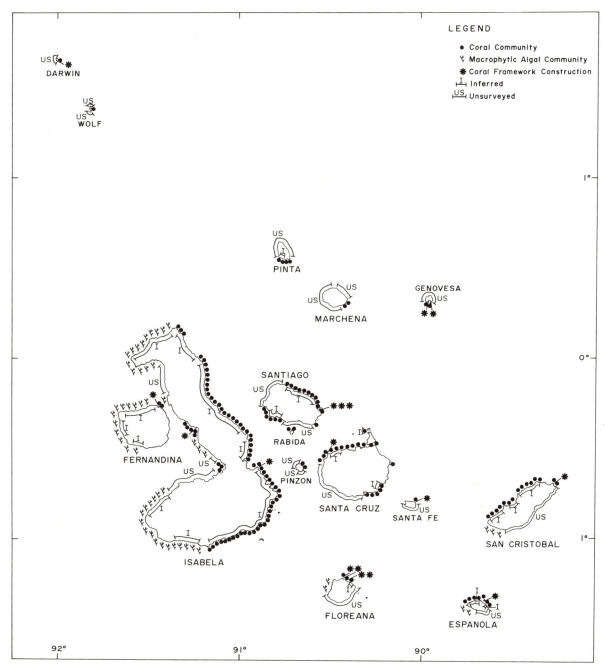

FIGURE 44. Summary map of observed and inferred distribution patterns of reef-coral communities, coral framework, and macrophytic algal communities in the Galápagos Archipelago. Coastal areas lacking symbols were mainly characterized by hard substrate assemblages containing coralline algae, algal mats, barnacles, and other epibenthic groups.

Santiago) exhibited coral community development in a variety of areas with no obvious distributional pattern*.

Perhaps the strongest pattern was evident in the sparse occurrence of hermatypic coral communities in the western sector (Isabela west and Fernandina). Here reef-building corals were largely confined to (a) the inner reaches of Elizabeth Bay, (b) the shore of Isabela on the leeward side of Fernandina (Urvina Bay), and (c) the lava rock pools at Espinosa Point. Exposed sites harbored species-rich and abundant macrophytic algal communities. Macrophytic algal floras were also present on the western sides of the southern islands, possibly due to the cool, nutrient-rich Equatorial Undercurrent, which we suspect reaches these areas periodically. Coral development in the northern islands, judging from this limited survey, seemed to extend deeper and to be confined chiefly to the southern exposures of these islands.

Reef framework construction is recorded at seventeen sites throughout the islands. Pocilloporid buildups, noted at twelve sites, were the most common; they reached modest proportions ($\geq$ 1 m in thickness and several hundred m^2 in area) within the southern, western, and northern island groups. Three of the pocilloporid patch reefs were killed in recent years. One reef, at Espinosa Point, has undergone a gradual exposure; and another, in Urvina Bay, was suddenly elevated. Both of these events were a result of volcanism and subsequent tectonic uplift. The third dead pocilloporid buildup, at Pinzón Island, was evidently buried by sand. *Pavona clavus* buildups, four in all, were present in the southern, central, and northern islands. The largest buildups were observed at Champion Island (Floreana), with approximate maximum dimensions of 10 m in thickness and 0.5 km long, and at Bartolomé Island (Santiago), with 6 m in thickness and $\sim$ 0.6 km long. The one buildup dominated by *Porites*, 4 to 5 m thick and $\sim$ 1 ha, was also present at Bartolomé.

We are now prepared to compare Joubin's (1912) locations of coral reefs in the Galápagos with the present findings. According to Joubin, the south, southeast, west, and part of the northwest (near Wreck Bay) coasts of San Cristóbal are fringed with coral reefs. While we did not survey most of the southern coast of San Cristóbal, reefs were not present in the other areas designated by Joubin; only small incipient reef structures were observed in the northeastern sector of the island (fig. 44). At Floreana Island, Joubin showed coral reefs present along the west coast, where we observed macro-

---

*Continuing marine surveys indicate an abundance of pocilloporid and pavonid corals at the northeastern end of Santa Cruz Island as well (G. R. Robinson). The coral formations are located directly in front of "coral rocks cove" (near 0° 30' S; 9° 15' W), so named because of the many coral boulders strewn along the high tide line. *Pocillopora damicornis* is the chief coral, forming patches at shallow depth along the sides of the cove, and *Pavona clavus* is the predominant species in deep water. Preliminary mapping shows *Pavona* present continuously between the 15- and 20-m isobaths and extending about 70 m parallel to the shore, suggesting incipient reef development. The maximum height of individual colonies is $\sim$ 1 m and many of them are undermined by *Eucidaris*.

phytic algal communities. Reef formations were most prevalent on the north-east coast of Floreana. The last area noted by Joubin to support reef growth was the northernmost coast of Isabela, at Punta Albemarle. We did not observe reef formations in this area; in fact, this point consists of numerous bold and rugged rock outcrops. Thus, Joubin's locations of coral reefs in the Galápagos Islands do not agree with the present findings. Considering the large size of the coral reefs shown by Joubin, it is unlikely that they have vanished in the past 100 years or so. Unfortunately, his sources are not clearly identified so that it is difficult to trace the origins of these discrepancies.

Eucidaris was generally abundant and preyed heavily on pocilloporid corals in the southern islands. It was common to locally abundant on the central and northern islands, but usually absent to rare and only occasionally common in the western sector of the Galápagos.

It should be noted that the above generalizations, while based on numerous and widely dispersed surveys, are the results of sampling and should therefore be accepted on provisional terms. The large subtidal areas that have not been surveyed (fig 44) indicate the magnitude of uncertainty that still remains.

CORAL GROWTH

Information on coral growth can be used in a variety of studies, for example, (a) understanding the developmental history of coral reefs, (b) studying the descriptive analysis of coral growth per se, (c) analyzing the effects of various physical and biological conditions such as light, water movement, temperature, and food availability, (d) assessing past environmental conditions from the growth record of the coral skeleton, and (e) investigating physiological and biochemical questions relating to the mechanism of calcification, and to other reef organisms in terms of predator-prey interactions, competition, and symbiosis (Buddemeier and Kinzie, 1976). Many of these approaches have a direct bearing on questions raised in the present study. The linear growth rates of branching (*Pocillopora*) and massive hemispherical (*Pavona*) corals were determined to assess the potential contribution of corals to reef growth, to investigate seasonal differences, to compare coral growth under different environmental regimes within the archipelago, to infer past environmental conditions, and to relate the amounts of coral that are produced and then consumed by corallivores.

While reef growth is a very complex process that depends upon coral growth and the growth of numerous calcareous organisms other than corals, erosion and depositional processes, and small- and large-scale disturbances of reef populations, the paucispecific nature of eastern Pacific reefs greatly simplifies the task of assessing reef accumulation rates. This is especially true for pocilloporid reefs where some sections of the reef frame are comprised of branches from the same colony from bottom to top. The prominence of pavonid corals in the Galápagos, whose skeletons typically show marked seasonal density banding, has permitted an analysis of varying environmental conditions (seasonally and spatially) on coral growth and of conditions that influenced coral growth during the recent past.

METHODS

Linear growth rates of *Pocillopora* were obtained by staining colonies with Alizarin Red S (Barnes, 1970, 1972) during warm and cool water periods.

Colony sizes ranged between 15–20 cm in diameter. The species selected for study were *P. elegans* at Onslow Island (Floreana Island) and *P. damicornis* at Punta Espinosa (Fernandina Island), which were the most abundant species at these sampling sites. The stained corals were placed on the bottom near their original sites of attachment and tagged with hookup wire (wrapped around the dead basal branches). Water depth at Punta Espinosa was about 1 m below mean tide level and 1–3 m below mean tide at Onslow Island. Two colonies of *P. elegans* were placed in wire enclosures (mesh size = 12 mm) at Onslow Island. Colonies were collected after periods ranging from one to nearly four months, cleaned with dilute sodium hypochlorite, and all live (at time of collection) branchtips measured. The growth data reported are the linear increments in the colony branches, measured from the uppermost (distal) stain line to the branchtips.

Density band widths in massive corals were analyzed from fragments 10–25 cm in length (measured along the growth axis) that were broken from the summits of large, healthy colonies at seven different localities where corals were abundant. Water depth ranged from 1–5 m relative to MLLW (mean lower low water tide datum). At the time of collection, January and February 1975 and 1976, these areas were not subject to strong wave action. Two species of *Pavona*, *P. clavus* and *P. gigantea*, were selected for this analysis because they are widely distributed in the Galápagos Islands, and preliminary inspection showed distinct skeletal banding. In addition, these two species produce clear skeletal banding in Panamá, and work in progress there indicates that the density bands are correlated with seasonally warm and cool water conditions. Galápagos corals were cut along the main growth axis into slabs 5 mm in thickness (two to four slabs per colony), and these were x-rayed in cardboard holders (0.7 sec, 46 KVP, 200 ma) with a GE 600 three-phase generator unit. Glossy prints were made from the x-ray negatives, and x-radiographs of sections showing most distinct banding were selected for measurement. The density bands were traced onto transparent overlays. A major criterion used for the identification of annual band couplets was their presence at the periphery or flanks of colonies. With the aid of the transparent overlay, the peripheral couplets on either side of a slab could be traced and matched medially along the main growth axis. The innermost (proximal) boundary of a particular dark (dense) band—equal seasonally to the transition warm/cool water periods (see section below on Calibration)—was selected as a reference point and then traced medially as described above. In order to avoid biased results, measurements were made with calipers and a rule only once *before* the statistical analyses and not repeated thereafter. The number of annual bands represented in the time series analysis was often less in the earlier years than would be expected from the total number of colonies examined because all colonies were not equally old.

Oxygen isotope (^{18}O) analyses were performed on carbonate (aragonite) material removed from coral slabs with a chisel in increments of three samples per year. Each sample contained approximately 1 gm of material, and 50–100 mg subsamples were analyzed. The standard employed was PDB-1 (PD Belemnite Limestone).

The incidence of growth discontinuities and bioerosional damage were also assessed from photographic prints of the 5-mm-thick slabs of *Pavona* colonies. While only the numbers of boring bivalves were determined, Highsmith (1981) has shown that the frequency of bore holes provides a valid estimate of the relative intensity of overall bioerosional damage, that is, total skeletal excavation due to bivalves, sponges, polychaetous annelids, sipunculans, and other boring organisms.

POCILLOPORA ELEGANS *AND* POCILLOPORA DAMICORNIS

The linear growth rates of sixteen colonies of *P. elegans* were assessed over six sampling periods on the Onslow Island patch reef from January through October 1975 (fig. 45). During the warm-water season, colony growth was sampled on the reef flat at ~ 1 m depth (thick lines) and on the deep reef edge at ~ 3 m depth (thin lines). Also shown are four colonies of *P. damicornis* from the semi-enclosed lava pools at Punta Espinosa, Fernandina Island. These data, except for two colonies at Onslow Island within enclosures (identified with asterisks), represent net coral growth, that is, the incremental linear growth of all branchtips regardless of obvious signs of attrition from corallivores. Estimates of gross coral growth will be considered later when the activities of corallivores are compared in the Galápagos and Panamá.

In the warm season (January to April), the linear growth rates of *P. elegans* on the reef flat and reef edge did not show any consistent differences. Reef flat colonies sampled at different times in the warm season showed higher, lower, and equal median growth compared to reef edge colonies. Overall, the median linear growth rates on the reef flat (n = 5) and reef edge (n = 6) were respectively 2.8 and 2.4 mm/mo. These median values do not differ significantly (P = 0.428, 2-tailed Mann-Whitney U-test). A statistically significant seasonal difference in the linear growth rate of *P. elegans* is evident (by inspection) with median growth centered between 2.0–3.0 mm/mo. during the warm-water period and about 1.0 mm/mo. in the cool period.

Pocillopora damicornis (n = 4) ranged in linear growth between about 1.5 to almost 3.0 mm/mo. in the lava pool habitat at Punta Espinosa. This high variability in growth may reflect the stressful conditions of exposure and extreme fluctuations in water temperature that occur periodically at this site. Compared with the growth rate of a single colony of *P. elegans* at Onslow Island (median = 1.2 mm/mo.), it appears that coral growth in the lava pool habitat was higher over the same general period.

The linear growth rates of two colonies maintained in enclosures dif-

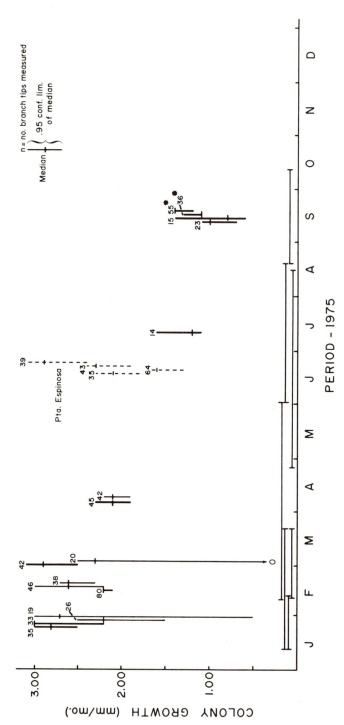

FIGURE 45. Incremental growth of *Pocillopora* during warm and cool periods. *Pocillopora elegans* was measured at Onslow Island and *P. damicornis* at Punta Espinosa, Fernandina Island. Growth rates at Onslow Island are noted for colonies on the reef flat (~1 m depth, thick lines) and on the reef edge (~3 m, thin lines). Colonies were measured in a lava pool patch reef at Punta Espinosa (~1 m). Each vertical line represents one colony; the number of branchtips measured in each colony is noted above. Two colonies on the reef flat at Onslow Island (asterisks) were maintained in enclosures. The lengths of growth periods are indicated by horizontal lines along the time axis; coral colonies are centered directly above the corresponding growth periods.

fered significantly from unprotected colonies (P $\ll$ 0.001, Kruskal-Wallis ANOVA). The growth of unprotected colonies was 67 percent of that of colonies protected from corallivores over a two-month period (August–October, fig. 45). Although the sample size is small, the data suggest that corallivores may significantly reduce the net linear growth rate.

Seasonal variations in the linear growth rate of *P. elegans* at Onslow Island generally appeared to track variations in seawater temperature and cloud cover. Coral growth (CG) was greatest from January to April when sea surface temperatures (SST) were high and cloud cover (CC) low; after April coral growth declined sharply with falling seawater temperatures and increasing cloud cover (fig. 46). The reason for the sharp decline in coral growth from February to March, when sea surface temperatures increased and cloud cover decreased, is not immediately apparent. The bivariate correlation coefficients for linear coral growth as a function of sea surface temperature and cloud cover are, respectively, $\tau_{CG\,SST} = 0.467$ (P = 0.136) and $\tau_{CG\,CC} = -0.333$ (P = 0.235).* With cloud cover partialled out ($\tau_{CG\,SST.CC} = 0.379$), the decline in τ_{CG} indicates that light probably also had some effect on coral growth. While these limited data fail to reach an acceptable significance level, they do suggest that coral growth is associated positively with sea surface temperature and negatively with cloud cover. Similar, but statistically significant, relationships were demonstrated for *Pocillopora damicornis* in Panamá (Glynn, 1977).

PAVONA CLAVUS *AND* PAVONA GIGANTEA

Linear growth rates of massive corals were assessed at seven localities utilizing *Pavona clavus* and *P. gigantea*, which are generally abundant in the Galápagos Islands. *Porites lobata* is also an abundant massive coral in the Galápagos but was not collected for growth analysis because the density bands in this species are often indistinct and difficult to interpret.** This condition has been observed in Panamá (Glynn, personal observations) and

---

*Because of the few observations available and certain important violations of the underlying assumptions of the method of least squares regression—notably heterogeneity of variances and high multicollinearity (temperature and cloud cover are highly correlated)—a nonparametric test, Kendall's method of rank correlation (τ) was used to determine the degree of association of temperature and cloud cover on *Pocillopora* growth rates at Onslow Island. (Transformation of these data to logarithms and arcsine indicated a greater departure from normality and possible problems with autocorrelation of the residuals.) Nonparametric statistics are used in all subsequent tests where appropriate.

**A few old, corroded colonies of *Porites lobata* were found on a beach at Pinta Island by JWW. The remaining dense bands in these colonies did show a distinct annual growth pattern. One colony showed 57 mm of linear skeletal growth in seven years, or 8.1 mm/yr. This growth rate falls within the range of values reported for this species, 6–13 mm/yr, in Hawaii and the central Pacific (Buddemeier and Kinzie, 1976).

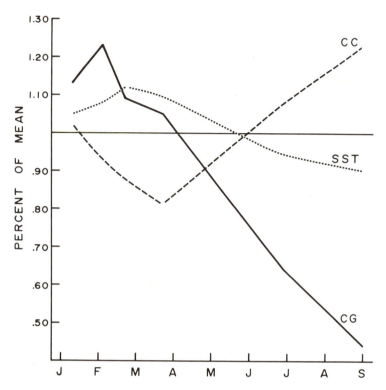

FIGURE 46. Seasonal variations in the growth of *Pocillopora elegans* (CG, n = 14 colonies, excluding two colonies in enclosures) at Onslow Island (Floreana Island), sea surface temperatures (SST), and cloud cover (CC) at Academy Bay (Santa Cruz Island) in 1975. Data are plotted as percentages of the mean of each series. The temperature and cloud cover curves are based on monthly mean values.

elsewhere (Buddemeier and Kinzie, 1976) as well, and is apparently due to the prominence of lateral-growing polyps in this genus. Two chief aspects of coral growth are herein considered, namely, (a) linear growth rate differences between islands, and (b) variations in coral growth in relation to environmental conditions, particularly sea temperature and cloud cover. First, however, it is necessary to establish the seasonal timing of density band formation.

Calibration: X-radiographic analyses of the skeletons of massive, hermatypic corals in the Gulf of Panamá (Macintyre and Smith, 1974; Macintyre and Glynn, unpublished data), indicate that density bands are formed there seasonally. Depending upon the species, high-density layers are produced by a thickening or coalescing of dissepiment structures (and closer bundling of sclerodermites) or by a thickening of the corallite walls (Macintyre and Smith, 1974; Emiliani et al., 1978). In *Pavona gigantea*, high-density bands are formed by a temporary thickening of the corallite walls (Macintyre and Smith, 1974). Live colonies of *Pavona gigantea* and *Gardineroseris planulata* were stained with Alizarin Red S bone stain and collected after several months of growth during nonupwelling and upwelling periods. A single dense band formed in both species under nonupwelling (warm water, high overcast) conditions and a low-density band formed during upwelling (cool water, low overcast) (fig. 47). The seasonal formation of density bands has been demonstrated at several other localities (largely nonupwelling environments) where high- and low-density band couplets are formed each year (e.g., Knutson et al., 1972; Buddemeier et al., 1974; Dodge and Thomson, 1974; Weber et al., 1975; Hudson et al., 1976; Stearn et al., 1977; Highsmith, 1979; Wellington and Glynn, 1983). As in Panamá, the density bands in massive Galápagos corals appear to form largely in response to seasonal variations in sea surface temperature and cloud cover. That is, a high-density band forms in Galápagos corals in the warm season and a low-density band in the cool season. However, the dense, warm season banding in Galápagos corals is more irregular than in corals in the Gulf of Panamá (fig. 48). In some years the high-density bands are prominent, in other years dense bands are faint, and some years show multiple dense banding (see Hudson, 1977; Highsmith, 1979). Dense "stress bands" (often associated with periods of severe winter cooling) have also been identified in corals (e.g., off Florida) (Hudson et al., 1976; Emiliani et al., 1978), but such bands were not seen in the Galápagos corals.

The annual pattern of formation of density bands in the Galápagos was determined by collecting corals in the different seasons and noting the condition of bands in the peripheral growth zone. *Pavona gigantea* and *P. clavus* collected in the Galápagos at the beginning of the warm season (February) usually showed a broad or thick low-density band that had formed during the preceding cool season. Corals collected from the Urvina shelf (fig. 49), which was uplifted during the 1954 warm season (probably sometime in March according to Richards, 1957), showed an incipient dense band. Colonies collected near the end of the warm season (April) typically have a dense band at their summits (fig. 48). These results appear to be in general agreement with the seasonal timing of band formation reported for massive corals from several other regions (Highsmith, 1979). In the majority of studies that found high-density bands forming during periods of high sea surface temperature, the seasonal light availability was low. In the Galápagos, high-density bands appeared to form during high SST and high insolation. These seasonal growth patterns are by no means invariant; high-density bands also form in some corals during seasons of low SST (Buddemeier and Kinzie, 1975; Dodge and Thomson, 1974).

Another way to test the relation between density bands and water temperature is by measuring the oxygen isotopic composition of the aragonite in the coral skeleton. This method is based on the fact that coralline aragonite is

FIGURE 47. X-radiographs of massive corals from Panamá and the Galápagos Islands. 1 - *Pavona gigantea*, Saboga Island, stained 17 August 1973, collected 25 October 1974. 2 - *Pavona gigantea*, Saboga Island, stained 17 August 1973, collected 25 October 1974. 3 - *Gardineroseris planulata*, Saboga Island, stained 14 June 1972, collected 5 May 1973. 4 - *Pavona gigantea*, Urvina Bay, collected 8 May 1977. 5 - *Pavona gigantea*, Urvina Bay, collected 8 May 1977. 6 - *Pavona gigantea*, Urvina Bay, collected 8 May 1977. 1, 2, and 3 are from the Pearl Islands, Gulf of Panamá. Arrows and broken lines indicate the upper limit of stain deposited in the coral skeletons. In 1 and 2 the stain lines are present in the lower one-third of the second dense bands, in 3 the stain line is present at the base of the uppermost, wide dense band; 4, 5, and 6 are from the west side of Isabela Island.

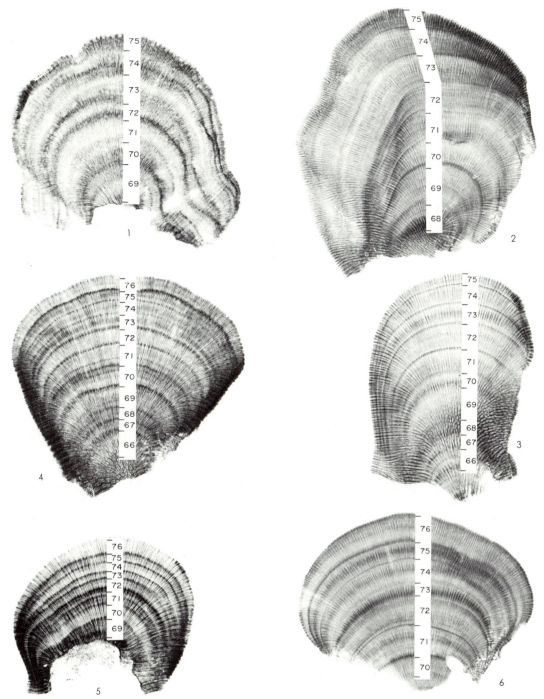

FIGURE 48. X-radiographs of massive corals from the Galápagos Islands. *1 - Pavona gigantea*, Cartago Bay, Isabela Island, collected 10 February 1976. *2 - Pavona clavus*, Cartago Bay, Isabela Island, collected 10 February 1976. *3 - Pavona clavus*, Floreana Island, along shore opposite Champion Island, collected 6 February 1976. *4 - Pavona gigantea*, Floreana Island, opposite Champion Island, collected 25 April 1977. *5 - Pavona gigantea*, Duncan Island, collected 3 May 1977. *6 - Pavona clavus*, Duncan Island, collected 3 May 1977.

FIGURE 49. Large colony of *Pavona clavus* at Urvina Bay uplift, 9 February 1976.

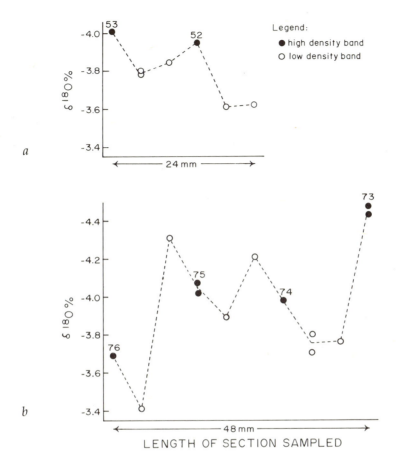

FIGURE 50. Oxygen isotope composition of skeletal carbonate of *Pavona clavus* at Urvina uplift (*a*) and Española Island (*b*). Plot *a* is a 24-mm transect equal to nearly two years of growth and plot *b* is a 48-mm transect equal to about three years growth. ^{18}O values are relative to the Chicago PDB standard.

enriched in ^{18}O relative to seawater and becomes more enriched with decreasing temperature during calcification (Faure, 1977). Weber and Woodhead (1972) demonstrated a simple linear depletion in $\delta^{18}O$ with increasing water temperature for whole coral colonies of a variety of species from numerous localities in the world's tropical seas. More detailed studies of individual colonies have shown seasonally related trends with a depletion in $\delta^{18}O$ in high-density bands formed during periods of high water temperatures (Emiliani et al., 1978; Fairbanks and Dodge, 1979). On the basis of these results, it is of interest to examine the oxygen isotopic composition of the density banding in Galápagos corals.

In figure 50, the oxygen isotope ($\delta^{18}O$ $^\circ/_{\circ\circ}$) composition is plotted along portions of the growth axes of two colonies of *Pavona clavus*.* The colony from the Urvina uplift was sampled over a period equal to approximately two years of growth, that is, during two warm and two cool seasons. In this case the high-density bands coincided with the lowest $\delta^{18}O$ values, which is the expected result if high-density bands form during warm-water periods (fig. 50a). The results from a colony collected at Española Island are equivocal (fig. 50b). Only in the high-density band formed in 1973 was the $\delta^{18}O$ level greatly depleted. Part of this apparent noncomformity could be due to the coarse sampling employed here (about three samples per year of growth). Even in the high-resolution sampling performed by Fairbanks and Dodge (1979), which was twelve to fifteen samples per year, low-density bands sometimes coincided with the lowest ^{18}O values. It also must be realized that the relationship between $^{18}O/^{16}O$ ratios and temperature may be affected by the photosynthetic rate of endosymbiotic zooxanthellae. Erez (1978) and Emiliani et al. (1978) have suggested that when photosynthesis increases (and the rate of calcification increases), the isotopic composition of the skeleton becomes lighter. This is because photosynthesis increases the amount of ^{16}O enriched metabolic CO_2 available during skeletogenesis. In support of this view, Land et al. (1975) have shown that within-colony and within-corallite variation in isotopic composition are closely correlated with growth rates, that is, faster growing areas tend to be isotopically lighter. During conditions of seasonal warm water and high insolation, photosynthetic rates should be high; which leads to the formation of an isotopically lighter skeletal layer. Thus, we may conclude that our analyses, while limited in scope, are in agreement with the above observations and tend to support the high-density/warm season relationship noted earlier.

While the formation of density bands can be correlated reasonably well with seasonal conditions, it is not now possible to determine linear growth increments or skeletal densities deposited per unit time for particular bands within yearly periods (e.g., per month). For this reason, annual growth measurements are based on the linear dimensions of band couplets, that is, one year's growth is equated to the combined thickness of one low- and one high-density band.

Growth Rate Differences Between Islands: Considering first *Pavona clavus*, the median (and mean) annual linear growth of this species was relatively low, 9.26 and 8.44 mm respectively, at Punta Pitt, San Cristóbal Island and Urvina Bay, Isabela Island, compared with five other localities that ranged from 11.57 mm (James Bay, Santiago Island) to 17.35 mm (Cartago Bay, Isabela Island) (table 9). Coral linear growth rates were significantly

---

*These analyses were performed by J. Killingley and R. Dunbar, in W. H. Berger's laboratory, Scripps Institution of Oceanography, and were made available by E. M. Druffel, Mount Soledad Radiocarbon Laboratory, La Jolla, California.

TABLE 9. Annual Growth Rates (mm/yr) of *Pavona clavus* and *P. gigantea* at Seven Localities in the Galápagos Islands. Colony growth is based on the thickness of density bands (one couplet per year) measured on photographic prints of x-radiographs. Sample statistics were calculated from the mean growth of individual colonies.

Locality	Species	Number Measured		Period	Median	Mean	Range of Mean Growth	Intercolony Variance	CV[a]
		Colonies	Annual Couplets						
San Cristóbal Island									
Punta Pitt	*Pavona clavus*	4	29	1963–1975	9.26	9.18	7.36–10.84	1.75	16.66
Española Island									
Gardner Bay	*Pavona clavus*	4	41	1961–1975	15.13	14.59	12.34–15.76	1.80	10.62
Floreana Island opposite	*Pavona clavus*	13	116	1963–1976	12.77	12.00	6.02–14.16	5.07	19.53
Champion Island	*Pavona gigantea*	10	99	1963–1976	9.70	9.10	5.01–12.97	7.45	31.63
Pinzón Island	*Pavona clavus*	7	51	1966–1976	12.94	12.12	7.83–15.07	5.42	20.75
	Pavona gigantea	4	50	1962–1976	8.56	8.47	7.33–9.43	0.56	10.21
Santiago Island	*Pavona clavus*	5	46	1963–1975	11.57	11.67	10.98–12.43	0.32	5.44
Isabela Island	*Pavona clavus*	5	41	1964–1975	17.35	17.41	15.40–19.39	1.62	8.17
Cartago Bay	*Pavona gigantea*	6	51	1964–1975	10.47	10.96	7.83–15.30	6.26	25.00
Isabela Island	*Pavona clavus*	14	175	1938–1953	8.44	8.36	5.98–10.24	1.67	16.05
Urvina Bay	*Pavona gigantea*	12	109	1938–1953	6.63	5.87	3.23–7.37	2.05	25.45

[a]Coefficient of variation, $CV = s(100)\bar{x}$, with s calculated to three decimal places.

different (P≪0.001) among the localities sampled (Kruskal-Wallis one-way ANOVA). Dunn's multiple comparison procedure ($\alpha = 0.05$) indicates that the linear growth rate of *P. clavus* was lower at Urvina than at Española, Floreana, and Cartago, and that growth at Punta Pitt was lower than at Cartago. It should be noted that the Urvina Bay coral samples did not overlap in time with those collected recently at all other localities (in 1975 and 1976). Urvina coral growth was assessed over a sixteen-year period from 1938 to 1953. However, there is no large-scale oceanographic evidence to indicate that environmental conditions were different across Isabela Island earlier or have changed later to alter these results (Garth, 1946*a*; Harris, 1969; Maxwell, 1974).

Pavona gigantea also showed a significant difference in annual linear growth between sites (Kruskal-Wallis test, $0.001 < P < 0.01$; table 9). The median rate of 6.63 mm/yr at Urvina Bay, west side of Isabela Island, is significantly ($\alpha = 0.05$) lower than at Floreana Island (9.70 mm/yr) or at Cartago Bay (10.47 mm/yr), east side of Isabela Island (Dunn's multiple comparison procedure).

Coral growth was highly variable at certain localities. At Floreana, Pinzón, and Isabela (Cartago Bay and Urvina Bay), for example, the coefficient of variation (CV) in growth among colonies exceeded 20.0 in four of eight cases (table 9). The interesting point here is the extent the variability in coral growth is related to fluctuations in environmental conditions. Evidence was presented earlier (fig. 6) showing that seasonal fluctuations in seawater temperature were markedly different among localities. Accordingly, we hypothesized that environments subject to high variations in thermal conditions would demonstrate high variability in coral growth. To test this possibility, we computed intracolony variances of the annual linear growth for all colonies of both species listed in table 9 (table 10). Because *P. gigantea* showed a lower linear growth rate and higher variance in growth than *P. clavus*, the two species are treated separately. (A median growth of 7.38 mm/yr, 6.92–8.92, 0.95 confidence limits of median, for thirty-two colonies of *P. gigantea* is different from 11.24 mm/yr, 10.20–12.77 representing the .95 confidence limits of the median, for fifty-two colonies of *P. clavus* at $P \ll 0.001$, Mann-Whitney U-test).

A difference in growth variability between sites is evident in both species with significance levels of $0.05 > P > 0.02$ for *P. clavus* and $0.02 > P > 0.01$ for *P. gigantea* (Kruskal-Wallis ANOVA). In *Pavona clavus*, this difference occurred between Floreana Island and Cartago Bay ($\alpha = 0.05$, Dunn's multiple comparison procedure). That is, growth was significantly more variable at Floreana than in Cartago Bay. The corresponding comparison for *P. gigantea* showed that annual linear growth was more variable at Pinzón Island than at Floreana. The variance in annual linear growth at Urvina Bay, which demonstrated low coral growth rates, was not significantly greater than that observed elsewhere.

TABLE 10. Intracolony Coefficients of Variation for Annual Growth in *Pavona clavus* and *P. gigantea*.

	Pavona clavus		Pavona gigantea	
Locality	Median	Range	Median	Range
Punta Pitt, San Cristóbal Island	23.66	11.02–30.32	—	—
Gardner Bay, Española Island	25.24	18.22–31.85	—	—
James Bay, Santiago Island	28.74	15.42–39.10	—	—
Champion, Floreana Island	31.22[a]	17.47–47.50	25.38[a]	11.98–34.12
Pinzón Island	26.07	12.48–29.45	36.56[a]	28.41–55.28
Cartago Bay, Isabela Island	15.89[a]	14.51–19.59	30.30	18.11–33.41
Urvina Bay, Isabela Island	28.16	11.24–58.38	32.97	14.08–53.14

[a]Significantly different from other median values at $\alpha = 0.05$, Dunn's multiple comparison procedure.

Finally, the correlation (Kendall rank correlation) between linear growth rate and intracolony variance was tested for all colonies and localities. For *Pavona clavus* (n = 52), the correlation coefficient ($\tau = -0.142$) just failed to reach significance (P > 0.068). The correlation for *P. gigantea* (n = 32) was considerably weaker with $\tau = -0.034$ (P > 0.390). In summary, corals occurring in areas of high temperature variation appear to show significantly higher intracolony variation in growth increment than those living under more stenothermal conditions. However, this variability is not well correlated with growth rate. This suggests that other exogenous and/or endogenous factors may regulate growth rates, perhaps in concert with temperature.

Growth Discontinuities: While the massive corals, *Pavona clavus*, *P. gigantea*, and *Porites lobata*, were relatively abundant at Urvina (pl. 1), a large number of these (especially *Pavona gigantea*) were small, encrusting in growth habit, and often showed signs of growth irregularities (fig. 47: 4, 5, 6). Many of these irregularities suggest that some areas on the colony surface were stressed or killed and then invaded by algae. Presumably, when more favorable conditions for coral growth returned, the dead areas were rapidly covered over with coral from surrounding live surfaces and growth then proceeded vertically in pace with the unaffected areas. Disturbances of this nature are henceforth referred to as growth discontinuities. Upwelling has been observed to affect adversely the growth of pocilloporid corals in a similar manner in the Gulf of Panamá (Glynn and Stewart, 1973). The incidence of growth discontinuities (observed in x-radiographs) at the seven sampling sites is summarized in table 11. Discontinuous growth was observed in *Pavona clavus* and *P. gigantea* at Floreana and Pinzón Islands and in Urvina Bay. Growth was interrupted most in *P. gigantea* at Urvina Bay where 6.8 skeletal discontinuities/10 colonies/10-year period occurred. No discontinuities were observed at Española Island or in Cartago Bay, sites where coral growth was high (table 9), suggesting that skeletal discontinuities reflect suboptimal growth conditions. This was tested in the two species by comparing median coral linear growth rates (table 9) with the incidence of growth discontinuities (table 11). Areas of the corallum crossed by these discontinuities were avoided in the sampling transects (fig. 47: 4, 5) so that linear growth rate estimates are not directly affected by them. Badly eroded colonies with discontinuities were omitted from the growth analysis because of uncertainties in identifying annual couplets but were included (four in number) in the analysis in table 11. For *Pavona clavus* (n = 7), Kendall's correlation coefficient ($\tau = -0.169$) was nonsignificant (P = 0.386). For *P. gigantea* (n = 4), Kendall's τ ($\tau = -1.00$) indicates that low linear growth rate and a high frequency of discontinuities are correlated (P = 0.042). These limited data suggest that growth conditions at Urvina are suboptimal for *P. gigantea*. While the linear growth rate of *P. clavus* was lowest at Urvina (8.44 mm/yr) and the number of growth discontinuities was relatively high (1.3/10 colonies/10 years ea.), colonies of this species attained 2 m in height (fig. 49).

Bioerosion: In addition to the negative responses of corals to upwelling (lower growth rate and localized injury), which appear to be largely a result of low water temperature stress, there is a body of data indicating that animals living in coral skeletons tend to erode and weaken coral colonies to a great extent in areas of high productivity (Highsmith, 1980*b*). The animals largely responsible for this damage are boring bivalves and sponges, which are filter feeders (planktivores) that depend upon food present in the water column. Highsmith (1980*b*) has demonstrated, on a global scale, a significant correlation between the abundance of boring organisms (and other coral-associated filter feeders such as ahermatypic corals, serpulid polychaetes, and pyrgomatine and acorn barnacles) and phytoplankton productivity.

In order to test whether bioerosion is related to differences in productivity within the Galápagos, the numbers of boring bivalves (*Lithophaga* spp.) were counted in all *Pavona* colonies available from seven localities (table 12). The apparent differences between localities, in terms of median number of lithophagine holes/100 cm² for each pavonid species, were not significant (*Pavona clavus*, $0.20 > p > 0.10$; *Pavona gigantea*, $0.10 > p > 0.05$). If the data from both species are pooled (N = 87), however, a significant difference between localities is evident. Dunn's multiple comparison procedure (with $\alpha = 0.25$) indicates that the number of borers were higher in corals from Urvina and Floreana than from Cartago. The pooled median abundances of

TABLE 11. Incidence of Skeletal Growth Discontinuities in *Pavona clavus* and *P. gigantea* at the Various Collecting Localities. Direct comparisons between sites can be made from the number of growth discontinuities per ten colonies per ten-year period.

Locality	Number Colonies	*Pavona clavus* Discontinuities			No. of Discontinuities 10 col^{-1} 10 yrs^{-1}	Number Colonies	*Pavona gigantea* Discontinuities			No. of Discontinuities 10 col^{-1} 10 yrs^{-1}
		0	1	2			0	1	2	
Punta Pitt, San Cristóbal Island	4	4	0	0	0	—	—	—	—	—
Española Island	4	4	0	0	0	3[a]	3	0	0	0
Floreana Island	13	12	1	0	0.6	10	9	1	0	1.0
Pinzón Island	7	6	1	0	2.8	5	4	1[a]	0	3.5
James Bay, Santiago Island	5	5	0	0	0	—	—	—	—	—
Cartago Bay, Isabela Island	5	5	0	0	0	5	5	0	0	0
Urvina Bay, Isabela Island	14	11	3	0	1.3	13	6	5	2	6.8

[a]Colony fragments less than 10 cm in length along growth axis.

Lithophaga spp. holes at Urvina and Floreana were 2.2 and 2.0 /100 cm² respectively; no bivalve bore holes were present in the majority of coral slabs examined from Cartago Bay, Punta Pitt, and Española Island. While no attempt was made to quantify the abundances of other planktivores associated with pavonid corals, it should be noted that the bases and margins of at least some colonies at all localities were riddled with boring sponges, and that gall-crab (hapalocarcinid) burrows and worm tubes were also present in many sections. Vermetid gastropod tubes, rock oysters (Chamidae), and acorn barnacles were especially abundant around the dead basal areas of coral at Urvina.

Although no data are available on the differences in primary productivity between island sites, it has been suggested that hermatypic coral abundance and water fertility are inversely related (Margalef, 1968). For a variety of reasons that are discussed below, we suspect that hermatypic corals should show relatively low rates of growth in areas of high plankton productivity. A significant inverse relationship between the linear growth of coral and frequency of *Lithophaga* borings is indicated (fig. 51) for the different localities sampled ($\tau = -0.564$, $P < 0.008$). Inspection of particular sites indicates that coral growth was low and bioerosion high at Urvina, Floreana, and Pinzón; corals at Española and Cartago demonstrated the opposite condition. Of all sites, Urvina is probably subject to the greatest upwelling influence and Cartago belongs to a low productivity area (Maxwell, 1974). As noted earlier (see chapter 3, *Nature and Distribution of Coral Communities and Coral Reefs*), the abundance of macrophytic algae along parts of the west coast of Floreana suggests that upwelling influences this island, but it is not presently known whether it reaches the northeastern corner. *Pavona clavus* at Punta Pitt and *P. gigantea* at Cartago did not follow the predicted trend. On one hand, the low numbers of *Lithophaga* in these corals are understandable since both sites do not appear to be subject to high levels of primary production. On the other hand, coral growth rates were lower than expected, a condition that could be due to several other factors.

Highsmith (1980b) has offered a summary of the mechanisms by which high primary productivity may restrict the distribution of reef corals. First of all, an increasing availability of food in the water column (dissolved and particulate organic matter, phytoplankton, and zooplankton) will lead to a proliferation of planktivores. As noted above, many of these planktivores are associated with corals and are active in bioerosion. They burrow into and weaken coral skeletons (Goreau and Hartman, 1963; Connell, 1973; Hein and Risk, 1975) and are in turn eaten by fish predators that damage corals in order to extract the boring organisms (Glynn et al., 1972; Highsmith, 1980b). Benthic animals that benefit from high levels of productivity will also compete with corals for space and possibly food (zooplankton). In addition, the high nutrient levels that are characteristically associated with fertile areas typically favor benthic algal productivity (Kinsey and Domm, 1974), which could lead

TABLE 12. Number of Boring Bivalve (*Lithophaga* spp.) Holes present in 5-mm-thick Slabs of *Pavona clavus* and *P. gigantea* at Various Localities (see fig. 51). Number of holes in each colony normalized to $(100 \text{ cm}^2)^{-1}$.

Locality	*Pavona clavus*				*Pavona gigantea*				
	Number Colonies	Minimum	Maximum	Median	Number Colonies	Minimum	Maximum	Median	Pooled Median
Punta Pitt									
San Cristóbal Island	4	0	3.6	0	—	—	—	—	0
Española Island	4	0	0.9	0	3	0	4.6	2.9	0
Floreana Island	13	0	5.3	0.6	10	0	12.9	2.8	2.0
Pinzón Island	7	0	3.5	1.2	5	0.6	2.1	1.6	1.4
James Bay									
Santiago Island	5	0	8.8	1.5	—	—	—	—	1.5
Cartago Bay									
Isabela Island	5	0	0.8	0	5	0	0.9	0	0
Urvina Bay									
Isabela Island	14	0	7.3	2.0	12	0	6.4	2.8	2.2

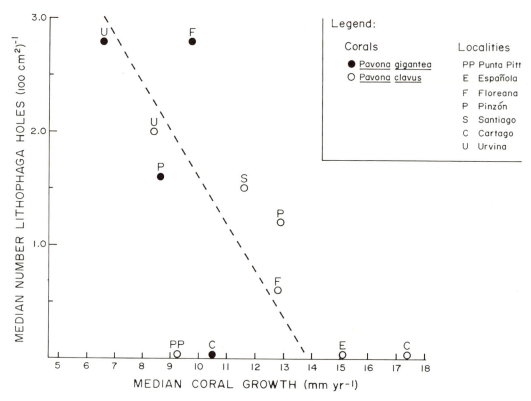

FIGURE 51. Inverse relationship between coral growth rates and density of lithopha-gine borers in coral. Regression line located by the approximate method of Brown and Mood (in Daniel, 1978).

to (a) increased competition with adult corals, and (b) possible interference with the settlement of coral larvae and overgrowth of juvenile corals (Adey et al., 1977; Birkeland, 1977; Rogers, 1979). In some areas supporting abundant benthic algae, coral mortality may also result from the "farming" activities of damselfish, which often kill nearby corals in order to expand their territories (Kaufman, 1977; Wellington, 1982b). While this activity has been shown to be significant on some reefs (eastern Pacific mainland and Caribbean), we do not believe that it is important in the Galápagos Islands (see chapter 6, *Biological Interactions: Damselfish Ejection Behavior*). Finally, it is possible that the high phosphate concentrations associated with environments of high productivity could reduce coral growth rates by inhibiting the formation of calcium car-bonate crystals (Kinsey and Davies, 1979).

Annual Variations in Coral Growth: Time series plots illustrating annual linear growth rates in *Pavona clavus* and *P. gigantea* show some long-term patterns that frequently coincide with major oceanographic and meteorologic events in the Galápagos Islands. These annual variations in coral growth will be examined first in relation to El Niño years and to the Panamá Current Influence, when the Galápagos area is temporarily under the influence of relatively warm, low saline, and nutrient-poor tropical waters. Since it is probable that the southerly movement of tropical waters (PCI) is at times felt mainly around the Galápagos Islands and not much further south (developing into major or minor Niño events), we have attempted to distinguish between these different phenomena in the following discussion. The various Niño events reported in the recent literature have been identifiable in Galápagos sea-surface temperature records (compare figs. 5, 52, and 53). A warming trend (PCI) was observed in the Galápagos in 1976, but this apparently did not have any appreciable influence along the South American mainland.

Annual linear growth rate trends in *P. clavus* were assessed at six sites, spanning periods from eleven to fifteen years (fig. 52). The variation in coral growth is expressed as percent deviation of the annual growth (linear radial growth = thickness of band couplets) from the grand mean growth at each site.

First, it is necessary to determine the existence of significant variations in growth in relation to particular years over the sampling period (1963–1976). The annual variations in the growth indices were found to differ significantly among years ($P \ll 0.001$, Kruskal-Wallis one-way ANOVA). Dunn's multiple comparison procedure indicates that growth in 1969 was significantly greater than in 1963 and 1975 ($\alpha = 0.05$). If the significance level is reduced to $\alpha = 0.10$, 1973 is also shown to be a year of low linear growth. High coral growth in 1969 was evident at all sites; however, at Pinzón and Española, linear growth was greatest in 1974 and 1965, respectively. Although the 1969 growth peak corresponds with a minor Niño year, a consistently high growth record is not evident in other Niño (major and minor) years. For example, the Galápagos area in 1965 experienced a warm-water period, but only two (Floreana and Española) of six sites showed above-average growth. The 1972 major Niño event was likewise correlated with high coral growth at only two sites (Cartago and Pinzón).

In addition to the significant variations in growth between years just examined, *P. clavus* annual linear growth rates demonstrated significant agreement between sites ($0.001 < P < 0.01$, Kendall test of concordance). This indicates that the long-term patterns of linear growth are probably controlled in large part by factors operating broadly throughout the islands.

A total of twenty colonies of *Pavona gigantea* were assessed similarly to the above at three localities during periods ranging from twelve to fourteen years (fig. 53). Coral growth did not show a significant difference among years ($0.20 > P > 0.10$, Kruskal-Wallis ANOVA). Kendall's test of concordance between sites just failed to reach a significant level ($0.05 < P < 0.10$). This is not surprising considering the high variance and small number of colonies sampled.

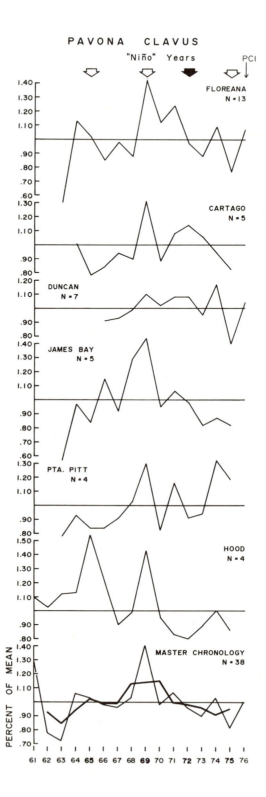

PAVONA CLAVUS

"Niño" Years

· 114 ·

In terms of the generality of coral growth response, it is of interest to compare the similarity of long-term patterns between the two species of *Pavona*. The results of this comparison are not clear-cut but suggest that the linear growth patterns in *Pavona* are in fair accordance with each other. The annual deviations in the master chronologies of *P. clavus* and *P. gigantea* (figs. 52 and 53, bottom plots, thin-lined curves) just failed to show a significant agreement ($0.10 > P > 0.05$, Kendall's test of concordance). However, agreement between species was significant ($0.05 > P > 0.02$) in the three-year moving average curves of the master chronologies (figs. 52 and 53, bottom plots, heavy-lined curves).

Variations in annual growth were also examined in dead *Pavona* colonies sampled at the Urvina Bay uplift. From these samples it was possible to determine variations in coral growth from 1938 to 1953, just prior to the emergence event. In both *P. clavus* and *P. gigantea*, growth during this period appeared greatest from about 1940 to 1945, and thereafter declined erratically to 1953 (fig. 54). However, statistical testing failed to show a significant difference in linear growth between years in either species ($0.10 > P > 0.05$, for both *P. clavus* and *P. gigantea*, Kruskal-Wallis ANOVA). The patterns of annual growth are similar in the two species over the sixteen year period ($\tau = 0.50$, $P \sim 0.003$, Kendall rank correlation). The correspondence between years of peak coral growth and El Niño events recorded in South America are suggestive, and therefore will be examined briefly.

The most reliable and relevant sea surface temperature data available appear to be those in Doberitz (1967) recorded at Puerto Chicama, Peru. Long-term observations in the Galápagos are not available prior to 1965. The strong El Niño invasion of 1941 and minor Niño events are noted in figure 54 (Wyrtki, 1973, 1975; Wooster and Guillen, 1974; Ramage, 1975). *Pavona gigantea* exhibited a growth index in 1941 that exceeded the long-term mean by 43 percent. Maximum linear growth in *P. clavus*, however, followed the 1941 El Niño event by one year. Growth was 6 percent and 8 percent above average in *P. clavus* and *P. gigantea* respectively in 1948 (a minor Niño year), and fell markedly in 1950, an exceptionally cool-water period. Growth then increased slightly in both species, but not above the mean, during the partial Niño developments in 1951 and 1953. Unexplained high linear growth rates occurred in several colonies of *P. clavus* in 1942 and 1945. These could have resulted from more local effects (PCI) in the Galápagos or from a minor Niño event that was not detected along the Peruvian mainland.

FIGURE 52. Annual variations in band widths (linear axial growth) of *Pavona clavus* at six localities in the Galápagos Islands. Data are plotted as a percentage of the mean of each series. The master chronology comprises all data and includes annual (thin curve) as well as three-year running average (thick curve) traces. Minor (1965, 1969, 1975) and major (1972) Niño years, and the Panama Current Influence (1976) in the Galápagos are identified.

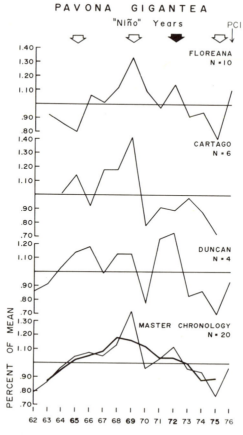

FIGURE 53. Annual variations in band widths (linear axial growth) of *Pavona gigantea* at three localities in the Galápagos Islands. Data are illustrated as in figure 52.

The degree of correlation between the linear axial growth of *Pavona* and the sea surface temperature and cloud cover observed in Academy Bay over the period 1965–1976 is summarized in table 13. Overall, sea surface temperature demonstrates a stronger correlation (positive) with coral growth than does cloud cover (negative). The partial correlation coefficients indicate the influence of temperature on growth, independent of cloud cover. With respect to the annual master chronologies, the effect of temperature on growth of *P. clavus* showed an appreciable increase with cloud cover partialled out ($\tau_{\text{CG SST}} = 0.639$, $\tau_{\text{CG SST.CC}} = 0.858$). The corresponding comparison in *P. gigantea* resulted in a decline in the correlation between temperature and growth when controlling for the effect of cloud cover ($\tau_{\text{CG SST}} = 0.483$, $\tau_{\text{CG SST.CC}} = 0.339$).

A recent study we conducted in Panamá on *Pavona gigantea* and *P. clavus*

TABLE 13. Kendall Rank Correlation Coefficients of *Pavona* Growth (Annual Band Widths) as a Function of Sea Surface Temperature ($\tau_{CG\ SST}$), Cloud Cover ($\tau_{CG\ CC}$), and Sea Surface Temperature with Cloud Cover Partialled Out ($\tau_{CG\ SST.CC}$). Correlation coefficients for cloud cover and temperature ($\tau_{CC\ SST}$) are also listed. These statistics are calculated from the data of the time series plots in figures 52 and 53.

Species and Sites	Correlation Coefficients			
	$\tau_{CG\ SST}$	$\tau_{CG\ CC}$	$\tau_{CC\ SST}$	$\tau_{CG\ SST.CC}$
Pavona clavus				
Floreana	0.199 P=0.181	0.030 P=0.444	−0.627** P=0.002	0.280
Cartago	0.282 P=0.113	−0.058 P=0.401	−0.651** P=0.003	0.303
Pinzón	0.422* P=0.035	−0.211 P=0.181	−0.575** P=0.007	0.376
James Bay	0.343+ P=0.071	−0.096 P=0.341	−0.651** P=0.003	0.372
Punta Pitt	0.128 P=0.291	0.020 P=0.464	−0.651** P=0.003	0.186
Española	0.153 P=0.255	−0.345+ P=0.069	−0.651** P=0.003	−0.101
Master chronology (yearly)	0.639** P=0.002	−0.164 P=0.230	−0.800** P<0.0002	0.858
Pavona gigantea				
Floreana	0.334+ P=0.066	−0.303+ P=0.085	−0.627** P=0.002	0.194
Cartago	0.283 P=0.113	−0.325+ P=0.082	−0.651** P=0.003	0.099
Pinzón	0.683** P=0.001	−0.381* P=0.043	−0.627** P=0.002	0.617
Master chronology (yearly)	0.483* P=0.014	−0.381* P=0.043	−0.627** P=0.002	0.339

+ = P<0.10, * = P<0.05, ** = P<0.01.

indicates that linear growth and calcification rates are accelerated in areas of moderate upwelling (Gulf of Panamá) compared to nonupwelling areas (Gulf of Chiriquí) (Wellington and Glynn, 1983). While upwelling may be important in terms of nutrient supply, the best correlate to pavonid coral growth in Panamá was light rather than temperature. The results presented here, indicating a positive correlation between linear growth and Niño years, may reflect a positive response to increased solar radiation even though our partial correlation analysis suggests that temperature is a more important factor.

In summary, the above analyses suggest that linear growth in massive Galapagan *Pavona* species is accelerated during the periodic occurrence of

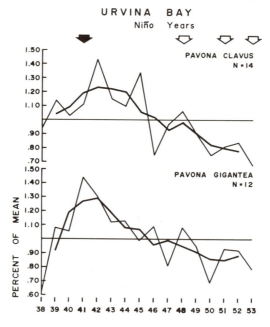

FIGURE 54. Annual variations in band widths (linear axial growth) of *Pavona clavus* and *Pavona gigantea* from the Urvina Bay (Isabela Island) uplift. Minor (1948, 1951, 1953) and major (1941) Niño years are identified.

Niño events, although a great deal of variance in growth is evident between years and sites. We expect that some of this is due to errors of measurement in the technique adopted in this study. Another important source of variation could arise from measuring linear-skeletal growth rather than mass deposition. Band width cannot be directly equated with the rate of calcification. For example, Dodge and Thomson (1974) demonstrated that the mass of $CaCO_3$ deposited depends on the density of the coral skeleton as well as its thickness. Differences in skeletal density were not measured in this study. Additional sources of variation between sites could result from local effects such as differences in temperature, cloud cover, sedimentation regimes, and food abundance.

CHAPTER FIVE

PHYSICAL CORRELATES OF CORAL DISTRIBUTION, ABUNDANCE, AND GROWTH

With the establishment of a broad, and admittedly tentative, picture of reef-coral distributions and growth rates, it is now possible to assess the relative importance of the various physical factors examined in this study. The following discussion, in part intended as a synthesis, will examine physical environmental conditions in relation to coral community development throughout the Galápagos Islands. Factors will be considered in the approximate order presented in Chapter 2 (*Physical Environment*).

CURRENTS, UPWELLING, AND ASSOCIATED CONDITIONS

Currents and their associated temperature and nutrient characteristics appear to have a major influence on the character of littoral marine communities in the Galápagos. The meager development of hermatypic corals on the west sides of Isabela and Fernandina corresponds closely with the occurrence of EUC (Equatorial Undercurrent) upwelling in this area. At the height of upwelling (August–September), the mean sea temperature at one exposed site (Caleta Iguana) was 15.4°C; the minimum temperature during this period was 14.3°C. These sustained low temperatures are well below the limits tolerated by reef-corals.

Some coral buildups are present in the western sector, however. The pocilloporid reefs at Punta Espinosa have formed in rock basins that are appreciably warmer (by ca. 4°C on the average) than the water offshore. We suspect that the uplifted coral formations in Urvina Bay and the live subtidal coral communities in the inner reaches of Elizabeth Bay were not subject to the full effect of the EUC regime. Urvina Bay, located east of Fernandina, is not exposed directly to the open sea, and both areas are situated well inside the 100 fathom (183 m) contour (fig. 1). The bottom off Caleta Iguana, however, drops away steeply; the 1,000 fathom (1,830 m) isobath here is located only 7.4 km offshore.

The prominence of ahermatypic corals at shallow depth in Tagus Cove is probably due in part to the cool, nutrient-rich and turbid waters in this area. (The darkness prevailing beneath the broad ledges must also play a role.) Similarly, macrophytic algal communities are best developed where the EUC surfaces. The luxuriant algal floras present on the western sides of Floreana, Española, and San Cristóbal may reflect the influence of easterly moving streams of the EUC (Pak and Zaneveld, 1973).

Comparative growth rates of two massive corals (*Pavona clavus* and *P. gigantea*) were significantly lower at Urvina than at sites to the east of Isabela Island. One massive species (*P. gigantea*) was generally small and exhibited a significantly higher incidence of growth discontinuities at Urvina compared with sampling sites removed from the EUC. In addition, the numbers of boring bivalve holes in coral skeletons (an index of primary productivity), was significantly higher in massive corals at Urvina (west side) than at Cartago (east side).

Another obvious distributional pattern was the strong development of reef corals on the northeastern sides of islands (San Cristóbal, Española, Floreana, and Santa Fe) located furthest south in the archipelago. This sector of the Galápagos is under the influence of the South Equatorial Current, with sea surface temperatures normally above 20°C during the coolest time of year. Moreover, upwelling is apparently absent here and the relatively low nutrient levels of the clear Peru oceanic waters, which sweep vigorously by the islands' northeastern coasts, do not support abundant plankton populations that would increase turbidity. The unexplained high incidence of borers in corals at Floreana, however, suggests the possible influence of some trophic enrichment in this area.

The substantial but shallow coral buildups at Urvina Bay (ca. 5 m depth before uplift) and Cartago Bay (2 m depth) suggest the limiting effect of turbidity on the depth of reef-frame development. Light penetration is low in these areas. Elsewhere in the archipelago where the water is usually clear (such as in the northern islands, the central islands [excluding Cartago Bay], and the southern islands), coral buildups occur to depths of 10–20 m.

CLOUD COVER

The high cloud densities observed over the eastern coast of Isabela and over the southwestern sectors of Santiago and Santa Cruz Islands are not logically correlated with coral abundance on these islands. Previous work generally (Stoddart, 1969*a*), and in the eastern Pacific in particular (Dana, 1975; Glynn, 1977), has indicated that reef-building corals attain maximum growth under high ambient light conditions (clear skies and high water transparency, for example). On Isabela, however, coral communities, and in one instance framework construction, are commonly present along the east shore where cloud cover (and turbidity) was consistently high, at least during 1977 and

1978. The same relationship was found at Santiago, that is, high cloud cover over the southwestern sector of the island where coral communities predominated. The extreme eastern end of Santiago, in the Bartolomé area, also showed high cloud cover associated with significant reef framework construction. Because the southwest coast of Santa Cruz is still unsurveyed, it is not possible to compare the high cloud cover there with coral abundance. Thus, it appears from the above observations that cloud cover is not a key factor in limiting coral community development on the larger islands of the Galápagos.

WATER TURBULENCE

The construction of pocilloporid frameworks usually takes place under conditions of limited wave action. On one hand, while isolated colonies of *Pocillopora* spp. offer little resistance to water flow, they can and do grow to a large size under conditions of high turbulence. On the other hand, the erect and fragile framework formed by the interlocking branches of numerous colonies offers high resistance to water movement, thus greatly increasing the chances for breakage. Therefore, rigid pocilloporid frames are usually restricted to protected sites. Two exposed locations with minor pocilloporid buildups, however, have been observed in Panamá (Glynn et al., 1972) and Colombia (Glynn et al., 1980). The northeastern sectors of the southerly islands are in the lee of the prevailing southeasterly seas, and six of the thirteen pocilloporid buildups observed in the islands occur at these locations. Pocilloporid frames elsewhere in the archipelago are also found at protected sites, such as in the lava basins at Punta Espinosa and in Urvina, Cartago, and Darwin bays.

Coral buildups formed of massive species (*Pavona* and *Porites*) do not appear to be so greatly influenced by wave action. Massive coral buildups occur outside of Darwin Bay and along the exposed south shore of Bartolomé Island.

GEOLOGIC DISTURBANCES

Tectonic Movements and Landslides: Tectonic movements associated with volcanism have been demonstrated to be locally important in the Galápagos. Two such events have occurred recently in the western section of the archipelago where volcanism is presently most active. An abrupt uplift on the west side of Isabela elevated coral communities above sea level ($\frown$ 5 m, pl. 1 and fig. 49), and a slow and slight emergence of lava basins at Punta Espinosa, Fernandina ($\frown$ 0.5 m, fig. 39), killed reef crest corals and halted further vertical growth.

Vertical earth movements may affect coral reefs with fair regularity in seismically active areas. Reefs that showed signs of tectonic uplift, with dead coral blocks in growth position and reef flats located above low water level, were described by Kuenen (1950) in Indonesia. Kuenen (1950) emphasized the importance of emergence events in reef building and concluded that they have occurred widely in Indonesia and in parts of the Indian Ocean. Stoddart (1969a) suggested that the dead, uppermost levels of coral reefs in the Solomon Islands also could have resulted from tectonic emergence.

Slides and slumping can be expected to occur on steep shores, especially where adjacent to land surfaces with sparse vegetation and periodic heavy rainfall. We observed three such sites: the eastern side of Darwin Bay (Genovesa Island) and the shores of Wolf and Darwin Islands. The effects of rock slides were particularly in evidence at Wolf Island, where coral abundance was low at shallow depth and massive coral colonies were small in size compared with identical species elsewhere on stable substrates. Rockfalls have apparently interfered with coral framework construction on Malpelo Island, Colombia, in a similar fashion (Birkeland et al., 1975). At Malpelo it was also noted that the effects of slides were exacerbated by boring organisms that erode the bases of corals, thus accelerating their breakage and downslope movement into deep water.

Volcanism: The occurrence of lava flows is probably better known than tectonic events and landslides. Lava flows of massive proportions that reach the sea could be expected to devastate all benthic life in the immediate area. While the Galápagos are one of the most active areas of volcanism known, the remoteness of the islands has resulted in an incomplete, and for some islands unknown, record of events. Volcanic activity has been recorded on Fernandina, Isabela, and Santiago (and possibly on Española, Pinta, and Floreana) since early in the eighteenth century (Smithsonian Institution summary of global volcanic activity during the last 12,000 years, courtesy T. Simkin).

Fernandina is the most active volcano, and three of its known eighteen eruptions since 1813 have reached the sea (table 14). The eruption of 1825 was observed by Captain Benjamin Morrell and the crew of the schooner *Tartar* (Morrell, 1832). This eruption was accompanied by a massive lava flow that reached the sea and raised the sea surface temperature to 66°C in the Bolivar Canal, several kilometers from the affected coastline. The exact location of the flow was not recorded, but T. Simkin (personal communication) believes that its most likely meeting point with the sea was about 5 km north of Mangle Point and not near the present-day Espinosa Point as stated in Brower (1968, p. 62). It is likely that any corals present in the Espinosa lava basins were killed at that time. We could not find any evidence (e.g., altered fossiliferous deposits) of previous coral destruction at Espinosa Point, however. This could mean that all corals now present at Espinosa have colonized this site since the 1825 eruption.

TABLE 14. Known Eruptions That Have Resulted in Lava Flows Reaching the Sea.

Island	Volcano	Locations	Year	Source
Fernandina	Fernandina	Possibly 5 km N of Mangle Point	1825	Morrell (1832)
		Unknown	1846	Townsend (1925)
		SE coast	1927	Richards (1962)
Isabela	Wolf	NE coast, immediately N of Cape Marshall	1925	Beebe (1926)
		NE coast, immediately N of Cape Marshall	1948	Richards (1954)
		NE coast, immediately N of Cape Marshall	1963	McBirney and Williams (1969)
	Sierra Negra	S shore, Elizabeth Bay	1953	Richards (1962)
		S shore, Elizabeth Bay	1963	McBirney and Williams (1969); Delaney et al. (1973)
		S shore, Elizabeth Bay	1979	Simkin; Smithsonian SEAN Bull. (1979)
Santiago	Santiago	Unknown	1904	T. Simkin (personal communication)
		James Bay	after 1684	Heyerdahl (1963); Swanson et al. (1974)
		SE coast and Sullivan Bay area	1897 1904–06	T. Simkin (personal communication) from Richards (1962) and Martinez (1934)

It is of interest to compare the thickness of the pocilloporid framework and its rate of growth at Espinosa with the time interval presumed favorable for colonization and growth since the 1825 event. The maximum framework thickness we observed (in five probe holes) was 1.52 m, and coral growth (measured over a 3.5 month period) ranged from 1.5–3.0 mm/month. In a 100-year period, the uninterrupted construction of a pocilloporid frame would amount to a buildup with a maximum thickness of 1.8–3.6 m. It is possible, however, that growth was occasionally interrupted since 1825, such as by tectonic events, a lava flow (1846), and other factors. In addition, Grigg and Maragos (1974) found that the recovery of coral communities to their initial state (including surface coverage) following destruction by lava flows in Hawaii required about fifty years in sheltered areas. A recovery period of this magnitude is realistic for the Espinosa site as well, considering the high coral density required to produce a continuous reef frame. While precise measurements of the sizes and growth rates of *Porites* colonies are not available, the 1-m-high colonies observed there, assuming an annual growth of 1 cm, are probably also on the order of 100 years old. Thus, we tentatively conclude that the coral formations in the Espinosa lava rock basins are about 100 years of age and developed after the major eruption of Fernandina in 1825.

It is probable that the lava flows that poured into the sea in 1846 and 1927 also had major local effects on the marine biota. A later study of the 1961 flow by Simkin, in which he assessed possible shoreline changes from aerial photographs, indicated that this flow probably did not reach the sea as noted by Léveque in a written communication to Richards (1962). One of these flows (1927) reached the southeast coast of Fernandina (the location of the 1846 flow is unknown) in the vicinity of Mangle Point. A massive fish mortality and other disturbances were noted in 1927 (Richards [1962] noted that this 1927 eruption was erroneously cited as occurring during 1937–1938 by Slevin [1959]) by members of an Allan Hancock expedition (Meredith, 1939). We suspect that the paucity of reef-building corals along the east coast of Fernandina is due in large part to the frequent volcanic disturbances on this island.

At least two coastal areas on Isabela Island have experienced frequent lava flows: the south shore of Elizabeth Bay and the northeast shore between Albemarle Point and Cape Marshall. Neither area was surveyed by us. The likelihood of substantial coral development in south Elizabeth Bay seems low considering the proximity of this area to EUC, upwelling and frequent (latest in 1979) disturbances from lava flows. Although the northeastern coastal area is in a favorable location relative to the EUC, we predict that the intensity and recency of the lava flows would have prevented significant coral colonization and growth in this area as well

Lava also poured into the sea at Santiago Island in 1904, but the location of this flow is unknown. The coral populations we observed on the north coast of Marchena appeared very youthful (highly dispersed and small colonies), perhaps indicative of recent but unrecorded lava flows at this site.

In summary, volcanism and upwelling appear to be the physical factors having the greatest effect on present-day coral distributions in the Galápagos with water turbulence, tectonic movements, and landslides also important at certain locations.

CHAPTER SIX

BIOLOGICAL INTERACTIONS

Until now our attention has been focused almost exclusively on how corals are affected by the physical environment. Physical environmental factors appear to influence the distribution of corals on a large scale (in terms of kilometers), for example, on particular islands within the archipelago or on sectors of shore of a given island. On a smaller scale (in terms of meters), as along a depth gradient or within particular communities, the distribution of corals seems to be determined less directly by physical environmental factors than by biological interactions.

One of the first adverse effects on coral we observed was the feeding of the club-spined sea urchin, *Eucidaris thouarsii*, on species of *Pocillopora* and other corals. Large numbers of the urchin, commonly more than thirty individuals per m² in certain bottom areas, were rasping live coral surfaces and ingesting both coral tissues and skeleton. This type of interaction, where animals feed directly on live corals, is referred to as predation (with certain qualifications, see below) and will be the first topic considered in this section. Predation is also defined to include omnivores and herbivores that feed on all or parts of other live organisms. Other kinds of biological interactions observed in the Galápagos and also considered in this section are (a) corallivore interference, (b) biotic disturbance, and (c) competition.

METHODS

The abundance of the club-spined sea urchin *Eucidaris* was determined from the numbers of individuals, counted in 0.25 m² quadrats, that were located by dropping the quadrat haphazardly from 1–2 m above the bottom, in different reef zones (shallow reef flat, slope, deep reef edge, and rubble-sand plain). Only urchins on or near the surface of the reef were counted because the destruction of corals is prohibited in Galapagan waters. In Panamá, rock and coral substrates were excavated and individual coral colonies were fragmented in order to expose the urchins.

Eucidaris test diameters (maximum diameters) were measured to the nearest mm with calipers and a rule. Urchins were first dried at 60°C (to a constant weight) and then dried briefly at 103°C (to drive off water of crystallization) to determine their mass.

The kinds of food consumed by *Eucidaris* were observed directly by noting the organisms on which the urchins were feeding (mucus strings were a useful sign of active feeding on corals), the abrasion marks on the feeding surface, the nature of particles between the urchin's teeth, and indirectly by the examination of gut contents.

Eucidaris were offered only live coral as food in laboratory aquariums in Panamá. Between twenty-five and twenty-eight urchins, collected from coral reefs in the Gulf of Chiriquí and ranging from 0.7–2.4 cm in test diameter, were placed in submerged bowls (12 cm diameter) in a tank supplied with continuously running seawater. The water was passed through polypropylene wool filters (100 microns or 140 mesh size, J. R. Bisho Company, Inc., San Francisco, California) to remove suspended particulate matter. A sprig of *Pocillopora damicornis,* 4–5 cm in length, was placed in each bowl containing an urchin. In one series of observations the urchins were allowed to move in and out of the bowls; in another, the urchins were confined to bowls containing a coral sprig by the placement of a plastic screen mesh tied across the mouth of the container. No shelter or structures were present in the tank other than the bowls (and plastic screen covers in some trials), corals, and a drain tube. In addition, the tank was scraped thoroughly beforehand, and intermittently during the observations, so that coral was the only food present. Each treatment was monitored at least twice daily for a period of one week. The feces produced by urchins confined to bowls (see below) was collected weekly, washed on a Millipore filter and dried (at 60°C and then briefly at 103°C) to constant weight. Empty bowls were used as controls to monitor the amount of nonfecal particulate matter settling from the water; this was found to be negligible.

To study the effects of corallivore grazing on the growth form of pocilloporid corals, colonies of *Pocillopora damicornis* and *P. capitata* were maintained in aquariums in Panamá in the absence or presence of the coral-eating pufferfish, *Arothron meleagris.* Ten colonies of each coral species were allowed to grow for periods ranging from two to three months in the absence or presence of the corallivore. Pufferfish were introduced (periodically one day per week); the corals realized a net gain in growth in spite of the presence of the fish.

Grain-size analyses were performed on the gut contents of *Eucidaris* and on surficial bottom sediments at the Onslow Island coral reef. Gut contents dissected from urchins were treated repeatedly with dilute sodium hypochlorite to remove organic matter. Bottom sediments were washed thoroughly with distilled water (avoiding loss of the finer particles) to remove salts. Samples were then dried to constant weight and sieved through eight screens ranging in mesh size from 2.00 mm (-1.00 ø) to 0.07 mm (3.75 ø). The phi (ø) scale is a logarithmic transformation of the Wentworth scale (mm). The particles were identified under a dissecting microscope up to $50 \times$ magnification.

Ingestion rates of coral and coralline algae by *Eucidaris* were determined by two methods: (a) urchins were removed while feeding from calcareous substrates and allowed to defecate for twenty-four hours; the dry mass of sediment produced (free of organic matter) was equated to one day's grazing; defecation occurred continuously, and some food still remained in the gut after twenty-four hours, and (b) urchins feeding on calcareous algae (far removed from coral) were placed on live coral and allowed to feed for twenty-four hours; the dry mass of coral grains (free of organic matter) dissected from the urchins' guts was equated to one day's grazing. The two methods produced similar results, in the range of 0.40–0.84 gm/individual/day. However, it is likely that these methods provide minimum grazing rates because feeding was interrupted. Further details can be found in Glynn et al. (1979).

The abundances of invertebrate corallivores other than *Eucidaris* were determined from the numbers observed in the sea urchin censuses and from the numbers observed on or near the surface of coral substrates. The under-surfaces of coral blocks and live colonies were examined when such substrates could be moved and replaced with minimal disturbance. Pufferfish were censused in coral communities by counting individuals over given time intervals while the observer was swimming.

Juvenile and adult *Eucidaris* were exposed to predation on open reef surfaces in the Galápagos and Panamá. Because the presence of a diver-observer (5–10 m distant) interfered with the feeding of fishes, the urchins were left on the bottom for periods of one to two hours before examination. Then the urchins were approached quietly from the surface. Urchins that found shelter were exposed again to predation. Observations were performed during the day and night.

Because the methods and materials varied greatly in the study of damselfish ejection behavior, the procedures are described below along with the results. The abundance of agonistic symbiotic crustaceans was determined by sampling six different colonies of *Pocillopora elegans*. Each colony was enclosed in a plastic bag at depth, dislodged, and then transported to the surface where the crustaceans were removed. The live corals were returned to the same area from which they were collected.

PREDATION

Feeding by many predators results in the death of the entire prey organism. However, predation of corals usually does not involve the death of the entire colony. Since at least some portions of corals usually remain after a feeding bout and are thus potentially capable of further reproduction, it is appropriate to distinguish between predators that kill and those that injure their prey. "Corallivores" will refer to the set of animals that feed on live corals; after feeding they typically leave behind live portions of the colony (Glynn et al., 1972). Some corallivores, however, notably the crown-of-thorns sea star *Acanthaster* (which is probably absent from the Galápagos at present), very often kill whole adult coral colonies. This is especially the case for small coral colonies. Also, the ovulid gastropod *Jenneria* will at times form dense aggregations on a single coral colony and kill the entire colony.

Generally it is possible to classify corallivores into three groups (Hiatt and Strasburg, 1960), depending on their manner of feeding and its effect on the colony: (a) "browsers" pass over corals lightly, feeding on living tissues only, without scraping the skeleton; (b) "grazers" feed on corals by abrading, scratching, or biting various parts of a colony; and (c) "croppers" break off the tips of branching corals. Grazers and croppers, therefore, remove both living tissues and skeleton. Skeletal particles, branches, branchtips, and knobs are the sorts of parts removed by grazing and cropping corallivores. The effects of grazing are often more destructive to the reef than those of browsing; although this is not true of the coral. However, in certain species such as *Acanthaster* and *Jenneria* (as noted above), intensive browsing can lead to complete colony death. Fourteen corallivore species were observed feeding, or were suspected of feeding at least occasionally, on live reef corals in the Galápagos: two echinoderms, four mollusks, two crustaceans, and six fishes.

Echinoderm Corallivores: The grazing of large numbers of *Eucidaris thouarsii* on live *Pocillopora* spp. is remarkable and possibly unique to the Galápagos environment (figs. 21 and 22). The only other echinoid known to feed naturally on live corals is *Diadema antillarum* Philippi in the Caribbean (Bak and van Eys, 1975), but the numbers involved (up to 8 percent of the population or 0.7 individual/m^2) are appreciably below those observed for *Eucidaris.* McPherson (cited in Lawrence, 1975) demonstrated a preference for animal food (a clionid sponge and mullet) by the Caribbean *Eucidaris tribuloides* (Lamarck) under laboratory conditions. A report on the impact of *Eucidaris* on coral communities in the Galápagos was published earlier (Glynn et al., 1979). Here we will summarize the salient features of the published report and elaborate on aspects of this work that have not yet received sufficient attention.

Galápagos *Eucidaris* attain extraordinary population densities, are large in size, occur on open surfaces, and move freely over the bottom while feeding during the day and night. Along the edges of *Pocillopora* patch reefs, *Eucidaris* is commonly present to the extent of twenty to fifty individuals per m^2 (fig. 23). Their numbers generally decline as live coral cover increases and as sand replaces live coral and coralline algae in deeper water. The lower abundance of urchins in areas with high coral cover, where the closely spaced vertical branches of *Pocillopora* form an almost flat (one-dimensional) table, possibly is due to the reduced number of crevices available for shelter in this habitat. Most of the urchins observed on the reef flat were present on the edges of holes or depressions in the coral framework. High population densities were typical of most areas in the Galápagos where pocilloporid corals were abundant. At Onslow, Pinta, and San Cristóbal, median urchin densities (and 0.95 confidence limits of the median, see footnote on page 39, with n = number of $0.25\ m^2$ quadrats) were respectively 34 (24–36, n = 40), 32 (24–36, n = 60), and 34 (24–48, n = 22). The Barrington Island patch reef, with a median density of 1.2 *Eucidaris* per m^2 (n = 4, 6.6 m^2 quadrats), was an exception, and the low numbers of urchins there might be related to the abundance of damselfishes at this site (see *Damselfish Ejection Behavior* under *Corallivore Interference* below). No *Eucidaris* were found in the *Pocillopora*-filled lava rock basins at Punta Espinosa, and they also appeared to be less abundant in the northern islands (Darwin and Wolf, 1975). Noncoral bottoms in the southern, central, and northern islands, such as rock paved with crustose coralline algae, often supported large populations of the urchin. However, on western island shores subject to upwelling, *Eucidaris* was uncommon to absent.

The test diameters of individuals from three populations of *Eucidaris* that were sampled in the Galápagos are illustrated in figure 55. These samples represent urchins that were largely visible to the collector. Modal test diameters ranged from 4.3–6.3 cm on the reef flat and deep reef flanks, respectively, at Onslow Island. Within the Onslow population, it is seen that the largest urchins occurred in deeper water (the two samples differed significantly at P < 0.001, Mann-Whitney U-test). Urchins from the Pinta and Bartolomé populations were intermediate in size compared to those at Onslow.

Eucidaris size distributions from two populations in Panamá are also shown in figure 55 for comparison. In Panamá, mainland Ecuador, Colombia, and Costa Rica, the urchins live secretively, wedged firmly within coral and rock. The modal sizes of *Eucidaris* found on coral reefs in Panamá, 0.7 –1.1 cm in test diameters, were considerably less than those in the Galápagos. Even the population with the largest urchins in Panamá, that at Paitilla where the urchins live in holes in hard rock, contained significantly smaller individuals (the two samples are nonoverlapping) than those on the reef flat at Onslow Island.

Limited sampling of population densities in comparable coral habitats indicated initially that *Eucidaris* was equally abundant in the Galápagos and Panamá (Glynn et al., 1979). The median density on the reef edge at Onslow was 34 individuals/m^2 (fig. 23) and in coral rubble on the reef edge (3–6 m) at Uva Island, Panamá (n = 6 quadrats) was 38 individuals/m^2 (P ⌐ 0.18, Mann-Whitney U-test). More extensive sampling in Panamá and Colombia indicates that *Eucidaris* is in general probably less numerous in mainland versus Galápagos coral communities. For example, in eighteen $0.25\ m^2$ quadrats obtained recently (22–23 May 1979) on a fringing reef at Gorgona Island,

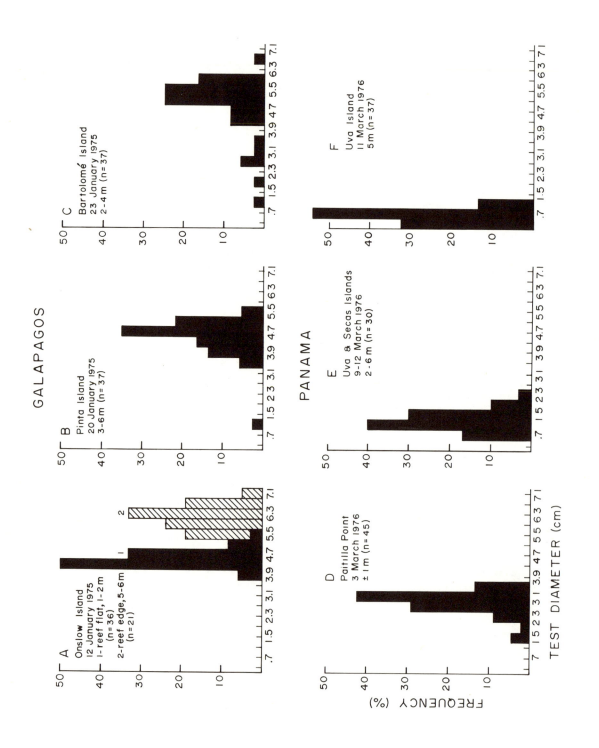

GALAPAGOS

PANAMA

A
Onslow Island
12 January 1975
1 - reef flat, 1 - 2 m
(n = 36)
2 - reef edge, 5 - 6 m
(n = 21)

B
Pinta Island
20 January 1975
3 - 6 m (n = 37)

C
Bartolomé Island
23 January 1975
2 - 4 m (n = 37)

D
Paitilla Point
3 March 1976
± 1 m (n = 45)

E
Uva & Secas Islands
9 - 12 March 1976
2 - 6 m (n = 30)

F
Uva Island
11 March 1976
5 m (n = 37)

TEST DIAMETER (cm)

FREQUENCY (%)

Colombia, *Eucidaris* abundances ranged from zero (in ten quadrats) to a maximum of 20 urchins/m² (Glynn et al., 1980). The sizes of the sea urchins, as in Panamá (see below), were small; the test diameters of most urchins were between 1–2 cm, and the size range was 0.4–4.1 cm. These numbers are more akin to those observed on the reef flat and are clearly less than those characteristic of the reef edge in the Galápagos (fig. 23). It is important to emphasize, moreover, that sampling in Panamá and Colombia was complete in the sense that it was permissible to break coral and thoroughly search the plots. The Galápagos samples must surely underestimate the numbers of smaller urchins, especially on bottom areas with high coral cover and relief.

As noted earlier, the prominence of club-spined urchins in Galápagos coral communities is remarkable. This is due to their abundance, noncryptic habit, and particularly to the bulk of individual urchins. Therefore, even if mainland and Galápagos urchin abundances are equal, the biomass of Galápagos urchins will exceed by far that on the mainland. We offer some calculations of the biomass of *Eucidaris* present in coral communities in the Galápagos, Panamá, and Colombia in order to demonstrate this difference in quantitative terms.

Regression curves relating urchin size and mass are shown in figure 56 for samples from the Galápagos and Panamá. Because the slopes differ significantly (P≪0.001, t-test), it is not possible to test for a difference in elevation or dry mass between the two linear regressions. It is permissible, however, to perform a t-test on the dry masses of Galápagos and Panamá urchins within the same size range (from 2.0–5.0 cm test diameter). Such a test indicates that Galápagos *Eucidaris* are greater in mass than Panamá *Eucidaris* of equal size (P≪0.001, t-test). Mean individual urchin masses for the Galápagos and Panamá respectively were 50.74 gm (n = 24) and 16.48 gm (n = 36). The greater mass of Galápagos urchins seems to be due to the skeleton more than to tissue; that is, the test and spines of Galápagos urchins appear thicker than those of Panamá urchins.

By applying the appropriate size/mass relationships to observed size-frequency distributions, it is possible to calculate estimates of urchin biomass as summarized in table 15. The differences in biomass of four samples from each region are clearly significant. The lowest biomass of *Eucidaris* on a Galápagos reef flat, where two urchins contributed 131 gm/m², is more than two times that of the highest biomass observed on a fringing reef in Colombia, where twenty urchins contributed 50 gm/m². At a median density of 34 urchins/m² on the reef edge, the biomass of *Eucidaris* in the Galápagos was 4.33 kg/m².

In the Galápagos, *Eucidaris* grazes chiefly on crustose coralline algae and

FIGURE 55. Size-class frequency distributions of *Eucidaris thouarsii* at three sites in the Galápagos Islands and on the Pacific coast and near-shore islands of Panamá. Urchin size is the maximum test diameter.

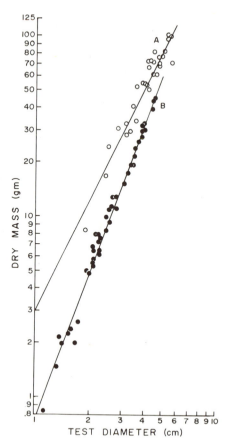

FIGURE 56. Linear (logarithmic) relationships between the test diameter and dry mass of *Eucidaris* from the Galápagos Islands (A) and Panamá (B). Test diameter is the maximum diameter and the mass was obtained by oven-drying the urchins to a constant dry weight. The Galápagos sample was collected in Academy Bay, 4 April 1976, and the Panamá sample was collected at Taboguilla Island, 28 June 1977. The sample size (n), estimated regression equation (natural logarithms), coefficient of determination (r^2), and significance level of the F-ratio for each population are, respectively: A - Galápagos Islands, n = 30, $\hat{Y} = 2.959\ X^{2.060}$, $r^2 = 0.917$, $p \ll 0.0005$; B - Panamá, n = 44, $\hat{Y} = 0.708\ X^{2.758}$, $r^2 = 0.984$, $p \ll .0005$.

reef-building corals. Urchins were frequently observed grazing on all species of *Pocillopora*, namely, *P. damicornis*, *P. elegans*, and *P. capitata*, and also on *Pavona clavus*. The fact that numerous urchins fed on the dead, and often algal-encrusted surfaces of *Porites lobata*, but never on this coral's tissues, suggests an active avoidance by *Eucidaris*. The most detailed feeding censuses were conducted on the Onslow Island patch reef inside the "crown." These demonstrated that from about one- to two-thirds of the *Eucidaris* sampled were, at any given time (day or night), feeding on live coral, primarily pocil-

TABLE 15. Estimated *Eucidaris* Biomass (Dry) in the Galápagos Islands and Mainland Eastern Pacific. Calculated from size-frequency distributions and regression curves relating size to mass.

Locality and Habitat	Number per m²	Biomass (gm)
Galápagos		
Onslow Island:		
Reef flat	2	131
	8	525
Reef edge	34	4,330
Pinta Island:		
Patch reef	8	534
Mainland eastern Pacific		
Panamá		
Paitilla Point:		
Rock, low intertidal zone	5	70
Uva Island:		
Reef edge	38	20[a]
Colombia		
Gorgona Island:		
Fringing reef	4	9
	20[b]	50

[a]Maximum estimate, allowing mass of 0.5 gm for all urchins < 1.0 cm in test diameter. The small urchins which dominated this sample lie outside of the range of the regression curve.
[b]Maximum number of urchins sampled; most plots contained considerably fewer urchins.

loporid corals. A single feeding census conducted on a pocilloporid patch reef at Cape Ibbetson, Pinta Island (20 January 1975, 0945–1030), indicated that fewer urchins were feeding on live coral there than at Onslow. Only 2.7 percent of the sample (n = 73 individuals), or two individuals, were feeding on live *Pocillopora*; the remainder were grazing on crustose coralline algae or not feeding.

Eucidaris rarely grazes on live coral in Panamá. No urchins have actually been observed feeding on live coral in the field, but the gut contents of occasional specimens contained fresh *Pocillopora* grains that may have been ingested alive. A few *Eucidaris* maintained in captivity also grazed heavily on a colony of the massive coral *Gardineroseris planulata*, but only after they were confined with the coral for over two months. Crustose coralline algae were also available. These observations prompted the question: Why are pocilloporid corals such an important dietary item of *E. thouarsii* in the Galápagos and not in Panamá? It is not likely that availability is a factor because *Pocillopora* is abundant in both areas. Some simple tests were designed to determine if Panamá *Eucidaris* would feed on *Pocillopora* under laboratory conditions.

Club-spined urchins were placed individually in open bowls (sub-merged in a large seawater tank) containing sprigs of live *Pocillopora*. The urchins moved seemingly at random inside and outside of the bowls. They did not show a close association with the coral, and no coral was grazed during the first week or subsequently in two replicates that spanned a total period of three weeks. This treatment was then modified by confining each urchin to a bowl (with plastic screen mesh tied across the mouth of the container) with a coral sprig. During the fourth week, after three weeks without feeding, the majority of the urchins began grazing; 60.0 percent (n = 25) had grazed on live *Pocillopora* by the end of the fourth week. By the end of the fifth week, 80.7 percent (n = 26, the extra individual was excluded from the previous treatment because it escaped from the bowl) of the urchins in the same population had fed on live coral. These observations demonstrate that *Eucidaris* in Panamá can also feed on live coral, although under quite artificial conditions, namely, when confined with coral in a no-choice situation and in the absence of predators.

The amount of coral-grit feces produced by the urchins showed a highly significant positive correlation ($\tau = 0.766$, $P \ll 0.00001$, Kendall rank correlation) with urchin size (fig. 57). Urchins not feeding or feeding only sparingly on coral were generally small in size with a test diameter ≤ 1.5 cm (dry mass < 2 gm). In order to test for a possible difference in the amount of coral eaten by urchins of different sizes, the twenty-seven urchins were divided into large and small groups above and below the median mass (1.79 gm). Their defecation rates were then adjusted (normalized) according to body mass (table 16). This adjustment indicates that small urchins had a median defecation rate of only 0.76 mg feces/gm urchin/day compared with large urchins whose median defecation rate was 3.95 mg feces/gm urchin/day. This is a statistically significant difference ($P \sim 0.001$, Mann-Whitney U-test), indicating that small urchins are ingesting disproportionately less coral than large urchins. These results suggest a size difference, where urchins must attain a certain size (about 2 gm dry weight or 1.5 cm test diameter) before they will feed on live coral in considerable amounts. The smallest *Eucidaris* observed feeding on coral in the Galápagos were also about 1.5 cm. Urchins smaller than this were secretive and presumably feeding on crustose coralline algae and other shade-tolerant organisms. It should be noted, however, that else-where some juvenile echinoids (< 1 cm) feed heavily on organisms with calcareous skeletons. Some urchin species in temperate waters have been reported to consume significant amounts of calcareous algae (Kawamura and Taki, 1965) and bryozoans (Elmhirst, 1922) when young, and later to include proportionately more fleshy algae and other items in their diets.

These differences in the feeding preferences of Galápagos and mainland *Eucidaris,* including the associated differences in concealment and diel activities mentioned earlier, illustrate some of the variations in behavior that are possible in geographically separated species populations and how they can lead to significant effects at the ecological level. Although *E. thouarsii* from the

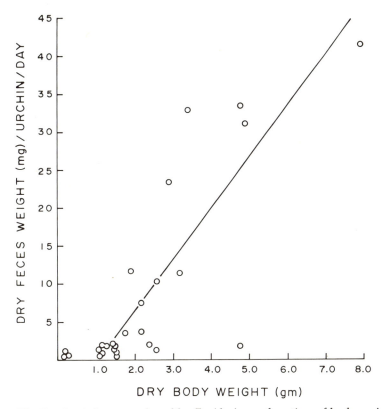

FIGURE 57. Coral grit feces produced by *Eucidaris* as a function of body weight. Body weights were calculated from test diameters according to the linear-mass relationship for Panamá in figure 56. The estimated regression equation is $\hat{Y} = -7.8 + 7.1\ X$. Approximate curve fit after the method of Brown and Mood (1951).

Galápagos is indistinguishable morphologically from those elsewhere in the eastern Pacific (Clark, 1925), it is possible that genetic divergence has occurred and is responsible for these differences.

An immediate result of *Eucidaris* grazing on live coral is the blanched and abraded surface left on the corallum after a feeding bout. Steady grazing on the branchtips of *Pocillopora* alters the growth form of the coral. Colonies growing in the presence of corallivores generally have clavate or flaring terminal branches. When these same colonies are allowed to grow in the absence of grazing corallivores, thin branchlets form on the summits of terminal branches (*Pocillopora damicornis*) or verrucae become more numerous on exposed peripheral branches (*Pocillopora capitata*). Examples of these effects are illustrated in figures 1 and 2 in the appendix. It should be noted that certain physical influences can also have an effect on the growth form of *Pocillopora*. An example of this is the shallow-occurring population of pocilloporid corals, with strongly clavate terminal branches, in the lava basins at

TABLE 16. Rate of Coral Grit Feces Produced by Small and Large Panamanian *Eucidaris* Supplied with Live Coral *(Pocillopora)* for Food. Urchin test diameters were converted to body weights according to the linear-mass relationship for Panamá in figure 56.

	Small Urchins		Large Urchins	
	Body Mass (gm)	Feces Mass (mg/gm urchin/day)	Body Mass (gm)	Feces Mass (mg/gm urchin/day)
	0.23	0	1.94	6.00
	0.23	3.44	2.25	1.64
	0.33	0	2.25	3.26
	1.12	0	2.46	0.83
	1.15	1.19	2.55	0.48
	1.25	0.53	2.59	3.95
	1.25	1.37	2.97	7.78
	1.31	1.33	3.26	3.50
	1.40	1.31	3.37	9.75
	1.49	0.76	4.79	0.34
	1.49	0.92	4.79	6.97
	1.62	0	4.93	6.29
	1.62	0.49	7.93	5.29
Median	1.25	0.76	2.97	3.95

Punta Espinosa. Corallivores are rare or absent from this habitat and the flaring growth form, which appears to be due to cropping, is probably a response to physical stress from the frequent subaerial exposures occurring at this location.

If damage caused by grazing is extensive and regeneration of the coral fails to cover the bare area, the latter can be colonized by a variety of sessile species. We observed the branchtips of numerous colonies of *Pocillopora* overgrown by barnacles (*Megabalanus galapaganus*) and crustose coralline algae. Crustose coralline algae most frequently invaded the bare areas produced by *Eucidaris* grazing on massive *Pavona* colonies. Adult *Pocillopora* normally are not killed by *Eucidaris* because, for mechanical reasons, the relatively large urchins cannot enter into the more central areas of the thickly branching colonies. Grazing is primarily confined to the outer branchtips. Colony death would result only if grazing were intense and prolonged, outstripping regeneration and coral growth, or if grazing were directed onto juvenile corals.

Whether or not *Eucidaris* grazes on live or dead coral, coralline algae, or whatever encrusting forms it encounters, the urchins inevitably generate sediments when feeding on a calcareous substrate. Food dissected from the guts of urchins grazing on coral and coralline algae contained skeletal grains chiefly in the size range of coarse (0.84 mm) to very coarse (2.00 mm) sand (fig. 58). Sediment resulting from the abrasion of *Pocillopora* was coarser than

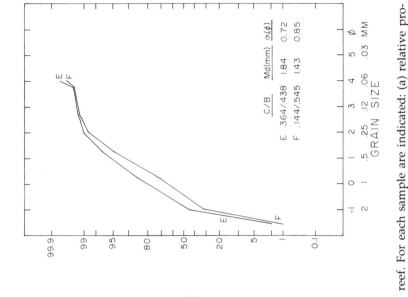

FIGURE 58. Sediment grain size distributions (cumulative probability curves) of gut contents of ten *Eucidaris* after removal of organic matter (A, 11 February 1975; B, 21 March 1975; C, 2 April 1975; and D, 21 March 1975) and in bottom samples in the *Psammocora* (E, 3 m depth, 12 January 1975) and *Pocillopora* (F, 1 m depth, 12 January 1975) zones, Onslow Island

reef. For each sample are indicated: (a) relative proportion of coral (C) and coralline algae (CA) or coral and barnacle parts (B), based on compositional analysis of 0.25 ϕ (0.84 mm) grain class; (b) median grain size (Md); and (c) σ_I, the Inclusive Graphic Standard Deviation (after Stoddart, 1978). The number of particles counted in each sample was ≥ 165.

that produced by the abrasion of crustose coralline algae. The coral skeleton breaks down at a comparatively large size, resulting in cubical or blocklike grains; the algal skeleton typically breaks down into platy or flaky grains. This difference in grain size is evident in a shift downward, in the direction of reduced median grain diameter (Md), as the proportion of calcareous algae in the gut increases (compare A and B with C and D, fig. 58). Gut contents with 80.5 percent coral (in the 0.25 ø or 0.84 mm size class) disclosed a median particle diameter of 1.78 mm that declined steadily to 1.09 mm in urchins with only 2.3 percent coral.

The dispersion in grain-size distribution is approximated by σ_1, the Inclusive Graphic Standard Deviation, which measures the degree of sorting. Sorting of the gut contents, bearing in mind that *Eucidaris* is the source of this particular class of sediment, was not especially high, ranging from 1.16 ø in A (poorly sorted) to 1.48 ø in D (poorly sorted). Neither was sorting high in sediments in Panamá generated by a cropping pufferfish (*Arothron*, ø = 1.09, poorly sorted) and by grazing hermit crabs (*Aniculus*, ø = 0.99, moderately sorted, and *Trizopagurus*, ø = 1.54, poorly sorted) (Glynn et al., 1972). Nonetheless, the median grain-sizes generated by these corallivores were sufficiently well separated (4.0 mm, 0.8 mm, and 0.4 mm, respectively) to allow a reasonable identification of the contributing source organisms.

Bottom samples from surface sediments at Onslow were also composed dominantly of coarse to very coarse calcareous sands (fig. 58, E and F). However, these samples were dominated by barnacle fragments, with coral grains ranking second in abundance. Panamá reef sediments also typically contain a high proportion of barnacle skeletal grains. In the Pearl Islands, Panamá, sediments surrounding a pocilloporid fringing reef contained from 10 percent to nearly 30 percent barnacle grains (Glynn et al., 1972). It appears that barnacle remains are much more abundant on coral bottoms in the eastern Pacific than in the reef sediments thus far reported in the western Atlantic and Indo-Pacific provinces (Stoddart, 1969a; Orme, 1977). Since barnacles are filter feeders it is reasonable to assume that they would prosper and contribute significantly to reef sediments in areas of high productivity, such as in the eastern Pacific (Highsmith, 1980; see chapter 4, *Coral Growth: Bioerosion*).

Although *Eucidaris* was not observed preying directly on live adult barnacles, they did frequently graze the outer skeletal surfaces of live and dead barnacles, and must therefore, in this manner, contribute toward the breakdown of this class of organisms. Known barnacle predators at Onslow include the asteroid *Heliaster cumingii* and the thaidid gastropod *Thais planospira*, both of which prey on the large and common barnacle *Megabalanus galapaganus*. The empty cups eventually may be eroded by echinoid and fish grazers and by various mechanical processes. It is reasonable to assume that *Eucidaris* is the chief generator of barnacle grains at Onslow by virtue of its abundance and intense grazing activities and the close correspondence in the size of ingested and surrounding bottom sediments. The hermit crab

TABLE 17. Calculated Amounts of Calcareous Sand Generated by *Eucidaris* on the Onslow Island Coral Reef.

Reef Section	Area (m²)[a]	Number of *Eucidaris*[b]	Sed./Day[c] (kg)	Sed./Year (tons)
Reef flat and shallow slope, nearly continuous *Pocillopora* cover, 1–2.5 m	7,200	36,000	18.0	6.6
Reef edge, scattered *Pocillopora*, 3–5 m	1,600	54,400	27.2	9.9
Total				16.5

[a]Determined from the base community map of Onslow Island, figure 18.
[b]Based on a population density of 5 urchins/m² for the reef flat, and 34 urchins/m² for the reef edge, figure 23.
[c]Calculated on basis of mean sediment defecation rate, including coral and calcareous algae, of 0.5 gm/individual/day (after Glynn et al., 1979).

grazer *Aniculus*, which also produces sediment in the 0.8 mm size grade, was not common on the Onslow reef (see below).

In light of the considerable impact of *Eucidaris* on carbonate substrates, it is of interest to examine in quantitative terms the contribution of the urchin toward the generation of sediments in a reef environment. Data on the numbers of urchins present on the two principal sections of the Onslow Island reef are summarized in table 17. On the basis of these urchin abundances, and a mean ingestion rate of 0.5 gm (dry weight) of coral skeleton per urchin per day (Glynn et al., 1979), calculated sediment generation rates were 6.6 and 9.9 metric tons per year respectively for the reef flat/shallow slope and reef edge section of the Onslow reef. Total estimated sediment production was 16.5 tons per annum for the immediate reef unit of 0.88 ha area or 18.8 tons per ha per annum. This is probably a conservative estimate because it does not take into account (a) all urchins, especially those present deep in the reef frame, and (b) skeletal carbonates broken down, but not ingested, by the feeding activities of grazing urchins. (This latter source of sediment production is probably not great, judging from the small amounts observed in urchins feeding on coral in aquariums.) Because the gut contents of urchins grazing on reef surfaces represented freshly abraded coralline algae and coral, all of the sediment recovered was treated as new material eroded from the reef.

The generation of new carbonate sediments by *Eucidaris* in the Galápagos, at a rate of 18.8 metric tons/ha/yr or 1.9 kg/m²/yr, is nearly three times the combined rate of sediment production (0.64 kg/m²/yr) due to a gastropod (*Jenneria*), hermit crabs (*Trizopagurus* and *Aniculus*), and fish (*Arothron*) corallivores on a patch reef in Panamá (table 18). Near the center of the Onslow Island (Galápagos) reef, where coral cover is high (60 percent to 80 percent of the planar surface), *Eucidaris* can reduce the gross $CaCO_3$ production of coral in this habitat (7–9 kg/m²/yr) by 10 percent to 20 percent (Glynn et al., 1979).

TABLE 18. New Sediment Production by Invertebrate and Fish Grazers on Carbonate Reef Substrates.

Locality	Species	Numerical and Biomass Abundance[a]	Habitat	New Sediment Production (kg/m²/yr)	Authority
Galápagos Islands (Pacific), Onslow Island	*Eucidaris thouarsii*	34 individuals/m² (Md)	Deep reef edge	1.9	Glynn et al., 1979; this study
		2–8 individuals/m² (Md)	Reef flat		
Panamá (Pacific), Pearl Islands, Gulf of Panamá	*Jenneria pustulata*[b]	1.4 individuals/m² (Md)	Patch reef, all zones	0.51	Glynn et al., 1972
	Trizopagurus magnificus	24.2 individuals/m² (Md)	Patch reef, all zones	0.10 ⎫ 0.64	
	Aniculus elegans	0.01 individuals/m²(Md)	Patch reef, all zones	0.01 ⎬	
	Arothron meleagris	40 individuals/ha (T)	Patch reef, all zones	0.02 ⎭	
Panamá (Caribbean), San Blas Islands	*Scarus croicensis* Bloch	6,000 individuals/ha (T) 4.7 gm/m²	Patch reef	0.5	Ogden, 1977
St. Croix (Caribbean), U.S. Virgin Islands	*Diadema antillarum* Philippi	87,500 individuals/ha 8.8 individuals/m² (T)	Patch reef	4.6	Ogden, 1977
	Echinometra lucunter (Linnaeus)	100 individuals/m² (x̄)	Algal ridge	3.9	
Barbados (Caribbean)	*Diadema antillarum*	23 individuals/m² (x̄)	Fringing reef	5.3	Scoffin et al., 1980
	Sparisoma viride (Bonnaterre)	0.43 gm/m² (x̄)		0.034[c]	

[a]Md = median, T = total number of individuals censused or estimated present, x̄ = mean.

[b]The gastropod *Jenneria* is a browser; when several individuals kill a colony of *Pocillopora* the coral skeleton is not immediately eroded but becomes a part of the reef sediments (or is incorporated into the reef frame) without a loss in size.

[c]The sediment production value given for *Sparisoma viride* is derived from Frydl (1977). It should be noted that this refers only to sediment produced at the Northern Bellairs Reef (or fringing reef-north lobe in Frydl's thesis). For the entire reef, Frydl calculated that *S. viride* produces 0.168 kg of sediment/m²/yr—a value five times that reported by Scoffin et al. (1980).

On the reef edge, where coral cover $\leq$ 30 percent and $CaCO_3$ production by corals $\leq$ 3 kg/m^2/yr, urchins are especially abundant ($\sim$ 40 individuals/m^2) resulting in zero coral growth. Thus, urchins impede horizontal reef growth along the deep reef edge. Corallivore activities on the patch reef in Panamá appeared to affect all portions of the reef equally, with cropping and mortality reducing the annual $CaCO_3$ production of corals on the entire reef (5.1 kg/m^2/yr) by about one-third. On reefs in Panamá (Gulf of Chiriquí), where *Acanthaster* is present at a population density of 26 individuals/ha, annual coral production (6.7 kg/m^2/yr, Glynn, 1977) is reduced by about 15 percent by this corallivore alone (Glynn, 1973).

Because coral reefs in the eastern Pacific are apparently subject to a greater range and intensity of corallivore activities than reefs in the Caribbean (Glynn et al., 1972; Glynn, in press), it is of interest to compare the rates of new sediment production among reef carbonate grazers in the two regions (table 18). While certain fish and urchin grazers generate large amounts of new sediment on Caribbean reefs—the urchins *Diadema antillarum* and *Echinometra lucunter* (Linnaeus) produce two to three times (Ogden, 1977) the amount of sediment produced by *Eucidaris* in the Galápagos (Glynn et al., 1979)—it is important to realize that most of the carbonate breakdown in the Caribbean involves dead coral. The algae associated with dead coral substrates (epibenthic and endolithic species) are the main items sought by Caribbean grazers. Some Caribbean parrotfishes and urchins do occasionally feed directly on live coral, but not to the extent that live coral is attacked by corallivores in the Pacific. At Onslow Island, for example, 52 percent of the *Eucidaris* population was found grazing on live coral during both the day and night. In Curaçao, 4.5 percent to 8.2 percent of a *Diadema* population was observed grazing on live coral only at night (Bak and van Eys, 1975). In St. Croix (Ogden, 1977) and Barbados (Scoffin et al., 1980), *Diadema* was rarely observed grazing on live coral.

Even though Caribbean grazers feed mainly on dead coral surfaces, their activities lead to the weakening of colonies through excavation and undercutting, and in time the affected corals fragment, collapse, and often die (Scoffin et al., 1980). Thus, it is evident that grazing in the Caribbean does play a significant role in coral reef development, but because it is largely directed toward dead carbonate surfaces its effects are perhaps less obvious than in the Pacific. It is also important to bear in mind that browsers, while they do not erode coral skeletons directly, produce dead coral surfaces that are more readily attacked by grazers and bioeroders (MacGeachy and Stearn, 1976; Scoffin et al., 1980; Highsmith, 1981).

The asteroid browser *Nidorellia armata* was also observed feeding on live coral in the Galápagos. Chesher (1972) noted that *Nidorellia* is a coral predator, but did not give any specific information on its diet. In Panamá, *Nidorellia* feeds on sponges and possibly algae but has never been observed feeding on live coral. In the Galápagos, the starfish was found feeding on several occasions, with stomach everted, on large (0.5–1 m diameter) colonies of *Pavona clavus.* Since the coral colonies attacked were usually large, the feeding scars small (2–5 cm in diameter), and the starfish not abundant (usually < 1 per m^2 in areas with coral), browsing by *Nidorellia* amounted to only minimal coral death. The greatest observable effect was the creation of small dead patches on *Pavona* that could presumably serve as local colonization sites for algae and various benthic animals.

The crown-of-thorns sea star *Acanthaster planci* (Linnaeus), which feeds almost exclusively on reef-building corals in Panamá (Glynn, 1976) and elsewhere in the eastern Pacific (Glynn, 1974*a*), has not been observed in the Galápagos Islands. *Pharia pyramidata* (Gray), another sea star that preys on *Pocillopora* corals at certain mainland localities (in the Gulf of California [Dana and Wolfson, 1970] and at Machalilla, Ecuador [personal observations]), is present in the Galápagos but was not seen feeding on coral.

Molluscan Corallivores: *Jenneria pustulata* (Lightfoot), an ovulid gastropod mollusk, is a specialist on corals, preying on pocilloporid corals and on small ahermatypic corals in Panamá (Glynn et al., 1972). *Jenneria* is uncommon in the Galápagos Islands, and only a few individuals have been observed. In contrast, *Jenneria* was always present in coral communities at various sites sampled in Panamá and Colombia (Glynn et al., 1980) where densities commonly ranged between 4 and 20–40 snails/m^2 at any particular site censused extensively.

Three additional gastropods that are closely associated with species of *Pocillopora,* living amongst the coral branches, are *Muricopsis zeteki* Hertlein and Strong, *Latiaxis (Babelomurex) hindsii,* and *Quoyula madreporarum* (Sowerby). These species are present in the Galápagos and the first two were observed browsing on live coral in groups of two to five snails per colony. However, no more than 10 percent of the surface of any given colony had been killed by these snails. The amount of live tissue damage caused by *Quoyula* is unknown, but appears to be largely confined to the point of attachment and is thus not great (Robertson, 1970). It is possible that colony collapse could result from the excavation of numerous *Quoyula* in the basal branches of *Pocillopora,* but this has not been observed.

Crustacean Corallivores: The two hermit crab corallivores *Trizopagurus magnificus* and *Aniculus elegans* Stimpson, which occasionally graze on the peripheral branches of *Pocillopora* in Panamá (Glynn et al., 1972), were not universally abundant in pocilloporid coral communities in the Galápagos Islands. Both species were observed in live *Pocillopora* colonies at Punta Pitt, San Cristóbal Island. It is possible that the hermits at Punta Pitt were scraping and ingesting live coral, although we did not observe this directly.

Fish Corallivores: While several fish species feed on live coral at least occasionally, or accidentally while preying on other organisms associated with coral, few fishes in the eastern Pacific rely predominantly on a live coral diet. The most noteworthy fish corallivore is *Arothron meleagris,* which usually crops *Pocillopora* (Glynn et al., 1972) and sometimes grazes on massive corals *(Porites)* as well (Porter in Vermeij, 1978). A few individuals of this pufferfish were observed cropping *Pocillopora* at three localities, namely, the Punta Pitt area, near Xarifa Island in Gardner Bay (Española Island) and the Punta Boquerizo area (Santiago Island). *Arothron meleagris,* however, was not present at these sites or elsewhere in the Galápagos at the population densities observed in mainland coral communities. Censuses carried out at Punta Pitt, Gardner Bay, and Punta Boquerizo disclosed *A. meleagris* abundances of 1.3 individuals/MH (man-hour), 1.0 individuals/MH, and 2.5 individuals/MH, respectively. In comparable coral habitats at Gorgona Island, Colombia, nine censuses revealed a median abundance of 6.0 individuals/MH (Glynn et al., 1980). Twenty-four puffers/MH were observed in two censuses at Gorgona. Thus, the relatively low level of cropping by this puffer probably has only a slight impact on Galápagos pocilloporid corals.

Arothron hispidus (Linnaeus) is more catholic in its feeding habits than *A. meleagris.* In addition to cropping corals *(Pocillopora),* this pufferfish also feeds heavily on sponges, polychaetous annelids, crustaceans, and other items (Glynn et al., 1972). More recently in Panamá it was observed cropping *Psammocora stellata* and feeding on encrusting tunicates. Like its congener, *A. hispidus* is also relatively uncommon in the Galápagos compared to mainland localities. Therefore, its effect on corals is probably even less than that of *A. meleagris.*

Some chaetodontids or butterfly fishes are notorious corallivores, feeding frequently, and in certain cases obligately, on coral mucus and polyps (Hobson, 1974; Reese, 1977; Neudecker, 1977, 1979). Though four Panamic chaetodontids occur in the Galápagos, only one, *Heniochus nigrirostris* (Gill) feeds on live coral in the eastern Pacific region. *Heniochus nigrirostris* was seen feeding by one of us (GMW) on the exposed tissues of *Pavona gigantea* in the Pearl Islands, Gulf of Panamá.

While several species of parrotfishes (Scaridae) undoubtedly graze on live coral at least occasionally (Randall, 1974), more often than not the feeding scars (usually paired furrows) found on corals are only assumed to be due to parrotfishes. In the absence of direct observation, it must be borne in mind that *Arothron* also grazes on live massive corals and produces scars that are similar in form to those left by scarids.

Our observations indicate that *Scarus ghobban, Scarus perrico,* and *Scarus rubroviolaceus* probably all occur commonly in coral habitats throughout the Galápagos Islands. While feeding scars (ca. 2-cm-long nicks) were frequently observed on massive corals in these areas, no parrotfishes were actually seen feeding on live coral. Since the three scarids were implicated in grazing live coral in Panamá (Glynn et al., 1972), it is likely that they are to some extent responsible for the scars observed on massive corals in the Galápagos. Even so, excessive scarring of *Porites lobata*, *Pavona clavus*, and *Pavona gigantea*, to the extent of forming dead patches, was rare. In addition, the affected coral surfaces appeared to be undergoing complete regeneration.

The importance of damselfish and their ecological significance on coral reefs is becoming evident. It has now been abundantly demonstrated that many species of damselfish maintain territories on reefs (e.g., Low, 1971; Vine, 1974; Brawley and Adey, 1977; Kaufman, 1977). These territories typically contain a high biomass of algae (and for this reason are termed algal mats or algal gardens) compared with adjacent bottom areas. The reason for this is that other herbivorous fishes (e.g., parrotfishes and surgeonfishes) and invertebrates (e.g., sea urchins and snails) are largely excluded by the damselfish, which are the principal consumers of the plant cover in the territory.

One of the results of the establishment of algal mats is the inhibition of settlement by coralline algae and various sessile invertebrates including corals (Vine, 1974; Potts, 1977). This is because many slow-growing benthic forms cannot keep pace with, and are outcompeted by, fast-growing algae (Dart, 1972; Birkeland, 1977). However, the abundance and diversity of small, motile invertebrates such as crustaceans, brittle stars, and worms, can be high within algal mats compared with surrounding areas (Lobel, 1980). It has also been shown that some damselfish increase the area of their territory by biting and killing portions of living corals (Kaufman, 1977; Wellington, 1982*b*). Thus, damselfish activities reduce live coral cover in two ways: (a) by promoting abundant algal growth with which juvenile corals have difficulty competing, and (b) by directly killing corals.

The latter phenomenon of direct killing has been observed on Pacific reefs in Panamá (Wellington, 1982*b*). Here, coral killing is chronic and differential with respect to species—massive corals, especially *Pavona*, suffer high mortality compared to branching *Pocillopora* species. This has an important effect in regulating the vertical zonation patterns of corals in Panamá. Surprisingly, coral killing by damselfish does not appear to occur on Galápagos reefs. The culpable species in Panamá is *Eupomacentrus acapulcoensis* (Fowler). This damselfish is rare or absent in the Galápagos, and *E. arcifrons* and *E. beebei* predominate instead.

Coral Reef Herbivores: The important role of fish and invertebrate herbivores on coral reefs has been amply demonstrated over the past two decades. It is highly probable that the pervasive grazing of parrotfishes, surgeonfishes, damselfishes, and sea urchins has a greater impact on reef corals than the direct consumption of corals by corallivores. Field experiments have demonstrated conclusively that if fish and urchin herbivores are excluded from reef surfaces, then the treated areas are quickly overgrown by algae

(Stephenson and Searles, 1960; Randall, 1961; Earle, 1972; Ogden et al., 1973; Sammarco et al., 1974; Vine, 1974; Birkeland, 1977; Wanders, 1977; Brock, 1979).

Algal turfs and frondose algae proliferate in the absence of grazers resulting in the exclusion of the low-growing and slower-growing forms, such as crustose coralline algae, corals, and prostrate colonial animals. There is some evidence indicating that the sediment trapped in algal mats also has a detrimental effect on young corals (Potts, 1977). Frequent grazing tends to limit the growth of algae and thus provides open surfaces for the colonization and subsequent growth of corals and crustose coralline algae. It is likely that many corals recently settled onto open surfaces are incidentally damaged and killed by grazers. Survivorship is probably higher among young corals that settle on inaccessible sites with adequate illumination, such as in fissures, depressions, and surfaces beneath overhanging projections. However, Birkeland (1977) has shown that parrotfish in the Caribbean (Panamá) graze around juvenile corals without touching or damaging them. Elsewhere in the Caribbean (Curaçao; Bak and Engel, 1979) and in the western Pacific (Guam; Neudecker, 1979), fish grazers have been observed killing juvenile corals.

This herbivore effect adds another dimension to the development of coral communities. We considered earlier the relationship between upwelling and the occurrence of macrophytic algal communities. If the abundances of warm-water fish and urchin herbivores are reduced in cool-water environments then this will favor the proliferation of algae, as nutrient enrichment accompanying upwelling would promote algal growth. Fish herbivores did not appear to be so plentiful in upwelling areas in the Galápagos, for example, in exposed sites on the western coast of Isabela, as they were in protected areas with coral communities. In general, tropical waters do seem to support a greater variety and abundance of fish herbivores than do temperate waters (Bakus, 1969). More data are needed before the effects of urchin herbivores can be compared in warm and cool-water environments.

Fish Predators of *Eucidaris*: The apparent low level of fish predation on *Eucidaris* (and other echinoids) in the Galápagos is probably an important factor in accounting for the high abundance and noncryptic habits of adult urchins in this region. We never observed adult *Eucidaris* being eaten by fish. However, juvenile (< 1.0 cm test diameter) *Eucidaris* removed from coral and placed on the reef bottom in the open were sometimes eaten by the Mexican hogfish *Bodianus diplotaenia* (Gill). Both juvenile and adult *Eucidaris* similarly exposed on coral reefs in Panamá (Gulf of Chiriquí) were quickly attacked by triggerfish and puffers.

In Panamá, within one to two hours after placing several groups of ten adult *Eucidaris* on the bottom (2–4 cm test diameter, and spaced linearly ca. 1 m apart), from one to three individuals were usually broken open and often two to three of the remainder would have their spines broken off. Upon approaching the exposed urchins quietly from the surface (without scuba), it was found that the triggerfish *Sufflamen verres* (Gilbert and Starks) and the puffer *Arothron meleagris* were the most frequent predators. Both fishes were observed biting at the urchins and removing soft parts from broken tests. The puffer was actually seen biting off the spines and then breaking open the test with its strong beaklike teeth. All urchin predation took place during the day and crepuscularly.

On other occasions, adult *Eucidaris* (3–4 cm test diameter) have been hand-fed to the puffer *Arothron hispidus* on coral reefs in Panamá. Juvenile *Eucidaris* (≤ 1 cm) were crushed whole by *A. hispidus*; adult urchins were first divested of several spines and then the test was crushed. Other triggerfishes that feed on *Eucidaris* are *Pseudobalistes naufragium* (Jordan and Starks) and *Balistes polylepis* Steindachner. On several occasions in the Pearl Islands, Panamá, *P. naufragium* was observed crushing large *Eucidaris*. The skeletal remains of *Eucidaris* sometimes occur in the middens of *P. naufragium* in the Pearl Islands.

Adult urchins exposed in the Galápagos did not seek concealment immediately. Urchins exposed in Panamá buried themselves in coral rubble or became lodged in the reef framework before the end of each observation period (in one to two hours). It seems reasonable to postulate that the strong concealment behavior demonstrated by mainland *Eucidaris* evolved in response to the high levels of predation observed in Panamá as compared with the Galápagos Islands. All of the pufferfish, triggerfish, and wrasse predators of *Eucidaris* are present at both localities, but there are obvious differences in their abundances (see *Fish Corallivores*). Pufferfishes and triggerfishes, with the possible exception of *Sufflamen verres*, are not numerous in the Galápagos. It is tempting to speculate that the abundance of sharks in the Galápagos (see e.g., Barlow, 1972) especially the Galápagos shark, *Carcharhinus galapagoensis* Snodgrass and Heller, might be responsible for the generally low standing stock of reef fishes that prey on sea urchins.

CORALLIVORE INTERFERENCE

The interactions herein considered are potentially more complex than a one-to-one predator-prey situation because they involve the insertion of additional species that may impede or prevent predation. We will examine here the possible role of (a) damselfishes in defending corals from attack by corallivores (notably *Eucidaris* and *Nidorellia*) and (b) the crustacean symbionts of *Pocillopora* in defending their coral host from *Eucidaris*.

Damselfish Ejection Behavior: As mentioned above, damselfish defend their algal mats from herbivorous competitors. The defending damselfish chase other fishes away (that is, conspecifics as well as congeneric and more distantly related species) or use their mouths to grasp slow-moving invertebrates that they expel from their territories. It is possible that damselfish may protect corals adjacent to their territories by preventing entry of omnivorous corallivores (e.g., *Eucidaris*). This possibility was suggested after observations were made on the *Pocillopora* patch reef at the northeastern anchorage of Santa Fe Island.

As stated earlier in the descriptive section (chapter 3, *Nature and Distribution of Coral Communities and Coral Reefs*), the Santa Fe reefs and coral communities contained small numbers of *Eucidaris* but high abundances of two damselfish species. This prompted us to collect sea urchins from the surrounding bottom area and to place them on various substrates in order to observe the outcome. Unexpectedly, within a matter of seconds, damselfishes grasped nearly all of the *Eucidaris* by their spines and ejected them from their territories. Urchins too large to be lifted by the damselfish were dragged and rolled along the bottom. The urchins were generally moved over distances of 0.5–2 m and were then ignored only after ejection from a given territory. Urchins that fell into holes or that became lodged in the coral framework were also subsequently ignored. This ejection behavior was then examined and quantified in terms of its intensity and specificity to other species and inanimate objects.

The test procedure involved placing different objects on the summits of live *Pocillopora* within damselfish territories (mostly *P. elegans* with some *P. damicornis*) simultaneously between 5–10 cm apart, and then noting the order of removal. These activities were viewed at a distance of 1.5–2.0 m and the observation time for each trial was fifteen or twenty seconds. The eight sets of observations, and their respective replicates, all involved different individual damselfish. However, the two damselfish species that participated in this behavior, *Eupomacentrus arcifrons* and *E. beebei*, were not identified for each trial. D. R. Robertson repeated some of these observations at Academy Bay and did record the responses of the two damselfishes (personal communication). Robertson's procedure involved placing one urchin on an algal mat and then observing the response for up to three minutes. Each replicate involved a different fish. Tables 19 and 20 summarize the results of our observations (13–14 February 1976) and those of Robertson (15 August 1976), respectively.

The rationale behind the experiments was (a) to quantify the strength of the ejection response to *Eucidaris*, and (b) to compare the intensity of the ejection response to an inanimate object and to various species that may pose varying degrees of harm to a damselfish's territory.

In experiment 1 (table 19), the objects ejected or not ejected in twenty seconds were tallied without regard to the order in which they were ejected. Of the four objects tested, *Eucidaris* was removed in every instance (100 percent ejection), the coral rock in less than one-half of the trials (43 percent), the sea urchin *Lytechinus semituberculatus* in 1 percent of the trials, and the snail

TABLE 19. Ejection of Various Objects from Live *Pocillopora* Coral by the Territorial Damselfishes *Eupomacentrus arcifrons* and *E. beebei*, Santa Fe Island.

Experiment	No. of Trials	Time (sec.)	Objects[a] (size cm)[b]	Ejections[c]		Not Ejected
				Ejected		
				First	Second	
1. Four objects presented 4 at a time; sea urchins and coral rock equal in size, snail ca. ½ size of above	14	20	*Eucidaris* (6–10)	14	—	0
			Coral rock (8)	6	—	8
			Lytechinus (5–9)	1	—	13
			Cerithium (3.5)	0	—	14
2. Two objects presented pairwise; small sea urchin versus large coral rock	11	20	*Eucidaris* (2.4–7.5)	10*	1**	0
			Coral rock (12.8)	1*	9**	1
3. Two objects presented pairwise; sea urchin and coral rock equal in size	12	20	*Eucidaris* (12.8)	10*	0**	2
			Coral rock (12.8)	0*	10**	2
4. Two objects presented pairwise; small versus large sea urchins	12	20	*Eucidaris* (1.4–3.6)	12*	0**	0
			Eucidaris (3.0–7.6)	0*	10**	2
5. Two objects presented pairwise; two different sea urchins of equal size	14	20	*Eucidaris* (3.0–7.6)	12*	2**	0
			Lytechinus (6.2)	2*	6**	6
6. Two objects presented pairwise; sea urchin and sea star of equal size	13	15	*Eucidaris* (6.5–12.6)	12*	2**	—
			Nidorellia (11.1)	1*	6**	—
7. Two objects presented pairwise; two sea stars of equal size	22	15	*Nidorellia* (12.1)	11*	—	—
			Pharia (15.7)	7*	—	—
8. Two objects presented pairwise; sea urchin and sea star of equal size	20	15	*Eucidaris* (5.5–10.0)	16*	—	—
			Pharia (15.7)	4*	—	—

[a] The objects employed were the sea urchins *Eucidaris thouarsii*, *Lytechinus semituberculatus*, the sea stars *Nidorellia armata*, *Pharia pyramidata*, the snail *Cerithium* sp. and a round, smooth, grey-white pebble of *Porites lobata*.

[b] All size measurements are the longest or maximum diameter of the item measured; for the sea urchins this is the test diameter and spine tip to spine tip diameter (italics); for the sea stars arm tip to arm tip (italics); for the snail the height of the shell.

[c] In experiment 1, the tally denotes the total number of objects ejected or not ejected (italics) irrespective of their order. In experiments 2–5, asterisks indicate the order of ejection, one asterisk first and two asterisks second. In experiments 6–8, observations were terminated after ejection of the first species.

TABLE 20. Ejection of Sea Urchins from Algal Mats by Territorial Damselfishes, Academy Bay, Santa Cruz Island.

Damselfish Species	No. of Trials[a]	Observation Time (min.)	Sea Urchin Species[b]	Ejections[c,d]
Eupomacentrus arcifrons	20	3	*Eucidaris*	20 < 10 sec.
	20	3	*Lytechinus*	1 < 10 sec.
				1 30 sec.
				18 —
Eupomacentrus beebei	20	3	*Eucidaris*	14 < 10 sec.
				2 30 sec.
				4 —
	20	3	*Lytechinus*	*20* —

[a]Sea urchins introduced one at a time; the same urchin was sometimes used repeatedly in different trials. Each sea urchin was introduced into the territory of a different fish.

[b]The sea urchins were not measured, but adults were used in every case and were similar in size to those listed in experiments 1 and 5, table 19.

[c]Numbers in italics indicate not ejected.

[d]Ejection time equals the time to removal after the sea urchin was first seen by the damselfish.

Cerithium sp. was not ejected (0 percent). *Eucidaris* would appear to pose the greatest threat in terms of altering the substrate, but *Lytechinus* and *Cerithium* might also be expected to feed in a damselfish's algal mat. If a rock remained in place long enough, it could kill the algae underneath. But algae eventually would grow on a stationary rock as well. It is fair to question whether the damselfishes were reacting to a rock (and possibly other objects) as a threat. For example, there was probably an element of a reaction to (a) the *movement* (indicating a live object) involved in placing an object in the territory, and (b) the *conspicuousness* of the object, that is, how it stood out from the rest of the objects in a territory.

In experiments 2–5, attention was paid to the order of ejection and the number of objects remaining after twenty seconds' observation time. Pairwise presentations of *Eucidaris* and coral rock, in experiments 2 and 3, showed a clear tendency for damselfish to eject initially either large or small *Eucidaris*. After the ejection of *Eucidaris*, the fish returned and then ejected the coral rock. Most objects were ejected after twenty seconds or at least inspected, mouthed, and carried or pushed toward the periphery of the territory.

Among small and large *Eucidaris* presented pairwise, in experiment 4, it is obvious that small urchins were ejected first. The damselfish then returned quickly and either ejected or attempted to eject the remaining large sea urchins.

In experiment 5, two different sea urchin species of comparable size were introduced pairwise. In twelve of fourteen trials, *Eucidaris* was ejected before *Lytechinus*. This result is significant ($X^2_{(1,14)} = 7.14, 0.01 > P > 0.005$).

The sea star *Nidorellia armata*, occasionally a corallivore, was tested against *Eucidaris* approximately equal in size (diameter) to the sea star in experiment 6. The pomacentrids ejected *Eucidaris* first at a highly significant level ($X^2_{(1,12)}$ = 9.30, 0.005>P>0.001). Two facultative sea star corallivores, approximately equal in size, were tested in experiment 7. (It should be recalled that while *Pharia pyramidata* feeds on live coral on the mainland, it has not yet been observed eating coral in the Galápagos.) In this treatment, the number of *Nidorellia* ejected first exceeded *Pharia* by four. This result was not significant, however ($X^2_{(1,22)}$ = 0.88, 0.50>P>0.25). In experiment 8, *Eucidaris* was ejected first significantly more frequently than *Pharia* ($X^2_{(1,20)}$ = 7.20, 0.01 > P > 0.005). The following hierarchical rankings summarize the order of ejection of objects placed in damselfish territories in this first set of experiments:

Experiments 1–5

  Eucidaris (small > large) > coral rock > *Lytechinus* > *Cerithium*

Experiments 6–8

  Eucidaris > *Nidorellia* > *Pharia*

The results summarized in table 20 allow a comparison of the two damselfish species in terms of the intensity of their ejection response. *Eupomacentrus arcifrons* ejected all *Eucidaris* in less than ten seconds after the sea urchins were first noticed by the damselfish. Two *Lytechinus* were ejected by *E. arcifrons* and eighteen were left in place after initial inspection and mouthing. *Eupomacentrus beebei* ejected a total of sixteen *Eucidaris* and left four in place. All *Lytechinus* were briefly inspected, mouthed, and then ignored. These data confirm the earlier observations that *Eucidaris* is ejected more vigorously than *Lytechinus*.

In order to test a possible difference in ejection intensity between the damselfishes, the ejection frequencies for each species were pooled as follows:

	Eucidaris	*Lytechinus*
E. arcifrons	20	2
E. beebei	16	0
Fisher exact probability*	P = 0.329, NS	

There is a high likelihood that the two damselfishes eject these sea urchins at equal rates.

These limited observations raise many questions. It seems reasonable to

---

*Since the *Lytechinus* cell frequencies are so small, only two ejections in one instance and none in the other, the appropriate test for these data is the Fisher exact probability test.

assume that the ejection response is an adaptation related to the defense and maintenance of an important resource. The demonstration of a strong ejection response toward invertebrates and other objects (Limbaugh, 1964; Clarke, 1970; Foster, 1972; Irvine, 1975; Williams, 1980; and present results) can hardly be considered an error in species recognition and thus nonadaptive as proposed by Murray (1971). If damselfish ejection behavior is adaptive, then one can postulate a direct relationship between the intensity of ejection and the harm a threatening species could bring to the defending damselfish. It is likely, however, that damselfish territories serve several important functions, such as food production, shelter from predators, a nesting site, and defense of eggs (Low, 1971; Myrberg and Thresher, 1974). An intruding species, then, must be evaluated in terms of its effect on the damselfish's food supply, shelter and breeding success, and possibly other factors. With these provisos in mind, it is worthwhile to speculate briefly on the relationship of the ejection response to the threats posed by the species tested.

Low (1971) and Ebersole (1977) demonstrated that the level of agonism elicited in damselfish was closely correlated with the dietary overlap of intruding fishes. That is, herbivorous fishes (competitors for algae) elicited a strong agonistic response and were prevented from entering damselfish territories whereas carnivorous fishes, except for a large labrid that disturbed shelter sites and presumably damselfish eggs (Low, 1971), were largely ignored. It has been suggested by Williams (1980) that the preferential ejection of the sea urchin *Diadema* over *Echinometra* by a Caribbean damselfish is due to the greater activity and competitive overlap of *Diadema* with the damselfish. Interestingly, *Echinometra* was more abundant than *Diadema*, but because of its sedentary habit apparently did not pose a serious threat. If it is more advantageous for the damselfish to protect its food resource than its shelter holes (see below), it is possible that the strict herbivores *Lytechinus* and *Cerithium* would offer a greater threat to the algal mat and therefore should have been ejected more vigorously than *Eucidaris*. But it is not certain that the echinoid and gastropod herbivores feed on the sorts of algae making up the algal mats. Furthermore, it appeared that *Eucidaris* were more numerous than *Lytechinus* and *Cerithium* in the areas inhabited by damselfishes, and entered into the territories more frequently than *Lytechinus* and *Cerithium*.

Live coral is commonly present in damselfish territories, but its benefit to the fish, if any, is unknown. It is possible that coral is an important supplemental food source (although we saw no evidence for this in the Galápagos, see p. 146) and that the coral colony provides a refuge from predation. When damselfish were pursued aggressively (by us) they invariably dived into holes formed by pocilloporid corals. Low's (1971) observations suggest that an Australian damselfish uses coral for shelter and defends cavities that it excavates under coral boulders. It is conceivable that the high level of agonism toward *Eucidaris* has evolved in part to keep coral holes clear of this urchin. *Eucidaris*, where abundant, do occupy coral holes. Interspecific fighting for shelter holes has been demonstrated among stomatopods (Kinzie, 1968; Dingle et al., 1973) and sea urchins (Grünbaum et al., 1978), although Ebersole (1977) has denied its importance in a Caribbean damselfish on the basis of indirect evidence (fish small enough to fit into damselfish shelter holes were not those most consistently attacked).

Of all the species examined in the present study, certainly *Eucidaris* has the greatest destructive impact on live coral. The removal of inanimate objects, such as the coral rock, would tend to allow for continued algal growth. Why small *Eucidaris* are ejected preferentially over large urchins is not immediately apparent unless the cryptic habit of small urchins leads to greater predation on damselfish eggs and the filling of shelter holes. One could argue that objects are ejected in the order of their ease of manipulation. But if this were true, the small snail should have been one of the first items ejected.

The preferential ejection of *Eucidaris* over the sea stars and then ejection of the occasional corallivore *Nidorellia* before *Pharia*, which was not found preying on coral in the Galápagos, suggests an order proportional to the damage the three species inflict on live coral. *Nidorellia* and *Pharia*, which prey predominantly on sponges, hydroids, bryozoans, and other sessile animal groups, would appear to pose a minor threat to damselfish algal mats or live coral within damselfish territories.

Whatever the true cause and effect relationship of the ejection response, it does appear that damselfishes are effective at clearing their territories of invertebrate corallivores, and in this capacity contribute positively to coral growth and survival. The overall effects of damselfishes, taking into account their direct impact on corals in feeding and clearing bottom areas and their indirect influence on corals through substrate modification (algal mat formation), remain to be clarified.

Crustacean Symbionts In Coral: Considering the effective role that crustacean symbionts play in averting *Acanthaster* attacks from their pocilloporid coral hosts (reported thus far in Panamá [Glynn, 1976] and the South Pacific region [Pearson and Endean, 1969; Weber and Woodhead, 1970]), it is interesting to note that no agonistic interactions were observed between the symbionts and *Eucidaris*. Except for the damselfish interference discussed above, *Eucidaris* grazed unhampered on *Pocillopora* in the Galápagos. Crabs in the genus *Trapezia* were present in Galápagos *Pocillopora* at similar densities, usually at least a single pair per coral colony, as observed in areas where they successfully repel attacks by *Acanthaster* (Abele and Patton, 1976; Preston, 1973; Patton, 1974). The species of *Trapezia* observed in the Galápagos and their respective numbers per coral colony are given in table 21. A pistol shrimp, *Alpheus lottini* Guérin, which behaves aggressively toward *Acanthaster* by snapping and pinching, was not found in the six colonies sampled. Sampling carried out by P. Castro and M. Huber (personal communication), however, did reveal *A. lottini* to be as abundant in Galápagos pocilloporid

TABLE 21. Numbers of Agonistic Crabs Present in Colonies of *Pocillopora elegans*, Academy Bay, Santa Cruz Island (26 January 1975, 2 to 4 m depth). Identifications by L. G. Abele.

Colony Number	Colony Volume[a] (cm^3)	*Trapezia* Symbionts	
		T. ferruginea[b]	*T. digitalis*
1	5525	8 M[c]	4 M
		6 F	1 F
2	5400	2 M	1 M
		4 F	2 F
3	4200	1 M	0
		1 F	
4	3825	2 M	1 M
			1 F
5	3315	2 M	1 M
		2 F	1 F
6	2520	3 M	1 M
		5 F	1 F

[a]Length × width × height.

[b]Castro (in press) has demonstrated that "*T. ferruginea*" is a complex of three species, viz., *T. corallina* Gerstaecker, *T. formosa* Smith, and *T. ferruginea* Latreille.

[c]M = male, F = female.

corals, that is, about one pair of shrimp per colony, as in Panamá. It is not presently known whether the relatively slow-moving and heavily armored urchin fails to elicit a defensive response on the part of the crustacean symbionts or simply ignores the aggressive actions of the crabs. In Panamá, introduced *Eucidaris* elicit low-level agonistic responses from crabs and shrimps (Glynn, in press). The sluggish and heavily armored asteroid *Culcita novaeguineae* Müller and Troschel also feeds successfully on *Pocillopora* in the central and western Pacific (Goreau et al., 1972; J. Flanigan and P. W. Glynn, personal observations). *Culcita* is attacked by the crustacean guards, at relatively low levels compared with *Acanthaster*, but usually continues to feed on a defended coral just the same (Glynn, in press).

BIOTIC DISTURBANCE

It is now recognized that various kinds of disturbance, biotic as well as abiotic, can have important effects on the structure of marine communities (e.g., on species diversity and succession; Dayton, 1971; Dayton and Hessler, 1972; Connell, 1978; Sousa, 1979). The activities of vagile animals associated with coral reefs can influence the survival and growth of corals. Some examples of the effects of herbivorous fishes and sea urchins were considered earlier (*Coral Reef Herbivores*). In this section we examine a variety of disruptive activities. Although some of these involve feeding, our interest here is not on the particular prey item attacked but rather the disturbing effect (often incidental) of the feeding activity on other associated or nearby reef organisms. In addition to feeding, other potentially disruptive activities are nest building by fishes, the excavation of permanent shelter holes, animal movements over and through unconsolidated reef material, and possibly the movements of fishes in and out of temporary (sleeping) shelter holes. While the above class of disturbances might seem minor—compared for example with storms, log damage, freshwater dilution, extreme tidal exposures, or outbreaks of *Acanthaster*—it is important to realize that they occur frequently, often daily.

The majority of the effects discussed below have been observed on Pacific coral reefs in Panamá or in other regions. Most of the disturbances have been reported in qualitative terms only. Quantitative and experimental studies on this subject still remain to be carried out. Because most of the species involved in the biotic disturbance of coral communities in Panamá also occur in the Galápagos, it is tentatively assumed that the individual effects of any given species will be the same in both areas. Certain species, however, such as triggerfish, puffers, and parrotfish, are less abundant on reefs in the Galápagos than in Panamá. Therefore, their combined effects (per species population) may be less in the former than in mainland localities.

Fishes that feed by grubbing or lifting, or those that break into corals in search of cryptic prey, can have a marked effect on local coral patches. Triggerfishes are especially effective in breaking apart corals in order to extract burrowing bivalves and other infaunal forms (Glynn et al., 1972; Highsmith, 1980). *Pseudobalistes naufragium* bites off 3- to 5-cm-long knobs from *Porites lobata* colonies and breaks apart pocilloporid patches (up to 30–40 cm diameter) in search of bivalves, notably *Periglypta multicostata* (Sowerby), and other cryptic invertebrates such as echinoids and gastropods (Rowley and Wellington, in prep.). It is also probable that the giant humphead wrasse (*Cheilinus*) breaks apart pocilloporid colonies in order to expose crabs in the western Pacific Ocean (Randall et al., 1978). Triggerfish are also noted for their ability to lift and rearrange bottom materials while feeding (Fricke, 1971). Some of the coral fragments generated by triggerfish continue to live (asexual propagation), but also many may be buried and then die, especially from colonies adjacent to sand.

Several fish species roam over the deep reef edge individually or in schools (often mixed schools containing several species) where they plough into reef sediments and/or overturn live and dead coral colonies in order to expose cryptic invertebrate prey (Hobson, 1968; Glynn, 1974b). The following species have been observed feeding in this manner on Panamanian reefs: Carangidae—*Caranx melampygus* Cuvier (in Cuvier and Valenciennes); *Gnathanodon speciosus* (Forskål); Mullidae—*Mulloidichthys dentatus* (Gill); and Labridae—*Hemipteronotus taeniourus* (Lacépède). Tetraodontid and diodontid puffers and triggerfish commonly join the schooling fishes when they are churning up bottom sediments. Herbivorous fish grazers, such as parrotfish and surgeonfish, also disturb reef substrates consisting of loose sediments. The chief effect of all such disruptive activities seems to be on young corals that are attached to the loose rubble. Their upright position, relative to light and water circulation, is frequently changed, and the corals are often buried beneath rubble and sand, at least temporarily. The significance of these sorts of disturbances are expected to diminish with increasing size of the coral colony.

The excavation of nesting or living holes by fishes can lead to marked rearrangements of reef rubble. For example, triggerfish construct nests up to 2 m in diameter and 0.7 m deep (Lobel and Johannes, 1980), and a single tilefish can transport up to 500 fragments as far as 9 m away from its burrow, in a period of eight days (Clifton and Hunter, 1972).

Large invertebrates, such as gastropods and sea stars, disturb reef sediments to some extent during their normal movements (Glynn, 1974b). On some reefs in Panamá, the daily movements of sea urchins (*Toxopneustes*) through rubble (burying during daylight hours and emerging at night) result in extensive mixing of the uppermost 10-cm layer.

It is likely that large parrotfish and other fishes seeking refuge in holes on pocilloporid reefs at night may also affect their shelter holes and surrounding areas. This would be especially so if a resting fish were discovered by a predator.

Finally, we note a potential form of disturbance that is perhaps unique to the Galápagos Islands. The Galápagos sea lion, *Zalophus wollebaeki* Sivertsen, was observed occasionally to rub its belly against the branchtips of *Pocillopora* corals. Some individuals from the rookery at Onslow Island were seen rocking to and fro, in rhythm with the surge, over the pocilloporid reef near shore. Some of the coral's branchtips appeared inflated and truncated at this site, but no tissue abrasion or skeletal breakage was noted. These activities are probably not important in limiting coral growth.

COMPETITION

Competition among species for space has been recognized as a potentially important force shaping the structure of coral reef communities (Gravier, 1910; Mayor, 1918; Glynn et al., 1972; Connell, 1973; Lang, 1973; Porter, 1974). As we have shown in previous chapters, the high densities of corals on many reefs in the Galápagos suggest that often space may be a limiting factor. In this section we will discuss two types of competitive interactions, direct (extracoelenteric aggression or digestion, and sweeper tentacle defense) and indirect (overtopping) interference competition, which have been described, and assess their relative importance on Galápagos reefs.

One direct interference mechanism termed "extracoelenteric aggression or feeding" involves the ability of an individual colony to extend its mesenterial filaments from the gut and kill the opposing tissues of an adjacent species (Gravier, 1910; Lang, 1973; Connell, 1973). The pioneering work of Lang (1973) established a transitive (linear) dominance hierarchy among Caribbean corals indicating that the most aggressive corals are those which grow slowly and are uncommon on the reef (in general, species of the suborder Faviina > Fungiina > Astrocoeniina). It was suggested by Lang that this relationship provides a mechanism by which slow growing species can counterbalance the advantage of rapidly growing corals, and thus may act to maintain local species diversity on reefs. Following Lang's experimental protocol (that is, short-term laboratory manipulations of interspecific pairs), Glynn (1974*b*) concluded that in the eastern Pacific the slow-growing massive coral *Pavona* (Fungiina) was dominant over *Pocillopora* (Astrocoeniina). These findings were, however, inconsistent with earlier field observations of naturally occurring contests—*Pocillopora* appeared to damage *Pavona* more frequently than the reverse (Glynn et al., 1972). A more recent study has shown that both of these reports are, in a sense, correct (Wellington, 1980). During the initial period of contact between *Pocillopora* and *Pavona* colonies, the latter species reacts first by extending its mesenterial filaments and partially killing the branches of *Pocillopora*. However, after a period of from seven to sixty days the undamaged tentacles of polyps near the affected area begin to elongate, extending up to thirty times their normal length of one millimeter. Also, the cnidom, or composition of nematocysts and spirocysts present in the acrospheres (minute swellings in the epidermis), shifts from one composed primarily of atoxic food-entangling spirocysts to a higher percentage of powerful nematocysts (mainly basitrichous isorhizae). These "sweeper tentacles" are passively swept by water currents onto the tissues of the adjacent *Pavona* colony where they inflict damage. This retaliation or defense maneuver permits *Pocillopora* to regenerate previously damaged areas and begin regrowth in the direction of the opposing coral. The eventual outcome is that *Pocillopora* prevails in direct conflicts with *Pavona*.

Other recent studies suggest that sweeper tentacle defense may be a widespread and important means of combating encroaching corals. For example, Richardson et al. (1979) found that the Caribbean massive coral, *Montastrea cavernosa* (Linnaeus), is able to deter mesenterial attacks from its more aggressive congener, *Montastrea annularis* (Ellis and Solander). It does so by the peripheral extension of sweeper tentacles that presumably attack the tissues of encroaching corals, thus preventing them from getting close enough to extend their mesenterial filaments. Also, a survey of naturally occurring coral-coral interactions in the Indian Ocean revealed that species predominance on the reef was directly related to the aggressiveness of a coral (that is, its ability to inflict damage on other species) and was independent of taxonomic grouping or corallum morphology (Sheppard, 1979). The high dominance ranking of *Pocillopora verrucosa* (Ellis and Solander) in Sheppard's study suggests that his results may involve sweeper tentacle interactions.

Another form of competition is indirect interference in which one species, by virtue of a higher linear growth rate and branching morphology, is able to overtop another species. This can eventually lead to mortality of the slower growing species by restricting access to light and water movement, increasing sedimentation, physical containment, or a combination of these factors. The linear growth rate data presented in chapter 4 (*Coral Growth*), and from other studies in the eastern Pacific (Glynn and Stewart, 1973; Maguire and Porter, 1977; and others), show that *Pocillopora* has a 1.5- to 3-fold advantage over massive corals, particularly *Pavona*. Because overtopping is a protracted process requiring many years to complete (Connell, 1973), it is difficult to assess experimentally its direct importance. Reefs in the Galápagos, as elsewhere in the eastern Pacific, commonly contain mostly *Pocillopora* spp. in shallow water, especially when coral density is high. Its competitive superiority with respect to both direct and indirect interference mechanisms no doubt contribute largely to their success. What accounts for their relative paucity in deep water? It appears that, in deep areas of the reef, competition between branching and massive species may be reduced by the activities of grazing fishes. It has been shown in Panamá, for example, that *Pocillopora* suffers differentially higher juvenile mortality from grazing fishes, particularly from the pufferfish *Arothron* spp., in deep water as compared to massive species (Wellington, 1982*b*).

In the Galápagos, massive corals often occur in high densities in deep reef zones, and it is noted that their peak abundances are often nonoverlapping (see figs. 35 and 43). It is unknown whether these patterns reflect the outcome of differential competitive abilities or some other mechanisms (for example, differential mortality or niche specialization) along a depth gradient. With respect to potential competitive abilities, these massive corals do possess some interspecific differences. For example, *Pavona clavus* has a higher growth rate than *Pavona gigantea* (see chapter 4); but there is no interference interaction exhibited, either involving mesenterial filaments or sweeper tentacles, when congeneric colonies are placed in direct contact (Wellington, 1980).

Competition involving interference between corals and other taxa, particularly interphyletic interactions, is generally uncommon in open-reef habitats. However, among the cryptofauna, competition for space is often intense among individuals from a variety of taxa (Jackson and Buss, 1975; Jackson, 1979). Overtopping and overgrowth of solitary or semicolonial corals by rapidly growing colonial sponges and tunicates was frequently observed (see chapter 3, *Nature and Distribution of Coral Communities: Western Sector*, and pls. 2, 4). Because of their indeterminate and rapid asexual growth, many sessile colonial organisms have a distinct advantage in space competition over slower-growing solitary organisms such as ahermatypic corals. As Jackson (1977) has pointed out, however, solitary organisms often prevail in spite of this competitive disadvantage by being differentially resistant to predation and physical disturbances. These factors probably account for the persistence of the diverse and abundant ahermatypic coral assemblages we observed in the western sector (western Isabela and Fernandina). For example, the sea star *Heliaster cumingii* was frequently observed (pl. 3) preying on colonial tubeworms and tunicates. In addition, fishes, especially wrasses, were noted to prey heavily on various encrusting colonial organisms. We saw little evidence of predation on corals in this environment.

In summary, high densities of corals, particularly in shallow water, suggest that space is often a limiting factor on Galápagos reefs. However, the degree to which coral-coral competition controls community structure on these reefs is presently unknown. From previous studies on direct and indirect interference mechanisms, we know that *Pocillopora* is potentially the superior space competitor, and this probably contributes to its predominance in shallow water. Further study is needed, however, to determine if vertical zonation among massive corals in deeper reef areas results from similar competitive interactions.

CHAPTER SEVEN

GALÁPAGOS CORAL COMMUNITIES: RELATIONSHIPS AND REGIONAL COMPARISONS

Before considering some of the similarities and differences among Galápagos coral reefs and coral reefs in other tropical seas, we review briefly the probable origin of the Galápagos Archipelago and then, in greater depth, the affinities of the Galapagan shallow-water marine biota in relation to other biogeographic regions. Since dispersal routes and the geologic history of a biota are so often important in understanding the provenance of present-day marine distributions (Valentine, 1973), these factors are also considered in the following discussion.

ORIGIN OF THE GALÁPAGOS ISLANDS

Two great submarine ridges diverge from the Galápagos platform in the form of a V, with each ridge extending toward the eastern Pacific mainland (fig. 59). One of these, the Cocos Ridge, extends northeast from the Galápagos and approaches mainland Central America near the Panamá-Costa Rican frontier. The second ridge, the Carnegie Ridge (including its western salient, the Galápagos platform), is oriented in an east-southeasterly direction and approaches mainland South America just north of the Gulf of Guayaquil, Ecuador. These ridges appear to have had their origin in the Galápagos "hot spot," which is presently extruding lava on the sea floor bordering the westernmost Galápagos Islands (Holden and Dietz, 1972). A "hot spot" is an upwelling center of molten basalt, a narrow plume or pipe of mantle material that rises and spreads out radially in the asthenosphere (Wilson, 1965; Morgan, 1971). As the oceanic plate moves over the upwelling center, a continuous outpouring of basalt produces a linear aseismic ridge on the sea floor. Lava issuing from the hot spot is presumably alternately spilled on the Cocos Plate and the Nazca Plate, which lie, respectively, to the north and south of the east-west-trending Galápagos Rift (fig. 59). Thus, seafloor spreading toward the northeast has given rise to the Cocos Ridge, and spreading to the east-southeast to the Carnegie Ridge. The relatively small Malpelo Ridge, which seems to have

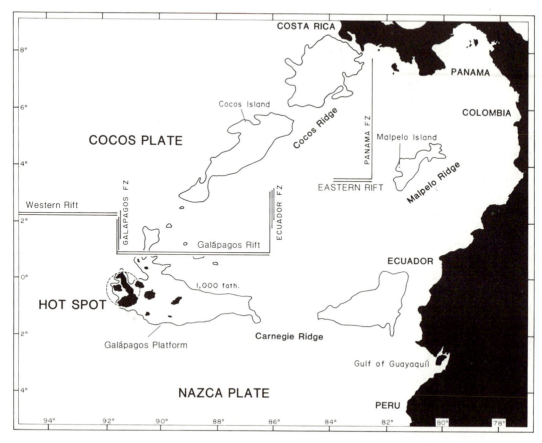

FIGURE 59. Schematic diagram of the major submarine features in the eastern equatorial Pacific. Location of melting anomaly (hot spot) from Johnson and Lowrie (1972).

separated from the north-moving Cocos Ridge, has remained in its present position since late Miocene time. Cocos Island is presently the only emergent portion of the Cocos Ridge. The Galápagos Islands represent the westernmost emergent section of the Carnegie Ridge, and Malpelo Island represents the emergent remnant of the Malpelo Ridge. According to Holden and Dietz (1972), this model assumes that the segments of the submarine ridges nearest the mainland are the oldest. Malpelo Ridge and the eastern section of the Carnegie Ridge were built first; then the Cocos and western Carnegie ridges were formed; and, finally, the Galápagos segment, which is still under active construction today (Lonsdale and Klitgord, 1978).

The dating of volcanic rocks from various islands in the Galápagos has confirmed that most of the volcanic terrain there was formed during a short interval from 2.4 to 3 million years ago to the present (Cox and Dalrymple, 1966; Bailey, 1976). However, evidence supporting a consistent age gradient away from the hot spot (with rocks increasing in age from west to east) is equivocal. The oldest fossiliferous beds thus far discovered, on Santa Cruz and Baltra Islands, are late Miocene (Durham and McBirney, 1976) and Pliocene (Hertlein, 1972) in age. According to Williams (1966b), those parts of the Galápagos volcanoes now exposed to view were built mainly during Pleistocene and Recent times.

BIOGEOGRAPHIC AFFINITIES

Considering the mode of origin of the Galápagos—from the Galápagos hot spot—and their essentially oceanic setting, it is usually assumed that the present-day littoral marine biota (and the terrestrial biota) was largely derived by dispersal via marine currents from the tropical and subtropical eastern Pacific mainland region. (See Holden and Dietz, 1972, for an alternative model explaining terrestrial dispersal and speciation.) The Galápagos have always been relatively close to northwestern South America and Central America (Panamá and Costa Rica) and have probably received currents regularly (seasonally) from both of these mainland areas since their formation. Communication with the Caribbean Sea had ended by the end of the Pliocene, sometime between 3.5 (Saito, 1976) and 3.1 (Keigwin, 1978) million years ago, and the great distances involved across the East Pacific Barrier (the deep-water expanse separating the Central Pacific from the eastern Pacific, Ekman, 1953) has probably not favored the immigration of numerous elements from the Central Pacific. A comparison of the character of some of the better-known shallow-water taxa of the Galápagos with the nearest mainland eastern Pacific area indicates a strong similarity (with some significant differences) in the biotic composition of the two regions. The mainland area, from the Gulf of Guayaquil (3°S) to the Gulf of Tehuantepec (16°N), is generally recognized as the Panamic Province and contains the highest diversity of tropical elements in the eastern Pacific region (fig. 60). The offshore islands of Malpelo and Cocos and Clipperton Island (the easternmost atoll in the Pacific) belong in the Panamic Province.

The Galápagos marine flora includes a significant number of species, about 15 percent, that are also found along the Pacific American coast and on adjacent islands from California to Chile (Silva, 1966). Many of the Galápagos marine algae are endemic with about 36 percent reported by Silva (1966).

Among the reef-building corals, all thirteen species present in the Galápagos are also members of the Panamic Province (*Annotated List of the Scleractinian Corals of the Galápagos* app., p. 215). A few hermatypic coral and hydrocoral species present on the American Pacific mainland (in the Panamic Province) are apparently absent from the Galápagos: two species of firecoral (*Millepora*), two species of *Pocillopora*, and one species of *Porites*. Of the thirty-two ahermatypic coral species, eight (25 percent) are also members of the

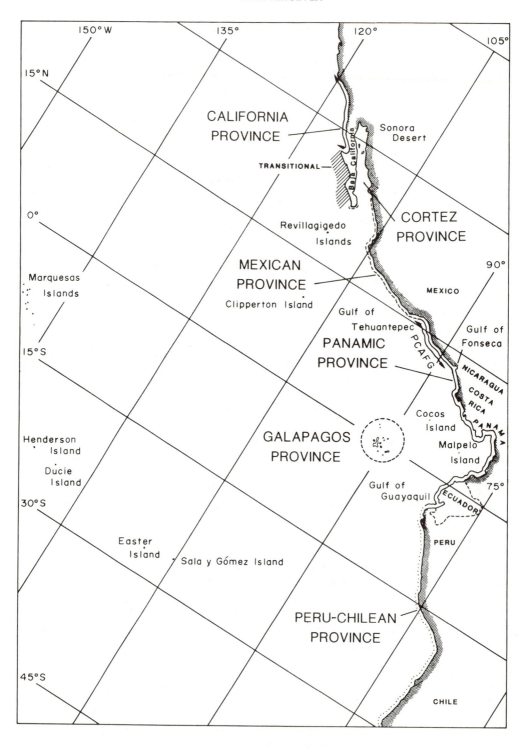

Panamic Province and nine (28 percent) are presently known only from the Galápagos Islands. The remaining fifteen ahermatypes are members of the Indo-Pacific fauna (twelve species, 38 percent) or are present in the Atlantic Ocean (three species, 9 percent). The large numbers of endemic species, and the strong ties with the eastern Pacific and Indo-Pacific regions are notable. However, faunal affinities inferred from the distributions of ahermatypic corals must be viewed cautiously due to their wide tolerance range for temperatures and depth conditions (Wells, 1956).

Among the other relatively well known marine invertebrate taxa, for example, spirorbid worms (Bailey and Harris, 1968), echinoderms (Chesher, 1972), mollusks (Emerson, 1961, 1978), and crustaceans (Garth, 1946a, b; Child and Hedgpeth, 1971), a strong affinity with the Panamic Province is also evident.

The marine inshore fishes of the Galápagos are well known and of these the largest segment (54 percent) is shared with the mainland eastern Pacific (Rosenblatt and Walker, 1963; Walker, 1966). The shallow-water fish fauna demonstrates a high degree of endemism as well, with 23 percent of the species known only from the Galápagos Islands.

Due to the high degree of endemism exhibited by most marine groups thus far studied, it is apparent that a substantial amount of speciation has occurred in the Galápagos. Thus, the Galápagos littoral marine biota is distinctive (as recognized by Ekman, 1953) and it is convenient to recognize this by referring to the area as the Galápagos Province (Briggs, 1974; Brusca and Wallerstein, 1979).

WARM-WATER EASTERN PACIFIC REGION

In addition to the Galápagos and Panamic provinces, the eastern Pacific warm-water region also encompasses a tropical (Mexican) and a subtropical (Cortez) province to the north (fig. 60). The essential features of these eastern Pacific biogeographic subdivisions were, according to Brusca and Wallerstein (1979), initially recognized by Dana (1853). Coral communities and small coral reefs have been reported from both of these provinces. The subtropical/warm-temperate transitional zone south of the Gulf of Guayaquil (3°S) is assumed to be relatively restricted due to the compression of surface isotherms at Cape Blanco near Talara, Peru where the Peru Coastal Current turns westward.

The southern boundary of the Mexican Province, based largely on ichthyological collections, is often given as Tangola-Tangola Bay (Briggs, 1955; Springer, 1958), just west of the Gulf of Tehuantepec, Mexico. The coastal

FIGURE 60. Major zoogeographic provinces in the eastern Pacific, shallow, warm-water region. PCAFG shows the location of the Pacific Central American Faunal Gap (Springer, 1958).

stretch from the Gulf of Tehuantepec southeast to the Gulf of Fonseca, within the Panamic Province, is dominated by sandy beaches and coastal lagoons. Springer (1958) referred to this segment of shoreline as the Pacific Central American Faunal Gap (PCAFG, fig. 60). No coral reefs have been reported from this area, a fact usually attributed to the absence of firm substrata along this stretch of coast. The reader is reminded, however, that coral patches have been reported south of Acajutla, El Salvador (Gierloff-Emden, 1976). The Mexican Province continues to the northwest along the Mexican mainland coast to the Gulf of California (the Cortez Province), and additionally encompasses the tip of Baja California (the Cabo San Lucas area) and eventually merges with the warm-temperate California Province along the southern half of the outer (west) coast of Baja California. The Revillagigedo Islands, located about 400 km (250 miles) south-southwest of Cabo San Lucas, show a strong resemblance to the Cape area (Walker, 1960), and hence to the Mexican Province. The warm-temperate/subtropical/tropical boundary on the outer coast of Baja California is ill defined because of the presence of shallow, protected bays and inlets that harbor tropical elements, and exposed promontories and areas of upwelling that support cool-water species (Dawson, 1960; Durham and Allison, 1960; Hubbs, 1960; Brusca and Wallerstein, 1979). This transitional zone has been referred to as the Surian Province (Valentine, 1966). Results of the Puritan Expedition (Squires, 1959) indicate that at least one hermatypic coral (*Porites*) occurs on the outer Baja coast as far north as Magdalena Bay (about 24°N).

The Cortez Province (Gulf of California) can probably best be characterized as a subtropical area. It is important to recognize, however, that the northern part of the Gulf, which is greatly influenced by the continental climatic conditions of the Sonoran Desert, is often subject to intense winter cooling. Seasonal ranges in near-shore sea surface temperatures around Puerto Peñasco (near the northern Gulf terminus) may vary from 30°–32°C in the summer and from 10°–12°C in the winter (Brusca, in press). During exceptionally cold winters, when shore temperatures drop to 8°–9°C, certain tropical and subtropical species experience mass mortalities (Brusca and Wallerstein, 1979). As one travels south in the Gulf, latitudinal warming increases and seasonal extremes in temperature are less pronounced (Hubbs and Roden, 1964). This change in the marine climate is reflected in the appearance of increasing numbers of hermatypic corals (Squires, 1959) and other tropical species (e.g., bryozoans [Soule, 1960]; brachyuran crabs [Garth, 1960]; fishes [Walker, 1960 and Thomson et al., 1979]) toward the south.

Besides the major biogeographic subdivisions in the eastern Pacific, an insular confinement pattern in species' distributions has also been recognized. This involves the occurrence of a high proportion of Indo-Pacific species on oceanic islands which are not present on the eastern Pacific mainland. An example from the mollusks, one of the best-studied groups, illustrates this pattern. Most of the fifty-two species of Indo-Pacific prosobranch gastropods and bivalves recorded in the eastern Pacific (thirty-eight species or 73 percent) are known only from offshore islands: the Galápagos Islands have nine such species; Cocos Island, four; Clipperton Atoll, thirty-eight; and the Revillagigedo Islands, six. Clipperton, the westernmost American outpost located in the path of the North Equatorial Countercurrent (figs. 60 and 61), has its marine molluscan fauna of seventy species about equally divided between Indo-Pacific and Panamic elements (Emerson, 1967, 1978). A similar pattern of insular confinement has been described for the marine shore fishes (Snodgrass and Heller, 1905; Rosenblatt and Walker, 1963; Briggs, 1967).

One explanation often given to account for the preponderance of Indo-Pacific species in insular situations is that requisite coral reef habitats are more prominent on offshore islands. Where coral communities and reefs have been examined more recently on the mainland, numerous Indo-Pacific fishes (Greenfield et al., 1970; Rosenblatt et al., 1972) and invertebrates (Glynn, 1972) have been found. If migrant Indo-Pacific species require corals (and in some cases they do, e.g., the gastropod *Quoyula*; corallicolous crustaceans such as *Hapalocarcinus*, *Trapezia* and *Alpheus*; and *Arothron meleagris*, a pufferfish) or simply require similar environmental conditions where corals live, it seems reasonable to expect that most Indo-Pacific species will also be found in mainland localities where coral communities are present.

HISTORICAL BIOGEOGRAPHY

Dispersal Routes and Barriers: Ocean currents can serve as an effective means of dispersal, allowing for the interchange of species between widely separated biotas. This is especially true for many tropical and subtropical benthic marine organisms that have a high proportion of species capable of long-distance dispersal (Scheltema, 1977; Soule and Soule, 1979; Zinsmeister and Emerson, 1979). Currents can also enhance the spread of benthic organisms (and some terrestrial groups) by rafting on floating debris and by transporting propagules to islands or shallow sea mounts and banks that might serve as stepping stones (Hamilton, 1956).

In addition to access, other factors that may influence the dispersal process are (a) the physical characteristics of the transporting medium (e.g., temperature, salinity, depth, light levels, current speeds, and constancy), (b) a source area with a biota producing a high proportion of long-lived larvae (that is, with indirect development), and (c) the timing and duration of reproductive events. For example, with reference to the properties of the water mass, the survival of larvae of warm- and shallow-water species would be highest in convergent surface currents flowing within the low latitudes. Further, currents from a source area would carry greater numbers of propagules if they originate there during the peak reproductive period. Abbott (1966) integrated these various factors and noted their relevance to the strong biotic

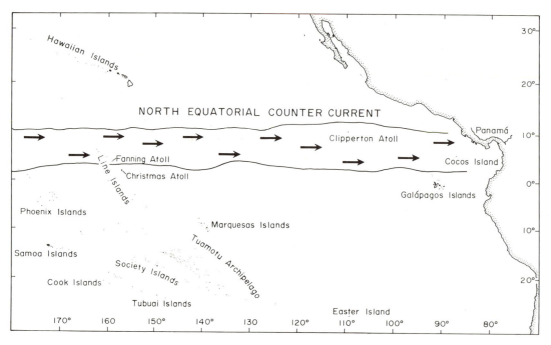

FIGURE 61. Path of North Equatorial Countercurrent across the central and eastern Pacific Ocean. Boundary limits are integrated from monthly surface current drift, 1980 (pilot chart of the north Pacific Ocean, DMA Stock No. Pilot 558110, Defense Mapping Agency Hydrographic/Topographic Center, Washington, D.C.).

affinities between the Galápagos and the Ecuador-Colombia-Panamá coastal faunas.

The Peru Coastal and Oceanic currents and the South Equatorial Current sweep past the Galápagos and are thus potential conveyors of organisms from Peru and Chile. These currents are best developed during the cool season when reproductive activities are expected to be lowest. Moreover, because these currents move constantly offshore, selection would not be expected to favor a pelagic larval stage in littoral species. It is expected that relatively few forms on the coast of Peru would produce larvae capable of long-distance transport. This situation should result in a small to moderate biotic affinity between the Galápagos and Peru.

The Equatorial Undercurrent could possibly transport larval forms from the Central Pacific (figs. 3-A and 61). This subsurface current passes through the Line Islands and exists at least as far west as the Gilbert Islands (173–177°E) (Tsuchiya, 1970). It is swift (2.9 knots or 150 cm/second at its core) and cool (15–17°C) (Knauss, 1960, 1963; Pak and Zaneveld, 1973) and therefore might supply ahermatypic coral larvae and other relatively deep-water tropical organisms to the Galápagos.

While the North Equatorial Countercurrent is probably an effective dispersal route for some shallow-water tropical forms between the central Pacific and eastern Pacific, it normally flows north of the Galápagos and would therefore be expected to have a greater influence between 4° and 10°N latitude (fig. 61). At higher latitudes, the North Equatorial Current and California Current move away from the American tropical Pacific coast (fig. 3-A). The California Current swings broadly away from the American coast south of Baja California. The Costa Rica Current moves in a northwest direction along the Pacific coast from Panamá to at least Baja California (in December) and could therefore transport tropical larval forms seasonally to the north.

Reference was made earlier to Springer's (1958) Pacific Central American Faunal Gap, the great stretch of sandy beaches and coastal lagoons extending from southern Mexico to Nicaragua. As suggested by Springer, this type of habitat might discourage the dispersal of organisms with direct or abbreviated indirect larval development that require hard substrates. Areas subject to seasonal upwelling can lead to significant changes in water quality (e.g., temperature, salinity, and nutrient levels) and in the trophic conditions (productivity and biomass) of local environments. Three well-known inshore upwelling areas in the eastern Pacific are centered in the Gulf of Tehuantepec, the Gulf of Papagayo, and the Gulf of Panamá (Hubbs and Roden, 1964). Upwelling and nonupwelling environments in Panamá demonstrate many differences in the composition of coral reef biotas (Glynn et al., 1972; Rosenblatt et al., 1972), extent and age of reef formations (Glynn and Macintyre, 1977), and growth rates of corals (Glynn, 1977). Some coral reef associates, such as the hydrocoral *Millepora* and the crown-of-thorns sea star *Acanthaster*, are absent from the Gulf of Panamá and apparently from all localities south (Glynn et al., in press). This difference in distribution could be due to the seasonally cool waters in the Gulf of Panamá, preventing the spread south of certain species found in western Panamá (Gulf of Chiriquí) outside of the upwelling area.

Probably the most effective barrier to influence the American tropical marine biota was the emergence of the Middle American land bridge at the end of the Pliocene (Whitmore and Stewart, 1965; Woodring, 1966; Vermeij, 1978). During the time that western Atlantic and eastern Pacific waters were in communication, the reef coral communities of the Middle American region were a mixture of many genera that are now characteristic of either the Caribbean (Bahamas and Florida, Caribbean and Gulf of Mexico) or Indo-Pacific faunas. For example, during Miocene time the following coral genera, which are today restricted to the Indo-Pacific region (including the eastern Pacific), were members of identical reef assemblages in the tropical American region: *Favites, Goniopora, Seriatopora, Psammocora, Galaxea, Pocillopora, Hydnophora, Leptoseris, Pavona, Stylophora*, and *Coscinaraea* (from Heck and McCoy, 1978, according to Durham, 1966; Frost and Langenheim, 1974; Frost, 1977). Some of the Miocene genera, such as *Acropora, Porites*, and *Favia*, still occur in both Pacific and Atlantic regions.* *Colpophyllia, Mycetophyllia, Solenastrea,* and *Stephanocoenia,* and three additional genera, are surviving Caribbean Miocene corals now restricted to tropical western Atlantic waters (Wells, 1969).

A current controversy concerns the historical biogeographic relationships of eastern Pacific coral communities since this area was isolated from the Caribbean at the end of the Pliocene. Two opposing views have emerged on this question: (a) *long-distance dispersal,* that is, extant eastern Pacific coral communities are modern and derived from the central Pacific by larval transport following periods of massive extinction after closure of Central American seaways (Garth, 1974; Dana, 1975; Zinsmeister and Emerson, 1979); and (b) *vicariance,* that is, eastern Pacific coral communities are derived from a previously widespread, pan-Tethyan biota that has since been modified by tectonic events, speciations, and extinctions (McCoy and Heck, 1976; Heck and McCoy, 1978). The former assumes the spread of species over long distances during short periods of time, and the latter over short distances during long periods of time. These two views have come into sharp focus since Dana (1975) proposed that eastern Pacific coral communities are youthful, a result of recolonization events from the central Pacific (Line Islands) following Pleistocene perturbations and extinctions. We explore below the principal arguments and evidence supporting these two hypotheses, and offer our suggestions for future work that might help test them.

The Fossil Record: The fossil record for hermatypic corals is woefully incomplete, and much of the information available is based on tenuous conclusions. The identifications of many of the genera reported from the eastern Pacific Tertiary, especially from the Eocene, are dubious indeed. Nonetheless, a strong early affinity between the coral fauna of Atlantic and Pacific American waters is evident.

Through the Cretaceous and early Tertiary (Paleogene), spanning about 100 million years, fully 89 percent of the known species of eastern Pacific fossil corals also occurred in the tropical Atlantic region (table 22). During the same period, only about 40 percent of the ancient eastern Pacific coral fauna is known from the Indo-West Pacific region. At that time the tropical waters of the Atlantic and Pacific oceans were connected by a great seaway, the Tethys Sea. This circumtropical sea in its early history harbored a pantropical

---

*Montastrea is omitted from this listing despite the insistence of Chevalier (1971), Veron et al. (1977), and Wijsman-Best (1977) that this genus occurs in the Indo-Pacific. The Indo-Pacific parallel of the Atlantic *Montastrea* is *Plesiastrea*. The polyps of *Montastrea* have directive mesenterial couples (Duerden, 1902) and hence the genus belongs to Group I of Matthai (1914). *Plesiastrea versipora* and *P. curta* ("*Montastrea*" *curta*) lack such couples and thus belong to Matthai's Group II. But until the anatomy of the polyps of more Indo-Pacific species of "*Montastrea*" is studied (regrettably so little has been done on the structure of scleractinian polyps since Matthai's work of seventy years ago), whether or not they are *Plesiastrea* will remain unsettled.

TABLE 22. Eastern Pacific Hermatypic Coral Genera Shared by Western Atlantic and Indo-West Pacific Regions During Two Geologic Intervals and at Present (After Durham, 1966, with Emendations by Heck and McCoy, 1978).

Interval	Regions	Genera	
		Number	Percent
Cretaceous-Oligocene	Eastern Pacific and western Atlantic	32	89
63 to 25 m.y. ago	Eastern Pacific and Indo-West Pacific	14	39
36 EP genera	Western Atlantic and Indo-West Pacific	15	42
Miocene-Recent	Eastern Pacific and western Atlantic	13	72
25 m.y. to present	Eastern Pacific and Indo-West Pacific	14	78
18 EP genera	Atlantic and Indo-West Pacific	15	83
Contemporary	Eastern Pacific and Western Atlantic	1	17
Present	Eastern Pacific and Indo-West Pacific	6	100
6 EP genera[a]	Western Atlantic and Indo-West Pacific	1	17

[a]Coral genera deleted from the listing of Heck and McCoy (1978), because of erroneous records, subgeneric status, or misclassification as hermatypes, are *Agaricia*, *Cladocora*, *Leptoseris*, *Madracis*, *Montipora*, *Polyastra*, and *Pseudocolumnastraea*.

reef-coral fauna (Wells, 1956, 1969; Newell, 1971, 1972). During Neogene to Holocene time (about 25 million years), communication between the Mediterranean Sea and the Indian Ocean was severed (Miocene) and all marine connections across Middle America finally disappeared (Pliocene) (Whitmore and Stewart, 1965; Woodring, 1966), thus isolating tropical western Atlantic and western Tethys from the remainder of the world's oceans. It was during this period that the two great modern reef-coral faunas originated, the Caribbean and the Indo-Pacific (Wells, 1956). The Indo-Pacific coral fauna underwent enormous expansion (ninety genera; Wells, personal communication), in large part due to diversification in the families Acroporidae, Poritidae, and Pocilloporidae. The Caribbean fauna became markedly reduced (twenty-six genera), perhaps as a result of its isolation from the Indo-Pacific realm and extinctions that occurred in the Caribbean during the Miocene. Active mountain building and an increase in the deposition of muddy sediments possibly extinguished many corals there (Newell, 1959, 1971). During the late Pliocene and Pleistocene, the tropical American region was severely affected by episodes of cooling (in the Caribbean, Emiliani [1971], reported a 7–8°C lowering, and Prell and Hays [1976], a 4°C lowering) and sea level fluctuations (with vertical excursions as great as 130 m [Fairbridge, 1973]) resulting from the glacial advances and retreats of the period (Stoddart, 1976; Stanley and Campbell, 1981). During this period many eastern Pacific corals became extinct (eighteen genera) and the affinity between Atlantic and eastern Pacific coral faunas weakened slightly, from 89 percent to 72 percent (table 22). Concurrently, the eastern Pacific and Indo-West Pacific relationships demonstrated a relative increase of about twofold, from 39 percent to 78 percent (due to the extinction of western Atlantic corals in both the Caribbean and eastern Pacific).

From the known fossil records of eastern Pacific corals, one can cautiously infer their origins. The earliest occurrences of two genera (*Cycloseris* and *Gardineroseris*) in the Miocene of the Indo-West Pacific, and then their appearances later in the eastern Pacific, suggest immigration from west to east (fig. 62). *Cycloseris* is also known from the early Tertiary in the Mediterranean region, and had disappeared there by the Miocene, without having reached the Atlantic-Caribbean region. *Cycloseris* flourished in the Indo-Pacific throughout the late Tertiary and is widespread today from the Red Sea to the eastern Pacific. Both eastern Pacific species of *Cycloseris*, *C. elegans* and *C. mexicana*, are very similar if not identical to, respectively, a *Cycloseris* species from off Dar es Salaam (Tanzania) and *Cycloseris distorta* (Michelin), which is widespread in the Red Sea, Indian Ocean, and central Pacific. It is highly probable that *Cycloseris* arrived in the eastern Pacific from the west. However, it is thus far known in the fossil record in the central Pacific only in the Miocene of the Bikini drill hole (Wells, 1954), possibly because sandy bottom habitats are not well represented in this region.

Pavona and *Pocillopora* may have persisted at low levels in the eastern Pacific since their extinctions in the Caribbean, but it is also possible that they immigrated to the eastern Pacific from the west. Small populations of *Pocillopora* now are known to have been present in the southern Caribbean about 120,000 years B.P., but evidently not during the earlier Pleistocene and much of the Pliocene (Geister, 1977). Since *Porites* and *Leptoseris* are pantropical in distribution, we cannot infer anything from these taxons at the generic level. *Psammocora* could be an example of long-distance dispersal from the eastern Pacific to the Indo-West Pacific region. This necessarily limited analysis suggests that the eastern Pacific coral fauna was largely derived from the west.

Currently known eastern Pacific fossil coral assemblages are few, scattered in distribution, and small in size compared with those in the tropical western Atlantic region. *Pocillopora* was present in the Galápagos Islands during late Pliocene to early Pleistocene time (Durham, 1979). The dredging of a suite of hermatypic corals (*Pocillopora*, *Porites*, *Leptoseris*, *Plesiastrea*, and *Stylophora*) from a guyot on the Nasca Ridge indicates that reef corals occurred much farther south than the Galápagos (about 2,700 km south) in late Tertiary or Quaternary time (Fisher, 1958; Allison et al., 1967).* This Nasca

---

Plesiastrea and *Stylophora* were also collected from the Nasca Ridge (J. W. Wells, personal communication). The confusion over the identity of *Stylophora* and *Madracis* (Fisher, 1958; Durham, 1979) arises from the fact that there are two different lots from the Ridge. One is Durham's lot (H73), which includes *Pocillopora*, *Porites*, *Leptoseris*, and originally *Stylophora*. The *Stylophora*, obviously Recent and growing on fossil *Porites*, is actually the ahermatype *Madracis* cf. *pharensis*. The second lot in Wells's possession (H72), collected a few km from H73, includes *Pocillopora*, *Porites* (two species: one massive and the other slender branching and possibly referable to *Porites compressa* Dana, present in Hawaii), *Stylophora*, and *Plesiastrea* cf. *versipora* (present in the Indo-Pacific, but not in Hawaii).

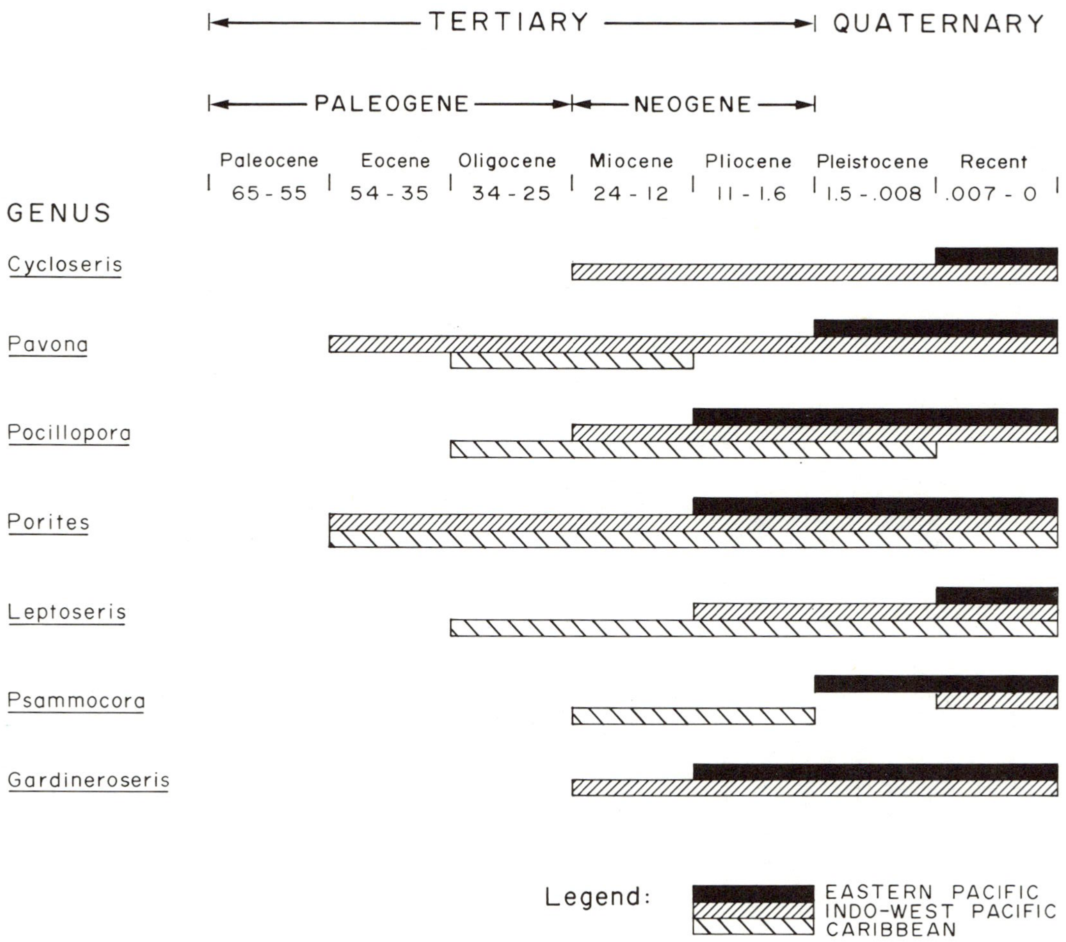

FIGURE 62. Contemporary eastern Pacific reef-building coral genera and their occurrences in the three major coral reef provinces since the beginning of Tertiary time.

Ridge occurrence is interesting because it is in line with a chain of islands (e.g., Easter, Ducie, and Pitcairn) and sea mounts extending eastward from the Tuamotu Archipelago, and may represent a former southerly connection between the central and eastern Pacific regions. The late Tertiary (lower Pliocene; Durham, 1947) Imperial formation (Vaughan, 1917), located inland from the extreme north end of the Gulf of California, probably represents the northernmost range extension of reef corals in the eastern Pacific. This assemblage primarily consists of Caribbean genera (Vaughan, 1917) and apparently marks the last significant Caribbean connection with the Pacific (Squires, 1959; Durham and Allison, 1960). Poritid and probably pavonid (Durham's *Solenastrea* from Ecuador is shown to be identical to *Pavona*, see *Pavona clavus*, appendix) coral formations occurred respectively in the Gulf of California (Squires, 1959) and at the Tres Marias Islands, Mexico (Jordan and Hertlein, 1926; Hanna, 1926) during the Pliocene. During the last interglacial period (Sangamon time, about 110,000 B.P.), *Pocillopora* was present as far north as Guadalupe Island (off the west coast of Baja California), about 1,100 km northwest of the nearest known outer coast occurrence of *Pocillopora* today (Durham, 1979). A taxonomically similar pocilloporid fossil deposit was described by Palmer (1928) on the Mexican mainland coast (near Escondido Bay, Oaxaca state), and Durham (1979) suggested that this occurrence and the Guadalupe assemblage may have been contemporaneous. Clearly, then, on one hand, it is evident that the same coral genera have had a long history of occurrence in this region. On the other hand, little evidence is available to support the claim that this has been a continuous fauna.

On the basis of recent geological evidence, it does not seem probable that the scarcity of fossil corals and reefs along the western American coast is due to seafloor consumption (or erosion of the continental margins) by the major subduction zone present in this region, as suggested by Heck and McCoy (1978). According to Lonsdale and Klitgord (1978) and Lowrie et al. (1979), the active subduction zone off the Pacific coast of Panamá has been located seaward (south) of the continental shelf since late Miocene time (twelve million years B.P.). The minimal separation distance between the axis of a trench and the volcanic front (arc-trench gap) in any subduction zone is 100–124 km (Dickinson, 1973). Contemporary reef-building corals, or such corals that might have been present during low sea level stands, are situated on the landward borders of the continental shelf, far to the north of the subduction zone.

Contemporary Coral Species Distributions: If we now examine the relationships of contemporary eastern Pacific coral genera, we find the strongest affinity with the Indo-West Pacific (100 percent), and a weak affinity with the western Atlantic (17 percent) (fig. 62). In the western Atlantic, on the Caribbean side of the Isthmus of Panamá, there are twenty-eight genera; on the Pacific side, eight. Of these, only three cosmopolitan forms, *Porites*,

· 174 ·

Leptoseris, and *Millepora* are common to both faunas, but there are no species in common.

Again, the Pacific character of the eastern Pacific hermatypic coral fauna is readily apparent from a listing of all valid taxons in relation to their nearest east-central Pacific occurrences (table 23). All eastern Pacific species are also found in the nearest sites to the west, except for four forms: *Pocillopora capitata, Cycloseris elegans, Porites nodulosa* Verrill, and *Porites panamensis* Verrill. These species could be endemic, but it is possible that the last three also occur in the Indo-Pacific region. None of the twenty-six species listed in table 23 occurs in the Caribbean-Atlantic region.

Thus the extant eastern Pacific coral fauna, and that of the Galápagos Islands, has extremely close ties with the central and western Pacific, several thousand kilometers distant, and only the feeblest of relations to the Caribbean, less than 100 km distant across the Isthmus of Panamá (Glynn, 1972; Porter, 1972).

Historically, the Caribbean fauna was derived from the Caribbean Miocene fauna, whereas that of the eastern Pacific can only be related to the still poorly known Miocene faunas of the central and western Pacific. If the present eastern Pacific coral fauna is a legacy of a pre-Pliocene assemblage that occurred on both American Pacific and Caribbean shores, as proposed by the vicariance school (Heck and McCoy, 1978), we may ask why no Atlantic species or their progenitors have survived in the eastern Pacific to the present day?

Long-distance Dispersal: If reef corals and associated organisms became extinct in the eastern Pacific during unfavorable Pleistocene glacial periods, following the Pliocene closure of the Panamá Portal, then the only species pool available for subsequent recolonization would be from the Central Pacific and from island stepping stones along the way. Heck and McCoy (1978) suggested, however, that all corals now present in the eastern Pacific are survivors of a once continuous Panamerican reef-coral assemblage. This notion is difficult to reconcile with the strong (nearly identical) affinity between eastern Pacific and Indo-West Pacific coral faunas noted earlier.

Proponents of long-distance dispersal claim that reef organisms can cross the East Pacific Barrier and colonize eastern Pacific shores. It is usually assumed that long-lived (teleplanic) larvae start this journey from the Line Islands (eastern Polynesia) and travel for 3.5 to 4 months (5,700 to 6,500 km) in the eastward-flowing North Equatorial Countercurrent (fig. 61) until reaching stepping-stone islands (Clipperton Atoll, Cocos Island) and/or submarine banks or the American mainland. The movement of settled coral colonies attached to floating pumice or logs is another suggested means of dispersal (McBirney and Williams, 1969). Richards (1958) traced the movements of pumice (in the North Equatorial Current) arising from a 1952 eruption in the Revillagigedo Islands to Hawaii, Johnston Island, the Marshall

TABLE 23. Eastern Pacific and Nearest Eastcentral Pacific Records of Hermatypic Corals.

Species	Panamá	Galápagos	Gulf of California	Cocos	Colombia	Ecuador	Central America	Clipperton	Malpelo	Easter	Hawaii	Line	Marquesas	Tuamotus	Pitcairn-Ducie	Tahiti
Pocillopora damicornis (Linnaeus)	x	x	x	-	x	x	x	-	-	x	x	x	x	x	x	x
Pavona varians Verrill	x	x	-	x	x	x	-	x	x	-	x	x	x	-	-	x
Pavona clavus Dana	x	x	x	x	x	x	x	x	-	-	x	x	x	x	x	x
Pavona gigantea Verrill	x	x	x	-	x	x	x	x	-	-	x	x	-	x	x	-
Pocillopora capitata Verrill	x	x	x	-	x	x	x	-	-	-	x	-	-	-	-	-
Psammocora stellata Verrill	x	x	x	x	x	x	x	-	-	-	x	-	-	-	-	-
Pocillopora elegans Dana	x	x	x	x	x	x	x	-	-	-	x	-	-	x	x	x
Gardineroseris planulata (Dana)	x	x	x	x	x	-	-	x	x	-	-	-	x	x	x	x
Pocillopora eydouxi Milne Edwards & Haime	x	x	-	-	x	x	x	-	x	-	-	x	x	x	-	x
Cycloseris elegans Verrill	x	x	-	-	-	-	-	-	x	-	-	x	-	-	-	x
Psammocora brighami Vaughan	x	x	-	-	x	-	-	-	-	-	x	-	x	x	-	-
Millepora intricata[a] Milne Edwards	x	-	-	-	-	-	-	-	-	-	-	-	-	-	-	-
Millepora platyphylla Ehrenberg	x	-	-	-	-	-	-	-	-	-	-	x	x	x	x	x
Porites panamensis Verrill	x	x	x	x	x	x	x	-	-	x	-	-	-	-	-	-
Porites lobata Dana	x	x	x	x	x	x	x	-	x	x	-	x	x	x	x	x
Leptoseris papyracea (Dana)	x	-	x	x	x	x	-	-	-	-	-	-	-	x	x	-
Cycloseris distorta (Michelin)	-	x	x	x	-	x	-	-	-	-	-	-	-	-	-	-
Psammocora superficialis (Gardiner)	-	x	x	x	-	x	-	x	-	-	-	-	-	-	-	x
Pocillopora meandrina Dana	-	x	x	x	x	x	x	x	-	x	x	x	x	-	x	x
Porites nodulosa Verrill	-	x	x	-	x	x	x	x	-	-	-	-	x	-	-	-
Leptoseris hawaiiensis Vaughan	-	-	x	x	-	-	-	-	-	-	x	-	-	-	-	-
Pocillopora danae Verrill	-	-	-	-	x	-	-	-	-	x	x	x	x	x	x	x
Pocillopora verrucosa (Ellis & Solander)	-	x	-	-	-	-	x	x	-	x	-	x	x	x	x	x
Cycloseris vaughani Boschma	-	x	-	-	-	-	-	-	-	x	x	-	x	x	-	-
Leptoseris solida (Quelch)	-	-	-	-	-	-	-	-	-	x	x	-	-	-	x	-
Pocillopora diomedeae Vaughan	-	-	-	-	-	-	-	-	-	x	-	x	-	-	-	x

[a]Not recorded, thus far, from east of the Caroline Islands.

Islands, and Wake Island. Small corals were attached to lumps of pumice that reached the Marshall Islands after 560 days and a distance of 8,700 km. It is not known, however, at which point during this journey the corals settled onto the pumice. Live coral attached to pumice also has come ashore at Cocos-Keeling from Krakatoa (Guppy, 1889) and on the Queensland coast from points unknown (Saville-Kent, 1893). Wells (personal communication) collected several bits of pumice on the Queensland coast in 1954, and some of this material contained small (2.5 cm maximum diameter) *Pocillopora* colonies. Rafting on kelp was proposed by Birkeland (1971) to explain the occurrence of a sea star and snail brooding their young on a sea mount, and by Gerrodette (1981) as one means to account for the latitudinal coastal spread of an ahermatypic coral with a short-lived planula larva. While some workers give importance to the Equatorial Undercurrent (Cromwell Current) as a mechanism for transporting Indo-Pacific species to the eastern Pacific (Zinsmeister and Emerson, 1979), one should be reminded that this is an essentially cool-water current (14°–17°C) and as such probably offers suboptimal conditions for reef-associated organisms.

The existence of an easterly moving countercurrent during the Tertiary has been questioned by Heck and McCoy (1978), on the basis of a simulation study of paleocurrents (Luyendyk et al., 1972). If reef organisms arrived to the eastern Pacific relatively recently, however, as proposed by Walker (1966), Rosenblatt and Hobson (1969), and Dana (1975), it is necessary to assume the existence of the North Equatorial Countercurrent only during Pleistocene (during interglacial spells) and perhaps Recent (Holocene) time.

There also exists a South Equatorial Countercurrent that has its origin at the sea surface near the Solomon Islands and extends all the way east to the coast of South America (Reid, 1961; Tsuchiya, 1970). The axis of this current is centered near 10°S, passing through the Marquesas Islands at 104°W, and extends as far east as 120°W, at which position it appears to shift southward. Rotschi (1970) noted an eastward drift, to 170°W, of euphausids from New Guinea (4,400 km) and young stomatopod larvae from the New Hebrides (2,200 km) by this countercurrent. As for its potential as a conveyor of reef organisms to the eastern Pacific, the South Equatorial Countercurrent is relatively slow (10–30 cm per second) and appears to enter subsurface layers east of 140°W (Wyrtki, 1965); its proximity to the eastern Pacific is favorable, but its fate after approaching South America is unknown.

The length of the larval life of corals under natural conditions is not well known. Dana (1975) calculated that a coral planula would need to remain in the water column for 125 days to reach the eastern Pacific from the Line Islands, assuming a high and steady current speed of 60 cm per second. From a laboratory study, under conditions that discouraged larval settlement (constantly changing water and removing organic films), Harrigan (1972a, b) found that the planula of *Pocillopora damicornis* could remain unattached for up to 212 days. Dana (1975) interpreted this result to suggest that this coral species can produce teleplanic larvae. Heck and McCoy (1978) challenged Dana's interpretation and cited studies showing that the planulae of *P. damicornis* spent a much shorter time, about three weeks, in the plankton (Edmondson, 1946; Atoda, 1947, 1951). In view of the capacity of many species with pelagic larvae to be able to postpone settlement and metamorphosis under unfavorable conditions, such as the absence of an appropriate substratum (Wilson, 1960; Crisp, 1974; Gray, 1974), it seems to us that Harrigan's findings are not necessarily an artifact of laboratory conditions. Coral larvae, and the larvae of shallow benthic species generally, would find it advantageous to delay settlement if present in currents over deep water. Richmond (in press) recently examined, in energetic terms, the larval dispersal potential of the planulae of *Pocillopora damicornis* and found that long-range dispersal may be possible: 13 percent to 27 percent of carbon fixed by symbiotic zooxanthellae is translocated to the larva, and the stored fat reserves of larvae are high. The competency of long-lived planktonic planulae, however, has yet to be demonstrated.

On the basis of distribution patterns of adult coral colonies and the position of a subtropical countercurrent, Grigg (in press) proposed post-Pleistocene recolonization events by larval dispersal to account for the extant occurrence of *Acropora* (three species) in the Hawaiian Islands. According to this view, larval dispersal occurred between Johnston Island and the French Frigate Shoals in the Hawaiian chain, a distance of 720 km. Grigg (1981) estimated that fifty days in the plankton were required to make this journey.

Since so little is known of the larval ecology of reef corals, we will discuss briefly some aspects of the larval ecology of other coral reef associates in order to gain some perspective to the problem of long-distance dispersal. It should be understood at the outset that the vast majority (80–85 percent) of presently known shallow-living, benthic marine species in the tropics have a pelagic larval stage in their development (Thorson, 1950, 1961; Mileikovsky, 1971; Scheltema, 1977). Furthermore, recent findings are showing that many groups of invertebrates produce larvae that can remain in the plankton for extended periods of time (teleplanic larvae); in some cases, for as long as a year (Scheltema, 1972; Zinsmeister and Emerson, 1979; these authors give several references to this literature).

Extensive sampling of the plankton within several major surface currents in the Atlantic Ocean has disclosed the presence of teleplanic larvae, from many invertebrate phyla (including the Mollusca, Arthropoda, Annelida, and Echinodermata), which are widely scattered across the Atlantic basin (Scheltema, 1977). There are also numerous descriptions in the literature of coelenterate larvae taken from plankton tows far at sea (e.g., Leloup, 1964), but the larvae are not usually related to the adult forms. Scheltema (personal communication) has observed that coelenterate larvae are quite common in offshore tropical waters. When the times required for transoceanic dispersal are compared with laboratory estimates of the duration of pelagic stages, it is seen that many larvae can be easily transported across the Atlantic Ocean. For example, the time required for transatlantic drift between Brazil and the Gulf of Guinea (this can be accomplished in both directions by two different currents) ranges from 60 to 150 days; ten gastropod species with teleplanic larvae have estimated pelagic stages ranging from 42 to 320 days (Scheltema, 1971, 1977). Additionally, almost all of the Atlantic species with teleplanic larvae have been found to have amphi-Atlantic distributions.

A distribution pattern that seems inexplicable by vicariance was noted by Newman (1979) with regard to barnacles. The argument is this: How does one account for the occurrence of littoral barnacles on oceanic islands too young and too distant ever to have been a part of a former land mass? Newman (1979) argued convincingly that the littoral barnacles present on certain islands associated with the mid-Atlantic Ridge and in the Indian Ocean must have reached those sites by epiplanktonic means (jump dispersal).* Bermuda, an oceanic island of volcanic origin, most likely received its reef-coral fauna by larval transport from the West Indies via the Gulf Stream. Laborel (1974) proposed that from the West Indies and Bermuda (stepping stone), Gulf Stream conveyance allowed transatlantic colonization of reef corals in the Cape Verde Islands. A south Atlantic stepping-stone route, via the oceanic islands of Martin Vaz (Brazil) and St. Helena was also suggested by Laborel (1974) to explain the derivation of the African Gulf of Guinea coral fauna from Brazil. Numerous similar examples could be cited, from all oceans and from a diversity of biotas, both terrestrial and marine.

Jump dispersal probably played a significant role in the eastern Pacific in the colonization of the Galápagos Islands, Cocos Island, Malpelo Island, Clipperton Atoll, and the Revillagigedo Islands. It is highly probable that the oceanic Hawaiian chain was formed from massive lava extrusions associated with the Pacific lithospheric plate, a hot spot origin similar to that proposed for the Galápagos Islands (Shaw, 1973; Van Andel, 1974). The Hawaiian chain, drifting and subsiding in a northwesterly direction, never seems to have been connected with a former land mass. Many workers (e.g., see Carlquist, 1981) have proposed that Hawaii's angiosperm flora, and the native land biota in general, reached the islands from a variety of areas by means of jump dispersal. Hawaii's littoral marine fauna has most likely been derived by jump dispersal from the southwest via the Marcus Necker Ridge (Kay, in Devaney and Eldredge, 1977) and/or the west via a southern branch extension of the Kuroshio Current (Zinsmeister and Emerson, 1979). Grigg (1981) also favors recolonization of *Acropora* into the Hawaiian Archipelago by way of Johnston Island (from the southwest), and has demonstrated how an east-

---

*Pielou (1979), in recognizing the importance of the time scale in dispersal, has proposed the term jump dispersal, which to us seems especially relevant to the long-distance dispersal of pelagic larvae produced by tropical, shallow-living benthic marine species: *jump dispersal*, "... the movement of individual organisms across great distances, followed by the successful establishment of a population of the original dispersers' descendants at the destination."

erly flowing subtropical countercurrent could serve as an effective means of conveyance.

Most of the Indo-Pacific coral reef fishes present in the eastern Pacific (about fifty species are presently known) possess larval stages adapted to long-distance pelagic transport or juveniles and adults that can live in association with floating debris in the open water for long periods of time (Hubbs and Rosenblatt, 1961; Rosenblatt et al., 1972). Unfortunately, very few quantitative data on the duration of the larval lives of reef fishes have been published. Available evidence indicates, however, that many reef fishes have pelagic larval stages of a few weeks or a few months (Moran and Sale, 1977; Johannes, 1980). Moreover, Johannes (1978) and Sale (1980) are of the opinion that many coral reef fishes will probably be shown to be capable of extending their larval lives in the absence of suitable settlement sites. *Acanthurus triostegus* Linnaeus, an Indo-Pacific reef fish present on offshore islands and at certain mainland sites in the eastern Pacific, has a pelagic larval life of 2.5 months (Randall, 1961). Randall (1961) presented indirect evidence, that is, a greater range of sizes of larvae settling between monthly peaks of settlement, that *A. triostegus* is capable of extending its usual larval life beyond 2.5 months.

At least some long-distance dispersal seems to be associated with the great variability in strength and direction of oceanic currents, most likely a response to major short-term climatic fluctuations. Abnormalities in circulation can produce peculiar patterns of settlement, leading to the establishment of species hundreds of kilometers beyond their normal range. Such sporadic episodes of transport have been termed "dispersal pulses" (an ephemeral mode of jump dispersal) by Zinsmeister and Emerson (1979). Dispersal pulses could provide relatively rapid transport, thus increasing the probability of long-distance dispersal. Anomalous occurrences of subtropical and tropical species in southern California (Zinsmeister, 1974) were correlated with periods of abnormal oceanic circulation. The club-spined sea urchin *Eucidaris thouarsii* and the Pinto lobster *Panulirus inflatus* (Bouvier), species that occur abundantly at Magdalena Bay and further south, were found in southern California (1,000 to 1,200 km north) during a large-scale warming trend in the late 1950s. The El Niño event has been directly implicated in the anomalous occurrence of Panamic fishes off Peru (Vildoso, 1976).

Dana's (1975) use of the high velocity of 60 cm/second or 52 km/day (Pickard, 1963) over a 125-day period, to account for rapid water transport from the Line Islands to Costa Rica (ca. 6,500 km), could be a realistic though infrequent rate associated with El Niño invasions. Volume transport from west to east is intensified during periods of hypothesized "backsloshing," that is when previously strong southeasterly trade winds off South America slacken and thus allow a hydrodynamic readjustment of sea level differences (Wyrtki, 1973, 1975; Wyrtki et al., 1976). Thus, long-distance dispersal would be favored by extreme or anomalous meteorological and oceanographic conditions. But even these anomalous conditions have occurred frequently in recent years; Quinn (1974) reported six such events during the last three decades.

The strong phylogenetic relationships existing among numerous marine taxa in the eastern Pacific and Caribbean cannot be denied (e.g., Ekman, 1953; Rosen, 1975). For example, strong affinities have been demonstrated among the algae (Earle, 1972), mollusks (e.g., Woodring, 1970), brachyuran crabs (Garth, 1946; Gore and Abele, 1976), echinoderms (Chesher, 1972; Lessios, 1981), and fishes (Rosenblatt, 1963; Rubinoff and Rubinoff, 1971). But neither can the strong relationship between eastern Pacific and Indo-Pacific coral reef communities be refuted. Could it be that most taxa showing strong transisthmian ties belong predominantly to inshore assemblages that are relatively tolerant of the physical perturbations associated with the Neogene? Reef coral assemblages, on the other hand, are known to be relatively intolerant of harsh environmental conditions (notably abrupt lowering of sea temperatures; Shinn, 1972; Glynn and Stewart, 1973), and therefore would be expected to be periodically exterminated, and reconstituted from the central Pacific during favorable interglacial periods. To summarize, then, in order to establish the true genetic relations of eastern Pacific coral communities we believe that it is essential to recognize a recent and predominantly Indo-Pacific connection.

Another mode of origin, which we have not touched upon, is the possibility that remnants of the more extensive Neogene fauna survived in the eastern Pacific and were augmented by dispersal from the west. In other words, the recent coral fauna is a result of both vicariance and dispersal. It is important to ask how the above hypotheses could be tested. In our minds, there are three avenues of research that might be explored: (a) determination of the genetic affinities between coral species common to the eastern and western Pacific regions. Given the rather marked differences in physical conditions between these two regions (e.g., water temperatures, nutrient levels, and turbidity), we would predict a measurable divergence in genotypes. If dispersal is occurring, then affinities should be high; especially in areas where transport is likely to occur (e.g., on distant offshore islands and continental areas in line with countercurrents), (b) a thorough study of fossil assemblages on the mainland and on offshore islands that might act as stepping stones for dispersal. For example, little work has been conducted on Clipperton Atoll—the only atoll in the eastern Pacific. The scleractinian corals known from this island are identical with eastern Pacific continental forms (in Sachet, 1962; Garth, 1965); however, drilling efforts on the reef may provide clues to the nature of past coral assemblages, and (c) in order to test the reality of the dispersal model, attempts should be made to demonstrate the potential competency of long-lived coral larvae. This, of course, would not provide conclusive evidence but could increase the probability of the correctness of the dispersal hypothesis.

GALÁPAGOS AND EASTERN PACIFIC COMPARISONS

Because the Galápagos Islands are located near the southern limit of distribution of reef corals in the eastern Pacific basin, it is of interest to compare them with the northernmost outpost of coral communities located in the Gulf of California. Subsequent comparisons will include coral development in upwelling areas within the Panamic Province, and the quintessence of eastern Pacific reef development in the nonupwelling areas of Panamá, Costa Rica, and Colombia. Each regional comparison will consider geographical, geological, and ecological (physical and biotic) conditions.

Gulf of California: From the standpoint of conditions suitable for reef growth, the Gulf of California is a somewhat harsher environment than the Galápagos. This is due in large part to the northerly location of the Gulf, spanning nearly 9° latitude between 23°N and 32°N, and a strong continental influence caused by the surrounding high terrain (1- to 3-km-high mountains in Baja California) and desert conditions (Schreiber, 1967; Brusca, 1980; Brusca and Wallerstein, 1979). Before the volume discharge of the Colorado River was severely reduced by irrigation and construction of the Hoover Dam, its effects (dilution and sediment transport) were discernible as far south in the Gulf as La Paz (Brusca, 1980). Approximately 50 percent of the sediments entering the Gulf in former years were derived from the Colorado River. The average annual river flow in the vicinity of Yuma, Arizona, was more than 18.5×10^9 m³ (15 million acre-feet) between 1902–1934; by 1963–1964 no permanent surface water from the Colorado River was reaching the Gulf (Thomson et al., 1969). The northern Gulf (north of Guaymas and Santa Rosalia) is subject to pronounced seasonal variations (especially thermal) and is best considered as subtropical; the southern Gulf experiences less pronounced seasonal changes and is more nearly tropical in nature (Hubbs and Roden, 1964; Brusca, in press). However, upwelling and high rates of primary productivity have been reported in all parts of the Gulf (Roden and Groves, 1959; Zeitzschel, 1969). Other physical factors affecting corals, such as currents, suspended sediments, tides, and habitat type, are discussed in Parker (1964), Roden (1964), Thomson et al. (1969, 1979), and Brusca (1980, in press). Several small coral patches have been reported in the Gulf (Steinbeck and Ricketts, 1941; Fraser, 1943; Durham, 1947; Squires, 1959; Dana and Wolfson, 1970; Barham et al., 1973) and these are located in the southern half of the Gulf, south of Concepción Bay. *Porites panamensis* is the only common reef coral present north of Concepción Bay, where it forms mainly small encrusting and nodular colonies.* The principal species in the coral communities and coral buildups in the southern Gulf are *Pocillopora elegans, Pocillopora damicornis, Porites panamensis, Pavona gigantea,* and *Pavona clavus.* Most of the fringing coral communities are formed by the columnar form of *Porites panamensis.* The primary reef-frame is *Pocillopora,* which erects an interlocking network of closely spaced, vertically oriented branches. El Pulmo reef, located inside the Gulf near the tip of Baja California, is the best known and largest coral formation reported in the literature (Squires, 1959; Brusca and Thomson, 1977).

The reef corals at Pulmo are growing on a series of submerged, parallel, rock (extruded igneous rock) ridges that extend offshore in a northeasterly direction. Corals occur from near the extreme low tide level to at least 10 m depth. The corals contributing most to the buildups at Pulmo are *Pocillopora elegans,* at shallow depth, and *Porites panamensis* and *Pavona gigantea* in deeper water. Macroscopic (noncalcareous) algae, gorgonians, crustaceans, and opisthobranch and bivalve mollusks (both boring and epibenthic species) are also common, living in close association with corals. According to Brusca and Thomson (1977), some parts of the Pulmo reef complex have undergone modest framework construction. While no vertical dimensions were noted, these workers reported that coral growth in two areas was equal to or considerably greater in volume than the underlying rock substrate.

A coral formation showing substantial vertical growth was discovered recently immediately south of the Pulmo reef, in the protected anchorage of Los Frailes Bay.** Two patch reefs with a combined area of 150 by 250 m are located at shallow depth (to 9 m) on the leeward side of Los Frailes Point. Surface inspection indicated that the main reef-frame, composed dominantly of *Pocillopora elegans,* is about 3 m in vertical thickness. Massive *Pavona* sp. colonies are scattered around the reef base. These observations were made in June, during a summer upwelling episode induced by southeasterly winds (Roden and Groves, 1959). Maximum-minimum thermometers placed on the reef crest (3 m depth) and base (9 m depth) recorded minimum temperatures of 14.8°C and 11.0°C respectively.

In San Gabriel Bay (east side of Espíritu Santo Island, northeast of La Paz), large isolated blocks of *Pocillopora elegans* occur at 2–5 m depth and form a barrierlike structure about 1 km long that parallels the sand beach. Some of

---

*Several specimens of *Porites californica* Verrill 1870 and *Porites panamensis* Verrill 1866 were studied in detail and found to show no significant morphological differences beyond the usual variation present within single colonies. Therefore, since *P. panamensis* has priority, this name will be used subsequently.

**Dustin D. Chivers kindly made this information available. The Frailes Bay coral reef complex was discovered during the Los Frailes Expedition (June 1979) of the California Academy of Sciences.

the pocilloporid blocks are 12 m in diameter and 1–2.5 m in height. Although this formation is structurally discontinuous, it does modify wave action and currents to leeward and thus produces the same result as the dampening effect of laminar algal beds in the northern Gulf (Squires, 1959). A coral community composed of *Porites panamensis* was also observed along the eastern rocky shore of San Gabriel Bay. Other occurrences of *Porites* communities in the lower Gulf region are given in Squires (1959).

Both Squires (1959) and Brusca and Thomson (1977) have remarked on the apparent youthfulness of coral reefs in the Gulf of California. Brusca and Thomson (1977) estimated that the Pulmo reef was probably less than 20,000 years old and possibly less than 5,000 years old. Assuming similar accumulation rates (~ net vertical reef growth) of pocilloporid reefs in the Gulf of California and the Gulf of Panamá, we may estimate the ages of the framework buildups of the Frailes Bay and San Gabriel Bay reefs from data in Glynn and Macintyre (1977). (Since the growth rates of *Pocillopora* in the Gulf of California are probably lower than in the Pearl Islands [Dana and Wolfson, 1970; Glynn and Stewart, 1973; Glynn, 1977], the framework accumulation rates in the Gulf of California may be slightly less [and the buildups older] than the following estimates.)

In the Pearl Islands (Saboga Island), Gulf of Panamá, 5- to 6-m-thick pocilloporid reefs have maximum ages of 3,800 to 4,500 years. Based on these accumulation rates, the Frailes Bay reef is probably no older than 2,300 years and the San Gabriel Bay reef no older than 1,900 years. If, however, the Gulf of California reefs had realized uninterrupted vertical growth, a condition observed on some pocilloporid reefs in Panamá (Glynn and Macintyre, 1977), it is possible that the Frailes Bay and San Gabriel Bay buildups formed only during the past 250 to 300 years. The vertical thicknesses of most of the coral buildups in the Galápagos are similar to those of the Frailes and San Gabriel bay reefs (table 24). Pocilloporid buildups are of the same order of magnitude in the two areas and thus presumably comparable in age. Galapagan pavonid reefs attain 6–10 m in thickness (at Champion and Bartolomé islands). It is possible that these kinds of reefs are somewhat older than pocilloporid reefs in the Gulf of California. While estimates of the accumulation rates of reefs composed of massive corals show a high variance, from 1–3 m/1,000 yr to 5–8 m/1,000 yr (e.g., see Macintyre et al., 1982), the largest Galapagan reefs are calculated to have been forming, on the average, during the past 1,000 to 5,000 years. In conclusion, Cortezian and Galapagan coral reefs appear equally youthful and have formed mainly during the latest Holocene time.

In terms of physical conditions favoring coral growth, Squires (1959) stressed the importance of the following: (a) availability of shallow firm substrates, (b) protection from extreme wave action, but receiving adequate circulation, (c) water column relatively free of fine, suspended sediments, and (d) position on northern portion of an embayment. Conditions a–c were also found to have important effects in the Galápagos. Condition b, in particular, was strongly in evidence in the Galápagos vis-à-vis the occurrence of rich coral communities and coral buildups on the northeastern sides of islands. The abundance of corals on the north sides of embayments, which must be partly a function of condition b, is a common pattern in the Gulf of California. The Pulmo reef faces north, where it occasionally is subject to strong wave action. The other north-facing coral formations noted by Squires (1959) are present in bays and thus to the leeward of strong wave action. The Frailes Bay reef is situated on the south side of an embayment (near an anchorage), and in this position may be subject to less buffeting than the Pulmo reef.

Squires (1959) also considered low water temperatures to be significant in limiting the northerly range extension of hermatypic corals in the Gulf. He demonstrated an attenuation of coral genera with increasing latitude in the Gulf, as Wells (1955) did in the opposite direction in the southern hemisphere along the Great Barrier Reef complex, and noted a changeover between corals and kelp between 26°N and 28°N latitude (Squires, 1959, Table 1). Judging from the low temperatures recorded during upwelling at the Frailes Bay reef (11.0°C at 9 m, and 14.8°C at 3 m), it is highly likely that such conditions can have a significant local effect in the Gulf. The coolest water conditions in the Galápagos occur on the west coast of Isabela Island, where sea surface temperatures of 14.3°–15.1°C were recorded. This Galápagos area lacks reef-building corals, but supports rich macrophytic algal communities. Since eastern Pacific hermatypic corals are stressed by water temperatures of 18°C (Glynn and Stewart, 1973; Glynn, 1977), it is likely that the Frailes Bay corals experience such low temperatures infrequently and only briefly (probably no more than a few days at a time). In Hawaii, *Pocillopora damicornis* dies in less than two weeks at 18°C (Jokiel and Coles, 1977), and in less than twenty-four hours at 15°C (Clausen, 1971). Upwelling need not kill corals directly, but could promote the growth of algae (and animal populations feeding on plankton and detritus) due to the higher levels of nutrients that accompany upwelling events. Squires (1959) repeatedly stressed the active competition observed between algae and reef-building corals in the Gulf of California.

Although the Pulmo reef contains nearly the same corals that erect impressive frameworks elsewhere in the eastern Pacific, Squires (1959) attributed the weak development of reefs in the Gulf to the depauperate nature of the coral fauna there.* This notion is probably partly correct. One can imagine more extensive consolidation of reefs, or reef building in new zones, for example, in wave-exposed habitats, if certain species present in the central and western Pacific (*Synaraea, Acropora, Montipora, Leptoria, Hydnophora*, inter alia) were present in the Gulf. However, species-poor, and in some instances, monospecific coral reefs have formed under a variety of conditions in

---

*No large, massive *Porites* species have been reported from the Gulf of California. *Porites lobata* is present in the Galápagos and in the Panamic Province where it often contributes significantly to reef building and, in some cases, forms virtually monospecific reefs.

TABLE 24. Variety of Eastern Pacific Reef-Frame Buildups, Vertical Thicknesses, and Statistical Comparisons.

Locations	Predominant Coral	Vertical Thickness (m)[a]	Number Observations	Median Thickness Pocilloporid Reefs (m)	Locality Comparisons[b]					
					GAL	CAL	PAP	PAN	CHI	GOR
Galápagos Islands										
Punta Pitt, San Cristóbal Island	*Pocillopora*	1	1							
Osborn Island, Española Island	*Pocillopora*	0.5–1	1							
Onslow Island, Floreana Island	*Pocillopora*	Md = 0.6(0.6–0.8)	5							
Cormorant Bay, Floreana Island	*Pocillopora*	Md = 1.2(1.1–2.7)	8							
Champion Island, Floreana Island	*Pavona*	4–5, max. = 10	1							
Champion Island, Floreana Island	*Pocillopora*	1	1							
Santa Fe Island	*Pocillopora*	0.5	1							
Santa Cruz Island, Conway Bay	*Pocillopora*	0.5–1	1	1.0(0.8–1.2)[c]	—	NS	NS	*	*	*
Cape Barrington, Isabela Island	*Pavona*	1	1							
Bartolomé Island, Santiago Island	*Porites*	4–5	1							
Bartolomé Island, Santiago Island	*Pavona*	2–3, max. = 6	1							
Urvina Uplift, Isabela Island	*Pocillopora*	0.5	1							
Punta Espinosa, Fernandina Island	*Pocillopora*	Md = 1.2(1.0–1.5)	5							
Darwin Bay, Genovesa Island	*Pocillopora*	1	1							
Darwin Bay, Genovesa Island	*Pavona*	2–3	1							
Darwin Island	*Pocillopora*	1	1							
Gulf of California										
Los Frailes Bay	*Pocillopora*	3	1							
San Gabriel Bay	*Pocillopora*	1–2.5	2	2.5(1–3)	NS	—	NS	NS	NS	NS
Gulf of Papagayo										
Santa Elena Bay	*Pocillopora*	Md = 2.2(1.8–2.4)	4							
Culebra Bay	*Pocillopora*	Md = 1.8(0.6–3.0)	3							

Gorda Point	*Pocillopora*	Md = 1.2(0.6–1.5)	5	1.8(1.2–2.4)	—	*	*	NS
Samara	*Pocillopora*	Md = 2.2 (2–2.5)	2					
Gulf of Panamá								
Iguana Island	*Pocillopora*	Md = 4.9(3.4–6.1)	3					
Saboga Island	*Pocillopora*	Md = 5.2(3.0–5.5), 5.6*	6					
Contadora Island	*Pocillopora*	Md = 2.8(1.8–4.6)	4					
Pedro Gonzáles Island	*Pocillopora*	Md = 3.8(3.4–4.3)	4	4.3(3.4–4.9)	*	—	NS	NS
Cañas Island	*Pocillopora*	Md = 4.9(4.3–4.9)	3					
Gulf of Chiriquí								
Uva Island	*Pocillopora*	Md = 5.2*(2.4*–11.0*)	4					
Secas study reef	*Pocillopora*	Md = 10.8*(8.2*–12.0*)	3					
		Md = 8.6(3.7–13.4)	2					
Cavada Island	*Pocillopora*	Md = 6.6(4.0–9.2)	2	7.9(6.2–10.4)	*	NS	—	NS
Coiba Island	*Pocillopora*	Md = 7.6(4.3–9.4)	3					
Canales de Tierra Island	*Pocillopora*	Md = 7.9(5.8–10.4)	3					
Ensenada de Muertos	*Pocillopora*	Md = 6.0(4.0–7.9)	2					
Secas (south island)	*Pavona*	max. = 5	1					
Golfito (Costa Rica)								
Los Mogos reef	*Porites*	Md = 10(9–11)	2					
Gorgona Island (Colombia)								
La Azufrada reef	*Pocillopora*	Md = 2.8(2.0–8.0)	3					
Playa Blanca reef	*Pocillopora*	8	1					
Pier reef	*Pocillopora*	6	1	4.4(2.5–8.0)	NS	NS	NS	—
La Camaronera	*Pocillopora*	2–3	1					

[a]Standard type denotes visual estimates, italic type reef probing, and asterisks core drilling. Framework thickness values from near shore or forereef talus slopes are omitted from this tabulation. Ranges (in parentheses) are given with median (Md) values.

[b]Statistical testing demonstrated highly significant differences in reef thicknesses between sites (P < 0.001, Kruskal-Wallis test). Multiple comparisons testing (α = 0.20) indicates where the differences occur (asterisks).

[c]Medians and 0.95 confidence limits are shown for pocilloporid reefs at various localities. The range in reef thickness is shown for the Gulf of California.

the eastern Pacific, thus leaving open the question of why reefs are absent from many seemingly favorable areas. Possibly time is a factor: if the eastern Pacific coral fauna was depleted or extirpated during cool periods and sea level fluctuations in the Pleistocene, and perhaps more recently (Glynn et al., ms.), the patchy occurrence of reefs today may represent an early stage of colonization and growth following large-scale disturbances (Goreau, 1969; Stoddart, 1976).

Of all the corallivores known from the Gulf, *Acanthaster* has received the most attention. Most species of corallivores discussed earlier occur in the Gulf, but little is known of their population sizes and effects. The regular five-armed sea star *Pharia pyramidata* was observed feeding on *Pocillopora* coral (Dana and Wolfson, 1970), and *Porites* colonies are broken into by balistids presumably (Barham et al., 1973, fig. 5); outside of these brief reports, little is known. While most workers have referred to the crown-of-thorns sea star in the Gulf as an American endemic, namely, *Acanthaster ellisii* (Gray), we do not believe that it can be separated morphologically from *A. planci*, and therefore recognize only the latter species in all eastern Pacific and Indo-Pacific populations.*

Acanthaster occurs most commonly in the southern half of the Gulf where corals are most abundant. The sea star is abundant locally; as many as forty-eight individuals were reported for one area (Barham et al., 1973), and population densities of at least one individual/200 m² were observed in several areas (Barham et al., 1973; Dana and Wolfson, 1970). *Acanthaster* feeds on hermatypic corals (*Porites, Pocillopora, Psammocora*), a gorgonian (*Pacifigorgia*), and algae (the brown alga *Padina* and coralline algae). *Porites panamensis* was the principal prey at northerly localities where this coral predominates, and *Pocillopora* was eaten frequently in the southern Gulf. *Acanthaster* tended to feed on small, encrusting colonies of *Porites* and on small colonies or broken branches of *Pocillopora*. Intact, erect colonies of *Pocillopora* are usually avoided by *Acanthaster*, mainly because of the coral's crustacean symbionts that attack and drive off the sea stars (Pearson and Endean, 1969; Weber and Woodhead, 1970; Glynn, 1976, 1980).

While *Acanthaster* does consume large amounts of coral locally, up to 87 percent of the standing crop annually, it is generally held that such levels of predation are not causing a decline in Gulf coral populations (Dana and Wolfson, 1970; Barham et al., 1973). Dana and Wolfson (1970), however, offered the suggestion that *Acanthaster* predation, combined with (a) slow

---

*The relevant references to this problem are: Madsen (1955), Caso (1962), Barham et al. (1973), and Glynn (1974a). Even the supposed behavioral differences reported by Dana and Wolfson (1970; see also Barham et al., 1973) were inconsistent for *Acanthaster* populations observed in Panamá, American Samoa, and Guam (Glynn, personal observations). At all three localities, numerous individuals were seen feeding on open bottom areas during the day, and feeding aggregations were present at comparable sea star abundances. *Acanthaster brevispinus* Fisher is a second valid species occurring in the western Pacific; however, it does not frequent coral reefs (Lucas and Jones, 1976).

coral growth (due to low water temperatures), (b) an abundance of boring organisms, and (c) a paucity of coralline algae to serve as a binding agent in reef consolidation, could be an important factor in limiting reef-frame construction in the Gulf. *Eucidaris*, the club-spined sea urchin, was responsible for most coral grazing in the Galápagos. The urchin concentrated on pocilloporid corals and, in its manner of scraping, reduced the branchtips to sand. In contrast, the skeletons of pocilloporid corals killed by *Acanthaster* are left intact. Given sufficient coral recruitment and regrowth, reef accumulation will continue.

The predominant corals in the Galápagos are pavonid species; no pavonid communities or buildups have been recorded from the Gulf. Since all species of *Pavona* are readily eaten by *Acanthaster*, it would be interesting to investigate a possible causal connection between the low abundance of *Pavona* and presence of *Acanthaster* in the Gulf, and the high abundance of *Pavona* and absence of *Acanthaster* in the Galápagos. A similar pattern of *Pavona* spp. abundance, examined again below, exists in the Gulf of Panamá and at Malpelo and Gorgona islands, Colombia (*Acanthaster* absent), and in the Gulf of Chiriquí (*Acanthaster* present).

Upwelling Centers: In terms of temperature conditions (means and seasonal ranges), the three upwelling centers off the Pacific Mexican and Central American coasts are similar to waters in the lower half of the Gulf of California and in the eastern sector of the Galápagos Islands. Upwelling occurs in the gulfs of Tehuantepec (Mexico), Papagayo (Nicaragua-Costa Rica), and Panamá (Panamá), and is brought about mainly by Atlantic winds that move seasonally across the mountain gaps and low passes in these areas (Hubbs and Roden, 1964). The winds are strongest during the northern winter season (from about November–April) and induce upwelling by moving surface water offshore, which is then replaced by cool subsurface water.

During the windy or dry season in the three gulfs, it is not unusual for sea surface temperatures to drop suddenly by 5°–6°C over a four-to eight-day period. Mean minimum temperature data for the three gulfs (Hubbs and Roden, 1964) indicate that upwelling may be strongest in the Gulf of Tehuantepec, somewhat less in the Gulf of Papagayo, and the least in the Gulf of Panamá. The number of months with mean minimum temperatures of 20°C or less in the three areas were five (November–March) for Tehuantepec, three (January–March) for Papagayo, and zero for Panamá. Significantly lower minimum temperatures were reported over a four-year period for Papagayo as compared with Panamá (Glynn et al., ms.). In spite of the seasonally cool and nutrient-rich conditions that occur in the upwelling centers, reef corals are found in at least two of them. While upwelling conditions in Tehuantepec probably periodically approach the limits of reef coral tolerance, the situation there is complicated by the fact that few, if any, suitable substrates are present for coral settlement. This area is composed predominantly of unconsolidated (sandy) sediments. No mention of corals has been reported for this segment of the Pacific Central American Faunal Gap. Some information is now available on coral development in the Gulf of Papagayo.

Several small, fringing, pocilloporid reefs are present on the northwestern Costa Rican coast. These reefs are all dead and presumably died between 150 to 300 years ago (Glynn et al., in press). Glynn and co-workers hypothesize that during the Little Ice Age an equatorward shift of the trade wind system caused an intensification of upwelling (lower water temperatures and longer periods of cool water) in this area which stressed corals and eventually led to the death of the Papagayo reef tract. The dead reefs attained median vertical framework thicknesses of 1.2–2.2 m (table 24) and developed at relatively shallow depths (median water depth of four reefs = 4 m). Papagayo pocilloporid buildups were slightly thicker than those in the Galápagos, but not significantly so. While scant coral communities are present in Papagayo today, probably as a consequence of recolonization processes since the cool water perturbation, no live coral buildups have been observed in the area. Some biological evidence indicative of cooler conditions today in Papagayo than in the Gulf of Panamá are (for Papagayo): (a) low live coral cover, (b) small coral colony sizes, (c) low coral growth rates, (d) high rates of bioerosion in coral skeletons, (e) high incidence of growth interruptions in coral skeletons, and (f) abundant macrophytic algal communities, especially *Sargassum* in the Punta Santa Elena area. These findings suggest that the Gulf of Papagayo is a truly marginal reef coral area. Nowhere else in the eastern Pacific have corals been found to be so greatly affected by the physical environment.

Extensive coral community development and live pocilloporid reefs are present in the Gulf of Panamá (Glynn and Stewart, 1973; Glynn and Macintyre, 1977). Core drilling and ^{14}C dating indicate that one of the largest reefs in the Pearl Islands (Saboga Island reef) is 5-6 m in vertical thickness and that it began to build between 3,800 and 4,500 years ago. Five pocilloporid reefs in the Gulf revealed 4-m-thick sections and one of them (Iguana Island reef) is at least 6 m in thickness (table 24). Thus, pocilloporid buildups in the relatively mild upwelling environment of the Gulf of Panamá have, in every instance, attained greater dimensions than in the Galápagos Islands. Statistical analysis indicates that Gulf of Panamá reefs are significantly thicker than reefs in Papagayo or the Galápagos. How do the growth rates of reef-building corals compare in these two regions?

The mean annual net growth (linear branch elongation) of pocilloporid corals in the Gulf of Panamá (3.1 cm/yr) and the Galápagos (2.0 cm/yr) were similar (P > 0.05, Mann-Whitney U-test). The apparent difference is less if a correction is made to account for corallivore grazing in the two areas. We assume that hermit crabs and pufferfish remove 7.3 percent of the annual growth in Panamá (Glynn et al., 1972) and that *Eucidaris* removes 33 percent of the annual growth in the Galápagos (Glynn et al., 1979). (*Jenneria* is excluded from consideration because the effects of this potentially important corallivore were minimal for the growth measurements obtained in Panamá. Also, any damage resulting from *Jenneria* was usually detectable and thus excluded.) These adjustments suggest mean skeletal growth rates in the Gulf of Panamá and the Galápagos were 3.3 cm/yr and 2.7 cm/yr respectively.

Neither is a significant difference apparent in the linear skeletal growth of massive corals in the Gulf of Panamá and the Galápagos. Ample data are available to test the growth rates of *Pavona gigantea* and *P. clavus* in the two areas: *P. gigantea*—thirty-three colonies from the Pearl Islands (Glynn, 1974*b*; Glynn et al., in press), twenty colonies from the Galápagos (see table 9; Urvina Bay data were omitted from this analysis because of the harsh conditions and low growth observed); *P. clavus*—seven colonies from the Pearl Islands (Wellington and Glynn, 1983), thirty-eight colonies from the Galápagos (from table 9, excluding Urvina Bay). Mean skeletal growth in *P. gigantea* was 0.92 cm/yr in the Gulf of Panamá and 0.99 cm/yr in the Galápagos (P~0.30, Mann-Whitney U-test). Mean skeletal growth in *P. clavus* was 1.37 cm/yr in the Gulf of Panamá and 1.24 cm/yr in the Galápagos (P~0.13, Mann-Whitney U-test).

It does not seem likely from the foregoing that coral growth rate differences can account for the differences in pocilloporid reef thicknesses observed in the Gulf of Panamá and the Galápagos. As suggested previously (Glynn et al., 1979), it is possible that the destructive grazing by *Eucidaris* on Galapagan pocilloporid reefs is responsible for the thin accumulations of corals there. Where *Eucidaris* is absent in the Galápagos (at the Espinosa lava pools), pocilloporid reef-frame construction occurred rapidly, on the order of 1.2 m/100 yr (12 m/1,000 yr), rivaling the highest rates known in the eastern Pacific (14–21 m/1,000 yr, Gulf of Chiriquí, Panamá; Glynn and Macintyre, 1977). Because *Eucidaris* tends not to feed on massive coral species, one would expect massive reef buildups to have approximately equal dimensions in the two areas. While massive corals are abundant in the Gulf of Panamá, reefs that are constructed chiefly of massive species are not known there. The two massive coral reefs measured in the mainland eastern Pacific are 5 m *(Pavona)* and 10 m *(Porites)* in vertical thickness (table 24). The massive reef buildups in the Galápagos are also of this size: *Pavona*, 6–10 m maximum; *Porites*, 4–5 m (table 24).

A study recently completed in the Pearl Islands, Gulf of Panamá, demonstrates the importance of certain biological interactions in affecting the development and zonation patterns of coral communities (Wellington, 1982*b*). Coral zonation on a fringing reef at Contadora Island is apparently controlled by differential mortality. Like the majority of eastern Pacific coral reefs, the Contadora study reef contains predominantly branching pocilloporid corals at shallow depth and massive pavonid corals along the reef base. Wellington (1982*b*) found that massive corals suffered higher rates of mortality in shallow areas than did branching species. The damselfish *Eupomacentrus acapulcoensis* was responsible for the observed differential coral mortality because of (a) its preference for killing massive corals while establishing and enlarging algal mats, and (b) its greater abundance at shallow depth due to the greater availability of shelter sites among pocilloporid corals. Relatively few damselfish are present in deep reef zones, because of a paucity of shelter sites, and it is here that smaller pavonid corals can escape the chronic nipping damage of damselfish. Wellington (1982b) also found that mortality among juvenile corals fell heaviest on pocilloporid species in deep areas. This difference was due to fish grazers, mainly from pufferfishes (*Arothron*) that attacked pocilloporid corals more frequently than pavonid corals. Moreover, at shallow depths damselfish territories appear to provide a settlement refuge for *Pocillopora*. Damselfish vigorously defend their territory from herbivorous grazers (mainly parrotfishes and surgeonfishes) and egg predators (particularly *Arothron*): both fish groups can cause coral mortality. Juvenile corals experimentally transplanted into damselfish territories (yet outside the algal mat) survived and grew well compared to transplants outside the territories. These results suggest that damselfish may have a potentially positive effect on juvenile coral survivorship. Workers outside of the eastern Pacific have found that damselfish generally exert a negative influence on reef development through (a) reducing grazing, which permits abundant algal growth and thus competitive interference with corals (Vine, 1974; Potts, 1977), and (b) killing coral, which promotes the growth of the algal mat (Kaufman, 1977).

In contrast, damselfishes in the Galápagos do not appear to kill any reef-building corals, whether branching or massive species. The interaction between damselfish and potential coral predators (e.g., *Arothron*), however, is probably similar to that in Panamá. That is, where damselfish occur they facilitate establishment of *Pocillopora*; where they are absent, *Pocillopora* suffers higher differential mortality from grazing fish compared with *Pavona*. Thus, zonation is equally marked in both the Galápagos and Panamá. The predominance of *Pocillopora* in shallow water in the Galápagos is, in part, due to its superior competitive ability, but may also be aided by damselfish, which repel important corallivores such as *Eucidaris* (see chapter 6). As would be expected, where damselfish do not kill coral to establish or extend their algal gardens, massive coral development is often substantial in the Galápagos. In Panamá larger *Pavona* in the deeper reef areas are eventually colonized and attacked by damselfish as colony surface area becomes sufficiently irregular to provide fish with a suitable shelter site. Thus, we suggest that damselfish have an effect on zonation at both localities; the absence of direct differential coral mortality induced by damselfish leads to a greater development of massive corals and a strong pattern of coral zonation in the Galápagos.

Tropical Waters: While several warm water areas supporting reef growth are now known in the eastern Pacific, the most thoroughly studied of these are located in the Gulf of Chiriquí, Panamá, and at Gorgona Island, Colombia. Numerous pocilloporid reefs occur in the Gulf of Chiriquí, on offshore islands, and along the mainland. By virtue of the high mountain range bisecting Panamá and Costa Rica, the seasonal trade winds are largely cut off from the Pacific, thus preventing upwelling (Glynn, 1972; Glynn et al., 1972; Glynn, 1977). The thermocline (e.g., using the 20°C isotherm for its location) undergoes a small but significant shoaling in the dry season in Chiriquí (from 36 m to 32 m), but it does not surface as in the Gulf of Panamá (Dana, 1975). Fringing pocilloporid reefs are present along much of the eastern leeward shore of Gorgona (Prahl et al., 1979). Gorgona Island is located south of the upwelling Gulf of Panamá and north of the cool, coastal Peru Current (Stevenson et al., 1970; Glynn et al., in press). It is also far enough removed (about 30 km) from the wet, mangrove-fringed mainland so that its waters are usually clear.

The near-shore, oceanographic conditions of Chiriquí and Gorgona are similar and some of the physical factors relevant to coral reef development in the two areas can be summarized briefly as follows: (a) shallow thermocline (~30 m depth), (b) mean sea surface temperature ranges slightly seasonally from 27°C to 30°C, (c) surface salinity is generally low, ranging from 31°/oo to 33°/oo, and (d) water clarity (lateral visibility) is generally relatively high (10–15 m), but may occasionally be reduced considerably (to 2–3 m) during the wet season. Water clarity, and hence light levels, increases significantly on offshore eastern Pacific islands (Malpelo, Cocos, Revillagigedo, and Clipperton islands). Dana (1975) compared these conditions with those of a western Pacific atoll (Marshall Islands) and concluded that the weak development of coral reefs in one of the most favorable of eastern Pacific environments was due in large part to a, c, and d above. However, Dana (1975) went on to predict accelerated coral reef development in the eastern Pacific given: (a) a continued relative stillstand of sea level for the next several thousand years, and (b) additional immigration of hermatypic corals and associated biota from the Indo-Pacific region.

Some reefs in the Gulf of Chiriquí have attained thicknesses of 12–13 m, and have formed at maximum rates of 14–21 m per 1,000 years (Glynn and Macintyre, 1977). These accumulation rates are of the same order of magnitude as the highest rates reported in the Indo-Pacific (10 m per 1,000 years) and Caribbean (9–15 m per 1,000 years) regions (Adey, 1978). A statistical comparison of median reef thicknesses indicates that live pocilloporid buildups in Chiriquí are significantly thicker than those in the Galápagos or the dead reef frameworks sampled in Papagayo (table 24). The Gorgona pocilloporid reefs are significantly thicker than the Galápagos reefs.

Three common patterns of reef-coral community development in the eastern Pacific, whether in subtropical (Galápagos, Gulf of California), low latitude upwelling (gulfs of Papagayo and Panamá), or strictly tropical non-upwelling environments (Gulf of Chiriquí, Gorgona Island), include: (a) reef flat or shoal with relatively low, live coral cover, and with a mixture of a few (usually less than five) coral species; (b) reef slope with high, live coral cover, and dominated by pocilloporid corals; and (c) reef base with relatively low, live coral cover, but with a relatively high, species diversity (sometimes as many as ten coral species are present in this zone). These patterns, and some processes that control or modify their development, are now considered for coral reefs present in Chiriquí and Gorgona, with occasional reference to subtropical and upwelling areas.

While *Pocillopora* spp. are strong competitors at shallow depths (Porter, 1974; Glynn, 1976; Wellington, 1980), they have been shown to be relatively sensitive to extreme low water exposures. On reef flats in upwelling and nonupwelling areas, *Pocillopora* suffers higher mortality rates than *Porites* or *Psammocora* (Glynn, 1976). This differential susceptibility, to a large extent, allows the development of mixed coral assemblages in shallow habitats.

On reef slopes, pocilloporid corals usually predominate. Occasionally, physical and biotic disturbances free portions of the slope substrate that may be subsequently colonized by pocilloporid corals (usually by the propagation of viable broken fragments), by other coral species, or by a variety of other benthic forms (algae, sponges, mollusks, inter alia). Triggerfishes (especially *Pseudobalistes naufragium*), in foraging for mollusks, can break apart large areas of *Pocillopora*. This activity may be more frequent in upwelling areas, which seem to support a higher biomass of infauna (living within the reef matrix) compared with nonupwelling areas (Wellington, unpub. obs.). Log damage can sometimes be significant. Neutrally buoyant or waterlogged tree stumps and logs have been observed to strike the bottom repeatedly, in a pile-driving manner, and also to be dragged over extensive areas of reefs by the action of tides and water turbulence. This kind of damage can produce patches (∼ 1 m in diameter) or swaths (5–10 m in length) of crushed coral. Log damage has been observed most commonly on seaward reef slopes, where floating objects first begin to shoal.

It is in the reef base zone that coral species diversity is greatest, and also where the frequency of interspecific interactions is highest. Biotic disturbance, predation, and symbiotic associations have all been recognized as important factors in controlling and regulating community structure in this zone. Since live coral cover is relatively low, presumably due to disturbance and predation, competition does not seem as important at the reef base as on the reef slope.

A variety of animal activities (e.g., the destructive effects of herbivores, predators foraging among corals for associated animal prey, diel movements through unconsolidated rubble, nest-building, and construction of shelters), probably play a significant role in affecting the survival and growth of coral populations in deep reef zones through their frequency and persistence. Many of these effects were discussed earlier (see chapter 6, *Biological Interactions*) and are also mentioned in Glynn (1974*b*, 1982*a*).

Three corallivores kill large amounts of coral: *Jenneria pustulata* and *Arothron meleagris* prey on pocilloporid corals, usually killing only portions of colonies; *Acanthaster* feeds preferentially on nonpocilloporid corals, and often kills entire colonies (especially small species and juvenile colonies of large species). Damselfish can also kill relatively large amounts of coral locally (within their territories) and in deep water they establish territories almost exclusively on massive corals. No one kind of coral (massive or branching) is spared from disturbance and/or predation along the reef base.

Another aspect of predation concerns the effects of a different class of predators that may control the population sizes of corallivores. For example, *Jenneria* and *Acanthaster* do not appear to be limited by the abundance of their coral prey (that is, resource limited), but rather by predation. Pufferfishes *(Diodon* and *Arothron)* prey commonly on adult *Jenneria* (see Glynn et al., 1978) and harlequin shrimps *(Hymenocera picta* Dana), and amphinomid polychaetous worms *[Pherecardia striata* (Kinberg)] are frequently found attacking and killing adult *Acanthaster* (see Glynn, 1982*b*). Damselfish abundances also seem to be controlled by predation (Wellington, 1982*b*). *Arothron* appears to be limited by the number of shelter holes, which suggests a predator-related effect as well, but it is also possible that intraspecific competition is involved in delimiting grazing areas (Glynn, personal observations).

The mutualism between pocilloporid corals and crustacean symbionts (xanthid crabs and an alpheid shrimp) has a pivotal effect on which coral species are killed by *Acanthaster* (Glynn, 1974*a*, 1976). Host corals are vigorously defended by the crustaceans, with the result that *Acanthaster* feeds preferentially on coral species lacking these agonistic symbionts. Pocilloporid corals are not entirely immune from predation, for example, broken (separated) branches with few or no symbionts are readily eaten by the crown-of-thorns, but this form of defense reduces predation substantially. This coral-crustacean mutualism is probably the main reason why some colonies of *Pocillopora* can persist in reef base areas frequented by *Acanthaster.*

Acanthaster is not present on Gorgona Island reefs, and the relatively high abundances of nonpocilloporid corals there may be due to the absence of this predator (Glynn et al., in press). While such patterns (and suggested causes) are intuitively appealing, we caution that they are merely correlations and must be viewed as such.

Many of the above-mentioned ecological processes are presented in summary form in relation to upwelling and nonupwelling environments in table 25.

GALÁPAGOS COMPARED WITH CENTRAL PACIFIC AREAS

Some brief remarks are now offered relative to the extent of coral community and reef development in the Galápagos and other areas in the central Pacific region. Some of the more obvious similarities and differences in reef mor-

TABLE 25. Some Major Features of Reef-Coral Community Development and Occurrences of Influential Animals in Upwelling and Nonupwelling Environments in the Eastern Pacific.

Thermal Regime	Geographic Area	Extent of Coral Development	Vertical Zonation Pattern Present	Distribution and Importance of Organisms with Potential Impact on Coral						
				Acanthaster	Eucidaris	Arothron	Jenneria	Trizopagurus	Eupomacentrus	Pseudobalistes
Upwelling										
Prolonged exposure to cool water (<18°C)	Western Galápagos (Ecuador)	Absent to low	No	—	* 3	Rare	—	—	* 8	—
	Gulf of Tehuantepec (Mexico)	Absent	No	—	X	—	—	—	X	—
	Gulf of Papagayo (Costa Rica)	Low	No	—	X	—	—	—	X	—
	Gulf of California-North (Mexico)	Absent to low	No	—	X	X	—	—	X	—
Periodic exposure to cool water (20°–22°C)	Gulf of Panamá (Panamá)	Low to moderate	Yes	—	* 3,4	* 5,6	** 5	* 5	*** 6	** 9
	Galápagos (Ecuador)	Moderate to high	Yes	—	*** 3	* 3	—	* 3	** 8	Rare
	Gulf of California-South (Mexico)	Low to moderate	Yes	X 1	X	X	—	X	X	Rare
Nonupwelling										
Constant high temperature (>25°C)	Gulf of Chiriquí (Panamá)	High to very high	Yes, but weak	*** 2	* 3,4	** 5	*** 5	* 5	** 6	* 9
	Gorgona (Colombia)	High	Yes	—	* 7	*** 7	*** 7	* 7	*** 7	* 7
	Golfito (Costa Rica)	High	No	—	X	—	X	—	—	—

— = absent
X = present but extent of impact unknown
* = present but with minimal impact
** = present with significant impact
*** = present with major impact

References: 1 = Dana and Wolfson (1970)
2 = Glynn, Stewart & McCosker (1972)
Glynn (1973, 1974a, 1976, 1977, 1982)
3 = Glynn, Wellington & Birkeland (1979)
4 = Wellington and Glynn (personal observations)

5 = Glynn, Stewart & McCosker (1972)
6 = Wellington (1982b)
7 = Glynn, Prahl & Guhl (1980)
8 = This report
9 = Rowley & Wellington (manuscript)

phology and community processes are noted, especially where such phenomena appear to demonstrate widespread generality.

Marquesas Islands: From the standpoint of reef coral species composition and geomorphology, the Marquesan reefs of French Polynesia (fig. 61) are notably similar to Galapagan reefs. The Marquesas Islands, high volcanic islands dating from Miocene to Pleistocene time, are also the nearest group of Polynesian Islands to the eastern Pacific (5,500 km west of the Galápagos). These islands, however, are mainly situated in the path of the South Equatorial Current, which flows in a westerly direction. As noted earlier, the South Equatorial Countercurrent also flows past the Marquesas, but its efficacy as a dispersal corridor to the eastern Pacific may not be very great.

Coral reefs in the Marquesas Islands are depauperate, but contain about twice the number of hermatypic coral species present in the Galápagos, that is, twenty-six versus thirteen species (Chevalier, 1978). One or a few corals (e.g., *Porites lobata, Pocillopora* spp.) often predominate as structural elements in Marquesan frameworks (Crossland, 1927; Chevalier, 1978). Reefs in the Marquesas, as everywhere in the eastern Pacific, are small, of fringing or patch morphology, mostly confined to shallow depths (usually 10 m or less), and are present in bays or along protected shores (Brousse et al., 1978; Chevalier, 1978). The contribution of crustose coralline algae to reef development in the Marquesas seems to be more prevalent than in the eastern Pacific (Chevalier, 1973). Although no chronological sequence has been reported, Chevalier's (1978) schematic reef profiles suggest that the Marquesan reefs are exceptionally youthful. The reef frameworks of surveyed reefs are only 3–5 m in thickness. In the Galápagos, pocilloporid reefs ranged from 1–3 m in thickness, and pavonid reefs from 2–3 m with a maximum vertical development of about 10 m.

The meager development of reefs in the Marquesas has been attributed to (a) a too rapid rate of subsidence (Dana, 1890), (b) a lack of erosion platforms and stable substrates suitable for reef growth, an amplification of (a) above (Agassiz, 1903), and (c) the negative effects on coral growth of regular upwelling (Crossland, 1927; Ranson, 1952; Ladd, 1971). More recent workers have emphasized the isolation and impoverishment of the coral fauna (Chevalier, 1978), especially following glacial periods (Davis, 1928), and the possibility that the high productivity of surrounding waters tends to interfere with coral growth indirectly through the competitive advantage gained by other benthic organisms under such conditions (Sournia, 1976; Brousse et al., 1978).

Line Islands: Further to the southwest of French Polynesia, in the Tuamotu Archipelago (Low or Dangerous Islands) and the Society Islands (fig. 61), coral diversity is high; reefs attain enormous dimensions; and several different reef types—barrier, atoll, and elevated and submerged reefs—

make their first appearance. It was in these seas (Tuamotu and Society Islands) that Darwin (1842) began to compare the morphologies of reef types with his theory of subsidence and the orderly development of reefs on slowly sinking ocean volcanoes. For purposes of comparing eastern and western Pacific coral development, we will focus on the Line Islands, since it is from there that the eastern Pacific may be more directly influenced.

The southernmost of the Line Islands, which lie astride the easterly moving North Equatorial Countercurrent, are located about 600 km north-northwest of the Society Islands and extend approximately linearly in the same direction, from 12°S–8°N latitude. The Line Islands are oceanic atolls, and the northern segment of this chain, from Christmas Island to Palmyra Island (2°–8°N), is in the path of the North Equatorial Countercurrent. These islands possibly have served as an important source for a large component of the coral reef biota of the eastern Pacific. Much has been learned of this area recently due to two expeditions to Fanning Island in 1970 and 1972 by the University of Hawaii (see *Pacific Science,* 1971, 25 [2], and 1974, 28[3]).

Virtually no studies have dealt in detail with the origin and development of coral reefs in the Line Islands. However, the hypothetical scheme suggested for the evolution of Christmas Island (Valencia, 1977), one of the largest of the Line Islands, may be generally representative of reef formation in the Line Islands's atolls, especially during later Pleistocene time (Wiens, 1962).*

Christmas Island undoubtedly rests on a volcanic basement and its overall shape probably is dependent largely on the morphology of the founding volcano. Reef limestone has accumulated to thicknesses of at least 120 meters and presumably has been in the process of development, although not necessarily continuously, since Cenozoic time. Deep drilling on Mururoa Atoll, Tuamotus, revealed reef limestones to about 400 meters, which is not an unusual thickness for oceanic atolls (Steers and Stoddart, 1977). On the basis of drilling and geophysical measurements, most atolls have demonstrated complex developmental histories, sometimes showing frequent discontinuities caused by tectonic events, emergence, sea level fluctuations, and changing water conditions (e.g., swell direction and seawater temperature variations). These findings have prompted Steers and Stoddart (1977) to develop an integrated theory of coral reef evolution which combines elements of Darwin's Subsidence Theory and Daly's (1934) Glacial Control Theory.

It is probable that the surface features of Christmas Atoll were altered appreciably during Pleistocene glacial episodes when reefs were exposed and subjected to marine erosion and rainwater solution (karst erosion). Maximum sea level regression during the Wisconsin glaciation, to about 130 m below present sea level (Donn et al., 1962), probably led to the emergence of Christ-

---

*Valencia (1977) noted that Christmas Island is the largest atoll in the world in terms of emergent (subaerial) surface area.

mas Island reefs. During this period, large portions of the exposed reef may have been dissolved and mechanically eroded. When sea level began to rise about 18,000 years B.P., during glacial retreat, new reef growth resumed on the old eroded reef foundations. This new reef growth kept pace with the rising sea level and accreted vertically until 4,000 to 5,000 years B.P. when present sea level stabilized (Hopley, 1974).

Maragos (1974*a*) has shown that the reef-coral fauna of Fanning Island is appreciably more diverse than formerly recognized (Stehli and Wells, 1971). Presently, seventy species of hermatypic corals belonging to thirty-two genera are known from Fanning. Coral communities occur in at least four different habitats: (a) turbid lagoon, (b) clear lagoon, (c) leeward ocean reef slopes, and (d) seaward ocean reef slopes. In the eastern Pacific and Marquesas Islands, coral communities and reefs are more restricted ecologically than at Fanning, being essentially confined to bays and protected shores. Framework construction at Fanning is taking place in habitats a, b, and c.

Due to suspended sediments ($CaCO_3$), the visibility in turbid lagoon waters is reduced to 2 m (compared with 10–15 m in clear lagoon areas), and the bottom is covered with calcareous mud. Still, the extent of coral knoll development (physical dimensions and presumably accretion rates) was about equal in turbid and clear lagoon areas (Roy and Smith, 1971). Coral knolls, however, are more abundant in clear lagoon waters. Ramose corals predominate in turbid lagoon waters and massive corals in clear lagoon areas. *Pocillopora damicornis*, so abundant on eastern Pacific reefs in turbid waters, is also abundant in turbid lagoon waters at Fanning. The coral diversity in these similar habitats, however, is considerably greater at Fanning (twenty-seven species) than in the eastern Pacific (six–eight species). The clear lagoon coral communities at Fanning, and the clear-water protected coral communities in the eastern Pacific (e.g., Galápagos Islands, offshore islands in the Gulf of Chiriquí, Cocos Island) contain a few species in common—*Pavona clavus, Pavona gigantea, Pavona varians, Pocillopora damicornis, Porites lobata,* and *Psammocora superficialis.* A total of forty-six coral species in the clear lagoon at Fanning contrasts sharply with the eight to ten species present under similar conditions in the eastern Pacific. Some notable differences in reef structure are apparent in turbid- and clear-water reefs due to differences in composition relative to the frame-building species. For example, turbid-water reefs tend to be open, have gentle slopes, and are subject to extensive infilling by fine sediments. This kind of reef is very similar to the pocilloporid reefs present in the eastern Pacific. The clear-water lagoonal reefs typically have vertical walls, overhangs, and are massive. Eastern Pacific pavonid and poritid reefs are similar, but generally lack steep walls.

Leeward ocean reef slopes are especially well developed in terms of coral diversity, abundance, and vertical zonation (Maragos, 1974*b*). A leeward ocean reef transect at Fanning contained forty reef-building corals, showed a mean surface coverage of 60 percent, and extended to 30–50 m depth. Water visibility approached 50 m or more on seaward reef slopes. Three depth assemblages were recognized: (a) deep (30–35 m), (b) intermediate (20–25 m), and (c) shallow (8–15 m). Briefly, these zones were characterized by (a) low coral cover, small average colony size, and high species diversity (deep zone); (b) high coral cover, large average colony size, and low species diversity (intermediate zone); and (c) relatively high coral cover, relatively small average colony size, and moderately high species diversity (shallow zone).

Maragos (1974b) proposed the influence of several factors to account for these differences in community structure. Wave action seemed to have little influence in the deep assemblage, but possibly low light levels and high sediment cover are important there. Physical environmental conditions were judged to be relatively stable and optimal at intermediate depths with biological interactions determining the nature of the assemblage. Wave action (and storm activity) was considered to have significant limiting effects in shallow reef zones.

Maragos (1974b) suggested that the abundance of Lobophyllia (a hermatypic mussid coral) and Sarcophyton (an alcyonacean octocoral) at intermediate depths, both forming the largest colonies observed, might be due to their superior competitive abilities. It was hypothesized that Lobophyllia could eliminate other corals by means of extracoelenteric digestion (extrusion of mesenterial filaments onto adjacent corals) and Sarcophyton could overgrow and smother other corals by virtue of a rapid growth rate. A comprehensive study of the digestive capacities of numerous corals in the Chagos Archipelago (Indian Ocean) revealed that Lobophyllia (and another mussid coral) occupied an intermediate position in the digestive hierarchy (Sheppard, 1979). Some agariciid corals that are present at intermediate depths at Fanning, and that probably compete for space with Lobophyllia, were not attacked (digested) by Lobophyllia at Chagos. It also has been observed that Lobophyllia is generally avoided by Acanthaster and eaten by the sea star only when preferred corals are in short supply (Goreau et al., 1972; Laxton, 1974; Nishihira and Yamazato, 1974). Soft corals are also avoided by Acanthaster (Endean, 1973). Although not mentioned by Maragos (1974b), Acanthaster has been observed at Fanning (Townsley and Townsley, 1973) and was noted by Edmondson (in Dana, 1970) to be "very common" to "abundant" at nearby Christmas Island. Thus, the possibility also exists that certain species attain large sizes and predominate because they are often avoided by predators.

Although species of Pocillopora, Porites, and Pavona are often important community members at Fanning, they do not predominate over extensive areas as in the eastern Pacific and the Marquesas. Pavona clavus, so conspicuous in Galapagan coral communities, is small and encrusting and occupies only the dead portions or small spaces on and between other species at Fanning.

Coral cover is severely reduced in shallow reef areas, with crustose coralline algae (Porolithon) assuming major prominence. Corals were also in low abundance at shallow depths on windward (seaward) reefs along the east and southeast coast of Fanning (Maragos, 1974a). Wave assault (due to the prevailing trades) is strong in this area, and the presence of rubble ramparts on reef flats and along the shore attest to significant storm damage. The predominance of calcareous algae (the existence of an algal ridge was not explicitly noted), and the presence of a well-developed, groove-and-spur system are features that are virtually absent in the eastern Pacific, except at Clipperton Island (Sachet, 1962).

Results of the Fanning studies indicate that the reef coral fauna there has closer similarities with islands to the south (Tuamotu, Society, and Cook islands) and west (Phoenix Islands) than with Hawaii (Maragos, 1974a; Maragos and Jokiel, 1978; Dana, 1979). Nevertheless, our next comparison will encompass the Hawaiian Archipelago, north of the Line Islands, because of its marginal (northern tropical to subtropical) location, isolation from the central and western Pacific coral reef centers, and comparable geologic history to that in the Galápagos.

Hawaiian Archipelago: Despite the impoverishment of the Hawaiian reef coral fauna, its diversity and extent of coral reef development is unequivocally greater than in the Galápagos or the eastern Pacific in general. Forty-two hermatypic corals are presently known from the Hawaiian Islands (Maragos, 1977; Grigg et al., 1981), including perhaps a half-dozen species shared with the eastern Pacific. *Pocillopora damicornis* occurs in Hawaii, but it is not an important frame-builder and behaves like a fugitive species (Maragos, 1972, 1974b; Highsmith, 1982). *Porites compressa* Dana, a ramose species, is the ecological equivalent of *Pocillopora damicornis* in the eastern Pacific in terms of its ability to spread, dominate coral communities, and contribute to reef construction (Maragos, 1972; Dollar, 1975; Stimson, 1978).

Fringing, barrier, and atoll reefs occur in the Hawaiian chain. Fringing reefs are well developed, with the highest percentage of coral cover, on the lee coasts of Hawaii (Kona) and Maui (Grigg, 1983), and are also present on the islands of Molokai, Oahu, and Kauai (Payne et al., 1970). Barrier reefs are present on the windward side of Oahu Island, extending across the mouth of Kaneohe Bay (Smith et al., 1973; Smith et al., 1981) and at Maro Reef, in the leeward Hawaiian Islands (Grigg, 1983). Maragos (1977) stated that many of the Hawaiian reef formations were built during prehistoric times because present-day reef growth is poor or declining. Grigg (1982a), however, has presented rates of carbonate production in the southeastern Hawaiian chain that rival the highest values reported for any tropical coral reef area (see below). Contemporary framework construction is most pronounced in bays and along leeward (southwestern exposures) coasts that are sheltered from the northeast trades and from long-period high waves generated by storms in the North Pacific (Grigg and Maragos, 1974; Grigg, 1983).

Geologically, the Hawaiian chain has formed in a comparable manner to the Galápagos Islands (Morgan, 1972). Both island groups appear to have arisen from a melting anomaly or "hot spot" by extrusions of lava from the seafloor. The linear northwest-to-southeast alignment of the Hawaiian Islands is due to a net northwesterly drift of the Pacific Plate during island formation. After initial formation, all of the Hawaiian islands underwent gradual subsidence and erosion. The oldest outlying islands are therefore the lowest in elevation, eventually forming atolls (e.g., Kure, Midway, Pearl and Hermes, and Lisianski atolls). Beyond Kure Atoll, the Pacific's most northern atoll (Dana, 1971), the Hawaiian chain continues toward the northwest (below the sea surface) as a series of drowned atolls (guyots) and seamounts, which merge with the Emperor Seamounts at approximately 32°N (Grigg, 1982a). The majority of the Hawaiian Islands, which have formed within the last twenty-seven million years (Rotondo, 1980; Rotondo et al., 1981), are considerably older than the Galápagos Islands, which have formed during the past three million years (Bailey, 1976).

Grigg (1982a, b) has postulated some interesting effects of coral reef development on islands arising in tropical waters and then drifting and subsiding into cooler seas. Based on the growth rates of a major reef-building Hawaiian species (*Porites lobata*) and coral coverage for all species, Grigg has demonstrated that colony accretion rates decrease steadily from the southeastern (19°–22°N) to the northwestern (28°N) islands in the Hawaiian chain. Gross $CaCO_3$ production due to corals in the southeastern and northwestern areas of the island chain were, respectively, 15kg $CaCO_3/m^2/yr$ and 11 mm/yr (vertical growth) and 0.3 kg $CaCO_3/m^2/yr$ and 0.2 mm/yr. Easton and Olson (1976) reported net reef accumulation rates for Hanauma Reef (Oahu, Hawaii) of 0.3 to 2.9 m/1,000 yr, which are relatively high and in line with Grigg's high values. Latitudinal differences in incident solar radiation and sea surface temperature were considered to be the main factors responsible for these divergent production rates; light and temperature combined accounted for 68 percent of the variability in calcification (Grigg, 1982b).

From the foregoing, it is seen that carbonate production at the northwestern end of the Hawaiian chain is, at the present time, just sufficient to offset erosion and subsidence. Atolls that are subsiding at about 28°N latitude therefore are unable to maintain their positions at sea surface. Grigg has termed this boundary or threshold where atoll reef growth and subsidence are in balance "the Darwin Point" (Grigg, 1982a). Rates of reef accretion at Kure Atoll, the northernmost atoll in the Hawaiian chain, are probably very close to threshold values. Continuing plate movement to the north would eventually result in atoll drowning and the formation of guyots. The discovery of remnant reef structures (e.g., fringing reefs, coral knolls, and lagoonal sediments) on the summits of guyots in the Emperor Seamounts, as far as 45°30' N, is strong evidence that coral reefs developed on these features at shallow depth in tropical to subtropical latitudes (Greene et al., 1978).

It is instructive to compare the extent of coral reef development in the

Galápagos with Hawaii, taking into account the geologic historical aspects outlined above. The development of fringing reefs in the Galápagos is weak, and barrier and atoll reefs are absent. To what extent has reef development in the Galápagos been influenced by geologic events, and how do these relate to (a) coral growth rates, (b) coral cover (abundance), (c) physical conditions (e.g., upwelling, volcanism, wave assault), (d) coral species diversity, and (e) biotic effects (such as grazing by corallivores). Each of these factors will be considered in turn.

Coral growth rates are not higher in Hawaii than in the Galápagos. Pocilloporid corals in the Galápagos showed a mean annual growth (branch elongation) of 2.2 cm/yr (Glynn et al., 1979, and chapter 4), and in the windward (southeastern) Hawaiian Islands, 1.0 cm/yr (Edmondson, 1928) and 1.3 cm/yr (Maragos, 1972). The higher Hawaiian growth rate of 1.3 cm/yr is not significantly different from the 2.2 cm/yr growth rate observed in the Galápagos (P>0.05, Mann-Whitney U-test). Median linear growth of *Porites lobata* in Hawaii (at four windward island localities on Hawaii, Maui, Oahu, and Kauai; Grigg, 1982*a*, *b*) and two species of *Pavona* in the Galápagos (data pooled) were essentially identical—both had rates of 1.1 cm/yr (P~0.35, Mann Whitney U-test).

Mean coral cover in the eastern warm-water sector of the Galápagos was 34 percent. This is approximately equivalent to the amount of coral reported by Grigg (in press) for Nihoa and Laysan Islands, located at 23°N and ~26°N respectively. Areas in the Galápagos with the highest abundance of coral, such as Floreana, Bartolomé, and the northern islands (Wolf and Darwin), with live coral cover often around 70 percent, are similar to the southeastern Hawaiian Islands of Oahu, Maui, and Hawaii, which ranged from 60 to 90 percent coral cover.

We may observe the following four conditions regarding the physical environment: seawater temperature, rainfall, wave action, and volcanic activity. Kaneohe Bay, located on the northeastern side of Oahu Island, will serve as the main site for comparisons with the eastern Galápagos Islands. The barrier reef and fringing and patch reefs in Kaneohe Bay are probably the most thoroughly studied reefs in the Hawaiian Islands.

In terms of sea temperatures, the eastern and northern Galápagos Islands and southern Hawaiian Islands are similar; both were classified as subtropical areas by Abbott (1966). On Waikiki reef (Oahu) the annual extreme variation in surface temperature is approximately 10°C, and the lowest daily temperature recorded over a two-year period was 21.5°C (Edmondson, 1928). The annual extreme variation at Academy Bay is approximately 8°C, and the lowest daily temperature recorded there over a nine-year period was 17.8°C. Mean sea surface temperatures in the Galápagos range from about 23°C (Academy Bay, fig. 5) to 24°C (overall area), compared with Hawaii where mean SSTs range from about 22°C (Hilo; Abbott, 1966) to 25°C (Kaneohe Bay; Smith et al., 1981).

In contrast with the Hawaiian Islands, the Galápagos receive little rainfall. The mean annual rainfall at Academy Bay over a ten-year period (1965–1974) was 360 mm; at Kaneohe Bay, Oahu, it was approximately 1,000–1,500 mm (Smith et al., 1973, Smith et al., 1981). Torrential rains are common at Kaneohe Bay; Banner (1968) reported 436 mm of rain falling in a single day. In spite of the large differences in rainfall, it does not appear that this had a debilitating effect on coral reefs until after the mismanagement of the Kaneohe Bay watershed.

Wave assault is apparently greater on exposed Hawaiian shores than in comparable environments in the Galápagos Islands. In both areas, active reef accretion is most pronounced at sheltered sites. Northeastern or windward exposures in the Hawaiian Islands receive nearly constant buffeting from high seas generated by the Northeast Trades and frequent severe wave assault generated by winter storms in the north Pacific. Southern and southeastern shores in the Galápagos are exposed seasonally to the Southeast Trades. The Hawaiian Islands are also subject to relatively frequent tsunamis, long-period waves often caused by seafloor faulting. Especially destructive tsunamis occurred in Hawaii in 1877 and 1946 (Shepard, 1959), and minor ones in 1952, 1957, and 1960 (Grigg and Maragos, 1974). The Kaneohe Bay barrier reef effectively blocked the shoreward progression of the 1946 tsunami (Shepard, 1959), but also experienced at least minor damage through the dislodgment of large corals from shoal reef zones (Maragos, 1972). Waves generated by tsunamis and violent storms can cause significant damage to reefs in Hawaii, and such disturbances may even limit reef development on windward (northern) island shores (Dollar, 1982a, b; Grigg, submitted). Grigg and Maragos (1974), and Dollar (1982a, b), have underlined the importance of severe storm disturbances in Hawaii, particularly with regard to their effects on the structure (successional stages and species diversity) of coral communities. Numerous coral reefs are present, however, on other Pacific islands located along major storm tracts, and they develop in adjustment to such conditions (Munk and Sargent, 1954; Wiens, 1962; Stoddart, 1971; Ogg and Koslow, 1978).

Volcanism appears to be of roughly equal frequency in the two areas. A comparison of the frequencies of lava flows that have reached the sea on the two largest islands indicate an incidence of 7.7 flows per 100 years for Hawaii (Grigg and Maragos, 1974) and 10.9 flows per 100 years for Isabela (see table 14).

Like Galapagan coral reefs, Hawaiian reefs are constructed of few coral species. The predominant reef-building corals in Hawaii belong primarily to one genus (*Porites*, including both massive and branching species) and in the Galápagos to three genera (*Porites, Pocillopora,* and *Pavona*). Coralline algae have also contributed significantly to the shoal sections of Hawaiian reefs, more so than in the Galápagos. Some reefs on Oahu actually contain more crustose coralline algae than coral (Pollock, 1928; Easton and Olson, 1976).

Both island groups seem to possess similar frame-building coral elements, but Hawaiian reefs apparently have a higher abundance of calcareous algae. Except for the center of the Hawaiian chain, certain coral hermatypes present on windward shores of reefs in the Pacific and Atlantic oceans are either rare *(Acropora)* or absent *(Millepora* and *Heliopora).* Maragos (1972) suggested that the absence of such forms could be the reason why windward reef building is so meager in Hawaii compared with other reef areas where they are present. Although Hawaii's scleractinian coral fauna is about twice as rich as that in the Galápagos, the essential frame-building species are about equal in number in both areas and have the potential to erect reef structures on sheltered or leeward shores. A major difference in terms of biotic composition would seem to be the preponderance of crustose coralline algae on shallow Hawaiian reefs; calcareous algae are not important as structural members of Galapagan coral reefs.

We will now examine some possible biotic differences that could limit hermatypic coral populations in the Hawaiian and Galápagos islands. Grazing by corallivores seems to be important in both areas, although interference competition can be significant locally in Hawaii. Algae have been observed to overgrow and kill corals on reefs off Waikiki (Edmondson, 1928), at Hanauma Bay (Easton and Olson, 1976), and at Kaneohe Bay (Maragos, 1972; Smith et al., 1973; Banner, 1974), Oahu Island, which are all areas that have been stressed by man. A variety of benthic invertebrates, such as barnacles, oysters, tunicates, bryozoans, and sponges, were observed to outcompete transplanted corals in the south basin of Kaneohe Bay, which formerly supported fringing reefs (Maragos, 1972).

Maragos (1972) noted that reef corals in Hawaii were frequently grazed by fishes. No obvious differences in the intensity of fish grazing is evident, however, between reefs in Hawaii (Maragos, 1972; Hobson, 1974) and the eastern Pacific (chapter 6; Glynn et al., 1972; Hobson, 1968; Thomson et al., 1979). Unlike the Galápagos, the corallivore *Acanthaster* is present throughout the major Hawaiian Islands (Edmondson, 1933; Branham et al., 1971). Although this corallivore can at times attain high population densities, approximately 20,000 individuals were observed feeding on coral along a 2-km stretch of coast off south Molokai, according to Branham et al. (1971); this large aggregation did not overwhelm its coral food source. A coral *(Montipora)* present in low abundance, but with a high growth rate, was preferred by *Acanthaster* over a more abundant but slower-growing coral *(Porites compressa).* Branham et al. (1971) suggested that such a feeding preference might be the reason why the nonpreferred coral is relatively abundant on the Molokai reefs. Coral death due to corallivores has not yet been related to reef growth in Hawaii.

Some estimates of reef growth, based on the production rates of calcium carbonate, are assembled in table 26 with values from the Galápagos and other areas. The estimates for gross production (that is, before losses from

TABLE 26. Estimates of CaCO$_3$ Production for Coral Reefs in the Galápagos, Hawaii, and Other Areas.

Geographic Area	Locality and Environmental Conditions	Production Rate		Apparent Production Type[a]	Reference
		gm/m²/yr	mm/yr		
Hawaiian Islands	Hanauma reef, Oahu Island, coralgal fringing reef				
	reef flat	(7,400)[b]	5.5	N	Easton (1969)
	entire reef	(4,400)[b]	3.3	N	Easton & Olson (1976)
	Kaneohe Bay barrier reef, Oahu Island	3,000	(2)[b]	G	Smith et al. (1970)
	Reef community on lava flow, Maui Island	1,400	(1)[b]	N	Oostdam in Chave et al. (1972)
	Leeward offshore reefs, 10 m depth				
	Hawaii Island	15,000	11	G	Grigg, 1982a
	Kure Atoll	300	0.2	G	Grigg, 1982a
Galápagos Islands	Onslow Island patch reef, Floreana Island				
	(70 percent coral cover)	8,000	(5.9)[b]	G	Glynn et al. (1979) and
	low Eucidaris density	7,600	(5.6)[b]	N	present study
	high Eucidaris density	6,600	(4.9)[b]	N	
	(30 percent coral cover)	3,400	(2.5)[b]	G	

low *Eucidaris* density	2,800	(2.1)[b]	N	
high *Eucidaris* density	0	0	N	Present study
Lava rock basin, Pt. Espinosa, Fernandina Island				
Eucidaris absent	(16,000)[b]	12	N	
Panamá				
Gulf of Chiriquí, nonupwelling area	6,700	(5.0)[b]	G	Glynn (1977)
	(2,200–10,000)[b]	1.6–7.5	N	Glynn & Macintyre (1977)
Gulf of Panamá, upwelling area	5,100	(3.8)[b]	G	Glynn (1977)
	(1,700)[b]	1.3	N	Glynn & Macintyre (1977)
Pacific Ocean				
Favorable conditions for coral reefs	10,000	(6.9)[c]	N	Kinsey (1979) in Grigg, 1982*a*
Caribbean Sea				
Barbados leeward fringing reef	10,700	(7.3)[c]	G	Stearn & Scoffin (1977)

[a] G, gross production, is the amount of CaCO₃ produced by the reef community per unit area of seafloor; N, net production, is the amount of CaCO₃ retained by the reef system, not counting losses due to physical and biotic processes (see Chave et al., 1972).

[b,c] Values in parentheses calculated from companion values assuming a porosity of 50 percent and coral skeletal density of 2.7 (Chave et al., 1972), b, or 2.9 (Grigg, 1982*a*), c, as a conversion factor between mm/yr and gm/m²/yr.

mechanical, chemical, and biological processes) suggest that production rates are of the same order of magnitude on Hawaiian (mean = 6,100 gm/m²/yr) and Galapagan (mean = 5,700 gm/m²/yr) reefs. The great range in values in Hawaii is due mainly to the latitudinal environmental differences (seawater temperature and light) noted by Grigg (1982a, b). Mean net production values for Hawaii (4,400 gm/m²/yr; Easton and Olson, 1976) and the Galápagos (6,600 gm/m²/yr; Glynn et al., 1979) are also rather similar. Losses due to *Eucidaris* grazing accounted for the large spread of values in the Galápagos. Where this urchin corallivore was absent, net production was 16,000 gm/m²/yr; where present in high abundance, no net $CaCO_3$ production occurred. While echinoid grazing may be a major agent of erosion in certain shallow, waveswept, reef-rock habitats in the northernmost leeward Hawaiian Islands (Russo, 1977, 1980), it does not appear to be as potent and pervasive in limiting reef growth as in the Galápagos.

Vertical production or accumulation rates (net values) also indicate comparable reef growth in the two regions: Hawaii, mean = 3.3 mm/yr; Galápagos, mean = 4.9 mm/yr (see table 26). The similar rates of net and gross (see above) reef growth raise the possibility that the initiation of reef development might be more difficult in the Galápagos than in Hawaii. The production rates listed for regions favoring coral reef growth elsewhere (nonupwelling Panamá, tropical Pacific Ocean, and Caribbean Sea) suggest that reef growth can be rapid under optimal conditions even in the subtropical waters of the Hawaiian and Galápagos Islands.

In light of the comparisons made above, it is now possible to examine in more depth why coral reefs are better developed and more widespread in Hawaii than in the Galápagos. While a definitive answer is not forthcoming, it does appear that an explanation may center around at least four considerations: time, localized upwelling, the presence of reef-forming and binding calcareous algae, and corallivore effects.

The oldest Galápagos Islands may be two to three million years in age, but most of them are youthful, having been formed during Pleistocene and Recent times. Thus, compared with Hawaii, coral reefs in the Galápagos have had relatively little time to become established and to develop. Time could have been even more restrictive in the Galápagos if the coral fauna there was extirpated during late Pleistocene time and only recently recolonized the islands from the Panamic Province.

Although mean sea surface temperatures are similar in the two regions where reefs are present, upwelling of cool nutrient-rich water has an important effect locally in the Galápagos. Upwelling of the Equatorial Undercurrent limits coral growth in the western sector of the Galápagos. Low water temperatures have an important effect on reef growth in Hawaii, but only in the northernmost leeward islands.

Many of the shallow reef zones in Hawaii contain abundant populations of calcareous red algae that are capable of building and consolidating reef structures. The contribution of coralline algae to reef building in the Galápagos is minimal.

Intense grazing by motile *Eucidaris* on live reef-building corals also appears to interfere with reef formation and expansion throughout much of the Galápagos Islands. No corallivore has been shown to reduce net $CaCO_3$ production to zero in Hawaii.

The recent dislocations at Kaneohe Bay represent an extreme example of man's impact on a marine ecosystem. Most of the Kaneohe Bay reef system, which only a few decades ago supported flourishing coral communities celebrated for their beauty, has shown a recent shift away from a predominance of coral populations (Smith et al., 1981). In the early 1970s, Banner (1974) observed that no coral was left growing in one-third of the bay, almost all coral had been overgrown by an alga in another one-third, and that only in the last third of the bay were the coral reefs reasonably intact. This upheaval is due to a variety of activities (most notably soil erosion, freshwater dilution, and sewage pollution) related to man's population growth around the bay and general disregard for the marine environment. It is encouraging to note that sewage diversion was initiated in 1977–1978 and some coral recovery has been detected (Smith et al., 1981). However, due to the disappearance of hard substratum (from sewage-mediated biological activity and siltation) and the long replacement times of corals, recovery of reefs may require several decades or be prevented altogether.

It seems almost paradoxical that any area in the world today with such natural beauty, intrinsic interest, and high popularity can still claim a marine environment of virtually pristine quality. This circumstance is not fortuitous, but is due in large measure to a model system of conservation and education promoted by the Charles Darwin Foundation for the Galápagos Isles and the Galápagos National Park Service of the government of Ecuador. Steps are currently being taken to insure the protection of near-shore marine environments in the Galápagos (Wellington, 1983). Our studies in the Galápagos have revealed the variety and significance of natural disturbances, both physical and biotic, that can influence the formation and development of coral communities and coral reefs. It seems important to us that an attempt be made to maintain Galápagos marine waters in as strictly a natural setting as feasible. Only under such conditions can we gain a meaningful understanding of the natural ecological processes that shape the evolution of coral reef communities.

APPENDIX

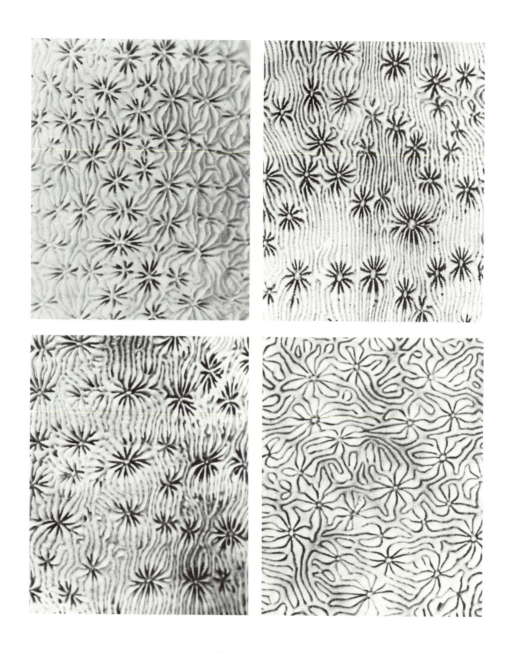

Pavoṅa gigantea, x4

ANNOTATED LIST OF THE SCLERACTINIAN CORALS OF THE GALÁPAGOS

JOHN W. WELLS

CONTENTS

ABSTRACT

The presence of scleractinian corals has been known in the Galápagos for more than a century since Darwin's visit in 1835, and the number of species and genera recorded has risen with practically each new visitor. In this listing the named taxons are enumerated, twenty of which are hermatypic species and forty-nine are ahermatypic, totals reduced by synonymy and reassignment to thirteen and thirty-one respectively. The hermatypic fauna of thirteen species and six genera is composed mostly of Indo-Pacific forms, only four being confined to the eastern Pacific. The rich ahermatypic fauna of thirty-one species and twenty-two genera includes ten as yet known only from the Galápagos, six others are Panamic, eleven are Indo-Pacific or cosmopolitan, four are Mediterranean-Atlantic-Caribbean, and two are doubtfully Galapagan. Six of the ahermatypes are newly described species (Wells, 1982), three of them known at present only in the Galápagos.

INTRODUCTION

Charles Darwin's visit to the Galápagos in 1835 lasted more than two months, but his published works contain few references to corals. Although he remarked on the apparent absence of reefs, he must have seen some corals in the shallow waters around the islands as well as the coral boulders and worn fragments of reef corals so common on many sandy beaches. He did collect at least one specimen (now lost) that was described forty-one years later by Peter Martin Duncan (1876) as *Placopsammia darwini* [= *Tubastraea coccinea* Lesson]. The earliest notice of corals in the Galápagos, however, came in 1848 when Milne Edwards and Haime described a new species, *Flabellum gallapagense* [*sic*], apparently a fossil (late Tertiary?) in the Stokes Collection, and in 1860, *Madrepora [Acropora] crassa*, but the latter was almost certainly not from the Galápagos. The next record was by Pourtalès in 1875 when he listed specimens picked up on beaches during the visit of the *Hassler* in 1872: *Oulangia bradleyi, Pavona gigantea, Pavona clivosa, Pavona* sp., *Astropsammia pedersenii* [*Tubastraea coccinea*], *Pocillopora capitata*, and *Porites* sp., all forms previously described by Verrill from the western coasts of Central America and Mexico. Subsequent notices and descriptions of Galápagos corals were reviewed by Durham (1966) who listed thirty-two species living in the islands, of which ten (five genera) are hermatypic and twenty-two (sixteen genera) are ahermatypic.

In the National Museum of Natural History (USNM) there are several miscellaneous lots of Galapagan corals collected by the *Albatross* in 1888 and on the cruises of the *Anton Bruun* in 1966. These and other materials collected in the Galápagos in January, 1975, by Charles Birkeland, P. W. Glynn, G. M. Wellington, and the writer, corals in the reference collections at the Charles Darwin Research Station, Galápagos (CDRS) and at the Smithsonian Tropical Research Institute, Naos Island, Panamá (STRI), specimens collected by Douglas Faulkner, and corals loaned by the California Academy of Sciences (CAS) and by the Peabody Museum of Natural History, Yale University

(YPM), have added several genera and species to the coral fauna. The total number of corals after revisions now stands at thirteen species (six genera) of hermatypes and thirty-one species (twenty-two genera) of ahermatypes, not including two doubtful or supposedly fossil records, although the latter are included in the systematic discussion. The following lists include all species taxons recorded from the Galápagos since 1848 with their present taxonomic status:

Hermatypic Coral Species Recorded from the Galápagos

** = Species recorded only from the Galápagos and extreme eastern Pacific (others, except as noted, are Indo-Pacific in distribution).

** *Acropora crassa* (Milne Edwards & Haime) (*non* Coryell 1929), doubtful record
** *Cycloseris elegans* (Verrill)
** *Cycloseris mexicana* Durham
Gardineroseris planulata (Dana)
Pavona clavus Dana
Pavona clivosa Verrill = *P. clavus*
** *Pavona gigantea* Verrill (and Fanning Island)
Pavona varians Verrill
Pavona (Polyastra) ponderosa Durham = *Gardineroseris planulata*
Pavona (Pseudocolumnastraea) galapagensis Durham & Barnard = *P. clavus*
** *Pocillopora capitata* Verrill
Pocillopora damicornis (Linnaeus)
Pocillopora elegans Dana
Pocillopora verrucosa Squires, and Durham & Barnard = *P. elegans?*
Porites excavata Verrill = *P. lobata*
Porites lobata Dana
Psammocora profundacella Durham = *P. (Plesioseris) superficialis*
Psammocora (Plesioseris) superficialis (Gardiner)
** *Psammocora (Stephanaria) brighami* Vaughan (and Hawaii)
Psammocora (Stephanaria) stellata Verrill

Ahermatypic Coral Species Recorded from the Galápagos

* = Species at present recorded only from the Galápagos.
** = Species recorded only from the Galápagos and extreme eastern Pacific (Panamic).
*** = Species Indo-Pacific or cosmopolitan in distribution.
**** = Species Mediterranean-Atlantic-Caribbean in distribution.

** *Astrangia browni* Palmer

* *Astrangia equatorialis* Durham & Barnard

Astrangia gardnerensis Durham & Barnard = *Astrangia browni*

Astrangia hondaensis Durham & Barnard = *Polycyathus hondaensis*

Astropsammia pedersenii Verrill = *Tubastraea coccinea*

*** *Balanophyllia eguchii* Wells

* *Balanophyllia galapagensis* Vaughan

* *Balanophyllia osburni* Durham & Barnard

Balanophyllia scheeri Durham & Barnard = *Rhizopsammia verrilli*

Bathycyathus consagensis Durham & Barnard = *Phyllangia consagensis*

** *Caryophyllia diomedeae* von Marenzeller

Cladocora arbuscula von Marenzeller (*non* Lesueur) = *Cladocora debilis*

**** *Cladocora debilis* Milne Edwards & Haime

*** *Culicia rubeola* (Quoy & Gaimard)

* *Cyathoceras avis* (Durham & Barnard)

*** *Dendrophyllia gracilis* Milne Edwards & Haime

*** *Desmophyllum cristagalli* Milne Edwards & Haime

Desmophyllum galapagense Vaughan = *Javania cailleti*

*** *Enallopsammia amphelioides* (Alcock)

*** *Endopachys grayi* Milne Edwards & Haime

Endopachys vaughani Durham = *Endopachys grayi*

* *Endopsammia pourtalesi* (Durham & Barnard)

* *Flabellum daphnense* Durham & Barnard

* *Flabellum gallapagense* Milne Edwards & Haime (fossil; doubtful)

*** *Javania cailleti* (Duchassaing & Michelotti)

Javania galapagensis Zibrowius = *J. cailleti*

**** *Javania* sp. cf. *J. pseudoalabastra* Zibrowius

Kionotrochus ? *avis* Durham & Barnard = *Cyathoceras avis*

Kionotrochus ? *hoodensis* Durham & Barnard = *Cyathoceras avis*

Lobopsammia darwini Durham = *Tubastraea coccinea*

Lophosmilia wellsi Durham & Barnard = *Phyllangia consagensis*

**** *Madracis asperula* Milne Edwards & Haime

**** *Madracis pharensis* (Heller)

* *Madrepora galapagensis* Vaughan

** *Oulangia bradleyi* Verrill

** *Paracyathus humilis* Verrill

** *Phyllangia consagensis* (Durham & Barnard)

Placopsammia darwini Duncan = *Tubastraea coccinea*

** *Polycyathus hondaensis* (Durham & Barnard), doubtful in Galápagos

* *Polycyathus isabela* Wells

*** *Rhizopsammia verrilli* van der Horst

* *Rhizopsammia wellingtoni* Wells

** *Sphenotrochus hancocki* Durham & Barnard

Thecopsammia pourtalesi Durham & Barnard = *Endopsammia pourtalesi*

*** *Tubastraea coccinea* Lesson

*** *Tubastraea faulkneri* Wells

* *Tubastraea floreana* Wells

*** *Tubastraea tagusensis* Wells

Tubastraea tenuilamellosa (Milne Edwards & Haime) = *Tubastraea coccinea*

The hermatypic fauna of thirteen species is composed mostly of widely distributed Indo-Pacific forms, only four being at present known only from the Panamic or extreme eastern Pacific region. Of the thirty-one ahermatypic species, ten are as yet known only in the Galápagos, six are Panamic, four (*Cladocora debilis*, *Javania cailleti*, *Madracis asperula*, and *M. pharensis*) are conspecific with Mediterranean-Atlantic-Caribbean forms, and the remaining eleven are Indo-Pacific or cosmopolitan in distribution.

SYSTEMATIC LIST OF GALÁPAGOS SCLERACTINIA

The following abbreviations are used for locations of collections; USNM = National Museum of Natural History, Washington, D.C.; BMNH = British Museum (Natural History), London; CDRS = Charles Darwin Research Station, Galápagos; STRI = Smithsonian Tropical Research Institute, Panamá; CAS = California Academy of Natural Sciences, San Francisco; YPM = Peabody Museum of Natural History, Yale University.

Order SCLERACTINIA
Suborder ASTROCOENIINA Vaughan & Wells 1943
Family THAMNASTERIIDAE Vaughan & Wells 1943
Genus *Psammocora* Dana 1846
Subgenus *Stephanaria* Verrill 1867
***Psammocora* (*Stephanaria*) *stellata* (Verrill) 1866**
Plate 1, Figures 1, 2

Stephanocora stellata Verrill 1866, p. 330
Stephanaria stellata Verrill 1870, p. 545, pl. 9, figs. 4, 4a
—— —— Quelch 1886, p. 129

—— —— Vaughan 1907, p. 142, pl. 43, figs. 2, 2a, b, 3, 3a

P. (Stephanaria) stellata Durham 1947, p. 19, pl. 8, figs. 1, 2; pl. 13, fig. 1

—— —— Durham 1950, p. 38, pl. 36, fig. 5

—— —— Durham & Barnard 1952, p. 29, pl. 2, fig. 8

—— —— Squires 1959, p. 406

Like *P. (S.) brighami*, this species is common in the Galápagos, never forming colonies more than a few centimeters in size.

Occurrence: Galápagos, shore to 23 m (Durham & Barnard); Onslow Island, inside "crown," 0–3 m; Wolf (Wenman) Island, 15–20 m; Genovesa (Tower) Island, Darwin Bay, 20 m; Bahía Urvina, Isabela Island, raised platform; La Paz to Pearl Islands; Cocos Island, La Libertad and Sucre Island, Ecuador. Hawaii, Palmyra Island, Canton Island, Pitcairn Island, Fiji.

Psammocora (Stephanaria) brighami Vaughan 1907
Plate 1, Figures 3, 4

Stephanaria brighami Vaughan 1907, p. 143, pl. 43, figs. 4, 4a, 5

P. (Stephanaria) brighami Durham & Barnard 1952, p. 29, pl. 2, figs. 7a, b

Nodular to subramose, distinguished from *P. (S.) stellata*, which has the same growth habit, by its smaller, superficial calices and single columellar tubercle.

Occurrence: Darwin (Culpepper) Island, near arch rock, 7–9 m; Pinzón (Duncan) Island, shallow water (Durham & Barnard). Hawaii; San Lorenzo Channel, Gulf of California, 3–6 m (Durham & Barnard).

Subgenus *Plesioseris* Duncan 1884
Psammocora (Plesioseris) superficialis (Gardiner) 1898
Plate 1, Figures 5, 6

Psammocora superficialis Gardiner 1898, p. 537, pl. 40, fig. 2

—— —— Hoffmeister 1925, p. 46

—— *profundacella* Yabe, Sugiyama & Eguchi 1936, p. 60, pl. 45, figs. 1, 4, 5, 7, 8

non —— *superficiales* [sic] *ibid.*, p. 60, pl. 41, figs. 4, 5

——— Ma 1959, p. 5, pl. 18, fig. 1

—— *profundacella* Durham 1962, p. 49, fig. 6

—— *superficialis* Veron & Pichon 1976, p. 27, figs. 25, 26

The supposed differences between *P.(P.) superficialis* and *P.(P.) profundacella* are slight. The latter has larger, deeper calices with thick, acute walls and thirty or more septa, of which about twelve are free to the columella (Vaughan 1918, pl. 59, figs. 4, 4a). *P. (P.) superficialis* has small (1.5–2 mm), very shallow calices with low, thin walls and about twenty septa, of which seven are free to the columella, but on the subramose upward extensions of specimens from the Galápagos and Cocos Island, the calices have acute walls like those of *P. (P.) profundacella*, and it is unlikely that more than one species is involved.

P. (P.) superficialis is distinguished from *P. (Stephanaria) stellata* and *P. (S.) brighami* by the acute collines and cerioid aspect of the calices.

Occurrence: Mosquera Island near Baltra Island, 5 m (Durham); Darwin (Culpepper) Island, off arch rock, 8 m; Cocos Island, Wafer Bay, 7–10 m (Durham). Funafuti; Samoa; Kyûsyû, Sikoku, Honshû.

Family POCILLOPORIDAE Gray 1840
Genus *Pocillopora* Lamarck 1816

The great intraspecific variability in species of this genus is well known and the taxonomic status of the fifty or more named taxons is chaotic: ". . . the clue to it [variation] has not yet been discovered, nor can be without observation on the reef, as well as in a marine laboratory" (Crossland, 1952, p. 109).

In addition to ecovariation, colony-form can be modified by predation (cropping or grazing) by corallivores, not only on the polyps, but also on the more accessible tips of the branches and branchlets of the corallum. The list of corallivores and their modes of predation is growing (Robertson, 1970; Bak & van Eys, 1975; Neudecker, 1977). Their activities in the Panamic region have been discussed recently by Glynn et al. (1972), and Glynn has kindly permitted the writer to mention here some of his recent field and laboratory observations.

Colonies of *P. damicornis* and *P. capitata* from Urabá Island, Bay of Panamá, were placed in aquariums without corallivores at the Smithsonian Tropical Research Institute laboratory on Naos Island. New growth of normal type of predator-maimed branches was evident even after a few months. Figure 1a shows a branch cluster of maimed *P. damicornis* as collected in the field. Figure 1b shows a cluster from a colony similarly maimed from the same site after three months, when the normal growth of small branchlets had resumed. In Figure 2a the tips of the branches of *P. capitata* have been deprived of their verrucae and become calvate and clavate. Figure 2b shows resumption of growth of terminal verrucae after four months of isolation.

In the Galápagos, predation by fish and sea urchins (*Eucidaris thouarsii*) is common, especially on *P. damicornis* (pl. 2, figs. 2–5) and *P. capitata* (Glynn et al., 1979).

The varieties of *P. damicornis* (*P. caespitosa*) illustrated by Vaughan (1907) from Hawaii seem to be in part due to the effects of predation. Specimens of *P. ligulata* Dana from Midway Island have normal, verrucae-tipped flabellate branches from one site, whereas the branches of colonies from another site are calvate. The calvate summits of other species such as *P. mean-drina, P. elegans,* and *P. eydouxi* have been taken to some degree as a species or varietal criterion, e.g., *P. meandrina* Dana, distinguished from *P. nobilis* Verrill by the calvate, non-verrucate summits of the thick, flabellate branches.

Pocillopora damicornis (Linnaeus) 1758
Plate 2, Figures 1-5

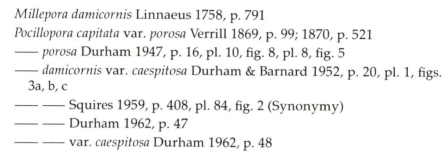

  Millepora damicornis Linnaeus 1758, p. 791

  Pocillopora capitata var. *porosa* Verrill 1869, p. 99; 1870, p. 521

  —— *porosa* Durham 1947, p. 16, pl. 10, fig. 8, pl. 8, fig. 5

  —— *damicornis* var. *caespitosa* Durham & Barnard 1952, p. 20, pl. 1, figs. 3a, b, c

  —— —— Squires 1959, p. 408, pl. 84, fig. 2 (Synonymy)

  —— —— Durham 1962, p. 47

  —— —— var. *caespitosa* Durham 1962, p. 48

Small colonies of this species occur at almost all sites in the Galápagos. Cropping of the tips of branches by predators causes the tips to expand laterally, becoming clavate, flabellate, even submeandrine (pl. 2, figs. 2, 3; also the type of *P. porosa*, figured by Durham, 1947), with some development of the normally absent verrucae. A more extreme modification is illustrated on plate 2, figures 4 and 5, where cropping of the tips has resulted in stout, stubby branches devoid of verrucae, closely resembling *P. mauritiana* Brueg-gemann (1878). This variant, occurring occasionally among more typical brown *P. damicornis* on the lagoon patch reef south of Punta Espinosa, was pinkish-brown.

Occurrence: Española (Hood) Island (Durham & Barnard); Osborn Island near Española Island, 3 m (Durham); Gardner Island near Española, 45–65 m (Durham & Barnard); Fernandina Island, lagoon patch reef south of Punta Espinosa, exposed at low tide; Darwin (Culpepper) Island, near arch, 10 m; Floreana Island; Stephens Bay, San Cristóbal (Chatham) Island; Academy Bay, Santa Cruz Island, 12–14 m *Anton Bruun* Sta. 66128, USNM. Gulf of California, Panamá, Ecuador, and west to Red Sea.

Pocillopora elegans Dana 1846
Plate 3, Figures 1, 2

  Pocillopora elegans Dana 1846, p. 532, pl. 51, fig. 1 (type figured by Vaughan 1918, pl. 23, figs. 3, 4, 4a; 1919, pl. 6)

  —— *robusta* var. *pumila* Durham & Barnard 1952, p. 26, pl. 1, fig. 6

—— *elegans* Squires 1959, p. 409 (in part); pl. 34, fig. 5
—— —— Durham 1962, p. 48

This is the dominant species of *Pocillopora* in the Galápagos, where it forms virtually monospecific banks. The typical form is shown on plate 3, figure 1. The observed variations strongly suggest that the species includes *P. danae* Verrill (see Vaughan, 1918, pl. 22, fig. 2, of the type). Plate 3, figure 2 shows a Galápagos specimen similar to Vaughan's illustration (1918, pl. 22, fig. 1) of a variant from Murray Island which is also identical with Verrill's type of *P. robusta* var. *pumila* from La Paz, figured by Durham (1947, pl. 7, fig. 2).

Occurrence: Pinzón (Duncan) Island; Osborn Island near Española, 3 m (Durham); west shore of Xarifa Island near Española (Hood) Island, 3 m; Galápagos, shore to 18 m (Durham & Barnard); Darwin (Culpepper) Island, off arch rock, 8 m ("pumila"-, and near arch rock, 9 m; Onslow Island, 4 m; Wolf (Wenman) Island, northeast side, 7 m. Gulf of California south to Ecuador; eastern and central Pacific.

Pocillopora capitata Verrill 1864
Plate 3, Figures 3, 4

Pocillopora capitata Verrill 1864, p. 60; 1869, p. 99; 1870, p. 520
—— —— Durham 1947, p. 16; pl. 7, fig. 3; pl. 8, fig. 4
—— *robusta* Durham 1950, p. 38, pl. 36, fig. 5
—— *robusta* Durham & Barnard 1952, p. 26, pl. 1, figs. 5, 5a (*non* fig. 6)
—— *elegans* Squires 1959, p. 409 (in part)

Colonies of *P. capitata* from the Panamic region have very weakly developed septa and columella, commonly only a small columella, and were grouped with *P. elegans* by Squires. The specimens from the Galápagos have very weak septa and usually a distinct columella, with notably acute verrucae that give the straggly branches a thorny aspect, whereas the branches of *P. elegans* are generally subflabellate to flabellate with smaller, less acute, more numerous verrucae.

Occurrence: Gardner Island near Española Island, 5–6 m (Durham 1962); Wolf (Wenman) Island, northeast side, about 8 m; Onslow Island, inside "crown," 3 m; Academy Bay, Santa Cruz Island, 8–12 m (*Anton Bruun* Sta. 66112, USNM); south of Academy Bay, 8–9 m (*Anton Bruun* Sta. 66111, USNM); Baltra Island (*Anton Bruun* Sta. 791–B, USNM). Gulf of California, Panamá, Cocos Island, south to Ecuador and west to Galápagos.

Genus *Madracis* Milne Edwards & Haime 1848
Madracis asperula Milne Edwards & Haime 1850

> *Madracis asperula* M. E. & H. 1850, p. 101, pl. 4, figs. 2, 2a
> —— —— Durham & Barnard 1952, p. 14, pl. 1, figs. 2a, 2b
> —— —— Zibrowius 1980, p. 16, pls. 1, 2 (Synonymy)

Comparison of Durham & Barnard's figures with topotypes from Madeira and specimens from the Caribbean reveals no significant differences between them, although it might be expected that the Galápagos examples would be distinct from Atlantic-Caribbean specimens.

Occurrence: Off Gardner Bay, Española (Hood) Island, 63 m (Durham & Barnard).

Madracis pharensis (Heller) 1868
Plate 16, Figures 1, 5, 6

> *Madracis* sp. Durham & Barnard 1952, p. 15, pl. 1, fig. 1
> —— *pharensis* Zibrowius 1980, p. 18, pl. 3, figs. A–M (Synonymy)

Zibrowius, in his elaborate analysis of this Mediterranean and eastern Atlantic species, is reluctant to concede the identity of similar forms from the western Atlantic and Caribbean, while acknowledging their very great similarity. Specimens from the Galápagos are equally indistinguishable from the typical examples figured by Zibrowius, as a comparison with the specimen illustrated on plate 16 will show.

Occurrence: Gardner Island near Santa Maria (Floreana) Island, 30 m on rock wall, coll. G. M. Wellington (CDRS, CAS); Gardner Bay, Española (Hood) Island, 63 m (Durham & Barnard); Gorgona Island, Colombia, 63 m (Durham & Barnard).

Family ACROPORIDAE Verrill 1902
Genus *Acropora* Oken 1815
Acropora crassa (Milne Edwards & Haime) 1860

> *Madrepora crassa* M. E. & H., 1860, v. 3, p. 135
> —— —— Brook 1893, p. 30

In their original description, Milne Edwards and Haime indicated the locality of this species as "patrie inconnue." Later Brook redescribed the specimen in the Paris Museum and noted that it was labeled as coming from the Galápagos. No examples of *Acropora* have yet been found in the Galápagos or in the Pacific east of a line extending from Johnston Island to Ducie Atoll.

Occurrence: Apparently erroneously recorded from the Galápagos.

Suborder FUNGIINA Verrill 1865
Family AGARICIIDAE Gray 1847
Genus *Pavona* Lamarck 1801
***Pavona varians* Verrill 1864**
Plate 4, Figures 1-6

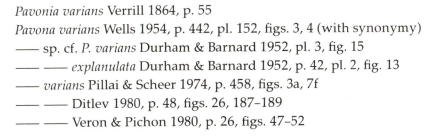

> *Pavonia varians* Verrill 1864, p. 55
> *Pavona varians* Wells 1954, p. 442, pl. 152, figs. 3, 4 (with synonymy)
> —— sp. cf. *P. varians* Durham & Barnard 1952, pl. 3, fig. 15
> —— —— *explanulata* Durham & Barnard 1952, p. 42, pl. 2, fig. 13
> —— *varians* Pillai & Scheer 1974, p. 458, figs. 3a, 7f
> —— —— Ditlev 1980, p. 48, figs. 26, 187–189
> —— —— Veron & Pichon 1980, p. 26, figs. 47–52

The aptness of the specific epithet of this widespread species is justified by the extreme variation found within the same corallum—massive to laminar sheets, short collines centrally on massive forms to elongate collines normal to the growing margins enclosing one or two series of centers, corallite walls rounded to acute, though along with all of this, the septa on long collines average 35 per 10 mm. The range of variation was well illustrated by Matthai (1948, pl. 12, fig. 1) from a specimen from Tahiti, and a large colony (pl. 4, figs. 4, 5) from Uva Island, Gulf of Chiriquí, Panamá, collected by P. W. Glynn, might equally have come from Tahiti.

Occurrence: Northeast side of Wolf (Wenman) Island, 15 m; Stephens Bay, San Cristóbal (Chatham) Island; west side of Champion Island, 10 m; Darwin Bay, Genovesa (Tower) Island, on rock walls, 12–18 m; Academy Bay, Santa Cruz Island, 3 m (CDRS 234); Academy Bay, 12–14 m (*Anton Bruun* Sta. 66128, USNM); Islas Plazas, Santa Cruz Island, 8 m (CDRS 113). Red Sea eastward through Indian Ocean and the Pacific northward to Bonin Islands and Hawaii; Pacific coast of Central and South America from the Gulf of Chiriquí south to La Plata Island, Ecuador; Cocos Island, Clipperton Island.

***Pavona clavus* Dana 1846**
Plate 5, Figures 1-5; Plate 6, Figures 1-5

> *Pavonia clavus* Dana 1846, p. 253, pl. 24, fig. 4
> —— *clivosa* Verrill 1869, p. 395; 1870, p. 544, pl. 9, fig. 8
> —— —— Bassett-Smith 1890, p. 445
> *Siderastrea clavus* Gardiner 1898, p. 525, pl. 44, fig. 1; 1905, p. 935
> —— —— *maldivensis* Gardiner 1905, p. 935, pl. 89, figs. 1, 2 (*non* fig. 3)

———— *micrommata* Felix 1913, p. 335, fig. 3

Pavona maldivensis Vaughan 1918, p. 138, pl. 56, figs. 3, 3a, 3b

—— *clavus* v. d. Horst 1922, p. 420, pl. 31, fig. 7

—— *gardineri* v. d. Horst 1922, p. 420, pl. 31, figs. 5, 6

—— *clavus* Umbgrove 1924, p. 12, pl. 2, fig. 8

—— *maldivensis* Ma 1937 (*non* Gardiner), p. 153, pl. 93, figs. 1, 2

—— *clavus liliacea* Ma 1937, p. 155, pl. 62, fig. 3

Progyrosmilia regularis Umbgrove 1950, p. 645, pl. 84, figs. 1, 2

Pavona clivosa Durham & Barnard 1952, p. 37, pl. 2, fig. 2

—— (*Pseudocolumnastraea*) *galapagensis* Durham & Barnard 1952, p. 44, pl. 3, figs. 16a, b

Solenastrea ecuadoriana Durham & Barnard 1952, p. 59, pl. 5, figs. 2, 3

Pavona clavus Wells 1954, p. 441, pl. 152, figs. 1, 2

—— *clivosa* Squires 1959, p. 412, pl. 32, fig. 1

—— *maldivensis* Ma 1959, p. 18, pl. 42, figs. 1, 2

—— *clavus liliacea* Ma 1959, p. 19, pl. 18, fig. 2 (*non* pl. 15, figs. 2, 2a)

—— *clavus* Scheer 1964, p. 458

? —— —— Scheer & Pillai 1974, p. 30, pl. 13, figs. 1, 2

—— *duerdeni* Scheer & Pillai 1974, p. 30, pl. 13, figs. 3, 4

—— *xarifae* Scheer & Pillai 1974, p. 31, pl. 14, figs. 1–3

Plocoastraea larochensis Chevalier 1968, p. 127, pl. 6, fig. 2; pl. 10, fig. 1; text fig. 10

Stylocoeniella paumotensis Chevalier 1976, p. 255, pl. 18, fig. 2; pl. 23, figs. 1–5

Pavona clavus Veron & Pichon 1980, p. 21, figs. 35–40

Comparison of topotype specimens of *P. clivosa* from the Pearl Islands with many specimens of *P. clavus* including Dana's type, from the Pacific, all of which show considerable variation within the same colony, affords no criteria for separating *P. clivosa* from *P. clavus*. *P. maldivensis* Gardiner seems to be a distinct species and, at most, *P. duerdeni* Vaughan from Hawaii is only a variety. *P. xarifae* Scheer & Pillai, based on a single specimen from the Nicobars, is the same as *P. duerdeni*.

Solenastrea ecuadoriana Durham & Barnard is only a beachworn fragment of *P. clavus* having the aspect of plocoid corallites. Such specimens are common on Galápagos beaches (pl. 6, fig. 3). *Progyrosmilia regularis* Umbgrove from the lower Pleistocene of Java, *Plocoastraea* Chevalier 1968 (type, *P. larochensis*) from the Pleistocene of Maré, New Caledonia, and *Stylocoeniella paumotensis* Chevalier, are also similarly worn *P. clavus*.

Occurrence: Santa Fe (Barrington) Island, 5 m (Durham & Barnard); Genovesa (Tower) Island, Darwin Bay, 12–18 m, laminar growth form; Champion Island, north side, 10m, nodular and laminar; Wolf (Wenman) Island, northeast side, 20 m, columniform; Darwin (Culpepper) Island, near arch rock, 10 m; Pinta (Abingdon) Island, southeast side near Punta Ibbetson; Marchena (Bindloe) Island, north side, 6 m; Bartolomé Island, shallow water; Española (Hood) Island, beach (*Albatross*, Sta. 1888, USNM); Santa Cruz Island, south of Academy Bay, 8–10 m (*Anton Bruun* Sta. 66112, USNM). Gulf of California; Pearl Islands; La Plata Island, La Libertad (35 m), and Sucre Island, Ecuador. Red Sea throughout tropical Indo-Pacific.

Pavona gigantea Verrill 1869
Plate 7, Figures 1-4; Plate 8, Figures 1, 2

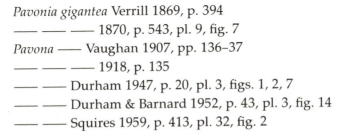

Pavonia gigantea Verrill 1869, p. 394
—— —— —— 1870, p. 543, pl. 9, fig. 7
Pavona —— Vaughan 1907, pp. 136–37
—— —— —— 1918, p. 135
—— —— Durham 1947, p. 20, pl. 3, figs. 1, 2, 7
—— —— Durham & Barnard 1952, p. 43, pl. 3, fig. 14
—— —— Squires 1959, p. 413, pl. 32, fig. 2

As in other massive or encrusting species of *Pavona*, there is much variation of growth form, depending on situation: massive or columnar colonies on open bottoms to thin, expanding laminae on steep slopes or walls where illumination is low. It is distinguished from *P. clavus* (*P. "clivosa"*) by the greater distance between centers—rarely less than 3 mm, and by the proportionally fewer septa, generally sixteen or less.

Although considered characteristic of the Panamic Province, the presence of this species at Fanning Island suggests that it ranges farther west.

Occurrence: Marchena (Bindloe) Island, north side, 6 m; Genovesa (Tower) Island, Darwin Bay, 13–18 m, on walls; Champion Island, 10–12 m, slanting down on rock walls; Bartolomé Island, 5 m; Gardner Island near Española (Hood) Island, 5–6 m (Durham & Barnard); Wolf (Wenman) Island, 6–30 m, columnar; Onslow Island, 3–5 m, laminar on rock walls; Mosquera Island near Baltra Island, 5 m (Durham & Barnard). Gulf of California; Bay of Panamá; Pearl Islands, 13 m; Sucre Island, Ecuador; Clipperton Island; Fanning Island (coll. J. E. Maragos).

Genus *Gardineroseris* Scheer & Pillai 1974

In 1905 Gardiner described and figured (pp. 937–938, pl. 89, fig. 5; pl. 90, fig. 7) a new coral from the Maldive Islands which he placed in the genus

Agaricia, A. ponderosa, with a variety *minikoiensis*. He noted variability in the thickness of the septa and growth form of the colony, *ponderosa* being massive and the variety a laminar expansion with shallower calices. He strongly doubted that the variety represented a distinct species and had some doubts that it was even a "true variety." A few years previously Verrill had redescribed Dana's *Agaricia* (*Undaria*) *planulata* (1901, p. 156, pl. 27, fig. 8) and made it the type of a new genus, *Asteroseris* (*non Asteroseris* de Fromentel 1867), based on a fragment of a thin, laminar expansion agreeing with Gardiner's variety *minikoiensis*. A specimen from Upolu, Samoa, was described by Wells (1936, p. 551, pl. 10, figs. 1–3) in which both the massive and laminar growth forms occurred in the same corallum showing the identity of *A. ponderosa* and *A. ponderosa minikoiensis*, as well as their identity with *A. planulata*, but placed the species incorrectly in *Polyastra*, a subgenus of *Pavona*. A massive corallum from Panamá illustrated here (pl. 9, figs. 3–5) similarly shows the *ponderosa* facies on the top and the *minikoiensis-planulata* facies on the sides.

In 1937 Ma figured (pl. 45, figs. 2, 3) a specimen from Kyûshû which Yabe, Sugiyama & Eguchi (1936) had incorrectly identified as *Agaricia ? minikoiensis* and without description placed it in a new subgenus of *Agaricia* (*Agariciella*). Two years later Umbgrove (1939) pointed out the close similarity of *Polyastra ponderosa, P. planulata, P. delicatula* (Felix), and *P. wahaiensis* (Umbgrove), the latter two being late Cenozoic forms inseparable from *planulata*. In 1959 Ma dropped the name *Agariciella* and listed his *minikoiensis* as *Leptoseris minikoiensis* (= *L. mycetoseroides* Wells).

Gardineroseris planulata (Dana) 1846
Plate 9, Figures 1–6

Agaricia (*Undaria*) *planulata* Dana 1846, p. 338
—— —— —— —— 1859, p. 55
—— ? *planulata* Milne Edwards & Haime 1860, p. 84
Asteroseris planulata Verrill *in* Dana 1872, p. 383 (in list); 1890, p. 424
Goniastrea sericea Ortmann 1888, p. 173, pl. 6, fig. 7
Asteroseris planulata Verrill 1901, p. 155, pl. 27, fig. 8
Agaricia ponderosa Gardiner 1905, p. 927, pl. 89, figs. 5, 6
—— —— var. *minikoiensis* Gardiner 1905, p. 938, pl. 90, fig. 7
—— —— Vaughan 1918, p. 140
Tichoseris delicatula Felix 1913, p. 337, pl. 27, figs. 4, 11
Agaricia ponderosa van der Horst 1922, p. 418
Tichoseris wahaiensis Umbgrove 1924, p. 13, pl. 1, figs. 6, 7
Agaricia ponderosa Faustino 1927, p. 200, pl. 65, figs. 1, 2
Tichoseris wahaiensis Umbgrove 1935, p. 49, pl. 14, fig. 4

Pavona (*Polyastra*) *planulata* Wells 1936, p. 551, pl. 10, figs. 1–3

non *Agaricia* ? *ponderosa* Yabe, Sugiyama & Eguchi 1936, p. 55, pl. 27, fig. 5; pl. 38, fig. 1; pl. 52, fig. 1

non ——? *minikoiensis* ibid., p. 55, pl. 42, figs. 5–7

non —— (*Agariciella*) *minikoiensis* Ma 1937, p. 149, pl. 45, figs. 2, 3

—— *ponderosa* Ma 1937, p. 148, pl. 93, fig. 3

Pavona ? aff. *P. varians* Montanaro-Gallitelli 1943, p. 54, pl. 11; pl. 12, figs. 1, 1a

Pavona (*Polyastra*) *ponderosa* Umbgrove 1943, p. 16

—— *ponderosa* Matthai 1948, p. 182, pl. 6, figs. 18, 19, 21–24

Agaricia ponderosa Ma 1959, p. 16, pl. 42, fig. 3

non *Leptoseris minikoiensis* Ma 1959, p. 18, pl. 27, figs. 2, 3

Pavona (*Polyastra*) *ponderosa* Durham 1962, p. 50, fig. 5

Polyastra planulata Chevalier 1968, p. 125

Agaricia ponderosa Loya & Slobodkin 1971, p. 123

—— —— Rosen 1971, p. 111

Pavona (*Polyastra*) *planulata* Nemenzo 1971, p. 159, pl. 6, fig. 2

Gardineroseris ponderosa Scheer & Pillai 1974, p. 32, pl. 15, figs. 1, 2

Agariciella planulata Birkeland et al. 1976, p. 66, fig. 25

Polyastra ponderosa Chevalier 1978, p. 247

Gardineroseris planulata Ditlev 1980, p. 48, figs. 29, 197–200

—— —— Veron & Pichon 1980, p. 68, figs. 121–125

This species is very widespread from the Gulf of Aqaba (Eilat) and the Red Sea throughout the Indian Ocean and eastward through the East Indies, the Philippines, the Great Barrier Reefs, and northward to Kyûshû and Honshû, eastward to Tahiti and Fanning Island, and now found in the extreme eastern Pacific (Gulf of Chiriquí, Gulf of Panamá, Cocos Island, Malpelo Island, and the Galápagos). Plio-Pleistocene: Java, Ceram, Celebes; Pleistocene: Hawaii (coll. 1980 by J. E. Maragos).

Occurrence: Galápagos: Academy Bay, Santa Cruz Island, 4 m.

Family FUNGIIDAE Dana 1846
Genus *Cycloseris* Milne Edwards & Haime 1849
***Cycloseris elegans* (Verrill) 1870**
Plate 11, Figures 3, 5

Fungia elegans Verrill 1870*a*, p. 100; 1870*b*, p. 542, pl. 10, figs. 1, 2

Cycloseris elegans Vaughan 1907, pp. 115, 116, 117, 128

—— —— Durham 1947, p. 24, pl. 9, figs. 1–3, 5, 6, 11, 12

—— —— Durham & Barnard 1952, p. 52, pl. 4, figs. 20a, b
—— —— Squires 1959, p. 414
—— —— Durham 1962, p. 52

This species occurs on sandy bottoms amongst abundant *Cycloseris mexicana*. Occasional *Diaseris* forms (pl. 11, figs. 3, 5), much larger (up to 60 mm) than nonregenerated individuals, are common. Polyps pale brown or bright green.

Occurrence: Southwest side, Gardner Island near Española (Hood) Island (Durham); beach, Punta Nunez, Santa Cruz Island (CDRS); east side of Onslow Island, 15 m, on sand. La Paz south to Panamá, 10–73 m.

Cycloseris mexicana Durham 1947
Plate 11, Figures 4, 6

Diaseris sp. Vaughan 1907, pp. 118, 119, 120
Cycloseris mexicana Durham 1947, p. 24, pl. 9, figs. 4, 7–10
—— —— Durham & Barnard 1952, p. 52, pl. 4, fig. 21

This species is very similar to, if not identical with, *C. distorta* (Michelin) 1842, which is widespread in the Red Sea, Indian Ocean, and central Pacific in depths from 10 to 90 m.

Occurrence: East side of Onslow Island, 15 m, on sandy bottom; Galápagos, 30–36 m (Durham & Barnard); Cocos Island, 25–85 m (Durham & Barnard); Gulf of California, 11–45 m, south to La Libertad, Ecuador, 15–64 m (Durham & Barnard).

Family PORITIDAE Gray 1840
Genus *Porites* Link 1807
Porites lobata Dana 1846
Plate 10, Figures 1–6

Porites lobata Dana 1846, p. 562, pl. 55, fig. 1
—— *excavata* Verrill 1870, p. 504
—— Sandwich Islands Bernard 1905, p. 100
—— *paschalensis* Vaughan 1906, p. 50, pl. 50, figs. 9, 10
—— *lobata* Vaughan 1907, pp. 196–207, pl. 81, figs. 1, 1a, 1b; pl. 82, figs. 1, 1a, 2; pl. 83, figs. 1, 1a, 2, 2a; pl. 84, figs. 1, 1a, b, 2; pl. 85, fig. 1; pl. 96, figs. 1–3
—— —— —— 1918, p. 192, pl. 85, figs. 2, 2a, 3
—— —— Hoffmeister 1925, p. 73, pl. 21, figs. 1a, b

? —— —— Crossland 1952, p. 242
—— —— Wells 1954, p. 452, pl. 166, figs. 1, 2
—— *excavata* Squires 1959, p. 420, pl. 33, figs. 1, 2 (Verrill's type)
—— *lobata* ? Durham 1962, p. 51
—— —— Wells 1972, p. 189, figs. 3–6

This common central Pacific coral appears to be the only species of *Porites* in the Galápagos, where it is common in depths from low water to at least 10 m. Colonies attain a considerable size—up to 2 m wide and 1 m thick. Growth bands on beach-worn masses indicate a yearly growth rate of 8–13 mm. The wide range of intraspecific variation was profusely illustrated by Vaughan (1907). An extreme example from a shallow lagoon reef patch on Fernandina Island south of Punta Espinosa, exposed at low tide, dominated by massed *Pocillopora* heads with rare *Porites*, is illustrated on plate 10, figure 3.

Occurrence: Eastern Pacific: Easter Island; Galápagos; Cocos Island (pl. 9, fig. 5), erroneously identified as *P. californica* Verrill by Wells, in Bakus (1975); Bay of Panamá, Pearl Islands (pl. 9, fig. 6). Elsewhere: Great Barrier Reefs eastward throughout the central Pacific, northward to Hawaii (type locality) and Midway Island (pl. 9, fig. 4), southward to Pitcairn Island.

Suborder FAVIINA Vaughan & Wells 1943
Family FAVIIDAE Gregory 1900
Genus *Cladocora* Ehrenberg 1834
Cladocora debilis Milne Edwards & Haime 1849
Plate 14, Figures, 9, 10

Cladocora debilis Milne Edwards & Haime 1849, p. 308; 1857, p. 599
—— *arbuscula* von Marenzeller 1904 (*non* Lesueur), p. 76, pl. 1, figs. 1a–e
—— *debilis* Durham & Barnard 1952, p. 58, pl. 4, figs. 22a–e
—— —— Zibrowius 1980, p. 31, pl. 11, figs. A, B, C (Synonymy)

No specimens of this species from the type locality (Madeira) or elsewhere in the Atlantic had been illustrated until recently, when the syntypes of Milne Edwards & Haime in the BMNH were described and figured by Zibrowius. The species is particularly characterized by the budding at nearly right angles from the main stems and by well-developed pali, as in *C. patriarca* Pourtalès of the south Atlantic, which is probably a synonym. The specimens figured by von Marenzeller, and Durham and Barnard from the eastern Pacific agree with typical *C. debilis* of the eastern Atlantic, as do specimens recently collected by A. De Roy in the Galápagos (pl. 14, figs. 9, 10). The species also occurs in the western Atlantic and Caribbean.

Occurrence: East of Cocos Island, 124–188 m (*Albatross* Stas. 3361, 3368) (von Marenzeller); Wolf (Wenman) Island, 180–270 m, off Gardner Bay, Española (Hood) Island, 45–78 m (Durham & Barnard); Galápagos, 100m (De Roy).

Family RHIZANGIIDAE d'Orbigny 1851
Genus *Culicia* Dana 1846
***Culicia rubeola* (Quoy & Gaimard) 1833**
Plate 11, Figures 1, 2

> *Dendrophyllia rubeola* Quoy & Gaimard 1833, p. 97, pl. 15, figs. 12–15
> *Culicia rubeola* Wells 1954, p. 464, pl. 185, figs. 3–6 (with synonymy)
> —— —— Squires 1960, p. 6, figs. 5, 6
> —— —— —— 1964, p. 3
> —— —— Squires & Keyes 1967, p. 21, pl. 1, fig. 1

This genus has not previously been reported from the far eastern Pacific.

Occurrence: Academy Bay, Santa Cruz Island, 4 m (CDRS 239); Cousin's Rock, Santiago Island, 21–27 m (polyps strong red in color); Wolf (Wenman) Island, 3 m on walls of cave (polyps nearly colorless); Onslow Island, inside "crown," 0–3 m; Darwin (Culpepper) Island, off arch rock, 7 m (corallites 1 per cm², on boulder 29X33 cm); Caleta Iguana, Isabela Island; Rábida (Jervis) Island, 1 m (CAS 018925); Bay of Panamá, Malpelo Island, 10 m on undersides of rocks (STRI, coll. C. Birkeland, 1972). Widespread in the central Pacific.

Genus *Astrangia* Milne Edwards & Haime 1848
***Astrangia browni* Palmer 1928**
Plate 12, Figures 1, 3

> *Astrangia browni* Palmer 1928, p. 27, pl. 1, figs. 1, 2
> —— *gardnerensis* Durham & Barnard 1952, p. 70, pl. 5, fig. 27

This species is distinguished from *A. equatorialis* by its larger calices (up to 4 mm), shallower calices, and well-developed columella.

Occurrence: Gardner bay, Española (Hood) Island, shore to 7 m (Durham & Barnard); Caleta Iguana, Isabela Island, 5 m (with *A. equatorialis*). Four miles west of Puerto Angel, Oaxaca, Mexico—polyps "dark sea green" (Palmer).

***Astrangia equatorialis* Durham & Barnard 1952**
Plate 12, Figures 1, 2

> *Astrangia equatorialis* Durham & Barnard 1952, p. 69, pl. 6, figs. 29a, b

This species has smaller calices (up to 2.5 mm) than *A. browni* , deeper calices, and a weakly developed columella.

Occurrence: Gardner Bay, Española (Hood) Island, 7 m (Durham & Barnard); Caleta Iguana, Isabela Island, 3–5 m (with *A. browni*); Onslow Island, 3–5 m (polyps pale pink); Onslow Island, inside "crown," 0–3 m; Bahía Urvina, Isabela Island, raised platform; Tagus Cove, Isabela Island, in caves 0–15 m (polyps pink); Darwin (Culpepper) Island, off arch rock, 7 m.

Genus *Oulangia* Milne Edwards & Haime 1848
Oulangia bradleyi Verrill 1866
Plate 12, Figures 4, 5

> *Oulangia bradleyi* Verrill 1866, p. 333; 1870, p. 534, pl. 9, fig. 10
> —— —— Durham & Barnard 1952, p. 77, pl. 8, fig. 39

Occurrence: 3.5 miles west of Punta Albemarle, Isabela Island (polyps brown with clear tentacles), 14m; Bahía Urvina, Isabela Island, raised platform; "Galápagos," large corallites: d = 14 × 16 mm, h = 8 mm, with 96 septa (V. & T. Williams, 1970) (STRI). Panamá, "rocky pools at low-water mark" (Verrill); San José Rock, near entrance to Panama Canal, 4 m (P. W. Glynn, 1974): on walls of Miraflores Locks, Panama Canal (P. W. Glynn, 1974); Ecuador, reef at Machalilla (P. W. Glynn, 1975).

Genus *Phyllangia* Milne Edwards & Haime 1848
Phyllangia consagensis (Durham & Barnard) 1952
Plate 12, Figures 6, 7

> *Bathycyathus consagensis* Durham & Barnard 1952, p. 79, pl. 8, figs. 40a–c,
>   pl. 9, fig. 40f
> *Lophosmilia wellsi* Durham & Barnard 1952, p. 90, pl. 12, fig. 52
> *Bathycyathus consagensis* Squires 1959, p. 422

Corallites similar to those of *P. dispersa* Verrill, common in the Bay of Panamá but larger (7–10 mm), approaching those of *P. americana* Milne Edwards & Haime of the Caribbean, but the corallite tissue is white rather than brownish, and as in *P. americana* the larger septa often bear flat paliform lobes, suggesting *Colangia*, but in that genus the lobes are regularly disposed. A related species was described as *Astrangia hayamaensis* by Eguchi (1968) from Sagami Bay, Japan. The specimens identified as *P. papuensis* Studer from Amboina and *P. dispersa* Verrill from Malacca by Ridley (1884) are a single species very close, if not identical, to *P. consagensis*.

Occurrence: Stephens Bay, San Cristóbal (Chatham) Island, 58 m (*L. wellsi* Durham & Barnard); Punta Espinosa, Fernandina (Narborough) Island, 4 m, under rock ledge (CDRS 117); Bahía Urvina, Isabela (Albemarle) Island, raised platform, in crevices; Tagus Cove, Isabela Island, in caves and over-hangs, 0–20 m (polyps brown to burnt orange with green tentacles); Geno-vesa (Tower) Island, 10–20 m (polyps pale pink, with vermilion planulae); Cousin's Rock, Santiago (James) Island (polyps strong red); Darwin (Culpep-per) Island, dredged in 30–50 m; Gulf of California, 18–82 m (Durham & Barnard, and Squires).

Family OCULINIDAE Gray 1847
Genus *Madrepora* Linnaeus 1758
***Madrepora galapagensis* Vaughan 1906**
Plate 13, Figures 1, 2

Madrepora galapagensis Vaughan 1906, p. 63, pl. 2, figs. 1, 1a, b

Vaughan's specimens, dredged by the *Albatross*, came from deep, cold (9°C) water, and the occurrence of the same species in temperate (ca. 18°C), shallow, and nearly lightless water is perhaps unexpected. In the *Albatross* specimens of *M. galapagensis* and the Hawaiian *M. kauaiensis* Vaughan (540–630 m, 7° C), the bottoms of the calices are solidly filled with stereome, whereas in the shallow water examples from Tagus Cove, illustrated herein, the skeletal structures are all light with very little internal filling and the third cycle of septa is very feebly developed. Both *M. galapagensis* and *M. kauaiensis* may prove to be synonyms of the cosmopolitan *M. oculata* (Linnae-us), according to Zibrowius (1974, p. 765). *M. oculata* was recorded from 742 m southeast of San Cristóbal (Chatham) Island (*Albatross* Sta. 3401).

Polyps very pale pink; corallum white, but one specimen from a cave ceiling, Española Island, 15 m, is tinted pink.

Occurrence: Five miles off southeast end of Española (Hood) Island, 550 m (*Albatross* Sta. 4642) (Vaughan); Española Island, 15 m, on cave ceiling (coll. Douglas Faulkner, 1973); Tagus Cove, Isabela Island, 18–24 m, abundant on cave ceilings.

Suborder CARYOPHYLLIINA Vaughan & Wells 1943
Family CARYOPHYLLIIDAE Gray 1847
Subfamily *Caryophylliinae* Gray 1847
Genus *Caryophyllia* Lamarck 1801
***Caryophyllia diomedeae* von Marenzeller 1904**

Caryophyllia diomedeae von Marenzeller 1904, p. 79, pl. 1, fig. 2
? —— —— Durham & Barnard 1952, p. 82, pl. 9, fig. 43

A small, worn specimen (d = 7 mm, h = 8 mm) was dredged in the Galápagos by the *Albatross* in 1888.

The shallow water specimens reported from the Galápagos by Durham and Barnard are not certainly the same as the bathyal form described by von Marenzeller.

Occurrence: *Albatross* Sta. 3358, off Panamá, 1,043 m (von Marenzeller); *Albatross* Sta. 2808, north of San Cristóbal (Chatham) Island, 1,160 m (USNM); Stephens Bay, San Cristóbal (Chatham) Island, Galápagos, and off Medidor Island, Bahía Honda, Panamá, 55–64 m (Durham & Barnard).

Genus *Cyathoceras* Moesley 1881
Cyathoceras avis (Durham & Barnard) 1952
Plate 13, Figures 3, 4

> *Kionotrochus* ? *avis* Durham & Barnard 1952, p. 88, pl. 11, figs. 50, a, b; pl. 12, fig. 50c
>
> —— ? *hoodensis* Durham & Barnard 1952, p. 89, pl. 12, figs. 51a–d

Durham & Barnard rightly doubted their reference of this coral to *Kionotrochus*, which is a typical turbinolian shown by Squires (1960) to possess pali. The turbinolian aspect of *C. avis* and *C. hoodensis*, which are identical species, suggested by the turbinate coralla with faint traces of early attachment, reflects the lack of suitable sites for larval fixation on a soft or sandy bottom.

  C. avis, with its lack of pali and presence of a well-developed columella of the *Caryophyllia* type, is distinguished by its septal arrangement in which 40 septa are grouped 10/10/20, not 48 septa grouped 12/12/24 as described by Durham and Barnard, although their figures show only 10/10/20.

Occurrence: Northeast of Floreana (Charles) Island, 110 m (*K*.? *avis* Durham & Barnard); north of Española (Hood) Island, 90–180 m (*K*.? *hoodensis* Durham & Barnard); Galápagos, ca. 100 m (V. & T. Williams, 1970)(STRI).

Genus *Paracyathus* Milne Edwards & Haime 1848
Paracyathus humilis Verrill 1870
Plate 13, Figures 5, 6

> *Paracyathus humilis* Verrill, 1870, p. 538
>
> —— —— Durham & Barnard 1952, p. 92, pl. 12, figs. 54a, b

Four specimens from the Galápagos, the largest of which is 10 mm in height, with a calicular diameter of 7 mm, have four complete cycles of septa. Septa of the first cycle exsert about 1 mm, the succeeding cycles regularly less so. Pali prominent, before all but the last cycle, elevated distinctly above the papillary columella. Corallum a light brown color.

Occurrence: Darwin Bay, Genovesa (Tower) Island, 23 m; Pearl Island (Verrill); Sulphur Bay, Clarion Island, 104 m (Durham & Barnard).

Genus *Polycyathus* Duncan 1876
***Polycyathus isabela* Wells 1982**
Plate 14, Figures 1, 2, 3

Polycyathus isabela Wells 1982, p. 211, fig. 1:1–3

This species differs from the only other eastern Pacific *Polycyathus, P. hondaensis* (Durham & Barnard) from Panamá, by its larger corallites with nearly twice as many septa and pali.

Occurrence: 3.5 miles west of Punta Albemarle, Isabela Island, 14–23 m, Holotype, USNM 46964.

***Polycyathus hondaensis* (Durham & Barnard 1952)**

Astrangia hondaensis Durham & Barnard 1952, p. 72, pl. 6, figs. 52a, b, c

"Questionably in the Galápagos Islands and Cocos Island, 210–276 m" (Durham and Barnard).

Occurrence: Off Medidor Island, Bahía Honda, Panamá, 180–210 m.

Subfamily TURBINOLIINAE Milne Edwards & Haime 1848
Genus *Sphenotrochus* Milne Edwards & Haime 1848
***Sphenotrochus hancocki* Durham & Barnard 1952**

Sphenotrochus hancocki Durham & Barnard 1952, p. 94, pl. 13, figs. 57a, b
? —— *intermedius* (Goldfuss) 1826 (Synonymy: Felix 1925, p. 173)
? —— *ralphae* Squires 1964, p. 5, pl. 1, figs. 1–4

This species is very close to, if not the same as *S. intermedius* of the European Cenozoic and the Miocene of Costa Rica, as are specimens from off Pratas Island, South China Sea (*Albatross* Sta. 5312, USNM), 256 m, and the Philippines (*Albatross* Sta. 5145, USNM), 41 m.

Occurrence: Galápagos, 18–275 m, from many stations (Durham & Barnard), most records being from 27–82 m. Lower California, 36 m (Durham & Barnard).

Subfamily *Desmophyllinae* Vaughan & Wells 1943
Genus *Desmophyllum* Ehrenberg 1834
***Desmophyllum cristagalli* Milne Edwards & Haime 1848**

Desmophyllum cristagalli Milne Edwards & Haime 1848a, p. 233, pl. 7, fig. 10

—— —— von Marenzeller 1904, p. 81

Zibrowius (1974a, p. 758 et seq.) has recently reviewed the distribution and synonymy of this cosmopolitan species.

Occurrence: Southeast of San Cristóbal (Chatham) Island, 742 m (*Albatross* Sta. 3401); northeast of Santa Cruz (Indefatigable) Island, 716 m (*Albatross* Sta. 2818, USNM).

Family FLABELLIDAE Bourne 1905
Genus *Flabellum* Lesson 1832
Flabellum gallapagense Milne Edwards & Haime 1848

Flabellum gallapagense [sic] Milne Edwards & Haime 1848, p. 87, pl. 4, figs. 3, 3a; 1848a, p. 264, 431

—— *Galapagosense* [sic] d'Orbigny 1852, 3:143

—— *gallapagense* de Fromentel 1861, p. 90

—— —— Felix 1927, p. 409

Milne Edwards & Haime based this species on a single specimen* in the Stokes Collection: "Fossile de Gallapagos" (p. 264) and "Miocène: Gallapagos" (p. 341), and in 1857: "Miocène? Gallapagos." Tertiary sediments do occur in the Galápagos. Dall (Dall & Ochsner, 1928) reported fossiliferous strata on Santa Cruz and Baltra and considered them to be Pliocene. Durham (1965) found beds on Santa Cruz that he believed to be late Miocene, a conclusion apparently accepted by McBirney & Williams (1969). It is barely possible that the supposed Miocene age of *F. gallapagense* may have been correct.

This species is very similar to, if not identical with, the Recent *F. thouarsii* M. E. & H. (1848, p. 265, pl. 8, fig. 5) of the South Atlantic (100–200 m).

Occurrence: Fossil (Miocene?), Galápagos (?).

Flabellum daphnense Durham & Barnard 1952

Flabellum daphnense Durham & Barnard 1952, p. 96, pl. 13, figs. 58a, b

---

*Unfortunately this specimen, the first coral to be reported from the Galápagos, appears to be lost. Milne Edwards and Haime (1860) noted that the Stokes Collection had been sold by Stokes's heirs and dispersed. Sherborn (1940) says that Stokes's material was bought by the British Museum, but a search by B. R. Rosen for the specimen in 1976 failed to locate it.

The granulation of the exterior of the corallum of this species, which is based on a single specimen, is like that found on some of the brown-tinted coralla of *Polymyces fragilis* (Pourtalès) of the Caribbean, on similarly colored examples of *F. autearoa* Squires 1964 from New Zealand, and on a subfossil *Flabellum* from the New Hebrides.

Occurrence: Southeast of Daphne Major Island, Galápagos, 100 m (Durham & Barnard).

Genus *Javania* Duncan 1876
Javania cailleti (Duchassaing & Michelotti) 1866

Desmophyllum cailleti Duchassaing & Michelotti 1866, p. 66, pl. 8, fig. 2
—— *galapagense* Vaughan 1906, p. 63, pl. 1, figs. 1–1b
Javania galapagensis Zibrowius 1974, p. 17
—— *cailleti* Cairns 1979, p. 153, pl. 28, figs. 8–12; pl. 30, figs. 1, 4
—— —— Zibrowius 1980, p. 157, pl. 82 (Synonymy)

A dead corallum dredged in 1888 by the *Albatross* has five cycles of septa; diameter of calice, 27 mm. The base is broken away and the present height is 39 mm, and diameter at the lower end is 6 mm. There are also three juvenile specimens from the same haul.

Occurrence: Off Bartolomé Island, 143 m (*Albatross* Sta. 2816, USNM); northeast of Santa Cruz Island, 716 m (*Albatross* Sta. 2818, USNM); five miles off southeast end of Española (Hood) Island, 540 m (*Albatross* Sta. 4642) (Vaughan). Western Mediterranean, eastern Atlantic, western Atlantic, and Caribbean, 150–1,500 m (Zibrowius, Cairns).

Javania sp. cf. *J. pseudoalabastra* Zibrowius 1974

Javania pseudoalabastra Zibrowius 1974, p. 10, pl. 2, figs. 7–12
—— —— Cairns 1979, p. 156, pl. 30, figs. 9–10
—— —— Zibrowius 1980, p. 156, pl. 81, figs. A–D

Three fragments, probably from one corallum, agree very closely with the three specimens from the Azores described by Zibrowius. A proximal piece is white, the other two distal bits are brownish-mauve in color. The major septa are strongly exsert, and all septa bear laterally stout, pointed granules arranged in rows concentric with the margins.

Occurrence: Northeast of Santa Cruz Island, 716 m (*Albatross* Sta. 2818, USNM). Azores, 784–1,577 m (Zibrowius). Western Atlantic, 1,089–1,234 m (Cairns).

Suborder DENDROPHYLLIINA Vaughan & Wells 1943
Family DENDROPHYLLIIDAE Gray 1847
Genus *Balanophyllia* S.V. Wood 1844
Balanophyllia galapagensis Vaughan 1906

Balanophyllia galapagensis Vaughan 1906, p. 67, pl. 4, figs. 2, 2a–b

A deeper water species, so far known from only one record.

Occurrence: 4.5 miles off Española (Hood) Island, 180 m (*Albatross* Sta. 4643).

Balanophyllia osburni Durham & Barnard 1952

Balanophyllia osburni Durham & Barnard 1952, p. 100, pl. 15, figs. 63a–d
—— —— Durham 1962, p. 52, figs. 2a, d

Occurrence: South of Santa Cruz (Indefatigable) Island, 110 m (Durham & Barnard); Osborn Island near Española Island, 3 m (Durham). Octavia Bay, Colombia (Durham & Barnard).

Balanophyllia eguchii Wells 1982
Plate 14, Figures 6, 7, 8

Balanophyllia affinis Wells (*non* Semper) 1964, p. 114, pl. 2
Dendrophyllia arbuscula var. *compressa* Eguchi & Sasaki 1973, p. 811, pl. 1, fig. 3 (*non B. compressa* Seguenza 1880, p. 303, pl. 17, figs. 26, 27)
Balanophyllia eguchii Wells 1982, p. 211, fig. 1:4–6

This is a common species at the Galápagos, distinguished from other shallow-water forms of *Balanophyllia* by the quasi-colonial habit ("*Rhodopsammia*") like that of *Rhizopsammia*, and by the compressed mature corallites with a distinctive septal arrangement.

The polyps of the Galápagos specimens were vermilion to pinkish-vermilion in color. Those from the Bay of Panamá were yellow; those from Hawaii pinkish-orange or orange; and those from Japan orange-brown or reddish.

Occurrence: North side of Marchena Island, 6 m (Holotype, USNM 46966); Rábida (Jervis) Island, 7.5 m; Champion Island, 1 m (CDRS 011); Academy Bay, Santa Cruz Island, 10 m (CDRS 227); Onslow Island under rocks and ledges, 3–5 m (CDRS 106, 225; CAS 0189928); Sombrero Chino, Santiago Island, under rock ledges (CDRS 224); Cousin's Rock, 21–27 m. Elsewhere: Wakayama-ken, Japan, 7 m (L. G. Harris); Shizuoka Prefecture, central Japan (Eguchi); outside Kaneohe Bay, Hawaii, ceiling of pocket in ledge,

26 m (L. G. Harris); off Southern Queensland, 85 m (Wells); northeast end of Punta Chame, Bay of Panamá, to 27 m (R. Stewart); Taboguilla Island, Bay of Panamá, 9–12 m (G. Hendler); Malpelo Island, 9 m (C. Birkeland).

Genus *Dendrophyllia* de Blainville 1830
Dendrophyllia gracilis Milne Edwards & Haime 1848
Plate 16, Figures 1-4

Dendrophyllia gracilis Milne Edwards & Haime 1848*b*, p. 100, pl. 1, fig. 13; 1860, vol. 3, p. 119

—— *coccinea* Dana 1846, p. 388, pl. 27, fig. 4 (*non Oculina coccinea* Ehrenberg 1834)

—— *danae* Verrill *in* Dana 1872, p. 384 (*pro D. coccinea* Dana *non* Ehrenberg)

—— *gracilis* Verrill 1866, p. 29, pl. 1, fig. 2, pl. 2, figs. 2, 2a

? —— ——Semper 1872, p. 267

? —— *conferta* Quelch 1886, p. 146, pl. 7, figs. 2, 2a, 2b

? —— *coarctata* Duncan 1886, p. 17, pl. 1, figs. 27, 28

—— *gracilis* Bourne 1905, p. 213, pl. 4, figs. 26–28 (anatomy)

? —— *ramea* Bedot 1907, p. 236, pl. 306, figs. 183–187

—— *elegans* v. d. Horst 1922a, p. 57, pl. 8, figs. 9, 10 (*non D. elegans* Duncan 1866)

—— *coccinea* v. d. Horst 1926, p. 45, pl. 3, figs. 1, 2, 3

—— *gracilis* Faustino 1927, p. 220

—— *sphaerica* Nemenzo 1960, p. 19, pl. 10, fig. 2

—— sp. Catala 1964, pl. 19, figs. 1, 2

—— sp. cf. *D. gracilis* Eguchi 1968, p. C60, pl. 23, figs. 4, 5, 6

Tubastraea coccinea titizimaensis Eguchi 1968, p. C71, pl. 33, figs. 1–4, pl. 31, figs. 1–4 (*non* pl. 17, fig. 16)

Dendrophyllia gracilis Faulkner 1974, p. 162, pl. 44

—— —— Faulkner & Chesher 1979, pp. 305–306, pls. 180–189

Van der Horst's *D. elegans* (not *D. elegans* Duncan 1866, an Eocene species), was said to be marked by the absence of a columella, but among a number of colonies of *D. gracilis* from Palau the columella was absent or nearly absent in some, and well-developed in other corallites of the same colony. This intracolonial variation, as well as variation in depth of the calices, suggests that *D. arbuscula* van der Horst (1922) and specimens identified with *D. arbuscula* by Eguchi (1968), Scheer & Pillai (1974), and Pillai & Scheer (1974), are within the limits of *D. gracilis*.

Verrill (1866) noted that the polyps of specimens from Hong Kong (45 m) were bright salmon in color, tentacles almost white, and oral disc with salmon-colored radii. The polyps of specimens from Cousin's Rock, Galápagos, collected by Douglas Faulkner, were pink or orange in color, and those of colonies from Palau (Faulkner, 1974; Faulkner & Chesher, 1979) were like those described by Verrill; others were orange or pink. *D. gracilis* is probably the yellow or pink *Dendrophyllia* noticed by Crossland (1927, p. 541) in his enthusiastic description of the marine garden at Tagus Cove.

Occurrence: Cousin's Rock, 12 m (Faulkner, 1973); Gardner Bay, Española (Hood) Island, low intertidal to 10 m (CDRS 008); Rábida (Jervis) Island, 7 m (CAS 018925); Santiago (James) Island, tide pools in Sullivan Bay (CAS 018926). Reported from the eastern Indian Ocean eastward through the Philippines and Great Barrier Reefs to Japan, to 45 m. Milne Edwards & Haime's type came from "China."

Genus *Endopachys* Lonsdale 1845
Endopachys grayi Milne Edwards & Haime 1848

> *Endopachys grayi* Milne Edwards & Haime 1848*b*, p. 81, pl. 1, figs. 2, 2a
> —— *oahense* Vaughan 1907, p. 147, pl. 44, figs. 3, 3a
> —— *vaughani* Durham 1947, p. 39, pl. 11, figs. 6, 7, 8, 10, 11
> —— —— Durham & Barnard 1952, p. 103, pl. 16, figs. 67a, b
> —— *grayi* Hickson 1922, p. 155, 2 figs.
> —— —— Umbgrove 1950, p. 648, pl. 82, figs. 1–10, pl. 83, fig. 7, tf. 2

Umbgrove demonstrated the unity of the supposed species *E. japonica*, *E. oahense*, and *E. vaughani*, with *E. grayi*.

Occurrence: North of Española (Hood) Island, 90–180 m (Durham & Barnard); Tagus Cove, Isabela Island, 45 m, dredged dead; Gulf of California and Lower California, 18–365 m; Cocos Island; Persian Gulf, 100 m; Hawaii, 53–211 m; Indonesia, 40–141 m; Philippines; Japan, 197–658 m; Late Tertiary and Pleistocene: Philippines, Taiwan, Japan, Java.

Genus *Rhizopsammia* Verrill 1870
Rhizopsammia verrilli van der Horst 1922
Plate 15, Figures 1, 2, 3, 4

> *Rhizopsammia verrilli* v. d. Horst 1922*a*, p. 64, pl. 8, figs. 1, 2
> *Balanophyllia scheeri* Durham 1962, p. 53, figs. 2b, c, 4, 7

Several mature corallites with diameters of 6.5 × 8 and 9 × 10mm, with five cycles of septa and a prominent spongy columella. Two young offsets from stolons, 2 mm in height, have calicular diameters of 3 mm, one with three cycles, the other with four cycles of septa, and epitheca extending to the margins of the calices.

Color of the polyps: vermilion.

Occurrence: Northeast side of Wolf (Wenman) Island, 15 m, on under surface of *Pavona varians*; north side of Marchena Island, 15 m; Champion Island; Wafer Bay, Cocos Island, 7–10 m (Durham). Elsewhere: between Nusa Besi and northeast point of Timor, 27–54 m (types, v. d. Horst), and off Paru Pandjang, west coast of Binongka, 278 m (broken pieces, v. d. Horst).

Rhizopsammia wellingtoni Wells 1982
Plate 15, Figures 5, 6, 7; Plate 16, Figure 1

Rhizopsammia wellingtoni Wells 1982, p. 213, fig. 2:1–3

R. wellingtoni is nearest to *R. chamissoi* Wells from the Marshall Islands, in which the calices have many fifth cycle septa developed and the polyps are brick-red or vermilion in color. *R. verrilli* van der Horst has larger corallites with five septal cycles.

The polyps of *R. wellingtoni* were deep purple-black.

Occurrence: Tagus Cove, Isabela Island, 16–25 m (holotype, USNM 46969); Tagus Cove under rock ledge, 2 m (CDRS 118, CAS 018995); Gardner Island, near Floreana Island, 30 m (CDRS 103); dredged off Onslow Island, 36–43 m.

Genus *Endopsammia* Milne Edwards & Haime 1848
Endopsammia pourtalesi (Durham & Barnard) 1952

Thecopsammia pourtalesi Durham & Barnard 1952, p. 104, pl. 16, fig. 68

This species is very close to, if not identical with *E. philippinensis* Milne Edwards & Haime, the type of the genus, widespread in shallow water (under stones or coral heads) to 80 m, from East Africa into the central Pacific (Wells, 1964, p. 118).

Occurrence: South Seymour Island near Baltra Island, no bathymetric data (Durham & Barnard).

Genus *Enallopsammia* Michelotti 1871
Enallopsammia amphelioides (Alcock) 1902

Enallopsammia amphelioides Zibrowius 1973, p. 45, pl. 3, figs. 16–23 (with synonymy).

A small fragment of the tip of a branch with two very deep calices 3 mm in diameter, with twenty-four septa.

Occurrence: Northeast of Santa Cruz Island, 716 m (*Albatross* Sta. 2818, USNM). Maldives, Indonesia, Tuamotus, Hawaii, 229–1,633 m.

Genus *Tubastraea* Lesson 1829

This genus and its type species *T. coccinea* were first described in 1829, although the date is usually cited as 1831 or 1834. Lesson's "Zoophytes" of the Zoologie of the Voyage . . . sur . . . la Coquille appeared in Volume 2, Part 2, the whole volume of which was finally issued in 1838, but, as Sherborn and Woodward showed (1906, p. 336), the author's copies of the section "Zoophytes" were sent out in 1829.

Tubastraea coccinea Lesson 1829
Plate 17, Figures 1, 2

Tubastraea coccinea Lesson 1829, p. 93; 1834, p. 515, pl. 1

This cosmopolitan tropical species has a worldwide distribution from the Red Sea to Panamá, the Atlantic and West Indies, under many names: *affinis* Duncan, *atrata* Dennant (?), *aurantiaca* Milne Edwards & Haime, *aurea* Quoy & Gaimard, *darwini* Duncan, *ehrenbergiana* Milne Edwards & Haime, *gaimardi* van der Horst, *klunzingeri* van der Horst, *manni* Verrill, *pedersenii* Verrill, *radiata* Verrill, *sibogae* van der Horst, *surcularis* Verrill, *tenuilamellosa* Milne Edwards & Haime, *turbinata* Nemenzo, *urvillei* Milne Edwards & Haime, *valida* Verrill, and *willeyi* Gardiner. "It is highly probable that at least all the other described species of *Tubastraea* are nothing but varieties of *T. aurea* (Quoy & Gaimard) [=*T. coccinea* Lesson]" (Boschma, 1953, p. 110). The polyps are commonly orange to vermilion in color but range from yellowish-green, yellow, pink, scarlet, to reddish brown.

Unfortunately, the fate of the solitary specimen of *Placopsammia darwini* Duncan 1876, "Galapagos Islands. Collected by Mr. Darwin" is unknown, like many of Duncan's types, but from the description and wretched figure it seems to have been *T. coccinea*, where it is placed here. The attribution to *Placopsammia*, a Tertiary form, is improbable indeed, and Duncan appears to have had doubts (1884, p. 179). Nor can the reference of *P. darwini* to *Lobopsammia*, an early Tertiary genus, be supported.

T. diaphana (Dana) is a closely related species distinguished by the black, greenish-black, or dark brown polyps. The same somber colors characterize the polyps of the dendroid species *T. micrantha* (Ehrenberg) (+*nigrescens* Dana and *viridis* Milne Edwards & Haime).

Occurrence: Cousin's Rock, Santiago Island, 21-27 m; Tagus Cove, Isabela Island, 15 m; Darwin (Culpepper) Island, 8-27 m; Wolf (Wenman) Island, 5-20 m; shore of Floreana Island, and Isabela Island (Durham 1947); Osborn Island near Española Island, 3 m (Durham 1962); Guy Fawkes Island near Santa Cruz Island, 5 m on "steep rock" (Durham 1962); south side of Daphne Minor Island, 27 m (USNM); tide pool, Sullivan Bay, Santiago Island (USNM); Academy Bay, Santa Cruz Island, 12-14 m (USNM). Late Pleistocene, raised beach, James Bay, Santiago Island (*Astropsammia pedersenii*, in Hertlein, 1939).

Tubastraea faulkneri Wells 1982
Plate 19, Figures 1-4

> *Dendrophyllia aurea* van der Horst 1926, p. 46, pl. 2, fig. 1 (non *aurea* Quoy & Gaimard)
>
> *Tubastrea aurea* Boschma 1953, p. 112, pl. 9, figs. 5, 6
>
> —— —— Nemenzo 1971, p. 182, pl. 12, fig. 3
>
> *Tubastraea* new species Faulkner & Chesher 1979, p. 307, pl. 192
>
> —— *faulkneri* Wells 1982, p. 216, fig. 3:1-3

This species is distinguished from *T. coccinea* (pl. 17, figs. 1, 2) by the widely spaced corallites partly sunken in thickened coenosteum and by the prominent fusion of the fourth cycle septa to those of the third. That *T. faulkneri* is only an ecovariant of *T. coccinea* seems to be negated by the occurrence of the two forms at the same site on the steep walls of Tagus Cove.

The polyps are orange in color (G. M. Wellington's and D. Faulkner's photographs; A. G. Hume's note to specimens from Banda).

Occurrence: Tagus Cove, Isabela Island, 3-5 m (G. M. Wellington); Great Reef, Bailechesengel Island, Palau Islands, 7.6 m (Holotype USNM 47145) (D. Faulkner); Goeneng Api, Banda Island, 5 m, USNM 62570 (A. G. Humes); Wainitu, Amboina (van der Horst); Puerto Galera, Oriental Mindoro, Philippines (Nemenzo).

Tubastraea tagusensis Wells 1982
Plate 20, Figures 1, 2, 3, 4, 5, 6

> *Tubastraea coccinea* Scheer & Pillai 1974, p. 64, pl. 30, figs. 1-3
>
> —— new species Faulkner & Chesher 1979, p. 307, pl. 193
>
> —— *tagusensis* Wells 1982, p. 216, fig. 4:1-4

This striking *Tubastraea* has smaller corallites than *T. coccinea* from which it is distinguished by the regularity of alternation of the two groups of septa—a single small septum lies between the twelve large, equal first and second cycle septa.

Color of polyps: lemon yellow with red peristomes; pale red-violet, pale red-violet with yellowish coenosarc.

Occurrence: Tagus Cove, Isabela Island, 4.5 m (Holotype USNM 46977); Tagus Cove, 7.6 m (paratype USNM 46979); Tagus Cove, 11–24 m (CDRS 107, 228, 229; CAS 018996); Cousin's Rock, Santiago Island, 3 m (CDRS 230); south side of Daphne Minor Island, 43 m (USNM). Nicobar Islands (Scheer & Pillai); Palau Islands (D. Faulkner).

Tubastraea floreana Wells 1982
Plate 18, Figures 3, 4, 5, 6

Tubastraea floreana Wells 1982, p. 218, fig. 4:5, 6

This species is like *T. tagusensis* and has the same characteristic septal arrangement, but the corallites are much smaller — 4–6 mm in *T. floreana* and 8–10 mm in *T. tagusensis.*

Polyps bright pink, drying to dark red-black.

Occurrence: Playa Prieta, west side of Floreana Island, shallow water (Holotype USNM 46974); Caleta Iguana, Isabela Island, from overhang at 5 m (USNM 46976); Gardner Island, near Española (Hood) Island, in cave at 2 m (USNM 46975) (G. M. Wellington); Pinzón (Duncan) Island (*Albatross*, USNM).

REFERENCES

Bak, R. P. M., and G. van Eys. 1975. Predation of the sea urchin *Diadema antillarum* Philippi on living coral. Oecologia, 20:111–115.

Bakus, G. J. 1975. Marine zonation and ecology of Cocos Island, off Central America. Atoll Res. Bull., 179, 9 pp., 7 figs.

Bassett-Smith, P. W. 1890. Report on the corals from Tizard and Macclesfield Banks, China Seas. Annals and Mag. of Nat. Hist., Ser. 6, 6:353–374; 443–458, pls. 12–14.

Bedot, M. 1907. Madréporaires d'Amboine. Revue Suisse de Zoologie, 15:143–292, 46 pls.

Bernard, H. M. 1905. The *Porites* of the Indo-Pacific region. Catalogue of the Madreporarian corals in the British Museum (Natural History), 5, 310 pp., 35 pls.

Birkeland, C., D. L. Meyer, J. P. Stames, and C. L. Buford. 1975. Subtidal communities of Malpelo Island. *Smithsonian Contribs. to Knowl., Zoology*, No. 176: 55–68, figs. 20–27, tables 5–8.

Boschma, H. 1953. On specimens of the coral genus *Tubastraea*, with notes on phenomena of fission. Studies of the Fauna of Curaçao and other Caribbean Islands, 4: 109–119, pls. 9–12.

Bourne, G. C. 1905. Report on the solitary corals collected by Dr. Herdman. Report to the Government of Ceylon on the Pearl Oyster Fisheries of the Gulf of Manaar (Royal Society of London), part 4, Supplemental Report Number 29: 187–242, pls. 1–4.

Brook, G. 1893. The genus *Madrepora*. Catalogue of the Madreporaria in the British Museum (Natural History), 1, 219 pp., 35 pls.

Brueggemann, F. 1878. Neue Korallen-Arten aus dem Rothen Meer und von Mauritius. Abhandlungen von Naturwissenschaftlichen Vereine Bremen, 5: 395–400, pls. 7, 8.

Cairns, S. D. 1979. The deep-water Scleractinia of the Caribbean Sea and adjacent waters. Studies on the Fauna of Curaçao and other Caribbean Islands, 57, 180: 1–341, 40 pls., 56 maps, 5 tables.

Catala, R. 1964. Carnival under the sea. Sicard, Paris, 141 pp., 27 pls., 48 figs.

Chevalier, J.-P. 1961. Recherches sur les madréporaires et les formations récifales Miocènes de la Méditerranée occidentale. Soc. Géol. France., Mém., n.s., v. 40: 562 pp., 26 pls, 199 figs.

———. 1968. Les madréporaires fossiles de Maré. Expédition française sur les récifs coralliens de la Nouvelle-Calédonie (Foundation Singer-Polignac, Paris), 3: 85–158, 10 pls.

———. 1976. Madréporaires actuels et fossiles du lagon de Taiaro. Cah. Pac., 19: 253–264, 4 figs., pls. 15, 18–23.

———. 1978. Coraux des Iles Marquises. Cah. Pac., 21: 243–278, 14 figs., 3 pls.

Crossland, C. 1927. Marine ecology and coral formations in the Panama region, Galapagos, and Marquesas Islands, and the atoll of Napuka. Roy. Soc. Edinburgh, Trans., 55 (2): 531–554, 11 figs., 1 pl.

Crossland, C. 1952. Madreporaria, Hydrocorallineae, *Heliopora* and *Tubipora*. Scientific Reports of the Great Barrier Reef Expedition, 1928–29 (British Museum, Natural History), 6, 3: 257 pp., 56 pls.

Dall, W. H., and W. H. Ochsner. 1928. Tertiary and Pleistocene mollusca from the Galapagos Islands. Calif. Acad. of Sci., Proc., 17: 89–139, 6 pls.

Dana, J. D. 1846. Report on the Zoophytes. United States Exploring Expedition . . . 7: vi, 740 pp.; atlas: 61 pls. (1849).

———. 1859. Synopsis of the report on the Zoophytes of the United States Exploring Expedition. New Haven: vi, 172 pp.

———. 1872. Corals and coral islands. New York. 398 pp. (and later editions).

Ditlev, H. 1980. A field-guide to the reef-building corals of the Indo-Pacific. Klampenborg: Scandinavian Science Press, 291 pp., 401 figs.

Duchassaing, P., and J. Michelotti. 1866. Mémoire sur les coralliaires des Antilles. Supplément. Mém. Acad. Sci. Turin, (2) 23: 97–206, pls. 1–11.

Duncan, P. M. 1866. A monograph of the British fossil corals. Being a supplement to the monograph of the British fossil corals by Messrs. Milne Edwards & Haime. Part 1. Introduction and corals from the Tertiary formations: 69 pp., 10 pls. Palaeontographical Society, London.

———. 1876. Notices of some deep-sea and littoral corals from the Atlantic Ocean, Caribbean, Indian, New-Zealand, Persian Gulf and Japanese, etc., Seas. Proc. of the Zool. Soc. of Lond. for 1876, pp. 428–442, pls. 38–41.

———. 1884. A revision of the families and genera of the sclerodermic Zoantharia, Edwards & Haime, or Madreporaria (Madreporaria rugosa excepted). J. Linnaean Soc. Lond., 18: 1–204.

———. 1886. On the Madreporaria of the Mergui archipelago collected for the trustees of the Indian Museum, Calcutta, by Dr. John Anderson. . . . J. Linnaean Soc. Lond. Zool., 21: 1–25, pl. 1.

Durham, J. W. 1947. Corals from the Gulf of California and the North Pacific coast of America. Mem. Geol. Soc. of Am., 20: 68 pp., 14 pls.

——. 1950. E. W. Scripps cruise to the Gulf of California, Part 2. Megascopic paleontology and marine stratigraphy. Geol. Soc. Am. Mem., 43, 216 pp., 48 pls., 3 figs., 10 tables.

——. 1962. Corals from the Galápagos and Cocos Islands. Proc. of the Calif. Acad. of Sci., 32: 41–56.

——. 1965. Geology of the Galapagos. Pac. Disc., 18(5):3–6, 8 figs.

——. 1966. Coelenterates, especially stony corals, from Galápagos and Cocos Islands. In The Galápagos. Berkeley and Los Angeles: University of California Press, 123–135.

Durham, J. W., and J. L. Barnard. 1952. Stony corals of the eastern Pacific collected by the Valero III and Valero IV. Allan Hancock Pac. Exped., 16(1): 110 pp., 16 pls.

Eguchi, M. 1968. The hydrocorals and scleractinian corals of Sagami Bay. Biol. Lab. of the Imper. House., Tokyo, 68 pp., 36 pls.; C1–C80, 33 pls.; A1–A2, 1 pl.

——. 1973. On some new or little known corals from Japan and Australia. Seto Mar. Lab., Publications, 20: 81–87, pl. 1, 2 text figs.

Faulkner, D. 1974. This living reef. New York: Quadrangle. 180 pp., 107 pls.

Faulkner, D. and R. Chesher. 1979. Living corals. New York: C. N. Potter. 310 pp., 193 col. pls.

Faustino, L. A. 1927. Recent Madreporaria of the Philippine Islands. Monographs of the Philippine Department of Agriculture and Natural Resources. Bur. of Sci., 22: 310 pp., 100 pls.

Felix, J. 1913. Die fossilen Anthozoen aus der Umgegend von Trinil. Palaeontographica, 60: 311–365, pls. 24–27.

——. 1925. Anthozoa Eocaenica et Oligocaenica. Fossilium Catalogus, Animalia, 28, 296 pp.

——. 1947. Anthozoa Miocaenica. Fossilium Catalogus, Animalia, 35: 27–488.

Fromentel, L. E. G. de. 1861. Introduction à l'étude des polypiers fossiles. Paris, 357 pp.

Gardiner, J. S. 1898. On the fungid corals collected by the author in the South Pacific. Proc. of the Zool. Soc. of Lond. for 1898: 525–539, pls. 43–45.

——. 1905. The fauna and geography of the Maldive and Laccadive Archipelagoes, vol. 2, supp. 1, Madreporaria: 933–957, pls. 89–93.

Glynn, P. W., R. H. Stewart, and J. E. McCosker. 1972. Pacific coral reefs of Panamá: structure, distribution and predators. Geologische Rundschau, 61: 483–519.

Glynn, P. W., G. M. Wellington, and C. Birkeland. 1979. Coral reef growth in the Galápagos: limitation by sea urchins. Science, 203: 47–49, 2 figs.

Goldfuss, A. 1826. Petrefacta Germaniae, 1 (1), 70 pp., 24 pls.

Hertlein, L. G. 1939. Marine Pleistocene molluscs from the Galapagos Islands. Proc. of Calif. Acad. of Sci., (4), 23:367–380, pl. 32.

Hickson, S. J. 1922. On two specimens of the genus Endopachys from the Persian Gulf. Bijdragen tot de Dierkunde, Amsterdam, 22: 155–160.

Hoffmeister, J. E. 1925. Some corals from American Samoa and the Fiji Islands. Pubs. of the Carnegie Inst. of Wash., 343: 89 pp., 23 pls.

Horst, C. J. van der. 1922. Madreporaria: Agariciidae. No. 9, Percy Sladen Trust Expedition. Linnaean Soc. of Lond. Transactions, (2) 18: 417–429, pls. 31–32.

——. 1922a. Madreporaria of the Siboga Expedition, Part 3: Eupsammidae. Siboga Expedition, Reports, Monograph 16c: 47–75, pls. 7, 8.

——. 1926 Madreporaria: Eupsammidae. No. 2, Percy Sladen Trust Expedition. Linnaean Soc. of Lond. Transactions, (2) 19: 43–53, pls. 2, 3.

Lesson, R. P. 1829. Voyage autour de Monde sur ... *La Coquille*, pendant les Années 1822, 1823, 1824, et 1825. Zoologie, 2, Part 2, Zoophytes, 151 pp., 16 pls.

———. 1834. *In:* C. Belanger, Voyage aux Indes-Orientales par le Nord de l'Europe ... pendant ... 1825–1829. Zoologie, 515–519; atlas, pls. 1, 2.

Linnaeus, C. 1758. Systema naturae, 1: 824 pp.

Loya, Y., and L. R. Slobodkin. 1971. The coral reefs of Eilat (Gulf of Eilat, Red Sea). Symp. of the Zool. Soc. of Lond., 28:117–139.

Ma, T. Y. H. 1937. On the growth rate of reef corals and its relation to sea water temperature. Mem. of the Nat. Inst. of Zool. and Bot. (Academia Sinica), Zool. Ser., 1: 226 pp., 100 pls.

———. 1959. Effect of water temperature on growth rate of reef corals. Oceanographica Sinica, special vol. 1: 116 pp., 321 pls.

McBirney, A. R., and H. Williams. 1969. Geology and petrology of the Galápagos Islands. Geol. Soc. of Am., Mem. 118.

Marenzeller, E. von. 1904. Stein-und-Hydro-Korallen. Reports of dredging operations off the west coast of Central America, etc., 33. Bull. of the Mus. of Comp. Zool., Harv. College, 43: 75–87, pls. 1, 2.

Matthai, G. 1948. Skeletal variation in two large coralla from Tahiti, one of *Pavona varians* Verrill and another of *Psammocora haimiana* Milne Edwards & Haime. Phil. Transactions of the R. Soc. of Lond., 233B: 197–199, pls. 15, 16.

Michelin, H. 1842. Déscription d'une nouvelle espèce du genre Fongie [*Fungia distorta*]. Revue Zoologique, 5: 316; Magasin de Zoologie, 5: pl. 5 (1843).

Milne Edwards, H. and J. Haime. 1848. Recherches sur les Polypiers. Premier Mémoire. Structure et développement des polypiers en général. Annales des Sciences Naturelles, (3)9: 37–89, pls. 4–6.

———. 1848a. Recherches sur les Polypiers. Deuxième Mémoire. Monographie des Turbinolides. Annales des Sciences Naturelles, (3)9: 211–344, pls. 7–10.

———. 1848b. Recherches sur les Polypiers. Troisième Mémoire. Monographie des Eupsammides. Annales des Sciences Naturelles, (3)10: 65–114, pl. 1.

———. 1849. Recherches sur les Polypiers. Quatrième Mémoire. Monographie des Astréides; Part 2. Annales des Sciences Naturelles, (3)11: 233–312.

———. 1850. Recherches sur les Polypiers. Cinquième Mémoire. Monographie des Oculinides. Annales des Sciences Naturelles, (3)13: 63–110, pls. 3, 4.

———. 1857–60. Histoire naturelle des Coralliaires. Paris. Vol. 2: 633 pp. (1857); vol. 3: 560 pp. (1860); Atlas, 31 pls. (1857).

Montanaro-Gallitelli, E. 1943. Coralli costruttori delle scogliere emerse di Massaua e Gibuti. Reale Accad. Italia: Miss. Geol. Dancalia Merid. Hararino, 4: 1–76, pls. 1–16.

Nemenzo, F. 1960. Systematic studies on Philippine shallow water scleractinians: Part 4, Suborder Dendrophylliida. Nat. and App. Sci. Bull., 18: 1–22, pls. 1–10.

———. 1971. Systematic studies on Philippine shallow-water scleractinians: VII, Additional forms. Nat. and App. Sci. Bull., 23: 141–209, 11 pls.

Neudecker, S. 1977. Transplant experiments to test the effect of fish grazing on coral distribution. Proc. of the Third. Int. Coral Reef Symp., 1: 317–324.

Orbigny, A. d'. 1850–1852. Prodrôme de paléontologie stratigraphique universelle des animaux mollusques et rayonnés. ... Paris, 3 vols.

Ortmann, A. 1888. Studien über Systematik und geographische Verbreitung der Steinkorallen. Zool. Jahrb., Abt. f. Syst., 3: 143–188, pl. 6.

Palmer, R. H. 1928. Fossil and Recent corals and coral reefs of western Mexico. Proc. of the Am. Phil. Soc., 67:21–31, pls. 1–3.

Pillai, C. S. G., and G. Scheer. 1974. On a collection of Scleractinia from the Strait of Malacca. Proc. of the Second Int. Coral Reef Symp., 2: 445–464.

Pourtalès, L. F. de. 1875. Corals at the Galapagos Islands. Am. J. of Sci., (3) 10: 282–283.

Quelch, J. J. 1886. Report on the reef corals. Reports on the Scientific Results of the Voyage of HMS *Challenger*, Zool., 16 (3): 203 pp., 12 pls.

Quoy, J. R. C. and J. P. Gaimard. 1833. Voyage de découverte de l'Astrolabe, Zoologie, 4: 390 pp.; 5 (Atlas): pls. 14–25.

Ridley, S. O. 1884. On some structures liable to variation in the subfamily Astrangiaceae (Madreporaria). Linn. Soc. Lond., Zool., 17: 395–399, pl. 16.

Robertson, R. 1970. Review of the predators and parasites of stony corals, with special reference to symbiotic prosobranch gastropods. Pac. Sci., 24:43–54.

Rosen, B. R. 1971. Provisional check list of corals collected during The Royal Society Expedition to Aldabra, Phase 6. *In* Regional Variation in Indian Ocean Coral Reefs. Sym. of the Zool. Soc. of Lond., 28: 109–114.

Rossi, L. 1961. Etudes sur le seuil Siculo-Tunisien, 6. Madréporaires. Annales de l'Institut Océanographique, 39: 32–48.

Scheer, G. 1964. Korallen von Abd-el-Kuri. Zoologische Jahrbuch, Systematische 91: 451–466, 4 pls.

Scheer, G. and C. S. G. Pillai. 1974. Report on the Scleractinia from the Nicobar Islands. Zool., 122: 75 pp., 33 pls.

Seguenza, G. 1880. Le formazione Terziarie nella provincia di Reggio (Calabria) Atti R. Accad. dei Lincei, (3) 6:446 pp., 17 pls., map.

Sherborn, C. D., and B. B. Woodward. 1906. Notes on the dates of publication of the natural history portions of some French voyages.— "Voyage autour du monde . . . sur . . . la Coquille pendant . . . 1822–25 par L. J. Duperrey, etc.—A correction. Ann. Mag. Nat. Hist., (7) 17:335–336.

Sherborn, C. D. 1940. Where is the—collection? Cambridge Univ. Press, 148 pp.

Squires, D. F. 1959. Corals and coral reefs in the Gulf of California. Bull. Am. Mus. Nat. Hist., 118: 371–431, pls. 28–34.

———. 1960. The scleractinian genera *Kionotrochus* and *Cylindrophyllia*. Records Dominion Museum, New Zealand, 3:283–288, 16 figs.

———. 1964. New stony corals (Scleractinia) from northeastern New Zealand. Records Auckland Institute Museum, 6: 1–9, 2 pls.

———. 1964a. Biological results of the Chatham Islands 1954 Expedition, Part 6: Scleractinia. Mem. New Zealand Ocean. Inst., 29: 31 pp., 4 pls.

Squires, D. F. and I. W. Keyes. 1967. The marine fauna of New Zealand: Scleractinian corals. Mem. New Zealand Ocean. Inst., 43: 46 pp., 6 pls.

Umbgrove, J. H. F. 1924. Report on Pleistocene and Pliocene corals from Ceram. Geological, Petrographical and Palaeontological Results of Explorations, . . . *In* . . . Ceram by L. Rutten and W. Hotz, ser. 2., Palaeontology 1: 22 pp., 2 pls.

———. 1939. Madreporaria from the Bay of Batavia. Zoologisch Mededeelingen, Rijksmuseum van Natuurlijke Historie, Leiden, 22: 1–64, pls. 1–18.

———. 1943. A revision of fossil corals from Celebes described by Dollfus. Tijdschr. Geol.-Mijnbouw Genoot Ned. Col. Geologie en Mijnbouw, 5: 15–16.

———. 1946. Corals from a Lower Pliocene patch reef in central Java. J. Paleon., 20: 521–542, pls. 77–82.

———. 1950. Corals from the Putjangan Beds (Lower Pleistocene) of Java. J. Paleont., 24: 637–651, pls. 81–84.

Vaughan, T. W. 1901. The stony corals of Porto Rican waters. Bull. U. S. Fish Comm. for 1900, 2: 289–320, pls. 1–38.

———. 1906. Reports on the scientific results of the expedition to the eastern tropical Pacific . . . 6. Madreporaria. Bull. Mus. Comp. Zool., Harv. College, 50(3): 61–72, pls. 1–10.

———. 1907. Recent Madreporaria of the Hawaiian Islands and Laysan. Bull. U.S. Nat. Mus., 59: 436 pp., 96 pls.

———. 1918. Some shoal-water corals from Murray Island, Cocos-Keeling Islands, and Fanning Island. Pubs. of the Carnegie Inst. of Wash., 213: 51–234, pls. 20–93.

———. 1919. Corals and the formation of coral reefs. Ann. Rep. of the Smithson. Inst. for 1917: 189–238, 38 pls.

Veron, J. E. N. and M. Pichon. 1976. Scleractinia of eastern Australia, part I. Families Thamnasteriidae, Astrocoeniidae, Pocilloporidae. Aust. Inst. Mar. Sci., Mon.1: 86 pp., 166 figs.

———. 1980. Scleractinia of eastern Australia, part III. Families Agariciidae, Siderastrei-dae, Fungiidae, Oculinidae, Mussidae, Merulinidae, Pectiniidae, Caryophyllii-dae, Dendrophylliidae. Aus. Inst. Mar. Sci., Mon.4: 453 pp., 487 figs.

Verrill, A. E. 1864. List of the polyps and corals sent by the Museum of Comparative Zoology to other institutions in exchange, with annotations. Bull. of the Mus. of Comp. Zool., Harv. Coll., 1(3): 29–60.

———. 1865. Classification of polyps: extracts condensed from a synopsis of the polypi of the North Pacific Exploring Expedition, part 1. Communications of the Essex Institute, 4(5): 145–152.

———. 1866. Synopsis of the polyps and corals of the North Pacific Exploring Expedition . . . with descriptions of some additional species from the west coast of North America, part 3, Madreporaria. Communications of the Essex Institute, 5: 17–50, pls. 1, 2.

———. 1866a. On the polyps and corals of Panama with descriptions of new species. Proc. of the Boston Soc. of Nat. Hist., 10: 323–333.

———. 1868. Synopsis of the polyps and corals of the North Pacific Exploring Expedition, part 4. Actinaria. Communications of the Essex Institute, 5: 315–330, pl. 3.

———. 1869. On some new and imperfectly known echinoderms and corals. Proc. of the Boston Soc. of Nat. Hist., 12: 381–396.

———. 1869a. Synopsis of the polyps and corals of the North Pacific Exploring Expedition. Additions and corrections. Communications of the Essex Institute, 6: 75–104.

———. 1870a (January). Contributions to zoology from the Museum of Yale College, no. 5. Descriptions of echinoderms and corals from the Gulf of California. Am. J. of Sci., 49: 93–100.

———. 1870b (December). Notes on radiata in the Museum of Yale College, no. 6. Review of the corals and polyps of the west coast of North America. Transac-tions of the Conn. Acad. of Arts & Sci., 1:500–546, pls. 9, 10.

———. 1901. Variations and nomenclature of Bermudian, West Indian, and Brazilian reef corals, with notes on various Indo-Pacific Corals. Transactions of the Conn. Acad. of Arts & Sci., 11: 63–168, 26 pls.

Wells, J. W. 1936. The madreporarian genus *Polyastra* Ehrenberg. Ann. Mag. Nat. Hist., (10)18: 549–552, pls. 9, 10.

———. 1954. Recent corals of the Marshall Islands. U. S. G. S. Prof. Pap. 260-I: 385–486, pls. 94–187.

———. 1964. Ahermatypic corals from Queensland. Univ. of Queensland Dep. of Zool. Pap., 2(6): 107–121, 3 pls.

———. 1972. Notes on Indo-Pacific scleractinian corals, part 8. Scleractinian corals from Easter Island. Pac. Sci., 26: 182–190, 14 figs.

———. 1982. Notes on Indo-Pacific scleractinian corals, part 9. New corals from the Galápagos Islands. Pac. Sci., 36:211–219, 4 figs.

Yabe, H., T. Sugiyama, and M. Eguchi. 1936. Recent reef-building corals from Japan and the south sea islands under the Japanese mandate. Tôhoku Imperial University Science Reports, Second Ser, special vol. 1: 66 pp., 59 pls.

Zibrowius, H. 1973. Revision des espèces actuelles du genre *Enallopsammia* Michelotti 1871. . . . *Beaufortia*, 21: 37–54, 23 figs.

———. 1974. Révision du genre *Javania* et considérations générales sur les Flabellidae (Scléractiniaires). Bull. Inst. Océanogr., Monaco, 71(1429): 48 pp., 5 pls.

———. 1974a. Scléractiniaires des Iles Saint Paul et Amsterdam (Sud de l'Océan Indien). Tethys, 5: 747–778, 3 pls.

———. 1980. Les Scléractiniaires de la Mediterranée et de l'Atlantique nord-central. Inst. Océanogr., Monaco, Mém. 11: 284 pp., 107 pls., 3 tables.

PLATE 1

Psammocora. Figures 1, 2.—*P. (Stephanaria) stellata* (Verrill), Onslow Island, Galápagos, 3 m, USNM 46921, x1, x16.

Figures 3, 4.—*P. (Stephanaria) brighami* (Vaughan), Culpepper Island, Galápagos, 8 m, USNM 46922, x1, x16.

Figures 5, 6.—*P. (Plesioseris) superficialis* (Gardiner), Culpepper Island, Galápagos, 8 m, USNM 46923, x0.5, x16.

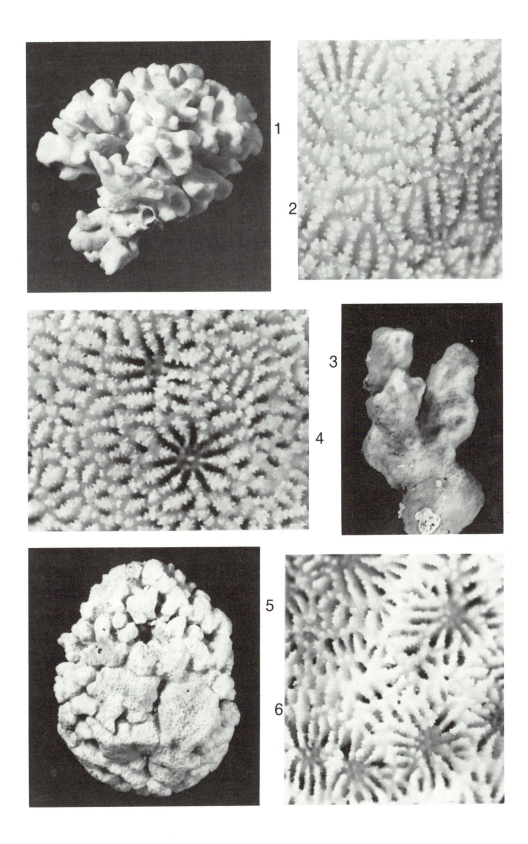

PLATE 2

Pocillopora damicornis (Linnaeus). Figure 1.—typical form, Pinta Island, Galápagos, 3 m, USNM 46924, x0.5.

Figure 2.—predator-cropped, near arch rock, Culpepper Island, Galápagos, 9 m, USNM 46925, x1.

Figure 3.—predator-cropped, patch reef in lagoon south of Punta Espinosa, Fernandina Island, Galápagos, 1 m, USNM 46926, x0.5.

Figure 4.—predator-cropped, subclavate form, patch reef in lagoon south of Punta Espinosa, Fernandina Island, Galápagos, 1 m, USNM 46927, x1.

Figure 5.—predator-cropped, extreme form, patch reef in lagoon south of Punta Espinosa, Fernandina Island, Galápagos, 1 m, USNM 46928, x1.

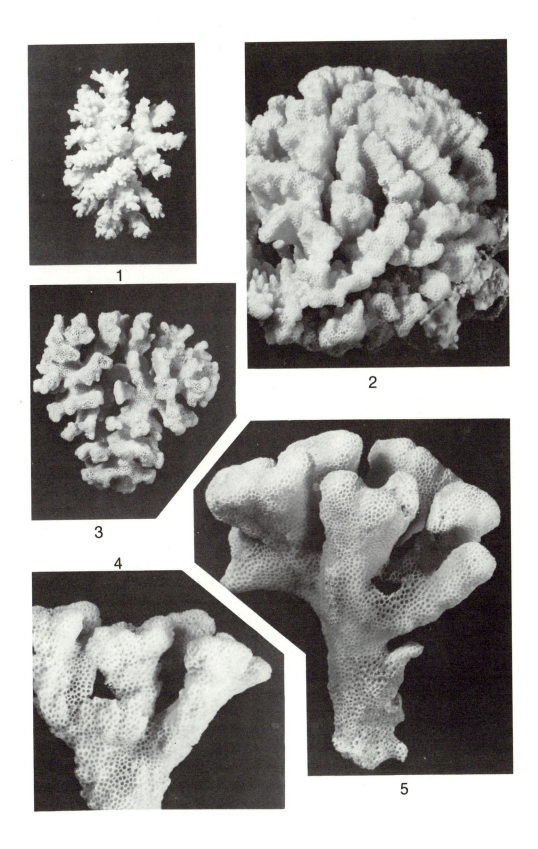

1

2

3

4

5

PLATE 3

Pocillopora. Figure 1.—*P. elegans* Dana, near arch rock, Culpepper Island, Galápagos, 9 m, USNM 46929, x0.5.

Figure 2.—*P. elegans* Dana, near arch rock, Culpepper Island, Galápagos, 8 m, USNM 46930, x0.5

Figure 3.—*P. capitata* Verrill, predator-cropped, northeast side, Wenman Island, Galápagos, 8 m, USNM 46931, x1.

Figure 4.—*P. capitata* Verrill, predator-cropped, inside "crown," Onslow Island, Galápagos, 3 m, USNM 46932, x0.5.

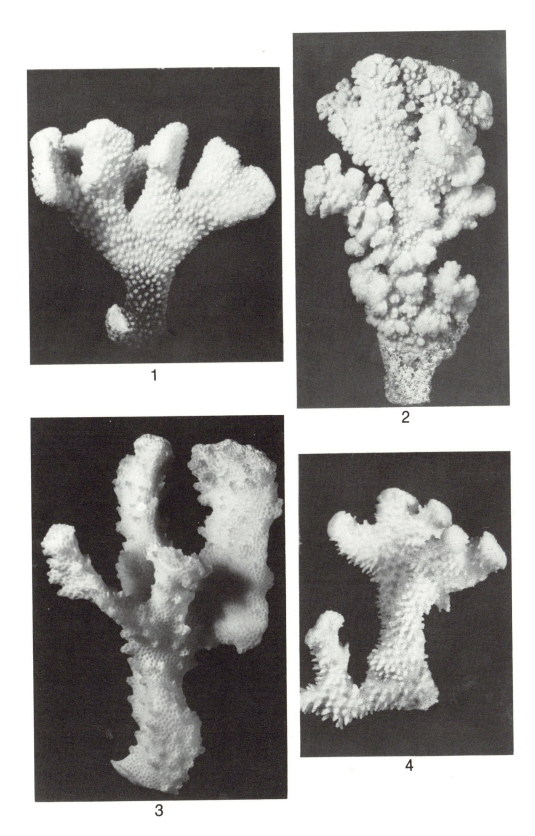

1

2

3

4

PLATE 4

Pavona varians Verrill. Figures 1, 2, 3.—northeast side, Wenman Island, Galápagos, 15 m, USNM 46933, x0.5, x4, x4.

Figures 4, 5.—Gulf of Chiriquí, Panamá (coll. P. W. Glynn), USNM 46934, x0.25, x4.

Figure 6.—Saboga Island, Pearl Islands, Panamá (coll. P. W. Glynn), USNM 46935, x4.

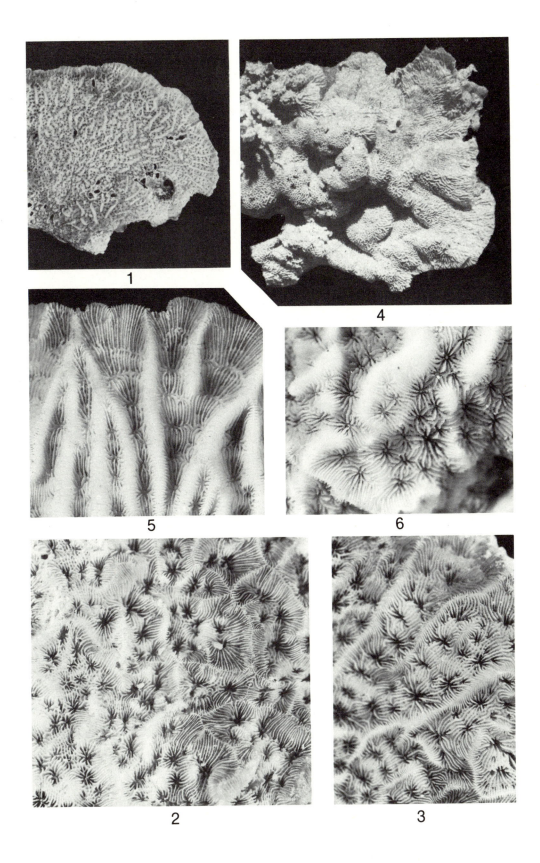

1

4

5

6

2

3

PLATE 5

Pavona clavus Dana. Figures 1, 2, 3.—holotype, Fiji Islands, USNM 221, x1, x4, x4.

Figures 4, 5.—normal clavate form, northeast side, Wenman Island, Galápagos, 15–18 m, USNM 46936, x1, x4.

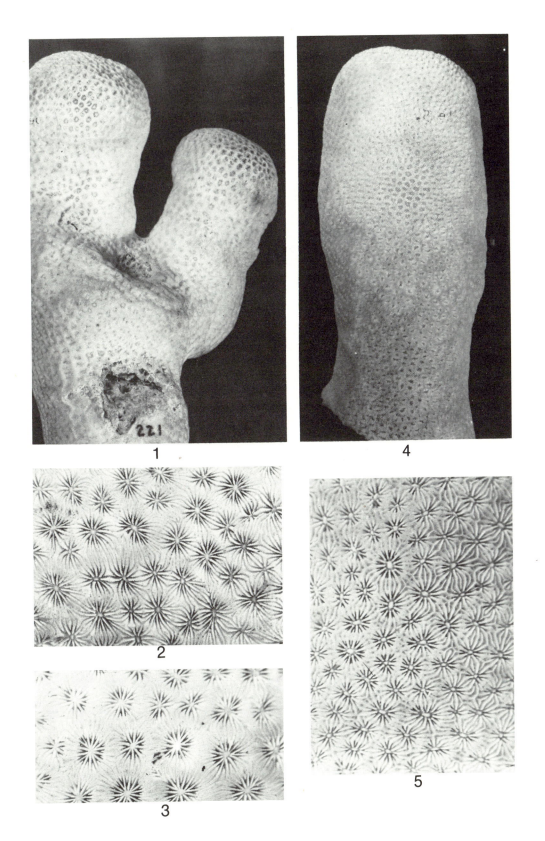

1

4

2

3

5

PLATE 6

Pavona clavus Dana. Figure 1.—laminar form, reef on west side, Champion Island, Galápagos, 10 m, USNM 46937, x4.

Figure 2.—nodular, subspherical form, Saboga Island, Pearl Islands, Panamá (coll. P. W. Glynn), USNM 46938, x4.

Figure 3.—*"Solenastrea ecuadoriana,"* worn, on beach, Stephens Bay, Chatham Island, Galápagos, USNM 46939, x4.

Figures 4, 5.—laminar form, reef on west side, Champion Island, Galápagos, 9–12 m, USNM 46940, x1, x4.

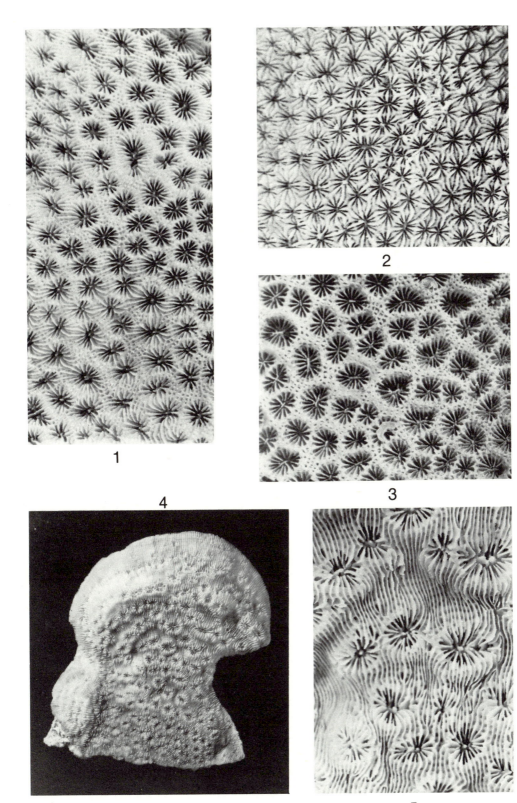

1

2

3

4

5

PLATE 7

Pavona gigantea Verrill. Figures 1, 2.—clavate form, northeast side, Wenman Island, Galápagos, 10 m, USNM 46941, x1, x4.

Figure 3.—laminar form, Darwin Bay, Tower Island, Galápagos, 12–18 m, USNM 46942, x4.

Figure 4.—laminar form, on rock wall, Onslow Island, Galápagos, 3–5 m, USNM 46943, x4.

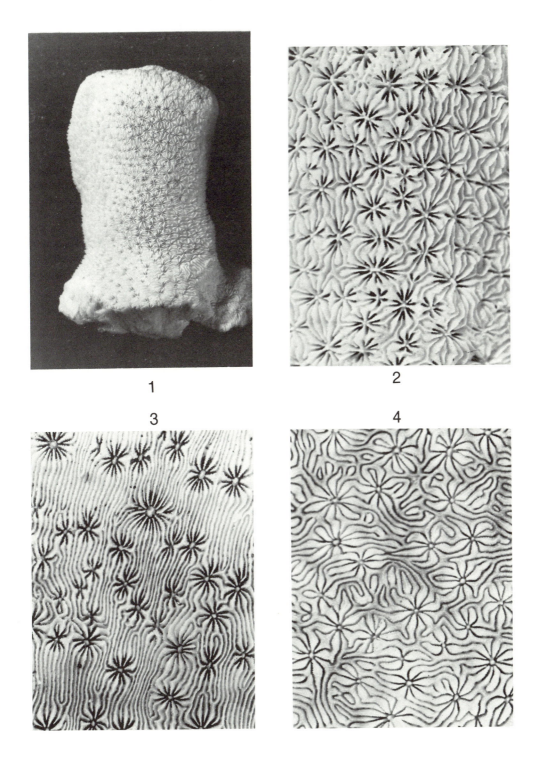

1

2

3

4

PLATE 8

Pavona gigantea Verrill. Figures 1, 2.—crateriform corallum, on wall, Darwin Bay, Tower Island, Galápagos, 12–18 m, USNM 46944, x0.5, x4.

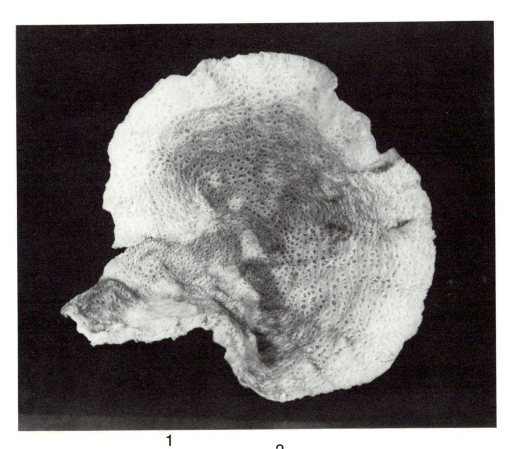

1

2

PLATE 9

Gardineroseris planulata (Dana). Figures 1, 2.—Academy Bay, Santa Cruz Island, Galápagos, 4 m, USNM 46945, x1, x4.

Figures 3, 4, 5.—Saboga Island, Pearl Islands, Panamá (coll. P. W. Glynn); Figure 4, calices on upper surface of corallum; Figure 5, calices on side of corallum, USNM 46946, x1, x4, x4.

Figure 6.—calices of typical form of *G. "ponderosa,"* Ongu Island, North Malosmadulu Atoll, Maldives (*Te Vega* Sta. 130), USNM 46947, x4.

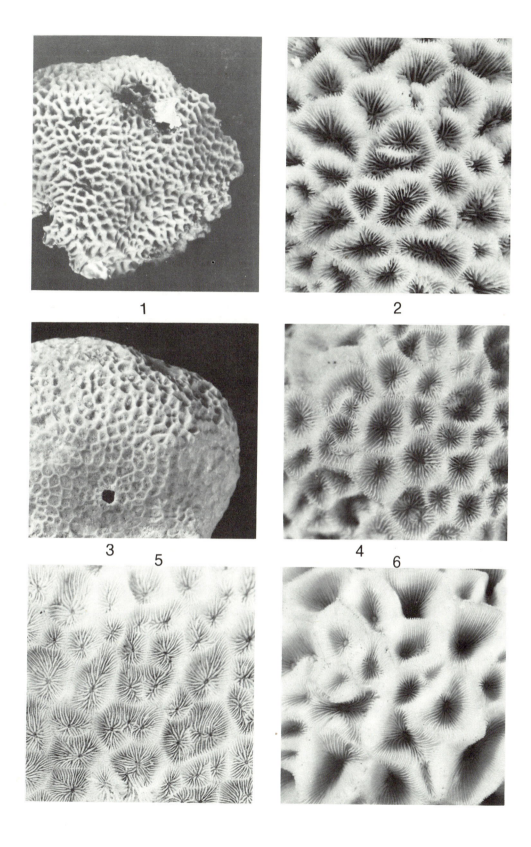

1

2

3

5

4

6

PLATE 10

Porites lobata Dana. Figure 1.—northeast side, Wenman Island, Galápagos, 8 m, USNM 46948, x16.

Figure 2.—northeast side, Onslow Island, Galápagos, 7 m, USNM 46949, x16.

Figure 3.—loose nodule, patch reef in lagoon south of Punta Espinosa, Fernandina Island, Galápagos, 1 m, USNM 46950, x16.

Figure 4.—typical form, Midway Island, USNM 46951, x16.

Figure 5.—Cocos Island (coll. J. Bakus), USNM 46952, x16.

Figure 6.—Pedro Gonzáles Island, Pearl Islands, Panamá (coll. P. W. Glynn), 5 m, USNM 46953, x16.

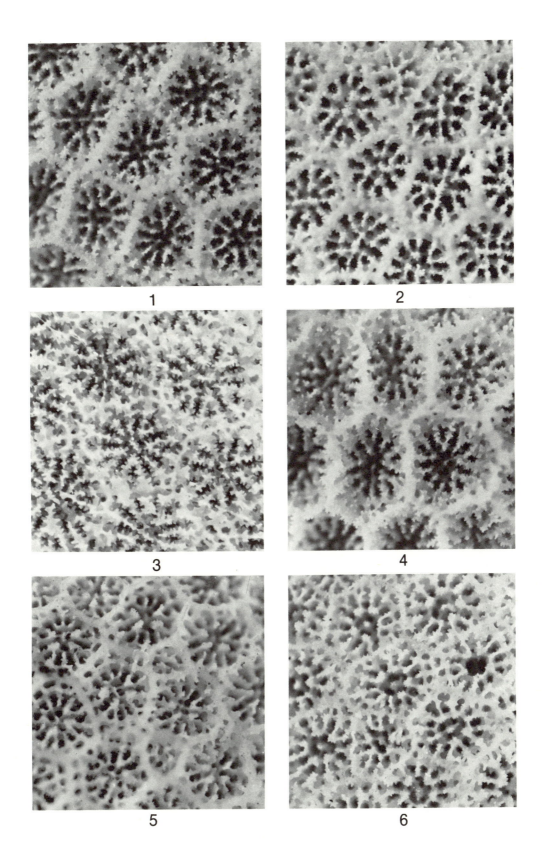

1

2

3

4

5

6

PLATE 11

Culicia and *Cycloseris*. Figure 1.—*Culicia rubeola* (Quoy & Gaimard), on wall of cave, northeast side, Wenman Island, Galápagos, 3 m, USNM 46954, x4.

Figure 2.—*C. rubeola* (Quoy & Gaimard), wall of aquarium, Nouméa, New Caledonia (R. L. A. Catala), USNM 46955, x4.

Figures 3, 5.—*Cycloseris elegans* (Verrill), *Diaseris*-form, oral and aboral aspects, east side, Onslow Island, Galápagos, 15 m, USNM 46956, x1.5.

Figures 4, 6.—*Cycloseris mexicana* Durham, *Diaseris*-form, oral and aboral aspects, east side, Onslow Island, Galápagos, 15 m, USNM 46957, x1.5.

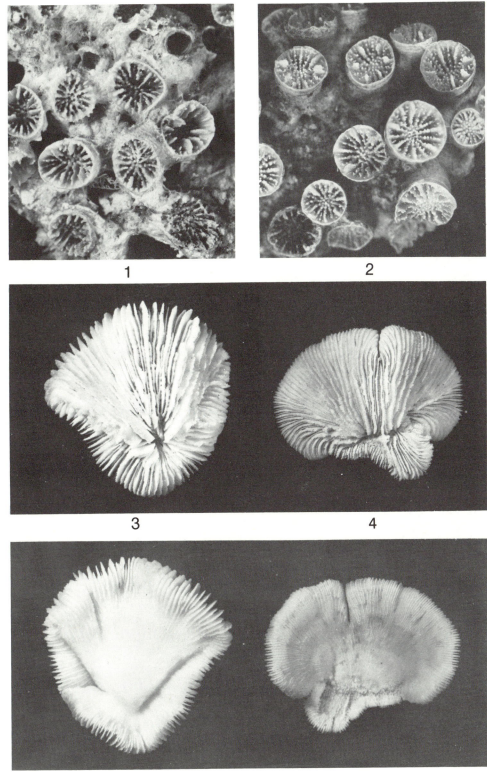

1

2

3

4

5

6

PLATE 12

Astrangia, Oulangia, and *Phyllangia.* Figure 1.—*Astrangia equatorialis* Durham & Barnard (left side of specimen), and *A. browni* Palmer (right side), Caleta Iguana, Isabela Island, Galápagos, 5 m, USNM 46958, x1.

Figures 2, 3.—calices of *A. equatorialis* and *A. browni,* x4, x4.

Figure 4.—*Oulangia bradleyi* Verrill, 3.5 miles west of Punta Albemarle, Isabela Island, Galápagos, 14 m, USNM 46959, x1.

Figure 5.—*O. bradleyi,* same locality as figure 4, CDRS (G. M. Wellington photo), x3.

Figures 6, 7.—*Phyllangia consagensis* (Durham & Barnard), Cousin's Rock, Galápagos, 20–27 m, USNM 46960, x1, x4.

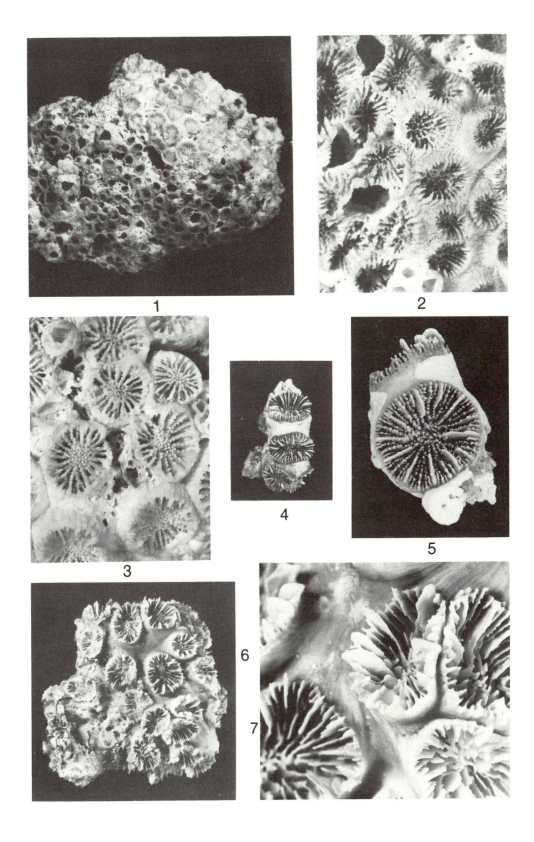

PLATE 13

Madrepora, Cyathoceras, and *Paracyathus.* Figures 1, 2.—*Madrepora galapagensis* Vaughan, cave ceiling, Tagus Cove, Isabela Island, Galápagos, 18–24 m, USNM 46961, x1, x4.

Figures 3, 4.—*Cyathoceras avis* (Durham & Barnard), calicular and lateral aspects, Galápagos, no data (coll. V. & T. Williams, 1970), USNM 46962, x4, x4.

Figures 5, 6.—*Paracyathus humilis* Verrill, lateral and calicular aspects, Darwin Bay, Tower Island, Galápagos, 23 m, USNM 46963, x1, x4.

1

2

3

4

5

6

PLATE 14

Cladocora, Polycyathus, and *Balanophyllia.* Figures 1, 2.—*Polycyathus isabela* Wells, holotype USNM 46964, 3.5 miles west of Punta Albemarle, Isabela Island, Galápagos, 14 m, x2, x4.

Figure 3.—*P. isabela* Wells, 3.5 miles west of Punta Albemarle, 15 m, x3.5 (G. M. Wellington photo).

Figures 4, 5.—*Balanophyllia galapagensis* Vaughan, dredged off Onslow Island, Galápagos, 36–45 m, USNM 46965, x2, x4.

Figures 6, 7, 8.—*Balanophyllia eguchii* Wells, north side of Marchena Island, Galápagos, 6 m, holotype USNM 46966, x1, x4, x4.

Figures 9, 10.—*Cladocora debilis* Milne Edwards & Haime, ca. 100 m, Galápagos, USNM 46967, x1, x4.

PLATE 15

Rhizopsammia. Figures 1, 2.—*R. verrilli* van der Horst, northeast side of Wenman Island, Galápagos, 15 m. Figure 1: note stolon from large corallite to offset. Figure 2: calice of offset, USNM 46933, x2, x8. Figures 3, 4.—north side of Marchena Island, Galápagos, 6 m, USNM 46968, x2, x4.

Figures 5, 6.—*R. wellingtoni* Wells, Tagus Cove, Isabela Island, Galápagos, 25 m, holotype USNM 46969, x1, x4.

Figure 7.—*R. wellingtoni* Wells, same locality as preceding, paratype USNM 46970, x4.

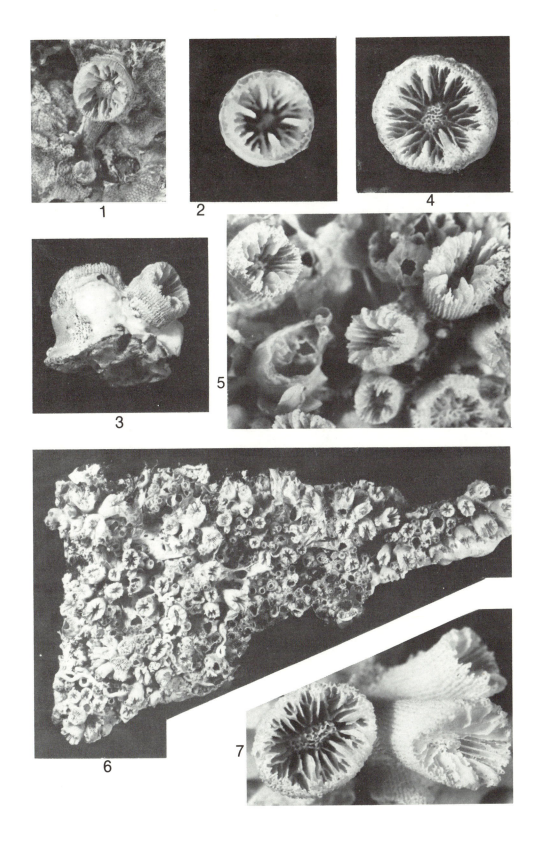

PLATE 16

Rhizopsammia and *Madracis.* Figure 1.—*R. wellingtoni* and *M pharensis,* Gardner Island, near Santa Maria (Floreana) Island, attached to rock wall, 30 m, CAS 018851, x1.

Figures 2, 3, 4.—*R. pulchra* Verrill, Pearl Islands, Panamá, extreme low water, holotype, YPM 5375, x2, x4, x4. (On a small rolled cobble with "*Oulangia bradleyi, Astrangia dentata, A. pulchella,* and a new species of *Paracyathus*" (Verrill 1870). Corallite at upper right of figures 2 and 3 is *A. pulchella.*

Figures 5, 6.—*Madracis pharensis,* same specimen as figure 1, x4, x10.

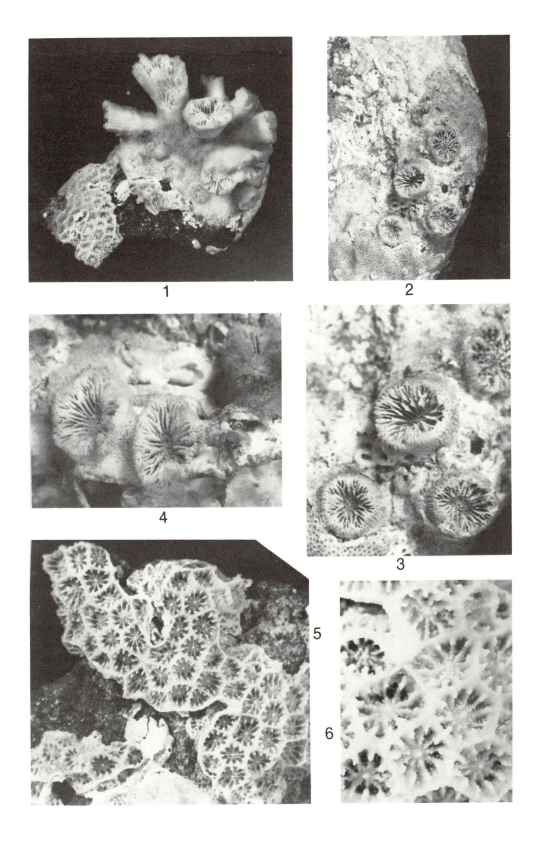

1

2

4

3

5

6

PLATE 17

Dendrophyllia gracilis Milne Edwards & Haime. Figures 1, 2.—Cousin's Rock, north of Bartolomé Island, Galápagos, 12 m (coll. D. Faulkner, 1973), USNM 46971, x1, x4.

Figures 3, 4.—Ulach Pass, Kayangel Atoll, Palau Islands (coll. D. Faulkner), USNM 46972, x1. Figure 4.—same corallum as figure 3, photographed *in situ* with polyps fully expanded, by D. Faulkner, x1.

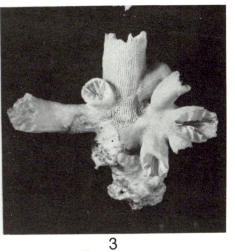

PLATE 18

Tubastraea. Figures 1, 2.—*T. coccinea* Lesson, Cousin's Rock, north of Bartolomé Island, Galápagos, 25 m, USNM 46973, x1, x4.

Figures 3, 4.—*T. floreana* Wells, west side of Floreana Island, Galápagos, shallow water, holotype USNM 46974, x1, x4.

Figures 5, 6.—*T. floreana* Wells, overhang at 5 m, Caleta Iguana, Isabela Island, Galápagos, USNM 46976, x1, x4.

PLATE 19

Tubastraea faulkneri Wells. Figures 1, 2.—Great Reef, Bailechesengel Island, Palau, 8 m, holotype USNM 47145, x1, x2.

Figure 3.—Goenoeng Api, Banda, 8 m, vertical section through corallites and coenosteum, USNM 62570, x1.

Figure 4.—Tagus Cove, Isabela Island, Galápagos, 3–5 m. Colony *in situ*, polyps retracted, x0.6 (from color photo by G. M. Wellington).

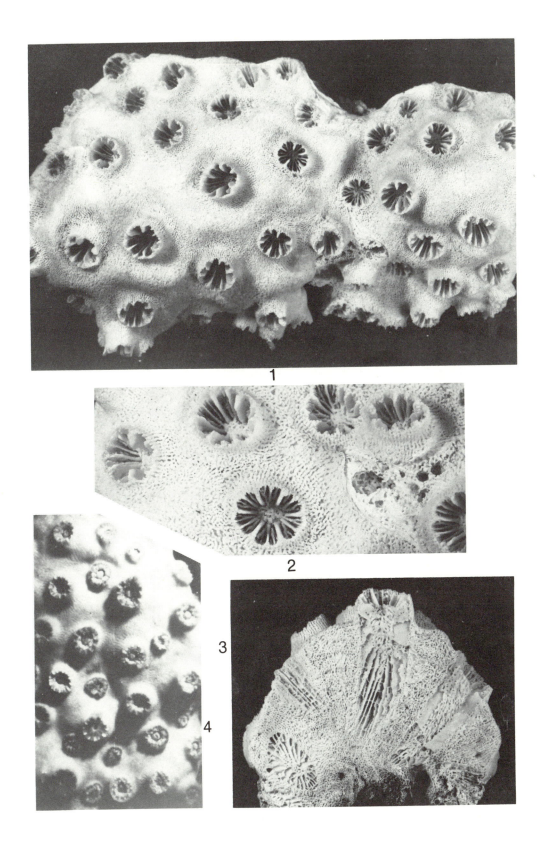

1

2

3

4

PLATE 20

Tubastraea tagusensis Wells. Figures 1, 2, 3.—Tagus Cove, Isabela Island, Galápagos, 4.5 m, holotype USNM 46977, x1, x2, x4.

Figure 4.—Tagus Cove, 4.5 m, USNM 46978, x1.

Figure 5.—Tagus Cove, 6 m, paratype USNM 46979, x0.5.

Figure 6.—same corallum as figure 5, polyps fully expanded at night, x1 (from color photo by D. Faulkner).

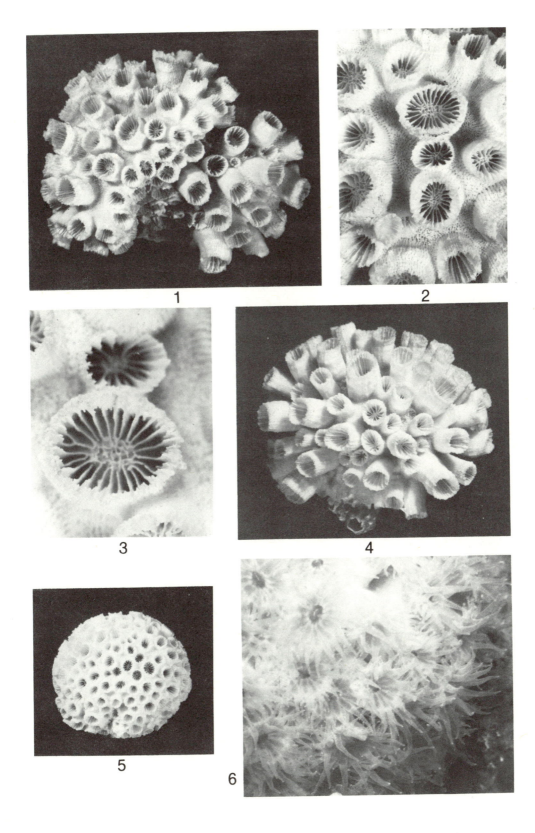

1

2

3

4

5

6

TAXONOMIC INDEX

New names are in CAPITAL letters; other names in valid use in *italic* letters. Page numbers of main references in **bold** face; pages with explanation of plates in *italics.*

LITERATURE CITED

Abbott, D. P. 1966. Factors influencing the zoogeographic affinities of the Galápagos inshore marine fauna. pp. 108–122. *In* R. I. Bowman, ed., The Galápagos, proceedings of the symposia of the Galápagos International Scientific Project. Berkeley and Los Angeles: University of California Press.

Abele, L. G., and W. K. Patton. 1976. The size of coral heads and the community biology of associated decapod crustaceans. J. Biogeogr., 3:35–47.

Adey, W. H. 1978. Coral reef morphogenesis: a multidimensional model. Science (Wash., D.C.), 202:831–837.

Adey, W. H., P. J. Adey, R. Burke, and L. Kaufman. 1977. The Holocene reef systems of eastern Martinique, French West Indies. Atoll Res. Bull., 218:1–40.

Agassiz, A. 1892. General sketch of the expedition of the "Albatross," from February to May, 1891. Bull. Mus. Comp. Zool. Harv. College, 23(1):1–89.

———. 1903. The coral reefs of the tropical Pacific. Mem. Mus. Comp. Zool. (Harv.), 28:443.

Allison, E. C., J. W. Durham, and L. W. Mintz. 1967. New southeast Pacific echinoids. Occas. Pap. Calif. Acad. Sci., 62:1–23.

Atoda, K. 1947. The larva and postlarval development of some reef-building corals. I. *Pocillopora damicornis cespitosa* (Dana). Sci. Rep. Tohoku Univ., 4th ser. Biol., 18:24–47.

———. 1951. The larva and postlarval development of the reef-building corals. IV. *Galaxea aspera* Quelch. J. Morphol., 89:17–35.

Bailey, J. H., and M. P. Harris. 1968. Spirorbinae (Polychaeta: Serpulidae) of the Galapagos Islands. J. Zool. (Lond.), 155:161–184.

Bailey, K. 1976. Potassium-argon ages from the Galapagos Islands. Science (Wash., D.C.), 192:465–467.

Bak, R. P. M. 1974. Available light and other factors influencing growth of stony corals through the year in Curaçao. Proc. Second Int. Coral Reef Symp. Brisbane, Australia, 2:229–233.

Bak, R. P. M., and M. S. Engel. 1979. Distribution, abundance and survival of juvenile hermatypic corals (Scleractinia) and the importance of life history strategies in the parent coral community. Mar. Biol. (Berl.), 54:341–352.

Bak, R. P. M., and G. van Eys. 1975. Predation of the sea urchin *Diadema antillarum* Philippi on living coral. Oecologia (Berl.), 20:111–115.

Bakus, G. J. 1969. Energetics and feeding in shallow marine waters. Int. Rev. Gen. and Exp. Zool., 4:275–369.

———. 1975. Marine zonation and ecology of Cocos Island, off Central America. Atoll Res. Bull., 179:1–9.

Ballard, R. D. 1977. Notes on a major oceanographic find. Oceanus, 20(3): 35–44.

Banner, A. H. 1968. A fresh water "kill" on the coral reefs of Hawaii. Univ. of Hawaii, Hawaii Inst. Mar. Biol. Tech. Rept. 15. 29pp.

———. 1974. Kaneohe Bay, Hawaii: urban pollution and a coral reef ecosystem. Proc. Second Int. Coral Reef Symp., Brisbane, Australia, 2:685–702.

Barham, E. G., R. W. Gowdy, and F. H. Wolfson. 1973. *Acanthaster* (Echinodermata, Asteroidea) in the Gulf of California. Fish. Bull. (Seattle), 71(4): 927–942.

LITERATURE CITED

Barlow, G. W. 1972. A paternal role for bulls of the Galapagos Islands sea lion. Evolution, 26:307–310.

Barnes, D. J. 1970. Coral skeletons: an explanation of their growth and structure. Science (Wash., D.C.), 170:1305–1308.

———. 1972. The structure and formation of growth-ridges in scleractinian coral skeletons. Proc. R. Soc. Lond. B. Biol. Sci., 182:331–350.

———. 1973. Growth of colonial scleractinians. Bull. Mar. Sci., 23:280–298.

Beebe, W. 1926. The Arcturus adventure. New York: G. P. Putnam's Sons, 439 pp.

Birkeland, C. 1971. Biological observations on Cobb Seamount. Northwest Sci., 45:193–199.

———. 1977. The importance of rate of biomass accumulation in early successional stages of benthic communities to the survival of coral recruits. Proc. Third Int. Coral Reef Symp., Miami, Florida, 1:15–21.

Birkeland, C., D. L. Meyer, J. P. Stames, and C. L. Buford. 1975. Subtidal communities of Malpelo Island. In The Biological Investigation of Malpelo Island, Colombia (J. B. Graham, ed.), Smithson. Contrib. Zool. 176:55–68.

Black, J. 1973. Galápagos, Archipielago del Ecuador. Quito, Ecuador: Imprenta Europa Cia. Ltda., 138 pp.

Bowman, R. I., ed. 1966. The Galápagos, proceedings of the symposia of the Galápagos International Scientific Project, 1964. Berkeley and Los Angeles: University of California Press, 318 pp.

Branham, J. M., S. A. Reed, J. H. Bailey, and J. Caperon. 1971. Coral-eating sea stars Acanthaster planci in Hawaii. Science (Wash., D.C.), 172:1155–1157.

Brawley, S. H., and W. H. Adey. 1977. Territorial behavior of threespot damselfish (Eupomacentrus planifrons) increases reef algal biomass and productivity. Environ. Biol. Fishes, 2(1): 45–51.

Briggs, J. C. 1955. A monograph of the clingfishes (Order Xenopterygii). Stanford Ichthyol. Bull., 6:1–224.

———1967. Relationship of the tropical shelf regions. Stud. Trop. Oceanogr. (Miami), 5:569–578.

———1974. Marine zoogeography. New York: McGraw-Hill, 475 pp.

Brock, R. E. 1979. An experimental study on the effects of grazing by parrotfishes and role of refuges in benthic community structure. Mar. Biol. (Berl.), 51:381–388.

Brousse, R., J. P. Chevalier, M. Denizot, and B. Salvat. 1978. Étude géomorphologique des Iles Marquises, pp. 9–74. In Les Iles Marquises, Géomorphologie, Climatologie, Faune et Flore, Cah. Pac., No. 21, Paris.

Brower, K., ed. 1968. Galápagos: the flow of wildness. Prospect. San Francisco: Sierra Club, 2:187.

Brown, G. W., and A. M. Mood. 1951. On median tests for linear hypotheses. Proceedings of the Second Berkeley Symposium on Mathematical Statistics and Probability. J. Neyman, ed., pp. 159–166. Berkeley and Los Angeles: University of California Press.

Brusca, R. C. 1980. A handbook to the common intertidal invertebrates of the Gulf of California. 2d (revised) ed. Tucson: University of Arizona Press, 513 pp.

———In press. Shallow-water ecology in the Gulf of California. In Schwartzlose, R., and A. Ayala-Castanares, eds., The Gulf of California: Origin, Evolution, Waters, Marine Life and Natural Resources. Univ. Auto. Nac. Mex.

Brusca, R. C., and D. A. Thomson. 1977. Pulmo Reef: The only "coral reef" in the Gulf of California. Ciencias Marinas, 1(3): 37–53.

Brusca, R. C., and B. R. Wallerstein. 1979. Zoogeographic patterns of idoteid isopods in the northeast Pacific, with a review of shallow water zoogeography of the area. Bull. Biol. Soc., Wash., 3: 67–105.

Buddemeier, R. W., and R. A. Kinzie III. 1975. The chronometric reliability of contemporary corals. *In* Growth rhythms and the history of the earth's rotation, G. D. Rosenberg and S. K. Runcorn, eds. London: John Wiley & Sons, pp. 135–147.
———1976. Coral growth. Oceanogr. Mar. Biol. Ann. Rev., 14: 183–225.
Buddemeier, R. W., J. E. Maragos, and D. W. Knutson. 1974. Radiographic studies of reef coral exoskeletons: rates and patterns of coral growth. J. Exp. Mar. Biol. Ecol., 14: 179–200.

Carlquist, S. 1965. Island life. Garden City, New York: The Natural History Press, 461 pp.
———1981. Chance dispersal. Am. Scientist, 69: 509–516.
Caso, M. E. 1962. Estudios sobre Astéridos de México: Observaciones sobre especies pacíficas del género *Acanthaster* y descripción de una subespecie nueva, *Acanthaster ellisii pseudoplanci*. An. Inst. Biol., México, 32(½): 313–331.
Castro, P. In press. Notes on symbiotic decapod crustaceans from Gorgona Island, Colombia, with a preliminary revision of the eastern Pacific species of *Trapezia* (Brachyura, Xanthidae), symbionts of scleractinian corals. An. Inst. Inv. Mar.—Punta Betín, 12.
Cavanaugh, C. M., S. L. Gardiner, M. L. Jones, H. W. Jannasch, and J. B. Waterburg. 1981. Prokaryotic cells in the hydrothermal vent tube worm *Riftia pachyptila* Jones: possible chemoautotrophic symbionts. Science (Wash., D.C.), 213:340–342.
Chave, K. E., S. V. Smith, and K. J. Roy. 1972. Carbonate production by coral reefs. Mar. Geol., 12:123–140.
Chesher, R. H. 1972. The status of knowledge of Panamanian echinoids, 1971, with comments on other echinoderms. *In* M. L. Jones, ed., The Panamic Biota: some observations prior to a sea level canal. Bull. Biol. Soc. Wash., 2:139–158.
Chevalier, J.-P. 1971. Les scléractiniaires de la Mélanésie Française. Ier Partie. Expedition Française sur les récifs de la Nouvelle-Calédonie, vol. 5, 307 pp., 38 pls., 182 figs.
———. 1973. Geomorphology and geology of coral reefs in French Polynesia, pp. 113–141, *In* O. A. Jones and R. Endean, eds., Biology and Geology of Coral Reefs, 1, Geology 1. New York and London: Academic Press.
———. 1978. Les coraux des Iles Marquises, pp. 243–283. *In* Les Iles Marquises, Géomorphologie, Climatologie, Faune et Flore, Cah. Pac., No. 21, Paris.
Child, C. A., and J. W. Hedgpeth. 1971. Pycnogonida of the Galápagos Islands. J. Nat. Hist., 5:609–634.
Chubb, L. J. 1933. Geology of Galapagos, Cocos, and Easter Islands. Bull. Bernice P. Bishop Mus., 110:1–44.
Clark, H. L. 1925. A catalogue of the recent sea urchins (Echinoidea) in the collection of the British Museum (Natural History). London: Oxford University Press, 263 pp., 12 pls.
Clarke, T. A. 1970. Territorial behavior and population dynamics of a pomacentrid fish, the garibaldi, *Hypsypops rubicunda*. Ecol. Monogr., 40:189–212.
Clausen, C. 1971. Effects of temperature on the rate of ^{45}Calcium uptake by *Pocillopora damicornis*. *In* H. M. Lenhoff, L. Muscatine, and L. V. Davis, eds., Experimental Coelenterate Biology. Honolulu: University of Hawaii Press, pp. 246–259.
Clausen, C. D., and A. A. Roth. 1975. Effects of temperature and temperature adaptations on calcification rate in the hermatypic coral *Pocillopora damicornis*. Mar. Biol. (Berl.), 33:93–100.

Clifton, H. E., and R. E. Hunter. 1972. The sand tilefish, *Malacanthus plumieri*, and the distribution of coarse debris near West Indian coral reefs. *In* B. B. Collette and S. A. Earle, eds., Results of the Tektite program: ecology of coral reef fishes. Bull. Los Ang. Cty. Mus. Nat. Hist. Sci., 14:87–92.

Connell, J. H. 1973. Population ecology of reef-building corals. *In* O. A. Jones and R. Endean, eds. Biology and geology of coral reefs. Biology 1. New York: Academic Press, 2:205–245.

———. 1978. Diversity in tropical rain forests and coral reefs. Science (Wash., D.C.), 199:1302–1310.

Corliss, J. B., J. Dymond, L. I. Gordon, J. M. Edmond, R. F. von Herzen, R. D. Ballard, K. Green, D. Williams, A. Bainbridge, K. Crane, and T. H. van Andel. 1979. Submarine thermal springs on the Galápagos Rift. Science (Wash., D.C.), 203:1073–1083.

Cox, A., and G. B. Dalrymple. 1966. Palaeomagnetism and potassium-argon ages of some volcanic rocks from the Galapagos Islands. Nature (Lond.), 209:776–777.

Crisp, D. J. 1974. Interspecies and intraspecies chemoreception by marine invertebrates, pp. 105–141. *In* P. T. Grant and A. M. Mackie, eds., Chemoreception in marine organisms. London and New York: Academic Press.

Cromwell, T., and E. B. Bennett. 1959. Surface drift charts for the eastern tropical Pacific Ocean. Bull. Inter-Am. Trop. Tuna Comm., 3(5): 217–237.

Crossland, C. 1927. Marine ecology and coral formations in the Panama region, the Galapagos and Marquesas Islands, and the Atoll of Napuka. The expedition to the South Pacific of the S. Y. *St. George.* Trans. Roy. Soc. Edinburgh, 55(2): 531–554.

Daly, R. A. 1934. The changing world of the Ice Age. New Haven, Connecticut: Yale University Press. 271 pp.

Dana, J. D. 1843. On the temperature limiting the distribution of corals. Am. J. Sci. & Arts, 45:130–131.

———. 1853. On the geographical distribution of Crustacea. *In* United States Exploring Expedition during the years 1838–1842, under the command of Charles Wilkes, U. S. N. Crustacea, 14(2):696–805.

———. 1890. Corals and coral islands. 3d ed., New York: Dodd, Mead, & Co., 440 pp.

Dana, T. F. 1970. *Acanthaster:* a rarity in the past? Science (Wash, D.C.), 169:894 only.

———. 1971. On the reef corals of the world's most northern atoll (Kure: Hawaiian Archipelago). Pac. Sci., 25:80–87.

———. 1975. Development of contemporary eastern Pacific coral reefs. Mar. Biol. (Berl.), 33:355–374.

———. 1979. Species-numbers relationships in an assemblage of reef-building corals: McKean Island, Phoenix Islands. Atoll Res. Bull., 228:1–27.

Dana, T., and A. Wolfson. 1970. Eastern Pacific crown-of-thorns starfish populations in the lower Gulf of California. Trans. San Diego Soc. Nat. Hist., 16(4): 83–90.

Daniel, W. W. 1978. Applied nonparametric statistics. Boston: Houghton Mifflin Co., 510 pp.

Dart, J. K. G. 1972. Echinoids, algal lawn and coral recolonization. Nature (Lond.), 239:50–51.

Darwin, C. R. 1839. Journal of researches into the geology and natural history of the various countries visited by H.M.S. *Beagle.* New York and London: Hafner Publishing Co., (facsimile reprint of 1st ed., 1952), 615 pp.

———. 1842. The structure and distribution of coral reefs. London: Smith, Elder & Co., 214 pp.

Davis, W. M. 1928. The coral reef problem. Am. Geogr. Soc., Spec. Publ., 9:1–596.

Dawson, E. Y. 1952. Circulation within Bahía Vizcaino, Baja California, and its effects on marine vegetation. Am. J. Bot., 39(7): 425–432.

———. 1960. A review of the ecology, distribution, and affinities of the benthic flora. Syst. Zool., 9:93–100.

Dayton, P. K. 1971. Competition, disturbance and community organization: the provision and subsequent utilization of space in a rocky intertidal community. Ecol. Monogr., 41:351–389.

Dayton, P. K., and R. R. Hessler. 1972. Role of biological disturbance in maintaining diversity in the deep sea. Deep-Sea Res., 19:199–208.

Delaney, J. R., W. E. Colony, T. M. Gerlach, and B. E. Nordlie. 1973. Geology of the Volcan Chico area on Sierra Negra Volcano, Galapagos Islands. Bull. Geol. Soc. Am., 84:2455–2470.

Devaney, D. M., and L. G. Eldredge. 1977. Reef and shore fauna of Hawaii, sec. I: Protozoa through Ctenophora. Honolulu: Bishop Museum Press, 278 pp.

Dickinson, W. R. 1973. Widths of modern arc-trench gaps proportional to past duration of igneous activity in associated magmatic arcs. J. Geophys. Res., 78:3395–3417.

Dingle, H., R. C. Highsmith, K. E. Evans, and R. L. Caldwell. 1973. Interspecific aggressive behavior in tropical reef stomatopods and its possible ecological significance. Oecologia, 13:55–64.

Doberitz, R. 1967. Zum Küstenklima von Peru. Teil I, Die Klimabeobachtungen der Jahre 1925 bis 1953 und die Wassertemperaturreihe der Jahre 1925 bis 1963 von Puerto Chicama. No. 59 Germany (Federal Republic) Seewetteraimt. Hamburg. Einzelveroeffen-Tlichungen, pp. 9–44.

Dodge, R. E., and J. Thomson. 1974. The natural radiochemical and growth records in contemporary hermatypic corals from the Atlantic and Caribbean. Earth Planet. Sci. Lett., 23:313–322.

Dollar, S. J. 1975. Zonation of reef corals off the Kona coast of Hawaii. M.S. thesis, University of Hawaii, Honolulu.

———. 1982a. Storm stress and coral community structure in Hawaii. Proc. Fourth Int. Coral Reef Symp., Manila, Philippines (1981), abstr.

———. 1982b. Wave stress and coral community structure in Hawaii. Coral Reefs, 1(2):71–81.

Donn, W. L., W. R. Farrand, and M. Ewing. 1962. Pleistocene ice volumes and sea-level lowering. J. Geol., 70:206–214.

Duerden, J. E. 1902. West Indian madreporarian polyps. N. Acad. Sci. (Wash.), Me. 8(7): 403–648.

Durham, J. W. 1947. Corals from the Gulf of California and the north Pacific coast of America. Mem. Geol. Soc. Am., 20:1–68.

———. 1962. Corals from the Galapagos and Cocos Islands. Proc. Calif. Acad. Sci., 4th ser., 32(2): 41–56.

———. 1966. Coelenterates, especially stony corals, from the Galápagos and Cocos Islands, pp. 123–135. In R. I. Bowman, ed., The Galápagos, proceedings of the symposia of the Galápagos International Scientific Project. Berkeley and Los Angeles: University of California Press.

———. 1979. A new fossil Pocillopora (coral) from Guadalupe Island, Mexico, pp. 63–70. In D. M. Power, ed., The California Islands: Proceedings of a Multidisciplinary Symposium. Santa Barbara, Calif., Santa Barbara Mus. Nat. Hist.

Durham, J. W., and E. C. Allison. 1960. The geologic history of Baja California and its marine faunas. Syst. Zool., 9:47–91.

Durham, J. W., A. R. V. Arellano, and J. R. Peck, Jr. 1955. Evidence for no Cenozoic Isthmus of Tehuantepec seaways. Geol. Soc. Am. Bull., 66:977–992.

Earle, S. A. 1972. The influence of herbivores on the marine plants of Great Lameshur Bay, with an annotated list of plants, pp. 17–44. *In* B. B. Collette and S. A. Earle, eds., Results of the Tektite program: ecology of coral reef fishes. Nat. Hist. Mus., Los Ang. Cty. Sci. Bull., 14.

Easton, W. H. 1969. Radiocarbon profile of Hanauma Reef, Oahu. abstr. Geol. Soc. Am. Spec. Pap., 121:86.

Easton, W. H., and E. A. Olson. 1976. Radiocarbon profile of Hanauma Reef, Oahu, Hawaii. Geol. Soc. Am. Bull., 87:711–719.

Ebersole, J. P. 1977. The adaptive significance of interspecific territoriality in the reef fish *Eupomacentrus leucostictus.* Ecology, 58(4):914–920.

Edmondson, C. H. 1928. The ecology of an Hawaiian coral reef. Bull. Bernice P. Bishop Mus., 45:1–64.

———. 1933. Reef and shore fauna of Hawaii. Spec. Pub. Bernice P. Bishop Mus., 22:1–295.

———. 1946. Behavior of coral planulae under altered saline and thermal conditions. Occas. Pap. Bernice P. Bishop Mus., 18:283–304.

Ekman, S. 1953. Zoogeography of the sea. London: Sidgwick & Jackson, 417 pp.

Elmhirst, R. 1922. Habits of *Echinus esculentus.* Nature (Lond.), 110:667 only.

Emerson, W. K. 1967. Indo-Pacific faunal elements in the tropical eastern Pacific, with special reference to the mollusks. Venus, 25(3 & 4): 85–93.

———. 1978. Mollusks with Indo-Pacific faunal affinities in the eastern Pacific Ocean. Nautilus, 92(2): 91–96.

Emiliani, C. 1971. The amplitude of Pleistocene climatic cycles at low latitudes and the isotopic composition of glacial ice, pp. 183–197. *In* K. K. Turekian, ed., The Late Cenozoic glacial ages. New Haven, Connecticut: Yale University Press, 618 pp.

Emiliani, C., J. H. Hudson, E. A. Shinn, and R. Y. George. 1978. Oxygen and carbon isotopic growth record in a reef coral from the Florida Keys and a deep-sea coral from Blake Plateau. Science (Wash., D.C.), 202:627–629.

Endean, R. 1973. Population explosions of *Acanthaster planci* and associated destruction of hermatypic corals in the Indo-West Pacific region, pp. 389–438. *In* O. A. Jones & R. Endean, eds. Biology and Geology of Coral Reefs, vol. 2, Biology 1. New York: Academic Press.

———. 1976. Destruction and recovery of coral reef communities, pp. 215–254. *In* O. A. Jones & R. Endean, eds., Biology and Geology of Coral Reefs, vol. 3, Biology 2. New York: Academic Press.

Enfield, D. B. 1975. Oceanography of the region north of the Equatorial Front: physical aspects. Topic No. 9, Workshop on The "El Niño" phenomenon. (IOC) Guayaquil, Ecuador, Dec. 9–12, 1974, pp. 35–55.

Enright, J. T., W. A. Newman, R. R. Hessler, and J. A. McGowan. 1981. Deep-ocean hydrothermal vent communities. Nature (Lond.), 289:219–221.

Erez, J. 1978. Vital effect on stable-isotope composition seen in foraminifera and coral skeletons. Nature (Lond.), 273:199–202.

Fairbanks, R. G., and R. E. Dodge. 1979. Annual periodicity of the $^{18}O/^{16}O$ and $^{13}C/^{12}C$ ratios in the coral *Montastrea annularis.* Geochim. Cosmochim. Acta, 43:1009–1020.

Fairbridge, R. W. 1973. Glaciation and plate migration. *In* D. H. Tarling and S. K. Runcorn, eds., Implications of continental drift to the earth sciences, vol. 1. New York: Academic Press.

Faure, G. 1977. Principles of isotope geology. New York: John Wiley & Sons, 464 pp.

Felbeck, H. 1981. Chemoautotrophic potential of the hydrothermal vent tube worm, *Riftia pachyptila* Jones (Vestimentifera). Science (Wash., D.C.), 213:336–338.

Fishelson, L. 1973. Ecological and biological phenomena influenc
composition and the reef tables at Eilat (Gulf of Aqaba, Red
(Berl.), 19:183–196.

Fisher, R. L., ed. 1958. Preliminary report on Expedition Downwir
California, Scripps Institution of Oceanography, IGY cruise
Pacific. IGY General Rept., ser. 2, 58 pp. N. A. S., Wash., D. C.

Forsbergh, E. D. 1969. On the climatology, oceanography and fisherie
Bight. Inter-Am. Trop. Tuna Comm. Bull., 14:49–385.

Foster, M. S. 1972. The algal turf community in the nest of the ocean
pops rubicunda. Proc. Seventh Int. Seaweed Symp., sec. 1. Sapp
gust, 1971.

Fraser, C. M. 1943. General account of the scientific work of the
eastern Pacific, 1931–41. Part II. Geological and biological ass
Hancock Found. Publ., University Southern California, 1:49–258

Fricke, H. W. 1971. Fische als Feinde tropischer Seeigel. Mar. Biol. (Ber

Frost, S. H. 1977. Miocene to Holocene evolution of Caribbean provin
corals. *In* D. L. Taylor ed., Proc. Third Int. Coral Reef Symp.,
Geology, 2:353–359.

Frost, S. H., and R. L. Langenheim, Jr., 1974. Cenozoic reef biofacies,
foraminifera and scleractinian corals from Chiapas, Mexico. D
Northern Illinois University Press, 388 pp.

Frydl, P. M. 1977. The geological effect of grazing by parrotfish (Scarid
dos coral reef. M. S. thesis, 136pp., McGill University, Montréal,

Garth, J. S. 1946a. Distribution studies of Galapagos Brachyura. Allan F
Exped., 5(11):603–638.

———. 1946b. Littoral brachyuran fauna of the Galapagos Archipelago.
Pacific Exped., 5(11):341–601.

———. 1960. Distribution and affinities of the brachyuran Crustacea. I
the biogeography of Baja California and adjacent seas, 2. Marin
Zool., 9:105–123.

———. 1965. The brachyuran decapod crustaceans of Clipperton Islan
Acad. Sci., 23:1–46.

———. 1974. On the occurrence in the eastern tropical Pacific of Ind
decapod crustaceans commensal with reef-building corals. Proc. Se
al Reef Symp., Brisbane, Australia, 1:397–404.

Garwood, N. C., D. P. Janos, and N. Brokaw. 1979. Earthquake-caused
major disturbance to tropical forests. Science (Wash., D.C.), 205:997

Geister, J. 1977. Occurrence of *Pocillopora* in late Pleistocene Caribbean cc
378–388. *In* Second Symposium international sur les coraux et réc
fossiles. Paris, Sept. 1975. B.R.G.M. (Paris) Mem. 89.

Gerrodette, T. 1981. Dispersal of the solitary coral *Balanophyllia elegans*
planular larvae. Ecology, 62:611–619.

Gierloff-Emden, H. G. 1976. La Costa de El Salvador, Monografia Morfólog
gráfica (1st Spanish ed.). Dirección de Publicacions, Ministerio de
San Salvador, 286 pp.

Glynn, P. W. 1968. Mass mortalities of echinoids and other reef flat organ
dent with midday, low water exposures in Puerto Rico. Mar. Biol. (E
243.

———. 1972. Observations on the ecology of the Caribbean and Pacific coa
ma. *In* M. L. Jones, ed. The Panamic Biota: Some observations prior t
canal. Bull. Biol. Soc. Wash., 2:13–30.

————. 1973. *Acanthaster:* effect on coral reef growth in Panama. Science (Wash., D.C.), 180:504–506.

————. 1974*a*. The impact of *Acanthaster* on corals and coral reefs in the eastern Pacific. Environ. Conserv., 1(4): 295–304.

————. 1974*b*. Rolling stones among the Scleractinia: mobile coralliths in the Gulf of Panamá. Proc. Second Int. Coral Reef Symp., Brisbane, Australia, 2:183–198.

————. 1976. Some physical and biological determinants of coral community structure in the eastern Pacific. Ecol. Monogr., 46(4): 431–456.

————. 1977. Coral growth in upwelling and nonupwelling areas off the Pacific coast of Panama. J. Mar. Res., 35:567–585.

————. 1980. Defense by symbiotic crustacea of host corals elicited by chemical cues from predator. Oecologia, 47:287–290.

————. 1982*a*. Coral communities and their modifications relative to past and prospective Central American seaways. Adv. Mar. Biol., 19:91–132.

————. 1982*b*. *Acanthaster* population regulation by a shrimp and a worm. Proc. Fourth Int. Coral Reef Symp., Manila, Philippines.

————. In press. Crustacean symbionts and the defense of corals: coevolution on the reef? *In* M. H. Nitecki, ed., Fifth Annual Spring Systematics Symposium on Coevolution, Field Mus. of Nat. Hist. Chicago and London: The University of Chicago Press.

Glynn, P. W., and I. G. Macintyre. 1977. Growth rate and age of coral reefs on the Pacific coast of Panama. Proc. Third Int. Coral Reef Symp., Miami, Florida, 2:251–259.

Glynn, P. W., and R. H. Stewart. 1973. Distribution of coral reefs in the Pearl Islands (Gulf of Panamá) in relation to thermal conditions. Limnol. Oceanogr., 18:367–379.

Glynn, P. W., E. M. Druffel, and R. B. Dunbar. In Press. A dead Central American coral reef tract: possible link with the Little Ice Age. J. Mar. Res.

Glynn, P. W., H. von Prahl, and F. Guhl. 1980. Coral reefs of Gorgona Island, Colombia with special reference to corallivores and their influence on community structure and reef development. An. Inst. Inv. Mar., Punta Betín 12.

Glynn, P. W., R. H. Stewart, and J. E. McCosker. 1972. Pacific coral reefs of Panamá: structure, distribution and predators. Geol. Rundschau, 61(2): 483–519.

Glynn, P. W., G. M. Wellington, and C. Birkeland. 1979. Coral reef growth in the Galápagos: limitation by sea urchins. Science (Wash., D.C.), 203(4375): 47–49.

Glynn, P. W., F. A. Oramas, C. A. Montaner, and J. B. Achurra. 1978. Speculations on the potential effects of molluscan corallivore introductions across the Isthmus of Panama. Assoc. Is. Mar. Lab., 14th Meeting, Santo Domingo. abstr.

Gore, R. H., and L. R. Abele. 1976. Shallow water porcelain crabs from the Pacific coast of Panama and adjacent Caribbean waters (Crustacea: Anomura: Porcellanidae). Smithson. Contrib. Zool., 237:1–30.

Goreau, T. F. 1961. Problems of growth and calcium deposition in reef corals. Endeavour, 20:32–39.

————. 1969. Post Pleistocene urban renewal in coral reefs. Micronesica, 5:323–326.

Goreau, T. F., and W. D. Hartman. 1963. Boring sponges as controlling factors in the formation and maintenance of coral reefs. *In* Mechanisms of Hard Tissue Destruction, Am. Assoc. Adv. Sci. Publ., 75:25–54.

Goreau, T. F., and N. I. Goreau. 1959. The physiology of skeleton formation in corals, 2. Calcium deposition by hermatypic corals under various conditions in the reef. Biol. Bull. (Woods Hole), 117:239–250.

————. 1960. The physiology of skeleton formation in corals, 3. Calcification rate as a function of colony weight and total nitrogen content in the reef coral *Manicina areolata* (Linn.). Biol. Bull. (Woods Hole), 118:419–429.

————. 1973. Coral Reef Project—Papers in Memory of Dr. Thomas F. Goreau, 17. The ecology of Jamaican coral reefs, 2. Geomorphology, zonation, and sedimentary phases. Bull. Mar. Sci., 23(2): 399–464.

Goreau. T. F., and C. M. Yonge. 1968. Coral community on muddy sand. Nature (Lond.), 217: 421–423.

Goreau, T. F., N. I. Goreau, and T. J. Goreau. 1979. Corals and coral reefs. Sci. Amer., 241(2): 124–136.

Goreau, T. F., J. C. Lang, E. A. Graham, and P. D. Goreau. 1972. Structure and ecology of the Saipan reefs in relation to predation by *Acanthaster planci* (Linnaeus). Bull. Mar. Sci., 22:113–152.

Gravier, C. 1910. Sur la lutte pour l'existence chez les madréporaires des récifs coralliens. Comptes rendus Académie des Sciences (Paris), 151:955–956.

Gray, J. S. 1974. Animal-sediment relationships. Oceanogr. Mar. Biol. Ann. Rev., 12:223–261.

Greene, H. G., G. B. Dalrymple, and D. A. Clague. 1978. Evidence for northward movement of the Emperor Seamounts. Geology, 6(1): 70–74.

Greenfield, D. W., D. Hensley, J. W. Wiley, and S. T. Ross. 1970. The Isla Jaltemba coral formation and its zoogeographical significance. Copeia, 1:180–181.

Grigg, R. W. 1981. *Acropora* in Hawaii. Part 2. Zoogeography. Pac. Sci., 35(1): 15–24.

————. 1982a. Darwin Point: a threshold for atoll formation. Coral Reefs, 1:29–34.

————. 1982b. Coral reef development at high latitudes in Hawaii. Proc. Fourth Int. Coral Reef Symp., Manila, Philippines.

————. 1983. Community structure, succession and development of coral reefs in Hawaii. Mar. Ecol. Prog. Ser., 11:1–14.

Grigg, R. W., and J. E. Maragos. 1974. Recolonization of hermatypic corals on submerged lava flows in Hawaii. Ecology, 55(2): 387–395.

Grigg, R. W., J. W. Wells, and C. Wallace. 1981. *Acropora* in Hawaii. Part I. History of the scientific record, systematics, and ecology. Pac. Sci., 35:1–13.

Grünbaum, H., G. Bergman, D. P. Abbott, and J. C. Ogden. 1978. Intraspecific agonistic behavior in the rock-boring sea urchin *Echinometra lucunter* (L.) (Echinodermata: Echinoidea). Bull. Mar. Sci., 28:181–188.

Guppy, H. B. 1889. The Cocos-Keeling Islands. Scott. Geogr. Mag., 5:181–197.

Hamilton, E. L. 1956. Sunken islands of the mid-Pacific mountains. Geol. Soc. Am. Mem., 64:1–97.

Hanna, G. D. 1926. Expedition to the Revillagigedo Islands, Mexico, in 1925. Part I. General account. Proc. Calif. Acad. Sci., ser. 4, 15:1–113.

Harrigan, J. F. 1972a. The planula larva of *Pocillopora damicornis*: lunar periodicity of swarming and substratum selection behavior. Ph.D. diss. 213 pp. University of Hawaii.

————. 1972b. Behavior of the planula larva of the scleractinian coral *Pocillopora damicornis* (L.). Am. Zool., 12: 723.

Harris, M. P. 1969. Breeding seasons of sea-birds in the Galapagos Islands. J. Zool. (Lond.), 159: 145–165.

————. 1979. Population dynamics of the Flightless Cormorant *Nannopterum harrisi*. Ibis, 121:135–146.

Heck, K. L., Jr., and E. D. McCoy. 1978. Long-distance dispersal and the reef-building corals of the eastern Pacific. Mar. Biol. (Berl.), 48:349–356.

Hedgpeth, J. W. 1969. An intertidal reconnaissance of rocky shores of the Galápagos. Wasmann J. Biol., 27:1–24.

Hein, F., and M. Risk. 1975. Bioerosion of coral heads: inner patch reefs, Florida reef tract. Bull. Mar. Sci., 25:133–138.

Hendler, G. 1977. The differential effects of seasonal stress and predation on the stability of reef-flat echinoid populations. Proc. Third Int. Coral Reef Symp., Miami, Florida, 1:217–223.

Hertlein, L. G. 1972. Pliocene fossils from Baltra (South Seymour) Island, Galapagos Islands. Proc. Calif. Acad. Sci., 4th ser., 39(3):25–46.

Heyerdahl, T. 1963. Archaeology in the Galápagos Islands. *In* Galápagos Islands, a unique area for scientific investigations, pp. 45–51. Occas. Pap. Calif. Acad. Sci. 44.

Hiatt, R. W., and D. W. Strasburg. 1960. Ecological relationships of the fish fauna on coral reefs of the Marshall Islands. Ecol. Monogr., 30(1): 65–127.

Highsmith, R. C. 1979. Coral growth rates and environmental control of density banding. J. Exp. Mar. Biol. Ecol., 37:105–125.

———. 1980. Geographic patterns of coral bioerosion: a productivity hypothesis. J. Exp. Mar. Biol. Ecol., 46:177–196.

———. 1981. Coral bioerosion at Enewetak: agents and dynamics. Int. Rev. Gesamten. Hydrobiol., 66:335–375.

———. 1982. Reproduction by fragmentation in corals. Mar. Ecol. Prog. Ser., 7:207–226.

Hobson, E. S. 1968. Predatory behavior of some shore fishes in the Gulf of California. Bur. Sports Fish. and Wildl., Res. Rep., 73:1–92.

———. 1974. Feeding relationships of teleostean fishes on coral reefs in Kona, Hawaii. Fish. Bull. (Seattle), 72(4): 915–1031.

Holden, J. C., and R. S. Dietz. 1972. Galapagos gore, NazCoPac triple junction and Carnegie/Cocos ridges. Nature (Lond.), 235:266–269.

Hopley, D. 1974. Investigations of sea level changes along the Great Barrier Reef coastline. Proc. Second Int. Coral Reef Symp., Brisbane, Australia, 2:551–562.

Houvenaghel, G. T. 1977. Description de la géomorphologie marine d l'archipel des Galapagos. Cah. Pac., 20:223–239.

———. 1978. Oceanographic conditions in the Galapagos archipelago and their relationships with life on the islands, pp. 181–200, *In* Upwelling Ecosystems, R. Boje and M. Tomczak, eds., New York: Springer-Verlag.

Houvenaghel, G. T. and N. Houvenaghel. 1974. Aspects écologiques de la zonation intertidale sur les côtes rocheuses des îles Galapagos. Mar. Biol. (Berl.), 26:135–152.

Hubbs, C. L. 1960. The marine vertebrates of the outer coast. Syst. Zool., 9:134–147.

Hubbs, C. L., and G. I. Roden. 1964. Oceanography and marine life along the Pacific coast of Middle America. *In* R. Wauchope (gen. ed.), and R. C. West (vol. ed.), Handbook of Middle American Indians. Natural Environment and Early Cultures. Austin: University of Texas Press, 1:143–186.

Hubbs, C. L., and R. H. Rosenblatt. 1961. Effects of the equatorial currents of the Pacific on the distribution of fishes and other marine animals. Tenth Pac. Sci. Cong., abstr., 1961:340–341.

Hudson, J. H. 1977. Long-term bioerosion rates on a Florida reef: a new method. Proc. Third Int. Coral Reef Symp., Miami, Florida, 2:491–497.

Hudson, J. H., E. A. Shinn, R. B. Halley, and B. Lidz. 1976. Sclerochronology: a tool for interpreting past environments. Geology (Boulder), 4:361–364.

Hughes, T. P., and J. B. C. Jackson. 1980. Do corals lie about their age? Some demographic consequences of partial mortality, fission and fusion. Science (Wash., D.C.), 209:713–715.

Hutchinson, G. E. 1950. Survey of contemporary knowledge of biogeochemistry, 3. The biogeochemistry of vertebrate excretion. Bull. Am. Mus. Nat. Hist., 96:1–554.

Hyman, L. H. 1940. The Invertebrates: Protozoa through Ctenophora. New York and London: McGraw-Hill, 726 pp.

Irvine, G. V. 1975. Damselfish territoriality: the maintenance of algal gardens and the removal of invaders. Student Reports, Doherty Found., Smithson. Trop. Res. Inst.

Jackson, J. B. C. 1977. Competition on marine hard substrata: the adaptive significance of solitary and colonial strategies. Am. Nat., 111:743–767.
———. 1979. Overgrowth competition between encrusting cheilostome ectoprocts in a Jamaican cryptic reef environment. J. Anim. Ecol., 48:805–823.
Jackson, J. B. C., and L. Buss. 1975. Allelopathy and spatial competition among coral reef invertebrates. Proc. Nat. Acad. Sci., U.S.A., 72(12):5160–5163.
Johannes, R. E. 1978. Reproductive strategies of coastal marine fishes in the tropics. Environ. Biol. Fishes, 3:65–84.
———. 1980. In press. In J. E. Bardach, J. J. Magnuson, R. C. May, and J. M. Reinhart, eds., Fish Behavior and Its Use in the Capture and Culture of Fishes. Int. Centre for Living Aquatic Resource Management, Manila, Philippines.
Johnson, G. L., and A. Lowrie. 1972. Cocos and Carnegie Ridges result of the Galapagos "hot spot"? Earth Planetary Sci. Lett., 14:279–280.
Jokiel, P. L., and S. L. Coles. 1977. Effects of temperature on the mortality and growth of Hawaiian reef corals. Mar. Biol. (Berl.), 43:201–208.
Jordan, E. K., and L. G. Hertlein. 1926. Expedition to the Revillagigedo Islands, Mexico, in 1925. Part 7. Contribution to the geology and paleontology of the Tertiary of Cedros Island and adjacent parts of Lower California. Proc. Calif. Acad. Sci., ser. 4, 15:409–464.
Joubin, L. 1912. Bancs et récifs de coraux (Madrépores). Ann. Inst. Océanogr., 4:1–7, 5 maps.

Kaufman, L. 1977. The Three Spot Damselfish: effects on benthic biota of Caribbean coral reefs. Proc. Third Int. Coral Reef Symp., Miami, Florida, 1:559–564.
Kawamura, K., and J. Taki. 1965. Ecological studies on the sea urchin, *Strongylocentrotus intermedius*, on the coast of Funadomari, in the north region of Rebun Island (III). Sci. Rep. Hokkaido Fish. Exp. Stn., 4:22–40.
Keigwin, L. D., Jr. 1978. Pliocene closing of the Isthmus of Panama, based on biostratigraphic evidence from nearby Pacific Ocean and Caribbean Sea cores. Geology (Boulder), 6(10):630–634.
Kinsey, D. W., and P. J. Davies. 1979. Effects of elevated nitrogen and phosphorous on coral reef growth. Limnol. Oceanogr., 24:935–940.
Kinsey, D. W., and A. Domm. 1974. Effects of fertilization on a coral reef environment—primary production studies. Proc. Second Int. Symp. Coral Reefs, Brisbane, Australia, 1:49–66.
Kinsman, D. J. J. 1964. Reef coral tolerance of high temperatures and salinities. Nature (Lond.), 202:1280–1282.
Kinzie, R. A. 1968. The ecology of the replacement of *Pseudosquilla ciliata* (Fabricius) by *Gonodactylus forcatus* (Forskål) (Crustacea: Stomatopoda) recently introduced into the Hawaiian Islands. Pac. Sci., 22:465–475.
Knauss, J. A. 1960. Measurements of the Cromwell Current. Deep-Sea Res., 6:265–286.
———. 1963. Equatorial current systems. In M. N. Hill, ed., The Sea: Ideas and Observations on Progress in the Study of the Seas. New York: Wiley-Interscience, 2:235–252.
Knutson, D. W., R. W. Buddemeier, and S. V. Smith. 1972. Coral chronometers: seasonal growth bands in reef corals. Science (Wash., D.C.), 177:270–272.
Kuenen, Ph. H. 1950. Marine Geology. New York: John Wiley & Sons, 568 pp.

Laborel, J. 1974. West African reef corals, an hypothesis on their origin. Proc. Second Int. Coral Reef Symp., Brisbane, Australia, 1:425–443.

Ladd, H. S. 1971. Existing reefs—geological aspects, pp. 1273–1300, Proc. North Am. Paleontol. Conv., Part J, Reef organisms through time.

Land, L. S., J. C. Lang, and J. Barnes. 1975. Extension rate: a primary control on the isotopic composition of West Indian (Jamaican) scleractinian reef coral skeletons. Mar. Biol. (Berl.), 33:221–233.

Lang, J. 1973. Interspecific aggression by scleractinian corals, 2. Why the race is not only to the swift. Bull. Mar. Sci., 23:260–279.

Lawrence, J. M. 1975. On the relationship between marine plants and sea urchins. Oceanogr. Mar. Biol. Ann. Rev., 13:213–286.

Laxton, J. H. 1974. Aspects of the ecology of the coral-eating starfish *Acanthaster planci*. Biol. J. Linn. Soc., 6 (1):19–45.

Leloup, E. 1964. Larves de Cerianthaires. Discovery Rep. 33:251–307.

Lessios, H. A. 1981. Divergence in allopatry: molecular and morphological differentiation between sea urchins separated by the Isthmus of Panama. Evolution, 35:618–634.

Lewis, J. B. 1976. Experimental tests of suspension feeding in Atlantic reef corals. Mar. Biol. (Berl.), 36:147–150.

Limbaugh, C. 1964. Notes on the life history of two California pomacentrids: garibaldis, *Hypsypops rubicunda* (Girard) and blacksmiths, *Chromis punctipinnis* (Cooper). Pac. Sci., 18:41–50.

Lobel, P. S. 1980. Herbivory by damselfishes and their role in coral reef community ecology. Bull. Mar. Sci., 30:273–289.

Lobel, P. S., and R. E. Johannes. 1980. Nesting, eggs and larvae of triggerfishes (Balistidae). Envir. Biol. Fishes, 5(3): 251–252.

Lonsdale, P., and K. D. Klitgord. 1978. Structure and tectonic history of the eastern Panama Basin. Geol. Soc. Am. Bull., 89:981–999.

Low, R. M. 1971. Interspecific territoriality in a pomacentrid reef fish, *Pomacentrus flavicauda* Whitley. Ecology, 52(4):648–654.

Lowrie, A., I. Aitken, P. Grim, and L. McRaney. 1979. Fossil spreading center and faults within the Panama fracture zone. Mar. Geophys. Res., 4:153–166.

Loya, Y. 1976. Recolonization of Red Sea corals affected by natural catastrophes and man-made perturbations. Ecology, 57:278–289.

Lucas, J. S., and M. M. Jones. 1976. Hybrid crown-of-thorns starfish (*Acanthaster planci* x *A. brevispinus*) reared to maturity in the laboratory. Nature (Lond.), 263:409–412.

Luyendyk, B. D., D. Foresyth, and D. Phillips. 1972. Experimental approach to the palaeocirculation of the oceanic surface waters. Geol. Soc. Am., Bull., 83:2649–2664.

MacArthur, R. H., and E. O. Wilson. 1963. An equilibrium theory of insular zoogeography. Evolution, 17:373–387.

———. 1967. The theory of island biogeography. Princeton: Princeton University Press, 203 pp.

McBirney, A. R., and K. Aoki. 1966. Petrology of the Galapagos Islands, pp. 71–77 *In* The Galápagos (R. I. Bowman, ed.). Berkeley and Los Angeles: University of California Press.

McBirney, A. R., and H. Williams. 1969. Geology and petrology of the Galápagos Islands. Geol. Soc. Am. Mem. 118, 197 pp.

McCoy, E. D., and K. L. Heck, Jr. 1976. Biogeography of corals, seagrasses, and mangroves: an alternative to the center of origin concept. Syst. Zool., 25:201–210.

MacGeachy, J. K., and C. W. Stearn. 1976. Boring by macroorganisms in the coral *Montastrea annularis* on Barbados reefs. Int. Rev. Gesamten. Hydrobiol., 61:715–745.

Macintyre, I. G., and S. V. Smith. 1974. X-radiographic studies of skeletal development in coral colonies. Proc. Second. Int. Coral Reef Symp., Brisbane, Australia, 2:277–287.

Macintyre, I. G., R. B. Burke, and R. Stuckenrath. 1982. Core holes in the outer fore reef off Carrie Bow Cay, Belize: a key to the Holocene history of the Belizean barrier reef complex. Proc. Fourth Int. Coral Reef Symp., Manila, Philippines. In press.

Madsen, F. J. 1955. A note on the sea-star genus *Acanthaster*. Vidensk. Medd. Dan. Naturhist. Foren., 117:179–192.

Maguire, L. A., and J. W. Porter. 1977. A spatial model of growth and competition strategies in coral communities. Ecol. Model., 3:249–271.

Maragos, J. E. 1972. A study of the ecology of Hawaiian reef corals. Ph.D. diss., University of Hawaii, Honolulu.

———. 1974*a*. Reef corals of Fanning Island. Pac. Sci., 28(3): 247– 255.

———. 1974*b*. Coral communities on a seaward reef slope, Fanning Island. Pac. Sci., 28(3):257–278.

———. 1977. Order Scleractinia, stony corals, pp. 158–241, *In* D. M. Devaney and L. G. Eldredge, eds., Reef and shore fauna of Hawaii, sec. 1: Protozoa through Ctenophora. Honolulu: Bishop Museum Press.

Maragos, J. E., and P. L. Jokiel. 1978. Reef corals of Canton Atoll: I. Zoogeography. Atoll. Res. Bull., 221:55–70.

Margalef, R. 1968. The pelagic ecosystem of the Caribbean Sea. *In* Symp. on investigations and resources of the Caribbean Sea and adjacent regions. UNESCO, Paris, France, pp. 483–498.

Marshall, S. M., and A. P. Orr. 1931. Sedimentation on Low Isles Reef and its relation to coral growth. Sci. Rep. Gt. Barrier Reef Exped., 1:93–133.

Martinez, N. G. 1934. Impresiones de un viaje al Archipiélago de Galápagos. Quito, Talleres Gráficos Nacionales, 3rd ed. Publicaciones del Observatorio de Quito, Sección de Geofísica.

Matthai, G. 1914. A revision of the Recent colonial Astraeidae possessing distinct corallites. Linn. Soc. Lond., Trans., ser. 2, 17:140 pp., 38 pls.

Maxwell, D. C. 1974. Marine primary productivity of the Galapagos Archipelago. 167 pp. Ph.D. diss. The Ohio State University.

Mayor, A. G. 1918. Ecology of the Murray Island coral reef. Carnegie Inst. Wash. Publ., 213:1–48.

Meredith, D. W. 1939. Voyages of the Velero III. 2d ed., Los Angeles: Bookhaven Press, 286 pp.

Mileikovsky, S. A. 1971. Types of larval development in marine bottom invertebrates, their distribution and ecological significance: a re-evaluation. Mar. Biol. (Berl.), 10:193–213.

Moran, M. J., and P. F. Sale. 1977. Seasonal variation in territorial response, and other aspects of the ecology of the Australian temperate pomacentrid fish *Parma microlepis*. Mar. Biol. (Berl.), 39:121–128.

Morgan, W. J. 1971. Convection plumes in the lower mantle. Nature (Lond.), 230:42–43.

———. 1972. Deep mantle convection plumes and plate motions. Am. Assoc. Pet. Geol. Bull., 56:203–213.

Morrell, B., Jr. 1832. A narrative of four voyages to the South Sea, north and south Pacific Ocean, Chinese Sea, Ethiopic and southern Atlantic Ocean, Indian and Antarctic Ocean from the year 1822 to 1831. New York: J. and J. Harper, 492 pp.

LITERATURE CITED

Munk, W. H., and M. C. Sargent. 1954. Adjustment of Bikini Atoll to ocean waves. Geol. Surv. Prof. Pap., 260-C:275–280.

Murphy, R. C. 1936. Oceanic birds of South America. vol. 1. Am. Mus. Nat. Hist., New York. 640 pp.

Murray, B. G. 1971. The ecological consequences of interspecific territorial behavior in birds. Ecology, 52:414–423.

Muscatine, L. 1973. Nutrition of corals, pp. 77–115. *In* O. A. Jones and R. Endean, eds., Biology and geology of coral reefs, 2, Biology 1. New York: Academic Press.

Muscatine, L., and E. Cernichiari. 1969. Assimilation of photosynthetic products of zooxanthellae by a reef coral. Biol. Bull. (Woods Hole), 137:506–523.

Muscatine, L., and J. W. Porter. 1977. Reef corals: mutualistic symbioses adapted to nutrient-poor environments. BioScience, 27:454–460.

Myrberg, A. A., Jr., and R. E. Thresher. 1974. Interspecific aggression and its relevance to the concept of territoriality in reef fishes. Am. Zool., 14:81–96.

Neudecker, S. 1977. Transplant experiments to test the effect of fish grazing on coral distribution. Proc. Third Int. Coral Reef Symp., Miami, Florida, 1:317–323.

———. 1979. Effects of grazing and browsing fishes on the zonation of corals in Guam. Ecology, 60(4):666–672.

Newell, N. D. 1959. Questions of coral reefs. Part I. Nat. Hist. Mag., 68:118–131.

———. 1971. An outline history of tropical organic reefs. Am. Mus. Novit., 2465:1–37.

———. 1972. The evolution of reefs. Sci. Am., 226:54–65.

Newman, W. A. 1979. On the biogeography of balanomorph barnacles of the Southern Ocean including new balanid taxa; a subfamily, two genera and three species. Proc. Int. Symp. Mar. Biogeogr. Evol. South. Hemisphere, Auckland, New Zealand, 1:279–305.

Nishihira, M., and K. Yamazato. 1974. Human interference with the coral reef community and *Acanthaster* infestation of Okinawa. Proc. Second Int. Coral Reef Symp., Brisbane, Australia, 1:577–590.

NOAA 1975–1976. Tide tables, high and low water predictions, west coast of North and South America, including the Hawaiian Islands. U.S. Department of Commerce.

Ogden, J. C. 1977. Carbonate-sediment production by parrot fish and sea urchins on Caribbean reefs, pp. 281–288. *In* S. H. Frost, M. P. Weiss and J. B. Saunders, eds., Reefs and related carbonates—ecology and sedimentology. Studies in Geology, No. 4, Am. Assoc. Pet. Geol., 421 pp.

Ogden, J. C., R. A. Brown, and N. Salesky. 1973. Grazing by the echinoid *Diadema antillarum* Philippi: formation of halos around West Indian patch reefs. Science (Wash., D.C.), 182:715–717.

Ogg, J. G., and J. A. Koslow. 1978. The impact of Typhoon Pamela (1976) on Guam's coral reefs and beaches. Pac. Sci., 32(2):105–118.

Orme, G. R. 1977. Aspects of sedimentation in the coral reef environment, pp. 129–182. *In* O. A. Jones and R. Endean, eds., Biology and Geology of Coral Reefs, vol. 4, Geology 2. New York: Academic Press, 337 pp.

Pak, H., and J. R. V. Zaneveld. 1973. The Cromwell Current on the east side of the Galapagos Islands. J. Geophys. Res., 78:7845–7859.

Palmer, R. H. 1928. Fossil and Recent corals and coral reefs of western Mexico. Three new species. Proc. Am. Philos. Soc., 67:21–31.

Palmer, C. E., and R. L. Pyle. 1966. The climatological setting of the Galápagos. *In* The Galápagos (R. I. Bowman, ed.), pp. 93–99. Berkeley and Los Angeles: University of California Press.

Parker, R. H. 1964. Zoogeography and ecology of macroinvertebrates of Gulf of California and continental slope of Western Mexico. *In* T. H. van Andel and G. G. Shore, Jr., eds., Marine Geology of the Gulf of California. Am. Assoc. Pet. Geol. Mem., 3:331–376.

Patton, W. K. 1974. Community structure among the animals inhabiting the coral *Pocillopora damicornis* at Heron Island, Australia, pp. 219–243. *In* W. B. Vernberg, ed., Symbiosis in the sea. Columbia University, South Carolina: Carolina Press, 276 pp.

Payne, M. M., M. B. Grosvenor, F. G. Vosburgh, and W. Chamberlin. 1970. National Geographic Atlas of the World. Revised 3d edition, Washington, D. C., 331 pp.

Pearson, R. G., and R. Endean. 1969. A preliminary study of the coral predator *Acanthaster planci* (L.) (Asteroidea) on the Great Barrier Reef. Fish. Notes (Depart. Harbours Mar., Queensland), 3:27–68.

Pickard, G. L. 1963. Descriptive physical oceanography. New York: MacMillan Co., 199 pp.

Pielou, E. C. 1979. Biogeography. New York: John Wiley & Sons, 351 pp.

Pollock, J. B. 1928. Fringing and fossil reefs of Oahu. Bull. Bernice P. Bishop Mus., 55:1–56.

Porter, J. W. 1972. Ecology and species diversity of coral reefs on opposite sides of the Isthmus of Panama, pp. 89–116. *In* M. L. Jones, ed., The Panamic biota: some observations prior to a sea-level canal. Bull. Biol. Soc. Wash. No. 2, Wash. D. C., 270 pp.

———. 1974. Community structure of coral reefs on opposite sides of the Isthmus of Panama. Science (Wash., D. C.), 186:543–545.

Potts, D. C. 1977. Suppression of coral populations by filamentous algae within damselfish territories. J. Exp. Mar. Biol. Ecol., 28:207–216.

Prahl, H. von, F. Guhl, and M. Grögl. 1979. Gorgona. Futura Grupo Editorial Ltda., Bogotá, 279 pp.

Prell, W. L., and J. D. Hays. 1976. Late Pleistocene faunal and temperature patterns of the Colombia Basin, Caribbean Sea. Mem. Geol. Soc. Am., 145:201–220.

Preston, E. M. 1973. A computer simulation of competition among five sympatric congeneric species of xanthid crabs. Ecology, 54:469–483.

Quinn, W. H. 1974. Monitoring and predicting El Niño invasions. J. Appl. Meteor., 13:825–830.

Ramage, C. S. 1975. Preliminary discussion of the meteorology of the 1972–73 El Niño. Bull. Am. Meteor. Soc., 56(2): 234–242.

Randall, J. E. 1961. A contribution to the biology of the convict surgeonfish of the Hawaiian Islands, *Acanthurus triostegus sandvicensis.*. Pac. Sci., 15:215–272.

———. 1961. Overgrazing of algae by herbivorous marine fishes. Ecology, 42:812.

———. 1974. The effect of fishes on coral reefs. Proc. Second Int. Coral Reef Symp., Brisbane, Australia, 1:159–166.

Randall, J. E., S. M. Head, and A. P. L. Sanders. 1978. Food habits of the giant humphead wrasse, *Cheilinus undulatus* (Labridae). Environ. Biol. Fishes, 3:235–238.

Ranson, G. 1952. Note sur la cause probable de l'absence de récifs coralliens aux îles Marquises et de l'activité réduite des coraux récifaux à Tahiti, aux Tuamotu, aux Hawaii, etc. . . . C. R. Somm. Soci. Biogéogr., 248:3–11.

Reed, J. K. 1980. Distribution and structure of deep-water *Oculina varicosa* coral reefs off central eastern Florida. Bull. Mar. Sci., 30(3): 667–677.

Reese, E. S. 1977. Coevolution of corals and coral feeding fishes of the family Chaetodontidae. Proc. Third Int. Coral Reef Symp., Miami, Florida, 1:267–274.

Reid, J. L., Jr. 1961. On the geostrophic flow at the surface of the Pacific Ocean with respect to the 1,000-decibar surface. Tellus, 13:489–502.

Richards, A. F. 1954. Volcanic eruptions of 1943 and 1948 on Isabela Island, Galápagos Islands, Ecuador. Volcano Letter (Hawaii), No. 525, pp. 1–3.

———. 1957. Volcanism in eastern Pacific ocean basin: 1945–1955. Cong. Geol. Int'l., 20th sess., sec. 1, Vulcanología del Cenozóico, 1:19–31.

———. 1958. Transpacific distribution of floating pumice from Isla San Benedicto, Mexico. Deep-Sea Res., 5:29–35.

———. 1962. Active volcanoes of the Archipelago de Colon (Galápagos). Part XIV, Catalogue of the active volcanoes of the world. Int. Assoc. Volcanol., Naples.

Richardson, C. A., P. Dustan, and J. C. Lang. 1979. Maintenance of living space by sweeper tentacles of *Montastrea cavernosa*, a Caribbean reef coral. Mar. Biol. (Berl.), 55:181–186.

Richmond, R. 1982. Energetic considerations in the dispersal of *Pocillopora damicornis* (Linnaeus) planulae. Proc. Fourth Int. Coral Reef Symp., Manila, Philippines.

Rinkevich, B., and Y. Loya. 1979a. The reproduction of the Red Sea coral *Stylophora pistillata*. I. Gonads and planula. Mar. Ecol. Prog. Ser., 1:133–144.

———. 1979b. The reproduction of the Red Sea coral *Stylophora pistillata*, II. Synchronization in breeding and seasonality of planula shedding. Mar. Ecol. Prog. Ser., 1:133–144.

Roberts, H. H. 1974. Variability of reefs with regard to changes in wave power around an island. Proc. Second Int. Coral Reef Symp., Brisbane, Australia, 2:497–512.

Robertson, R. 1970. Review of the predators and parasites of stony corals, with special reference to symbiotic prosobranch gastropods. Pac. Sci., 24:43–54.

Roden, G. I. 1964. Oceanographic aspects of Gulf of California. *In* T. H. van Andel and G. G. Shore, Jr., eds., Marine Geology of the Gulf of California. Am. Assoc. Pet. Geol. Mem., 3:30–58.

Roden, G. I., and G. W. Groves. 1959. Recent oceanographic investigations in the Gulf of California. J. Mar. Res., 18(1):10–35.

Rogers, C. S. 1979. The effect of shading on coral reef structure and function. J. Exp. Mar. Biol. Ecol., 41:269–288.

Rosen, B. R., and J. D. Taylor. 1969. Reef coral from Aldabra: new mode of reproduction. Science (Wash., D. C.), 166:119–120.

Rosen, D. E. 1975. A vicariance model of Caribbean biogeography. Syst. Zool., 24:431–464.

Rosenblatt, R. H. 1963. Some aspects of speciation in marine shore fishes, pp. 171–180. *In* J. P. Harding and N. Tebble, eds., Speciation in the Sea. The Systematics Association, London.

Rosenblatt, R. H., and B. W. Walker. 1963. The marine shore-fishes of the Galapagos Islands. Occas. Pap. Calif. Acad. Sci., 44:97–106.

Rosenblatt, R. H., and E. S. Hobson. 1969. Parrotfishes (Scaridae) of the eastern Pacific, with a generic rearrangement of the Scarinae. Copeia, 3:434–453.

Rosenblatt, R. H., J. E. McCosker, and I. Rubinoff. 1972. Indo-West Pacific fishes from the Gulf of Chiriqui, Panama. Nat. Hist. Mus. Los Ang. Cty. Contrib. Sci., 234:1–18.

Rotondo, G. M. 1980. A reconstruction of linear island chain positions in the Pacific: a case study using the Hawaiian Emperor chain. M.S. thesis, University of Hawaii. 58 pp.

Rotondo, G. M., V. G. Springer, G. A. J. Scott, and S. O. Schlanger. 1981. Plate movement and island integration: A possible mechanism in the formation of endemic biotas, with special reference to the Hawaiian Islands. Syst. Zool., 30(1): 12–21.

Rotschi, H. 1970. Variations of equatorial currents, pp. 75–83. *In* W. S. Wooster, ed., Scientific Exploration of the South Pacific. Nat. Acad. Sci., Wash., D. C. 257 pp.

Roy, K. J., and S. V. Smith. 1971. Sedimentation and coral reef development in turbid water: Fanning lagoon. Pac. Sci., 25(2):234–248.

Rubinoff, R. W., and I. Rubinoff. 1971. Geographic and reproductive isolation in Atlantic and Pacific populations of Panamanian *Bathogobius*. Evolution, 25:88–97.

Russo, A. R. 1977. Water flow and the distribution and abundance of echinoids (genus *Echinometra*) on an Hawaiian reef. Aust. J. Mar. Freshwater Res., 28:693–702.

———. 1980. Bioerosion by two rock boring echinoids *(Echinometra mathaei* and *Echinostrephus aciculatus)* on Enewetak Atoll, Marshall Islands. J. Mar. Res., 38(1): 99–110.

Sachet, M. H. 1962. Geography and land ecology of Clipperton Island. Atoll Res. Bull., 86:1–115.

Saito, T. 1976. Geologic significance of coiling direction in the planktonic Foraminifera *Pullenatina*. Geology (Boulder), 4:305–309.

Sale, P. F. 1980. The ecology of fishes on coral reefs. Oceanogr. Mar. Biol. Annu. Rev., 18:367–421.

Sammarco, P. W., J. S. Levinton, and J. C. Ogden. 1974. Grazing and control of coral reef community structure by *Diadema antillarum* Philippi (Echinodermata: Echinoidea): a preliminary study. J. Mar. Res., 32(1): 47–53.

Saville-Kent, W. 1893. The Great Barrier Reef of Australia; its products and potentialities. London: W. H. Allen & Co., 387 pp.

Scheer, G. 1971. Coral reefs and coral genera in the Red Sea and Indian Ocean, pp. 329–367. *In* D. R. Stoddart and M. Yonge, eds., Regional variation in Indian Ocean coral reefs. Symp. Zool. Soc. Lond. No. 28. London: Academic Press.

Scheltema, R. S. 1971. Larval dispersal as a means of genetic exchange between geographically separated populations of shallow-water benthic marine gastropods. Biol. Bull. (Woods Hole), 140:284–322.

———. 1972. Eastward and westward dispersal across the tropical Atlantic Ocean by larvae belonging to the genus *Bursa* (Prosobranchia, Mesogastropoda, Bursidae). Int. Revue Ges. Hydrobiol., 57(6):863–873.

———. 1977. Dispersal of marine invertebrate organisms: paleobiogeographic and biostratigraphic implications, pp. 73–108. *In* E. G. Kauffman and J. E. Hazel, eds., Concepts and Methods of Biostratigraphy. Stroudsburg, Pennsylvania: Dowden, Hutchinson & Ross.

Schmidt, H. 1974. On evolution in the Anthozoa. Proc. Second Int. Coral Reef Symp., Brisbane, Australia, 1:533–560.

Schreiber, J. F., Jr. 1967. Inventory of research on desert coastal zones. Office of Arid Lands Research, University of Arizona, Tucson, 76 pp.

Scoffin, T. P., C. W. Stearn, D. Boucher, P. Frydl, C. M. Hawkins, I. G. Hunter, and J. K. MacGeachy. 1980. Calcium carbonate budget of a fringing reef on the west coast of Barbados. Bull. Mar. Sci., 30:475–508.

Shaw, H. R. 1973. Mantle convection and volcanic periodicity in the Pacific: evidence from Hawaii. Bull. Geol. Soc. Am., 84: 1505–1526.

Shepard, F. P. 1959. The earth beneath the sea. Baltimore: The Johns Hopkins Press, 275 pp.

Sheppard, C. R. C. 1979. Interspecific aggression between reef corals with reference to their distribution. Mar. Ecol. Prog. Ser., 1:237–247.

Shinn, E. A. 1972. Coral reef recovery in Florida and in the Persian Gulf. Environ. Conserv. Dep., Shell Oil Co., Houston, Texas, 9 pp.

Silva, P. C. 1966. Status of our knowledge of the Galapagos benthic marine algal flora prior to the Galápagos International Scientific Project, pp. 149–156. *In* R. I. Bowman, ed., The Galápagos, proceedings of the symposia of the Galápagos International Scientific Project. Berkeley and Los Angeles: University of California Press.

Simkin, T., and K. A. Howard. 1970. Caldera collapse in the Galapagos Islands, 1968. Science (Wash., D. C.), 169:429–437.

Slevin, J. R. 1959. The Galápagos Islands, a history of their exploration. Occas. Pap. Calif. Acad. Sci., 25:1–150.

Smith, D. C., L. Muscatine, and D. M. Lewis. 1969. Carbohydrate movement from autotrophs to heterotrophs in parasitic and mutualistic symbiosis. Biol. Rev., 44:17–90.

Smith, S. V., K. J. Roy, K. E. Chave, J. E. Maragos, A. Seogiarto, G. Key, M. J. Gordon, and D. T. O. Kam. 1970. Calcium carbonate production and deposition in a modern barrier reef complex. Abstr., Paper presented to Ann. Meet. Geol. Soc. Am., Milwaukee, Wisc., 1970: 688–689.

Smith, S. V., K. E. Chave, and D. T. O. Kam. 1973. Atlas of Kaneohe Bay: a reef ecosystem under stress. University of Hawaii Sea Grant Program, 128 pp.

Smith, S. V., W. J. Kimmerer, E. A. Laws, R. E. Brock, and T. W. Walsh. 1981. Kaneohe Bay sewage diversion experiment: perspectives on ecosystem responses to nutritional perturbation. Pac. Sci., 35(4):279–395.

Smithsonian Institution. 1979. Sierra Negra (Galápagos). SEAN (Scientific Event Alert Network) Bull., 4(11):17–20.

Snodgrass, R. E., and E. Heller. 1905. Shore fishes of the Revillagigedo, Clipperton, Cocos and Galápagos Islands. Proc. Wash. Acad. Sci., 6:333–427.

Sorokin, Y. I. 1973. On the feeding of some scleractinian corals with bacteria and dissolved organic matter. Limnol. Oceanogr., 18:380–385.

Soule, D. F., and J. D. Soule. 1979. Marine zoogeography and evolution of Bryozoa in the southern hemisphere. *In* Proceedings of the International Symposium on Marine Biogeography and Evolution in the Southern Hemisphere, Auckland, New Zealand, 1:317–336.

Soule, J. D. 1960. The distribution and affinities of the littoral marine Bryozoa (Ectoprocta). *In* Symposium: the biogeography of Baja California and adjacent seas, 2. Marine biotas. Syst. Zool., 9:100–104.

Sournia, A. 1976. Abondance du phytoplancton et absence de récifs coralliens sur les côtes des îles Marquises. C. R. Acad. Sc., Paris, 282 (Ser. D.): 553–555.

Sousa, W. P. 1979. Experimental investigations of disturbance and ecological succession in a rocky intertidal algal community. Ecol. Monogr., 49:227–254.

Springer, V. G. 1958. Systematics and zoogeography of the clinid fishes of the subtribe Labrisomini Hubbs. Publ. Inst. Mar. Sci. Univ. Tex., 5:417–492.

Squires, D. F. 1959. Results of the Puritan-American Museum of Natural History Expedition to western Mexico, 7. Corals and coral reefs in the Gulf of California. Bull. Am. Mus. Nat. Hist., 118(7):367–432.

Stanley, S. M., and L. D. Campbell. 1981. Neogene mass extinction of western Atlantic molluscs. Nature (Lond.), 293:457–459.

Stead, J. A. 1975. Field observations on the geology of Malpelo Island. *In* The Biological Investigation of Malpelo Island, Colombia (J. B. Graham, ed.), pp. 17–20. Smithson. Contrib. Zool., 176:1–98.

Stearn, C. W., and T. P. Scoffin. 1977. Carbonate budget of a fringing reef, Barbados. Proc. Third Int. Coral Reef Symp., Miami, Florida, 2:471–476.

Stearn, C. W., T. P. Scoffin, and W. Martindale. 1977. Calcium carbonate budget of a fringing reef on the west coast of Barbados. Bull. Mar. Sci., 27(3):479–510.

Steers, J. A., and D. R. Stoddart. 1977. The origin of fringing reefs, barrier reefs and atolls, pp. 21–57. *In* O. A. Jones and R. Endean, eds., Biology and Geology of Coral Reefs, vol. 4, Geol. 2. New York: Academic Press.

Stehli, F. G., and J. W. Wells. 1971. Diversity and age patterns in hermatypic corals. Syst. Zool., 20:115–126.

Steinbeck, J., and E. F. Ricketts. 1941. Sea of Cortez. New York: The Viking Press, 598 pp.

Stephenson, W., and R. B. Searles. 1960. Experimental studies on the ecology of intertidal environments at Heron Island. Aust. J. Mar. Freshwater Res., 11:241–267.

Stevenson, M. R., O. Guillen G., and J. Santoro de Ycaza. 1970. Marine atlas of the Pacific coastal waters of South America. Berkeley, Los Angeles, London: University of California Press, 23 pp. plus numerous charts.

Stimson, J. S. 1978. Mode and timing of reproduction in some common hermatypic corals of Hawaii and Enewetak. Mar. Biol. (Berl.), 48:173–184.

Stoddart, D. R. 1969a. Ecology and morphology of recent coral reefs. Biol. Rev. Camb. Philos. Soc., 44:433–498.

––––––. 1969b. Post-hurricane changes in the British Honduras reefs and cays. Atoll Res. Bull., 131:1–25.

––––––. 1971. Coral reefs and islands and catastrophic storms, pp. 155–197. In J. A. Steers, ed., Appl. Coastal Geomorphol. London: Macmillan.

––––––. 1976. Continuity and crisis in the reef community. Micronesica, 12:1–9.

––––––. 1978. Mechanical analysis of reef sediments, pp. 53–66 In D. R. Stoddart and R. E. Johannes, eds., Coral reefs: research methods. Monogr. Oceanogr. Methodol., Unesco, Paris.

Swanson, F. J., H. W. Baitis, J. Lexa, and J. Dymond. 1974. Geology of Santiago, Rábida, and Pinzón Islands, Galápagos. Bull. Geol. Soc. Am., 85:1803–1810.

Taft, B. A., B. M. Hickey, C. Wunsch, and D. J. Baker, Jr. 1974. Equatorial Undercurrent and deeper flows in the central Pacific. Deep-Sea Res., 21:403–430.

Taylor, D. L. 1977. Intra-colonial transport of organic compounds and calcium in some Atlantic reef corals. Proc. Third Int. Coral Reef Symp., Miami, Florida, 1:431–436.

Taylor, W. R. 1945. Pacific marine algae of the Allan Hancock expeditions to the Galápagos Islands. Allan Hancock Pacific Expeditions, 12 (1):1–528.

Teichert, C. 1958. Cold- and deep-water coral banks. Bull. Am. Assoc. Pet. Geol., 42:1064–1082.

Thomassin, B. A. 1971. Les facies d'epifaune et d'epiflore des biotopes sédimentaires des formations coralliennes dans la région de Tuléar (sud-ouest de Madagascar), pp. 371–396. In D. R. Stoddart and M. Yonge, eds., Regional variation in Indian Ocean coral reefs. Symp. Zool. Soc. Lond. 28, London: Academic Press.

Thomson, D. A., L. T. Findley, and A. N. Kerstitch. 1979. Reef fishes of the Sea of Cortez. New York: John Wiley & Sons, 302 pp.

Thomson, D. A., A. R. Mead, and J. F. Schreiber, Jr., eds., 1969. Environmental impact of brine effluents on Gulf of California. O. S. W. Res. & Dev. Prog. Rept., 387:1–196.

Thorson, G. 1950. Reproduction and larval ecology of marine bottom invertebrates. Biol. Rev. Camb. Philos. Soc., 25:1–45.

––––––. 1961. Length of pelagic larval life in marine bottom invertebrates as related to larval transport by ocean currents, pp. 455–474. In M. Sears, ed., Oceanography. Am. Assoc. Adv. Sci., Wash., D. C.

Townsend, C. H. 1925. The Galápagos tortoises in their relation to the whaling industry, a study of old logbooks. Zoologica (N.Y.), 4:55–135.

Townsley, S. J., and M. P. Townsley. 1973. A preliminary investigation of the biology and ecology of the holothurians at Fanning Island, pp. 173–186. In K. E. Chave and E. Alison Kay (principal investigators), Fanning Island Expedition, July and August 1972, HIG-73-13, Hawaii Institute of Geophysics, University of Hawaii, Honolulu.

Trench, R. K. 1971. The physiology and biochemistry of zooxanthellae with marine coelenterates, I. The assimilation of photosynthetic products of zooxanthellae by two marine coelenterates. Proc. R. Soc. Lond. B. Biol. Sci., 177:225–235.

Tsuchiya, M. 1970. Equatorial circulation of the South Pacific, pp. 69–74. *In* W. S. Wooster, ed., Scientific Exploration of the South Pacific. Nat. Acad. Sci., Wash., D. C., 257 pp.

Valencia, M. J. 1977. Christmas Island (Pacific Ocean): reconnaissance geologic observations. Atoll Res. Bull., no. 197, 19 pp.

Valentine, J. W. 1966. Numerical analysis of marine molluscan ranges on the extratropical northeastern Pacific shelf. Limnol. Oceanogr., 11:198–211.

———. 1973. Evolutionary paleoecology of the marine biosphere. Englewood Cliffs, New Jersey: Prentice-Hall Inc., 511 pp.

Van Andel, T. J. H. 1974. Cenozoic migration of the Pacific Plate, northward shift of the axis of deposition and paleobathymetry of the Central Equatorial Plate. Geology (Boulder), 2:507–510.

Vaughan, T. W. 1906. Reports on the scientific results of the expedition to the eastern tropical Pacific . . . 6. Madreporaria. Bull. Mus. Comp. Zool., Harv. College, 50(3): 61–72.

———. 1917. The reef-coral fauna of Carrizo Creek, Imperial County, California and its significance. Prof. Pap. U. S. Geol. Surv., no. 98-T:355–395.

Vermeij, G. J. 1978. Biogeography and adaptation, patterns of marine life. Cambridge, Massachusetts: Harvard University Press, 332 pp.

Veron, J. E. N., M. Pichon, and M. Wijsmann-Best. 1977. Scleractinia of Eastern Australia, II. Families Faviidae and Trachyphylliidae. Aust. Inst. Mar. Sci. Monogr. Ser., vol. 3:233 pp.; 477 figs.

de Vildoso, A. Ch. 1976. Aspectos biológicos del fenómeno El Niño 1972–73. Parte I. Distribución de la fauna. (Reunion de trabajo sobre el fenómeno conocido como "El Niño," Guayaquil, Ecuador, 4–12 diciembre de 1974.) FAO Informes de pesca, 185:62–79.

Vine, P. J. 1974. Effects of algal grazing and aggressive behaviour of the fishes *Pomacentrus lividus* and *Acanthurus sohal* on coral-reef ecology. Mar. Biol. (Berl.), 24:131–136.

Wainwright, S. A. 1965. Reef communities visited by the Israel South Red Sea Expedition, 1962. Israel South Red Sea Expedition, 1962, Rep., No. 9, Bull. Sea Fish. Res. Sta. Haifa, 38:40–53.

Walker, B. W. 1960. The distribution and affinities of the marine fish fauna of the Gulf of California. *In* Symposium: the biogeography of Baja California and adjacent seas, II. Marine biotas. Syst. Zool., 9:123–133.

———. 1966. The origins and affinities of the Galápagos shorefishes, pp. 172–174. *In* R. I. Bowman, ed., The Galápagos, proceedings of the symposia of the Galápagos International Scientific Project. Berkeley and Los Angeles: University of California Press.

Wanders, J. B. W. 1977. The role of benthic algae in the shallow reef of Curaçao (Netherland Antilles), 3. The significance of grazing. Aquat. Bot., 3:357–390.

Weber, J. N., and P. M. J. Woodhead. 1970. Ecological studies of the coral predator *Acanthaster planci* in the South Pacific. Mar. Biol. (Berl.), 6:12–17.

———. 1972. Temperature dependence of oxygen-18 concentration in reef coral carbonates. J. Geophys. Res., 77:463–473.

Weber, J. N., P. Deines, E. W. White, and P. H. Weber. 1975. Seasonal high and low density bands in reef coral skeletons. Nature (Lond.), 255:697–698.

Wellington, G. M. 1980. Reversal of digestive interactions between Pacific reef corals: mediation by sweeper tentacles. Oecologia (Berl.), 47:340–343.

———. 1981. The role of competition, niche diversification and predation on the structure and organization of a fringing coral reef in the Gulf of Panama. Ph.D. diss. 181 pp. University of California, Santa Barbara.

———. 1982a. An experimental analysis of the effects of light and zooplankton on coral zonation. Oecologia (Berl.), 52:311–320.

———. 1982b. Depth zonation of corals in the Gulf of Panama: control and facilitation by resident reef fishes. Ecol. Monogr., 52 (3):223–241.

———. 1983. Marine environment and protection. In Key environments: Galápagos Islands, J. E. Treherne, gen. ed., and R. Perry, vol. ed. Pergamon Press, Oxford, England.

Wellington, G. M., and P. W. Glynn. 1983. Environmental influences on annual banding in eastern Pacific (Panama) corals. Coral Reefs (in press).

Wells, J. W. 1933. Corals of the Cretaceous of the Atlantic and Gulf coastal plains and western interior of the United States. Bull. Am. Paleontol., 18:85–288.

———. 1954. Fossil corals from Bikini Atoll. U. S. Geol. Surv. Prof. Pap. 260-P:609–617, pls. 223–224.

———. 1955. A survey of the distribution of reef coral genera in the Great Barrier Reef region. Repts. Great Barrier Reef Comm., 6:1–9.

———. 1956. Scleractinia, pp. F328–F444. In R. C. Moore, ed., Treatise on Invertebrate Paleontology. Part F. Coelenterata. Geol. Soc. Am. New York. Lawrence, Kansas: University of Kansas Press.

———. 1957. Corals. In "Treatise on Marine Ecology and Paleoecology" (J. W. Hedgpeth, ed.), Ecology, Mem. 67, Geol. Soc. Am., 1:1087–1104.

———. 1969. Aspects of Pacific coral reefs. Micronesica, 5:317–322.

Wells, J. W. 1982. Notes on Indo-Pacific scleractinian corals. Part 9. New corals from the Galápagos Islands. Pac. Sci., 36(2):211–219.

Wells, J. W., and J. C. Lang. 1973. Systematic list of Jamaican shallow-water Scleractinia. Bull. Mar. Sci., 23:55–58.

Whitmore, F. C., Jr., and R. H. Stewart. 1965. Miocene mammals and Central American seaways. Science (Wash., D. C.), 148:180–185.

Wiens, H. J. 1962. Atoll environment and ecology. New Haven and London: Yale University Press. 532 pp.

Wijsman-Best, M. 1977. Indo-Pacific coral species belonging to the subfamily Montastreinae Vaughan & Wells 1943, 2. The genera Montastrea and Plesiastrea. Zool. Meded. (Leiden), no. 7:81–97, 4 pls.

Williams, A. H. 1980. The threespot damselfish: a noncarnivorous keystone species. Am. Nat., 116:138–142.

Williams, H. 1966a. Volcanic history of the Galápagos Archipelago. Abstr., Bull. Volcanol., 29:27–28.

———. 1966b. Geology of the Galápagos Islands, pp. 65–70. In R. I. Bowman, ed., The Galápagos, proceedings of the symposia of the Galápagos International Scientific Project. Berkeley and Los Angeles: University of California Press.

Williams, P. M., K. L. Smith, E. M. Druffel, and T. W. Linick. 1981. Dietary carbon sources of mussels and tubeworms from Galápagos hydrothermal vents determined from tissue ^{14}C activity. Nature (Lond.), 292:448–449.

Wilson, D. P. 1960. Some problems in larval ecology related to the localized distribution of bottom animals, pp. 87–103. In A. A. Buzzati-Traverso, ed., Perspectives in Marine Biology. Berkeley and Los Angeles: University of California Press.

Wilson, J. T. 1965. Evidence from ocean islands suggesting movement in the earth. Phil. Trans. Roy. Soc. (London) 258, Symposium on Continental Drift 145.

Wood-Jones, F. 1912. Coral and atolls. London: Lovell Reeve & Co., 392 pp.

Woodley, J. D., E. A. Chornesky, P. A. Clifford, J. B. C. Jackson, L. S. Kaufman, N. Knowlton, J. C. Lang, M. P. Pearson, J. W. Porter, M. C. Rooney, K. W. Rylaarsdam, V. J. Tunnicliffe, C. M. Wahle, J. L. Wulff, A. S. G. Curtis, M. D. Dallmeyer, B. P. Jupp, M. A. R. Koehl, J. Neigel, and E. M. Sides. 1981. Hurricane Allen's impact on Jamaican coral reefs. Science (Wash., D. C.), 214:749–755.

Woodring, W. P. 1966. The Panama land bridge as a sea barrier. Proc. Amer. Phil. Soc., 110:425–433.

———. 1970. Geology and paleontology of Canal Zone and adjoining parts of Panama. U. S. Geol. Surv. Prof. Pap. 306-D (Eulimidae, Marginellidae to Helminthoglyptidae), pp. 299–452.

Wooster, W. S., and Guillen, G. O. 1974. Characteristics of El Niño in 1972. J. Mar. Res., 32:387–404.

Wooster, W. S., and J. W. Hedgpeth. 1966. The oceanographic setting of the Galápagos. In The Galápagos, R. I. Bowman, ed., pp. 100–107. Berkeley and Los Angeles: University of California Press.

Wyrtki, K. 1965. Surface currents of the eastern tropical Pacific Ocean. Bull. Inter-Am. Trop. Tuna Comm., 9:269–304.

———. 1966. Oceanography of the eastern equatorial Pacific. Oceanogr. Mar. Biol. Annu. Rev., 4:33–68.

———. 1973. Teleconnections in the equatorial Pacific Ocean. Science (Wash., D.C.), 180:66–68.

———. 1975. El Niño—the dynamic response of the Equatorial Pacific Ocean to atmospheric forcing. J. Phys. Oceanogr., 5(4):572–584.

Wyrtki, K., E. Stroup, W. Patzert, R. Williams, and W. Quinn. 1976. Predicting and observing El Niño. Science (Wash., D. C.), 191:343–346.

Yamaguchi, M. 1975. Sea level fluctuations and mass mortalities of reef animals in Guam, Mariana Islands. Micronesica, 11(2):227–243.

Yonge, C. M. 1940. The biology of reef-building corals. Brit. Mus. (Nat. Hist.), Great Barrier Reef Expedition, 1928–1929, Sci. Repts., 1(13):353–391.

Zeitzschel, B. 1969. Primary productivity in the Gulf of California. Mar. Biol. (Berl.), 3:201–207.

Zinsmeister, W. J. 1974. A new interpretation of the thermally anomalous molluscan assemblages of the California Pleistocene. J. Paleontol., 48:84–94.

Zinsmeister, W. J., and W. K. Emerson. 1979. The role of passive dispersal in the distribution of hemipelagic invertebrates, with examples from the tropical Pacific Ocean. Veliger, 22:32–40.

INDEX

Italicized page numbers refer to illustrations or tables. Page numbers in **boldface** refer to species accounts in the appendix.

Designer: Marvin R. Warshaw
Compositor: Computer Typesetting Services, Inc.
Printer: Malloy Lithographing, Inc.
Binder: Malloy Lithographing, Inc.
Text: 10 pt. Palatino
Display: Palatino